T0203487

Constraint Networks

Constraint Networks

Techniques and Algorithms

Christophe Lecoutre

Series Editor
Narendra Jussien

First published in Great Britain and the United States in 2009 by ISTE Ltd and John Wiley & Sons, Inc.

ISTE Ltd
27-37 St George's Road
London SW19 4EU
UK

www.iste.co.uk

John Wiley & Sons, Inc.
111 River Street
Hoboken, NJ 07030
USA

www.wiley.com

Library of Congress Cataloging-in-Publication Data

Lecoutre, Christophe.
 Constraint networks : techniques and algorithms / Christophe Lecoutre.
    p. cm.
 Includes bibliographical references and index.
 ISBN 978-1-84821-106-3
 1. Constraint programming (Computer science) 2. Computer algorithms. 3. Computer networks.
I. Title.
 QA76.612.L43 2009
 004.6--dc22
                                                                              2009016652

British Library Cataloguing-in-Publication Data
A CIP record for this book is available from the British Library
ISBN: 978-1-84821-106-3

Printed and bound in Great Britain by CPI Antony Rowe, Chippenham and Eastbourne.

Contents

Acknowledgements

First of all, I would very much like to thank Julian Ullmann, Emeritus Professor at King's College London, for his valuable support. Julian made an impressively careful reading of the entire book, giving me a lot of suggestions and amending the text in countless places. It was a great honor to me to benefit from Julian's help. Thanks to him, the manuscript has been considerably improved.

I am very grateful to people who have contributed comments, corrections and suggestions in various parts of the manuscript: Gilles Audemard, Christian Bessiere, Lucas Bordeaux, Frédéric Boussemart, Hadrien Cambazard, Sylvie Coste-Marquis, Marc van Dongen, Fred Hemery, Philippe Jégou, Mouny Samy Modeliar, Olivier Roussel, Thomas Schiex, Radoslaw Szymanek, Sébastien Tabary, Vincent Vidal, Richard Wallace, Ke Xu and Yuanlin Zhang. Thank you to all of you.

Notation

$\mathbb{N}$	set of natural integers	
$\mathbb{Z}$	set of integers	
D	used to denote sets of values	
X	used to denote sets of variables	
X_{evt}	used to denote sets of variables subject to recent events	
C	used to denote sets of constraints	

Main Acronyms

List of Algorithms

Introduction

The concept of *constraint* is central to a number of human activities. A constraint limits the field of possibilities in a certain universe. For example, a school timetable that coordinates students, teachers, lessons, rooms and time slots, must satisfy many constraints. Typically, for each group of students, the objective is to fill up one sheet such as the one shown[1] in Figure 1. In each time slot, you have to indicate who the teacher is, what the lesson is, and where it is located. Obviously, not all combinations are possible, since the constraints are numerous and various:

– no teacher can teach more than one class at the same time;

– different classes cannot be taught in the same room at the same time;

– classes cannot be taught in rooms that are too small, and preferably should not be taught in rooms that are much too big;

– some classes require specialized rooms such as science laboratories;

– some classes require consecutive periods in the same room with the same teacher;

– some part-time teachers need to have certain entire days off;

– students cannot have too far to travel between consecutive classes.

Besides school timetabling, constraint satisfaction problems arise in many enterprise and industrial tasks, ranging from scheduling to configuration, circuit design and molecular biology.

Constraint programming (CP) is a general framework providing simple, general and efficient models and algorithms for solving real-world and academic problems. The appeal of constraint programming mainly relates to the clear distinction between, on the one hand, its formalism, which facilitates the representation of various

---

1. All figures can be downloaded at http://www.iste.co.uk/Lecoutre/cn.zip

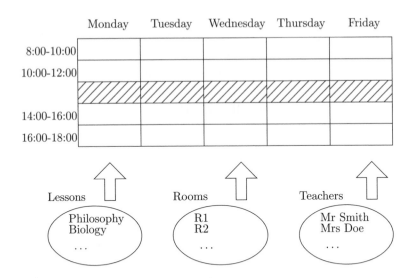

Figure 1. *The timetable assigned to a group of students. Filling timetable sheets is a constraint satisfaction problem*

problems by means of constraints, and, on the other hand, a vast range of algorithms and heuristics to solve them. Practical use of this framework involves two main stages. In the first of these, the user represents the problem abstractly by a *constraint network*, which is a set of variables together with a set of constraints, and perhaps also one or more objective functions. Ideally, this first stage is purely declarative, but in practice, some limited form of programming may be required (using e.g. an object-oriented or logic programming language). In the second stage, the problem represented by the constraint network is tackled by an available software tool, known as a *constraint solver*, that automatically obtains one solution, or all solutions, or an optimal solution, to the given problem. A *solution* is an assignment of values to all variables such that all constraints are satisfied.

A constraint network is a formulation of an *instance* of the *constraint satisfaction problem* (CSP) which is at the core of constraint programming. In a *discrete* instance, the domains, which are the sets of allowed values of variables, are finite. The discrete constraint satisfaction problem is not known to admit polynomial running time algorithms to solve its instances. More precisely, unless $P = NP$ (which is very unlikely to be the case), no such general algorithm can exist, since CSP is NP-hard[2]. This means that the worst-case time complexity of any algorithm for solving CSP instances is expected to be exponential. However, the worst case actually arises only

---

2. Complexity analysis is briefly introduced in Appendix A.2

within a limited range of situations, and outside this range efficient algorithms are already available. Efficiency is achieved by exploiting the structure of instances.

Although this book is focused on CSP, this problem or framework has many derivatives, mainly extensions, as indicated in Figure 2: temporal CSP (TCSP), weighted CSP (WCSP), valued CSP (VCSP), quantified CSP (QCSP), constraint optimization problem (COP), Max-CSP, distributed CSP (DisCSP), etc. Quite often, a concept or technique introduced for basic CSP has turned out to be relevant to its extensions. For example, the concept of arc consistency has been applied to most of these extensions.

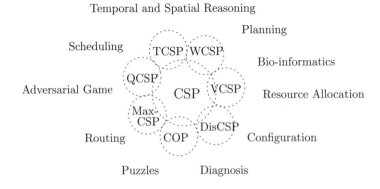

Figure 2. *The CSP framework and some of its extensions*

I. *Toward simplicity of use*

The ability to take heterogeneous constraints into account under a unifying framework has contributed to growing commercial interest in constraint programming since the 1990s. Modeling a problem may, however, turn out to be very difficult for the uninitiated user, as, for example, the number of specific patterns of constraints, called *global constraints*, may be unexpectedly large. In some cases, there is a need for specialized expertise to take full advantage of the efficiency of available techniques and algorithms.

A solver applies constraints so as to avoid exploring combinations of values that cannot possibly belong to any solution. Ideally, the operation of a solver should be totally transparent to the user: the user should not be aware of specific short-cuts used by the solver. Unfortunately, this idyllic vision is not exactly correct in reality because most of the currently available constraint toolkits require the user to guide search, to select algorithms to filter the search space, to break symmetries, etc. As pointed out by Puget [PUG 04], an important challenge for constraint programming is to achieve greater simplicity of use: constraint programming should be made easier for non-specialist users. Enhanced ease of use will boost the impact of constraint programming on industry and academia, and will establish it more firmly as a key software technology for solution of combinatorial problems.

To take up the "simplicity of use" challenge, there is a need for robust and efficient solvers that users can regard as *black-boxes*. A black-box is a system such that the user sees only its input and output data, while its internal structure or mechanism remains invisible. This approach has recently been emphasized by some position papers [PUG 04, GEN 06a] as well as the holding of constraint solver competitions[3]. The black-box approach partially addresses the requirement for simplicity since the user does not have to be aware of (or modify or extend) embedded techniques and algorithms. However, a black-box constraint solver must have a default configuration that in most cases yields the best behavior that could be obtained by fine tuning of available options. This can be achieved by making the solver *robust*.

A solver is robust when it is able to produce similar results, consuming similar resources (time and space), given different but equivalent models of the same problem. It is important to note that the user of an ideally robust solver does not need to provide carefully chosen constraint network models. Robustness compensates for bad modeling by providing sophisticated solving techniques. Some of these certainly remain to be invented, but others are presented in this book: inferences from strong consistencies, adaptive heuristics, nogood recording, automatic symmetry breaking, state-based search, etc. These techniques enable a particularly clever exploration of the search space, learning much useful information before or during search so as to avoid exploring fruitless combinations of values of variables. Given different formulations of the same CSP instance, advanced learning and inference techniques reduce behavior disparities by increasing the efficiency of the solver. Thus robustness and efficiency are intimately interrelated.

II. *Conceptual simplicity of techniques and algorithms*

Robust and efficient black-box solvers are intended to simplify the life of users. However, identifying and implementing appropriate state-of-the-art techniques and algorithms can be quite a hard task for black-box designers and developers. It is not easy to distinguish the most important algorithms among the large number that have been published. Moreover, certain algorithms require complex data structures and procedures that have not been disclosed in complete detail, so re-implementation is hazardous. Luckily, many of the substantial new developments that have appeared during the last decade are characterized by conceptual simplicity of techniques

---

3. See http://www.cril.univ-artois.fr/CPAI08/

and algorithms. This book attempts to present these developments comprehensively and rigorously, offering you a gentle introduction to this active field of research. Pragmatically, the book concentrates on general-purpose approaches that have proven to be effective in practice. These approaches are the source of a nascent generation of robust constraint solvers accessible to the average user.

If we insist on (conceptual) simplicity, this is because it has many nice features. Although these may be obvious, they deserve brief comment as follows. First, simplicity may be understood primarily as ease of comprehension. An easily understood principle is, from the master's point of view, easy to explain and, from the disciple's point of view, quick to assimilate. The difficulty in the comprehension of the world or of nature certainly lies in finding the elementary principles that enable explanation of the Creation. Modestly, in our context, the difficulty lies in finding the basic recipes that are at the origin of the efficiency of algorithms.

Another comment about simplicity is that it tends to make development easier. Proposed algorithmic solutions eventually become procedures written in programming languages. Software development time can be reduced, and more robust code can be written, if an algorithm is easy to code. Ease of coding usually depends on the complexity of the data structures that are employed. Generally, the shorter the code that implements an algorithm, the less the risk of bugs therein.

A final comment about simplicity concerns its impact on the reproduction of experiments. If a method is simple to understand and to implement, this simplicity substantially increases the probability that two people independently evaluating the method will develop similar (source) code and consequently obtain similar experimental results. Surely, science is nothing without the possibility of reproducing experiments (and, more generally, without the possibility of checking theoretical results).

III. *Organization of this book*

In the first chapter, constraint networks are introduced with the formalism that surrounds them. Formal foundations are then given, and several examples of constraint satisfaction problems are presented. In the second chapter, we study the nature of constraint networks, essentially discussing the presence or absence of structure in problems. The remainder of the book is divided into two parts.

The first part describes general inference methods based on local consistencies, which are relational and structural properties of constraint networks. The principle is to simplify the problem instance that must be solved by discarding some useless portions of the search space. This is made possible by propagating constraints following a targeted consistency that allows identification of inconsistent instantiations. Chapter 3 provides an overview of the consistencies usually studied in constraint satisfaction. Following usual practice, we concentrate mainly on first-order (or domain-filtering) consistencies that identify globally inconsistent values. Chapter 4 describes generic algorithms proposed to enforce the central consistency in constraint programming, namely (generalized) arc consistency; such algorithms are universal, as they can theoretically be used for any type of constraints. In Chapter 5, we restrict our attention to table constraints, that is to say, constraints defined by explicitly listing allowed (or forbidden) combinations of values. We describe very recent propagation schemes that have led to significant progress. In Chapter 6, we are interested in singleton arc consistency, a consistency built upon (generalized) arc consistency. We introduce some recent approaches that make use of the incrementality of arc consistency algorithms in different ways. Finally, in Chapter 7, we study dual consistency, which is a consistency related to path consistency.

The second part of the book presents general search methods that cleverly explore the search space of combinatorial problems. The basic idea of these methods is to gather useful information, before and especially during a search, so as to guide the search efficiently. Chapter 8 presents the concept of backtrack search, together with classical look-back and look-ahead schemes. Chapter 9 explains how dead-ends encountered during a search can be quite helpful in guiding the search toward sources of conflicts. The guidance heuristics involve constraint weighting and last-conflict reasoning. Chapter 10 investigates nogood recording, in conjunction with the idea of regularly restarting search. Nogoods can easily be extracted from the current state of search before each restart, and exploited in subsequent runs to discard portions of the search space that have already been explored. Chapter 11 introduces the promising related approach of exploiting partial states extracted, using sophisticated operators, throughout the search. Finally, Chapter 12 addresses the automatic breaking of symmetries. This is an important reasoning mechanism that allows symmetric portions of the search space to be discarded.

We wish to emphasize that many algorithms presented in this book have been implemented in our constraint solver Abscon. This solver is primarily intended to serve as a platform for the scientific development of research ideas. Incidentally, it participates in constraint solver competitions. We also wish to emphasize that this book does not attempt exhaustive coverage of all topics in the constraint processing field. It is intended mainly to promote the artificial intelligence approach to constraint programming, and is unsurprisingly built upon the experience of the author, making some sections rather personal.

IV. *Introductory example*

Most of the concepts introduced in this book refer to either inference or search. Nevertheless, sometimes concepts refer to both principles of inference and search.

This is the reason why we propose[4] an example to gently introduce the central notions of consistency and backtrack search. Map coloring is the problem chosen for this example.

The goal of a *map coloring problem* is to color a map so that adjacent regions, i.e. regions sharing a common border, have different colors. Figure 3(a) shows a map that has nine regions which need to be colored. The four color map theorem (e.g. see [WIL 05]) states that given any plane separated into regions, such as a political map of the states of a country, the regions can be colored using no more than four colors. Thus, we propose to color the map shown in Figure 3(a) with the four colors shown in Figure 3(b).

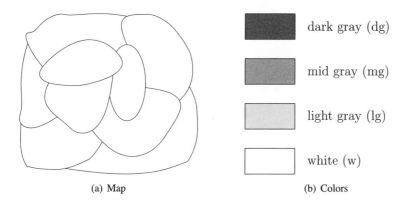

(a) Map   (b) Colors

dark gray (dg)

mid gray (mg)

light gray (lg)

white (w)

Figure 3. *A map with nine regions to be colored using four colors*

The map together with the colors shown in Figure 3 is an *instance* of the map coloring problem. We can represent this instance by a *constraint network* P which is a structure composed of variables and constraints. A *variable* is an unknown, which must be given, or *assigned*, a value from an associated *domain*. Naturally, the variables of our constraint network correspond to the nine regions of the map, and the domain of each variable contains the four available colors. The variables are $\{x_1, x_2, \ldots, x_9\}$ and the domains are $\{dg, mg, lg, w\}$, where dg stands for dark gray, mg stands for mid gray, etc. Figure 4 illustrates this. A *constraint* restricts the possible combinations of values of some variables. Since adjacent regions must be colored differently, we introduce a constraint on every pair of variables that represent adjacent regions. Such a *binary* constraint states that the values assigned to the two variables involved in this constraint must be different. We just use inequation constraints. For example, we have

---

4. I would like to thank Julian Ullmann for having suggested this to me.

$x_1 \neq x_2$ since x_1 and x_2 represent two adjacent regions located in the north of the map.

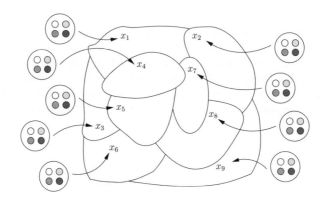

Figure 4. *Each region of the map is represented by a variable x whose domain is the set $\{dg, mg, lg, w\}$, that is, the four available colors*

It may be useful to associate a *constraint graph* with a (binary) constraint network so as to benefit from well-known results from graph theory. A constraint graph is an undirected graph built from a constraint network such that there is a vertex per variable, and there is an edge per pair of variables involved in a constraint. Figure 5 shows the constraint graph for our example. Using the constraint graph of the map coloring problem, we obtain an equivalent *graph coloring problem*: color the vertices of the graph such that adjacent vertices, i.e. vertices linked by an edge, have different colors.

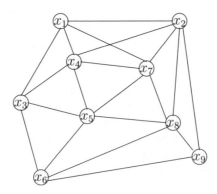

Figure 5. *The constraint graph associated with the constraint network partially depicted in Figure 4. Here, vertices are labeled with the variable names they represent*

To find a solution for this problem, we need *search*. In its complete form, search performs an exhaustive exploration of the search space. The *search space* is basically the Cartesian product of the domains of the variables; here, as we have nine variables and four values per domain, we obtain a search space whose size is 4^9. This represents 262,144 different configurations, or *complete instantiations*, for the constraint network. Enumerating every complete instantiation in turn and checking each one to see whether it satisfies all the constraints appears to be quite inefficient; this is a method called *generate and test*.

To improve the performance of the "generate and test" approach, it is possible to perform a depth-first exploration of the search space, verifying at each step that it may still be possible to find a solution. Variables are assigned, or *instantiated*, in turn, thereby forming *partial* instantiations. At each step, the local consistency of the partial instantiation can be checked: the partial instantiation is *locally consistent* iff each constraint *covered* by it (i.e. each constraint only involving instantiated variables) is satisfied.

For our example, a *depth-first search* (DFS) starts by assigning dg to x_1; see Figure 6(a). The partial instantiation $\{x_1 = dg\}$ is locally consistent because no constraint is covered by it (all constraints are binary). Then, DFS assigns dg to x_2; see Figure 6(b). This time, the partial instantiation is not locally consistent because the constraint $x_1 \neq x_2$ is covered and violated. No solution can be found by extending this partial instantiation, which corresponds to a *dead-end* situation and is called a *nogood*. This is why another value for x_2 is tried by the search; see Figure 6(c).

Assume now that the (locally consistent) partial instantiation $\{x_1 = dg, x_2 = mg, x_3 = mg, x_4 = w, x_5 = lg, x_6 = dg\}$ must be extended over x_7; see Figure 7(a). It is easy to see that any assignment to x_7 yields an inconsistent instantiation because x_1, x_2, x_4 and x_5 are adjacent to x_7 and have all been assigned different colors. Otherwise stated, no color remains possible for x_7. Consequently, after four tentative assignments for x_7 (because the domain of x_7 is composed of four values), the search has to return to the variable that was instantiated before x_7, which is x_6. When the search returns to a previous variable, we say that the search algorithm backtracks; this general principle is called *backtracking*. Depth-first search (with backtracking) is also called *backtrack search*. In our example, after backtracking from x_7, another value for x_6 must be tried; this is color mg as shown in Figure 7(b). This new assigned color is immediately discarded because the constraint $x_3 \neq x_6$ is violated. For a similar reason, lg is discarded, and so the only remaining possibility is to try w for x_6; see Figure 7(c). However, after assigning w to x_6, the algorithm again performs the same useless tentative instantiations of x_7, although the value of x_6 has no bearing on these failures. Rediscovering the same failure situations during search is called *thrashing*.

Finally, it seems reasonable to prevent conflicts that can easily be anticipated (so as to prevent, or at least reduce, thrashing). For example, if at the beginning of

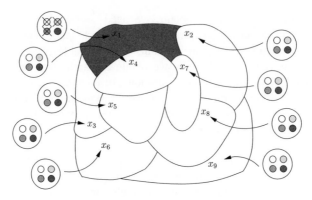

(a) DFS assigns dg to x_1

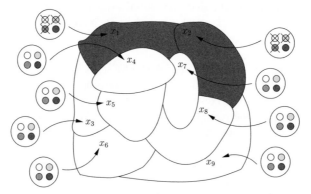

(b) DFS assigns dg to x_2. The partial instantiation is not locally consistent because the constraint $x_1 \neq x_2$ is violated.

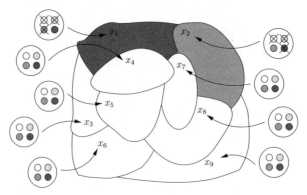

(c) DFS tries another assignment for x_2 (mg is assigned to x_2). The new partial instantiation is locally consistent.

Figure 6. *The early steps performed by DFS (depth-first search)*

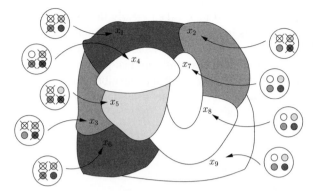

(a) The partial instantiation $\{x_1 = dg, x_2 = mg, x_3 = mg, x_4 = w, x_5 = lg, x_6 = dg\}$ must be extended over x_7. No extension is locally consistent: search has to backtrack to x_6.

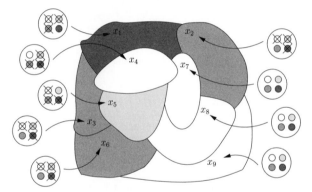

(b) After backtracking to x_6, a new value has been assigned to x_6. This value (as well as lg) is immediately discarded because the new partial instantiation is not locally consistent.

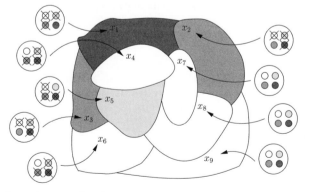

(c) The value w is now assigned to x_6. Four useless tentative assignments to x_7 will be performed again. This is a phenomenon called thrashing.

Figure 7. *Illustration of backtracking and thrashing*

search the value dg is assigned to x_1, then clearly this value can be removed from the domain of the variables in the neighborhood of x_1, namely x_2, x_3, x_4 and x_7; see Figure 8. A value for an uninstantiated variable is incompatible with the value of the last instantiated variable if there is a constraint that prevents these two variables from taking these values simultaneously. Such incompatible values are not *arc-consistent* and can be safely deleted without losing any solutions. Deletion of inconsistent values is called *filtering* of the domains.

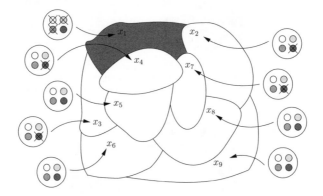

Figure 8. *By reasoning locally from constraints after dg is assigned to x_1, we deduce (infer) that the value dg can be safely removed from the domains of x_2, x_3, x_4 and x_7*

Sophisticated backtrack search algorithms interleave search steps and filtering inference processes that can identify inconsistent partial instantiations of arbitrary size. Before starting search, constraint networks are usually processed during a so-called *preprocessing* stage. Typically, inferences such as removing inconsistent values are performed at preprocessing time. Sometimes preprocessing alone is sufficient to solve a problem instance.

Chapter 1

Constraint Networks

This chapter introduces the formalism of constraint networks, which can abstractly represent many academic and real-world problems. Section 1.1 introduces variables and constraints, which are the main ingredients of constraint networks. This introduction includes different representations of constraints as well as the vital concept of constraint support. In section 1.2, we formally define constraint networks. Moreover, we present the (hyper)graphs that can be associated with any constraint network, and introduce instantiations. Section 1.3 provides some illustrative examples of problems that can be easily represented by means of constraint networks. For simplicity and entertainment, these examples are based on logic puzzles. Section 1.4 is concerned with partial orders in constraint networks, decisions and general properties of values and variables. Finally, section 1.5 introduces some data structures that can be employed to represent constraint networks in computer programs.

1.1. Variables and constraints

Here we will define variables and constraints, which are the main ingredients of constraint networks. They constitute the surface part of a problem representation, whereas domains and relations constitute the underlying part. In object-oriented design, we would certainly build up a class for variables and another for constraints, and represent all relevant information about variables and constraints in terms of attributes (maybe introducing additional classes) for these objects: identifier, domain, scope, relation, etc.

DEFINITION 1.1.– *[Variable] A variable, which is a component of an abstract system, is an object that has a name and is able to take different values. In our context, a* variable *(whose name is) x must be given a value from a set, which is called the* current domain *of x and is denoted by* $\mathrm{dom}(x)$. *The domain of a variable x may evolve over time, but it is always included in a set called the* initial domain *of x.[1] This initial domain, which is denoted by* $\mathrm{dom}^{\mathrm{init}}(x)$, *represents the full universe of the variable x.*

A *continuous* variable has an infinite initial domain, usually defined in terms of real intervals. Continuous variables are outside the scope of this book, which only considers discrete variables. A *discrete variable* is a variable whose initial domain contains a finite number of values.

We use letters x, y, z (and when necessary u, v, w), possibly subscripted or primed, to denote variables. Without any loss of generality, our variables can be assumed to have integer values in their domains when necessary. Quite often, letters a, b, c, possibly subscripted or primed, will be used to denote values. For example, x and y such that $\mathrm{dom}^{\mathrm{init}}(x) = \{a, b\}$ and $\mathrm{dom}^{\mathrm{init}}(y) = \{1, 2, \ldots, 100\}$ are two discrete variables whose initial domains contain 2 and 100 values, respectively.

Domains are dynamic sets, i.e. they may change over time. A variable is said to be *fixed* when its current domain only contains one value, and *unfixed* otherwise. A variable can be fixed either explicitly or implicitly (incidentally). When a variable x is explicitly given a value a from its current domain $\mathrm{dom}(x)$ during the progression of a scenario or an algorithm, every other value $b \neq a$ is considered to be removed from $\mathrm{dom}(x)$. In this case we say that the variable x is *instantiated*; otherwise, we say that x is *uninstantiated*. We also say that the variable x is *assigned* (the value a) or that the value a is assigned to x. Assigning a value to a variable is called a *variable assignment*. Implicitly fixed variables occur when deduction (inference) mechanisms are used. For example, consider the equality $x = y$ between two variables x and y whose (common) current domain is $\{1, 2\}$. If the variable x is assigned the value 1, by reasoning from the equality we can deduce that y must also be equal to 1, i.e. the value 2 can be removed from $\mathrm{dom}(y)$ by deduction. The two variables are then fixed, the first one explicitly and the second one implicitly. However, only the first variable is considered to be instantiated (or assigned).

A value a is said to be *valid* for a variable x iff $a \in \mathrm{dom}(x)$. Because of changes in $\mathrm{dom}(x)$, a value that is valid for x at time t may be invalid at another time t'. To keep track of those changes, it can be helpful to use a superscript t to denote the time at which we refer to a domain: $\mathrm{dom}^{t}(x)$ is the domain of x at time t. With t_0 representing the time origin we have, for every variable x, $\mathrm{dom}^{t_0}(x) = \mathrm{dom}^{\mathrm{init}}(x)$. Actually, as we shall see later, instead of using time, we use constraint networks as superscript for domains. Indeed, when we reason about several related constraint networks, it is

---

1. We can imagine situations where initial domains could be enlarged. However, no technique presented in this book allows us to do that.

expedient to write $\mathrm{dom}^P(x)$ to denote the domain of x in constraint network P. When the context is unambiguous, we simply use $\mathrm{dom}(x)$.

In this book, without any loss of generality, we assume that (names of) discrete variables belong to an infinite totally ordered set, with the (strict) total order denoted by $\lhd$; thus $x \lhd y$ means that variable x (strictly) precedes y within this order. Consequently, any set of variables handled in the remainder of this book is assumed to be totally ordered by $\lhd$.

REMARK 1.2.– *[Total Order on Variables] Any set X of variables is totally ordered according to the relation $\lhd$.*

Similarly, without any loss of generality, we assume that values are always taken from a totally ordered set, with the (strict) total order denoted by $<$; thus $a < b$ means that the value a (strictly) precedes b within this order. Consequently, any set of values handled in the remainder of this book is assumed to be totally ordered by $<$.

REMARK 1.3.– *[Total Order on Values] Any set V of values is totally ordered according to the relation $<$.*

To define constraints, we introduce *tuples*, *Cartesian product* and *relations*. More information about sets, relations, etc. can be found in Appendix A.1.

DEFINITION 1.4.– *[Tuple] A tuple τ is a sequence, usually enclosed between parentheses, of values separated by commas. A tuple containing r values is called an r-tuple. The ith value of an r-tuple, with $1 \leq i \leq r$, is denoted by $\tau[i]$.*

As values are taken from a totally ordered set, r-tuples can be lexicographically ordered by extending the relation $<$. The new strict total order is denoted by $<_{\mathrm{lex}}$, and the corresponding non-strict total order is denoted by $\leq_{\mathrm{lex}}$.

DEFINITION 1.5.– *[Lexicographic Order] Let τ and τ' be two r-tuples.*
  $-\ \tau <_{\mathrm{lex}} \tau'$ *iff* $\exists i \in 1..r$ *such that* $\tau[i] < \tau'[i]$ *and* $\forall j \in 1..i-1, \tau[j] = \tau'[j]$.
  $-\ \tau \leq_{\mathrm{lex}} \tau'$ *iff* $\tau <_{\mathrm{lex}} \tau'$ *or* $\tau = \tau'$.

EXAMPLE.– Considering values taken from $\mathbb{N}$, we have:
  $-\ (2, 4, 7, 6) <_{\mathrm{lex}} (3, 3, 3, 8)$;
  $-\ (2, 4, 7, 6) <_{\mathrm{lex}} (2, 4, 8, 2)$;
  $-\ (2, 4, 7, 6) <_{\mathrm{lex}} (2, 4, 7, 8)$.

A Cartesian product is a set composed of all tuples that can be built from a sequence of sets.

DEFINITION 1.6.– *[Cartesian Product] Let $D_1, D_2, \ldots, D_r$ be a sequence of r sets. The* Cartesian product $D_1 \times D_2 \times \cdots \times D_r$, *also written* $\prod_{i=1}^{r} D_i$, *is the set* $\{(a_1, a_2, \ldots, a_r) \mid a_1 \in D_1, a_2 \in D_2, \ldots, a_r \in D_r\}$. *Each element of* $\prod_{i=1}^{r} D_i$ *is an r-tuple.*

EXAMPLE.– We can define Cartesian products of domains of variables. For example, if x, y and z are three variables such that $\mathrm{dom}(x) = \mathrm{dom}(y) = \{a, b\}$ and $\mathrm{dom}(z) = \{a, c\}$, we have:

$$\mathrm{dom}(x) \times \mathrm{dom}(y) \times \mathrm{dom}(z) = \left\{ \begin{array}{l} (a, a, a), \\ (a, a, c), \\ (a, b, a), \\ (a, b, c), \\ (b, a, a), \\ (b, a, c), \\ (b, b, a), \\ (b, b, c) \end{array} \right\}$$

A relation is simply a subset of a Cartesian product.

DEFINITION 1.7.– *[Relation] A relation R defined over a sequence of r sets* $D_1, D_2, \ldots, D_r$ *is a subset of the Cartesian product* $\prod_{i=1}^{r} D_i$, *so* $R \subseteq \prod_{i=1}^{r} D_i$.

We also say that R is defined on $\prod_{i=1}^{r} D_i$.

EXAMPLE.– Here is a relation defined on $\mathrm{dom}(x) \times \mathrm{dom}(y) \times \mathrm{dom}(z)$:

$$R_{xyz} = \left\{ \begin{array}{l} (a, a, c), \\ (b, a, a), \\ (b, a, c), \\ (b, b, c) \end{array} \right\}$$

We can now introduce the central concept of *constraint*.

DEFINITION 1.8.– *[Constraint] A constraint, which is a component of an abstract system, is represented by a name and is a restriction on combinations of values that can be taken simultaneously by a set of variables. In our context, a* constraint *(whose name is) c is defined over a (totally ordered) set of variables, which constitute the* scope *of c and are denoted by* $\mathrm{scp}(c)$. *A constraint c is defined by a relation, denoted by* $\mathrm{rel}(c)$, *comprising exactly the set of tuples allowed by c for the variables of its* scope; *we have* $\mathrm{rel}(c) \subseteq \prod_{x \in \mathrm{scp}(c)} \mathrm{dom}^{\mathrm{init}}(x)$.

The letter c, possibly subscripted with the sequence of scope variables, or possibly primed, is used to denote a constraint. For example, the constraint c_{xyz} is such that

$\mathrm{scp}(c_{xyz}) = \{x, y, z\}$. Sometimes we use the symbol c to denote a value for a variable, but the context is always sufficient to distinguish between a constraint and a value.

A tuple τ allowed by c is also said to be *accepted* by c, and we say that τ *satisfies* c. A tuple that is not allowed by c is said to be *disallowed* or *forbidden* by c, and we say that c is unsatisfied, or *violated*, by τ. For example, if c_{xyz} is a constraint such that $\mathrm{rel}(c_{xyz}) = R_{xyz}$, where R_{xyz} is the relation introduced above, then (b, a, c) is an allowed tuple, whereas (a, b, a) is disallowed by c_{xyz}.

A variable x that belongs to $\mathrm{scp}(c)$ is said to be *involved* in c. Note that $\mathrm{scp}(c)$ is totally ordered according to the relation $\lhd$; see Remark 1.2. Consequently, in Definition 1.8 the order of the domains in the Cartesian product corresponds to the order of the variables for which they are the domains. We use $\mathrm{scp}(c)[i]$ in some algorithms to denote the ith variable involved in $\mathrm{scp}(c)$, with $1 \leq i \leq |\mathrm{scp}(c)|$. Two constraints c and c' such that $\mathrm{scp}(c) \cap \mathrm{scp}(c') \neq \emptyset$ are said to *intersect*. For example, c_{xyz} and c_{wy} are two constraints that intersect on variable y. The *arity* of a constraint c is the number of variables involved in c, i.e. $|\mathrm{scp}(c)|$. A constraint is:

– unary iff its arity is 1;

– binary iff its arity is 2;

– ternary iff its arity is 3;

– non-binary iff its arity is strictly greater than 2.

Notice that a non-binary constraint is considered as being neither binary nor (more surprisingly) unary. The reason is that, as we shall see later, unary constraints defined on discrete variables can easily be discarded (and so ignored).

Definition 1.8 is a little bit more general than the one usually employed, which is confined to *tailored constraints*. This has to do with the concept of embedded constraint networks introduced in [BES 06].

DEFINITION 1.9.– *[Tailored Constraint] A constraint c is said to be* tailored *iff* $\mathrm{rel}(c) \subseteq \prod_{x \in \mathrm{scp}(c)} \mathrm{dom}(x)$.

When a constraint is tailored, every allowed tuple only involves valid values, i.e. values in current domains. When it is not tailored, we may have $\mathrm{rel}(c) \not\subseteq \prod_{x \in \mathrm{scp}(c)} \mathrm{dom}(x)$, but by definition we know that $\mathrm{rel}(c) \subseteq \prod_{x \in \mathrm{scp}(c)} \mathrm{dom}^{\mathrm{init}}(x)$. The general definition 1.8 is useful in dynamic situations, as we shall see later. In practice, constraints are tailored when they are defined; but when domains of variables change, constraints do not systematically remain tailored.

It is important to note that constraint relations may also change over time; this is a feature of various approaches such as enforcing path consistency or pairwise consistency, which are introduced later. The state of a constraint c at time t is given by the state of $\mathrm{rel}(c)$ at time t, and also, indirectly, by the state of the domains of the variables involved in c at time t. To keep track of changes, if any, in a constraint relation, we can use a superscript t so that $\mathrm{rel}^t(c)$ is the relation of c at time t.

EXAMPLE.– Figure 1.1 illustrates the dynamic aspect of constraint relations with a ternary constraint c_{xyz} (with $\mathrm{scp}(c_{xyz}) = \{x, y, z\}$). We have $\mathrm{dom}^{\mathrm{init}}(x) = \mathrm{dom}^{\mathrm{init}}(y) = \mathrm{dom}^{\mathrm{init}}(z) = \{a, b, c\}$. At time t_0, the initial tailored constraint is defined. At time t_1, two allowed tuples of the initial relation have here been (arbitrarily) removed. At time t_2, some values have been (arbitrarily) removed from the domains of the variables involved in c_{xyz}, making c_{xyz} no longer tailored. For example, $(b, a, a) \in \mathrm{rel}^{t_2}(c_{xyz})$ but $(b, a, a) \notin \mathrm{dom}^{t_2}(x) \times \mathrm{dom}^{t_2}(y) \times \mathrm{dom}^{t_2}(z)$.

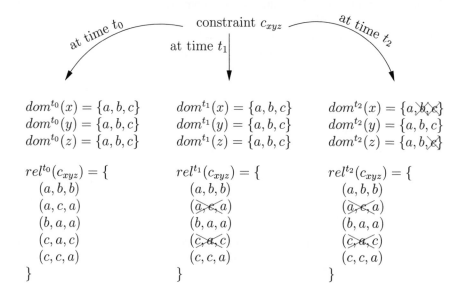

Figure 1.1. *Three (arbitrary) successive states of a constraint c_{xyz}*

The initial relation of c is denoted by $\mathrm{rel}^{\mathrm{init}}(c)$; this is the relation defined at the time origin t_0. As for domains, when we are concerned with constraints in more than one constraint network, e.g. when analyzing the dynamic behavior of an algorithm, we write $\mathrm{rel}^P(c)$ to denote the relation of c in constraint network P. When the context is unambiguous, we simply use $\mathrm{rel}(c)$.

Although we have defined a constraint in terms of an associated relation, this imposes no restriction on the practical prescription of constraints. In practice, a constraint may be defined either intensionally or extensionally.

DEFINITION 1.10.– *[Intensional Constraint] A constraint c is* intensional, *or defined in intension, iff* rel(c) *is implicitly described by a predicate[2], i.e. by a characteristic function that is defined from* $\prod_{x \in \text{scp}(c)} \text{dom}^{\text{init}}(x)$ *to* {*false, true*} *and based on a Boolean expression or formula.*

Examples of Boolean expressions are $x \neq y$ and $|x * y| < |z|$. Clearly, the semantics of constraints intensionally defined by Boolean expressions is immediately understood. We usually refer to an intensional constraint c as $c : expr$ where $expr$ is the predicate expression of c (also denoted by $expr[c]$).

DEFINITION 1.11.– *[Extensional Constraint] A constraint c is* extensional, *or defined in extension, iff* rel(c) *is explicitly described, either positively by listing the tuples allowed by c or negatively by listing the tuples disallowed by c.*

For an extensional constraint c, we use $table[c]$ and $\overline{table}[c]$ to denote the set of tuples allowed and disallowed by c, respectively. Of course, we have $table[c] = \text{rel}(c)$ and $\overline{table}[c] = \prod_{x \in \text{scp}(c)} \text{dom}^{\text{init}}(x) \setminus \text{rel}(c)$. The use of these special terms shows clearly that we are dealing with extensional constraints.

EXAMPLE.– Consider a ternary constraint c_{xyz}. Imagine that this constraint means that the values which can be assigned simultaneously to x, y and z must all be different. The constraint c_{xyz} can be defined in intension by using $x \neq y \wedge x \neq z \wedge y \neq z$ as a predicate expression, denoted by $c_{xyz} : x \neq y \wedge x \neq z \wedge y \neq z$. Note that this representation remains stable, irrespective of the initial domains of variables in scp(c_{xyz}). If $\text{dom}^{\text{init}}(x) \times \text{dom}^{\text{init}}(y) \times \text{dom}^{\text{init}}(z) = \{0,1,2\} \times \{0,1,2\} \times \{0,1,2\}$, then c_{xyz} can be represented in extension by one of the two following sets:

$$
table[c_{xyz}] = \left\{ \begin{array}{l} (0,1,2), \\ (0,2,1), \\ (1,0,2), \\ (1,2,0) \\ (2,0,1), \\ (2,1,0) \end{array} \right\} \qquad \overline{table}[c_{xyz}] = \left\{ \begin{array}{l} (0,0,0), \\ (0,0,1), \\ (0,0,2), \\ \dots \\ (2,2,1), \\ (2,2,2) \end{array} \right\}
$$

The number of allowed tuples is 6, whereas the number of disallowed tuples is 21. For simplicity and for space efficiency, it is better in this case to employ a representation of allowed tuples. If we generalize the ternary constraint c_{xyz} to an r-ary constraint c such that the initial domain of any involved variable is $\{0, 1, \dots, r-1\}$ while keeping the same semantics, the number of allowed and disallowed tuples become $r!$ and $r^r - r!$, respectively. It is then essential to represent such a constraint in

---

2. Note that an intensional constraint cannot always easily be defined by a Boolean formula, because it sometimes corresponds to use of a computer function.

intension, and even better, by a so-called global constraint whose meaning is implicit. Actually, the constraint introduced in our example is (an instance of) the well-known global constraint (pattern) allDifferent.

DEFINITION 1.12.– *[Global Constraint] A global constraint is a constraint pattern that captures precise relational semantics and can be applied over an arbitrary number of variables.*

For example, the semantics of allDifferent is that every variable must take a different value. When the allDifferent constraint pattern is applied to three variables x, y and z, we obtain a constraint denoted by c_{xyz} : allDifferent(x, y, z). Clearly, the allDifferent constraint pattern can be applied to any number of variables. For more information about global constraints, see e.g. [HOE 06, BEL 08].

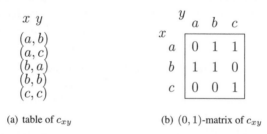

(a) table of c_{xy} (b) $(0, 1)$-matrix of c_{xy}

Figure 1.2. *Extensional representation of a binary constraint c_{xy} by a table and a $(0, 1)$-matrix*

An alternative representation for extensional constraints is to use multi-dimensional Boolean arrays, also called $(0, 1)$-matrices when constraints are binary. For example, assume that x and y are two variables such that $\mathrm{dom}(x) = \mathrm{dom}(y) = \{a, b, c\}$, and c_{xy} is a binary constraint defined in extension by the table[3] given in Figure 1.2(a). The constraint c_{xy} can equivalently be represented by the $(0, 1)$-matrix given in Figure 1.2(b). An entry of 0 (resp. 1) means that the tuple composed of the value labeling the row and the value labeling the column is disallowed (resp. allowed) by the constraint. For example, we find 1 at the intersection of row b and column a, meaning that (b, a) is allowed by c_{xy}. The space complexity of a table representation is $O(tr)$, where t denotes the number of tuples in the table, and r the arity of the constraint[4]. The space complexity of a multi-dimensional array representation is $O(d^r)$, where d denotes the greatest domain size, which shows that arrays can be used

---

3. Henceforth, tables are presented as a simple enumeration (list) of tuples.
4. Asymptotic notation is presented in Appendix A.2.1.

only for small-arity constraints. In the remainder of the book, we always consider extensional constraints implemented by tables.

As explained above, when constraints are not tailored we have $\text{rel}(c) \nsubseteq \prod_{x \in \text{scp}(c)} \text{dom}(x)$. For example, consider a binary intensional constraint $c_{xy} : x = y$ such that $\text{dom}^{\text{init}}(x) = \text{dom}^{\text{init}}(y) = \{0, 1, \ldots, 9\}$. We have $\text{rel}(c_{xy}) = \{(i, j) \in \text{dom}^{\text{init}}(x) \times \text{dom}^{\text{init}}(y) \mid i = j\}$. When the membership of domains is changed, we can implicitly update the relation associated with c_{xy}, e.g. as in [BAC 02a], so that $\text{rel}(c_{xy}) = \{(i, j) \in \text{dom}(x) \times \text{dom}(y) \mid i = j\}$, and constraints always remain tailored. However, it may not be practical to update a constraint relation represented in extension; in our example, an extensional representation of c_{xy} is $table[c_{xy}] = \text{rel}^{\text{init}}(c_{xy}) = \{(0, 0), \ldots, (9, 9)\}$. If 0 and 1 are removed from $\text{dom}(x)$, then in principle, (the table associated with) the relation of c_{xy} can be reduced to $\text{rel}(c_{xy}) = \{(2, 2), \ldots, (9, 9)\}$. In practice, updating $table[c_{xy}]$ may be expensive and not very helpful, and implicitly considering such an update may be unsafe in the development and/or complexity analysis of some algorithms. Therefore, unless explicitly mentioned, constraint relations will be considered as invariant, i.e. $\text{rel}(c) = \text{rel}^{\text{init}}(c)$ for all constraints c.

The distinction between what is allowed (i.e. what can be accepted by a constraint) and what is valid (i.e. what can be built from the variable domains of a constraint) is important for understanding the dynamic aspect of some algorithms.

Let $\tau = (a_1, \ldots, a_r)$ be an r-tuple of values of a (totally ordered) set of r variables $X = \{x_1, \ldots, x_r\}$. The value a_i will be denoted by $\tau[x_i]$. By extension, for any subset $X' \subseteq X$, the restriction of τ to the variables in X' will be denoted by $\tau[X']$. For example, let $X = \{w, x, y, z\}$ and $\tau = (a, b, b, c)$. We have $\tau[w] = a$, $\tau[x] = b$, ..., and $\tau[\{w, z\}] = (a, c)$. A valid tuple for a constraint is a tuple containing a valid value for every variable in the scope of the constraint.

DEFINITION 1.13.– *[Valid Tuple] Let c be an r-ary constraint. An r-tuple τ is valid on c iff $\forall x \in \text{scp}(c)$, $\tau[x] \in \text{dom}(x)$. The set of valid tuples on c is $\text{val}(c) = \prod_{x \in \text{scp}(c)} \text{dom}(x)$.*

By definition of variables, we always have $\text{val}(c) \subseteq \prod_{x \in \text{scp}(c)} \text{dom}^{\text{init}}(x)$. Moreover, when c is tailored, we have $\text{rel}(c) \subseteq \text{val}(c)$. Recall that a tuple τ is allowed by a constraint c iff $\tau \in \text{rel}(c)$. Supports and conflicts are defined as follows.

DEFINITION 1.14.– *[Support and Conflict] Let c be an r-ary constraint. An r-tuple τ is a support (resp. a conflict) on c iff τ is a valid tuple on c which is allowed (resp. disallowed) by c.*

If τ is a support (resp. a conflict) on a constraint c involving a variable x and such that $\tau[x] = a$, we say that τ is a support (resp. a conflict) for (x, a) on c; we also say that (x, a) is supported (resp. not supported) by c. When (a, b) is a support on a binary constraint c_{xy}, we sometimes say that (x, a) *supports* (y, b) on c_{xy}, and symmetrically that (y, b) supports (x, a) on c_{xy}.

NOTATION 1.15.– *Let c be a constraint.*

– *The set of supports on c is* $\sup(c) = \mathrm{val}(c) \cap \mathrm{rel}(c)$.

– *The set of conflicts on c is* $\mathrm{con}(c) = \mathrm{val}(c) \setminus \sup(c)$.

For a tailored constraint c, we have $\sup(c) = \mathrm{rel}(c)$ since $\mathrm{rel}(c) \subseteq \mathrm{val}(c)$. Determining if a tuple is allowed is called a *constraint check*, and determining if a tuple is valid is called a *validity check*. We often need to make such checks when looking for supports; search of supports represents a basic operation in constraint reasoning. Figure 1.3 summarizes the different sets introduced so far; Figure 1.4 provides a detailed example.

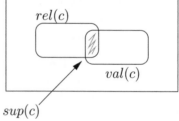

Figure 1.3. *A constraint c whose "universe" is $\prod_{x \in scp(c)} \mathrm{dom}^{\mathrm{init}}(x)$. The set of tuples allowed by c is $\mathrm{rel}(c)$. The set of valid tuples on c is $\mathrm{val}(c)$. The set of supports on c is* $\sup(c) = \mathrm{rel}(c) \cap \mathrm{val}(c)$

The following notation will be useful in situations where we need to deal with tuples that involve a particular value.

NOTATION 1.16.– *Let c be a constraint, $x \in \mathrm{scp}(c)$ and $a \in \mathrm{dom}(x)$.*

– *The set of valid tuples for (x, a) on c is* $\mathrm{val}(c)_{x=a} = \{\tau \in \mathrm{val}(c) \mid \tau[x] = a\}$.

– *The set of supports for (x, a) on c is* $\sup(c)_{x=a} = \mathrm{val}(c)_{x=a} \cap \mathrm{rel}(c)$.

– *The set of conflicts for (x, a) on c is* $\mathrm{con}(c)_{x=a} = \mathrm{val}(c)_{x=a} \setminus \sup(c)$.

– *The set of strict supports for (x, a) on c is* $\sup(c)\!\downarrow_{x=a} = \{\tau[\mathrm{scp}(c) \setminus \{x\}] \mid \tau \in \sup(c)_{x=a}\}$.

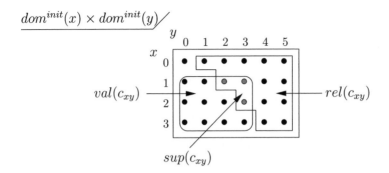

Figure 1.4. *A constraint $c_{xy} : x < y$ whose "universe" is*
$\mathrm{dom}^{init}(x) \times \mathrm{dom}^{init}(y) = \{0, \ldots, 3\} \times \{0, \ldots, 5\}$. *The set of tuples allowed by c_{xy} is*
$\mathrm{rel}(c_{xy}) = \{(i,j) \in \mathrm{dom}^{init}(x) \times \mathrm{dom}^{init}(y) \mid i < j\}$. *When $\mathrm{dom}(x) = \{1,2,3\}$ and*
$\mathrm{dom}(y) = \{0,1,2,3\}$, *the set of valid tuples on c_{xy} is* $\mathrm{val}(c_{xy}) = \{1,2,3\} \times \{0,1,2,3\}$.
The set of supports on c_{xy} is $\mathrm{sup}(c_{xy}) = \mathrm{rel}(c_{xy}) \cap \mathrm{val}(c_{xy}) = \{(1,2),(1,3),(2,3)\}$

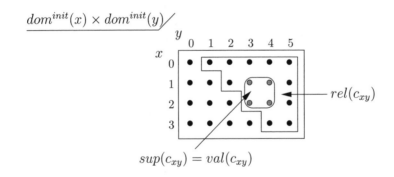

Figure 1.5. *The constraint from Figure 1.4 in a different state, since we now have*
$\mathrm{dom}(x) = \{1,2\}$ *and* $\mathrm{dom}(y) = \{3,4\}$. *Here, we have*
$\mathrm{sup}(c_{xy}) = \mathrm{val}(c_{xy}) = \{1,2\} \times \{3,4\}$. *Hence, c_{xy} is entailed: we have*
a guarantee that $x < y$

When we have $\mathrm{sup}(c)_{x=a} \neq \emptyset$, we say that c (currently) supports (x,a).
Note here that a strict support for a value (x,a) on a constraint c is a tuple
composed of $|\mathrm{scp}(c)| - 1$ values, whereas a "classical" support contains $|\mathrm{scp}(c)|$
values. We need strict supports to define some properties later. For example,
if c_{xyz} is such that $\mathrm{sup}(c_{xyz}) = \{(a,b,a),(a,b,c),(b,a,b),(c,c,b)\}$, then
$\mathrm{sup}(c_{xyz})_{x=a} = \{(a,b,a),(a,b,c)\}$, and $\mathrm{sup}(c_{xyz}){\downarrow}_{x=a} = \{(b,a),(b,c)\}$.

We can now introduce constraint *tightness* (and *looseness*), which is an important feature. The greater the tightness of a constraint, the more difficult it is to satisfy the constraint.

DEFINITION 1.17.– *[Constraint Tightness and Looseness] Let c be a constraint.*

– *The* looseness *of c is equal to the ratio*

$$\frac{|\operatorname{rel}^{\text{init}}(c)|}{|\prod_{x \in \text{scp}(c)} \operatorname{dom}^{\text{init}}(x)|}.$$

– *The* tightness *of c is equal to the ratio*

$$\frac{|\prod_{x \in \text{scp}(c)} \operatorname{dom}^{\text{init}}(x) \setminus \operatorname{rel}^{\text{init}}(c)|}{|\prod_{x \in \text{scp}(c)} \operatorname{dom}^{\text{init}}(x)|}.$$

Looseness and tightness above are defined from initial domains and relation; this corresponds to the classical usage. Sometimes it is useful to compute tightness or looseness from current domains and relation. The *current* constraint tightness (resp. looseness) of a constraint c is the ratio $|\operatorname{con}(c)|/|\operatorname{val}(c)|$ (resp. $|\sup(c)|/|\operatorname{val}(c)|$). Current constraint tightness corresponds to the ratio "number of conflicts on c over number of valid tuples on c". For example, the constraint tightness of the constraint c_{xy} depicted in Figure 1.4 is $\frac{10}{24}$, assuming that $\operatorname{rel}(c_{xy}) = \operatorname{rel}^{\text{init}}(c_{xy})$, and its current constraint tightness is $\frac{9}{12}$.

Universal and *empty* constraints correspond to extreme values of $\operatorname{rel}(c)$. A universal constraint can be safely ignored (but may be introduced for special purposes), whereas an empty constraint can never be satisfied.

DEFINITION 1.18.– *[Universal and Empty Constraints] Let c be a constraint.*

– *c is* universal *iff* $\operatorname{rel}^{\text{init}}(c) = \prod_{x \in \text{scp}(c)} \operatorname{dom}^{\text{init}}(x)$.

– *c is* empty *iff* $\operatorname{rel}^{\text{init}}(c) = \emptyset$.

After domains have been reduced, constraints sometimes seem to be universal or empty; they are said to be *entailed* or *disentailed*:

DEFINITION 1.19.– *[Entailed and Disentailed Constraints] Let c be a constraint.*

– *c is* entailed *iff* $\sup(c) = \operatorname{val}(c)$.

– *c is* disentailed *iff* $\sup(c) = \emptyset$.

As long as no value is restored to any domain, an entailed constraint is guaranteed to be satisfied (provided that at least one value remains in each domain). Similarly, a disentailed constraint is guaranteed to be unsatisfied. An illustration of an entailed constraint is given in Figure 1.5.

1.2. Networks of variables and constraints

Constraint satisfaction was introduced[5] and formalized in the the 1960s [DAV 62, ULL 65, GOL 65, ULL 66] and 1970s [WAL 72, MON 74, GAS 74, WAL 75, ULL 76, BIT 75, MAC 77a, STA 77, ULL 77, FRE 78, MCG 79, GAS 79]. Surprisingly, there are almost as many equivalent definitions of constraint networks (sometimes called constraint satisfaction problems) as papers about the topic. In the following definition, variables and constraints constitute the "interface" of constraint networks.

1.2.1. *Basic definitions*

A structure composed of variables and constraints is called a *constraint network* or, more simply, a network, when the context is unambiguous.

DEFINITION 1.20.– *[Constraint Network] A finite* constraint network P *is composed of a finite set of variables, denoted by* vars(P), *and a finite set of constraints, denoted by* cons(P), *such that* $\forall c \in \mathrm{cons}(P), \mathrm{scp}(c) \subseteq \mathrm{vars}(P)$.

Usually and unless stated otherwise, we will take as given both an initial constraint network denoted by P^{init} and a current constraint network denoted by P. The constraint network P is defined on the same[6] variables and constraints as P^{init}, and is derived from P^{init} by modification (reduction) of domains and/or relations. Informally, P^{init} is the constraint network specified by the user at time origin t_0; this is a formulation of a specific problem for which the user requires a solution. At time t during the solution process, P is the network obtained from P^{init} by application of various transformations. The initial domain of a variable x is $\mathrm{dom}^{\mathrm{init}}(x)$, whereas the current domain of x will be denoted by $\mathrm{dom}^{P}(x)$, or more simply $\mathrm{dom}(x)$ if the context is unambiguous. Similarly, we denote the initial relation associated with a constraint c by $\mathrm{rel}^{\mathrm{init}}(c)$, and the current relation by $\mathrm{rel}^{P}(c)$ or $\mathrm{rel}(c)$. In summary, when necessary we use constraint networks that are time-referential for domains and relations.

In this book, the set vars(P), any subset of vars(P) and consequently the scope of any constraint are totally ordered according to the relation $\lhd$; see Remark 1.2. We assume that $\lhd$ is implicitly given by the sequence of variables in listed sets. For example, for P such that $\mathrm{vars}(P) = \{v, w, x, y, z\}$ and $\mathrm{cons}(P) = \{c_{vwx}, c_{vyz}, c_{wxz}\}$ with $\mathrm{scp}(c_{vwx}) = \{v, w, x\}$, $\mathrm{scp}(c_{vyz}) = \{v, y, z\}$ and $\mathrm{scp}(c_{wxz}) = \{w, x, z\}$, we implicitly assume that $v \lhd w \lhd x \lhd y \lhd z$.

---

5. A good introduction to the emergence of constraint satisfaction is [FRE 06].

6. Two variables or two constraints are the same if they share the same name (identifier).

A *binary constraint network* is a network only involving binary constraints, whereas a *non-binary constraint network* is a network involving at least one non-binary constraint. From now on, unless stated otherwise, we shall only consider constraint networks involving no unary constraints. In the context of finite constraint networks, this is not a real limitation because for every unary constraint c_x such that $\text{scp}(c) = \{x\}$, we can simply replace $\text{dom}^{\text{init}}(x)$ by $\text{dom}^{\text{init}}(x) \cap \text{rel}^{\text{init}}(c_x)$ and discard c_x (since after this operation, c_x is an entailed constraint). This replacement enforces a property called node consistency, which was introduced in [MAC 77a].

EXAMPLE.– P such that

- vars$(P) = \{x, y\}$ with $\text{dom}^{\text{init}}(x) = \text{dom}^{\text{init}}(y) = \{a, b, c\}$, and
- cons$(P) = \{c_x, c_{xy}, c_y, \}$ with $\text{rel}^{\text{init}}(c_x) = \{a, b\}$ and $\text{rel}^{\text{init}}(c_y) = \{b, c\}$

can be transformed into P' such that

- vars$(P') = \{x, y\}$ with $\text{dom}^{\text{init}}(x) = \{a, b\}$ and $\text{dom}^{\text{init}}(y) = \{b, c\}$, and
- cons$(P') = \{c_{xy}\}$.

Another restriction that we impose is the *normalization* of constraint networks. From a formal point of view, it is better to deal with normalized networks because this avoids some form of non-determinism (for example, when recording so-called nogoods) and improves the filtering capabilities of various algorithms.

DEFINITION 1.21.– *[Normalized Constraint Network [APT 03, BES 06]] A constraint network P is said to be* normalized *iff* $\forall c_1 \in \text{cons}(P), \forall c_2 \in \text{cons}(P), c_1 \neq c_2 \Rightarrow \text{scp}(c_1) \neq \text{scp}(c_2)$.

Constraint networks can easily be normalized by merging constraints that share the same scope. More specifically, a non-normalized constraint network P can be normalized as follows. Each pair of constraints c_1 and c_2 such that $\text{scp}(c_1) = \text{scp}(c_2)$ is replaced by a new constraint c_3 such that $\text{scp}(c_3) = \text{scp}(c_1)$ and $\text{rel}(c_3) = \text{rel}(c_1) \cap \text{rel}(c_2)$.

EXAMPLE.– P such that

- vars$(P) = \{x, y\}$ and cons$(P) = \{c_1, c_2\}$,
- scp$(c_1) = \{x, y\}$ and rel$(c_1) = \{(a, a), (a, b), (b, b)\}$, and
- scp$(c_2) = \{x, y\}$ and rel$(c_2) = \{(a, b), (b, a), (b, b)\}$

can be transformed into P' such that

- vars$(P') = \{x, y\}$ and cons$(P') = \{c_3\}$, and
- scp$(c_3) = \{x, y\}$ and rel$(c_3) = \{(a, b), (b, b)\}$.

Such transformation is immediate when constraints are given in extension. For intensional constraints, the predicate expressions can simply be merged with a logical and ($\wedge$).

EXAMPLE.– P such that

– $\text{vars}(P) = \{x, y\}$ and $\text{cons}(P) = \{c_1, c_2\}$,

– $c_1 : x \le y$, and

– $c_2 : x + y < 10$

can be transformed into P' such that

– $\text{vars}(P') = \{x, y\}$ and $\text{cons}(P') = \{c_3\}$, and

– $c_3 : (x \le y) \wedge (x + y < 10)$.

Other cases can be addressed by converting if necessary some intensional constraints into extension.

To summarize, the space of constraint networks that we shall consider is the following.

NOTATION 1.22.– *[$\mathscr{P}$] The set of finite normalized constraint networks with no unary constraints is denoted by $\mathscr{P}$.*

When we want to limit constraints to a unique arity, we use the following space. For example, $\mathscr{P}_2$ represents the set of normalized binary constraint networks.

NOTATION 1.23.– *[$\mathscr{P}_k$] Let k be an integer such that $k \ge 2$. The set of finite normalized constraint networks of $\mathscr{P}$ only involving constraints of arity k is denoted by $\mathscr{P}_k$.*

The following space will also be useful. For $k = 2$, it guarantees that there exists exactly one constraint per pair of variables.

NOTATION 1.24.– *[$\mathscr{P}_{k^*}$] Let k be an integer such that $k \ge 2$. The set of finite normalized constraint networks of $\mathscr{P}_k$ with a k-ary constraint for each k-combination of variables is denoted by $\mathscr{P}_{k^*}$.*

From now on, whenever we refer to a constraint network without any other precision, we consider an element of $\mathscr{P}$.

The *degree* of a variable is a characteristic that may be useful (e.g. when devising variable ordering heuristics).

DEFINITION 1.25.– *[Degree] The* degree *of a variable is the number of constraints involving it. The* dynamic degree *of a variable x is the number of constraints involving x and at least one unfixed variable distinct from x.*

Remember that a variable is unfixed iff its domain is not singleton. Two variables x and y are said to be *neighbors* if there exists a constraint c such that $\{x, y\} \subseteq \mathrm{scp}(c)$. Throughout this book we use the following notation.

NOTATION 1.26.– *[n, e, d and r] For a given constraint network P, we denote by:*

- *n the number of variables,* $n = |\,\mathrm{vars}(P)|$;
- *e the number of constraints,* $e = |\,\mathrm{cons}(P)|$;
- *d the greatest domain size,* $d = \max_{x \in \mathrm{vars}(P)} |\,\mathrm{dom}(x)|$;
- *r the greatest constraint arity,* $r = max_{c \in \mathrm{cons}(P)} |\,\mathrm{scp}(c)|$.

When studying complexities, we shall assume that each variable is not *isolated*, i.e. involved in at least one constraint, which implies that $n \leq er$. For binary constraint networks ($r = 2$), this means that n is $O(e)$.

To simplify discourse in this book, we define *v-values* and *c-values*.

DEFINITION 1.27.– *[v-value]*

- *A v-value is a variable–value pair* (x, a) *where x is a variable and* $a \in \mathrm{dom}^{\mathrm{init}}(x)$.

- *A v-value of a constraint network P is a v-value* (x, a) *such that* $x \in \mathrm{vars}(P)$ *and* $a \in \mathrm{dom}^{P}(x)$.

Using this abbreviation, saying that a v-value (x, a) is removed (or deleted) is equivalent to saying that a is removed from $\mathrm{dom}(x)$. Note that in some (general) contexts, we shall refer to v-values simply as values because these two notions are quite close.

DEFINITION 1.28.– *[c-value]*

- *A c-value is a constraint-variable-value triplet* (c, x, a) *where c is a constraint,* $x \in \mathrm{scp}(c)$ *and* $a \in \mathrm{dom}^{\mathrm{init}}(x)$.

- *A c-value of a constraint network P is a c-value* (c, x, a) *such that* $c \in \mathrm{cons}(P)$ *and* $a \in \mathrm{dom}^{P}(x)$.

Recall that a tuple τ is a support on a constraint c for a v-value (x, a) when $x \in \mathrm{scp}(c)$ and τ is a support on c such that $\tau[x] = a$. In this case, we also say that τ is a *support* for the c-value (c, x, a). Two v-values (x, a) and (y, b) are said to be *compatible* iff either no binary constraint exists between x and y, or $(a, b) \in \mathrm{rel}(c_{xy})$ where c_{xy} is the binary constraint between x and y.

NOTATION 1.29.– *Let P be a constraint network.*

– v-vals(P) *denotes the set of* v-values *of P.*

– c-vals(P) *denotes the set of* c-values *of P.*

Figure 1.6 provides an example.

$$P$$

$$\begin{array}{ll} vars(P) = \{w, x, y, z\} \quad n = 4 & cons(P) = \{c_{wx}, c_{wyz}, c_{xz}\} \quad e = 3 \\ \left.\begin{array}{l} dom(w) = \{a, b\} \\ dom(x) = \{a, b, c\} \\ dom(y) = \{a\} \\ dom(z) = \{a, b, c\} \end{array}\right] d = 3 & \left.\begin{array}{l} scp(c_{wx}) = \{w, x\} \\ scp(c_{wyz}) = \{w, y, z\} \\ scp(c_{xz}) = \{x, z\} \end{array}\right] r = 3 \end{array}$$

v-values of P

$$\begin{array}{l} (w, a) \\ (w, b) \\ (x, a) \\ (x, b) \\ (x, c) \\ (y, a) \\ (z, a) \\ (z, b) \\ (z, c) \end{array}$$

c-values of P

$$\begin{array}{lll} (c_{wx}, w, a) & (c_{wyz}, w, a) & (c_{xz}, x, a) \\ (c_{wx}, w, b) & (c_{wyz}, w, b) & (c_{xz}, x, b) \\ (c_{wx}, x, a) & (c_{wyz}, y, a) & (c_{xz}, x, c) \\ (c_{wx}, x, b) & (c_{wyz}, z, a) & (c_{xz}, z, a) \\ (c_{wx}, x, c) & (c_{wyz}, z, b) & (c_{xz}, z, b) \\ & (c_{wyz}, z, c) & (c_{xz}, z, c) \end{array}$$

Figure 1.6. *A constraint network P involving $n = 4$ variables and $e = 3$ constraints. The greatest domain size is $d = 3$ and the greatest constraint arity is $r = 3$. The set of v-values and c-values of P are listed*

To conclude this introduction to constraint networks, we highlight an important class of constraint networks, wherein variables are Boolean and constraint predicates are logic clauses. Here constraint predicates are expressed as propositional formulae in conjunctive normal form (CNF). For example, the CNF formula:

$$(x \vee y \vee \neg z) \wedge (\neg w \vee \neg x) \wedge (w \vee \neg y \vee z)$$

is defined over four variables w, x, y, z that are Boolean, which means that their initial domains are $\{false, true\}$. This formula is a conjunction (operator $\wedge$) of three clauses. A clause is a disjunction (operator $\vee$) of literals where a literal is either a Boolean variable or its logical negation (operator $\neg$).

Any CNF formula can be directly "encoded" as a CSP instance expressed as a constraint network with the Boolean variables of the formula as variables and the CNF clauses as non-binary constraints of the network. This is called non-binary encoding in [WAL 00]. For our CNF formula above, the constraint network P is such that:

– vars$(P) = \{w, x, y, z\}$ with dom$(w) = \cdots = $ dom$(z) = \{false, true\}$;
– cons$(P) = \{c_{xyz} : x \vee y \vee \neg z, c_{wx} : \neg w \vee \neg x, c_{wyz} : w \vee \neg y \vee z\}$.

1.2.2. Associated (hyper)graphs

It is usual to refer to some properties of the (hyper)graphs that can be associated with any constraint network. Graphs and hypergraphs are formally defined in Appendix A.1.

The *constraint hypergraph*, also called *macro-structure*, associated with a (normalized) constraint network P consists of n vertices corresponding to the variables of P and also e hyperedges corresponding to the constraints of P; the vertices in a hyperedge correspond to the variables in the scope that it represents.

DEFINITION 1.30.– *[Constraint Hypergraph] The* constraint hypergraph *of a constraint network P is the pair (V, E) where $V = $ vars(P) and $E = \{$scp$(c) \mid c \in$ cons$(P)\}$.*

The *primal graph* of a constraint network P is the primal graph of the constraint hypergraph of P. It has n vertices corresponding to the variables of P and one edge for each pair of variables residing in the same constraint scope. For binary constraint networks, the primal graph is identical to the constraint hypergraph. The *dual graph* of a constraint network P is the dual graph of the constraint hypergraph of P. It has e vertices corresponding to the constraints of P and one edge for each pair of constraints sharing at least one variable. Figure 1.7 provides an example of a constraint hypergraph. Figures 1.8 and 1.9 show the primal and dual graphs for this hypergraph.

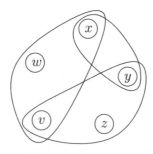

Figure 1.7. *The constraint hypergraph of a constraint network P such that* vars$(P) = \{v, w, x, y, z\}$ *and* cons$(P) = \{c_{vwx}, c_{vyz}, c_{xy}\}$. *The hyperedges represent the scopes of the three constraints in P*

The dual graph of a constraint network can be regarded as the transformation of a non-binary constraint network into a binary one. Such a transformation, called

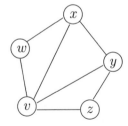

Figure 1.8. *The primal graph of the constraint hypergraph depicted in Figure 1.7. There is an edge between two vertices (variables) in the primal graph when there is a hyperedge (constraint) involving them in the hypergraph*

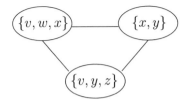

Figure 1.9. *The dual graph of the constraint hypergraph depicted in Figure 1.7. There is an edge between two vertices (constraint scopes) in the dual graph when their intersection is not empty*

dual encoding or dual graph encoding, comes from the relational database community and was introduced for constraint networks in [DEC 89b]. In the dual encoding, the variables are swapped with constraints. Each constraint c of the original non-binary constraint network is represented by a variable called a dual variable. The domain of each dual variable consists of the set of allowed tuples in the original constraint c. A binary constraint between two dual variables ensures that shared initial variables must be given the same values. Other encodings of non-binary constraint networks into binary ones exist (see e.g. [BAC 02a, SAM 05]).

We now introduce the *density* of a constraint network since this is a notion that can be related to (hyper)graphs.

DEFINITION 1.31.– *[Density] Let $P \in \mathscr{P}_k$ be a constraint network (only involving constraints of arity k). The* density *of (the constraint hypergraph associated with) P is equal to $e/\binom{n}{k}$.*

For $k = 2$ (the usual case) the network density is equal to $2e/(n^2 - n)$. For example, for a binary network involving 10 variables and 15 constraints, the density is $30/90 \approx 33\%$.

Finally, the *compatibility hypergraph*, also called *micro-structure* [JÉG 93], associated with a normalized constraint network P contains one vertex per v-value of P and one hyperedge per constraint support. It corresponds to a n-partite hypergraph with one partition for each variable.

DEFINITION 1.32.– *[Compatibility Hypergraph] The* compatibility hypergraph *of a constraint network P, denoted by $\mu(P)$, is the pair (V, E) where:*

- $V = $ v-vals(P);
- $E = \bigcup_{c \in \text{cons}(P)} \{\{(x_1, a_1), \ldots, (x_r, a_r)\} \mid \text{scp}(c) = \{x_1, \ldots, x_r\} \wedge (a_1, \ldots, a_r) \in \text{sup}(c)\}$.

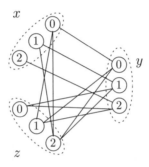

Figure 1.10. *The compatibility graph $\mu(P)$ of the constraint network P such that* vars$(P) = \{x, y, z\}$, *with* dom$(x) = $ dom$(y) = $ dom$(z) = \{0, 1, 2\}$, *and* cons$(P) = \{c_{xy} : x = y, c_{xz} : x < z, c_{yz} : y \neq z\}$

Due to the complexity of managing compatibility hypergraphs, they are usually introduced only for the binary case. Moreover, such graphs are usually given for networks involving tailored constraints. In this case the set of (hyper)edges can be equivalently defined from $\bigcup_{c \in \text{cons}(P)} \text{rel}(c)$. Some authors prefer to handle incompatibility hypergraphs, which differ from compatibility hypergraphs only in that hyperedges correspond to conflicts instead of supports.

An advantage of compatibility hypergraphs is their natural representation of constraints: an edge corresponds to a support. A drawback is that in certain circumstances implicit universal constraints must also be represented, at least in theory. Typically, when compatibility (hyper)graphs are used as a formal tool to make inferences (e.g. see [GAU 97, CHM 03]), this is for binary complete constraint networks, i.e. constraint networks in $\mathscr{P}_{2^*}$. However, in this book, compatibility graphs will be used only for illustrative purposes and implicit universal constraints will not be represented. Instead the reader should assume that, when there is no edge between (values of) two distinct variables, this implicitly signifies that there is a universal constraint between these variables. Figure 1.10 shows an example of a compatibility graph.

1.2.3. *Instantiations and solutions*

Before formally defining solutions to constraint networks, we need to introduce the concept of *instantiation*. To make this intuitive, you can just imagine that instantiations on a constraint network are analogous to paths in a labyrinth; see Figure 1.11. Starting from the entrance, a path through a labyrinth corresponds to a sequence of decisions taken at branch points. An instantiation on a constraint network is a sequence (or rather set) of v-values that corresponds to the assignment of distinct variables. If the current path cannot be extended to find an exit, we are at a dead-end. For an instantiation, we say that the current instantiation is globally inconsistent.

Figure 1.11. *A path in a labyrinth is analogous to an instantiation on a constraint network*

DEFINITION 1.33.– *[Instantiation]*

– *An* instantiation I *of a (potentially empty) set* $X = \{x_1, \ldots, x_k\}$ *of variables is a totally ordered[7] set* $\{(x_1, a_1), \ldots, (x_k, a_k)\}$ *such that* $a_1 \in \text{dom}^{\text{init}}(x_1), \ldots, a_k \in \text{dom}^{\text{init}}(x_k)$; *the value* a_i *with* $1 \leq i \leq k$ *is denoted by* $I[x_i]$ *and the set* X *of variables covered by* I *is denoted by* $\text{vars}(I)$.

– *An instantiation* I *is* valid *iff* $\forall (x, a) \in I, a \in \text{dom}(x)$.

---

7. The total order on variables is naturally extended to instantiations.

– *An instantiation I* on a constraint network P *is an instantiation of a set $X \subseteq$* vars(P); *I is* valid *on P iff $\forall (x, a) \in I, a \in \text{dom}^P(x)$; I is* complete *(on P) if* vars$(I) = $ vars(P), partial *otherwise.*

Sometimes, an instantiation $\{(x_1, a_1), \ldots, (x_k, a_k)\}$ is denoted by $\{x_1 = a_1, \ldots, x_k = a_k\}$, as in the introductory example of this book. Search algorithms usually handle valid instantiations on constraint networks. Often, instantiations are extended over additional variables or restricted over some variables.

DEFINITION 1.34.– *[Extension of Instantiation] Let I and I' be two instantiations. If* vars$(I) \cap$ vars$(I') = \emptyset$ *then $I'' = I \cup I'$ is an instantiation of* vars$(I) \cup$ vars(I'), *called an* extension *of I over* vars(I'), *or similarly, an* extension *of I' over* vars(I).

DEFINITION 1.35.– *[Restriction of Instantiation] Let I be an instantiation and X be a set of variables. $I' = I[X]$ is an instantiation of* vars$(I) \cap X$ *defined as $\{(x, a) \in I \mid x \in X\}$ and called the* restriction *of I over X.*

The extension of an instantiation I over a variable x is simply an extension of I over $\{x\}$. A constraint c is satisfied by an instantiation I iff I provides a value for every variable in scp(c) and the tuple obtained after restricting I over scp(c) is allowed by c.

DEFINITION 1.36.– *[Satisfying Instantiation] Let I be an instantiation.*

– *I covers a constraint c iff* scp$(c) \subseteq$ vars(I).

– *I satisfies a constraint c iff I covers c and the tuple $(a_1, \ldots, a_r)$, such that $I[\text{scp}(c)] = \{(x_1, a_1), \ldots, (x_r, a_r)\}$, is allowed by c.*

We can now introduce an important definition that is central to the development of many properties, called consistencies, which are exploited to reduce the combinatorics of constraint networks.

DEFINITION 1.37.– *[Locally Consistent Instantiation] An instantiation I on a constraint network P is* locally consistent *(on P) iff a) I is valid on P and b) every constraint of P covered by I is satisfied by I. It is* locally inconsistent *otherwise.*

EXAMPLE.– If P is a constraint network such that

– vars$(P) = \{x, y, z\}$ with dom$(x) = $ dom$(y) = $ dom$(z) = \{0, 1, 2\}$, and

– cons$(P) = \{c_{xy} : x = y, c_{xz} : x < z, c_{yz} : y \neq z\}$

then:

– $\{(x, 1)\}$ is a locally consistent instantiation, since there is no constraint covered by it;

– $\{(x,1),(y,0)\}$ is not a locally consistent instantiation, since the constraint c_{xy} covered by it is not satisfied by it ($1 \neq 0$);

– $\{(x,1),(y,1)\}$ is a locally consistent instantiation, since the constraint c_{xy} covered by it is satisfied by it ($1 = 1$);

– $\{(x,1),(y,1),(z,0)\}$ is an extension over z of $\{(x,1),(y,1)\}$ that is not locally consistent, since the constraint c_{xz} is not satisfied by it ($1 \not< 0$);

– $\{(x,1),(y,1),(z,2)\}$ is a complete and locally consistent instantiation, since all variables are covered, and all constraints are satisfied.

Note that $\emptyset$ is always a locally consistent instantiation. When an instantiation is complete and locally consistent, it constitutes a *solution*[8]. This is the case of the last instantiation in the example above.

DEFINITION 1.38.– *[Solution] Let P be a constraint network. A solution of P is a complete instantiation on P that is locally consistent. The set of solutions of P is denoted by* sols(P).

In other words, a solution to a network P is an assignment of values to all the variables such that all the constraints are satisfied. P is said to be *satisfiable* if it admits at least one solution, i.e. if sols$(P) \neq \emptyset$, *unsatisfiable* otherwise. The classical *constraint satisfaction problem* (CSP) is the task of determining whether or not a given constraint network is satisfiable, showing one solution if any. Other tasks, not addressed in this book, may be of interest: computing or counting all solutions, computing an optimal solution according to a given cost function, etc. A *CSP instance* is defined by a constraint network, and solving it means (in this book) finding one solution or instead proving that it is unsatisfiable. In the remainder of this book, we shall indifferently use constraint networks or CSP instances.

Similarly, a CNF formula is satisfiable iff there exists a complete instantiation of the variables of the formula such that each clause evaluates to *true*. Propositional satisfiability (SAT) is the general problem of deciding whether or not a given CNF formula, called a *SAT instance*, is satisfiable. This was the first problem shown to be NP-complete; see Appendix A.2.2 for more information about complexity classes. Clearly, as CSP is a generalization of SAT (see page 55), CSP is NP-hard. Considering that constraint checks are performed in polynomial time, certificates (solutions) can be checked in polynomial time. Consequently, CSP is NP-complete. Note that polynomial encodings (reductions) of CSP to SAT have been proposed; see e.g. [KLE 89, GEN 02a]. In fact, SAT is one of the most studied problems because of its theoretical and practical importance. Encouraged by impressive progress in

---

8. A locally consistent partial instantiation is called a partial solution by some authors.

practical solving of SAT, various applications ranging from formal verification to planning are encoded and solved using SAT.

Equivalent constraint networks are defined on the same variables and represent the same set of solutions.

DEFINITION 1.39.– *[Equivalence] Let P and P′ be two constraint networks such that* vars(P) = vars(P'). *P and P′ are equivalent, or* solution-equivalent, *iff* sols(P) = sols(P').

Note that a CSP instance is trivially unsatisfiable when a domain or a relation is empty. We regard all such instances as equivalent, and we denote by $\perp$ the representative of this implicit equivalence class.

NOTATION 1.40.– *Let P be a constraint network. We write* $P = \perp$ *iff* $\exists x \in$ vars(P) | dom(x) = $\emptyset$ *or* $\exists c \in$ cons(P) | rel(c) = $\emptyset$.

Equivalent constraint networks may differ considerably because, for instance, any unsatisfiable constraint network is equivalent to $\perp$.

To find solutions in practice we often handle supports. Recall that a support on a constraint is a tuple that is both valid (i.e. can be built from current domains) and allowed by this constraint (i.e. belongs to the associated relation). Recall also that a solution is a complete instantiation that is locally consistent. Therefore the restriction of a solution to the scope of a constraint c is a support on c.

The counterpart of locally consistent instantiation is *globally inconsistent instantiation*, which is instantiation doomed to failure because it cannot possibly lead to any solution. A globally inconsistent instantiation is also known as a *nogood*. Efficiently detecting, recording and exploiting nogoods is one of the keys to success in solving CSP instances.

DEFINITION 1.41.– *[Globally Inconsistent Instantiation] An instantiation I on a constraint network P is* globally inconsistent *iff it cannot be extended to a solution of P. It is* globally consistent *otherwise*.

REMARK 1.42.– *[Nogood] A globally inconsistent instantiation is also called a* nogood.

Obviously, an instantiation that is not locally consistent is necessarily globally inconsistent. However, the reverse is not true: a globally inconsistent instantiation is not necessarily locally inconsistent.

EXAMPLE.– Considering again the network P described above, we have:

- $\{(x, 1), (y, 0)\}$ is globally inconsistent since it is locally inconsistent;
- $\{(x, 1), (y, 1)\}$ is globally consistent since it can be extended to a solution;
- $\{(y, 2), (z, 1)\}$ is globally inconsistent while being locally consistent;
- $\{(x, 2)\}$ is also globally inconsistent while being trivially locally consistent.

It is sometimes helpful to employ a homogeneous representation of a constraint network, wherein domains and also constraints are replaced by nogoods. The *nogood representation* of a constraint network is a set of nogoods, one for every value removed from the initial domain of a variable and one for every tuple disallowed by a constraint.

DEFINITION 1.43.– *[Nogood Representation]*

– *The nogood representation* $\widetilde{x}$ *of a variable* x *is the set of instantiations* $\{\{(x, a)\} \mid a \in \mathrm{dom}^{\mathrm{init}}(x) \setminus \mathrm{dom}(x)\}$.

– *The nogood representation* $\widetilde{c}$ *of a constraint* c, *with* $\mathrm{scp}(c) = \{x_1, \ldots, x_r\}$, *is the set of instantiations* $\{\{(x_1, a_1), \ldots, (x_r, a_r)\} \mid (a_1, \ldots, a_r) \in \prod_{x \in \mathrm{scp}(c)} \mathrm{dom}^{\mathrm{init}}(x) \setminus \mathrm{rel}(c)\}$.

– *The nogood representation* $\widetilde{P}$ *of a constraint network* P *is the set of instantiations*

$$\left(\bigcup_{x \in \mathrm{vars}(P)} \widetilde{x} \right) \cup \left(\bigcup_{c \in \mathrm{cons}(P)} \widetilde{c} \right).$$

Instantiations in $\widetilde{P}$ are *explicit nogoods* of P (recorded through domains and constraints). Figure 1.12 provides an illustration. Here, we have a constraint network P composed of two variables x and y, with $\mathrm{dom}(x) = \{a_2, a_3\}$ and $\mathrm{dom}(y) = \{b_1\}$, and a binary constraint c_{xy} with $\mathrm{rel}(c_{xy}) = \{(a_1, b_1), (a_1, b_2), (a_2, b_1), (a_2, b_2), (a_3, b_3)\}$. Initially, we had $\mathrm{dom}^{\mathrm{init}}(x) = \{a_1, a_2, a_3\}, \mathrm{dom}^{\mathrm{init}}(y) = \{b_1, b_2, b_3\}$ and $\mathrm{rel}^{\mathrm{init}}(c_{xy}) = \mathrm{rel}(c_{xy}) \cup \{(a_3, b_2)\}$. The nogood representations of x, y, c_{xy} and P are given.

Such nogood representations will be useful later when studying closure properties of consistencies. Notice that when a nogood is larger than an another one, it is said to be *subsumed*; this will be developed in section 1.4.2. For example, $\{(x, a_2), (y, b_3)\}$ is subsumed by $\{(y, b_3)\}$. Intuitively, a nogood that is subsumed is not relevant as it is less general than (at least) another one, and two constraint networks are *nogood-equivalent* (a related definition is given in [BES 06]) when they have the same canonical form, i.e. represent exactly the same set of "unsubsumed" nogoods. Figure 1.12 shows the canonical nogood representation of a constraint network.

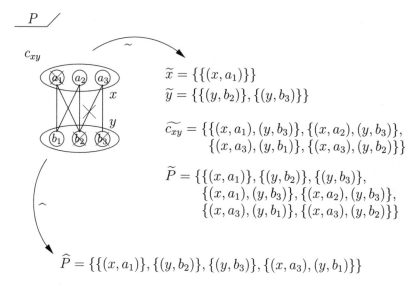

$$\widetilde{x} = \{\{(x, a_1)\}\}$$

$$\widetilde{y} = \{\{(y, b_2)\}, \{(y, b_3)\}\}$$

$$\widetilde{c_{xy}} = \{\{(x, a_1), (y, b_3)\}, \{(x, a_2), (y, b_3)\},$$
$$\{(x, a_3), (y, b_1)\}, \{(x, a_3), (y, b_2)\}\}$$

$$\widetilde{P} = \{\{(x, a_1)\}, \{(y, b_2)\}, \{(y, b_3)\},$$
$$\{(x, a_1), (y, b_3)\}, \{(x, a_2), (y, b_3)\},$$
$$\{(x, a_3), (y, b_1)\}, \{(x, a_3), (y, b_2)\}\}$$

$$\widehat{P} = \{\{(x, a_1)\}, \{(y, b_2)\}, \{(y, b_3)\}, \{(x, a_3), (y, b_1)\}\}$$

Figure 1.12. *The nogood representation $\widetilde{P}$ and canonical nogood representation $\widehat{P}$ of a constraint network P. $\widehat{P}$ is built from $\widetilde{P}$ by discarding subsumed nogoods*

DEFINITION 1.44.– *[Canonical Nogood Representation] The* canonical nogood representation $\widehat{P}$ *of a constraint network P is the set* $\{I \in \widetilde{P} \mid J \in \widetilde{P} \Rightarrow J \not\subset I\}$.

DEFINITION 1.45.– *[Nogood-equivalence] Let P and P' be two constraint networks such that* vars$(P) =$ vars(P'). *P and P' are* nogood-equivalent *iff* $\widehat{P} = \widehat{P'}$.

We are often interested in constraint networks that result from the instantiation of some variables:

NOTATION 1.46.– *[P|$_I$] Let P be a constraint network and I be a valid instantiation on P. P|$_I$ denotes the constraint network obtained from P by restricting, for each value (x, a) in I, the domain of x to $\{a\}$.*

If $P' = P|_I$ and $(x, a) \in I$, then we have $\text{dom}^{P'}(x) = \{a\}$. Notice that I is a nogood of P iff $P|_I$ is unsatisfiable.

It will also be useful to build *sub-networks* by discarding some variables and/or constraints.

DEFINITION 1.47.– *[Sub-network] Let P be a constraint network. A sub-network of P is a constraint network obtained from P by removing some variables of P and some constraints of P.*

By definition, a sub-network P' of P is such that $\forall c \in \text{cons}(P'), \text{scp}(c) \subseteq \text{vars}(P')$ since P' is a constraint network. Also, the state of variables and constraints is unchanged: we have $\forall x \in \text{vars}(P'), \text{dom}^{P'}(x) = \text{dom}^P(x)$ and $\forall c \in \text{cons}(P'), \text{rel}^{P'}(c) = \text{rel}^P(c)$. Figure 1.13 is an illustration of a sub-network.

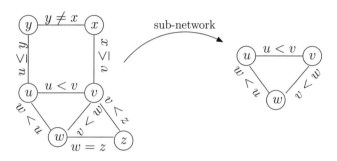

Figure 1.13. *A constraint network P and a sub-network P' of P*

1.3. Examples of constraint networks

We now give several examples of problems that can easily be represented using the formalism of constraint networks. Both for simplicity and for entertainment, all these problems correspond to logic puzzles. Specifically, these are the queens problem, the crossword problem, the Sudoku problem and the edge-matching puzzle.

1.3.1. *Queens problem*

The classical queens problem is easy to understand and illustrates the three main forms of constraints: extensional, intensional and global. The problem can be stated as follows: can we put eight queens on a chessboard such that no two queens attack each other? Two queens attack each other iff they belong to the same row, the same column or the same diagonal. Note that each queen must necessarily be in a different column, as in Figure 1.14. By considering boards of various size, the problem can be generalized as follows: can we put n queens on a board of size $n \times n$ such that no two queens attack each other?

We shall consider several representation models that only differ in terms of constraints. For all these models, there is one variable per queen (and column), and the values are row numbers. If the ith variable x_i is assigned the value j, it means that the ith queen is put in the square at the intersection of the ith column and the jth row. For the n-queens instance, we have a constraint network P such that $\text{vars}(P) = \{x_1, \ldots, x_n\}$ with $\text{dom}(x_i) = \{1, \ldots, n\}, \forall i \in 1..n$.

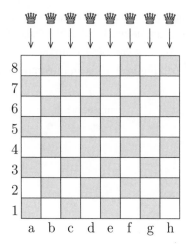

Figure 1.14. *The 8-queens instance: eight queens must be put on a chessboard such that no two queens attack each other*

As a tentative first model, we might impose a constraint to guarantee that no two queens are put on the same row, and another constraint to guarantee that no two queens are put on the same diagonal. Consequently, we have $\mathrm{cons}(P) = \{c_{ij} : x_i \neq x_j \mid i \in 1..n, j \in 1..n, i < j\} \cup \{c'_{ij} : |i - j| \neq |x_i - x_j| \mid i \in 1..n, j \in 1..n, i < j\}$. For example, for the 3-queens instance[9], we obtain $\mathrm{vars}(P) = \{x_1, x_2, x_3\}$ with $\mathrm{dom}(x_1) = \mathrm{dom}(x_2) = \mathrm{dom}(x_3) = \{1, 2, 3\}$ and $\mathrm{cons}(P)$ that contains:

$$c_{12} : x_1 \neq x_2 \qquad\qquad c'_{12} : |x_1 - x_2| \neq 1$$
$$c_{13} : x_1 \neq x_3 \qquad\qquad c'_{13} : |x_1 - x_3| \neq 2$$
$$c_{23} : x_2 \neq x_3 \qquad\qquad c'_{23} : |x_2 - x_3| \neq 1$$

This instance is not normalized since there are two distinct constraints on one pair of variables. This can cause inefficiency in a process that seeks a solution. We know that a v-value (x, a) is globally inconsistent (and can therefore be removed) if there exists a constraint c that does not support (x, a). In the 3-queens instance we can see that both c_{12} and c'_{12} independently support $(x_1, 2)$. However, the respective sets of strict supports, $\{1, 3\}$ and $\{2\}$, are disjoint. Consequently there is no support for $(x_1, 2)$ when these two constraints are merged. The second model is obtained by normalizing networks. For the normalized 3-queens instance, $\mathrm{cons}(P)$ contains:

---

9. This is a quite elementary (unsatisfiable) instance, but it is sufficient for our purpose.

$$c_{12}'' : x_1 \neq x_2 \wedge |x_1 - x_2| \neq 1$$
$$c_{13}'' : x_1 \neq x_3 \wedge |x_1 - x_3| \neq 2$$
$$c_{23}'' : x_2 \neq x_3 \wedge |x_2 - x_3| \neq 1$$

Here the constraint semantics are more complex, so we may less easily see how to apply specialized algorithms to filter the search space by removing values detected as locally inconsistent. Besides, it is known that filtering is more efficient with a global constraint allDifferent than with a clique[10] of binary inequation constraints (constraints of the form $x \neq y$). In an alternative formulation, $\mathrm{cons}(P)$ contains:

allDifferent(x_1, x_2, x_3)
$$c_{12}' : |x_1 - x_2| \neq 1$$
$$c_{13}' : |x_1 - x_3| \neq 2$$
$$c_{23}' : |x_2 - x_3| \neq 1$$

Yet another formulation converts the merged constraints into extension. In this case, for the 3-queens instance, $\mathrm{cons}(P)$ contains:

c_{12}''' such that $table[c_{12}'''] = \{(1,3),(3,1)\}$
c_{13}''' such that $table[c_{13}'''] = \{(1,2),(2,1),(2,3),(3,2)\}$
c_{23}''' such that $table[c_{23}'''] = \{(1,3),(3,1)\}$

This simple problem illustrates the importance of *modeling* in constraint programming (CP). Unluckily, modeling often demands a certain amount of expertise from the user. Our ambition in this book is to emphasize some techniques that render constraint solvers more robust, thus (partially) liberating the user from significant prerequisites. A bad model for the n-queens problem would allow each queen to be put on any square of the board, thus introducing variables whose domain contains n^2 values instead of n. The search space would be far larger. However, it is possible to translate this bad model automatically into one where domains only contain n values by exploiting a reformulation technique based on a property called interchangeability [FRE 97].

On the other hand, generating a constraint allDifferent on each set (clique) X of variables such that irreflexivity is guaranteed on each pair $\{x, y\}$ of variables of X (that is, at least $x \neq y$ is guaranteed) can also be envisioned as an automatic process[11]. It would lead here, for the n-queens problem, to a single additional constraint allDifferent involving all n variables, which could achieve better pruning of the search space. Automatically breaking variable and/or value symmetries is

---

10. See section A.1.2.

11. To the best of our knowledge, the constraint solvers Abscon, Choco and Mistral, which participated in the 2008 constraint solver competition, all include such a mechanism.

another important issue that may be helpful, as discussed in Chapter 12. Finally, automatically detecting constraints of similar scope, merging them and potentially converting them into extension (if the solver is equipped with an efficient filtering procedure for extensional constraints) is not particularly complex. To summarize, even if the user provides the constraint solver with badly modeled instances, the solver can automatically enrich (reformulate) a bad model to make the resolution more efficient.

Finally, we provide examples illustrating notions introduced earlier with the 8-queens instance. We employ the first model introduced above and denote the variables by $x_a, \ldots, x_h$ to clarify the correspondence with columns. Figure 1.15 shows one

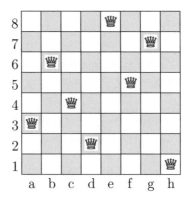

Figure 1.15. *One solution for the 8-queens instance. This is the complete instantiation* $\{(x_a, 3), (x_b, 6), (x_c, 4), (x_d, 2), (x_e, 8), (x_f, 5), (x_g, 7), (x_h, 1)\}$

solution to the 8-queens instance. A locally inconsistent instantiation is shown in Figure 1.16, and a globally inconsistent one is shown in Figure 1.17.

1.3.2. *Crossword problem*

A crossword is a word puzzle that normally takes the form of a square or rectangular grid of black and white squares. Playing crosswords is a very popular activity. The well-known goal is to fill the white squares with letters, forming words suggested by clues. We now adopt a totally different viewpoint: we do not wish to solve crosswords but instead to conceive them.

Conceiving a crossword puzzle requires two things: a grid and a dictionary. Indeed, given a grid, one can try to fill it up using words contained in the dictionary, as in Figures 1.18 and 1.19. Let us consider a simple and natural model for this problem (the one identified as m1 in [BEA 01]). First, we associate a variable with

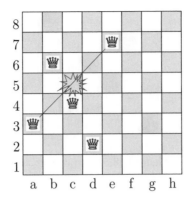

Figure 1.16. *The instantiation* $\{(x_a, 3), (x_b, 6), (x_c, 4), (x_d, 2), (x_e, 7)\}$ *is not locally consistent since the binary constraint* $|x_a - x_e| \neq 4$ *covered by it is not satisfied*

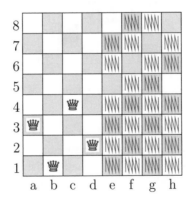

Figure 1.17. *The instantiation* $\{(x_a, 3), (x_b, 1), (x_c, 4), (x_d, 2)\}$ *is globally inconsistent (a nogood). By discarding positions that cannot be occupied without violating a constraint, one can indeed check that there are no more possibilities to put four additional queens on the chessboard. This is this kind of filtering that is performed by the algorithm called forward checking (presented later)*

each white square of the grid; the domain of a variable consists of the 26 letters of the Latin alphabet. For any maximal sequence of adjacent white squares in the grid, we introduce a constraint involving the variables associated with these squares such that the values assigned to these variables correspond to a word in the dictionary. Such a constraint is extensionally defined. Potentially (as in model m1), we introduce additional constraints to ensure that the same word does not appear more than once on the grid.

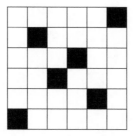

Figure 1.18. *A crossword grid*

Figure 1.19. *A solution to the crossword grid of Figure 1.18. It has been obtained with the dictionary "words"*

For example, assuming that we have three variables x, y and z corresponding to a maximal sequence of three adjacent white squares in the grid, we have an extensional constraint c_{xyz} such that $table[c_{xyz}] = \text{rel}(c_{xyz}) = \{(a,c,e),(a,i,d),\ldots,(z,o,o)\}$ contains tuples corresponding to all 3-length words in the given dictionary. Independently of any constraint, we have $\text{dom}^{init}(x) = \text{dom}^{init}(y) = \text{dom}^{init}(z) = \{a,b,\ldots,z\}$. The reader interested in this problem can consult e.g. [GIN 90, BEA 01, SAM 05, KAT 05, ULL 07, LEC 08a, ANB 08].

1.3.3. *Sudoku problem*

A Sudoku player aims to fill, using numbers from 1 to 9, a 9×9 grid so that the values are pairwise different in each column, in each row, and in each 3×3 (major) block. Sudoku commences with a partially filled grid, for example as in Figure 1.21, where the major blocks are demarcated by bold lines.

Solving a Sudoku grid is not difficult at all when a constraint solver is used, but people enjoy playing Sudoku without a computer. Techniques from constraint programming may help to explain how players reason, and also to measure the

S	A	C	C	A	G	E	N	T
A	E	R	O	L	O	G	I	E
C	R	A	I	N	D	R	A	S
C	O	I	T	E	R	A	I	T
A	L	N	E	L	O	I	S	E
G	O	D	R	O	N	N	E	R
E	G	R	A	I	N	E	R	A
N	I	A	I	S	E	R	A	I
T	E	S	T	E	R	A	I	S

Figure 1.20. *A symmetric French solution to the blank crossword grid* 9×9 *obtained by S. Tabary and the author, and published at http://pagesperso-orange.fr/ledefi*

	4							
5	3	9			1		6	
		1			2		5	
4		7	2		9			6
		6				5		
8			6		3	1		7
	8		7			2		
	6		3			4	1	8
							7	

Figure 1.21. *A Sudoku grid*

difficulty of Sudoku grids [SIM 05, LAB 06]. We now briefly introduce a CSP model that represents instances of this game. Modeling Sudoku illustrates the simplicity and declarativity of the constraint satisfaction approach.

To keep things simple, let us assume that we have a Sudoku grid that is is not filled at all, i.e. we have a blank grid. Then, the problem of filling this basic grid can be represented by the following constraint network P:

– $\text{vars}(P) = \{x_{1,1}, x_{1,2}, \ldots, x_{9,9}\}$ with $\text{dom}(x_{i,j}) = \{1, 2, \ldots, 9\}$ $\forall i, j \in 1..9$;

– $\text{cons}(P) = \{\text{allDifferent}(x_{i,1}, x_{i,2}, \ldots, x_{i,9}) \mid i \in 1..9\}$
$\cup \{\text{allDifferent}(x_{1,j}, x_{2,j}, \ldots, x_{9,j}) \mid j \in 1..9\}$
$\cup \{\text{allDifferent}(x_{v+i,h+j} \mid i \in 1..3, j \in 1..3) \mid v \in \{0, 3, 6\}, h \in \{0, 3, 6\}\}$.

2	4	8	5	7	6	9	3	1
5	3	9	4	8	1	7	6	2
6	7	1	9	3	2	8	5	4
4	1	7	2	5	9	3	8	6
3	2	6	8	1	7	5	4	9
8	9	5	6	4	3	1	2	7
1	8	3	7	6	4	2	9	5
7	6	2	3	9	5	4	1	8
9	5	4	1	2	8	6	7	3

Figure 1.22. *A solution to the Sudoku grid from Figure 1.21*

where $x_{i,j}$ is the variable associated with the square of the grid located at the intersection of row i and column j. The set of constraints only contains allDifferent constraints and can be divided into three subsets that correspond to rows, columns and blocks. It is easy to adapt this model to any partially filled grid since it suffices to assign appropriate values to some variables initially. A solution to the constraint network is of course a solution to the Sudoku problem. Figure 1.22 shows an example of a solution. Further information about the theory behind Sudoku, its origins, and its relationships with constraint programming can be found in [JUS 07].

1.3.4. *Edge-matching puzzles*

An edge-matching puzzle is a logic puzzle where a set of pieces whose edges are distinguished with colors or patterns must be assembled on a board in such a way that the edges of adjacent pieces match. Sometimes, pieces have four sides as in the puzzle depicted in Figure 1.23. Framed puzzles additionally present a special color (or pattern) that must necessarily be put on the outside border of the puzzle; the black color plays this role in our illustration. Figure 1.24 shows a solution to this framed edge-matching puzzle.

We now consider an instance of this problem in which pieces are four-sided, a frame is present, and the size of the board is $k \times k$. With $k \times k$ pieces numbered from 1 to k^2, a possible model is as follows. With each square of the board at the intersection of row i and column j ($1 \le i \le k, 1 \le j \le k$), we associate two variables denoted by p_{ij} and r_{ij}. The value of the variable p_{ij} indicates which piece must be put in the square at location (i, j) and r_{ij} indicates which rotation must be applied. You might think that the domain $\text{dom}(p_{ij})$ of each variable p_{ij} is initially the set $\{1, 2, \ldots, k^2\}$ composed of k^2 values, one per piece. However, in order to guarantee

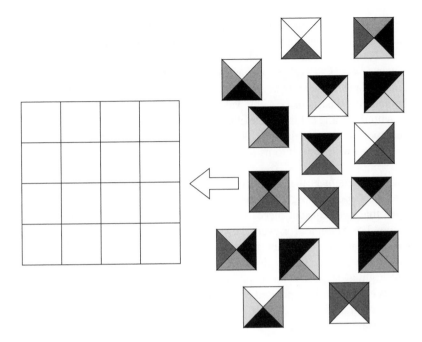

Figure 1.23. *A framed edge-matching puzzle*

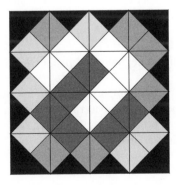

Figure 1.24. *The solution to the edge-matching puzzle from Figure 1.23*

the presence of a frame, the domains of p_{00}, p_{0k}, p_{k0} and p_{kk} must only contain four values. Indeed, such variables represent the four corners of the frame and only four pieces are compatible (have two sides with the frame color). Similarly, we can reduce the domain of $4 \times (k-2)$ other p_{ij} variables to $4 \times (k-2)$ values since this is exactly the number of pieces having one side with the frame color. For the remaining variables p_{ij}, the domain consists of $(k-1)^2$ values since this is the number of pieces having no side with the frame color. On the other hand, the domain $\text{dom}(r_{ij})$ of each variable r_{ij} is composed of four values $\{0, 90, 180, 270\}$ that represent the possible rotations of the piece p_{ij} with respect to its initial position.

A first constraint is that each piece must be selected only once. This is easily guaranteed by applying a global constraint allDifferent involving all p_{ij} variables. To guarantee that two adjacent pieces have edges that correspond, we need quaternary constraints. For example, for every $1 \leq i \leq k$ and every $1 \leq j \leq k-1$, we have a horizontal matching constraint involving p_{ij}, p_{ij+i}, r_{ij} and r_{ij+1}. This constraint checks that the left side of the piece p_{ij} after considering its rotation r_{ij} must match with the right side of the piece p_{ij+1} after considering its rotation r_{ij+1}. Such constraints can be easily expressed extensionally. Of course, we apply similar vertical matching constraints. Furthermore, we apply binary constraints to ensure that the frame is present.

Edge-matching puzzles are NP-complete problems and are therefore challenging benchmarks for both the SAT and CSP communities [ANS 08]. Currently, the most famous edge-matching puzzle is undoubtedly Eternity II. Indeed, a \$2 million prize is offered to the first person who succeeds in completing the 256-piece puzzle. After the first scrutiny date in December 2008, organizers are still searching for a winner. Eternity II is the follow up to Eternity I, which captured the imagination of thousands of people in the UK when a check for £1 million was handed over to a student who successfully solved the puzzle 18 months after launch.

1.4. Partial orders, decisions, nogoods and properties

This section introduces several important definitions and concepts that are useful in the remainder of this book. They concern partial orders on constraint networks, decisions taken by inference procedures or by search, generalized forms of nogoods and properties on values and variables.

1.4.1. *Partial orders*

To relate constraint networks, we introduce some partial orders. When two constraint networks P and P' are such that $\text{vars}(P) = \text{vars}(P')$ (resp. $\text{cons}(P) = \text{cons}(P')$), this implies that P and P' are defined on the same set of variables (resp.

the same set of constraints). Of course, the states of variables (resp. constraints) in both networks may differ substantially.

DEFINITION 1.48.– *[Partial Order $\preceq_d$] Let P and P' be two constraint networks such that* $\mathrm{vars}(P) = \mathrm{vars}(P')$ *and* $\mathrm{cons}(P) = \mathrm{cons}(P')$.

– $P' \preceq_d P$ *iff* $\forall x \in \mathrm{vars}(P)$, $\mathrm{dom}^{P'}(x) \subseteq \mathrm{dom}^P(x)$ *and* $\forall c \in \mathrm{cons}(P)$, $\mathrm{rel}^{P'}(c) = \mathrm{rel}^P(c)$.

– $P' \prec_d P$ *iff* $P' \preceq_d P$ *and* $\exists x \in \mathrm{vars}(P) \mid \mathrm{dom}^{P'}(x) \subset \mathrm{dom}^P(x)$.

DEFINITION 1.49.– *[Partial Order $\preceq_r$] Let P and P' be two constraint networks such that* $\mathrm{vars}(P) = \mathrm{vars}(P')$ *and* $\mathrm{cons}(P) = \mathrm{cons}(P')$.

– $P' \preceq_r P$ *iff* $\forall x \in \mathrm{vars}(P)$, $\mathrm{dom}^{P'}(x) = \mathrm{dom}^P(x)$, *and* $\forall c \in \mathrm{cons}(P)$, $\mathrm{rel}^{P'}(c) \subseteq \mathrm{rel}^P(c)$.

– $P' \prec_r P$ *iff* $P' \preceq_r P$ *and* $\exists c \in \mathrm{cons}(P) \mid \mathrm{rel}^{P'}(c) \subset \mathrm{rel}^P(c)$.

$P' \prec_d P$ means that P' can be obtained from P by removing some values from domains while keeping intact relations, whereas $P' \prec_r P$ means that P' can be obtained from P by removing some allowed tuples from relations while keeping intact domains. Clearly, $\preceq_d$ and $\preceq_r$ are partial orders since these relations are reflexive, anti-symmetric and transitive; see Appendix A.1. In other words, $(\mathscr{P}, \preceq_d)$ and $(\mathscr{P}, \preceq_r)$ are partially ordered sets (posets).

These partial orders may seem quite restrictive since networks must necessarily be defined on the same sets of variables and constraints. However, they are adapted to so-called domain-filtering and relation-filtering consistencies[12] that are prominent in the literature and are presented in Chapter 3. Besides, these two partial orders can be generalized when considering nogood representations as follows:

DEFINITION 1.50.– *[Partial Order $\preceq$] Let P and P' be two constraint networks such that* $\mathrm{vars}(P) = \mathrm{vars}(P')$.

– $P' \preceq P$ *iff* $\widetilde{P'} \supseteq \widetilde{P}$.

– $P' \prec P$ *iff* $\widetilde{P'} \supset \widetilde{P}$.

---

12. Even path consistency can be considered as relation-filtering, provided that the networks are completed with universal binary constraints.

Clearly, $(\mathscr{P}, \preceq)$ is a poset. It allows us not to keep the same set of constraints when comparing networks. This new partial order generalizes $\preceq_d$ and $\preceq_r$ as shown by the following proposition.

PROPOSITION 1.51.– *Let P and P' be two constraint networks. If $P' \preceq_d P$ or $P' \preceq_r P$ then $P' \preceq P$.*

An illustration of the three introduced partial orders is given in Figure 1.25.

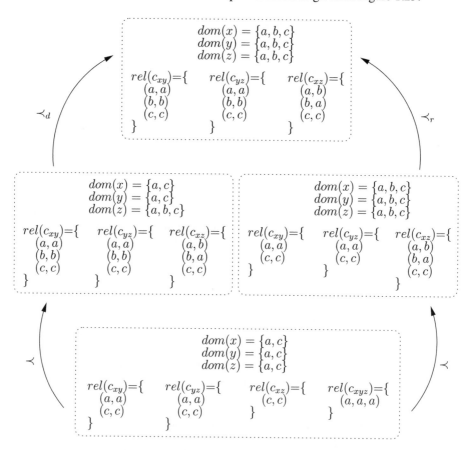

Figure 1.25. *Illustration of partial orders $\preceq_d$, $\preceq_r$ and $\preceq$. A constraint network is represented inside each dotted rectangle (variables and constraints are implicitly given by their associated domains and relations)*

Note that we can further generalize this last partial order by considering canonical nogood representations. The relation $\overset{\frown}{\preceq}$ is defined as follows: $P' \overset{\frown}{\preceq} P$ iff vars$(P) =$

vars(P') and $\widehat{P'} \supseteq \widehat{P}$. Clearly, we can easily build two distinct constraint networks P and P' such that $P' \stackrel{\sim}{\supseteq} P$ and $P \stackrel{\sim}{\supseteq} P'$. It suffices that $\widehat{P'} = \widehat{P}$ but $\widetilde{P'} \neq \widetilde{P}$, meaning that P and P' differ by subsumed nogoods. In other words, $\stackrel{\sim}{\supseteq}$ is a preorder (related to the one defined on page 33 in [BES 06]) but not a partial order because the relation is not antisymmetric. Nevertheless, using this relation, it is possible to construct a partial order on the quotient set of $\mathscr{P}$ by the nogood-equivalence relation introduced in Definition 1.45.

As explained previously, constraint networks are normalized and unary constraints are invisible after they have been applied to initial domains. There is therefore only one manner to discard (or remove) an instantiation from a given constraint network, or equivalently to "record" a new explicit nogood in a constraint network. A set of variables together with a set of nogoods determines a unique constraint network involving no universal constraints. To simplify the definition, but without any loss of generality, we assume that neither P nor $P \setminus I$ contains any universal constraint.

DEFINITION 1.52.– $[P \setminus I]$ *Let P a constraint network, and I be an instantiation on P. $P \setminus I$ denotes the constraint network P' such that* vars(P') = vars(P) *and* $\widetilde{P'} = \widetilde{P} \cup \{I\}$.

$P \setminus I$ is an operation that retracts I from P. Such an operation is likely to be performed when I has just been identified as a nogood (although this is not absolutely necessary). It can be seen as an operation that builds a new constraint network from P and I, not necessarily with the same set of constraints. Such an operation will be useful for reasoning on the theoretical impact of consistencies, as in Chapter 3. Let us show how P' is built. If $I \in \widetilde{P}$, of course we have $P' = P \setminus I = P$: this means that the instantiation I was already an explicit nogood of P. The interesting case is when $I \notin \widetilde{P}$. If I corresponds to a value a for a variable x, i.e. $I = \{(x,a)\}$, it suffices to remove a from dom(x). If I corresponds to a tuple allowed by a constraint c of P, it suffices to remove this tuple from rel(c). Otherwise, we must introduce a new constraint whose associated relation contains all possible tuples (built from initial domains) except the one that corresponds to the instantiation.

EXAMPLE.– If x, y and z are three variables whose initial domain is $\{a, b\}$, and if P is a constraint network such that

- vars$(P) = \{x, y, z\}$ with dom(x) = dom(y) = dom(z) = $\{a, b\}$, and
- cons$(P) = \{c_{xy}, c_{xz}\}$ with rel$(c_{xy}) = \{(a,a),(b,b)\}$ and rel$(c_{xz}) = \{(b,a)\}$

then $P' = P \setminus \{(x,a)\} \setminus \{(x,a),(y,a)\} \setminus \{(y,a),(z,a)\}$ is the network such that

- vars$(P) = \{x, y, z\}$ with dom$(x) = \{b\}$ and dom(y) = dom(z) = $\{a, b\}$, and
- cons$(P) = \{c_{xy}, c_{xz}, c_{yz}\}$ with rel$(c_{xy}) = \{(b,b)\}$, rel$(c_{xz}) = \{(b,a)\}$ and rel$(c_{yz}) = \{(a,b),(b,a),(b,b)\}$.

Here, we have successfully discarded three arbitrary instantiations.

1.4.2. *Decisions and nogoods*

In order to be able to define some properties (e.g. singleton arc consistency in Chapter 6) and a generalization of nogoods, we introduce *decisions*:

DEFINITION 1.53.– *[Positive and Negative Decision] A* positive decision δ *is a restriction on a variable* x *of the form* $x = a$, *whereas a* negative decision *is a restriction of the form* $x \neq a$, *where* $a \in \mathrm{dom}^{\mathrm{init}}(x)$. *A decision* δ *on a constraint network* P *is a positive or negative decision involving a pair* (x, a) *such that* $x \in \mathrm{vars}(P)$; δ *is* valid *on* P *iff* $a \in \mathrm{dom}^P(x)$.

A (valid) positive decision is a *variable assignment* and a (valid) negative decision a *value refutation*. Of course, $\neg(x = a)$ is equivalent to $x \neq a$ and $\neg(x \neq a)$ is equivalent to $x = a$. Hereafter, *decision* alone means either a positive or a negative decision. When decisions are taken on a network, we obtain a new network defined as follows:

DEFINITION 1.54.– *[P|$_\Delta$] Let P be a constraint network and Δ be a set of decisions on P. P|$_\Delta$ is the network obtained (derived) from P such that, for each positive decision* $x = a \in \Delta$, *each value* $b \in \mathrm{dom}(x)$ *with* $b \neq a$ *is removed from* $\mathrm{dom}(x)$, *and, for each negative decision* $x \neq a \in \Delta$, *a is removed from* $\mathrm{dom}(x)$.

In other words, $P|_\Delta$ is the greatest network $P' \in \mathscr{P}$ such that $P' \preceq_d P$ and P' entails[13] Δ. For any set Δ of decisions, $\mathrm{vars}(\Delta)$ denotes the set of variables occurring in decisions of Δ. For convenience, $P|_{\{x=a\}}$ and $P|_{\{x \neq a\}}$ will be simply denoted by $P|_{x=a}$ and $P|_{x \neq a}$, respectively. Figure 1.26 provides an illustration.

Not all sets of decisions are well-formed; those that systematically lead to failure are usually not relevant.

DEFINITION 1.55.– *[Well-formed Set of Decisions] A set Δ of decisions is said to be well-formed iff there exists at least one constraint network P such that* $\mathrm{vars}(P) = \mathrm{vars}(\Delta)$ *and* $P|_\Delta \neq \bot$.

Intuitively, when a set of decisions is not well-formed, it means that a domain wipe-out (i.e. an empty domain) is unavoidable. If Δ only involves positive decisions, then Δ is well-formed iff no two decisions in Δ involve the same variable. For example,

---

13. This is formalized by Definition 1.60.

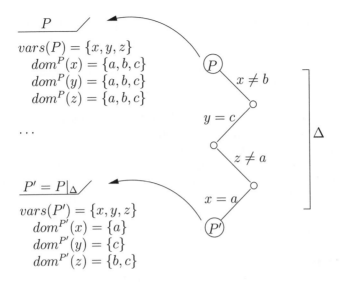

$$vars(P) = \{x, y, z\}$$
$$dom^P(x) = \{a, b, c\}$$
$$dom^P(y) = \{a, b, c\}$$
$$dom^P(z) = \{a, b, c\}$$

$$P' = P|_\Delta$$
$$vars(P') = \{x, y, z\}$$
$$dom^{P'}(x) = \{a\}$$
$$dom^{P'}(y) = \{c\}$$
$$dom^{P'}(z) = \{b, c\}$$

Figure 1.26. *The constraint network $P' = P|_\Delta \preceq_d P$ obtained from P after taking into account the decisions in $\Delta = \{x \neq b, y = c, z \neq a, x = a\}$; we have* vars$(\Delta) = \{x, y, z\}$. *No consistency is enforced*

$\{x = a, x = b\}$ is clearly badly formed. Moreover, a well-formed set cannot include a decision and also its negation. For example, $\{x = a, x \neq a\}$ is not well-formed. Finally, if all values in the initial domain of a variable are refuted, we have a badly formed set of decisions. For example, if $dom^{init}(x) = \{a, b, c\}$ then $\{x \neq a, x \neq b, x \neq c\}$ is not well-formed. Henceforth we shall only consider well-formed sets of decisions.

The concept of nogood has already been introduced in section 1.2.3; see Definition 1.42. A nogood is defined as a globally inconsistent instantiation. Such nogoods are sometimes said to be *standard* and they correspond to the definition proposed by Dechter in [DEC 03]. Conflict sets [DEC 90, FRO 94] are standard nogoods identified when a partial instantiation cannot be extended. In some cases, a nogood justification (which is usually a subset of constraints of the original problem) is associated with a nogood [SCH 94a]; this can be useful for non-chronological backtracking and is also particularly relevant in a dynamic context (adding and removing constraints dynamically). Eliminating explanations [GIN 93, JUS 00b, JUS 00a] provides a different way of considering nogoods.

Recognizing that instantiations and (well-formed) sets of positive decisions are fundamentally equivalent, we obtain an alternative definition for standard nogoods: a standard nogood of P is a set Δ of positive decisions on P such that $P|_\Delta$ is unsatisfiable. We will use both definitions interchangeably.

Consideration of positive and negative decisions as in [FOC 01, KAT 03, KAT 05] leads to a generalization of standard nogoods, called *generalized* nogoods:

DEFINITION 1.56.– *[Generalized Nogood] A set of decisions Δ on a constraint network P is a generalized nogood of P iff $P|_\Delta$ is unsatisfiable.*

Clearly, a (standard) nogood is generalized but the opposite is not necessarily true. For example, $\Delta = \{x = a, y = b\}$ such that $P|_\Delta$ is unsatisfiable is a standard nogood of P, and consequently by definition a generalized nogood of P. But $\Delta = \{x = a, z \neq c\}$, such that $P|_\Delta$ is unsatisfiable, is a generalized nogood of P which is not standard. In fact a generalized nogood can represent an exponential number of standard nogoods [KAT 05]. If, for example, we have r variables $x_1, x_2, \ldots, x_r$ such that $\text{dom}(x_i) = \{1, 2, \ldots, d\}, \forall i \in 1..r$, then the generalized nogood $\{x_1 \neq 1, x_2 \neq 1, \ldots, x_r \neq 1\}$ captures $d^r - 1$ standard nogoods.

It may be important to compare the relative pruning capabilities of nogoods. For example, identifying subsumed nogoods allows us to discard them.

DEFINITION 1.57.– *[Subsumption] Let P be a constraint network, and Δ_1, Δ_2 be two generalized nogoods of P.*

- *Δ_1 and Δ_2 are equivalent iff $P|_{\Delta_1} = P|_{\Delta_2}$.*
- *Δ_1 is subsumed by Δ_2 iff $P|_{\Delta_1} \preceq_d P|_{\Delta_2}$.*

$P|_\Delta$ indicates which part of the search space is forbidden by Δ. As an illustration, $\Delta_1 = \{x = a, y = b\}$ and $\Delta_2 = \{x \neq b, x \neq c, y = b\}$ are equivalent if $\text{dom}(x) = \{a, b, c\}$. If now Δ_1 and Δ_2 are such that $\Delta_2 \subseteq \Delta_1$, then Δ_1 is subsumed by Δ_2. Moreover, if Δ_1 and Δ_2 are standard and only involve unfixed variables, then Δ_1 is subsumed by Δ_2 iff $\Delta_2 \subseteq \Delta_1$.

We can use *membership decisions* to handle representatives of equivalence classes of nogoods. Membership decisions are decisions of the form $x \in D_x$. Note that such decisions are usually not taken by backtrack search algorithms (at least, not when tackling discrete CSP instances).

DEFINITION 1.58.– *[Membership Decision] A membership decision δ is a restriction on a variable x of the form $x \in D_x$, where $\emptyset \subset D_x \subseteq \text{dom}^{\text{init}}(x)$; δ is strict iff $D_x \subset \text{dom}^{\text{init}}(x)$. A membership decision δ on a constraint network P is a membership decision $x \in D_x$ such that $x \in \text{vars}(P)$; δ is valid on P iff $D_x \subseteq \text{dom}^P(x)$ and δ is strict on P iff $D_x \subset \text{dom}^P(x)$.*

For a set Δ of membership decisions on P, we can define $P|_\Delta$ in a manner similar to the definition introduced for positive and negative decisions. Specifically, we define $P|_\Delta$ to be the network obtained (derived) from P such that, for each membership decision $x \in D_x$, each value $b \in \mathrm{dom}(x)$ with $b \notin D_x$ is removed from $\mathrm{dom}(x)$. A set Δ of membership decisions is *well-formed* iff each variable occurs at most once in Δ (consequently, Δ is also well-formed according to Definition 1.55).

PROPOSITION 1.59.– *Let P be a constraint network. For every well-formed set Δ of (positive and/or negative) decisions on P, there exists a unique well-formed set Δ^m of strict membership decisions on P such that $P|_\Delta = P|_{\Delta^m}$.*

The proof is omitted. As an example, if $\mathrm{dom}^{\mathrm{init}}(x) = \mathrm{dom}^{\mathrm{init}}(y) = \mathrm{dom}^{\mathrm{init}}(z) = \{a, b, c\}$ and $\Delta = \{x = a, y \neq b, y \neq c, z \neq b\}$, then we have $\Delta^m = \{x \in \{a\}, y \in \{a\}, z \in \{a, c\}\}$.

Finally, note that a set of decisions is *entailed* by a constraint network P when decisions contained in this set have no more impact on P.

DEFINITION 1.60.– *[Entailed Decisions] Let Δ be a set of (positive and/or negative) decisions or a set of membership decisions on a constraint network P. P entails Δ iff $P|_\Delta = P$.*

A decision δ is entailed by P if $\{\delta\}$ is entailed by P.

1.4.3. Properties on values and variables

Constraint networks possibly have properties that may be used to simplify the search for a solution, typically by reducing the size of the search space. Some of these properties are more powerful than others; in this sense there are stronger and weaker properties. Network properties concerning values and variables are the most important. As a matter of fact, properties on values are defined from properties on v-values. However, recall that the distinction is thin between values and v-values. Here, when a property φ holds on a v-value (x, a), we also say that φ holds on the value a (for variable x).

Inconsistency of a single value is a centrally important property. Whereas an *inconsistent* value belongs to no solution and so can be discarded, an *implied* value belong to all solutions (if any) and so can be assigned. A set of implied values constitutes a *backbone* (briefly described in section 2.2.1).

DEFINITION 1.61.– *[Inconsistent/Implied Value] Let P be a constraint network and (x, a) be a v-value of P.*

- (x, a) *is* inconsistent *on P iff there is no solution S of P such that $S[x] = a$.*
- (x, a) *is* implied *on P iff every solution S of P is such that $S[x] = a$.*

In other words, (x, a) is inconsistent iff the instantiation $I = \{(x, a)\}$ is globally inconsistent, i.e. a nogood. Of course, a v-value not inconsistent is said to be (globally) consistent. If a v-value (x, a) is implied, then every v-value (x, b) with $b \neq a$ is inconsistent. Clearly the removal of inconsistent values preserves solutions. The purpose of domain-filtering consistencies, which are introduced later in this book, is to identify and remove inconsistent values. Figure 1.27 provides examples of inconsistent and implied values.

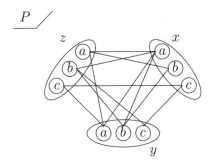

Figure 1.27. *A constraint network P such that $\mathrm{vars}(P) = \{x, y, z\}$ and $\mathrm{sols}(P) = \{(a, a, a), (a, b, b)\}$. The v-value (x, a) is implied, which means that (x, b) and (x, c) are inconsistent. (y, c) and (z, c) are also inconsistent*

Interchangeability is another important property introduced by Freuder [FRE 91]. Full interchangeability has been refined into several weaker forms, including neighborhood interchangeability, k-interchangeability, partial interchangeability and substitutability. Relational interchangeability (i.e. neighborhood interchangeability according to one constraint) [HAS 93] and neighborhood partial interchangeability [CHO 98] are further weak forms. Interchangeability and substitutability have been used in many contexts; see e.g. [BEN 92, HAS 93, CHO 95, FRE 97, BEL 94, COO 97, PET 03a, LAL 05].

A v-value (x, a) is *substitutable* for a v-value (x, b) iff substituting (x, a) for (x, b) in every solution involving (x, b) yields another solution. Two v-values are *interchangeable* iff each is substitutable for the other. Before defining these properties more formally we need to introduce some notation. When I is an instantiation such that $(x, a) \in I$, we denote by $I[x/b]$ the instantiation $(I \setminus \{(x, a)\}) \cup \{(x, b)\}$, which is the instantiation obtained from I by replacing the value assigned to x in I by b.

DEFINITION 1.62.– *[Substitutable/Interchangeable Value] Let P be a constraint network, and let (x, a) and (x, b) be two v-values of P.*

– (x, a) *is substitutable for (x, b) on P iff for every solution S of P such that $S[x] = b$, $S[x/a]$ is also a solution of P.*

– (x, a) *is (fully)* interchangeable *with* (x, b) *on P iff (x, a) is substitutable for* (x, b), *and* (x, b) *is substitutable for* (x, a).

For example, consider a constraint network P such that $\text{vars}(P) = \{x, y, z\}$ and $\text{sols}(P) = \{(a, a, a), (a, b, b), (b, a, a), (c, a, a), (c, b, b)\}$. The v-values (x, a) and (x, c) are interchangeable and both are substitutable for (x, b). When only a single solution is sought, we can remove a value that is interchangeable with another value (or for which a value is substitutable). Such removal preserves the satisfiability of the problem instance but not the full set of solutions[14]. In this spirit, we define *replaceable* values from substitutability.

DEFINITION 1.63.– *[Replaceable Value] Let P be a constraint network. A v-value* (x, a) *is* replaceable *on P iff there exists a v-value (x, b) of P such that (x, b) is* substitutable *for* (x, a).

Removable and *fixable* values, which have been defined more recently [BOR 04, BOR 08], are values that can be safely removed and assigned, respectively, preserving the satisfiability of instances.

DEFINITION 1.64.– *[Removable/Fixable Value] Let P be a constraint network and* (x, a) *be a v-value of P.*

– (x, a) *is* removable *on P iff for every solution S of P such that $S[x] = a$, there exists a value $b \neq a$ in $\text{dom}(x)$ such that $S[x/b]$ is also a solution of P.*

– (x, a) *is* fixable *on P iff for every solution S of P, $S[x/a]$ is also a solution of* P.

For example, consider a constraint network P such that $\text{vars}(P) = \{x, y, z\}$ and $\text{sols}(P) = \{(a, a, a), (a, b, b), (b, a, a), (c, b, b)\}$. The v-value (x, a) is fixable. The v-values (x, b) and (x, c) are removable; it is certainly surprising that (x, a) is also removable.

A value is clearly fixable iff it is substitutable for every other value in the domain. It is also easy to see that removability is a weaker property than replaceability because a replaceable value is necessary removable. Yet weaker properties are defined as follows:

DEFINITION 1.65.– *[Eliminable/Assignable Value] Let P be a constraint network and* (x, a) *be a v-value of P.*

– (x, a) *is* eliminable *on P iff either $\text{sols}(P) = \emptyset$ or there exists a solution S of P such that $S[x] \neq a$.*

---

14. However, by reasoning from equivalence classes or bundles, all solutions can be computed and represented compactly [HAS 93, BEC 01, CHO 02, LAL 05].

– (x, a) *is* assignable *on P iff either* sols$(P) = \emptyset$ *or there exists a solution S of P such that $S[x] = a$.*

Figure 1.28 shows relationships between network properties that concern values. A property φ is stronger than a property φ' iff whenever φ holds on a v-value of a constraint network P, φ' also holds on it. φ is strictly stronger than φ' iff φ is stronger than φ' and there exists at least one constraint network P such that φ' holds on a v-value of P but not φ. Note further that a value which is not implied is eliminable, and also that a (globally) consistent value is assignable.

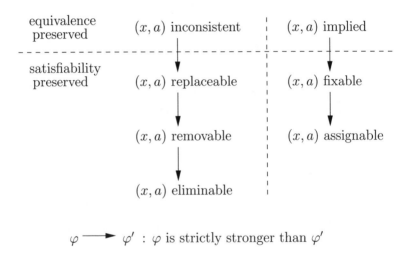

$$\varphi \longrightarrow \varphi' \; : \; \varphi \text{ is strictly stronger than } \varphi'$$

Figure 1.28. *Relationships between properties on values. We assume here that there are at least two values in the domain of x*

If there was a cheap way to identify eliminable values, then an instance could be solved by iteratively identifying and removing eliminable values. But no cheap way is available; checking whether a value is inconsistent, replaceable, removable, eliminable, implied, fixable or assignable is a co-NP-complete task (see [BOR 08] for a general proof). However, it is possible to make use of most of these properties locally, because there are polynomial time algorithms that determine whether a general property holds for some values by reasoning locally on some subproblems. An interesting result in [BOR 08] shows that local reasoning is not sound for the removability property. This leads to the practical use of local forms of stronger properties such as arc inconsistency and neighborhood substitutability.

We have hitherto been concerned with network properties of values; properties can also be defined for variables. As mentioned in [BOR 08], network properties of variables have been widely studied in several contexts (e.g. SAT) but have been rather neglected in the domain of constraint satisfaction. Two antithetical concepts are defined as follows:

DEFINITION 1.66.– *[Determined/Irrelevant Variable] Let P be a constraint network and x be a variable of P.*

  – x is determined *on P iff for every solution S of P and every value $b \neq S[x]$ in* $\text{dom}(x)$, $S[x/b]$ *is not a solution of P.*

  – x is irrelevant *on P iff for every solution S of P and every value $b \neq S[x]$ in* $\text{dom}(x)$, $S[x/b]$ *is also a solution of P.*

For example, consider a constraint network P such that $\text{vars}(P) = \{x, y, z\}$ with $\text{dom}(x) = \text{dom}(y) = \text{dom}(z) = \{a, b\}$ and $\text{sols}(P) = \{(a, a, a), (a, a, b), (b, b, a), (b, b, b)\}$. The variable x is determined and z is irrelevant.

Dependencies between variables on the entire network are important properties that can also be simply defined between variables within a single constraint (e.g. [CAM 08]). Several notions of dependency have been introduced [LAN 98] in the general context of propositional logic. For example, definability is a property which stipulates that some variables are fixed whenever some other variables are also fixed; this has been used [OST 02, PHA 07] for both complete and local search procedures in SAT. Functional dependencies among variables in declarative problem specifications have also been studied in [MAN 07].

DEFINITION 1.67.– *[Dependent Variable] Let P be a constraint network, x be a variable of P and X be a subset of variables of P such that $x \notin X$.*

  – x is dependent *of X on P iff for every two solutions S_1 and S_2 of P such that $S_1[y] = S_2[y], \forall y \in X$, we have $S_1[x] = S_2[x]$.*

  – x is minimally dependent *of X on P iff x is dependent of X on P, and there is no set of variables $Y \subset X$ such that x is* dependent *of Y on P.*

Interchangeability is a property that has been defined above on values. However, this property can also be defined on variables (see e.g. [LAW 07]). Note that if I is an instantiation containing the two v-values (x, a) and (y, b) then $I_{x \leftrightarrow y}$ denotes $(I \setminus \{(x, a), (y, b)\}) \cup \{(x, b), (y, a)\}$, i.e. the instantiation obtained from I by swapping values of x and y.

DEFINITION 1.68.– *[Interchangeable Variables] Let P be a constraint network and x, y be two variables of P. x is (fully)* interchangeable *with y on P iff for every solution S of P, $S_{x \leftrightarrow y}$ is also a solution of P.*

Variable and value interchangeability is sometimes called pairwise or piecewise variable and value symmetry (e.g. [FLE 06]). This property is useful for breaking symmetries in constraint networks.

Finally, an *eliminable* variable is one that, together with all constraints involving it, can be eliminated safely from a constraint network. This is a strong property that may be useful when constraint networks are composed of several connected components (independent sub-networks). Chapter 11 will refer to this property.

DEFINITION 1.69.– *[P⊖X] Let P be a constraint network and X be a set of variables of P. P ⊖ X is the constraint network P' obtained from P by removing all variables in X as well as every constraint c of P such that* $\mathrm{scp}(c) \cap X \neq \emptyset$.

DEFINITION 1.70.– *[Eliminable Variable] Let P be a constraint network and x be a variable of P. x is* eliminable *on P iff the satisfiability of P is equivalent to the satisfiability of* $P \ominus \{x\}$.

1.5. Data structures to represent constraint networks

Subsequent chapters introduce algorithms that find constraint network solutions. In preparation, we now precisely describe (in the context of backtrack search) some data structures that can serve to represent domains and constraints. This description is also required for our study of algorithm complexity analysis. Exhaustive presentation of all variants and alternatives is beyond the scope of this book.

1.5.1. *Representation of finite domains*

A CSP instance can be solved by a backtrack search algorithm in which, at each step, a decision is made. This decision is immediately followed by a filtering process called constraint propagation. This is introduced in detail in Chapter 8. Constraint propagation removes values, which must be restored upon backtracking. To achieve restoration we need, for each removed value, to record the level at which it was removed. Usually, the level (or depth) is given by the number of positive decisions, i.e. variable assignments, currently taken by the search algorithm. The current level, denoted by p, is then the current number of instantiated variables (also called past variables). In what follows, we introduce *trailing*, which is a domain representation and save/restore technique that is used in many constraint solvers. Copying and recomputation are known alternatives to trailing [SCH 99, CHO 01, SCH 06], but these will not be considered in this book.

During the search, trailing can use the following structures[15] to represent the current state of a domain (which is initially composed of d values).

---

15. As already stated, the initial domain of a variable can never be enlarged. This is quite a reasonable assumption, valid for all algorithms presented in this book.

– *values* is an array of size d that contains the set of values.

– *absent* is an array of size d that indicates which values are currently removed from the domain. More precisely, $absent[i] = -1$ indicates that $values[i]$ belongs to the current domain, whereas $absent[i] = k$ (≥ 0) indicates that $values[i]$ has been removed at level k of search.

– *next* is an array of size d that allows us to link (from first to last) all values of the current domain. When $absent[i] = -1$, $next[i]$ gives the index $j > i$ of the next value in the current domain (we have $absent[j] = -1$ and $\forall k \in i+1..j-1, absent[k] \neq -1$), or -1 if $values[i]$ is the last value.

– *prev* is an array of size d that allows us to link (from last to first) all values of the current domain. When $absent[i] = -1$, $prev[i]$ gives the index $j < i$ of the previous value in the current domain (we have $absent[j] = -1$ and $\forall k \in j+1..i-1, absent[k] \neq -1$), or -1 if $values[i]$ is the first value.

– *prevAbsent* is an array of size d that allows us to link all values that do not belong to the current domain. When $absent[i] \neq -1$, $prevAbsent[i]$ gives the index j of the value removed during search just before $values[i]$, or -1 if $values[i]$ is the first removed value.

We also need three variables denoted *head*, *tail* and *tailAbsent*, which indicate the indices of the first value, the last value and the last removed value, respectively. Using *head* and *tail* variables in conjunction with *next* and *prev* arrays, we obtain a behavior similar to a doubly linked list. Using *tailAbsent* and *prevAbsent*, we obtain a behavior similar to a stack (last-in first-out structure). The initialization of these structures is rather straightforward, as in Figure 1.29.

You may wonder how to find the position (index) of a given value. In fact, in the context of many consistency algorithms (e.g. generic algorithms such as GAC3 described in Chapter 4), this is never required as we can always reason about the indices of values. Nevertheless, in a more general context, we can always introduce a hash map which allows, under reasonable assumptions, the index of a given value to be obtained in constant time. For more information, see section 4 in [HEN 92] and implementation details in [BES 99]. From now on, to simplify the presentation of algorithms and without any loss of generality, we assume[16] that values and indices (of values) match, i.e. $\forall i \in 1..d$, $values[i] = i$; we then prefer to use symbols a and b (for values) instead of symbols i and j (for indices).

When a value is removed by constraint propagation (or search decision), the function removeValue, Algorithm 1, is called. This updates both the stack of removed values and also the doubly linked list of remaining values. Figure 1.30 illustrates this

---

16. However, observe that values and indices do not match in Figures 1.29 and 1.30 since, for example, $values[1] = 0$.

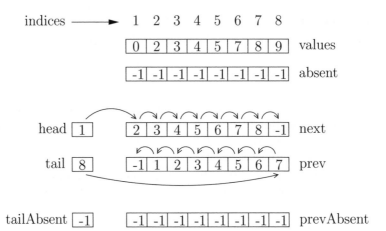

Figure 1.29. *The structures initialized for a domain composed of eight values* $\{0, 2, 3, 4, 5, 7, 8, 9\}$

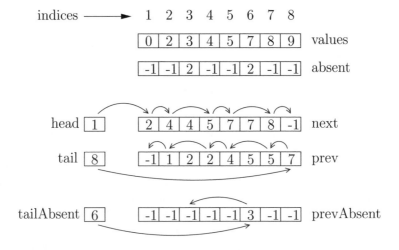

Figure 1.30. *The structures from Figure 1.29 after the successive removals of values* 3 *and* 7 *(at index* 3 *and* 6*) at level* 2. *The current domain is* $\{0, 2, 4, 5, 8, 9\}$

(for the second call to Algorithm 1, the formal parameter a is set to 6, and not 7, since for our illustration, indices and values do not match). When an assignment is performed during search, the function reduceTo, Algorithm 2, is called to remove all values distinct from the given one. When the solver backtracks up to level p, the function restoreUpto, Algorithm 4, is called. This function restores values, which have been removed at a level greater than or equal to p, back into the domains whence they came. Restoration of a value is achieved by calling function addValue which updates the stack as well as the doubly linked list. This use of a last-in first-out structure (stack) ensures that indexes at $prev[a]$ and $next[a]$ are correct when a value is restored. This is a technique known as dancing links [KNU 00].

Algorithm 1: removeValue(a: value, p: integer)

    // p is the current level (number of instantiated variables)
1 $absent[a] \leftarrow p$
2 $prevAbsent[a] \leftarrow tailAbsent$
3 $tailAbsent \leftarrow a$
4 **if** $prev[a] = -1$ **then**
5 | $head \leftarrow next[a]$
6 **else**
7     $next[prev[a]] \leftarrow next[a]$
8 **if** $next[a] = -1$ **then**
9 | $tail \leftarrow prev[a]$
10 **else**
11    $prev[next[a]] \leftarrow prev[a]$

Algorithm 2: reduceTo(a: value, p: integer)

---

1 $b \leftarrow head$
2 **while** $b \neq -1$ **do**
3 | **if** $b \neq a$ **then**
4 | removeValue(b, p)
5     $b \leftarrow next[b]$

The space complexity of this representation is $\Theta(|\operatorname{dom}(x)|)$ for any variable x, which is optimal. The time complexity of all elementary operations (determining if a value is present, getting next value, previous value, etc.) is $O(1)$. As a consequence, the time complexity of removeValue and addValue is $O(1)$. Of course, there are other representations of domains that may be quite useful. For example, if the order of values in domains is not important, we can use a sparse set data structure [BRI 93]. This allows restoration of all values removed at a given level in constant time. A bit vector, which is basically a structure that contains a collection of bits and provides constant-time access to each bit, is also an attractive data structure. In practice, we may select the domain representation that is best for the instance at hand [HEB 08].

Algorithm 3: addValue(a: value)

// a is the last removed value that needs to be restored
1 $absent[a] \leftarrow -1$
2 $tailAbsent \leftarrow prevAbsent[a]$
3 **if** $prev[a] = -1$ **then**
4 | $head \leftarrow a$
5 **else**
6 | $next[prev[a]] \leftarrow a$
7 **if** $next[a] = -1$ **then**
8 | $tail \leftarrow a$
9 **else**
10 | $prev[next[a]] \leftarrow a$

Algorithm 4: restoreUpto(p: integer)

---

1 $b \leftarrow tailAbsent$
2 **while** $b \neq -1 \land absent[b] \geq p$ **do**
3 | addValue(b)
4 | $b \leftarrow prevAbsent[b]$

In subsequent chapters, we sometimes simplify presentation by describing algorithms using more general representations of some instructions. For example, we shall implicitly take account of the parameter p when:

- $\mathrm{dom}(x)$.reduceTo(a, p) is simplified into: $x \leftarrow a$ or $x = a$;
- $\mathrm{dom}(x)$.removeValue(a, p) is simplified into: remove a from $\mathrm{dom}(x)$ or $x \neq a$.

1.5.2. *Representation of constraints*

We know that a constraint can be represented extensionally or intensionally (we do not discuss about global constraints in this section). When a generic filtering algorithm[17] is employed, one has to be able to perform a constraint check, that is to say, to determine if a given tuple is accepted by a constraint. If c is a constraint and τ a tuple to be checked against c, then the constraint check corresponds to the test $\tau \in \mathrm{rel}(c)$.

---

17. When specific filtering algorithm(s) or propagator(s) is(are) associated with the constraint, there is usually no need to have this functionality.

If the constraint c is defined in intension, one has just to write a Boolean function that accepts any tuple τ in parameter. For example, let us assume that c is defined by the predicate expression $x \neq y$, then the body of a function to be associated with c could simply be:

return $\tau[x] \neq \tau[y]$

When the constraint is given in extension, it is possible to represent its associated relation by:

– a multi-dimensional array of Boolean;

– a table, i.e. a list (or array) of arrays of integers;

– a hash map;

– bit vectors.

Using a multi-dimensional array allows us to perform a constraint check in $O(r)$, where r is the arity of the constraint, but the worst-case space complexity exponentially grows with the arity since it is in $O(d^r)$. This kind of representation can only be used for constraints of small arity and/or constraints involving variables with domains of small size. For example, assume that c is a ternary constraint such that $\mathrm{scp}(c) = \{x, y, z\}$ and that a 3-dimensional array m has been defined from the initial list of allowed or disallowed tuples given for c. The body of the function to be associated with c could simply be:

return $m[\tau[x], \tau[y], \tau[z]]$

When for space reasons, it is not possible to use a multi-dimensional array of Booleans, one can just record the given list of allowed or disallowed tuples (i.e. what we call a table). With binary search, it is possible to perform a constraint check in $O(\log(t)r)$, where t is the number of tuples, while the worst-case space complexity is $O(tr)$. An alternative, which can be worthwhile, is to adopt a hash map. With some assumptions, one can expect to check a tuple in $O(r)$. More information will be given in sections 5.1.1 and 5.6.1 of Chapter 5. Finally, bit vectors can be a good solution to save space and time for binary networks. This is discussed in section 4.5.3 of Chapter 4.

Chapter 2

Random and Structured Networks

It is conceptually very difficult to determine, either qualitatively or quantitatively, the extent to which any given object is randomly shaped. Shapes of (sufficiently large) randomly generated objects are characteristically irregular. This irregularity may be contrasted with the considerable regularity of structured objects fashioned directly or indirectly by human processes. We may ask: to what extent can shapes be considered to be regular? Assessing randomness is equivalent to assessing irregularity, and this has been explored in different ways.

In algorithmic information theory (e.g. see [COV 06]), the *Kolmogorov complexity* of an object corresponds to a measure of the computational resources needed to specify it. Kolmogorov randomness (also called algorithmic randomness) defines a sequence of bits as being random if and only if it is shorter than any computer program that can produce it. Unluckily, this measure is not readily computable and is not applicable to short sequences because the shortest way to deal with small sequences, whatever they are, is to write a program that simply prints them.

In [PIN 97], *approximate entropy*, which must not be confounded with *information entropy* [SHA 48], is introduced to measure the irregularity of a sequence of digits. This explicitly computable entropy quantifies the extent to which non-random sequences differ from maximally irregular sequences. Hogg [HOG 98] has proposed to extend the scope of approximate entropy to quantify the randomness of any discrete structure, i.e. any structure composed of a finite number of components. In particular, he has shown that this measure can be applied to constraint search processes. He has illustrated this with graph coloring and 3-SAT solution-seeking search processes.

Less formally, the reader should intuitively understand what characterizes the structure of a constraint network. A constraint network is structured if it is composed of one or more general components (sub-networks), each having a certain regularity. Quite often, such components correspond to clusters of variables and constraints that can be identified at modeling time. Typically, the more complex the context of the problem, the more numerous the components. For example, problems from enterprise or industry usually combine abstractions representing different aspects of the reality. The interconnection between components may be more or less regular, but except for very regular problems, variables and constraints usually do not play a similar role, nor do they have the same impact within the network. Consequently, some components of a constraint network are more difficult to satisfy than others. Therefore a challenge for a constraint solver is to recognize underlying structure and to exploit it.

People have recently focused their attention on ideas for capturing the hidden structure of problem instances. Structure can sometimes be characterized by *backbones* and *backdoors*. A backbone is a set of variables that always have the same value in any solution, while a (strong) backdoor is a set of variables that concentrate the combinatorics of a problem instance. Exploiting such features facilitates solving constraint networks. Minimal unsatisfiable cores, which are related to strong backdoors, provide further examples. Minimal unsatisfiable cores represent unsatisfiable sub-networks that cannot be reduced without becoming satisfiable. They are useful, for example, to explain sources of unsatisfiability. Yet another example is that identification of cliques in the (primal) constraint graph provides strong structural information that can be useful in practice. Finally, the amount of acyclicity in a constraint network indicates the extent to which the network can be handled (or transformed) as a tree.

This chapter is organized in two main sections dealing respectively with random and structured networks.

2.1. Random constraint networks

For some purposes, we may wish to generate instances on demand. In particular it is usual to generate random CSP instances automatically. This enables experimentation on a large set of instances with an unlimited number of different parameter settings (e.g. density of the network, tightness of the constraints, etc.). In this section, we present classical models used in the generation of random instances. In particular, we focus on two models, denoted by RB and RD, which, while guaranteeing inherent difficulty, can produce random instances having both extensional and intensional constraints.

2.1.1. *Classical models*

Here is a quick overview of the different classical models for random constraint network generators. There are four different classical models denoted by A, B, C and

D [SMI 96, GEN 01]. Each of these models proceeds in two steps. The first step builds network macro-structure, which is the constraint hypergraph. The second step builds network micro-structure, which is the compatibility hypergraph; see section 1.2.2. Actually, the two steps can be interleaved. Recall that the density of a normalized constraint network, assuming that all constraints have arity k, is equal to $e/\binom{n}{k}$, and that the tightness of a constraint corresponds to the proportion of disallowed tuples in the associated relation. For randomly generated constraints, tightness can also be defined as the probability that a tuple be disallowed.

Each random CSP instance is characterized by a 5-tuple (k, n, d, p_1, p_2) where k denotes the arity of the constraints, n the number of variables, d the uniform domain size, p_1 a measure of the density of the constraint network and p_2 a measure of the tightness of the constraints. There are four models since p_1 and p_2 can be either a probability or a proportion. p_1 is a probability in models A,C and is a proportion in models B,D. p_2 is a probability in models A,D and is a proportion in models B,C. Note that, for binary instances, k is usually omitted.

Model B is defined as follows:

DEFINITION 2.1.– *[Model B] A class of random CSP instances of* model B *is denoted by* $B(k, n, d, p_1, p_2)$ *where, for each instance:*

– $k \geq 2$ *denotes the arity of each constraint;*

– $n \geq 2$ *denotes the number of variables;*

– $d \geq 2$ *denotes the size of each domain;*

– $1 \geq p_1 > 0$ *determines the number* $e = p_1\binom{n}{k}$ *of constraints;*

– $1 > p_2 > 0$ *determines the number* $t = p_2 d^k$ *of disallowed tuples of each relation.*

To generate one instance $P \in B(k, n, d, p_1, p_2)$, *the generator constructs* e *constraints, each one formed by randomly selecting (without repetition) a scope of* k *(distinct) variables and randomly selecting (with repetition) a relation of* t *distinct disallowed tuples.*

For example, a CSP instance from class $B(2, 20, 10, 0.5, 0.3)$ has 20 variables whose domains contain exactly 10 values, and $0.5 \times \binom{20}{2} = 95$ binary constraints whose associated relations forbid exactly $0.3 \times 10^2 = 30$ tuples. Note that $p_1\binom{n}{k}$ and $p_2 d^k$ may have to be rounded to the nearest integer. Note also that we are free to use the number of constraints e and the number of disallowed tuples t directly instead of proportions.

Model D is defined as follows:

DEFINITION 2.2.– *[Model D] A class of random CSP instances of* model D *is denoted by* $D(k, n, d, p_1, p_2)$ *where, for each instance:*

- $k \geq 2$ *denotes the arity of each constraint;*
- $n \geq 2$ *denotes the number of variables;*
- $d \geq 2$ *denotes the size of each domain;*
- $1 \geq p_1 > 0$ *determines the number* $e = p_1\binom{n}{k}$ *of constraints;*
- $1 > p_2 > 0$ *denotes the constraint tightness in terms of probability.*

To generate one instance $P \in D(k, n, d, p_1, p_2)$, *the generator constructs* e *constraints, each one formed by randomly selecting (without repetition) a scope of k (distinct variables) and randomly selecting (with repetition) a relation such that each one of the d^k tuples is forbidden with probability p_2.*

It has been shown [CHE 91] that the hardest random instances occur at a so-called *phase transition* between an *under-constrained region* where all instances are almost surely satisfiable and an *over-constrained region* where all problems are almost surely unsatisfiable. This phase transition is associated with a range of values of a control parameter. This parameter is usually p_2 (or κ which measures the constrainedness of an instance [GEN 96b]). The peak of difficulty occurs close to the *threshold* or *crossover point*, which is where 50% of instances are satisfiable. The *mushy region* [SMI 96, PRO 96] is the range of values of the control parameter over which the phase transition takes place. Locating the phase transition has been addressed in [WIL 94, SMI 96]. An illustration is given in Figure 2.1.

To illustrate phase transition, we consider three series of classes of model D: $D(2, 20, 11, 180, p_2)$, $D(2, 30, 15, 306, p_2)$ and $D(2, 40, 19, 443, p_2)$. The difficulty of solving instances is increased with the number of variables, the uniform domain size and the number of (binary) constraints. Note that instead of being a proportion, the fourth parameter is the number of constraints. Here tightness p_2 is the control parameter that can be varied to cause the phase transition. Figure 2.2 shows the effort (CPU time) required for solution of instances from these three different classes. This is the effort required by a solver implementing the algorithm MAC that will be presented in Chapter 8. Figure 2.2 is limited to tightness values between 0.14 and 0.36 where the most difficult instances occur. From bottom to top, successive curves in Figure 2.2 are for $n = 20$, $n = 30$ and $n = 40$. As we shall see later, the threshold (or crossover point) for these three classes is theoretically located at $p_2 \approx 0.233$, which corresponds closely to the threshold observed experimentally (although for small problem instances, this is not always the case). Figure 2.3 shows the actual phase transitions: at $p_2 = 0.19$, all instances are satisfiable, while at $p_2 = 0.25$, all instances are unsatisfiable. Phase transition occurs between these two values.

At this stage, models A, B, C and D seem to be simple and equivalent tools for generating random instances. However, Achlioptas *et al.* [ACH 97] have identified a shortcoming of all four standard models. This is that random problem instances generated using these models suffer from (trivial) insolubility as problem size

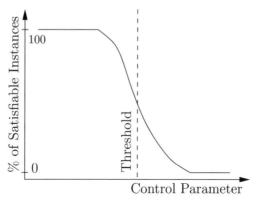

(a) Evolution of the proportion of satisfiable instances.

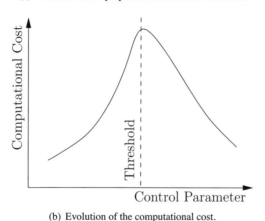

(b) Evolution of the computational cost.

Figure 2.1. *Phase transition, computational cost and threshold (crossover point)*

increases. Achlioptas *et al.* [ACH 97] have shown that, asymptotically, if $p_2 \geq 1/d$, such instances almost surely contain a flawed variable when the number of variables increases while other parameters are kept constant. A flawed variable is such that each value from its associated domain is flawed, i.e. not supported by a constraint of the instance. Therefore, an instance involving a flawed variable is trivially unsatisfiable and this can be discovered in polynomial time.

To overcome the deficiency of standard models, several alternatives have been proposed. In [ACH 97], a model E (for generating binary constraint networks) is introduced by selecting, with probability p, each one of the $d^2\binom{n}{2}$ tuples (x, y, a, b) where x and y are two distinct variables, $a \in \text{dom}(x)$ and $b \in \text{dom}(y)$. This new model is proved to be asymptotically interesting. However, it provides less flexibility in the construction of the network and quickly yields a complete constraint graph

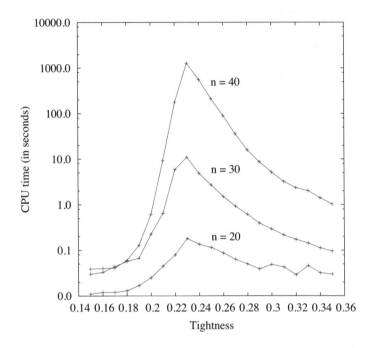

Figure 2.2. *Mean search cost of solving 50 instances of classes $D(2, 20, 11, 180, p_2)$,*
$D(2, 30, 15, 306, p_2)$ and $D(2, 40, 19, 443, p_2)$ with the complete search algorithm MAC

even when p is small. A generalized model has been proposed by Molloy [MOL 03]
with the introduction of a probability distribution in order to select constraints directly
(instead of selecting allowed tuples, one by one). Molloy [MOL 03] proves that *very
well behaved* sets of constraints obtained with a probability distribution certainly show
a phase transition. Because such distributions can be awkward to use in practice,
[MOL 03] also addresses the generation of difficult instances.

There has been some work that incorporates some "structure" into generated
random instances. One idea is to ensure that the generated instances are arc-consistent
[GEN 01] or (strongly) path-consistent [GAO 04]; local consistencies, such as arc
consistency and path consistency, are properties described in Chapter 3. More
precisely, Gent *et al.* [GEN 01] propose variants, called flawless models, of standard
models with flawed values prevented. They consider that "each value must be
supported by at least one unique value, i.e. one value that is not also required to
support another value" and achieve this by including, in each binary constraint,
a set S of d allowed tuples such that any pair τ_1, τ_2 of tuples of S is such that
$\tau_1[1] \neq \tau_2[1] \wedge \tau_1[2] \neq \tau_2[2]$. Then, the instances generated according to flawless

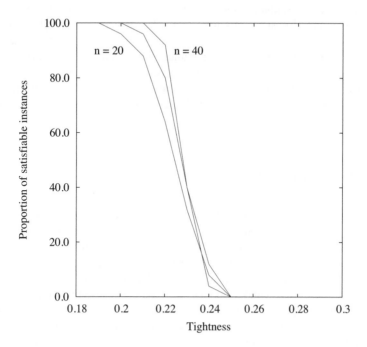

Figure 2.3. *Phase transitions for* $D(2, 20, 11, 180, p_2)$, $D(2, 30, 15, 306, p_2)$ *and* $D(2, 40, 19, 443, p_2)$

models are guaranteed to be arc-consistent and, at any value of $p_2 < 1/2$, do not suffer asymptotically from trivial insolubility". Unluckily, they can be solved in polynomial time as they embed easy subproblems [GAO 04]. A generalization of this approach has then been proposed by Gao and Culberson [GAO 04], who show that if each relation is chosen in such a way that the generated instances are strongly path-consistent, then such instances have exponential resolution complexity no matter how tight the constraints. By ensuring the presence of a l-regular bipartite graph in each generated relation (with a sufficiently large l), the instances are guaranteed to be strongly path-consistent. The main drawback is that generating random instances is no longer a fairly natural and easy task.

Finally, in [XU 00, SMI 01, XU 03, FRI 03] standard models have been revised by controlling the way parameters change as the problem size increases. The alternative model D scheme proposed by Smith in [SMI 01] guarantees the occurrence of a phase transition when some parameters are controlled and when the constraint tightness is within a certain range. The two revised models RB and RD introduced by Xu and Li in [XU 00, XU 03] provide the same guarantee by varying one of two control parameters around a critical value that can be computed. In the next section, we shall see that almost all instances of models RB and RD are hard, i.e. do not present resolution proofs of size less than exponential size. Also, Frieze and Molloy [FRI 03] identify a range of suitable parameter settings in order to show a non-trivial threshold of satisfiability. Their theoretical results apply to binary instances taken from model A and also to "symmetric" binary instances from a so-called model B, which, not corresponding to the standard one, associates the same relation with every constraint.

2.1.2. *Models RB and RD*

This section introduces some theoretical results concerning two models defined in [XU 00, XU 03]. Firstly, model RB is an alternative to model B. To simplify analysis, model RB, unlike model B, allows more than one constraint to have the same scope (but nothing prevents us from normalizing random instances generated by model RB). Results introduced below may possibly hold also for Model B (i.e. when selection of scopes is performed without duplicates). This is because the number of duplicate constraints is asymptotically much smaller than the total number of constraints and thus can be neglected in the analysis. But the main difference between models RB and B is that in model RB the domain size of each variable grows polynomially with the number of variables.

DEFINITION 2.3.– *[Model RB] A class of random CSP instances of* model RB *is denoted by* $RB(k, n, \alpha, r, p)$ *where, for each instance:*

– $k \geq 2$ *denotes the arity of each constraint;*

– $n \geq 2$ *denotes the number of variables;*

– $\alpha > 0$ *determines the domain size* $d = n^\alpha$ *of each variable;*

– $r > 0$ *determines the number* $e = r.n. \ln n$ *of constraints;*

– $1 > p > 0$ *determines the number* $t = pd^k$ *of disallowed tuples of each relation.*

To generate one instance $P \in RB(k, n, \alpha, r, p)$, *the generator constructs* e *constraints, each one formed by randomly selecting (with repetition) a scope of* k *(distinct) variables and randomly selecting (with repetition) a relation of* t *distinct disallowed tuples.*

Because $d = n^\alpha$ and $e = rn \ln n$, the parameters α and r determine the values of d and e for a given value of n. This makes it possible to determine the *critical value* p_{cr} of p where the hardest instances must occur. Specifically, $p_{cr} = 1 - e^{-\alpha/r}$ which is equivalent to the expression of p_{cr} given in [SMI 96]. Note that n^α, $r.n. \ln n$ and pd^k may have to be rounded to the nearest integer.

Model RD is similar to model RB except that p denotes a probability instead of a proportion.

DEFINITION 2.4.– *[Model RD] A class of random CSP instances of* model RD *is denoted by* $RD(k, n, \alpha, r, p)$ *where, for each instance:*

    – $k \geq 2$ *denotes the arity of each constraint;*

    – $n \geq 2$ *denotes the number of variables;*

    – $\alpha > 0$ *determines the domain size* $d = n^{\alpha}$ *of each variable;*

    – $r > 0$ *determines the number* $e = r.n. \ln n$ *of constraints;*

    – $1 > p > 0$ *denotes the constraint tightness in terms of probability.*

To generate one instance $P \in RD(k, n, \alpha, r, p)$, *the generator constructs* e *constraints, each one formed by randomly selecting (with repetition) a scope of* k *(distinct) variables and randomly selecting (with repetition) a relation such that each one of the* d^k *tuples is not allowed with probability* p.

The following analysis refers exclusively to model RB, although the results also hold for model RD. In [XU 00], it is proved that model RB, under certain conditions, not only avoids trivial asymptotic behavior but also guarantees exact phase transitions. More precisely, with Pr denoting a probability distribution, the following theorems hold:

THEOREM 2.5.– *If* $k, \alpha > \frac{1}{k}$ *and* $p \leq \frac{k-1}{k}$ *are constants then*

$$\lim_{n \to \infty} Pr[P \in RB(k, n, \alpha, r, p) \text{ is satisfiable}] = \begin{cases} 1 & \text{if } r < r_{cr} \\ 0 & \text{if } r > r_{cr} \end{cases}$$

where $r_{cr} = -\frac{\alpha}{\ln(1-p)}$.

THEOREM 2.6.– *If* $k, \alpha > \frac{1}{k}$ *and* $p_{cr} \leq \frac{k-1}{k}$ *are constants then*

$$\lim_{n \to \infty} Pr[P \in RB(k, n, \alpha, r, p) \text{ is satisfiable}] = \begin{cases} 1 & \text{if } p < p_{cr} \\ 0 & \text{if } p > p_{cr} \end{cases}$$

where $p_{cr} = 1 - e^{-\frac{\alpha}{r}}$.

The condition $p_{cr} \leq \frac{k-1}{k}$ is equivalent to $ke^{-\frac{\alpha}{r}} \geq 1$ given in [XU 00]. Theorems 2.5 and 2.6 guarantee a phase transition provided that the domain size is not too small and the constraint tightness, or the threshold value of the constraint tightness, is not too large.

EXAMPLE.– When the constraints are binary, the domain size must be greater than the square root of the number of variables (as $\alpha > 1/2$ and $d = n^{\alpha}$) and the constraint tightness or threshold value of the tightness is required to be at most 50%. The following table gives the limits of Theorems 2.5 and 2.6 for different arities.

k	α	p or p_{cr}
2	$> 1/2$	$\leq 1/2$
3	$> 1/3$	$\leq 2/3$
4	$> 1/4$	$\leq 3/4$
5	$> 1/5$	$\leq 4/5$

In practice, we shall certainly prefer to use Theorem 2.6 since the classical way of experimenting with random instances is to use the constraint tightness (here p) as a control parameter. Importantly, what is interesting with Models RB and RD is that once values of parameters k, α and r have been chosen so that Theorem 2.6 holds, we can generate more and more difficult instances (as shown below by Theorem 2.7) by simply increasing the value of n (the number of variables). We can be sure that the phase transition exists and stays at the same place. This allows observation of the *scaling behavior* of algorithms, which is important in the practical comparison of algorithms.

EXAMPLE.– When, $k = 2$, $\alpha = 0.8$ and $r = 3$, we see that $\alpha > 1/2$ and $p_{cr} = 1 - e^{-\frac{\alpha}{r}} \approx 0.233 \leq 1/2$, so Theorem 2.6 holds. Harder and harder instances, can be generated by increasing the value of n. For a given value of n, values of d and e are automatically determined, and rounding to the nearest integers, we obtain:

n	d	e	p_{cr}
10	6	69	0.229
20	11	180	0.234
30	15	306	0.233
40	19	443	0.233
50	23	587	0.234

After rounding, from series to series, the critical theoretical values p_{cr} may be slightly shifted, but this is really limited. Note also that the classes of model D introduced earlier in section 2.1.1 followed the scheme (i.e. parameters) of model RD. The only difference is that more than one constraint on the same scope was disallowed during generation. Models RB and RD can be perceived as a kind of framework, having proven good properties, wherein a classical series of random instances can be generated.

EXAMPLE.– It is worthwhile to check that for $k = 3$, $\alpha = 1$ and $r = 1$, Theorem 2.6 holds and that we can generate a series defined by:

n	d	e	p_{cr}
12	12	30	0.630
16	16	44	0.635
20	20	60	0.632
24	24	76	0.633
28	28	93	0.633

The next theorem establishes that unsatisfiable instances of model RB are almost surely guaranteed to be hard. The proof is based on a strategy following some results of [BEN 01, MIT 02] and can be found in [XU 03]. A similar result for model A has been presented in [FRI 03] with respect to binary instances (i.e. $k = 2$). Mitchell [MIT 00] has described similar behavior for instances where constraints have fewer than $d/2$ disallowed tuples.

THEOREM 2.7.– *If* $P \in RB(k, n, \alpha, r, p)$ *and* k, α, r *and* p *are constants, then, almost surely*[1], *P has no tree-like resolution of length less than* $2^{\Omega(n)}$.

To summarize, model RB guarantees exact phase transitions and hard instances at the threshold. This contradicts the statement in [GAO 04] about the requirement of an extremely low tightness for all existing random models to obtain non-trivial threshold behaviors and guaranteed hard instances at the threshold. Information about random instances forced to be satisfiable, as well as a vast range of experimental results, can be found in [XU 05, XU 07].

2.1.3. *Random constraint networks in intension*

In previously published literature, most of the experimental work with random constraint networks has been with binary instances. This is mainly due to space limitations, because the space needed for explicitly storing the tuples allowed (or disallowed) by a constraint grows exponentially with its arity. For instance, at least 10^9 memory words are needed to store 1% of the tuples of a 10-ary constraint that has 10 values per variable domain since 10^8 tuples, each one composed of 10 values, must be stored. It is not practical to represent large non-binary random networks with constraints given in extension.

We now present a variant [LEC 03b] of model RD that generates networks which have intensional constraints. This development enables experimentation with randomly generated networks of any arity.

We give each constraint c a unique identifier $id(c)$. The function isConsistent, Algorithm 5, defines the set of tuples allowed (disallowed) by constraint c. More precisely, for any given values of $(id(c), \tau)$, isConsistent(c, τ, p) determines if the tuple τ is allowed by c while considering tightness p. The function computeRandomValue always returns the same real random value between 0 and 1 (exclusive). The function isConsistent compares this random value with the constraint tightness p serving as an acceptance boundary.

---

1. We say that a property holds almost surely when this property holds with probability tending to 1 as the number of variables tends to infinity.

Algorithm 5: isConsistent(c: constraint, τ: tuple, p: 0..1): Boolean

---

Output: *true* iff $\tau \in \text{rel}(c)$ according to probability p

1 $realRandomValue \leftarrow$ computeRandomValue($id(C), \tau$)
2 **return** $realRandomValue \geq p$

Algorithm 6: computeRandomValue(id: integer, τ: tuple): real

Output: a real random value computed from id and τ

// variable *document*: array of bytes
// variable *fingerprint*: array of bytes
// variable b: byte
1 $document \leftarrow$ createDocumentWith(id, τ)
2 $fingerprint \leftarrow$ MD5($document$)   // SHA is an alternative
3 $b \leftarrow fingerprint[1]$
4 **for** i *ranging from* 2 *to* $fingerprint.length$ **do**
5 $\quad \lfloor \; b \leftarrow b \oplus fingerprint[i]$
6 **return** $b/256$

A simple implementation of the function computeRandomValue computes a seed from the parameters, and uses this to obtain a real value using a pseudo-random number generator. An alternative implementation uses a message digest algorithm like M5 [RIV 92] or SHA [NIS 02]. These algorithms correspond to secure one-way hash functions that take arbitrary-sized data, called documents, and output fixed-length hash values called *fingerprints* or *message digests*. For any bit changed in a document, the best hash functions modify at least 50% of the bits occurring in the computed fingerprint. In the present context, the document consists of the actual parameters of computeRandomValue, namely, the identification number of the constraint and the given tuple.

Real values of hash function can be obtained as shown in Algorithm 6. The function createDocumentWith, which is not described in detail here, creates a document that is simply a concatenation of all values of its actual parameters. Algorithm 6 then calls a hash function such as MD5 to generate a fingerprint. The exclusive-or operation ($\oplus$) is iteratively applied to each byte of the fingerprint. Finally, Algorithm 6 obtains a real value between 0 and 1 by dividing the resulting byte by 256.

This approach is correct, firstly because isConsistent always produces the same result for a given set of parameter values. Second, the decision whether each tuple τ is not allowed by c is made independently with probability p. By having the constraint identification number as a parameter of computeRandomValue, we obtain distinct constraints with the same arity.

It is now possible to define a variant, RD^{int}, of model RD that will work in practice with any required arity.

DEFINITION 2.8.– *[Model RD^{int}] A class of random CSP instances of* model RD^{int} *is denoted by* $RD^{int}(k, n, \alpha, r, p)$ *where, for each instance:*

- *$k \geq 2$ denotes the arity of each constraint;*
- *$n \geq 2$ denotes the number of variables;*
- *$\alpha > 0$ determines the domain size $d = n^{\alpha}$ of each variable;*
- *$r > 0$ determines the number $e = r.n. \ln n$ of constraints;*
- *$1 > p > 0$ denotes the constraint tightness in terms of probability.*

To generate one instance $P \in RD^{int}(k, n, \alpha, r, p)$, the generator constructs e intensional constraints, each one formed by randomly selecting (with repetition) a scope of k (distinct) variables and (implicitly) defined by the function isConsistent described above.

It is easy to implement this new model, which has no space requirement and allows experimentation with large arity constraints. To demonstrate the practical validity of this model, we have compared the instances generated by models RD and RD^{int}. More precisely, we have compared three approaches, as follows.

– Extension: the model RD is used, and the constraints are defined in extension using a pseudo-random number generator based on a linear congruential method.

– SHA: the model RD^{int} is used, and the constraints are defined in intension using SHA.

– MD5: the model RD^{int} is used, and the constraints are defined in intension using MD5.

We have experimented with classes $RD^{int}(2, 25, 15, 150, p)$ and $RD^{int}(3, 50, 5, 80, p)$. In the description of these classes, we have directly mentioned the domain size d (instead of α) and the number of constraints e (instead of r). In fact, for the first classes, $\alpha \approx 0.84$ and $r \approx 1.86$, whereas for the second classes, $\alpha \approx 0.41$ and $r \approx 0.41$. The former classes yield dense instances with 25 variables, 15 values per domain and 150 binary constraints, whereas the latter classes yield sparse instances with 50 variables, 5 values per domain and 80 ternary constraints. We limit our study to constraints of small arity because of the approach that expresses constraints in extension. For each value of p, varied from 0 to 1 with a step equal to $1/256$, and for each approach, 50 instances have been generated and solved by the algorithm MAC (presented in Chapter 8). Tables 2.1 and 2.2 show the results for several values of p located in the mushy region. Results are given in terms of the number of satisfiable instances (#sat), the average number of constraint checks (#ccks), and the average CPU time in seconds.

Tightness	SHA			MD5			Extension		
p	#sat	#ccks	CPU	#sat	#ccks	CPU	#sat	#ccks	CPU
85/256	49	52,636	0.26	50	68,405	0.33	48	50,071	0.07
86/256	49	71,620	0.39	48	96,090	0.46	48	62,774	0.09
87/256	47	106,283	0.51	46	108,863	0.63	47	91,855	0.13
88/256	44	142,706	0.71	40	125,014	0.60	42	130,379	0.19
89/256	34	189,478	0.91	32	165,009	0.81	29	195,430	0.29
90/256	21	211,338	1.01	25	182,229	0.86	22	193,591	0.28
91/256	12	197,716	0.95	14	196,004	0.92	15	196,428	0.28
92/256	4	185,203	0.89	9	200,059	0.97	11	187,122	0.27
93/256	1	169,795	0.81	5	193,020	0.90	7	180,506	0.26
94/256	0	151,028	0.72	1	174,125	0.82	2	163,857	0.23
95/256	0	131,131	0.62	0	156,439	0.73	1	144,739	0.20

Table 2.1. *Phase transition for $RD^{\text{int}}(2, 25, 15, 150, p)$*

Tightness	SHA			MD5			Extension		
p	#sat	#ccks	CPU	#sat	#ccks	CPU	#sat	#ccks	CPU
149/256	46	70,256	0.33	47	88,442	0.40	47	72,845	0.09
150/256	42	84,746	0.40	46	108,605	0.49	47	83,132	0.09
151/256	40	136,544	0.64	44	113,136	0.51	44	113,386	0.13
152/256	35	148,010	0.70	39	136,536	0.62	37	128,164	0.14
153/256	30	139,460	0.65	33	137,865	0.63	33	147,407	0.16
154/256	23	149,839	0.70	26	176,143	0.79	26	138,698	0.15
155/256	19	150,383	0.70	23	168,319	0.75	22	140,998	0.15
156/256	15	152,153	0.71	15	159,181	0.71	15	154,094	0.17
157/256	11	151,910	0.70	12	150,633	0.67	8	146,423	0.16
158/256	7	134,474	0.63	6	135,822	0.60	5	138,864	0.15
159/256	5	121,855	0.56	4	116,854	0.52	3	121,424	0.13

Table 2.2. *Phase transition for $RD^{\text{int}}(3, 50, 5, 80, p)$*

These results clearly show that the three approaches give similar results in terms of numbers of satisfiable instances and constraint checks. However, we observe that solving intensional random instances needs more CPU time than solving extensional ones. Indeed, the CPU time required to perform a constraint check is from 3 to 4 times longer; computing a fingerprint with MD5 or SHA is expensive. Nevertheless, these results confirm that a door is opened to realize experimentations with (intensional) random instances of large arity.

The location of each experimentally identified crossover point can be compared with its theoretical value. Table 2.1 shows experimental evidence that for the $RD^{\text{int}}(2, 25, 15, 150, p)$ classes, the crossover point is located between $p = 89/256 \approx 0.347$ and $p = 91/256 \approx 0.355$. This can be compared with the theoretically computed $p \approx 0.363$. Table 2.2 shows experimentally that for the $RD(3, 50, 5, 80, p)$ classes, the crossover point is located between $p = 153/256 \approx 0.597$ and $p = 155/256 \approx 0.605$. Again, this can be compared with the theoretically computed $p \approx 0.634$. A slight difference between experimental and theoretical values is more pronounced for the second classes.

2.1.4. Benchmarks

This section briefly presents some series of random instances that have been generated in format XCSP 2.1, briefly described in Appendix B. Many of these have been selected for use in various constraint solver competitions. In some experiments that will be reported later, we will refer to these series. This section is succinct[2].

2.1.4.1. Random series

2.1.4.1.1. Random instances from Model D

Seven classes of binary instances near crossover points have been generated following Model D. For each class $\langle 2, n, d, e, p_2 \rangle$, the number of variables n is fixed at 40, the domain size d lies between 8 and 180, the number of constraints e lies between 753 and 84 (so the density between 0.96 and 0.1) and the tightness p_2 lies between 0.1 and 0.9. Here, tightness p_2 is the probability that a pair of values is disallowed by a relation. The first class, $\langle 2, 40, 8, 753, 0.1 \rangle$, corresponds to dense instances involving constraints of low tightness, whereas the seventh one, $\langle 2, 40, 180, 84, 0.9 \rangle$, corresponds to sparse instances involving constraints of high tightness. It is important that a significant sampling of domain sizes, densities and tightnesses is provided.

2.1.4.1.2. Random instances from Model RB

As already mentioned, a desirable property of models RB and RD is that they can generate more and more difficult instances simply by increasing the value of n, once k, α and r have been fixed so that Theorem 2.6 holds. The scaling behavior of algorithms can easily be observed by increasing the number of variables. With $k = 2$, $\alpha = 0.8$ and $r = 3$, we have generated three series of random binary instance for $n \in \{30, 40, 50\}$.

---

2. Further information can be found at http://www.cril.fr/~lecoutre

With the same parameters, we have also generated three series of instances forced to be satisfiable (see [XU 07]). Similarly, with $k = 3, \alpha = 1$ and $r = 1$, we have generated three series of random ternary instance for $n \in \{20, 24, 28\}$, together with three additional series forced to be satisfiable.

2.1.4.1.3. Random instances from Model RB forced to be satisfiable

Using model RB, Ke Xu has encoded some forced binary CSP instances with $k = 2, \alpha = 0.8, r = 0.8$ and n varying from 40 to 59. Each such instance is prefixed by frb-n.

2.1.4.1.4. Random instances of large arity

Two series of non-binary instances with positive table constraints of arity 8 and 10 have been generated to illustrate [LEC 06d].

2.1.4.2. *Random series containing a small structure*

2.1.4.2.1. Ehi

A 3-SAT instance is defined to be a SAT instance in which each clause contains exactly three literals. Two series of 3-SAT unsatisfiable instances, originated in [BAY 97], have been converted into CSP instances using the dual method as described in [BAC 00]. Each instance is obtained by embedding a small unsatisfiable SAT formula into an easy random 3-SAT instance. The instance names of these series are prefixed by ehi-85 and ehi-90.

2.1.4.2.2. Geometric

Richard Wallace has proposed geometric random generation of constraint scopes as follows. Instead of a density parameter, a "distance" parameter, dst, is used such that $dst \leq \sqrt{2}$. For each variable, two coordinates are chosen randomly within the range $0, \ldots, 1$. Then for each pair (x, y) of variables, if the distance between their associated points is less than or equal to dst, the edge $\{x, y\}$ is added to the constraint graph. Constraint relations are generated in the same way as for homogeneous random CSP instances. Each such instance is prefixed by geo.

2.1.4.2.3. Composed

Nine series of 10 random binary CSP instances have been generated as follows. Each instance comprises a main (under-constrained) fragment together with some auxiliary fragments, each of these grafted to the main fragment by means of additional binary constraints. The series composed-25-10-20 contains 10 satisfiable instances, whereas all other series contains 10 unsatisfiable instances. Such classes have appeared in [LEC 04] and related instances have been used experimentally in [JUS 00b].

2.2. Structured constraint networks

This section is concerned with structures that can be found in problem instances arising in real life. Most of the concepts that characterize structure refer to subsets of variables. These concepts include backbones, backdoors, (minimal) unsatisfiable cores, cliques and cycles. We also consider the so-called small-world structure and morphing technique.

2.2.1. *Backbones and backdoors*

Backbones and *backdoors* are structurally significant sets of variables. A backbone [MON 99] is a set of variables (strictly speaking, an instantiation) that have the same values in every solution, or stated otherwise, a set of implied values:

DEFINITION 2.9.– *[Backbone] The* backbone *of a satisfiable constraint network P is the greatest instantiation I on P such that* $\mathrm{sols}(P|_I) = \mathrm{sols}(P)$.

Figures 2.4 and 2.5 show examples of backbones.

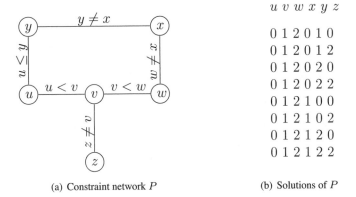

(a) Constraint network P (b) Solutions of P

Figure 2.4. *A constraint network P and the set* $\mathrm{sols}(P)$ *of its solutions. The domain of each variable of P is* $\{0, 1, 2\}$

The hardness of an instance seems to depend (at least partially) on the relative size of the backbone, i.e. the ratio of the size of the backbone to the number of variables. This ratio is called the *backbone fraction*. When an instance has a non-negligible backbone fraction, wrong decisions are easily made during the search for a solution. Wrong decisions taken at the beginning of search (near the top of the search tree) can punitively reduce the efficiency of backtrack search. For local search, solutions can be particularly difficult to find since they are clustered (they all extend the backbone).

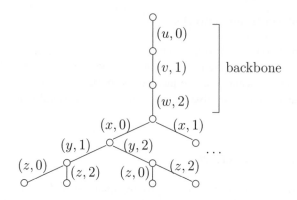

Figure 2.5. *The backbone of the constraint network depicted in Figure 2.4 is*
$\{(u, 0, (v, 1), (w, 2)\}$. *This is emphasized here with a tree structure (called a trie)*

Nevertheless, if the backbone fraction gets closer to 1, incorrect decisions may be detected more quickly as the instance is becoming highly constrained. We suspect that instances having a backbone set of moderate (but not negligible) size are the hardest, corresponding approximately to the transition threshold inherent to these instances [MON 99, ACH 00].

A backdoor is also a set of variables: when all the variables in a (strong) backdoor have been assigned values, the resulting instance can be solved in polynomial time. Small backdoors attempt to capture the overall combinatorics of problem instances, and also help to explain the heavy-tailed behavior of backtrack search algorithms [WIL 03a, WIL 03b]. To define backdoors, we need first to introduce *subsolvers*. Informally, a subsolver is an incomplete algorithm that runs in polynomial time and is able to solve certain instances. For example, a subsolver can be defined to recognize and solve the instances belonging to a tractable class; tractability is addressed in section 3.5.2 of Chapter 3. If a given instance does not belong to this class, the subsolver simply returns "I don't know" (in polynomial time). A backdoor is always defined with respect to a certain subsolver, or a certain tractable class.

DEFINITION 2.10.– *[Weak Backdoor] Let P be a satisfiable constraint network, and A be a subsolver. A weak backdoor of P is a set $X \subseteq \mathrm{vars}(P)$ of variables such that there exists an instantiation I of X on P such that A returns a solution of $P|_I$.*

By definition, unsatisfiable instances do not have any weak backdoor set. This is why a stronger form is proposed.

DEFINITION 2.11.– *[Strong Backdoor] Let P be a constraint network, and A be a subsolver. A strong backdoor of P is a set $X \subseteq \mathrm{vars}(P)$ of variables such that for*

every instantiation I of X on P, A solves P|$_I$, that is, A either returns a solution of
P|$_I$ or indicates that P|$_I$ is unsatisfiable.

There is one trivial backdoor: vars(P). This is a weak backdoor if P is satisfiable, and in any case, this is a strong backdoor[3]. The advantage of identifying small (strong) backdoors should be clear: search can be focused only on the variables of a (strong) backdoor instead of all variables of the instance. If a strong backdoor set of size k is known, the instance can be solved by enumerating and testing each instantiation of the backdoor variables. The overall complexity is then $O(\lambda d^k)$ where λ denotes the polynomial complexity of the subsolver [WIL 03b]. Figure 2.6 illustrates this.

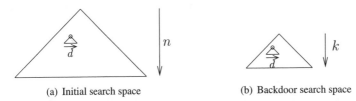

(a) Initial search space   (b) Backdoor search space

Figure 2.6. *The search space of the initial constraint network is $O(d^n)$, whereas the search space "delimited" by a backdoor of size k is $O(d^k)$. At each leaf of the backdoor search tree, a subsolver which runs in polynomial time is executed*

Many empirical studies (essentially conducted for SAT) have shown that structured instances usually admit a (very) small backdoor. Indeed, in the experiments, the *backdoor fraction*, i.e. the ratio of the size of the detected backdoor to the number of variables, is less than 1%, possibly less than 0.1% [WIL 03b]. This is not the case for random instances: the smallest backdoor sets obtained for 3-SAT with respect to 2-SAT and HORN-SAT (tractable classes of propositional formulae) represent at least 30% of the total number of variables [INT 03]. In practice, variable ordering heuristics appear to search implicitly for small backdoor sets, but there has been no comparative study of this.

Unsurprisingly, computing *a priori* small, minimal (i.e. backdoors that cannot be reduced) or, even better, minimum (i.e. backdoors of minimal size) backdoors can be quite expensive. For example, Szeinder shows [SZE 05] that the detection of backdoor sets (for SAT using a subsolver performing unit propagation and pure literal elimination) of size bounded by a fixed integer is of high parametrized complexity (W[P]-complete).

In [KIL 05], it is shown that there is little overlap between backbones and backdoor sets. Besides, in experiments (on SAT instances using a Davis Putnam

---

3. Naturally, the subsolver is assumed to solve the instance when the instantiation is complete.

procedure) problem hardness appears to be correlated with strong backdoor size, weakly correlated with backbone size, and not correlated with weak backdoor size. The fact that problem hardness is not a simple function of weak backdoor size was already shown in [RUA 04]. However, by considering a certain form of dependencies among backdoor variables, we arrive at the refined notion of a *backdoor key*. This is the ratio of the number of dependent variables to the size of the backdoor, and this appears to be closely related to problem hardness. *Backdoor trees* [SAM 08] represent another way to refine the concept of strong backdoor sets by taking into account the relationship between backdoor variables. Backdoor trees are decision trees on backdoor variables such that each leaf is tractable (i.e. solved by the subsolver). The hardness of instances can be ranked according to the number of leaves in backdoor trees.

2.2.2. *Cores and cliques*

On the practical side, when inconsistency is encountered, circumscription of the conflict can help the user to understand, explain, diagnose and restore consistency. A constraint network is said to be *minimally unsatisfiable* iff it is unsatisfiable and arbitrary deletion of one constraint makes it satisfiable. A (minimal) unsatisfiable core is related to strong backdoor.

DEFINITION 2.12.– *[Unsatisfiable Core] An* unsatisfiable core *of a constraint network P is an unsatisfiable sub-network of P.*

DEFINITION 2.13.– *[Minimal Unsatisfiable Core] An unsatisfiable core P' of a constraint network P is minimal iff there is no unsatisfiable core P'' of P such that $P'' \subset P'$.*

To check whether an unsatisfiable core P' is minimal, we check the satisfiability of every sub-network P'' obtained from P' by removing exactly one constraint. However, deciding whether a set of constraints is minimally unsatisfiable is known to be DP-Complete [PAP 88]. In the example in Figure 2.7, it is easy to check that the sub-network P' of P such that vars$(P') = \{u, v, w\}$ and cons$(P') = \{c_{uv} : u < v, c_{vw} : v < w, c_{uw} : u > w\}$ is unsatisfiable. Removing any additional constraint clearly makes the network satisfiable.

In the case of Boolean constraints, finding minimal unsatisfiable sub-formulae is an active research area. For example, some recent advances in satisfiability checking have allowed successful extensions of SAT solvers for handling such a hard computational problem [BRU 00, ZHA 03a, LYN 04b, OH 04, GRE 06]. In the context of constraint satisfaction, although there is a significant amount of work dealing with the identification of conflict sets of constraints, there is only a small amount of work really dedicated to the extraction of minimal unsatisfiable cores from

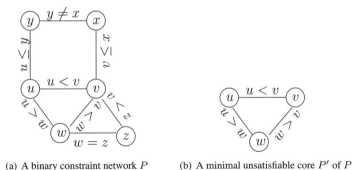

(a) A binary constraint network P (b) A minimal unsatisfiable core P' of P

Figure 2.7. *Illustration of a minimal unsatisfiable core*

constraint networks. An approach toward diagnosis of over-constrained networks has been proposed in [BAK 93] and [HAN 99, BAN 03] have contributed a method for finding all minimal unsatisfiable cores from a given set of constraints. To extract from an over-constrained problem an explanation (or relaxation) using preferences given by the user, a divide and conquer approach has also been proposed in [JUN 04]. Finally, the extraction of minimal unsatisfiable cores from constraint networks has been addressed by exploiting an adaptive variable heuristic [HEM 06], and has been shown to be effective for many problems. A finer-grained approach has been proposed in [GRE 07]: this allows the identification and removal of forbidden tuples that are not part of the cause of unsatisfiability.

A direct relationship between unsatisfiable cores and strong backdoors deserves to be mentioned. From an unsatisfiable core, one can extract a strong backdoor with respect to an elementary subsolver [LYN 04a]. The strong backdoor is the set of variables belonging to the unsatisfiable core, and the subsolver simply ensures that any constraint covered by the current instantiation is satisfied. Of course, whenever the current instantiation covers all variables present in the unsatisfiable core, the subsolver detects an unsatisfied constraint. Interestingly, it has been shown [HEM 06] that many structured problems admit small minimal unsatisfiable cores. Indeed, the ratio of number of variables in the detected minimal unsatisfiable cores to the total number of variables is usually far less than 1%. This confirms that small strong backdoors do exist in many structured problems.

The minimal unsatisfiable core P' extracted from the binary constraint network P in Figure 2.7 has a special property: its constraint graph is a clique. Besides, for every pair (x, y) of variables of this sub-network, we can see that the relation associated with the constraint involving x and y is irreflexive, i.e. we have $\forall (a, b) \in \text{dom}(x) \times \text{dom}(y), (a, b) \in \text{rel}(c_{xy}) \Rightarrow a \neq b$. In other words: $\forall \{x, y\} \subset \text{vars}(P')$, we have $x \neq y$. Hence we can infer an additional global constraint allDifferent over vars(P')

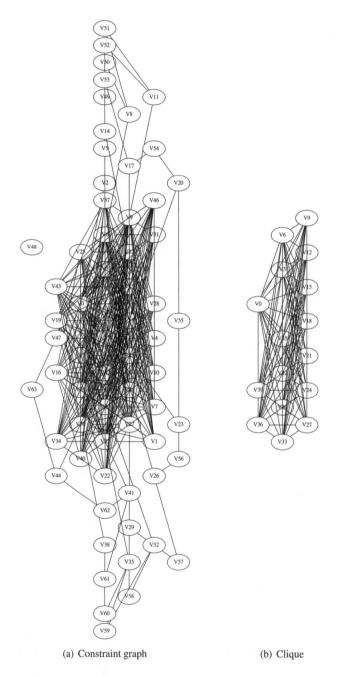

(a) Constraint graph   (b) Clique

Figure 2.8. *The constraint graph of the instance* **blackHole-4-4-e-0** *contains a 16-clique. A constraint* **allDifferent** *generated from this clique can be shown to be disentailed*

that improves pruning of the search space. In some constraint solvers, the filtering procedure (propagator) attached to allDifferent achieves a local consistency weaker than generalized arc consistency (presented in Chapter 3). Even in this case, inferring allDifferent global constraints can be quite effective provided that the following (trivial) proposition is exploited.

PROPOSITION 2.14.– *Let* c : *allDifferent*$(x_1, \ldots, x_r)$ *be a constraint. If* $|\cup_{i=1}^{r} \text{dom}(x_i)| <$ r, *then* c *is disentailed (i.e.* $\sup(c) = \emptyset$).

The presence of cliques is a structural feature that deserves careful study. Properties other than irreflexivity may also be exploitable (for example, see [TEA 08]). Interestingly, it is not so rare to find cliques in non-random problems. For example Figure 2.8 shows the constraint graph of the instance blackHole-4-4-e-0 which contains a 16-clique that enables us to infer a global constraint allDifferent. As this additional constraint is disentailed (this is shown from Proposition 2.14), the instance is directly proved to be unsatisfiable.

2.2.3. *Acyclicity*

It is well-known that binary constraint networks whose constraint graph is *acyclic* (i.e. forms a tree) can be solved in polynomial time; this is discussed in section 3.5.2. However, the macro-structure associated with a non-binary constraint network is not a graph but a hypergraph. So the question of acyclicity for hypergraphs arises. In fact, acyclicity turns out to be a fundamental structural property. This has been introduced in the context of relational databases [BEE 83, GOO 83, GYS 94].

In the dual graph D of a hypergraph $H = (V, E)$, each node represents a hyperedge of H and so corresponds to a subset of V; see section 1.2.2. An edge in D between vertices v and v' connects "shared" variables, those in $v \cap v'$. Such an edge is *redundant* iff there exists an alternate path between v and v' formed of edges each connecting (at least) variables in $v \cap v'$. If D is regarded as the dual graph of a constraint hypergraph, a redundant edge corresponds to a redundant constraint that can be eliminated because the other constraints in the dual graph enforce the equality between shared variables [DEC 06].

An acyclic subgraph of the dual graph resulting from the removal of redundant edges is called a *join-tree*. The set of vertices in a join-tree in which a node of the initial hypergraph occurs induces a connected subtree. This is called the *connectedness condition* of join trees. A hypergraph is *acyclic* iff it has a join-tree. Note that there are various equivalent characterizations of acyclic hypergraphs. For example, a hypergraph is acyclic iff its primal graph is *triangulated* or *chordal* (i.e. every cycle of length at least four has an edge connecting two non-adjacent nodes of the cycle) and *conformal* (i.e. there is a one-to-one mapping between maximal cliques of the primal graph and hyperedges of the hypergraph).

EXAMPLE.– Consider a constraint network P involving six variables u, v, w, x, y and z, and four ternary constraints c_{uvw}, c_{wxy}, c_{uyz} and c_{uwy} (this example is similar to the one presented in [DEC 92a]). Figures 2.9(a) and 2.9(b) show the constraint hypergraph and dual graph of P, respectively. Note that the three edges labeled with u, w, and y are redundant. Hence they can be removed. We obtain the join-tree depicted in Figure 2.9(c), which demonstrates that the constraint hypergraph of P is acyclic. Figure 2.9(d) shows the connected subtree of the join-tree of P induced by u.

Acyclic constraint networks are those whose constraint hypergraph is acyclic. Checking the satisfiability of acyclic constraint networks is tractable and highly parallelizable [GOT 01]. Besides, for identifying acyclic constraint networks and for finding a representative join-tree several efficient procedures have been developed in the area of relational databases [MAI 83]. Although in practice constraint networks are usually cyclic, structured instances often have several main components which are more or less independent. The intention of *structural decomposition methods* is to transform cyclic constraint networks into acyclic ones. This can be achieved by grouping variables (and constraints) into *clusters* that represent subproblems for which all solutions can be computed. Replacing each cluster with its set of solutions yields an acyclic equivalent constraint network. We provide more detail in the following paragraphs.

The definition of *tree decomposition* [ROB 86] is central in several structural decomposition methods.

DEFINITION 2.15.– *[Tree Decomposition] A* tree decomposition *of a graph* $G = (V, E)$ *is a tree* $T = (W, F)$ *such that:*

– *each vertex of* T *is a non-empty set (called cluster) of vertices of* G: $\forall w \in W, w \subseteq V$;

– *each vertex of* G *belongs to (at least) one cluster:* $\forall v \in V, \exists w \in W \mid v \in w$;

– *each edge of* G *belongs to (at least) one cluster:* $\forall e \in E, \exists w \in W \mid e \subseteq w$;

– *each vertex of* G *must induce a connected subtree of* T: $\forall w, w', w'' \in W$, *if there is a path in* T *from* w *to* w'' *traversing* w', *then* $w \cap w'' \subseteq w'$.

DEFINITION 2.16.– *[Tree-width] The* width *of a tree decomposition* $T = (W, F)$ *of a graph* G *is equal to* $\max_{w \in W} |w| - 1$. *The* tree-width *of a graph* G *is the minimum width over all tree decompositions of* G.

A tree decomposition of a constraint network P is a tree decomposition of the primal graph of P. Given such a tree decomposition, the challenge is to solve each subproblem identified by a cluster. This task dominates the overall worst-case time

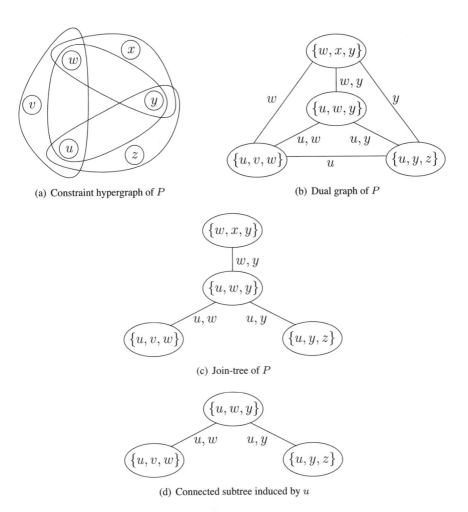

(a) Constraint hypergraph of P

(b) Dual graph of P

(c) Join-tree of P

(d) Connected subtree induced by u

Figure 2.9. *The constraint network P involving four ternary constraints is acyclic. By removing redundant edges from the dual graph of P, we obtain a join-tree. Edges in the dual graph and in the join-tree are labeled with shared variables*

complexity which is traditionally given by $O(ed^{w+1})$ for a tree decomposition whose tree-width is w. The space complexity is similar but can be reduced to become exponential in the maximal separator size (which is the size of the biggest intersection between clusters). It is interesting to compare these complexities with those of backtrack search algorithms. Although backtrack search is often efficient in practice (benefiting from constraint propagation and adaptive heuristics presented later in this book), its worst-case time complexity is $O(ed^n)$ and, without nogood recording, its worst-case space complexity is linear. Of course, we have $w < n$, and even on some cases $w \ll n$.

Tree-clustering [DEC 89b] is a well-known method for obtaining tree-decompositions. The two first steps are the triangulation of the primal graph and the search of maximal cliques.

EXAMPLE.– In the example in Figure 2.10, which is taken from [GOT 00], there is a constraint network P involving six variables u, v, w, x, y and z, two ternary constraints c_{uvw} and c_{xyz}, and two binary constraints c_{uz} and c_{wx}. Figures 2.10(a) and 2.10(b) show the constraint hypergraph of P and the dual graph of P. There is no redundant edge in the dual graph of P, which shows that P is not acyclic. To "render" P acyclic, the primal graph of P is first triangulated. In this example, inserting one edge is sufficient to obtain a triangulated graph; see Figure 2.10(d). Next, maximal cliques are identified in the triangulated primal graph. These maximal cliques define an acyclic hypergraph whose hyperedges correspond to clusters or subproblems. Figure 2.10(f) shows a tree decomposition for the hypergraph in Figure 2.10(a).

For real-world problems, tree decomposition may turn out to be quite attractive, as in the example in Figure 2.11 (kindly provided by Simon de Givry and Thomas Schiex).

Tree clustering is one of a number of structural decomposition methods. The main structural decomposition methods have been arranged in a hierarchy [GOT 00], which includes biconnected components [FRE 82], hinge decomposition [GYS 94], tree clustering [DEC 89b], cycle cutset [DEC 92a], cycle hypercutset [GOT 00] and hypertree decomposition [GOT 02]; see Figure 2.12. Jégou, Ndiaye and Terrioux have shown [JÉG 08, JÉG 09] that by separating decomposition from solution, new hybrid structural methods can be naturally devised. For example, a constraint network can be solved with an "optimal" time complexity by using tree clustering on one tree-decomposition induced by a hypertree-decomposition. This result provides a theoretical explanation of experimental results observed so far by the community, specifically, the good performance of tree decomposition methods. This result is partly derived from a new theoretical bound for backtrack search algorithms such as FC (the non-binary variant called nFC2 [BES 02]) and MAC. With S denoting the size of a given constraint network P, the worst-case time complexity of nFC2 to solve P is $O(Sr^k)$ where r is the maximum size of relations associated with constraints of P and k is the size of the minimum cover of vars(P) by scopes of constraints of P. Roughly speaking, a structural decomposition method D_1 strongly generalizes a structural decomposition method D_2 if D_1 allows more efficient decompositions than D_2. There is a rigorous definition in [GOT 02].

Using a hybrid of enumerative search and structural-driven approaches seems a good compromise because backtrack search can operate in linear memory, while tree

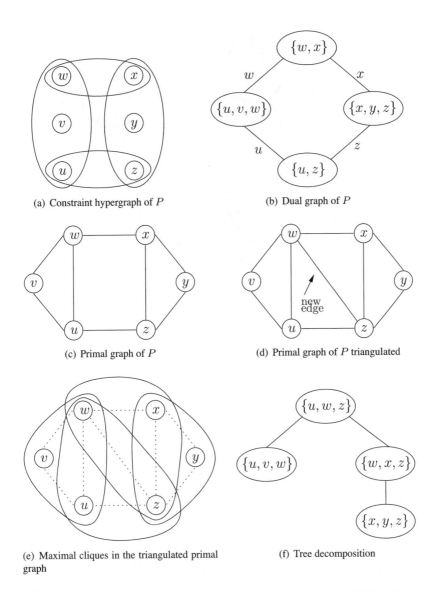

(a) Constraint hypergraph of P

(b) Dual graph of P

(c) Primal graph of P

(d) Primal graph of P triangulated

(e) Maximal cliques in the triangulated primal graph

(f) Tree decomposition

Figure 2.10. *The constraint network P is not acyclic. A tree decomposition is computed*

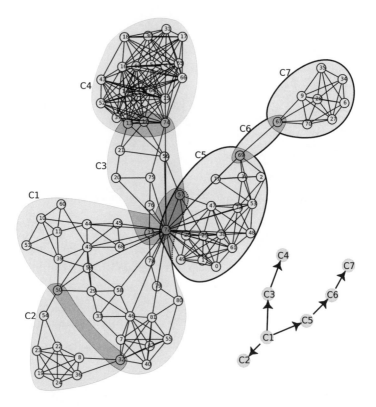

Figure 2.11. *Tree decomposition of the constraint graph of the preprocessed* scen-06 *instance*

decomposition guarantees good time complexity bounds. Among hybrid methods, we can cite backtracking with tree-decomposition (BTD) [JÉG 03] and AND/OR search [MAR 05b, MAR 05a], which are also related to pseudo-tree search [FRE 85b]. BTD computes a tree decomposition that is used as a partial variable ordering by the search heuristic. The essential property of tree decomposition is that after instantiating the variables in a separator, we obtain two independent subproblems that can be solved independently. During search, BTD focuses on separators (intersection of clusters) by recording structural goods and nogoods and thereby avoids visiting similar portions of the search space. BTD has been shown effective for both decision and optimization problems [JÉG 03, JÉG 04, GIV 06]. On the other hand, AND/OR search spaces display the independencies in the constraint graph and sometimes yield exponential saving compared to the traditional search space. AND/OR search spaces provide a unifying paradigm for advanced algorithmic schemes for graphical models.

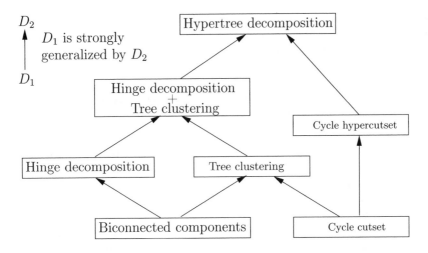

Figure 2.12. *The hierarchy of decomposition methods of [GOT 02]*

2.2.4. *Small world structure and morphing technique*

The structure of graphs, which are fundamental mathematical structures, has also been investigated. To quantify the structural properties of a graph, two *a priori* independent measures have been introduced in [WAT 98]: the *characteristic path length* and the *clustering coefficient*. The former is defined as the number of edges in the shortest path between two vertices, averaged over all pairs of vertices, and indicates the typical separation between two vertices in the graph. The latter is defined as the density of the subgraph (vertex-)induced[4] by the neighbors of a vertex (itself included), averaged over all vertices, and indicates the cliquishness of a typical neighborhood. While random graphs have a small characteristic path length and a low clustering coefficient, quite regular graphs (such as lattices) have a large characteristic path length and a high clustering coefficient.

We can interpolate between these extremes by introducing a certain amount of disorder in a regular graph: we can tune a probability parameter p so the resulting graph lies between regular and random. This way of artificially generating new graphs offers the opportunity to build graph-based problems (such as constraint networks) that can be used as benchmarks. For some intermediate values of p, the generated graph has a *small-world* structure: the graph has a small characteristic path length like random graphs and a high clustering coefficient like regular graphs. These structures seem to be surprisingly widespread since, for example, the neural network of the

---

4. Let $G = (V, E)$ be a graph and $X \subseteq V$, the subgraph vertex-induced by X is $G' = (X, \{(v, v') \in E \mid v \in X \land v' \in X\})$.

worm *caenorhabditis elegans*, the power grid of the western United States and the collaboration graph of film actors are shown to be small worlds. Walsh [WAL 99] has shown that (many) classical search problems have small world topology. This is the case for graph-coloring, timetabling and quasi-group problems. The distribution of time taken by search algorithms to solve small-world problems is likely to be heavy-tailed. Therefore a randomization strategy with geometric restarts (discussed later in this book) is suggested to tackle such problems more efficiently.

On the other hand, a general technique called *morphing* [GEN 99] can introduce structure or randomness in a wide variety of problems. In particular, morphing provides a simple mechanism for constructing small world graphs. The basic principle is that, given two structures S_1 and S_2, a new structure S_3 is built by taking components of S_1 with probability p and components of S_2 with probability $1 - p$ (proportions can also be considered). Many types of structures can be morphed, including graphs, matrices, vectors and relations. Moreover, morphing can be used to build new challenging benchmarks containing a mixture of structure and randomness.

Finally, in addition to the small-world model of graphs, and the classical random graph model [ERD 59] extensively studied during the last century, *scale-free* graphs have been proposed [ALB 99] as a new generic model of network topologies. In this model, the arity of vertices follows a power-law distribution. The world wide web, viewed as a graph, has such a structure as well as some social and metabolic networks. Scale-free networks, because of their heterogeneity, have been shown to be fairly robust to errors (random loss of vertices) although very vulnerable to attacks (targeted loss of the most important vertices) [ALB 00, CRU 04]. This latter property has been termed the "Achilles' heel" of scale-free networks. In [LI 05], topological features of scale-free graphs are discussed and a structural metric is proposed as a possible measure of the extent to which a graph is scale-free. To the best of our knowledge, the study of constraint networks with scale-free topologies has not been specifically investigated.

2.2.5. *Benchmarks*

In recent years, the community has collected many series of structured instances from different backgrounds. Some of these are briefly introduced below[5]. These clearly identified series (in format XCSP 2.1; see Appendix B) allow anybody to control and reproduce experimental results based on them.

---

5. There is further information about benchmark instances at http://www.cril.fr/~lecoutre

2.2.5.1. *Main series*

2.2.5.1.1. Crosswords

Given a grid and a dictionary, the problem is to fill the grid with words in the dictionary. To generate crossword instances, three series of grids (Herald, Puzzle, Vg) and four dictionaries (Lex, Uk, Words, Ogd) have been used. Herald refers to crossword puzzles taken from the Herald Tribune (Spring, 1999), Puzzle refers to crossword puzzles mentioned in [GIN 93, GIN 90], and Vg refers to blank grids. Lex is a dictionary used in [SAM 05], Uk is the UK cryptic solvers dictionary, Words is the dictionary in /usr/dict/words under Linux, and Ogd is a French dictionary[6]. Lex and Words are small dictionaries, whereas Uk and Ogd are large. The model used to generate the instances is the one identified by $m1$ in [BEA 01]. For the Vg grids, all instances involve only extensional constraints, because it is permissible to put the same word on the grid several times.

2.2.5.1.2. Haystacks

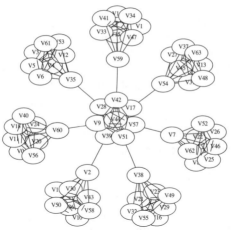

Figure 2.13. *The constraint graph of the binary instance* haystacks-08

The Haystacks instances are binary unsatisfiable instances created by Marc van Dongen. The instance haystacks-p is called the haystack instance of size p: it has $p \times p$ variables and each variable has domain $\{0, \dots, p-1\}$. The constraint graph is highly regular, consisting of p clusters: one central cluster and $p-1$ outer clusters, each one being a p-clique. The instances are designed so that if the variables in the central cluster are instantiated, only one of the outer clusters contains an inconsistency: this cluster is the haystack. The task is to find the haystack and decide that it is

---

6. See http://pagesperso-orange.fr/ledefi

unsatisfiable, thereby providing a proof that the current instantiation of the variables in the central cluster is inconsistent. The structure of the instance haystacks-08 is shown in Figure 2.13,

2.2.5.1.3. FAPP

The frequency assignment problem with polarization constraints (FAPP) is an optimization problem[7] that was part of the ROADEF'2001 challenge[8]. In this problem, there are constraints concerning frequencies and polarizations of radio links. Progressive relaxation of these constraints is explored: the relaxation level is between 0 (no relaxation) and 10 (the maximum relaxation). Progressive relaxation produces eleven CSP instances from any single original FAPP optimization instance. Series of instances are denoted by fappNB with $NB \in \{01, \ldots, 40\}$ while individual instances are denoted by fappNB-n-r where n is the number of variables and r is the relaxation level. The higher the value of r, the less constrained the instance.

2.2.5.1.4. QCP/QWH/BQWH

The quasi-group completion problem (QCP) is the task of determining whether the remaining entries of a partial Latin square can be filled in such a way that we obtain a complete Latin square, ie. a full multiplication table of a quasi-group [GOM 02]. The quasi-group with holes problem (QWH) is a variant of the QCP wherein instances are generated so as to be guaranteed satisfiable [GOM 02]. The eight series of instances generated by Radoslaw Szymanek for the 2005 constraint solver competition are denoted by qcp-p and qwh-p where $p \in \{10, 15, 20, 25\}$ corresponds to the order (size) of the Latin square. Two series of 100 satisfiable balanced quasi-group instances with holes, series denoted by bqwh-p with $p \in \{15, 18\}$, are also available.

2.2.5.1.5. Radar surveillance

The Swedish Institute of Computer Science (SICS) has proposed a model of realistic radar surveillance[9]. The problem is to adjust the signal strength (from 0 to s) of a given number of fixed radars with respect to six geographic sectors. Each cell of the geographic area of size $p \times p$ must be covered exactly by k radar stations, except for a number, i of forbidden cells that must not be covered. Three sets of 50 instances with non-binary constraints have been generated artificially. Each instance is denoted by radar-p-k-s-i.

2.2.5.1.6. Renault

This is a CSP instance obtained from a Renault Megane configuration problem [AMI 02] that has been converted from symbolic domains to numeric ones. This

---

7. This is an extended subject of the CALMA European project.
8. See http://uma.ensta.fr/conf/roadef-2001-challenge/
9. See http://www.ps.uni-sb.de/~walser/radar/radar.html

instance (which is available in two forms, one normalized and one not), denoted by renault, involves large table constraints of high arity. The series modifiedRenault contains instances generated (by Kostas Stergiou) from the original configuration instance. These are interesting for evaluating, for example, GAC algorithms for table constraints.

2.2.5.1.7. RLFAP

The radio link frequency assignment problem (RLFAP) is the task of assigning frequencies to a set of radio links satisfying a large number of constraints and using as few distinct frequencies as possible. In 1993, the CELAR (the French "centre d'electronique de l'armement") built a suite of simplified versions of radio link frequency assignment problems starting from data on a real network. These benchmarks have been made available to the public in the framework of the European EUCLID project CALMA (combinatorial algorithms for military applications). For more information, see [CAB 99]. There are five series of binary RLFAP instances, identified as either scen or graph. Following the approach of [BES 01a], some RLFAP instances have been modified by removing some constraints (w followed by a value) and/or some frequencies (f followed by a value). For example, scen07-w1-f4 corresponds to the instance scen07 without the constraints which have weight greater than one and also without the four highest frequencies. The most difficult instances belong to the series scen11-fNB with NB $\in$ 1..12. These real-world instances are highly structured as illustrated in Figure 2.14.

2.2.5.1.8. Scheduling job-shop and open-shop instances

Job-shop scheduling aims to find a schedule minimizing the overall completion time for a set of jobs requiring shared resources. Open-shop scheduling differs in that the operations of each job are not required to be ordered. Five series of satisfiable job-shop instances, denoted by js-e0ddr1, js-e0ddr2, etc. have been proposed by Norman Sadeh and experimental results are reported in [SAD 96]. Figure 2.15 shows the structure of the instance e0ddr1-10-by-5-1; sub-networks corresponding to five jobs are clearly identifiable. Naoyuki Tamura proposed another series of 10 instances for the 2006 constraint solver competition. This series, whose instance names are prefixed with gp10, corresponds to open-shop instances developed by Christelle Guéret and Christian Prin. Further series of job-shop and open-shop instances have been generated by Julien Vion in accordance with the description in [TAI 93]. Here, instances are only considered for satisfaction: instead of looking for an optimal solution, a time window is fixed, and one has to decide if a solution exists within this time window. To do this, when considering the original optimization problem, the time window has been set to the best known value (100 occurring in the name of the instances), a smaller value (95 occurring in the name of the instances) and a greater value (105 occurring in the name of the instances). Of course, all "100" and "105" instances are satisfiable. The instance names of the series are prefixed with js-taillard and os-taillard.

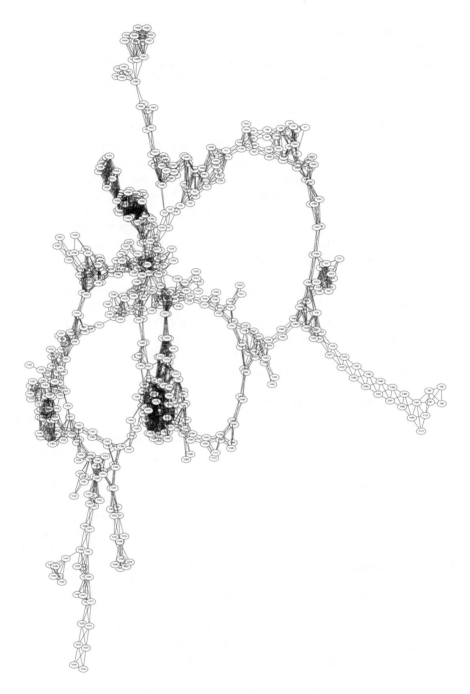

Figure 2.14. *The constraint graph of the binary instance* scen11

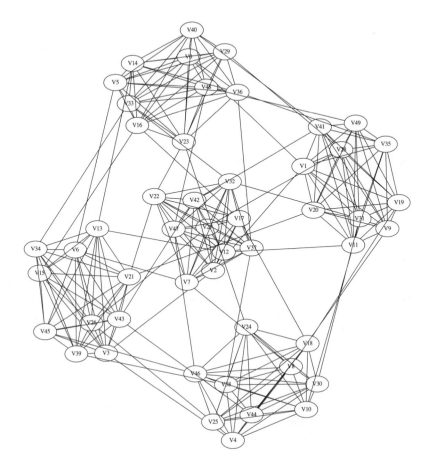

Figure 2.15. *The constraint graph of the binary instance e0ddr1-10-by-5-1*

2.2.5.1.9. Traveling salesperson

The object of the traveling salesperson problem is to determine a tour, of minimal length, that visits each in a given set of cities exactly once. Radoslaw Szymanek has generated two series of 15 ternary instances (all satisfiable) for the 2005 constraint solver competition. Names of these instances are prefixed by tsp-p with $p \in \{20, 25\}$.

2.2.5.2. *Other series*

2.2.5.2.1. All-interval series

The problem[10] is to find a vector $s = (s_1, \ldots, s_p)$, such that:

---

10. See prob007 at http://www.csplib.org

– s is a permutation of $\{0, 1, \ldots, p - 1\}$; and

– the interval vector $v = (|s_2 - s_1|, |s_3 - s_2|, \ldots, |s_p - s_{p-1}|)$ is a permutation of $\{1, 2, \ldots, p - 1\}$.

Each instance is ternary and denoted by series-p.

2.2.5.2.2. Black hole

The Black Hole problem is to move all cards in 17 fans of 3 cards each to the center pile, the Black Hole, which initially only contains the ace of spades. Radoslaw Szymanek has generated three series of binary instances (which correspond to a simplification of the original problem) for the 2005 constraint solver competition. These are prefixed by BlackHole-4-p with $p \in \{4, 7, 13\}$.

2.2.5.2.3. Chessboard coloration

The problem is to color all squares of a chessboard composed of r rows and c columns. There are exactly k available colors and the four corners of no rectangle of chessboard squares may be assigned the same color. Each instance is quaternary and denoted by cc-r-c-k.

2.2.5.2.4. Domino

This problem was introduced in [ZHA 01b] to emphasize the sub-optimality of the algorithm AC3. Each instance, denoted by domino-n-d, is binary and corresponds to an undirected constraint graph with a cycle. More precisely, n denotes the number of variables, the domains of which are $\{1, \ldots, d\}$, and there exist $n - 1$ equality constraints $x_i = x_{i+1}$ ($\forall i \in \{1, \ldots, n - 1\}$) and a trigger constraint $(x_1 = x_n + 1 \wedge x_1 < d) \vee (x_1 = x_n \wedge x_1 = d)$.

2.2.5.2.5. Golomb ruler

The problem[11] is to put k marks on a ruler of length p such that the distance between any two pairs of marks is distinct. Each instance from the model involving ternary (resp. quaternary) constraints is denoted by ruler-p-k-a3 (resp. ruler-p-k-a4). Figure 2.16 shows the primal constraint graph of the ternary instance ruler-17-6-a3.

2.2.5.2.6. Pigeons

The pigeonhole problem is to put p pigeons into $p - 1$ boxes, one pigeon per box. All instances are clearly unsatisfiable. Each instance is binary and denoted by pigeons-p.

---

11. See prob006 at http://www.csplib.org

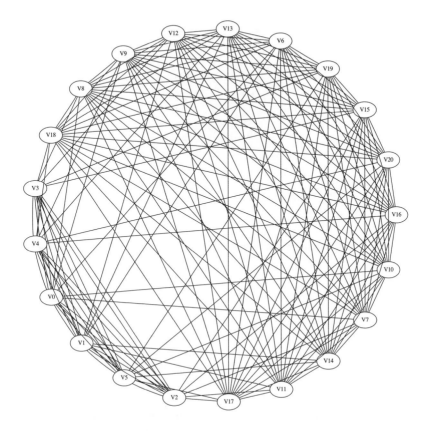

Figure 2.16. *The primal constraint graph of the ternary instance* ruler-17-6-a3

2.2.5.2.7. Queen attacking

The queen attacking problem[12] is to put a queen and the p^2 numbers $1, \ldots, p^2$, on a $p \times p$ chessboard so that:

– no two numbers are on the same cell;

– each number $i + 1$ is reachable by a knight move from the cell containing i;

– no cell that contains a prime number is not attacked by the queen (for satisfaction).

Each instance is binary and denoted by queenAttacking-p (qa-p in tables when the name must be shortened). The constraint graph of the binary instance queenAttacking-4 is shown in Figure 2.17.

---

12. See prob029 at http://www.csplib.org

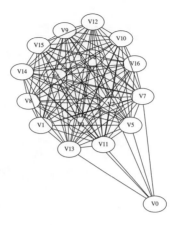

Figure 2.17. *The constraint graph of the binary instance* **queenAttacking-4**

2.2.5.2.8. Queens-knights

On a chessboard of size $q \times q$, the queens-knights problem is to put q queens and k knights such that no two queens can attack each other and all knights form a cycle (when considering knight moves) [BOU 04b]. In one version of this binary problem (identified by "add"), a square of the chessboard can be shared by both a queen and a knight and in another (identified by "mul"), this is not allowed. Each instance is denoted by queensKnights-q-k-add for the first version, or, for the second version, by queensKnights-q-k-mul (qk-... in tables when the name must be shortened). More information about this problem can be found in section 8.5.

2.2.5.2.9. Langford

The (generalized version of the) Langford's problem[13] is to arrange p sets of numbers ranging from 1 to k, so that each appearance of the number m is m numbers on from the last. Each instance is binary and is denoted by langford-p-k.

2.2.5.2.10. Primes

The Primes instances are non-binary intensional satisfiable instances created by Marc van Dongen. Domains of variables consist of prime numbers and all constraints are linear equations. The coefficients and constants in the equations are also prime numbers. Each instance is prefixed by primes.

---

13. See prob024 at http://www.csplib.org

2.2.5.2.11. Ramsey

Given a complete graph that has p nodes, the Ramsey problem[14] is to color, using k colors, the edges so that there is no monochromatic triangle in the graph, which means that in each triangle at most two edges may have the same color. Each instance is ternary and denoted by ramsey-p-k.

2.2.5.2.12. Schur's Lemma

The problem[15] is to put n balls labeled from 1 to n into three boxes so that for any triple of balls (x, y, z) such that $x + y = z$ are not all in the same box. The available series comprise ternary instances whose name is prefixed by lemma and suffixed by mod for the variant proposed in [BES 02].

---

14. See prob017 at http://www.csplib.org
15. See prob015 at http://www.csplib.org

PART ONE

Inference

Techniques and algorithms to solve constraint satisfaction problem (CSP) instances belong mainly (e.g. see [DEC 03, FRE 06]) to two main categories: *inference* and *search*[1]. Inference methods aim to simplify a problem so as to make it easier to solve, while preserving its semantics, i.e. its set of solutions. Simplification can be achieved by transforming the set of variables and constraints, or by discarding useless parts of the search space, or by other means. Exploration of the search space is required in the general case where it is impossible to solve a given CSP instance purely by inference. This exploration is called search.

The first part of this book is focused on inference – more precisely on *constraint propagation*, which uses semantics of constraints to identify and discard incompatible combinations of values. Such combinations, which are instantiations that cannot be part of any solution, are called (standard) *nogoods*. A constraint propagation (or filtering) algorithm is usually described in terms of *(local) consistencies*, which are properties of constraint networks. The classical way to "propagate constraints" is to enforce a given consistency on a given constraint network. Typically, this means reducing the domains of variables or the relations of constraints in order to obtain a more explicit network that satisfies the consistency. The resulting network does not lose any solutions, because only nogoods are "recorded" in the network. It is also simpler because recorded nogoods can be used to avoid exploration of useless parts of the search space.

For more than three decades, constraint propagation has received much attention because it is recognized as a very important component of complete efficient solvers. Many of the published filtering algorithms are dedicated to specific types of constraints (typically, global ones). Unfortunately, implementation of a large number of different algorithms requires substantial development effort, so experimental comparison of constraint solvers is not easy. General-purpose algorithms are centrally important in the development of robust black-box solvers. Generic filtering algorithms that can be used with all kinds of constraint provide a universal filtering mechanism which has a privileged place in the development of such solvers.

The following chapters present recent techniques and algorithms that improve or extend generic filtering capabilities. This work is based on simple consistencies: generalized arc consistency, singleton arc consistency and path/dual consistency.

---

1. The frontier between inference and search is not always quite distinct because inference is sometimes conducted by a limited form of search (e.g. when singleton arc consistency, described later, is enforced).

Chapter 3

Consistencies

A *consistency*, which is a general property of a constraint network (or a general condition on a constraint network), usually indicates a certain level of (local) coherence. It has to do with constraint (hyper)graphs and/or compatibility (hyper)graphs. In most cases, a *local* consistency is a property defined from particular subsets of variables and/or constraints. In contrast, *global* consistency is a precise property that refers to the entire network, guaranteeing in particular that a solution exists. Absence of a local consistency enables us to make deductions, also called *inferences*, that reveal some (standard) nogoods, i.e. reveal some instantiations that cannot lead to any solution.

By taking account of nogoods identified by inference, constraint networks can be modified so that they become more explicit and simpler to solve. This involves *constraint propagation*, which means the iterative collection of nogoods by a *filtering algorithm* that enforces a given consistency. In the worst case, a constraint satisfaction problem (CSP) instance cannot be solved in polynomial time, but the vast majority of filtering algorithms that perform constraint propagation run in polynomial time. Constraint propagation is central to constraint reasoning and has contributed to the success of constraint programming because it is an appealing concept yielding practical efficiency.

Although constraint propagation alone is usually not sufficient to solve a problem instance (e.g. by detecting unsatisfiability), it can simplify an instance before commencement of search. In practice constraint propagation is applied at each basic step during backtrack search. Thus backtrack search and inference (processes) are interleaved. Identification of nogoods allows some useless portions of the search space to be avoided. In other words, some fruitless branches of the search tree built by the backtracking algorithm are pruned so as to save much search effort.

In many cases, consistencies on which filtering algorithms are based allow the identification of inconsistent instantiations of a certain size. Specifically, a *kth-order* consistency is a consistency that permits identification of nogoods of size k. In practice, most of the consistencies that are studied or exploited are first- and second-order consistencies. A first-order consistency is associated with *domain-filtering* because identified nogoods are of size 1 and correspond to inconsistent values that can be removed from domains of variables. A second-order consistency enables identification of inconsistent pairs of values. When binary constraints are extensional, their associated tables can be easily updated to record some of these new nogoods, but unfortunately some missing constraints may also have to be included in the constraint network. This is why, in general and in practice, higher-order consistencies are *relation-filtering* consistencies, which means that they can be applied (conservatively) to existing constraints.

The chapter is organized as follows. Section 3.1 formulates basic variable-based consistencies. This provides a gentle introduction to the concept of consistencies and also to the role that they play. Next, section 3.2 states a stability principle for consistencies. When this holds for a consistency ϕ, we have an important guarantee for any constraint network P. Specifically, the existence of a unique greatest ϕ-*consistent* constraint network smaller than P is guaranteed. Section 3.3 introduces the most commonly studied (and used) domain-filtering consistencies; section 3.4 deals with higher-order consistencies. Finally, section 3.5 explains that, under certain conditions, the ideal global consistency can be identified, and even better, can be reached by simple polynomial transformations.

3.1. Basic consistencies

The class of consistencies called *k-consistencies*, introduced by Freuder in [FRE 78], provides a good starting point for a study of consistencies. This class generalizes early consistencies proposed by Mackworth [MAC 77a], which are introduced later in this chapter. Informally, a constraint network is k-consistent iff every locally consistent instantiation of $k - 1$ variables can be extended to a locally consistent instantiation involving any additional variable.

DEFINITION 3.1.– *[k-consistency] Let P be a constraint network and k be an integer such that $1 \leq k < n = |\operatorname{vars}(P)|$. P is k-consistent iff for every set X of $k - 1$ variables of P and every additional variable y of P, every locally consistent instantiation of X on P can be extended to a locally consistent instantiation of $X \cup \{y\}$ on P.*

If P is k-consistent and I is a locally consistent instantiation of X, then for every variable y, there exists a value b in $\operatorname{dom}(y)$ such that $I \cup \{(y, b)\}$ is a locally consistent instantiation on P. Note that the empty instantiation $I = \emptyset$ is deemed to be locally consistent. This means that no domain can be empty in a 1-consistent network.

As illustrated later in this section, a constraint network that is k-consistent is not necessarily j-consistent with $1 \leq j < k$. This is why a stronger form has been introduced:

DEFINITION 3.2.– *[Strong k-consistency] Let P be a constraint network and k be an integer such that $1 \leq k < n$. P is strongly k-consistent iff P is j-consistent for every integer j such that $1 \leq j \leq k$.*

In section 3.2, we will show that it is always possible to transform a constraint network into an equivalent one which is strongly k-consistent. The optimal time and space complexities for establishing strong k-consistency are $O(n^k d^k)$ and $O(n^{k-1} d^{k-1})$, respectively [COO 89, BES 06].

In terms of these consistencies, we can define what can be considered to be the ultimate consistency:

DEFINITION 3.3.– *[Global Consistency] A constraint network is globally consistent iff it is strongly n-consistent.*

A globally consistent network is maximally explicit. This is a very appealing consistency because we not only have the guarantee that a globally consistent constraint network is satisfiable (i.e. admits at least one solution) but also that any partial locally consistent instantiation can always be extended to a solution of the network [FRE 82].

THEOREM 3.4.– *A globally consistent constraint network is satisfiable, and a solution can be found by a backtrack-free depth-first search.*

EXAMPLE.– We now illustrate different consistencies in terms of constraint networks that have three variables x, y, z and three binary constraints, one per each pair of variables. The domains of the three variables are $\text{dom}(x) = \text{dom}(y) = \text{dom}(z) = \{a, b\}$. As there is no unary constraint and no domain is empty, all of these constraint networks are 1-consistent. The network shown in Figure 3.1 is satisfiable but not 2-consistent. Here $\{(x, b)\}$ is a locally consistent instantiation of size 1 that cannot be extended to a locally consistent instantiation that includes the variable z. Moreover, this network is not 3-consistent: $\{(y, b), (z, a)\}$ is a locally consistent instantiation of size 2 that cannot be extended to a locally consistent instantiation that includes the variable x. A constraint network on which a consistency other than global consistency holds is obviously not necessarily satisfiable. Figure 3.2 shows a constraint network that is 2-consistent but not satisfiable. On the other hand, Figure 3.3, shows a network that is 3-consistent but not 2-consistent, emphasizing the fact that k-consistency does not necessarily entail j-consistency for $j < k$. Finally, Figure 3.4 shows a constraint network that is 1-consistent, 2-consistent and 3-consistent, and is therefore strongly 3-consistent. As the number, n, of variables is equal to 3, this network is globally consistent.

Consistencies are of interest for two reasons. Firstly, consistencies can yield inferences that simplify the task of finding a solution. Networks can be made more explicit by identifying and recording instantiations (called *nogoods*) that cannot lead to any solution. A search procedure may thereby avoid visiting some useless portions of the search space. For example, in Figure 3.1 $\{(x, b)\}$ is an instantiation that cannot be consistently extended. We can take account of this directly by removing b from $\mathrm{dom}(x)$; (y, b) and (z, a) can be removed similarly to (x, b). Furthermore, the instantiation $\{(y, b), (z, a)\}$ cannot be extended consistently. We can take account of this by removing $\{(y, b), (z, a)\}$ from the y, z constraint relation. The result is a new network that is equivalent to the original one, but far easier to solve; see Figure 3.5.

A second good reason for interest in consistencies is that they enable identification of tractable classes of problem instances. The simplest case is (see Theorem 3.4) that a globally consistent constraint network can be solved in a *backtrack-free* manner by a simple depth-first search algorithm, whatever its variable ordering. Backtrack-free means that the search algorithm never has to reconsider an instantiation shown to be locally consistent: Chapters 8 and 9 deal with backtrack search and search-guiding heuristics.

EXAMPLE.– At the present stage, the following example concerning backtrack-free search can easily be understood. The search procedure works step-by-step. At each step, the current locally consistent instantiation is extended by selecting an unassigned variable and assigning to this variable a "locally consistent" value (we know that such a value exists). This procedure can be applied, for example, to the constraint network shown in Figure 3.4 using the variable ordering x, y, z. This means that values are assigned to variables in the sequence x, y, z. For the first variable, x, the first value a of $\mathrm{dom}(x)$ is considered. Because the network is 1-consistent, the instantiation $\{(x, a)\}$ is locally consistent. Next, y is selected and the first value a in $\mathrm{dom}(y)$ is considered. The search algorithm finds that the pair $\{(x, a), (y, a)\}$ is 2-consistent, so $\{(x, a), (y, a)\}$ is a locally consistent extension of the initial instantiation $\{(x, a)\}$. Next, the variable z is selected; the locally consistent instantiation (z, a) is checked against $\{(x, a), (y, a)\}$ but does not satisfy the binary constraints. Therefore the second value (z, b) is selected and is found to satisfy the binary constraints. The result is that $\{(x, a), (y, a), (z, b)\}$ is a final locally consistent instantiation which is therefore a solution of the constraint network.

The worst-case time complexity of the backtrack-free search procedure is $O(erd)$ where r denotes the greatest constraint arity. Unfortunately, even though it is theoretically possible to make any constraint network globally consistent, this process

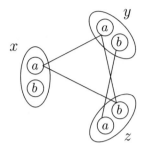

Figure 3.1. *A constraint network which is satisfiable although it is neither 2-consistent nor 3-consistent*

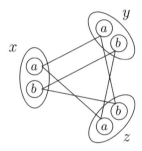

Figure 3.2. *A constraint network which is not satisfiable, although it is 2-consistent (but not 3-consistent)*

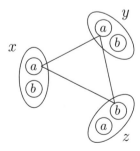

Figure 3.3. *A constraint network which is 3-consistent but not 2-consistent*

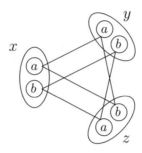

Figure 3.4. *A constraint network which is globally consistent as it is strongly 3-consistent*

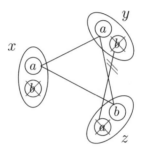

Figure 3.5. *Filtered constraint network of Figure 3.1*

is generally combinatorially explosive. This is because it is usually necessary to compute and record a huge number of inconsistent instantiations (nogoods) of various sizes.

In [FRE 85a], Freuder has generalized k-consistency into (i, j)-*consistency*. Informally, a constraint network is (i, j)-consistent iff every locally consistent instantiation of i variables can be extended to a locally consistent instantiation involving any j additional variables.

DEFINITION 3.5.– *[(i, j)-consistency] Let P be a constraint network and i, j be two integers such that $0 \le i < n$, $1 \le j \le n$ and $i + j \le n$. P is (i, j)-consistent iff for every set X of i variables of P and every additional set Y of j variables of P, every locally consistent instantiation of X on P can be extended to a locally consistent instantiation of $X \cup Y$ on P.*

If P is (i, j)-consistent and I is a locally consistent instantiation of X, and if $Y = \{y_1, \ldots, y_j\}$, then there exist a value $b_1 \in \text{dom}(y_1), \ldots$, a value $b_j \in \text{dom}(y_j)$ such that $I \cup \{(y_1, b_1), \ldots, (y_j, b_j)\}$ is a locally consistent instantiation on P.

The strong form of (i, j)-consistency is unsurprisingly defined as follows.

DEFINITION 3.6.– *[Strong (i, j)-consistency] Let P be a constraint network and i, j be two integers such that $0 \leq i < n$, $1 \leq j \leq n$ and $i + j \leq n$. P is strongly (i, j)-consistent iff P is (k, j)-consistent for every integer k such that $0 \leq k \leq i$.*

Clearly, k-consistency is equivalent to $(k - 1, 1)$-consistency. One particular consistency of this vast class allows us to introduce *minimal* networks [MON 74].

DEFINITION 3.7.– *[Minimal Constraint Network] A constraint network is minimal iff it is $(2, n - 2)$-consistent.*

When a constraint network (even involving non-binary constraints) is minimal, this means that every locally consistent instantiation of two variables can be extended to a solution. A minimal constraint network is maximally explicit in terms of binary constraints. In this case, an unsatisfiable minimal constraint network has an empty binary constraint for each pair of variables. For Montanari [MON 74] the central problem is to make a constraint network minimal. This problem is NP-complete [MAC 77a] and seeking a solution of a minimal network is not backtrack-free (unless $\prod_2^P = \Sigma_2^P$) [BES 06].

Finally, it may be interesting to relax the requirement that a locally consistent instantiation of size i must be extendable to every additional set of j variables. The existence of just one such additional set is sufficient in the following *weak consistency* [DON 06].

DEFINITION 3.8.– *[Weak (i, j)-consistency] Let P be a constraint network and i, j be two integers such that $0 \leq i < n$, $1 \leq j \leq n$ and $i + j \leq n$. P is weakly (i, j)-consistent iff for every set X of i variables of P, there exists an additional set Y of j variables of P such that a) $X \cap Y = \emptyset$ and b) every locally consistent instantiation of X on P can be extended to a locally consistent instantiation of $X \cup Y$ on P.*

This definition can be weakened further as follows: for every set X of i variables of P and every locally consistent instantiation I of X on P, there exists an additional set Y of j variables of P such that a) $X \cap Y = \emptyset$ and b) I can be extended to a locally consistent instantiation of $X \cup Y$ on P. In other words, when this property holds on a constraint network, it is always possible to find a way of extending a locally consistent instantiation of i variables into a locally consistent instantiation of $i + j$ variables. The theoretical or practical benefits of such weak forms remain to be demonstrated.

3.2. Stability of consistencies

Consistencies currently studied in the literature are those that identify nogoods. With a simple additional property, called *stability*, we obtain, for any constraint network P and any stable consistency ϕ, the guarantee that there exists a unique greatest ϕ-consistent network, denoted by $\phi(P)$, smaller than or equal to P, and equivalent to P. Such a consistency is said to be *well-behaved* and *enforcing* ϕ on P means computing $\phi(P)$. An algorithm that enforces a consistency ϕ on constraint networks is called a ϕ *algorithm*.

Recall that a consistency is simply a general property (or condition) of a constraint network. For a given network, either it holds or it doesn't.

DEFINITION 3.9.– *[ϕ-consistent Network] Let ϕ be consistency. A constraint network P is said to be ϕ-consistent iff the property ϕ holds on P.*

Sometimes, properties are combined as follows:

DEFINITION 3.10.– *[$\phi+\psi$-consistent Network] Let ϕ and ψ be two consistencies. A constraint network P is $\phi+\psi$-consistent iff P is both ϕ-consistent and ψ-consistent.*

It is usually possible to enforce ϕ on a network P by computing the greatest ϕ-consistent network smaller than or equal to P, according to a partial order, while preserving the set of solutions. Without a great loss of generality, from now on, we stipulate that any poset[1] $(\mathscr{P}, \preccurlyeq)$ is such that $\forall P_1 \in \mathscr{P}, \forall P_2 \in \mathscr{P}, P_1 \preccurlyeq P_2 \Rightarrow \text{vars}(P_1) = \text{vars}(P_2)$; constraint networks that are comparable are defined on the same variables.

DEFINITION 3.11.– *[Well-behaved Consistency] A consistency ϕ is* well-behaved *for a poset $(\mathscr{P}, \preccurlyeq)$ iff for every constraint network $P \in \mathscr{P}$:*

– there exists a ϕ-consistent constraint network $P' \in \mathscr{P}$ equivalent to P such that $P' \preccurlyeq P$; and

– for every ϕ-consistent constraint network $P'' \in \mathscr{P}$ such that $P'' \preccurlyeq P$, we have $P'' \preccurlyeq P'$.

P' is called the ϕ-closure of P for $(\mathscr{P}, \preccurlyeq)$, and is denoted by $\phi(P)$.

In other words, $\phi(P)$ is equivalent to P and is the greatest element of the set $\{P'' \in \mathscr{P} \mid P'' \text{ is } \phi\text{-consistent and } P'' \preccurlyeq P\}$. A well-behaved consistency is valuable if its enforcement simplifies (the resolution of) constraint networks. This is the case for *nogood-identifying* consistencies which are, so far as we are aware, the only ones studied in the literature.

---

1. Note that the symbol $\preccurlyeq$ is different from $\preceq$ used in Definition 1.50. The strict order associated with $\preccurlyeq$ is designated by $\prec$, but must not be confounded with the one associated with $\preceq$.

DEFINITION 3.12.– *[Nogood-identifying Consistency] A consistency ϕ is nogood-identifying iff the reason why a constraint network P is not ϕ-consistent is that some instantiations, which are not in $\widetilde{P}$, are identified as globally inconsistent by ϕ. Such instantiations correspond to (new) nogoods and are said to be ϕ-inconsistent (on P).*

Instantiations that are not in $\widetilde{P}$ (i.e. are not current explicit nogoods; see Definition 1.43) and are not ϕ-inconsistent are said to be ϕ-*consistent* (on P). The nice feature of nogood-identifying consistencies is that they can be exploited to make a constraint network more explicit by discarding ϕ-inconsistent instantiations. An instantiation I is discarded from a constraint network P by applying the operation $P \setminus I$ described on page 77; stated otherwise, a new explicit nogood I is stored in P. Enforcing a consistency ϕ on a network means taking into account (recording inside the network) nogoods identified by ϕ in order to make it ϕ-consistent. It is important that a nogood-identifying consistency can only identify new nogoods; this is a quite reasonable assumption.

It is not necessary to define a consistency in a uniform manner. This means that the property may integrate different levels of local coherence provided that it remains a nogood-identifying consistency. For example, as we shall see, generalized arc consistency is an important property defined uniformly on each constraint. We can imagine a mixed consistency that holds if certain constraints are generalized arc-consistent, and others are partially generalized arc-consistent. What is important is the "stability" of any consistency that is introduced. Indeed, this property, defined below, is useful for proving that a nogood-identifying consistency is well-behaved.

DEFINITION 3.13.– *[Stable Consistency] A nogood-identifying consistency ϕ is stable for a poset $(\mathscr{P}, \preccurlyeq)$ iff for every constraint network $P \in \mathscr{P}$, every constraint network $P' \in \mathscr{P} \mid P' \preccurlyeq P$ and every ϕ-inconsistent instantiation I on P, we have: $P' \setminus I \preccurlyeq P \setminus I \prec P$, and either $I \in \widetilde{P'}$ or I is ϕ-inconsistent on P'.*

The fact that $P' \setminus I \preccurlyeq P \setminus I \prec P$ ensures that the partial order is large enough to allow computation of ϕ-closures. On the other hand, the fact that either $I \in \widetilde{P'}$ or I is ϕ-inconsistent on P' guarantees that no ϕ-inconsistent instantiation on a constraint network can be missed when the network is made tighter: either it is discarded (has become an explicit nogood of P') or it remains ϕ-inconsistent.

We can now prove that a nogood-identifying consistency which is stable for a poset $(\mathscr{P}, \preccurlyeq)$ is necessarily well-behaved for $(\mathscr{P}, \preccurlyeq)$.

THEOREM 3.14.– *Any nogood-identifying consistency stable for a poset $(\mathscr{P}, \preccurlyeq)$ is well-behaved for $(\mathscr{P}, \preccurlyeq)$.*

Proof. Let $P \in \mathscr{P}$ be a constraint network and let us consider a network P' obtained from P by iteratively discarding (in any order) the ϕ-inconsistent instantiations identified by ϕ. If I_1 is the first discarded ϕ-inconsistent instantiation (on P) and $P_1 = P \setminus I_1$, we have (by stability) $P_1 \prec P$; if I_2 is the second discarded ϕ-inconsistent instantiation (on P_1) and $P_2 = P_1 \setminus I_2$, we have $P_2 \prec P_1, \ldots$, With k denoting the number of instantiations successively discarded (k must be finite since there are a finite number of possible instantiations), we have $P' = P_{k-1} \setminus I_k$ with $P' \prec P_{k-1}$. At the end, we have a) $P' \preccurlyeq P$ (more precisely, $P' \preccurlyeq P$ if $k = 0$ and $P' \prec P$ otherwise) by using the transitivity of $\prec$, b) P' ϕ-consistent since there are no more ϕ-inconsistent instantiations, and c) P' equivalent to P since only nogoods have been recorded.

Now, let us consider $P_0 = P$, $P_k = P'$ and the following induction hypothesis H(i): every ϕ-consistent constraint network $P'' \preccurlyeq P$ is such that $P'' \preccurlyeq P_i$. Let us show that H(i) holds for $0 \leq i \leq k$. First, H(0) clearly holds since $P_0 = P$. Now, with $i < k$, let us assume that H(i) holds and let us show H(i+1). As H(i) holds, by hypothesis, we know that any ϕ-consistent constraint network $P'' \preccurlyeq P$ is such that $P'' \preccurlyeq P_i$. We also know that $P_{i+1} = P_i \setminus I_{i+1}$ where I_{i+1} is the $(i + 1)$th discarded ϕ-inconsistent instantiation (on P_i). As I_{i+1} is ϕ-inconsistent on P_i, we know (by stability) that I_{i+1} is either discarded or ϕ-inconsistent on every constraint network smaller than or equal to P_i. If a constraint network $P'' \preccurlyeq P_i$ is ϕ-consistent, this means that I_{i+1} is an explicit nogood of P'' and we have $P'' = P'' \setminus I_{i+1}$. As ϕ is stable, we know that $P'' \setminus I_{i+1} \preccurlyeq P_i \setminus I_{i+1}$, whence $P'' \preccurlyeq P_{i+1}$. Hence H(i+1) holds and we can deduce that P' is the ϕ-closure of P. $\square$

Interestingly, the stability of a nogood-identifying consistency ϕ provides a general procedure for computing the ϕ-closure of any constraint network: iteratively discard (in any order) ϕ-inconsistent instantiations until a fixed point is reached (as shown in the previous proof). Provided that the procedure is sound (each removal corresponds to a ϕ-inconsistent instantiation) and complete (each ϕ-inconsistent instantiation is removed), the procedure is guaranteed to compute ϕ-closures. More generally, when different reduction rules are used, each must be shown to be correct, monotonic and inflationary. We can then benefit from the generic iteration algorithm given in [APT 03] (see Lemmas 7.5 and 7.8 and Theorem 7.11). Stability under union can also be proved for a domain-filtering consistency (introduced later), thus guaranteeing the presence of a fixed point [BES 06]. In our context, we obtain:

THEOREM 3.15.– *Let ϕ be a nogood-identifying consistency stable for a poset $(\mathscr{P}, \preccurlyeq)$. Any procedure iteratively discarding ϕ-inconsistent instantiations from a constraint network P computes $\phi(P)$. ϕ is said to be* iteration-free.

Proof. The proof of Theorem 3.14 shows that such a procedure, necessarily yields $\phi(P)$. $\square$

Another nice consequence of stability is *monotonicity*. Any nogood-identifying consistency that is stable for a poset $(\mathscr{P}, \preccurlyeq)$ is monotonic, i.e. preserves $\preccurlyeq$.

THEOREM 3.16.– *Let ϕ be a nogood-identifying consistency stable for a poset $(\mathscr{P}, \preccurlyeq)$. For any two constraint networks $P \in \mathscr{P}$ and $P' \in \mathscr{P}$, we have: $P' \preccurlyeq P \Rightarrow \phi(P') \preccurlyeq \phi(P)$. ϕ is said to be* monotonic.

Proof. Let $S = \{P'' \in \mathscr{P} \mid P''$ is ϕ-consistent and $P'' \preccurlyeq P\}$ and $S' = \{P'' \in \mathscr{P} \mid P''$ is ϕ-consistent and $P'' \preccurlyeq P'\}$. From $P' \preccurlyeq P$, we have $S' \subseteq S$. By definition, $\phi(P')$ is the greatest element of S' so $\phi(P') \in S'$. $S' \subseteq S$ implies $\phi(P') \in S$. Finally, as $\phi(P)$ is the greatest element of S, we necessarily have $\phi(P') \preccurlyeq \phi(P)$. ☐

The three foregoing theorems are given with respect to an abstract partial order. This book specifically considers the three partial orders $(\mathscr{P}, \preceq_d)$, $(\mathscr{P}, \preceq_r)$ and $(\mathscr{P}, \preceq)$ introduced in section 1.4.1. However, to relate to these, we need to introduce a couple of definitions.

DEFINITION 3.17.– *[kth-order Consistency] Let $k \geq 1$ be an integer. A kth-order consistency is a nogood-identifying consistency that allows the identification of nogoods of size k.*

kth-order consistency should not be confused with k-consistency. As seen earlier, k-consistency holds iff every locally consistent instantiation of a set of $k-1$ variables can be extended to a locally consistent instantiation involving any additional variable. In our terminology, this is a $(k-1)$th-order consistency. Furthermore, kth-order consistencies may possibly identify nogoods that do not correspond to locally consistent instantiations. This happens when such new nogoods are subsumed by existing ones.

Domain-filtering and *relation-filtering* consistencies are the main topic of the first part of this book. A domain-filtering consistency allows identification of inconsistent values, which can then be removed from domains. Similarly, a relation-filtering consistency can be enforced by removing some tuples from some (existing) constraint relations. These consistencies are defined as follows.

DEFINITION 3.18.– *[Domain-filtering Consistency] A domain-filtering consistency is a first-order consistency.*

DEFINITION 3.19.– *[Relation-filtering Consistency] A relation-filtering consistency ϕ is a nogood-identifying consistency such that, for every given constraint network P, every ϕ-inconsistent instantiation on P corresponds to a tuple allowed by a (non-implicit) constraint of P.*

The following corollaries can be derived from Theorems 3.14, 3.15 and 3.16:

COROLLARY 3.20.– *Any domain-filtering consistency stable for* $(\mathscr{P}, \preceq_d)$ *is well-behaved, iteration-free and monotonic for* $(\mathscr{P}, \preceq_d)$.

COROLLARY 3.21.– *Any relation-filtering consistency stable for* $(\mathscr{P}, \preceq_r)$ *is well-behaved, iteration-free and monotonic for* $(\mathscr{P}, \preceq_r)$.

COROLLARY 3.22.– *Any nogood-identifying consistency stable for* $(\mathscr{P}, \preceq)$ *is well-behaved, iteration-free and monotonic for* $(\mathscr{P}, \preceq)$.

These properties hold because there is a unique way of discarding ϕ-inconsistent instantiations; this shows the importance of normalizing constraint networks and removing unary constraints. Note also that Corollary 3.21 can be extended to every kth-order consistency if we consider networks completed with missing k-ary universal constraints. Importantly, to the best of our knowledge, all consistencies in the current literature are stable with respect to one of these posets. We shall essentially benefit from Corollary 3.20 because, for practical reasons, mainly first-order consistencies are studied.

Sometimes, by enforcing a (stable) consistency ϕ, we can demonstrate the unsatisfiability of a constraint network P, in which case $\phi(P) = \bot$. By definition, $\phi(P)$ is ϕ-consistent and corresponds to a precise network (not necessarily one with all domains or relations empty). In practice, when P is found unsatisfiable (because of a domain or relation wipe-out) while enforcing ϕ, the procedure enforcing ϕ is immediately stopped, thereby indicating failure (symbolized by $\bot$); by *domain wipe-out* or *relation wipe-out*, we mean a domain or relation that has become empty. In other words, $\phi(P)$ is not exactly computed when it corresponds to $\bot$ but this is not a problem because P has been shown to be unsatisfiable. When the ϕ-closure of a constraint network P is trivially unsatisfiable, i.e. when $\phi(P) = \bot$, we say that P is ϕ-inconsistent.

DEFINITION 3.23.– *[ϕ-inconsistent Constraint Network] Let ϕ be a well-behaved consistency. A constraint network is ϕ-inconsistent iff $\phi(P) = \bot$.*

Note that "P is not ϕ-consistent" is not equivalent to "P is ϕ-inconsistent". The first of these statements simply means that some instantiations are ϕ-inconsistent, whereas the second means that P is proved unsatisfiable by means of ϕ. Although this may seem disconcerting, this is the current usage.

In order to compare the pruning capability of different consistencies, we need to introduce a preorder as in [DEB 01]. When some consistencies cannot be ordered (none is stronger than another), we say that they are *incomparable*.

DEFINITION 3.24.– *[Preorder on Consistencies] Let ϕ and ψ be two consistencies.*

– *ϕ is stronger than ψ iff whenever ϕ holds on a constraint network P, ψ also holds on P.*

– *ϕ is strictly stronger than ψ iff ϕ is stronger than ψ and there exists at least one constraint network P such that ψ holds on P but not ϕ.*

An interesting result follows:

THEOREM 3.25.– *Let ϕ and ψ be two well-behaved nogood-identifying consistencies for a poset $(\mathscr{P}, \preccurlyeq)$. ϕ is stronger than ψ iff for every constraint network $P \in \mathscr{P}$, we have $\phi(P) \preccurlyeq \psi(P)$.*

Proof. ($\Rightarrow$). As ϕ and ψ are well-behaved, for every constraint network $P \in \mathscr{P}$, $\phi(P)$ and $\psi(P)$ exist; by definition $\phi(P)$ is ϕ-consistent. By hypothesis, ϕ is stronger than ψ, which means that $\phi(P)$ is also ψ-consistent. As $\phi(P)$ is ψ-consistent and such that $\phi(P) \preceq P$, we necessarily have $\phi(P) \preccurlyeq \psi(P)$. ($\Leftarrow$). If we have $\phi(P) \preccurlyeq \psi(P)$ for every constraint network $P \in \mathscr{P}$, then $\phi(P) = P$ entails $\psi(P) = P$. Therefore ϕ is stronger than ψ.   □

This result can, of course, be exploited for posets $(\mathscr{P}, \preceq_d)$, $(\mathscr{P}, \preceq_r)$ and $(\mathscr{P}, \preceq)$.

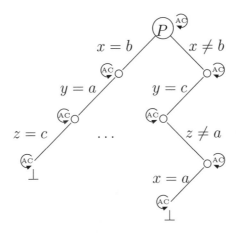

Figure 3.6. *Two branches leading to dead-ends in a search tree built by maintaining arc consistency (MAC)*

Finally, we introduce a definition connecting nogoods and consistencies. Indeed nogoods can be identified by means of a well-behaved consistency ϕ:

DEFINITION 3.26.– *[φ-nogood] Let P be a constraint network, Δ be a set of decisions on P and φ be a well-behaved consistency.*

- *Δ is a φ-nogood of P iff $\phi(P|_\Delta) = \bot$.*
- *Δ is a minimal φ-nogood of P iff $\nexists \Delta' \subset \Delta$ such that $\phi(P|_{\Delta'}) = \bot$.*

As an illustration, Figure 3.6 shows two branches of a search tree built by the algorithm MAC (presented in Chapter 8) which maintains arc consistency (AC for short, presented later in this chapter) during search. In Figure 3.6 the branch $\{x = b, y = a, z = c\}$ is a (standard) nogood and is also (standard) AC-nogood; we have $AC(P|_{\{x=b,y=a,z=c\}}) = \bot$. The other branch $\{x \neq b, y = c, z \neq a, x = a\}$ is a generalized nogood and also a generalized AC-nogood.

3.3. Domain-filtering consistencies

As already mentioned, a domain-filtering consistency is a *first-order consistency*, i.e. a consistency that permits identification of inconsistent values. This has the advantage that it does not modify the structure of the constraint network since existing constraints are not modified and new constraints are not introduced. Figure 3.7 illustrates the practical effect of enforcing a domain-filtering consistency. Here, nogoods (of size 1) that correspond to inconsistent v-values are supposed to be identified by reasoning from the constraints of P that are not depicted.

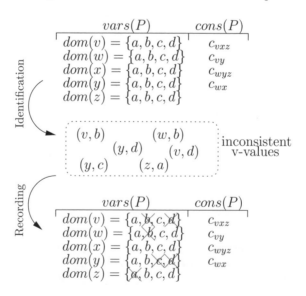

Figure 3.7. *Identification and recording of inconsistent v-values in a constraint network P. Only domains are modified*

To define a domain-filtering consistency ϕ completely, it is sufficient to specify the conditions under which a v-value (x, a) is considered as ϕ-inconsistent. Indeed, once it is known, the concept of local consistency can automatically be extended to variables, constraints and constraint networks as follows:

DEFINITION 3.27.– *[ϕ-consistency] Let P be a constraint network, and let ϕ be a domain-filtering consistency.*

 – *A v-value (x, a) of P is ϕ-consistent on P iff $\{(x, a)\}$ is ϕ-consistent on P.*

 – *A value a in the domain of a variable x of P is ϕ-consistent on P iff (x, a) is ϕ-consistent on P.*

 – *A variable x of P is ϕ-consistent on P iff every value in the domain of x is ϕ-consistent on P, i.e. $\forall a \in \mathrm{dom}(x)$, (x, a) is ϕ-consistent on P.*

 – *A constraint network P is ϕ-consistent iff every v-value of P is ϕ-consistent on P, i.e. $\forall x \in \mathrm{vars}(P), \forall a \in \mathrm{dom}(x)$, (x, a) is ϕ-consistent on P.*

Starting from previous definitions, we can henceforth restrict our definitions of domain-filtering consistencies to v-values only. But for *generalized arc consistency* (GAC), which is currently the most important consistency, we prefer to reintroduce all items (v-values, variables and constraint networks). We focus first on constraints because the usual way to perceive/enforce GAC is to iterate over each constraint. When generalized arc consistency (also called hyper-arc consistency, e.g. in [APT 03], and sometimes called domain consistency) holds, this guarantees the existence of a support for each value on each constraint:

DEFINITION 3.28.– *[Generalized Arc Consistency]*

 – *A constraint c is generalized arc-inconsistent, or GAC-consistent iff $\forall x \in \mathrm{scp}(c), \forall a \in \mathrm{dom}(x)$, there exists a support for (x, a) on c.*

 – *A constraint network P is generalized arc-inconsistent iff every constraint of P is generalized arc-inconsistent.*

Additionally, we have for any constraint network P:

 – *a v-value (x, a) of P is generalized arc-inconsistent on P iff for every constraint c of P involving x, there is a support for (x, a) on c;*

 – *a variable x of P is generalized arc-inconsistent on P iff $\forall a \in \mathrm{dom}(x)$, (x, a) is generalized arc-inconsistent on P.*

For unary and binary constraints, this property is classically known as *node consistency* (NC) and *arc consistency* (AC), respectively. For binary constraint networks, arc consistency is equivalent to $(1, 1)$-consistency. It is helpful that generalized arc consistency is defined for constraints of any arity. The acronym GAC plays the role of the symbol ϕ in Definition 3.27. For example, "generalized arc-consistent" can be systematically replaced by "GAC-consistent". Following Definition

3.12, a value[2] found to be globally inconsistent by generalized arc consistency is said to be *generalized arc-inconsistent* or *GAC-inconsistent*. In short, a value is not GAC-consistent iff it is GAC-inconsistent.

EXAMPLE.– For a (non-binary) constraint, Figures 3.8 and 3.9 illustrate generalized arc consistency. Here we have a major block extracted from a Sudoku square (see section 1.3.3) with its associated global allDifferent constraint. In Figure 3.8, the constraint is clearly generalized arc-consistent since we can fill up the entire block after inserting any remaining value. In Figure 3.9, the domains have already been reduced by application of other Sudoku constraints. In this case, some values cannot be put in the grid without leading to a failure. This is immediate for $(w, 3)$ and $(z, 8)$ since 3 and 8 are already present in the block (e.g. if we choose 3 for w, we obtain two occurrences of 3 in the block, violating the allDifferent constraint). If we choose $(w, 5)$, we must then choose $(x, 2)$ followed by $(z, 9)$, so there are no more possibilities left for y. Hence, there is no support for $(w, 5)$ on the global constraint, and so, $(w, 5)$ is GAC-inconsistent.

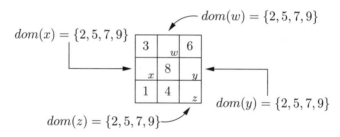

Figure 3.8. *An allDifferent constraint involving nine variables, of which w, x, y and z are unfixed. The other five variables are fixed. This constraint is generalized arc-consistent*

It is not surprising that generalized arc consistency is stable for $(\mathscr{P}, \preceq_d)$. To see that the conditions for stability hold (see Definition 3.13), consider two constraint networks $P \in \mathscr{P}$ and $P' \in \mathscr{P}$ such that $P' \prec_d P$, and consider a v-value (x, a) of P that is GAC-inconsistent on P. Clearly, $P' \setminus \{(x, a)\} \preceq_d P \setminus \{(x, a)\} \prec_d P$. Besides, if (x, a) is a v-value of P' then (x, a) is necessarily GAC-inconsistent on P' because for each constraint c involving x, the set of supports for (x, a) on c in P' is included in the set of supports for (x, a) on c in P. Other consistencies discussed in this book can also be proved to be stable, but these proofs will be omitted henceforth.

Because generalized arc consistency is stable, Corollary 3.20 implies that the *GAC-closure* of any network P exists. This network, denoted by $GAC(P)$, can

---

2. Strictly speaking, we should refer to an instantiation of size 1, but this is basically equivalent, as seen in Definition 3.27.

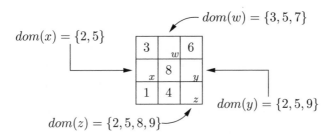

Figure 3.9. *An allDifferent constraint involving nine variables, of which w, x, y and z are unfixed. The other five variables are fixed. This constraint is not generalized arc-consistent. The v-values $(w, 3)$, $(w, 5)$ and $(z, 8)$ have no support on this constraint (and are said to be GAC-inconsistent)*

be computed by iteratively removing from P (in any order) all values that are not generalized arc-consistent. Following Definition 3.23, if $GAC(P) = \bot$ then P is said to be *generalized arc-inconsistent* or *GAC-inconsistent*. Contrary to what is the case for values, a constraint network that is not GAC-consistent is not necessarily GAC-inconsistent since we do not necessarily have $GAC(P) = \bot$. Note that Schiex *et al.* [SCH 96] compute an arc-consistent network P' smaller than (or equal to) a binary constraint network P with P' not necessarily being the AC-closure of P. This lazy form of arc consistency filtering can be applied when we simply wish to detect unsatisfiability of a constraint network.

An alternative to the foregoing definition is: "P is generalized arc-consistent iff every variable of P is generalized arc-consistent". Some authors also require that no variable has an empty domain, but this additional restriction may distort the theoretical foundations. If a constraint network cannot be considered as generalized arc-consistent because it has a variable with an empty domain, how can we define the GAC-closure? Of course, when $GAC(P) = \bot$, we obtain a constraint network equivalent to $\bot$ that is (considered to be) GAC-consistent although P is GAC-inconsistent. This may appear disconcerting but, as mentioned previously, these two notions are not contradictory. Systematically making explicit in definitions the cases where a domain or a relation is wiped-out when enforcing a consistency would just make things more complicated.

GAC is the highest level of local consistency that can be defined when considering constraints independently to make deductions (that are propagated from constraint to constraint through shared variables). Enforcing GAC on a constraint network P is equivalent to enforcing GAC on each constraint c of P, and enforcing GAC on a constraint c means removing all values without any support on c. GAC enforcement on a constraint c is denoted by $GAC(c)$, and $GAC(c) = \bot$ when a domain wipe-out is detected. Because of propagation, enforcing GAC on a constraint network may require enforcing GAC several times on the same constraint. We can associate a specific filtering algorithm, achieving generalized arc consistency, with certain types of constraints. Many such *GAC algorithms* have appeared in the literature; their number and diversity make it difficult to identify the most important or efficient ones. Their number and diversity also make difficult the practical comparison of complete constraint solvers. Fortunately, there also exist some generic procedures for establishing generalized arc consistency. These can be used on all kinds of constraints and their efficiency has been greatly improved (in particular, on extensional constraints). They will be studied in Chapters 4 and 5.

We can now introduce *singleton arc consistency* (SAC) which is built upon generalized arc consistency. SAC is stable, and as expected, the SAC-closure of a constraint network P is denoted by $SAC(P)$. This consistency stronger than GAC consists of looking one step in advance in all directions. Each value in turn is assigned to each variable in turn. After each assignment, generalized arch consistency is enforced and the satisfiability of the resulting constraint network is checked. This is a technique commonly employed in many fields of automated reasoning [BES 06].

DEFINITION 3.29.– *[Singleton Arc Consistency] A v-value (x, a) of a constraint network P is* singleton arc-consistent, *or* SAC-consistent, *iff $GAC(P|_{x=a}) \neq \bot$.*

Of course, it is possible to generalize the principle of checking one step in advance if a given local consistency holds as follows:

DEFINITION 3.30.– *[Singleton ϕ] A v-value (x, a) of a constraint network P is* singleton ϕ-consistent, *or* Sϕ-consistent, *iff $\phi(P|_{x=a}) \neq \bot$, where ϕ is a well-behaved consistency.*

We shall generally use the acronym $S\phi$ to refer to a consistency which is singleton ϕ. However, as it can be observed above, we do not make a real distinction between singleton arc consistency and singleton generalized arc consistency in this book: we only use the acronym SAC even if GAC is referred to (some authors employ the acronym SGAC). Note that $S\phi$ identifies nogoods of size 1 (so is domain-filtering) even if ϕ is not domain-filtering. Nevertheless, to prove directly (in particular, from Theorem 3.16) that the consistency built on top of ϕ is stable, the following proposition assumes that ϕ is first-order.

PROPOSITION 3.31.– *If ϕ is a first-order consistency stable for $(\mathscr{P}, \preceq_d)$, then singleton ϕ, denoted by $S\phi$, is stable for $(\mathscr{P}, \preceq_d)$. Furthermore, $S\phi$ is stronger than ϕ.*

From this proposition we deduce directly that SAC is stronger than (G)AC. As is the case for GAC, "singleton ϕ-consistent" can be replaced by "$S\phi$-consistent". A value that is not singleton ϕ-consistent is said to be *singleton ϕ-inconsistent* or *Sϕ-inconsistent*. Using different terminology, e.g. in the operations research literature, such a value is said to be ϕ-shavable (or simply shavable when the local consistency enforced is implicit). A constraint network P such that its $S\phi$-closure, denoted by $S\phi(P)$, is $\perp$ is also said to be *singleton ϕ-inconsistent* or *Sϕ-inconsistent*. Again, differing to what is the case for values, a constraint network that is not $S\phi$-consistent is not necessarily $S\phi$-inconsistent. Finally, for a given v-value (x, a), checking whether $S\phi(P|_{x=a}) \neq \perp$ is called a singleton ϕ-check on (x, a) or more simply, when $\phi = GAC$ (or when ϕ can be ignored), a *singleton check* on (x, a); we also say that (x, a) is *singleton checked* when $GAC(P|_{x=a}) \neq \perp$ is checked.

Singleton ϕ consistencies represent a class of consistencies that is vast and indeed infinite because it is possible to define a singleton consistency upon another singleton consistency. In [PRO 00] some insight into this class is provided from theoretical comparisons of various singleton consistencies, and also (i, j)-consistencies. For example, if ϕ is stronger than ψ then $S\phi$ is stronger than $S\psi$, and strong $(i + 1, j)$-consistency is strictly stronger than singleton (i, j)-consistency. Moreover, Prosser *et al.* [PRO 00] observe that enforcing a singleton consistency $S\phi$ may require several passes, i.e. iterating over all values several times, and may be expensive. In practice, they propose to limit constraint propagation to a single pass and to call this a *restricted Sϕ enforcing procedure*; but this is only an operational point of view and is not a new consistency.

Another well-known consistency is *path inverse consistency* (PIC) [FRE 96] which is just an alias name for $(1, 2)$-consistency. It is the weakest original consistency of the class of $(1, j)$-consistencies for $j \geq 2$; recall that $(1, 1)$-consistency corresponds to arc consistency. This class contains so-called *inverse* consistencies[3] that are all domain-filtering. Of course, in this class path-inverse consistency is the most cheaply enforceable since the horizon is limited to two additional variables. We now provide a refined definition for this special case of (i, j)-consistency.

DEFINITION 3.32.– *[Path Inverse Consistency] A v-value (x, a) of a constraint network P is* path-inverse consistent, *or* PIC-consistent, *iff for every set $\{y, z\}$ of two additional variables of P, there exist $b \in \text{dom}(y)$ and $c \in \text{dom}(z)$ such that $\{(x, a), (y, b), (z, c)\}$ is locally consistent.*

On binary networks, path inverse consistency is strictly stronger than arc consistency[4] but is strictly weaker than *max-restricted path consistency* (MaxRPC), which is another classical domain-filtering consistency [DEB 97a], itself strictly

---

3. An inverse consistency can be understood as a consistency defined from an existing one by taking a different (or inverse) angle. Most of the time, inverse is considered as a synonym for domain-filtering.
4. This is the case for constraint networks with less than three variables if we assume that y or z in the definition may be equal to x.

weaker than singleton arc consistency. Contrary to established usage, the definition given below for MaxRPC is for general constraint networks, i.e. networks involving constraints of any arity. However, even if non-binary constraints are involved, they are simply ignored (as for path consistency introduced in section 3.4.1).

DEFINITION 3.33.– *[Max-restricted Path Consistency] A v-value (x, a) of a constraint network P is* max-restricted path-consistent, *or* MaxRPC-consistent, *iff for every binary constraint c_{xy} of P involving x, there exists a locally consistent instantiation $\{(x, a), (y, b)\}$ of $\mathrm{scp}(c_{xy}) = \{x, y\}$ such that for every additional variable z of P, there exists a value $c \in \mathrm{dom}(z)$ guaranteeing that $\{(x, a), (z, c)\}$ and $\{(y, b), (z, c)\}$ are both locally consistent.*

EXAMPLE.– The following examples (some being taken from [DEB 01]) illustrate the differences between (some of) these consistencies. Figure 3.10 shows a simple constraint network that is arc-consistent but not path-inverse consistent. For example, the v-value (x, a) cannot be simultaneously successfully extended to y and z. Figure 3.11 shows a constraint network that is path-inverse consistent but not max-restricted path-consistent. To provide a clear picture, the constraint network is demarcated into two main parts: a first part where (w, a) is not max-restricted path-consistent (but path-inverse consistent) and a second where (w, a) has no additional support. Hence, for the v-value (w, a) it is not possible to find a support on x that can be successfully extended independently to y and z. Figure 3.12 shows a constraint network that is max-restricted path-consistent but not singleton arc-consistent.

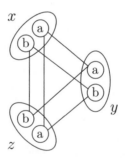

Figure 3.10. *A constraint network with three binary constraints. Each value is arc-consistent but no one is path-inverse consistent*

In addition to PIC, another consistency has been proposed in [FRE 96]. This defines a level of local consistency that is a function of the neighborhood of each variable: the neighborhood of a variable consists of all variables that are constrained with it. Such a consistency is strictly stronger than MaxRPC, but the time complexity

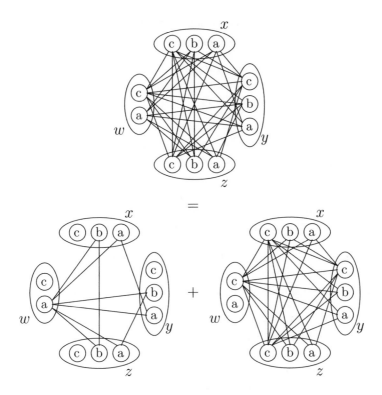

Figure 3.11. *A constraint network with six binary constraints. Each value is path-inverse consistent but* (w, a) *is not max-restricted path-consistent*

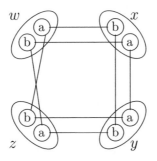

Figure 3.12. *A constraint network with four binary constraints. Each value is max-restricted path-consistent, but none is singleton arc-consistent*

of its enforcement is unfortunately exponential in the size of the largest neighborhood, which makes it inappropriate for dense problems.

DEFINITION 3.34.– *[Neighborhood Inverse Consistency] A v-value (x,a) of a constraint network P is* neighborhood-inverse consistent, *or* NIC-consistent, *iff there exists a locally consistent instantiation I on P of $\cup_{c\in\text{cons}(P)|x\in\text{scp}(c)}\text{scp}(c)$ with $(x,a)\in I$.*

Some consistencies introduced above are naturally orientated toward binary constraint networks. This is the case with path-inverse consistency and max-restricted path consistency which are completely useless for networks that have constraint arity that is not less than four. This may partially explain why they are not usually implemented in constraint solvers. Another reason is certainly the simplicity of implementing SAC compared to the relative complexity of implementing triangle-based local consistencies (such as PIC and MaxRPC), for which 3-cliques of binary constraints have to be managed. Moreover, because SAC is stronger, a user who wishes a strong consistency to be enforced during the early steps of search (or during preprocessing) may naturally be attracted by SAC.

In [STE 06, BES 08c], several domain-filtering consistencies have been proposed specifically for non-binary constraints. The first is called *relational path inverse consistency* (rPIC) by analogy with the variable-based path inverse consistency: instead of trying to extend a value to two variables, try to extend it to two constraints. This is another name for relational $(1,2)$-consistency, which will be presented in section 3.4.2. Roughly speaking, a value is rPIC-consistent when it can be extended over the scope of any two constraints to become a valid instantiation that satisfies them. More formally:

DEFINITION 3.35.– *[Relational Path Inverse Consistency] A v-value (x,a) of a constraint network P is* relational path-inverse consistent, *or* rPIC-consistent, *iff for every set $\{c_1,c_2\}$ of two constraints of P such that $x\in\text{scp}(c_1)\cup\text{scp}(c_2)$, there exists an instantiation I of $\text{scp}(c_1)\cup\text{scp}(c_2)$ such that $(x,a)\in I$, I is valid on P, and I satisfies both c_1 and c_2.*

This definition assumes that P involves at least two constraints, thus guaranteeing that rPIC is strictly stronger than GAC. Another domain-filtering consistency, which is inspired by the variable-based consistency MaxRPC (and follows the same scheme), is called *max-restricted pairwise consistency* (MaxRPWC). Roughly speaking, a value is MaxRPWC-consistent when a support for it can be found on each constraint and extended over the scope of any other constraint to constitute a valid instantiation that satisfies it. More formally:

DEFINITION 3.36.– *[Max Restricted Pairwise Consistency] A v-value (x,a) of a constraint network P is* max-restricted pairwise consistent, *or* MaxRPWC-consistent, *iff for every constraint c of P involving x, there exists an instantiation I of* scp(c) *such that* $(x, a) \in I$, *I is valid on P, I satisfies c, and for every additional constraint c' of P, there exists an extension I' of I over* scp(c')\scp(c) *that is valid on P and satisfies c'.*

The definition can equivalently be limited to consider each constraint $c' \neq c$ of P such that $|\operatorname{scp}(c) \cap \operatorname{scp}(c')| \geq 2$.

EXAMPLE.– Figure 3.13 provides examples of rPIC and MaxRPWC: there are three non-binary constraints c_1, c_2 and c_3 that intersect on the variables x and y, i.e. such that $\operatorname{scp}(c_1) \cap \operatorname{scp}(c_2) = \operatorname{scp}(c_1) \cap \operatorname{scp}(c_3) = \operatorname{scp}(c_2) \cap \operatorname{scp}(c_3) = \{x, y\}$. We also have $\operatorname{dom}(x) = \{a, b\}$ and $\operatorname{dom}(y) = \{a, b, c\}$. The v-values (y, b) and (y, c) are clearly rPIC-inconsistent. For example, the v-value (y, b) is rPIC-inconsistent because for $\{c_1, c_2\}$ there is no valid instantiation involving (y, b) that satisfies both c_1 and c_2. On the other hand, although rPIC-consistent, the v-value (x, a) is not MaxRPWC-consistent. To see this, consider the constraint c_1. The first support[5] for (x, a) on c_1 is $(a, a, \dots)$. This support can be extended to c_2 but not to c_3 since there is no support on c_3 involving (x, a) and (y, a). The second support for (x, a) on c_1 is $(a, b, \dots)$. This support can be extended to c_3 but not to c_2 since there is no support on c_2 involving (x, a) and (y, b). As a consequence, (x, a) is detected MaxRPWC-inconsistent.

$$rel(c_1) \qquad rel(c_2) \qquad rel(c_3)$$

$$x\ y\ \dots \qquad\qquad x\ y\ \dots \qquad\qquad x\ y\ \dots$$

$$\begin{pmatrix} a, a, \dots \\ a, b, \dots \\ b, a, \dots \\ b, c, \dots \end{pmatrix} \qquad \begin{pmatrix} a, a, \dots \\ a, c, \dots \\ b, a, \dots \\ b, b, \dots \end{pmatrix} \qquad \begin{pmatrix} a, b, \dots \\ a, c, \dots \\ b, a, \dots \end{pmatrix}$$

Figure 3.13. *Three non-binary constraints c_1, c_2 and c_3 that only intersect on $\{x, y\}$. The v-values (y, b) and (y, c) are rPIC-inconsistent (and consequently MaxRPWC-inconsistent). The v-value (x, a) is rPIC-consistent but MaxRPWC-inconsistent*

MaxRPWC is strictly stronger than rPIC which is itself strictly stronger than GAC. However, on networks where constraints intersect on at most one variable, MaxRPWC and rPIC collapse down to GAC [BES 08c]. Additional domain-filtering consistencies for non-binary constraints have been introduced in [STE 07]. For example, by increasing the horizon to three constraints, rPIC and MaxRPWC

---

5. A support for (x, a) on c is basically equivalent to a valid instantiation of scp(c) involving (x, a) and satisfying c.

can be adapted to become relational $(1,3)$-consistency and max-restricted 3-wise consistency, respectively. Inspired by w-consistency [NAG 03], a new consistency called *inverse w-consistency* (IwC) is identified:

DEFINITION 3.37.– *[Inverse w-consistency] A v-value (x,a) of a constraint network P is* inverse w-consistent, *or* IwC-consistent, *iff for every constraint c of P involving x, there exists an instantiation I of* $\mathrm{scp}(c)$ *such that* $(x,a) \in I$, *I is valid on P, I satisfies c, and for every additional constraint c' of P, there exists an extension I' of I over* $\mathrm{scp}(c') \setminus \mathrm{scp}(c)$ *that is locally consistent.*

Comparison of Definitions 3.36 and 3.37 reveals that the definition of inverse w-consistency is similar to the definition of MaxRPWC. The (important) difference is that the extension I' of a valid instantiation I over an additional constraint c' must correspond to a locally consistent instantiation. This means that, contrary to MaxRPWC, any constraint c'' covered by I', i.e. such that $\mathrm{scp}(c'') \subseteq \mathrm{vars}(I') = \mathrm{scp}(c) \cup \mathrm{scp}(c')$ must also be satisfied by I'. Clearly, IwC is strictly stronger than maxRPWC. An extension of IwC, called extended inverse w-consistency, can be made by recognizing that any constraint intersecting with both c and c' (in the definition), must be satisfied. In general, enforcement of the following relational adaptation of neighborhood inverse consistency may appear quite utopian, but this provides a nice upper bound in terms of filtering strength.

DEFINITION 3.38.– *[Relational Neighborhood Inverse Consistency] A v-value (x,a) of a constraint network P is* relational neighborhood inverse-consistent, *or* rNIC-consistent, *iff for every constraint c of P involving x, there exists an instantiation I of* $\cup_{c' \in \mathrm{cons}(P) | \mathrm{scp}(c) \cap \mathrm{scp}(c') \neq \emptyset} \mathrm{scp}(c')$ *such that* $(x,a) \in I$, *and I is locally consistent.*

EXAMPLE.– The following example illustrates the differences between the last three consistencies. Figure 3.14 shows successive steps that would (at least) be performed by a Max-RPWC algorithm to prove that a v-value (x,a) is Max-RPWC-consistent. As x belongs to the scopes of two constraints (a "horizontal" and a "vertical" one), in a first stage an instantiation I on the horizontal constraint is (successfully) extended over the scope of any other intersecting constraint. This corresponds to Figures 3.14(b) to 3.14(e). In a second stage, an instantiation I on the vertical constraint is (successfully) extended over the scope of any other intersecting constraint; this corresponds to Figures 3.14(f) to 3.14(h). This example assumes that no failure occurs, and does not consider constraints that do not intersect with the current constraint involving x since these can be ignored.

Let us now consider the first successive steps that would (at least) be performed by an IwC algorithm to prove that (x,a) is IwC-consistent. Figure 3.15 shows the behavior of this algorithm for the first stage (i.e. the horizontal constraint). Here, instead of systematically checking two constraints as for MaxRPWC, the IwC algorithm simultaneously checks three constraints at Figure 3.15(d) because one of these is covered by the two initial constraints. Figure 3.16, shows the two (successful)

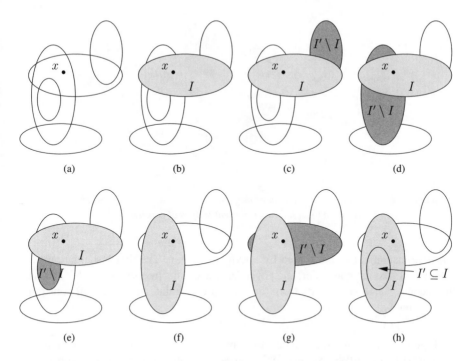

Figure 3.14. *Illustration of successive steps performed by a MaxRPWC algorithm when checking a v-value (x, a). Ovals represent scopes of constraints*

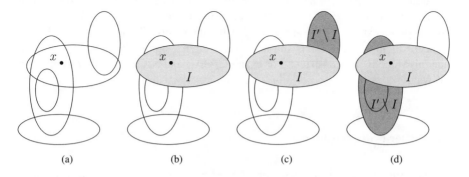

Figure 3.15. *Illustration of the first steps performed by an IwC algorithm when checking a v-value (x, a). Ovals represent scopes of constraints*

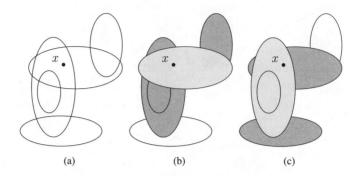

Figure 3.16. *Illustration of the first steps performed by a rNIC algorithm when checking a v-value (x, a). Ovals represent scopes of constraints*

tentative instantiations performed by a rNIC algorithm. The first instantiation starts from the horizontal constraint, and covers all constraints intersecting with it, whereas the second instantiation starts from the vertical constraint, and covers all constraints intersecting with it.

Figure 3.17 shows the relationships between consistencies introduced in this section. sPC and sPWC respectively represent the strong form of path consistency and pairwise consistency introduced in the next section. This means that these properties are combined with (generalized) arc consistency. More about this hierarchy of consistencies can be found in [DEB 01, BES 06, BES 08c, STE 07].

Finally, it is worth mentioning that several domain-filtering consistencies can be captured by a general framework which allows the definition of such inverse local consistencies [VER 99]. Each consistency ϕ in this framework is defined by describing a sub-network extracted from any given constraint network. The *viability* of each value is checked with respect to this sub-network: if after assigning it there is no solution, then this value is ϕ-inconsistent. For example, GAC and NIC can easily be defined in this way.

3.4. Higher-order consistencies

The previous section has dealt with first-order consistencies, which are also known as domain-filtering or inverse consistencies. We now move on to consider higher-order consistencies which permit identification of nogoods of size greater than one. Before going further we note that algorithms enforcing higher-order consistencies have potentially major drawbacks:

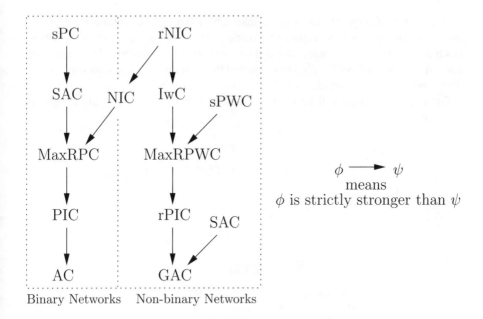

Figure 3.17. *Relationships existing between some domain-filtering consistencies*

– these algorithms modify the general structure of constraint networks: recording identified nogoods requires either adding new extensional constraints or modifying existing ones;

– the number of nogoods that may be identified increases exponentially with their size. For example, with a kth-order consistency, i.e. a consistency that only detects nogoods of size k, there may be as many as $\binom{n}{k}d^k$ distinct nogoods.

Figure 3.18 illustrates what nogood recording can do to the "structure" of a constraint network. This figure illustrates four possible effects when nogoods are of size greater than one:

– the negative table (i.e. table of forbidden tuples) of an extensional constraint is modified by adding some nogoods – see constraint c_{vxz};

– the positive table (i.e. table of allowed tuples) of an extensional constraint is modified by removing some nogoods – see constraint c_{vy};

– the semantics of an intensional constraint is modified by the addition of nogoods – see constraint c_{wyz};

– a new extensional constraint is introduced by using a negative table – see constraint c_{xy}.

Of course, if data structures other than tables (i.e. simple enumerating arrays) assumed here are used to represent extensional constraints, then these structures (such as matrices or hash maps) are updated appropriately. Another idea is to collect nogoods in a special pool (called base) so that the structure of the network can be left unchanged. This idea stretches the formalism but it can be seen as a very particular global constraint. This will be considered further in Chapter 10 in the context of restarting search.

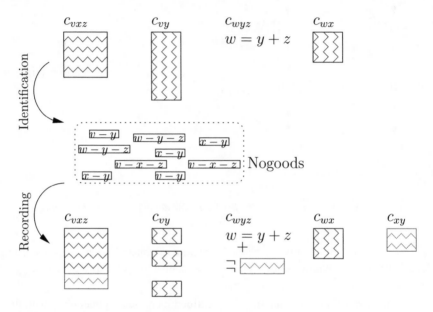

Figure 3.18. *Identification and recording of nogoods. Rectangles with an horizontal (resp. vertical) zigzagging pattern represent negative (resp. positive) tables*

There are basically two pragmatic approaches to deal with higher-order consistencies. One of these approaches avoids combinatorial space explosion by deliberately limiting the size of identified nogoods to a small value k. For example, *second-order consistencies* identify inconsistent pairs of values[6], and to record them the worst-case space complexity is "only" $O(n^2 d^2)$. Path consistency is a famous representative of this class. Another approach avoids making drastic changes in the structure of constraint networks by restricting identified nogoods to tuples allowed by existing constraints. This *conservative* approach amounts to using relation-filtering consistencies, which are particularly appropriate for extensional constraints. Pairwise

6. Strictly speaking, globally inconsistent instantiations composed of exactly two v-values, or nogoods of size 2.

consistency is a representative example of the relation-filtering class of consistencies. In practice, we may be tempted to combine both approaches as, for example, with conservative path consistency.

In this section, our first topic is path consistency; we hopefully address a common misunderstanding about it. We then present some higher-order relation-based consistencies; some of these underlie certain domain-filtering consistencies.

3.4.1. *Taking the right path*

Among the consistencies that allow us to identify inconsistent pairs of values, *path consistency* plays a central role. Introduced by Montanari [MON 74], its definition has often been misinterpreted. The problem is that a path in this context must be understood as any sequence of variables and not as a sequence of variables that corresponds to a path in the constraint graph. A footnote in the original paper indicates that "A path in a network is any sequence of vertices. A vertex can occur more than once in a path even in consecutive positions". There is no need for two successive variables in a path to be linked by a constraint. In this section, we introduce path consistency and show that the original definition is the right choice.

We require a precise definition of "path". The first definition below is given in [MON 74] and used implicitly in [MAC 77a, DEB 98] while the second is used, for example, in [TSA 93, BLI 99]. A *graph-path* is defined to be a sequence of variables such that there exists a binary constraint between any two variables adjacent in the sequence. A path in a binary constraint graph is a graph-path. If all non-binary constraints are discarded (i.e. ignored) then a path in the resulting constraint graph is also a graph-path. Note that any given variable may occur several times in a path. Figure 3.19 gives an illustration.

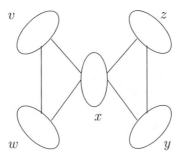

Figure 3.19. *The constraint graph of a binary constraint network* P. $\langle v, z, x \rangle$ *is a path of* P. $\langle v, y, w, y \rangle$ *is another one.* $\langle v, z, y, w \rangle$ *is a closed path of* P. $\langle v, x, y \rangle$ *is a graph-path of* P. $\langle v, x, w \rangle$ *and* $\langle z, x, v, w, x, y \rangle$ *are two closed graph-paths of* P

DEFINITION 3.39.– *[Path] Let P be a constraint network.*

– A path of P is a sequence $\langle x_1, \ldots, x_k \rangle$ of variables of P such that $x_1 \neq x_k$ and $k \geq 2$; the path is from variable x_1 to variable x_k, and $k - 1$ is the length *of the path.*

– A graph-path *of P is a path $\langle x_1, \ldots, x_k \rangle$ of P such that $\forall i \in 1..k - 1, \exists c \in \mathrm{cons}(P) \mid \mathrm{scp}(c) = \{x_i, x_{i+1}\}$.*

– A closed *path of P is a path $\langle x_1, \ldots, x_k \rangle$ of P such that $\exists c \in \mathrm{cons}(P) \mid \mathrm{scp}(c) = \{x_1, x_k\}$.*

The central concept is that of *consistent path* defined as follows:

DEFINITION 3.40.– *[Consistent Path] Let P be a constraint network.*

– An instantiation $\{(x_1, a_1), (x_k, a_k)\}$ on P is consistent *on a path $\langle x_1, \ldots, x_k \rangle$ of P iff there exists a tuple $\tau \in \prod_{i=1}^{k} \mathrm{dom}(x_i)$ such that $\tau[x_1] = a_1$, $\tau[x_k] = a_k$ and $\forall i \in 1..k - 1, \{(x_i, \tau[x_i]), (x_{i+1}, \tau[x_{i+1}])\}$ is a locally consistent instantiation[7] on P. The tuple τ is said to be a* support *for $\{(x_1, a_1), (x_k, a_k)\}$ on $\langle x_1, \ldots, x_k \rangle$ (in P).*

– A path $\langle x_1, \ldots, x_k \rangle$ of P is consistent *iff every locally consistent instantiation of $\{x_1, x_k\}$ on P is consistent on $\langle x_1, \ldots, x_k \rangle$.*

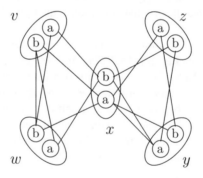

Figure 3.20. *The compatibility graph of a binary constraint network P. $\langle v, z, x \rangle$ is a consistent path of P. The closed graph-path $\langle v, x, w \rangle$ is not consistent contrary to $\langle z, x, v, w, x, y \rangle$*

EXAMPLE.– In the example in Figure 3.20, $\langle v, z, x \rangle$ is a consistent path of P since for the locally consistent instantiation $\{(v, a), (x, b)\}$ we can find b in $\mathrm{dom}(z)$ such that $\{(v, a), (z, b)\}$ is locally consistent (this is trivial since there is an implicit universal binary constraint between v and z) and $\{(x, b), (z, b)\}$ is locally consistent. Similarly, the second locally consistent instantiation $\{(v, b), (x, a)\}$ can be extended to z. The

---

7. If $x_i = x_{i+1}$, then necessarily $\tau[x_i] = \tau[x_{i+1}]$ because an instantiation cannot contain two distinct v-values involving the same variable.

closed graph-path $\langle v, x, w \rangle$ is not consistent; the locally consistent instantiation $\{(v, b), (w, a)\}$ cannot be extended to x. You might be surprised that $\langle z, x, v, w, x, y \rangle$ is consistent. It is important to note that we are free to select different values for x along the path (if this was not the case, a path-consistent binary constraint network would necessarily be minimal). For example, for the locally consistent instantiation $\{(z, b), (y, a)\}$, we can find the support $\tau = (b, b, a, b, a, a)$ on $\langle z, x, v, w, x, y \rangle$. This tuple belongs to $\mathrm{dom}(z) \times \mathrm{dom}(x) \times \mathrm{dom}(v) \times \mathrm{dom}(w) \times \mathrm{dom}(x) \times \mathrm{dom}(y)$, satisfies $\tau[z] = b$, $\tau[y] = a$ and all encountered binary constraints along the path. Along this path we have first (x, b) and subsequently (x, a).

We can now introduce the historical definition of *path consistency* (PC) [MON 74, MAC 77a].

DEFINITION 3.41.– *[Path Consistency] A constraint network P is* path-consistent, *or* PC-consistent, *iff every path of P is consistent.*

We shall ignore paths of length one (i.e. sequences of two variables) because, by definition, these are consistent. Montanari has shown that it is sufficient to consider paths of length two (i.e. sequences of three variables) only. Note that it is not necessary for the constraint graph to be complete (but, when path consistency is enforced, the resulting network may become complete).

THEOREM 3.42.– *[Montanari [MON 74]] A constraint network P is path-consistent iff every 2-length path of P (i.e. every sequence of three variables) is consistent.*

This leads to the following classical definition:

DEFINITION 3.43.– *[Path Consistency] Let P be a constraint network.*

   – *A locally consistent instantiation $\{(x, a), (y, b)\}$ on P (with $x \neq y$) is* path-consistent, *or* PC-consistent, *iff it is 2-length path-consistent, that is to say, iff there exists a value c in the domain of every third variable z of P such that $\{(x, a), (z, c)\}$ and $\{(y, b), (z, c)\}$ are both locally consistent; if $\{(x, a), (y, b)\}$ is not path-consistent, it is said to be* path-inconsistent *or* PC-inconsistent.

   – *P is* path-consistent *iff every locally consistent instantiation $\{(x, a), (y, b)\}$ on P is path-consistent.*

The question is: can we restrict our attention to graph-paths (see Definition 3.39)? Consider, for example, a constraint network composed of three variables x, y and z such that $\mathrm{dom}(x) = \{a, b\}, \mathrm{dom}(y) = \{a\}$ and $\mathrm{dom}(z) = \{a\}$ and a single constraint c_{xy} such that $\mathrm{rel}(c_{xy}) = \{(a, a)\}$. This network is not path-consistent since the locally consistent instantiation $\{(x, b), (z, a)\}$ is not consistent on the path $\langle x, y, z \rangle$. If we now limit our attention to graph-paths, these consist only of the variables x and y and there is no local inconsistency. However, for a binary constraint network that has a connected constraint graph (i.e. a constraint graph composed of a single connected component), the restriction to graph-paths is valid.

PROPOSITION 3.44.– *Let P be a binary constraint network such that $P \neq \perp$ and the constraint graph of P is connected. P is path-consistent iff every graph-path of P is consistent.*

Proof. For one direction ($\Rightarrow$), this is immediate. If P is path-consistent, then by definition every path of P is consistent, including graph-paths. For the other direction ($\Leftarrow$), we show that if every graph-path of P is consistent, then every 2-length path of P is consistent (and so P is path-consistent using Theorem 3.42). In practical terms, we consider a locally consistent instantiation $\{(x, a), (y, b)\}$ and show that for each third variable z of P, the following property $Pr(z)$ holds: $\exists c \in \operatorname{dom}(z)$ such that $\{(x, a), (z, c)\}$ and $\{(y, b), (z, c)\}$ are both locally consistent instantiations. For each variable z three cases must be considered, depending of the existence of the constraints c_{xz}, between x and z, and c_{yz}, between y and z. a) Both constraints exist: so there exists a graph-path $\langle x, z, y \rangle$ and as this path is consistent by hypothesis, the property $Pr(z)$ holds. b) Neither of the constraints exists: $P \neq \perp$ implies $\operatorname{dom}(z) \neq \emptyset$, so $Pr(z)$ holds because c_{xz} and c_{yz} are implicit and universal. c) Only the constraint c_{xz} exists (similarly, only the constraint c_{yz} exists): as the constraint graph is connected, there exists at least one graph-path from z to y, and consequently a graph-path from x to y of the form $\langle x, z, \ldots, y \rangle$. This means that there is a value in $\operatorname{dom}(z)$ which is compatible with (x, a), by using the hypothesis (every graph-path is consistent). This value is also compatible with (y, b) because there is an implicit universal constraint between z and y. Hence, $Pr(z)$ holds.   □

Note that a constraint network P such that every 2-length graph-path of P is consistent, is not necessarily path-consistent. In the special case where the constraint graph is complete, the constraint network is path-consistent because every path of P is also a graph-path of P.

PROPOSITION 3.45.– *For some constraint networks, the following properties are not equivalent.*

(a) Every graph-path is consistent.

(b) Every 2-length graph-path is consistent.

Proof. See Figure 3.21.   □

We have the following proposition for 2-length graph-paths:

PROPOSITION 3.46.– *Let P be a binary constraint network such that $P \neq \perp$ and P is arc-consistent. P is path-consistent iff every 2-length graph-path of P is consistent.*

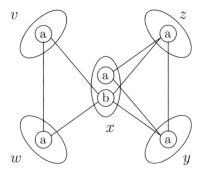

Figure 3.21. *Every 2-length graph-path of this constraint network is consistent. The graph-path* $\langle x, w, v, x, z \rangle$ *is not consistent for* $\{(x, a), (z, a)\}$

Proof. The proof is similar to the proof of Proposition 3.44 by considering 2-length graph-paths instead of graph-paths. Only case c) in the demonstration differs. c) Only the constraint c_{xz} exists (similarly, only the constraint c_{yz} exists): as P is arc-consistent, there exists a value in $\mathrm{dom}(z)$ that is compatible with (x, a). Because there is an implicit universal constraint between z and y, this value is also compatible with (y, b). Hence, $Pr(z)$ holds.   □

Theorem 3.42 and Propositions 3.44 and 3.46 suggest that the historical definition of path consistency is appropriate since this is the only one that is unrestricted (even if considering graph-paths seems more natural than considering paths). In practice, to check path consistency we only need to consider 2-length graph-paths, provided that binary constraints are arc-consistent.

Two different relation-filtering consistencies can be defined in terms of closed graph-paths. The first is *partial path consistency* (PPC) [BLI 99] and the second is *conservative path consistency* (CPC) [DEB 99].

DEFINITION 3.47.– *[Partial Path Consistency] A constraint network P is* partially path-consistent, *or* PPC-consistent, *iff every closed graph-path of P is consistent.*

DEFINITION 3.48.– *[Conservative Path Consistency] A constraint network P is* conservative path-consistent, *or* CPC-consistent, *iff every closed 2-length graph-path of P is consistent.*

For binary constraints, PPC and CPC are equivalent when the constraint graph is triangulated. Recall that a graph is triangulated (or chordal) if every cycle composed of four or more vertices has a chord, which is an edge joining two vertices that are not adjacent in the cycle.

PROPOSITION 3.49.– *[PPC on triangulated constraint graphs [BLI 99]] Let P be a binary constraint network P with a triangulated constraint graph. P is PPC-consistent iff P is CPC-consistent.*

Enforcing path consistency simply means discarding instantiations that are path-inconsistent (i.e. recording new explicit nogoods of size 2), since we know that the PC-closure, denoted by $PC(P)$, of any constraint network P exists (path consistency is well-behaved). To enforce path consistency, it may be necessary to introduce some new binary constraints, and so path consistency is not a relation-filtering consistency. PPC and CPC differ in that only existing constraints are altered. Two further relation-filtering forms can be derived from path consistency, the first by considering only closed paths, and the second by considering only closed 2-length paths. These will not be developed in this book.

3.4.2. *Relation-based consistencies*

Pairwise consistency [JAN 89] is a simple and natural relation-filtering consistency that allows reasoning about connections between constraints through shared variables. Pairwise consistency, which is also sometimes called inter-consistency [JÉG 91], is based on relational database work [BEE 83]. The following definition is in the spirit of nogood identification:

DEFINITION 3.50.– *[Pairwise Consistency]*

– *Given a constraint c, a valid instantiation of* $\mathrm{scp}(c)$ *that satisfies c is* pairwise-consistent, *or* PWC-consistent, *with respect to an additional constraint c' iff it can be extended over* $\mathrm{scp}(c') \setminus \mathrm{scp}(c)$ *into a valid instantiation that satisfies c'.*

– *A constraint network P is* pairwise-consistent *iff for every constraint c of P, every valid instantiation of* $\mathrm{scp}(c)$ *that satisfies c is pairwise-consistent with respect to every additional constraint c' of P.*

Equivalently, a valid tuple τ allowed by a constraint c, i.e. a support $\tau \in \sup(c)$, is pairwise-consistent with respect to a constraint c' iff $\exists \tau' \in \sup(c') \mid \tau[\mathrm{scp}(c) \cap \mathrm{scp}(c')] = \tau'[\mathrm{scp}(c) \cap \mathrm{scp}(c')]$. Note that any normalized binary constraint network which is arc-consistent is necessarily pairwise-consistent because there is not more than one shared variable between any two binary constraints. Therefore pairwise consistency should only be used with non-binary constraint networks. More precisely, pairwise consistency should be applied only to pairs (c, c') of constraints such that $c \neq c'$ and $|\mathrm{scp}(c) \cap \mathrm{scp}(c')| \geq 2$.

A natural generalization of pairwise consistency considers k constraints instead of two [JÉG 91].

DEFINITION 3.51.– *[k-wise Consistency]*

 – *Given a constraint c, a valid instantiation of $\mathrm{scp}(c)$ that satisfies c is k-wise-consistent, or kWC-consistent, with respect to a set C of $k-1$ additional constraints iff it can be extended over $\cup_{c' \in C} \mathrm{scp}(c') \setminus \mathrm{scp}(c)$ into a valid instantiation that satisfies every constraint in C.*

 – *A constraint network P is k-wise-consistent iff for every constraint c of P, every valid instantiation of $\mathrm{scp}(c)$ that satisfies c is k-wise-consistent with respect to every set C of $k-1$ additional constraints of P.*

For $k > 2$, k-wise consistency can be applied successfully to binary constraint networks. For binary constraint networks, 3-wise consistency is strongly related to conservative path consistency; see Definition 3.48. Figure 3.22 illustrates pairwise and 3-wise consistencies.

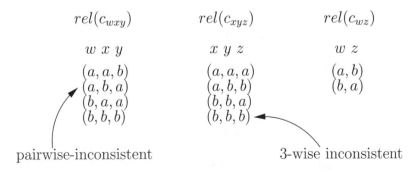

$$rel(c_{wxy}) \qquad rel(c_{xyz}) \qquad rel(c_{wz})$$

$$w \; x \; y \qquad\qquad x \; y \; z \qquad\qquad w \; z$$

$$\begin{pmatrix} a,a,b \\ a,b,a \\ b,a,a \\ b,b,b \end{pmatrix} \qquad \begin{pmatrix} a,a,a \\ a,b,b \\ b,b,a \\ b,b,b \end{pmatrix} \qquad \begin{pmatrix} a,b \\ b,a \end{pmatrix}$$

pairwise-inconsistent   3-wise inconsistent

Figure 3.22. *Three constraints "intersecting". The tuple (a, b, a) in $\mathrm{rel}(c_{wxy})$ is PWC-inconsistent since it cannot be extended to c_{xyz}. The tuple (b, b, b) in $\mathrm{rel}(c_{xyz})$ is 3WC-inconsistent since it cannot be extended to the two other constraints*

Relational (i, m)-consistencies constitute another important class of consistencies defined in terms of (existing) constraints. Recall that (i, j)-consistencies are basically expressed in terms of variables: given a set (locally consistent instantiation) of i variables, is it true that for every additional set of j variables there exists a locally consistent instantiation involving the $i + j$ variables? Except when $i = 1$, such variable-based consistencies may modify the structure of the constraint hypergraph by inserting new constraints whose arity depends on i. It may be desirable, in some cases, to preserve the structure of the network and also to avoid referring to a precise arity. This is why relational consistencies have been introduced [BEE 95, BEE 94b, DEC 97]. Let us begin with the the general class of relational (i, m)-consistencies:

DEFINITION 3.52.– *[Relational (i, m)-consistency] Let P be a constraint network and i, m be two integers such that $0 \leq i \leq n$ and $1 \leq m \leq e$. P is relationally (i, m)-consistent iff for every set X of i variables of P and every set C of m constraints of P such that $X \subseteq \bigcup_{c \in C} \mathrm{scp}(c)$, every locally consistent instantiation of X can be extended to a solution of the constraint network $(\bigcup_{c \in C} \mathrm{scp}(c), C)$.*

Note that an instantiation I extended to a solution of the constraint network $(\bigcup_{c \in C} \mathrm{scp}(c), C)$ is a valid extension of I over $\bigcup_{c \in C} \mathrm{scp}(c) \setminus \mathrm{vars}(I)$ that satisfies all constraints in C. It is important to emphasize similarities and differences between (i, j)-consistency and relational (i, m)-consistency. In both cases, we start with a set X of i variables and try to extend a locally consistent instantiation of this set of variables. However, while j refers to an additional disjoint set Y of variables, m refers to a set C of constraints involving the variables in X. In (i, j)-consistency we have to find a locally consistent instantiation of $X \cup Y$ on P; in relational (i, m)-consistency we have to find a locally consistent instantiation of $\bigcup_{c \in C} \mathrm{scp}(c)$ on a new network composed of constraints in C.

DEFINITION 3.53.– *[Strong Relational (i, m)-consistency] Let P be a constraint network and i, m be two integers such that $0 \leq i \leq n$ and $1 \leq m \leq e$. P is strongly relationally (i, m)-consistent iff P is relationally (j, m)-consistent for every integer j such that $0 \leq j \leq i$.*

Further (classes of) consistencies have been introduced: relational m-consistency, relational arc consistency and relational path consistency. Definitions given in the literature may slightly differ and are not always equivalent. Some definitions of relational arc, path and m-consistency refer to a strong form (as above), while others refer to the extension of a locally consistent instantiation to a unique variable (possibly within the scope of any given constraint). The reader is invited to compare definitions given in [BEE 95, BEE 94b, DEC 97, DEC 03, WAL 01, BES 06, BES 08c].

Relational consistencies capture [APT 03] various local consistencies introduced in the literature. For example:

– a constraint network is generalized arc-consistent iff it is relationally $(1, 1)$-consistent;

– a (normalized) binary constraint network is path-consistent if it is relationally $(2, 3)$-consistent;

– a constraint network is relationally path-inverse-consistent [BES 08c] iff it is relationally $(1, 2)$-consistent;

– a constraint network is satisfiable iff it is relationally $(0, e)$-consistent.

Moreover, relational consistencies are useful for characterizing relationships between properties of constraint networks and the level of local consistency needed to ensure global consistency (e.g. see [BEE 95, DEC 97, ZHA 03b]).

3.5. Global consistency

Global consistency (see Definition 3.3) is the ideal property. It guarantees not only that a constraint network is satisfiable, but also that any locally consistent partial instantiation can be extended to a solution in a backtrack-free manner by a simple depth-first search algorithm; see Theorem 3.4. As would be expected, the tasks of enforcing global consistency and of finding whether a constraint network is globally consistent are generally intractable. Nevertheless, for some structured problems under certain conditions, global consistency can be identified, and even better, can be reached by simple polynomial transformations.

3.5.1. *Identifying global consistency*

There has been much work on identification of conditions for a constraint network to be guaranteed to be globally consistent. A first interesting result [DEC 92b] has established a relationship between the size of the domains, the arity of the constraints and the level of local consistency. In the following, a constraint network P is *d-valued* iff the greatest domain size in P is equal to d and *r-ary* iff the greatest constraint arity in P is equal to r.

THEOREM 3.54.– *If a d-valued r-ary constraint network is strongly $d(r-1)+1$-consistent, then it is globally consistent.* There are two immediate corollaries.

COROLLARY 3.55.– *If a d-valued binary constraint network is strongly $d+1$-consistent, then it is globally consistent.*

COROLLARY 3.56.– *If a bi-valued binary constraint network is strongly 3-consistent, then it is globally consistent.*

This last corollary suggests that any bi-valued binary constraint network can be solved efficiently (i.e. in polynomial time). Strong 3-consistency can be enforced in polynomial time, yielding a network that is still bi-valued and binary.

Theorem 3.54 can be refined by taking account of the tightness of the constraints. Theorem 3.58 [BEE 97] specifies a level of strong consistency that is always less than or equal to the level of strong consistency required by Theorem 3.54.

DEFINITION 3.57.– *[m-tight]*

– *A constraint c is m-tight iff for every variable $x \in \text{scp}(c)$ and every valid instantiation I of $\text{scp}(c) \setminus \{x\}$, there are at most m valid extensions of I over x that satisfy c, or there are exactly $|\text{dom}(x)|$ such extensions.*

– *A constraint network P is m-tight iff every constraint of P is m-tight.*

THEOREM 3.58.– *If an m-tight r-ary constraint network is strongly $(m+1)(r-1)+1$-consistent, then it is globally consistent.*

If m^* is the smallest value such that the constraint network P is m^*-tight, then the smaller the value of m^* the stronger Theorem 3.58. Definition 3.57 implies that $m^* \leq d - 1$ since the case where, in the condition, d extensions exist imposes no restriction on m-tightness (see also the definition for binary constraints introduced in [BEE 94b]). Consequently, any constraint network is at least $d - 1$-tight, so Theorem 3.58 is a refinement of Theorem 3.54.

COROLLARY 3.59.– *If an m-tight binary constraint network is strongly $m + 2$-consistent, then it is globally consistent.*

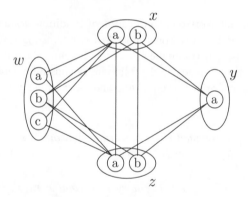

Figure 3.23. *A 1-tight binary constraint network which is strongly 3-consistent and consequently, globally consistent*

EXAMPLE.– The binary constraint network P in Figure 3.23, which illustrates these last two results, has four variables and five constraints; there is a constraint between each pair of variables, except between w and y. With Theorem 3.54, we can deduce that P is globally consistent if it is strongly 4-consistent since P is 3-valued (the greatest domain size is 3). This is not very helpful here since by definition, P is globally consistent iff it is strongly 4-consistent ($n = 4$). With Theorem 3.58, we can deduce that P is globally consistent if it is strongly 3-consistent since P is 1-tight. Checking strong 3-consistency is then sufficient to prove global consistency. To show that P is 1-tight, we only need to observe that every value of every variable involved in a constraint c is either compatible with exactly 1 value of the second variable involved in c or compatible with all values of the second variable involved in c.

Before identifying another connection between constraint tightness and global consistency [ZHA 03b, ZHA 06], we need the following definitions:

DEFINITION 3.60.– *[Properly m-tight] A constraint c is* properly *m-tight iff for every variable $x \in \mathrm{scp}(c)$ and every valid instantiation I of $\mathrm{scp}(c) \setminus \{x\}$, there are at most m valid extensions of I over x that satisfy c.*

DEFINITION 3.61.– *[Weakly m-tight] A constraint network P is* weakly *m-tight at level k, with $1 \leq k < n$, iff for every set X of variables of P such that $k \leq |X| < n$ and every additional variable x of P not present in X, there exists a properly m-tight constraint in $\{c \in \mathrm{cons}(P) \mid x \in \mathrm{scp}(c) \subseteq X \cup \{x\}\}$.*

THEOREM 3.62.– *If an r-ary constraint network is weakly m-tight at level $(m+1)(r-1)+1$ and strongly $(m+1)(r-1)+1$-consistent, then it is globally consistent.*

Whereas Theorem 3.58 requires every constraint to be m-tight, Theorem 3.62 does not require all constraints to be properly m-tight.

Some complementary results can be obtained by taking account of the looseness of constraints [BEE 94a, BEE 97]. These results indicate a lower bound of the inherent level of local consistency of any constraint network, and this may, for example, be useful for adjusting the preprocessing stage before searching for a solution.

DEFINITION 3.63.– *[m-loose]*

– *A constraint c is* m-loose *iff for every variable $x \in \mathrm{scp}(c)$ and every valid instantiation I of $\mathrm{scp}(c) \setminus \{x\}$, there are at least m valid extensions of I over x that satisfy c.*

– *A constraint network P is* m-loose *iff every constraint of P is m-loose.*

Here is the revised version by Zhang and Yap [ZHA 03c] of Theorem 4.2 in [BEE 97]:

THEOREM 3.64.– *A d-valued m-loose r-ary constraint network, with $r \geq 2$, is strongly k-consistent where k is the minimum value such that the following inequality holds:* $\binom{k-1}{r-1} \leq \lceil d/(d-m) \rceil - 1$

COROLLARY 3.65.– *A d-valued m-loose binary constraint network is strongly $\lceil d/(d-m) \rceil$-consistent.*

EXAMPLE.– To illustrate the significance of this last result, let us consider the n-queens problem (each instance being modeled as a normalized binary constraint network – see the second model in section 1.3.1). For this, the number of supports of every c-value is at least $d - 3$, so the network is at least strongly $\lceil d/3 \rceil$-consistent. Table 3.1, which is taken from [BEE 94a], allows us to compare the level of strong consistency predicted by Corollary 3.65 with the actual one.

level of strong consistency	n											
	4	5	6	7	8	9	10	11	12	13	14	15
predicted	2	2	2	3	3	3	4	4	4	5	5	5
actual	2	2	2	3	4	4	5	5	6	6	7	7

Table 3.1. *Predicted and actual level of strong consistency for* **n-queens** *instances*

Tree-convexity [ZHA 03b, ZHA 04, ZHA 06, ZHA 08] is another important property of constraints. It shows how some relationships between local and global consistencies can be established through the properties of set intersection on special sets. We will not go into the details of this general approach, which is based on a proof schema whence many consistency results can be derived. We first define *tree-convex sets* and *tree-convex constraints*.

DEFINITION 3.66.– *[Tree-convex Set] Let X be a finite set and T be a tree on X, i.e. the set of vertices of T is X. A subset $X' \subseteq X$ is* tree-convex *under T if the subgraph of T vertex-induced by X' is a tree.*

An illustration is given in Figure 3.24.

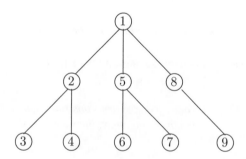

Figure 3.24. *A tree T on a set $X = \{1, 2, \ldots, 9\}$. As examples of tree-convex subsets of X under T, we have $\{1, 2, 3, 4\}$, $\{1, 2, 5\}$ and $\{5, 6\}$. $\{1, 2, 9\}$ and $\{6, 7\}$ are not tree-convex under T*

DEFINITION 3.67.– *[Tree-convex Constraint]*

 – *A constraint c is tree-convex under a tree T on $\cup_{x\in\text{scp}(c)}\text{dom}(x)$ iff for every variable $x \in \text{scp}(c)$ and every valid instantiation I of $\text{scp}(c) \setminus \{x\}$, the set $\{a \in \text{dom}(x) \mid I \cup \{(x,a)\}$ satisfies $c\}$ is either empty or tree-convex under T.*

 – *A constraint network P is* tree-convex *if there exists a tree T on $\cup_{x\in\text{vars}(P)}\text{dom}(x)$ such that every constraint of P is tree-convex under T.*

An alternative definition is proposed in [ZHA 08], in which domains are considered independently: tree convexity is then defined under a forest instead of a tree. Tree-convexity, which may occur naturally in some contexts (e.g. scene labeling), generalizes *row-convexity* introduced in [BEE 92, BEE 95]. Indeed, by noticing that a total ordering corresponds to a tree in which each node has at most one child, we obtain the following definition:

DEFINITION 3.68.– *[Row-convex Constraint] A constraint network P is* row-convex *if there exists a total order T on $\cup_{x\in\text{vars}(P)}\text{dom}(x)$ such that every constraint of P is tree-convex under T.*

Hence a binary constraint is row-convex when its $(0,1)$-matrix is such that in each row and in each column[8], all the ones are consecutive. In the example shown in Figure 3.25 a total order on $\text{dom}(x) \cup \text{dom}(y)$ can be obtained by considering for example $a_4 < b_1$.

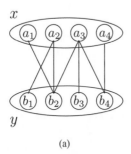

	y	b_1	b_2	b_3	b_4
x					
a_1		0	1	0	0
a_2		1	1	0	0
a_3		0	1	1	1
a_4		0	0	0	1

(a)   (b)

Figure 3.25. *A binary constraint c_{xy} between variables x and y, and its representation by a $(0,1)$-matrix using the total orderings $a_1 < a_2 < a_3 < a_4$ and $b_1 < b_2 < b_3 < b_4$. This constraint is row-convex (and then tree-convex)*

---

8. The fact that the condition also holds on columns is sometimes implicit in the literature because some authors consider the presence of two symmetric and equivalent constraints c_{xy} and c_{yx} (or relations) between any two constrained variables x and y.

Using the property of set intersection on tree-convex sets and the proof schema described in [ZHA 06], the following result is obtained:

THEOREM 3.69.– *If an r-ary tree-convex constraint network is strongly* $2(r-1)+1$*-consistent, then it is globally consistent.*

COROLLARY 3.70.– *If a binary tree-convex constraint network is strongly 3-consistent, then it is globally consistent.*

Interestingly, Jeavons *et al.* [JEA 98] show that a simple algebraic property characterizes all possible constraint relations for which k-consistency is sufficient to ensure global consistency (for $k > 2$). Before presenting this result, we need to introduce the closure property of relations as well as "near-unanimity operations".

DEFINITION 3.71.– *[Closure of Relations] Let* D *be a set (domain) and* φ : $D^k \rightarrow D$ *be a* k*-ary operation defined on* D. *For any list* $\tau_1 \ldots \tau_k$ *of* k r*-ary tuples not necessarily distinct of* D^r, $\varphi(\tau_1, \ldots, \tau_k)$ *defines the* r*-ary tuple* $(\varphi(\tau_1[1], \ldots, \tau_k[1]), \ldots, \varphi(\tau_1[r], \ldots, \tau_k[r]))$. *An* r*-ary relation* $R \subseteq D^r$ *defined on* D *is* closed *under* φ *iff* $\varphi(R) \subseteq R$ *where* $\varphi(R) = \{\varphi(\tau_1, \ldots, \tau_k) \mid \tau_1 \in R, \ldots, \tau_k \in R\}$.

DEFINITION 3.72.– *[Near Unanimity Operation] Let* D *be a set (domain) and* $\varphi : D^k \rightarrow D$ *be a* k*-ary operation defined on* D *with* $k \geq 3$. φ *is a near-unanimity operation iff* $\forall a \in D, \forall b \in D, \varphi(a, b, \ldots, b) = \varphi(b, a, b, \ldots, b) = \cdots = \varphi(b, \ldots, b, a) = b$.

A near-unanimity k-ary operator φ is such that whenever $k - 1$ arguments are equal to a value b, this value is necessarily returned by φ. In all other cases, any value can be returned by φ. We can now establish a link between closure of relations under near-unanimity operations and global consistency. Note that [JEA 98] also establishes a connection with a concept of decomposability.

THEOREM 3.73.– *Let* D *be a set (domain),* Γ *be a set of relations defined on* D, *and* $r \geq 3$ *be an integer. Every relation in* Γ *is closed under a near-unanimity operation of arity* r *iff for every constraint network* P *such that for every variable* x *of* P, $\text{dom}(x) = D$ *and for every constraint* c *of* P, $\text{rel}(c) \in \Gamma$, *establishing strong* r*-consistency ensures global consistency.*

Of course, this result can be generalized to take into account distinct domains of variables.

3.5.2. *Toward tractability*

The theory in the previous section does not enable precise circumscription of tractable CSP classes. *A CSP class is a set of CSP instances usually characterized* by a structural or relational property. The definition of a *structural class* is based on the constraint hypergraph; for example, the set of CSP instances whose hypergraph is acyclic is a structural class. A *relational class* is defined in terms of a given set of constraint relations, also called a constraint language. For example, the set of CSP instances confined to monotonic constraints [HEN 92] is a relational class.

A problem is *tractable* if there exists a polynomial algorithm to solve it. For a given CSP instance there are, in fact [GRE 08], two tractability problems. First, we have to determine whether the given CSP instance belongs to a specified tractable class: this is the *identification problem*. Second, we have to solve the given instance and show a solution if one exists: this is the *search problem*. A CSP class is said to be tractable iff both its identification problem and its search problem are tractable, intractable otherwise.

3.5.2.1. *Relational CSP classes*

Relational classes of CSP instances are defined in terms of constraint relations and/or variable domains (which can be considered as unary constraints). Even if theorems in section 3.5.1 seem attractive, they do not always lead to efficient solving procedures. We now discuss this aspect and introduce some well-known tractable relational classes.

First, the "class" of bi-valued binary constraint networks is tractable. Recognition of bi-valued binary networks is immediate, and enforcing strong 3-consistency (in polynomial time) ensures that modified networks are bi-valued and binary. On the other hand, the class of d-valued r-ary constraint networks is obviously intractable when $d > 2$ or $r > 2$. The reason is that enforcing strong $d(r - 1) + 1$-consistency (see Theorem 3.54) may induce new constraints of arity strictly greater than r. Consequently we have to enforce a new strong level of consistency that may induce new constraints of arity still higher, and so on (see also the discussion in [DEC 92b] about recursive classes of tractability). The class of m-tight r-ary constraint networks is not tractable either. In this case, both the value of m and the value of r may change when enforcing the strong level of consistency. Similarly, the class of weakly m-tight r-ary constraint networks is not tractable.

In [ZHA 06] the authors claim that there exists a polynomial algorithm to recognize a tree-convex constraint network. Moreover, [BEE 95] provides a method for efficient identification of a row-convex binary constraint network. But even if a given constraint network is tree-convex (or simply row-convex), there is no guarantee that it can be solved efficiently (i.e. in polynomial time). Enforcement of strong $2(r - 1) + 1$-consistency may disrupt convexity: the resulting network may not be more tree-convex (row-convex). In other words, the class of tree-convex (row-convex) constraint networks is not tractable. Although [ZHA 04] has shown that tree-convex constraint networks which are locally chain convex and union closed can be made globally consistent in polynomial time, the identification problem for such networks remains an open question.

Various subclasses of row-convex binary constraint networks have been studied. First, the class of binary *0/1/all* constraints [COO 94] (equivalent to implicational relations [KIR 93]) has been identified as a tractable subclass of the row-convex constraints class. This follows from Theorem 3.73 because the relations associated with these constraints are all closed under a near-unanimity operator called the majority operator [JEA 95a]. Because this operator is ternary, strong 3-consistency is sufficient to ensure global consistency. The *connected row-convex* (CRC) constraints [DEV 99] are a further special case of row-convex constraints; they have the nice features of being closed under composition, intersection and transposition, which are the basic operations of 3-consistency algorithms. Thus enforcement of strong 3-consistency preserves row convexity, so it is possible to make any CRC network globally consistent in polynomial time. Since connected row-convex constraints can be identified in polynomial time when domains are 3-valued, the class of CRC 3-valued constraint networks is also tractable. However, the connected row convex identification problem is intractable for domains of size four or more [GRE 08].

Finally, *max-closed* constraints [JEA 95b] constitute another important relational class. An r-ary constraint c is max-closed iff $\forall \tau_1 \in \text{rel}(c)$, $\forall \tau_2 \in \text{rel}(c)$, the tuple $\tau = (\max(\tau_1[1], \tau_2[1]), \dots, \max(\tau_1[r], \tau_2[r])) \in \text{rel}(c)$. Informally, the constraint is also satisfied by the tuple in which the value of each variable is the maximum of the values of this variable in two accepted tuples. Identification of a max-closed constraint is tractable if the constraint is given in extension; a max-closed constraint network can be solved[9] by establishing generalized arc consistency [COH 03b]. It is sufficient to check that no domain is empty and to select the maximum value in each domain to build a solution. A similar result holds for the class of *min-closed* constraints.

Tractable relational classes can be enlarged by *domain permutation* [GRE 08]. This mechanism independently permutes the domain of each variable of a CSP instance so that the resulting instance belongs to a tractable class. Finding such a permutation with respect to a targeted tractable relational class (or constraint language) is called the *reduction problem*. This amounts to solving, for any CSP instance P, an associated *lifted* instance whose solutions are the domain permutations that transform P into a tractable one. When the reduction problem is itself tractable, we obtain a new tractable class. The elegant theory in [GRE 08] allows definition of new tractable classes and unifies disparate known results. This work addresses the challenge of discovering domain permutations that make instances row-convex, connected row-convex or max-closed. Reduction tractability is proved for row-convex constraints (also proved in [BEE 95]), but row convex constraints do not form a

---

9. Initially, it was shown [JEA 95b] with pairwise consistency.

tractable language. Reduction intractability is shown (in general) for connected row-convex and max-closed constraints (also proved differently in [BES 08b]). Among other things, it is also shown that triangulated [COH 03a] and stable marriage instances are reducible, via domain permutations, to max-closed instances. Readers interested in tractability are invited to consult the paper of Green and Cohen [GRE 08].

3.5.2.2. *Structural CSP classes*

There has been much work on identification of structural properties of constraint networks that guarantee global consistency, or more simply, guarantee backtrack-free search. Some classical results are as follows.

First, Freuder [FRE 82, FRE 85a] identified a relationship between the width of the primal graph and the level of local consistency which ensures that a solution can be found without backtracking. The variable ordering used during search must be "compatible" with the width of the primal graph.

DEFINITION 3.74.– *[Width wrt $\lhd$] Let $G = (V, E)$ be a graph and $\lhd$ be a total order on V. The width of a node of G wrt $\lhd$ is the number of edges that connect it to previous (in the order) nodes of G. The width of G wrt $\lhd$ is the the maximum width of the nodes of G with respect to $\lhd$.*

DEFINITION 3.75.– *[Width] Let $G = (V, E)$ be a graph. The* width *of G is the minimum width of G with respect to all total orders of V.*

THEOREM 3.76.– *Let P be a constraint network and w be the width of the primal graph of P. A solution of P can be found by backtrack-free depth-first search if P is strongly $w + 1$-consistent.*

To guarantee this result, the width of the primal graph of P with respect to the variable ordering used during search must be equal to w.

COROLLARY 3.77.– *If the width of the primal graph of P is 1 (i.e. the primal graph is a tree or more generally a forest) and P is strongly 2-consistent, a solution of P can be found by a backtrack-free depth-first search.*

EXAMPLE.– For example, Figure 3.26 shows the constraint graph of a constraint network P. As this network only has binary constraints, the primal graph of P is equivalent to the constraint graph of P, which is a tree: its width is equal to 1. This minimum width is obtained for instance with the total variable ordering $x_6 \lhd x_5 \lhd x_4 \lhd x_3 \lhd x_2 \lhd x_1$. Strong 2-consistency can be enforced on such a network: Figure 3.27 shows the result. Enforcing strong 2-consistency does not modify the width of the constraint graph of P: it remains a tree since only domains are modified. It is easy to verify that a solution of P can be found by a backtrack-free depth-first search that selects variables according to $\lhd$ (defined above). A search process that

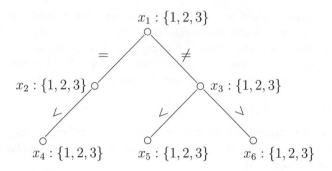

Figure 3.26. *A constraint network whose constraint graph is a tree*

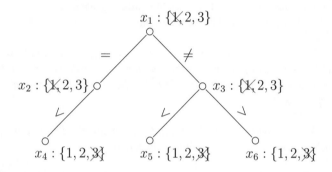

Figure 3.27. *The constraint network of Figure 3.26 made strongly 2-consistent*

employs a "non-optimal" variable ordering is not backtrack-free. For example, if the search procedure selects x_2, next x_3, next x_1, etc., the locally consistent instantiation $\{(x_2, 2), (x_3, 2)\}$ cannot be extended: every value of x_1 is incompatible and therefore backtrack occurs.

You might imagine that when the width of the primal graph of a given network P is 2, enforcement of strongly 3-consistency could be sufficient to solve P efficiently. However, unlike 2-consistency, enforcement of 3-consistency may modify the constraint (hyper)graph: some new binary constraints may be added to the network, thus increasing its width. This is discussed in [DEC 88], which also considers some directional forms of 2- and 3-consistency that make Theorem 3.76 slightly more applicable.

The class of CSP instances whose structure is *acyclic* is a tractable structural class. Structural tractability can be extended by decomposition methods that polynomially make "nearly acyclic" structures acyclic. This is the subject of section 2.2.3.

3.5.2.3. *Hybrid CSP classes*

Some tractable classes of CSP instances are called *hybrid* because they do not fall into one of the two main categories introduced above. This means that the underlying properties of instances of such classes depend both on the structure of the networks and also on the nature of the constraints. A first example of a tractable hybrid class is the class of triangulated CSP instances [COH 03a], i.e. instances for which the complement of the compatibility (hyper)graph is triangulated. For such instances, arc consistency is a decision procedure for satisfiability, and a domain permutation reduction exists to max-closed constraints. A new general property has more recently been introduced [COO 08]:

DEFINITION 3.78.– *[Broken-triangle Property] Let P be a binary constraint network.*

– *P satisfies the* broken-triangle property *with respect to a total order $\lhd$ on* vars(P) *iff for every set $\{x, y, z\}$ of three variables of P, with $x \lhd y \lhd z$, if $\{(x, a), (y, b)\}$, $\{(x, a), (z, c)\}$ and $\{(y, b), (z, c')\}$ are locally consistent then either $\{(x, a), (z, c')\}$ or $\{(y, b), (z, c)\}$ is locally consistent.*

– *P satisfies the* broken-triangle property *iff there exists a a total order $\lhd$ on* vars(P) *such that P satisfies the broken-triangle property with respect to $\lhd$.*

Figure 3.28 illustrates this.

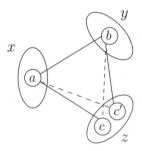

Figure 3.28. *If the broken-triangle property holds, at least one of the dotted edge is present, i.e. corresponds to a locally consistent instantiation*

The class of binary CSP instances satisfying the broken-triangle property (BTP) has been shown to be tractable. More precisely, there is a polynomial time procedure that finds a variable ordering which makes a binary CSP instance satisfying the broken-triangle property with respect to that ordering, or finds that no such ordering exists. An instance that satisfies the broken-triangle property can be solved in $O(ed^2)$. Note also that the broken-triangle property is closed under domain reduction. Thus enforcement of any domain-filtering consistency on a constraint network cannot destroy the broken-triangle property. The class of BTP instances is hybrid because it generalizes (contains) both the tractable structural class of tree-structured instances and the tractable relational class of renamable right monotone instances.

3.6. Caveats about node, arc and path consistencies

There is often confusion, in the literature, between classical node, arc and path consistencies and 1-, 2- and 3-consistencies. This deserves mention even if, under certain assumptions, the consistencies are equivalent. In particular, when constraint networks are binary and normalized, arc and path consistency do correspond to 2- and 3-consistencies.

REMARK 3.79.– *Node consistency is different from 1-consistency.*

This is true at least with our definitions and assumptions: in this book, we assume that 1-consistency is equivalent to $(0, 1)$-consistency and we assume that $\emptyset$ is a locally consistent instantiation. A constraint network P is node-consistent when each v-value (x, a) of P has a support on each unary constraint involving x, whereas P is 1-consistent when there is no empty domain in P. This is quite different. This difference is clear in $\mathscr{P}$, even if networks do not have unary constraints.

REMARK 3.80.– *[BES 06] Arc consistency is different from 2-consistency.*

Let us consider a constraint network P such that $\text{vars}(P) = \{x, y\}$ with $\text{dom}(x) = \text{dom}(y) = \{1, 2\}$ and $\text{cons}(P) = \{c_1 : x \leq y, c_2 : x \neq y\}$. P is arc-consistent since each value has a support on each constraint; but P is not 2-consistent since for example the locally instantiation $\{(x, 2)\}$ cannot be extended to y. The problem here is that P is not normalized. Normalization yields a unique constraint $c_3 : x < y$ and both consistencies become equivalent. In $\mathscr{P}_2$, it is always true that arc consistency is equivalent to 2-consistency because networks are normalized. However, generalized arc consistency and 2-consistency are completely different for non-binary constraints.

REMARK 3.81.– *[DEC 03] Path consistency is different from 3-consistency.*

For binary constraint networks, and more generally for networks that have no ternary constraints, both consistencies are equivalent. The presence of ternary constraints may make a difference. Consider, for example, a constraint network P such that $\text{vars}(P) = \{x, y, z\}$ with $\text{dom}(x) = \text{dom}(y) = \text{dom}(z) = \{1, 2\}$ and $\text{cons}(P) = \{c : x + y + z = 0\}$. Every valid instantiation of two variables of P is locally consistent since there are no binary (and no unary) constraints. P is therefore path-consistent. For example, $\{(x, 1), (y, 1)\}$ is locally consistent and we can find a value in the domain of z, e.g. $(z, 1)$, such that both $\{(x, 1), (z, 1)\}$ and $\{(y, 1), (z, 1)\}$ are locally consistent. But P is not 3-consistent.

Chapter 4

Generic GAC Algorithms

Generalized arc consistency (GAC) is the key property in constraint programming. When constraints are considered independently, GAC corresponds to the strongest form of local reasoning. Each constraint c can be regarded as an elementary sub-network $P_c = (\mathrm{scp}(c), \{c\})$, comprising the variables in $\mathrm{scp}(c)$ and the unique constraint c. Any v-value (x, a) of P_c that participates in at least one solution of P_c is said to be generalized arc-consistent on c. Generalized arc consistency of a constraint network guarantees the existence of a support for each c-value.

Reasoning locally at the level of each constraint facilitates integration of propagation algorithms into constraint solvers. Algorithms for enforcing generalized arc consistency, called *GAC algorithms*, are interesting in that they basically correspond to associating one filtering procedure with each constraint. Among such algorithms, some are specifically developed for certain types of constraints, whereas others can be applied to any type of constraints and are therefore said to be *generic* or *general-purpose*. Although specialized algorithms are attractive for solving particular problems, general-purpose algorithms are intended to simplify the life of developers and engineers/researchers who aim to generate scientific results, i.e. results that can be reproduced easily. Moreover, when a constraint has unknown semantics (or has no known features that can be exploited efficiently) a generic filtering algorithm is the only practical option. Hence the value of generic GAC algorithms presented in this chapter.

Generally speaking, constraint propagation is guided by events concerning variables. Examples of these events are an assignment of a value to a variable, a change in the membership of the domain of a variable, or a change in the smallest value in the domain. A *coarse-grained* filtering algorithm simply stores the identity of the variable that is involved, without storing an indication of what has happened to the variable or to its domain. For example, if values are deleted from a variable's domain, a coarse-grained algorithm stores the variable's identity but does not store the values that have been deleted. A *fine-grained* filtering algorithm actually records which values of which variables have changed. Examples of coarse-grained algorithms are (G)AC3 [MAC 77a, MAC 77b] and (G)AC2001 [BES 01b, ZHA 01b, BES 05c], while examples of fine-grained algorithms are (G)AC4 [MOH 86, MOH 88] and AC6 [BES 94]. Recall that when AC is used instead of GAC, this means that the constraints are binary.

This chapter is organized as follows. For enforcing generalized arc consistency, section 4.1 presents two coarse-grained propagation schemes that are basically equivalent. Of these, the variable-oriented propagation scheme is used predominantly in this book. In section 4.2, we introduce functions related to the support-seeking scheme called GAC-valid, while in section 4.3, this scheme is instantiated to produce two important coarse-grained GAC algorithms, namely GAC3 and GAC2001. Next, in section 4.4, we introduce general ideas concerning GAC and briefly review classical (G)AC algorithms, including fine-grained ones. Finally, before presenting a few experimental results, we explain in section 4.5 how the performance of general-purpose GAC algorithms can be improved by a) avoiding useless revisions and constraint checks, b) using residual supports and c) using the natural parallelism of bitwise operations.

4.1. Coarse-grained propagation schemes

To enforce a consistency[1] on a constraint network, local deductions or inferences are iteratively performed until a fixed point is reached or more generally a certain stopping condition is met. Quite often in practice, a local inference is made possible by reasoning from a single constraint, and corresponds to the removal of a value belonging to the domain of a variable involved in this constraint – the targeted consistency being domain-filtering. Interestingly, as soon as a local inference is performed, the conditions to trigger new inferences may hold since variables are typically shared by several constraints. This mechanism of propagating the results of local inferences from constraints to constraints is called *constraint propagation* and is achieved by *filtering algorithms*.

Classically, constraint propagation is guided by events concerning variables. In the context of generic (coarse-grained) filtering, where a unique procedure is used no matter what the constraints are, the only kind of events considered are when

---

1. Some constraint solvers may enforce different levels of local consistency in different parts of the constraint networks, but the principle of constraint propagation described here remains the same.

the domain of a variable changes (i.e. when it loses one or more values). In the context of specialized filtering, where one or even several dedicated procedures, called *propagators*, can be associated with each type of constraints, three other kinds of events are usually considered [SCH 06]:

- the variable becomes fixed (i.e. its domain becomes a singleton);
- the minimum value of a variable domain is modified;
- the maximum value of a variable domain is modified.

On the other hand, generic fine-grained filtering is guided by (deleted) values. We shall discuss this alternative in section 4.4.2 and, more generally, discuss the advantages and disadvantages of generic filtering in the conclusion of this chapter.

In this section, we describe two generic coarse-grained *propagation schemes* that can be employed to enforce generalized arc consistency on a given constraint network. Coarse-grained essentially means that the algorithms apply successive revisions of *arcs*, as described below. These schemes are so closely related that they collapse into a unique form when we simplify them to enforce a limited form of (generalized) arc consistency that corresponds to the amount of filtering performed at each search step by the backtracking algorithm called forward checking (FC). Nevertheless, we believe that it is worthwhile to present both of them. The former is the well-known *arc-oriented scheme*, and the latter is the *variable-oriented scheme*, which has some nice features.

4.1.1. *Arc-oriented propagation scheme*

We first introduce a classical *arc-oriented* coarse-grained propagation scheme for enforcing GAC on a given constraint network. An *arc* is a pair (c, x) where c is a constraint and x a variable in $\text{scp}(c)$. An arc of a constraint network P is an arc (c, x) such that $c \in \text{cons}(P)$. An arc-oriented propagation scheme records arcs in a dedicated set called the *queue*[2] of the propagation, although propagation is actually determined by events concerning variables. The arc-oriented approach is characterized by *revision* of arcs that are successively picked from the queue.

Revisions are at the heart of generic coarse-grained filtering algorithms. The revision of an arc (c, x), which means revision of $\text{dom}(x)$ with respect to constraint c, removes from $\text{dom}(x)$ all values that are not compatible with c, or more formally all values for which no support exists on c. We also say that x is revised against c. A revision is said to be *effective* or *fruitful* if it removes at least one value; otherwise, it

---

2. Following the usage, the queue must be seen as a set here, even if the term classically refers to a particular data structure in computer science.

is said to be *fruitless*. A revision is *useless* if we can predict that it will be fruitless. Obviously, we avoid wasting time by not performing useless revisions.

Stand-alone enforcement of generalized arc consistency means enforcement that is not done during backtrack search. The call enforceGAC$^{\mathrm{arc}}(P, \mathrm{vars}(P))$, Algorithm 7, achieves stand-alone enforcement of generalized arc consistency on a given constraint network P, and returns *false* if P is detected GAC-inconsistent, i.e. if $GAC(P) = \bot$. The set past(P) is the set of past variables of P, i.e. the variables of P that have been explicitly instantiated by a backtrack search algorithm such as FC or MAC, which are described in Chapter 8. When enforcement is stand-alone, we have past$(P) = \emptyset$ because there has been no variable assignment, and enforceGAC$^{\mathrm{arc}}(P, \mathrm{vars}(P))$ simply computes the GAC-closure of P. Moreover, when enforcement is stand-alone the formal parameter X_{evt} is set to $\mathrm{vars}(P)$, and in this case the initialization part (lines 1 to 3) of the algorithm is equivalent to:

$$Q \leftarrow \{(c, x) \mid c \in \mathrm{cons}(P) \wedge x \in \mathrm{scp}(c)\} \qquad \text{// all arcs are put in } Q$$

Algorithm 7 iteratively selects arcs from Q and calls revise, Algorithm 8, to perform revisions of arcs. For a given arc (c, x), the function revise returns *true* if at least one value has been removed from $\mathrm{dom}(x)$, i.e. if the revision of (c, x) has been effective. For each value a in $\mathrm{dom}(x)$ the function seekSupport determines whether or not there exists a support for (x, a) on c. Various implementations of seekSupport have been published; some of these will be discussed later in this chapter. When revision is effective, Algorithm 7 at lines 9 to 11 inserts into Q all arcs that need to be revised due to the modification of $\mathrm{dom}(x)$. Note that some useless revisions are avoided by not inserting the arcs involving x, because these have just been processed. If a domain becomes empty, known as *domain wipe-out*, Algorithm 7 returns *false* at line 8.

This algorithm can also be used during search. Then the set X_{evt} only contains the variables for which a recent event has occurred (evt is an abbreviation for event). A classical backtrack search algorithm iteratively considers two subproblems after a v-value (x, a) is selected: the first one is obtained from P by posting a branching constraint of the form $x = a$ and the second one by posting a branching constraint of the form $x \neq a$. To enforce GAC on P after instantiating a variable x, i.e. after taking the positive search decision $x = a$ (consequently, x belongs to past(P)), we must call enforceGAC$^{\mathrm{arc}}(P, \{x\})$. After refuting the value a from the domain of x, i.e. after taking the negative search decision $x \neq a$ (x does not belong to past(P)), we must also call enforceGAC$^{\mathrm{arc}}(P, \{x\})$. In both cases, X_{evt} is only composed of the variable x since x is the only variable concerned by the search decisions (that can be perceived as events). Chapter 8 provides more information, which is not required now, about backtrack search (MAC, binary branching, etc.) and about the statements between square brackets.

Algorithm 7: enforceGAC^{arc}(P: $\mathscr{P}$, X_{evt}: set of variables): Boolean [nogood]

Output: *true* iff $GAC(P) \neq \bot$

// Initialization of Q; Q contains arcs

1   $Q \leftarrow \emptyset$

2   **foreach** *arc (c, x) of P such that $x \notin \text{past}(P) \wedge \exists y \in \text{scp}(c) \cap X_{\text{evt}} \mid y \neq x$* **do**

3     $\lfloor$ $Q \leftarrow Q \cup \{(c, x)\}$

// Propagation through Q

4   **while** $Q \neq \emptyset$ **do**

5   pick and delete (c, x) from Q

6   **if** *revise*(c, x) **then**

      // dom(x) has been reduced

7   **if** dom$(x) = \emptyset$ **then**

8         $\lfloor$ **return** *false*   [**return** *handleEmptyDomain*(x)]

9   **foreach** *constraint $c' \in \text{cons}(P) \mid c' \neq c \wedge x \in \text{scp}(c')$* **do**

10   **foreach** *variable $x' \in \text{scp}(c') \mid x' \neq x \wedge x' \notin \text{past}(P)$* **do**

11           $\lfloor$ $Q \leftarrow Q \cup \{(c', x')\}$

12   **return** *true*   [**return** *nil*]

Algorithm 8: revise(c: constraint, x: variable): Boolean

Output: *true* iff the revision of the arc (c, x) is effective

1   $nbElements \leftarrow |\text{dom}(x)|$

2   **foreach** *value $a \in \text{dom}(x)$* **do**

3   **if** $\neg$*seekSupport*(c, x, a) **then**

4       $\lfloor$ remove a from dom(x) [expl$(x \neq a) \leftarrow$ *getExplanation*(c, x, a)]

5   **return** $nbElements \neq |\text{dom}(x)|$

EXAMPLE.– To illustrate constraint propagation, the domino-4-4 instance has a constraint network P such that:

   – vars$(P) = \{w, x, y, z\}$ with dom$(w) = \cdots = \text{dom}(z) = \{0, 1, 2, 3\}$;

   – cons$(P) = \{c_{wx}: w = x, c_{xy}: x = y, c_{yz}: y = z, c_{wz}: w = z + 1 \vee w = z = 3\}$.

In this example, Algorithm 7 is used stand-alone, and Q has first-in first-out (FIFO) structure, meaning that the oldest arc is always selected from Q. All arcs are put in Q initially, and then each in turn is selected as follows.

   – Step 0: initialization

$\Rightarrow Q = \{(c_{wx}, w), (c_{wx}, x), (c_{xy}, x), (c_{xy}, y), (c_{yz}, y), (c_{yz}, z), (c_{wz}, w), (c_{wz}, z)\}$

– Step 1: pick (c_{wx}, w) from Q
revise(c_{wx}, w) is fruitless
$\Rightarrow Q = \{(c_{wx}, x), (c_{xy}, x), (c_{xy}, y), (c_{yz}, y), (c_{yz}, z), (c_{wz}, w), (c_{wz}, z)\}$
– Step 2: pick (c_{wx}, x) from Q
revise(c_{wx}, x) is fruitless
$\Rightarrow Q = \{(c_{xy}, x), (c_{xy}, y), (c_{yz}, y), (c_{yz}, z), (c_{wz}, w), (c_{wz}, z)\}$
– Step 3: pick (c_{xy}, x) from Q
revise(c_{xy}, x) is fruitless
$\Rightarrow Q = \{(c_{xy}, y), (c_{yz}, y), (c_{yz}, z), (c_{wz}, w), (c_{wz}, z)\}$
– . . .

– Step 7: pick (c_{wz}, w) from $Q = \{(c_{wz}, w), (c_{wz}, z)\}$
revise(c_{wz}, w) is fruitless
$\Rightarrow Q = \{(c_{wz}, z)\}$
– Step 8: pick (c_{wz}, z) from Q
revise(c_{wz}, z) removes $(z, 0)$
$\Rightarrow Q = \{(c_{yz}, y)\}$
– Step 9: pick (c_{yz}, y) from Q
revise(c_{yz}, y) removes $(y, 0)$
$\Rightarrow Q = \{(c_{xy}, x)\}$
– . . .

The first effective revision occurs at Step 8, where (c_{wz}, z) is picked from Q. Then, (c_{yz}, y) is included in Q because $z \in c_{yz}$ and $y \neq z$. Subsequent steps remove values until a fixed point is reached, which means that further iterations make no further change. Figure 4.1 shows the compatibility graphs of:

– the initial constraint network P;

– the constraint network obtained after the first inference (Step 8);

– the constraint network after the second inference (Step 9);

– the final constraint network that corresponds to the AC-closure of P.

4.1.2. *Variable-oriented propagation scheme*

A second approach to enforcing GAC on a given constraint network is based on *variable-oriented* coarse-grained propagation, initially introduced in [MCG 79]. Here the propagation queue Q is a set of variables that capture *any(x)* events [SCH 06]: when a value is deleted from the domain of a variable, this variable is included in the set Q. A variable-oriented scheme can avoid unnecessary work by using time-stamps. A *time-stamp* is a value denoting the time at which a certain event occurred; time-stamps allow the progress of algorithms to be tracked over time. The practice

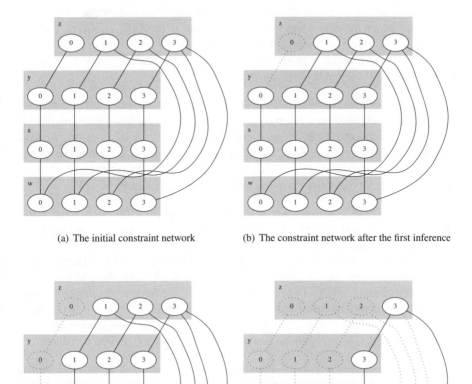

(a) The initial constraint network

(b) The constraint network after the first inference

(c) The constraint network after the second inference

(d) The constraint network made (G)AC

Figure 4.1. *Evolution of the constraint network during propagation. Dotted circles indicate deleted values*

of recording time-stamps consistently is called *time-stamping*; this will be useful for determining whether or not a given revision is useless.

By introducing a global counter *time* and by associating a time-stamp $stamp[x]$ with every variable x and a time-stamp $stamp[c]$ with every constraint c, it is possible to determine which revisions are relevant. The value of $stamp[x]$ indicates at which moment a value was most recently removed from $\mathrm{dom}(x)$, while the value of $stamp[c]$ indicates at which moment c was most recently made to be GAC-consistent. Initially, variables $time$, $stamp[x]$ for each variable x and $stamp[c]$ for each constraint c are set to 0. The value of $time$ is incremented whenever a variable is added to Q and whenever a constraint made GAC-consistent.

The call enforceGAC$^{\mathrm{var}}(P, \mathrm{vars}(P))$, Algorithm 9, enforces generalized arc consistency stand-alone on a given constraint network P. The Boolean value $false$ is returned if P is detected GAC-inconsistent, i.e. if $GAC(P) = \bot$. As before, we have $\mathrm{past}(P) = \emptyset$ for stand-alone GAC enforcement. To maintain GAC during the search, we can call enforceGAC$^{\mathrm{var}}(P, \{x\})$ after having taken a positive or negative decision on a variable x; for a positive decision, we know that x belongs to $\mathrm{past}(P)$.

To enforce GAC, variables are selected iteratively from Q. Each constraint c involving the selected variable x must be considered if $stamp[x] > stamp[c]$. In this case, every uninstantiated variable $y \neq x$ in $\mathrm{scp}(c)$ is revised with respect to c. Each revision is accomplished by function revise, Algorithm 8, which returns $true$ if at least one value has been removed. If the revision is effective, the y is inserted in the Q. To guarantee that c is made GAC-consistent, we have to determine whether the domain of a variable other than x in c has been modified since c was last made GAC-consistent. This is managed by the second part of the condition at line 8 of Algorithm 9. If this second part is satisfied then x is one of the revised variables.

Instructions shown in gray in Algorithm 9 are used when GAC is enforced[3] on c using a specific filtering procedure (propagator) that is not revision-based. The special function denoted here by enforceGAC-type, where type stands for the name of the filtering approach related to the type of c, specifically enforces GAC and returns the set of variables whose domain has been reduced. For example, enforceGAC-case and enforceGAC-str, which are described in Chapter 5, are two filtering procedures dedicated to table constraints. Such procedures are not revision-based because they *globally* enforce the local consistency GAC. Additional (input and/or output) information may be required to manage the incrementality/decrementality of some propagators, but this is clearly beyond the scope of this book, which is focused mainly on generic approaches.

The following examples are intended to enhance understanding of the role of time-stamps. First, consider a binary constraint c_{xy} involving the variables x and y. If the selection of the variable x from Q entails effective revision of (c_{xy}, y), and if later the selection of y from Q entails effective revision of (c_{xy}, x), then necessarily x is inserted again in Q. However, there is no need to perform the revision of (c_{xy}, y)

---

3. In practice, this may be some partial form of GAC, in which case the computation of GAC-closure of P is not guaranteed.

Algorithm 9: enforceGAC^{var}(P: $\mathscr{P}$, X_{evt}: set of variables): Boolean [nogood]

Output: *true* iff $GAC(P) \neq \bot$

// Initialization of Q; Q contains variables

1   $Q \leftarrow \emptyset$
2   **foreach** *variable* $x \in X_{\text{evt}}$ **do**
3 | insert(Q, x)

// Propagation through Q

4   **while** $Q \neq \emptyset$ **do**
5 | pick and delete x from Q
6 | **foreach** *constraint* $c \in \text{cons}(P) \mid x \in \text{scp}(c) \wedge stamp[x] > stamp[c]$ **do**
7 | | **foreach** *variable* $y \in \text{scp}(c) \mid y \notin \text{past}(P)$ **do**
8 | | | **if** $y \neq x$ *or* $\exists z \in \text{scp}(c) \mid z \neq x \wedge stamp[z] > stamp[c]$ **then**
9 | | | | **if** *revise*(c, y) **then**
                    // $\text{dom}(y)$ has been reduced
10   **if** $\text{dom}(y) = \emptyset$ **then**
11 | **return** *false*   [**return** *handleEmptyDomain*(y)]
12   insert(Q, y)

        // If enforcing GAC on c is not revision-based, the
        // foreach construct above (lines 7 to 12) is replaced by:
        $Y_{\text{evt}} \leftarrow$ enforceGAC-type(P, c)
        foreach *variable* $y \in Y_{\text{evt}}$ **do**
          | **if** $\text{dom}(y) = \emptyset$ **then**
          | | **return** *false*
          insert(Q, y)

13 | | $time \leftarrow time + 1$
14 | | $stamp[c] \leftarrow time$

15   **return** *true*   [**return** *nil*]

Algorithm 10: insert(Q: set of variables, x: variable)

---

1   $Q \leftarrow Q \cup \{x\}$
2   $time \leftarrow time + 1$
3   $stamp[x] \leftarrow time$

---

again when x is selected from Q provided that the domain of x has not been modified by propagating another constraint. In this case, all supports found for values of y

when revising (c_{xy}, y) are still valid because of a property of constraints called *bi-directionality*: if a v-value (y, b) is supported by (x, a) on c_{xy}, we know that (x, a) is symmetrically supported by (y, b) on c_{xy}, and is therefore not deleted when revising (c_{xy}, x). Here (y, b) is guaranteed to remain supported after revision of (c_{xy}, x). Further revision of (c_{xy}, y) will be useless so long as no new event concerning x occurs.

As another example (as given in [BES 01b]), let c_{xyz} be a ternary constraint whose scope is $\{x, y, z\}$. If selection of the variable x entails effective revision of (c_{xyz}, y) and of (c_{xyz}, z) then there is no need to perform again the revision of (c_{xyz}, z) if the variable y is selected and if the domains of x and y have not been modified elsewhere. Time-stamps allow identification of useless revisions. An important and desirable feature of time-stamping is that it is a *backtrack-stable* mechanism, meaning that no restoration or additional treatment is required when a tree search algorithm such as MAC backtracks. Time-stamps can safely remain unchanged by backtrack.

EXAMPLE.– To illustrate variable-oriented propagation, let us again consider stand-alone propagation for the domino-4-4 instance. Initially, to enforce GAC, all variables are put in Q; each variable is then selected in turn. In this example Q is again a FIFO structure, and successive steps in the execution of Algorithm 9 are as follows.

– Step 0: initialization
$\Rightarrow Q = \{w, x, y, z\}$

– Step 1: pick w from Q
constraint c_{wx}: revise(c_{wx}, w) is fruitless – revise(c_{wx}, x) is fruitless
constraint c_{wz}: revise(c_{wz}, w) is fruitless – revise(c_{wz}, z) deletes $(z, 0)$
$\Rightarrow Q = \{x, y, z\}$

– Step 2: pick x from Q
constraint c_{wx}: no revisions
constraint c_{xy}: revise(c_{xy}, x) is fruitless – revise(c_{xy}, y) is fruitless
$\Rightarrow Q = \{y, z\}$

– Step 3: pick y from Q
constraint c_{xy}: no revisions
constraint c_{yz}: revise(c_{yz}, y) deletes $(y, 0)$ – revise(c_{yz}, z) is fruitless
$\Rightarrow Q = \{z, y\}$

– Step 4: pick z from Q
constraint c_{yz}: no revisions
constraint c_{wz}: no revisions
$\Rightarrow Q = \{y\}$

– Step 5: pick y from Q
constraint c_{xy}: revise(c_{xy}, x) deletes $(x, 0)$
constraint c_{yz}: no revisions
$\Rightarrow Q = \{x\}$

– Step 6: pick x from Q
constraint c_{wx}: revise(c_{wx}, w) deletes $(w, 0)$

constraint c_{xy}: no revisions
$\Rightarrow Q = \{w\}$
  – Step 7: pick w from Q
constraint c_{wx}: no revisions
constraint c_{wz}: revise(c_{wz}, z) deletes $(z, 1)$
$\Rightarrow Q = \{z\}$
  – ...

Where there are no revisions in this example, useless work has been avoided by time-stamping. Figure 4.1 shows the evolution of the compatibility graph of P during propagation.

Arc-oriented and variable-oriented approaches are basically equivalent. These approaches differ in the instructions that must be executed when an element from the queue has just been selected and also when the queue is updated. This difference can be seen clearly by comparing lines 9 and 10 of Algorithm 7 with lines 6 and 7 of Algorithm 9. Note that, although not described in this book, a *constraint-oriented* propagation scheme [BOU 04a] is also possible.

There are many reasons for judging that the variable-oriented propagation scheme is better than the other two schemes. First, the space complexity of managing the queue is only $O(n)$ while it is (er) for the arc-oriented scheme and $O(e)$ for the constraint-oriented scheme. Second, if selecting an element from the queue requires iterating over all elements, then the worst-case time complexities of selecting an element are $O(n), O(er)$ and $O(e)$ for the variable-oriented, arc-oriented and constraint-oriented schemes, respectively, assuming that each element is evaluated in constant time. Third, since the seminal work of Wallace and Freuder [WAL 92], it has been shown that the variable-oriented approach provides the best practical results when combined with the *revision ordering heuristic dom* [BOU 04a] which selects from the queue the variable with the minimum domain size, or more recently the heuristic *dom/wdeg* [BAL 08a]. Fourth, the algorithm given here to enforce GAC using a variable-oriented propagation scheme is simpler than the one proposed in [BOU 04a], making it almost as simple as the arc-oriented scheme. Finally, the variable-oriented approach facilitates simultaneous management of generic and specific filtering algorithms.

4.1.3. *Applying forward checking*

In the following, we shall refer to *forward checking* (FC), which is a backtrack search algorithm [MCG 79, HAR 80] that maintains a partial form of (generalized) arc consistency. For binary constraint networks, whenever a variable x is instantiated during search, only uninstantiated variables connected to it are revised. Given a constraint network P, $FC(P, x)$ denotes the constraint network obtained from P after removing all values that have (initially) no support on a constraint involving x;

this can be regarded as enforcing a particular consistency. Of course, if a domain is wiped-out, we have $FC(P, x) = \perp$. To apply FC to a given constraint network P after a variable x has been instantiated, we call applyFC(P, x), Algorithm 11. This function is never called before search (i.e. at preprocessing time when no variable has been instantiated) and is never called after a value refutation. The overloaded function applyFC, Algorithm 12, differs from that in Algorithm 11 in that the second parameter is a set of variables instead of a variable. Calling applyFC(P, x) means calling applyFC$(P, \{x\})$. In this case, the formal parameter X_{evt} of Algorithm 12 is set to $\{x\}$ and the instruction at line 1 of Algorithm 12 is equivalent to:

foreach constraint $c \in \text{cons}(P) \mid x \in \text{scp}(c)$ **do**

There is no propagation queue, meaning that FC does not involve either of the propagation schemes introduced earlier in this section. For non-binary constraint networks, applyFC corresponds to nFC2 [BES 02] which is a generalization of binary forward checking: for each constraint c that involves the variable which has just been instantiated, we revise every uninstantiated variable in $\text{scp}(c)$ against c. The second parameter of Algorithm 12 is a set of variables because it will allow us to simulate several simultaneous variable instantiations in a dynamic backtracking context; see Algorithm 73 of Chapter 8. Statements between square brackets will also be useful in Chapter 8.

Algorithm 11: applyFC$(P: \mathscr{P}, x$: variable): Boolean [nogood]

Require: the variable x is instantiated, i.e. $x \in \text{past}(P)$
Output: *true* iff $FC(P, x) \neq \perp$

1 **return** *applyFC$(P, \{x\})$*

Algorithm 12: applyFC$(P: \mathscr{P}, X_{\text{evt}}$: set of variables): Boolean [nogood]

Require: all variables in X_{evt} are instantiated, i.e. $X_{\text{evt}} \subseteq \text{past}(P)$

1 **foreach** *constraint $c \in \text{cons}(P) \mid X_{\text{evt}} \cap \text{scp}(c) \neq \emptyset$* **do**
2   **foreach** *variable $y \in \text{scp}(c) \mid y \notin \text{past}(P)$* **do**
3   **if** *revise(c, y)* **then**
4   **if** $\text{dom}(y) = \emptyset$ **then**
5   **return** *false*   [return *handleEmptyDomain(y)*]

6 **return** *true*   [return *nil*]

EXAMPLE.– To illustrate forward checking, Figure 4.2 shows compatibility graphs for an example in which there are two binary constraints involving a variable y that has just been instantiated with the value c. The two constraints and the reduction of dom(y) to $\{c\}$ are shown in Figure 4.2(a). The call applyFC(P, y) removes all values from dom(x) and dom(z) that are not compatible with (y, c), as can be seen in Figure 4.2(b).

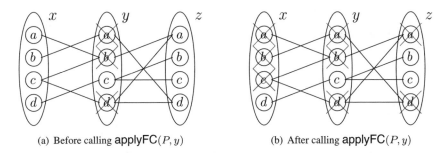

(a) Before calling applyFC(P, y)   (b) After calling applyFC(P, y)

Figure 4.2. *Illustration of FC: y has just been instantiated with c, and there are two binary constraints involving y*

On a binary constraint network, the cost of forward checking is limited:

PROPOSITION 4.1.– *The function* applyFC *admits a worst-case space complexity in* $O(1)$, *and on a binary constraint network, a worst-case time complexity in* $O(ed)$.

Proof. We only consider specific data structures of algorithms. For FC, there is none, so the worst-case space complexity in $O(1)$. On the other hand, there are at most k revisions where k denotes the number of constraints involving the last instantiated variable, and the revision of a variable against an instantiated variable is $O(d)$. As k is $O(e)$, we obtain $O(ed)$.   □

4.2. Iterating over valid tuples

At the heart of many filtering algorithms there is a search for supports of values, as in Algorithm 8. A support for a c-value (c, x, a), i.e. a support for (x, a) on c, can be sought by iterating over the set of valid tuples until an allowed one is found. When the targeted consistency is GAC, this *support-seeking* scheme is called *GAC-valid*. This is an universal approach since it can be theoretically used with all kinds of constraints, assuming that it is always possible to check that a given tuple is accepted by a constraint[4]. In this section, we present several functions related to GAC-valid.

---

4. We assume in this book that a constraint check is $O(r)$ where r is the constraint arity.

These functions will be used later to describe some filtering algorithms such as GAC3 and GAC2001.

Algorithm 13: getFirstValidTuple$((c, x, a)$: c-value): tuple

---

Require: $\mathrm{val}(c)_{x=a} \neq \emptyset$
Output: the smallest tuple $\tau \in \mathrm{val}(c)_{x=a}$

// let τ be an array of size $|\,\mathrm{scp}(c)|$
1 $\tau[x] \leftarrow a$
2 **foreach** *variable* $y \in \mathrm{scp}(c) \mid y \neq x$ **do**
3 $\quad \lfloor \; \tau[y] \leftarrow \mathrm{dom}(y).head$
4 **return** τ

Algorithm 14: getNextValidTuple$((c, x, a)$: c-value, τ: tuple): tuple

---

Require: $\tau \in \mathrm{val}(c)_{x=a}$
Output: the smallest tuple $\tau' \in \mathrm{val}(c)_{x=a}$ such that $\tau' >_{\mathrm{lex}} \tau$, or nil

1 **for** i *ranging from* $|\,\mathrm{scp}(c)|$ *down-to* 1 **do**
2 $\quad$ $y \leftarrow \mathrm{scp}(c)[i]$ $\hspace{2cm}$ // y is the ith variable of $\mathrm{scp}(c)$
3 $\quad$ **if** $y \neq x$ **then**
4 $\quad\quad$ **if** $\mathrm{dom}(y).next[\tau[y]] = -1$ **then**
5 $\quad\quad\quad$ $\lfloor \; \tau[y] \leftarrow \mathrm{dom}(y).head$
6 $\quad\quad$ **else**
7 $\quad\quad\quad$ $\tau[y] \leftarrow \mathrm{dom}(y).next[\tau[y]]$
8 $\quad\quad\quad$ **return** τ
9 **return** nil

Valid tuples are reviewed in the search for a support. Recall that $\mathrm{val}(c)_{x=a}$ is the set of valid tuples involving (x, a) on c; see Notation 1.16. If, for example, we have a ternary constraint c_{xyz} such that $\mathrm{dom}(x) = \{1, 4, 5\}$, $\mathrm{dom}(y) = \{2, 4\}$ and $\mathrm{dom}(z) = \{1, 2\}$, then:

$$\mathrm{val}(c_{xyz})_{y=4} = \{(1, 4, 1), (1, 4, 2), (4, 4, 1), (4, 4, 2), (5, 4, 1), (5, 4, 2)\}.$$

To iterate over valid tuples, we may employ functions getFirstValidTuple and getNextValidTuple, assuming, as always, a total order on values and a total order on the scope of each constraint such that tuples can be processed in a lexicographic order $\leq_{\mathrm{lex}}$. Moreover, we have a linked list of elements present in each domain, implemented using the variable *head* and the array *next*; see section 1.5.1. The call getFirstValidTuple$((c, x, a))$, Algorithm 13, returns the smallest tuple τ in $\mathrm{val}(c)_{x=a}$, i.e. the smallest valid tuple τ built from current domains of variables in $\text{scp}(c)$ such that $\tau[x] = a$; it is assumed that $\text{val}(c)_{x=a} \neq \emptyset$. The time complexity is $\Theta(r)$ where r is the arity of the constraint c. Tuple τ, is composed of the first element in the domain of each variable (except x) in $\text{scp}(c)$. The call getNextValidTuple$((c, x, a), \tau)$, Algorithm 14, either returns the smallest tuple τ' in $\text{val}(c)_{x=a}$ such that $\tau' >_{\text{lex}} \tau$, or returns the special value nil if there is no such tuple. The worst-case time complexity is $O(r)$. Here getNextValidTuple is always assumed to be called with a parameter τ in $\text{val}(c)_{x=a}$.

EXAMPLE.– For our most recent example:

- getFirstValidTuple$((c, y, 4))$ returns $(1, 4, 1)$;
- getNextValidTuple$((c, y, 4), (1, 4, 1))$ returns $(1, 4, 2)$;
- getNextValidTuple$((c, y, 4), (1, 4, 2))$ returns $(4, 4, 1)$;
- ...
- getNextValidTuple$((c, y, 4), (5, 4, 2))$ returns nil.

It is sometimes necessary to check the validity of a support found earlier during propagation. This is called a *validity check* and it is implemented by checking that each value in the tuple is present in the appropriate domain, as in Algorithm 15. As before, nil is a special value. This special value is not valid. On the other hand, within a given tuple, we sometimes need to locate the first (starting from the left) invalid value, if there is one. For this, we employ function getFirstInvalidPosition, Algorithm 16, which takes as input a tuple $\tau \neq nil$ and returns -1 when the tuple is valid.

Algorithm 15: isValidTuple(c: constraint, τ: tuple): Boolean

Output: *true* iff $\tau \in \text{val}(c)_{x=a}$

1 **if** $\tau = nil$ **then**
2 | **return** *false*
3 **foreach** *variable* $x \in \text{scp}(c)$ **do**
4 | **if** $\tau[x] \notin \text{dom}(x)$ **then**
5 | | **return** *false*
6 **return** *true*

Finally, the overloaded function getNextValidTuple, Algorithm 17, differs from that in Algorithm 14 in that there is an additional parameter; furthermore, the tuple τ that is given as parameter is not valid. The third parameter is assumed to indicate the position of the first invalid value in τ, as it would be computed by getFirstInvalidPosition. It is also assumed that $\text{val}(c)_{x=a} \neq \emptyset$. In Algorithm 17, each variable y whose position in $\text{scp}(c)$ is strictly greater than $limit$ is given in τ the first value in $\text{dom}(y)$; see lines 1

Algorithm 16: getFirstInvalidPosition(c: constraint, τ: tuple): integer

---

Require: $\tau \neq nil$
Output: the position of the first variable $y \in \mathrm{scp}(c)$ s.t. $\tau[y]$ invalid, or -1

1 **for** i *ranging from* 1 *to* $|\mathrm{scp}(c)|$ **do**
2 $\quad$ $y \leftarrow \mathrm{scp}(c)[i]$ $\qquad\qquad\qquad\qquad\qquad$ // y is the ith variable of $\mathrm{scp}(c)$
3 $\quad$ **if** $\tau[y] \notin \mathrm{dom}(y)$ **then**
4 $\quad\quad$ $\lfloor$ **return** i

5 **return** -1

---

to 4. To find a valid tuple strictly greater than τ, lines 5 through 14 seek the next value following $\tau[y]$ where y is the first encountered variable such that $\tau[y] < \mathrm{dom}(y).tail$. In our implementation (see section 1.5.1), we know that if $\tau[y] \in \mathrm{dom}(y)$ then $dom[y].next[\tau[y]]$ is the smallest value of $\mathrm{dom}(y)$ strictly greater than $\tau[y]$, but we also know that if $\tau[y] \notin \mathrm{dom}(y)$ then $dom[y].next[\tau[y]]$ is less than or equal to the smallest value of $\mathrm{dom}(y)$ strictly greater than $\tau[y]$. If there is no valid tuple strictly greater than τ then getNextValidTuple returns nil.

EXAMPLE.– If, for example, we have a 5-ary constraint c such that $\mathrm{scp}(c) = \{v, w, x, y, z\}$, and

- $\mathrm{dom}(v) = \{1, 3\}$,
- $\mathrm{dom}(w) = \{3, 4\}$,
- $\mathrm{dom}(x) = \{1, 4, 5\}$,
- $\mathrm{dom}(y) = \{2, 4\}$, and
- $\mathrm{dom}(z) = \{1, 2\}$

then the effects of function calls are as follows.

- getFirstInvalidPosition($c, (3, 4, 4, 2, 2)$) returns -1 (all values are valid).
- getFirstInvalidPosition($c, (3, 4, 6, 2, 2)$) returns 3 (the position of x).
- getNextValidTuple($(c, y, 2), (3, 4, 6, 2, 2), 3$) returns nil, since there is no valid tuple strictly greater than $(3, 4, 6, *, *)$, where a * symbol stands for any value.
- getFirstInvalidPosition($c, (3, 3, 6, 2, 3)$) returns 3.
- getNextValidTuple($(c, y, 2), (3, 3, 6, 2, 3), 3$) returns $(3, 4, 1, 2, 1)$.

4.3. GAC3 and GAC2001

GAC3 and GAC2001 are classical generic coarse-grained algorithms for establishing generalized arc consistency. Together with GAC3^{rm}, which is introduced later, these algorithms are certainly implemented in most general-purpose constraint

---

Algorithm 17: getNextValidTuple((c, x, a): c-value, τ: tuple, $limit$: int): tuple

---

Require: $\tau[x] = a, \tau \notin \text{val}(c)_{x=a}$ and $\text{val}(c)_{x=a} \neq \emptyset$
Require: $limit = \text{getFirstInvalidPosition}(c, \tau)$
Output: the smallest tuple $\tau' \in \text{val}(c)_{x=a}$ such that $\tau' >_{\text{lex}} \tau$, or nil

1 **for** i *ranging from* $limit + 1$ *to* $|\text{scp}(c)|$ **do**
2 | $y \leftarrow \text{scp}(c)[i]$ // y is the ith variable of $\text{scp}(c)$
3 | **if** $y \neq x$ **then**
4 | | $\tau[y] \leftarrow \text{dom}(y).head$

5 **for** i *ranging from* $limit$ *down-to* 1 **do**
6 | $y \leftarrow \text{scp}(c)[i]$ // y is the ith variable of $\text{scp}(c)$
7 | **if** $y \neq x$ **then**
8 | | **if** $\tau[y] \geq \text{dom}(y).tail$ **then**
9 | | | $\tau[y] \leftarrow \text{dom}(y).head$
10 | | **else**
11 | | | $\tau[y] \leftarrow \text{dom}(y).next[\tau[y]]$
12 | | | **while** $\text{dom}(y).absent[\tau[y]] \neq -1$ **do**
13 | | | | $\tau[y] \leftarrow \text{dom}(y).next[\tau[y]]$
14 | | | **return** τ

15 **return** nil

---

solvers. We can arrive at these algorithms by specifying the precise manner of seeking supports for values in the propagation schemes presented in the first section of this chapter. We will define GAC3 and GAC2001 in this way. The basic seeking-support scheme followed by these two algorithms is GAC-valid. Hence functions introduced in section 4.2 will be useful.

The simplest generic GAC algorithm is undoubtedly GAC3 [MAC 77a, MAC 77b], if we disregard the inefficient (G)AC1 [MAC 77a]. GAC3 can employ either of the two propagation schemes described in section 4.1. For example, in [MCG 79, CHM 98] AC3 has a variable-oriented propagation scheme. To formulate GAC3, we need only to provide an implementation of the function seekSupport called by revise, Algorithm 8, which is called in Algorithms 7 and 9. Specifically, GAC3 uses seekSupport-3, Algorithm 18, which calls functions getFirstValidTuple and getNextValidTuple described in the previous section. Recall that the idea is to iterate over the valid tuples for (x, a) on c until one is accepted by c, which is tested by means of a *constraint check*. A constraint check is of the form $\tau \in \text{rel}(c)$, and this can be implemented in different ways (by evaluating a Boolean expression, querying a database, looking for a tuple in a list, etc.). Whatever the implementation, a constraint check is simply executing a Boolean function.

Algorithm 18: seekSupport-3((c, x, a): c-value): Boolean

Output: $true$ iff $\sup(c)_{x=a} \neq \emptyset$

1 $\tau \leftarrow$ getFirstValidTuple((c, x, a))
2 **while** $\tau \neq nil$ **do**
3   **if** $\tau \in \text{rel}(c)$ **then**
4   **return** $true$
5      $\tau \leftarrow$ getNextValidTuple($(c, x, a), \tau$)
6 **return** $false$

Algorithm 19: seekSupport-2001((c, x, a): c-value): Boolean

Output: $true$ iff $\sup(c)_{x=a} \neq \emptyset$

1 **if** $last[c, x, a] = nil$ **then**
2      $\tau \leftarrow$ getFirstValidTuple((c, x, a))
3 **else**
4      $j \leftarrow$ getFirstInvalidPosition($c, last[c, x, a]$)
5   **if** $j = -1$ **then**
6   **return** $true$
7   **else**
8         $\tau \leftarrow$ getNextValidTuple($(c, x, a), last[c, x, a], j$)
9 **while** $\tau \neq nil$ **do**
10   **if** $\tau \in \text{rel}(c)$ **then**
11        $last[c, x, a] \leftarrow \tau$
12   **return** $true$
13     $\tau \leftarrow$ getNextValidTuple($(c, x, a), \tau$)
14 **return** $false$

A development of (G)AC3 [BES 05c] has appeared in [BES 01b] and [ZHA 01b], which refer to it as (G)AC2001 and (G)AC3.1, respectively. The important difference between GAC3 and GAC2001/3.1 is that when a support is sought for a value, GAC3 starts the search from scratch, whereas GAC2001/3.1 resumes the search from the point where the last support was found for this value. This simple modification makes GAC2001 optimal for binary constraints. GAC2001 has an array, denoted by $last$, that stores (the identity or reference of) the last support which has been found for each c-value (c, x, a): $last[c, x, a]$ is the last support found for (x, a) on c. Initially, all elements of this three-dimensional array $last$ must be initialized to the special value nil.

GAC2001 uses seekSupport-2001, Algorithm 19, which is called by revise, Algorithm 8, which is itself called in Algorithms 7 and 9. Revision of an arc involves checking the validity of the last support, for each c-value, and if necessary seeking a new support. This does not affect the first call: when $last[c, x, a] = nil$, seekSupport-3 and seekSupport-2001 behave identically. When $last[c, x, a] \neq nil$, a validity check is performed by calling getFirstInvalidPosition. If -1 is the integer value returned by this function, the tuple $last[c, x, a]$ is still a support; this is why $true$ is returned at line 6. Otherwise, the smallest valid tuple τ such that $\tau >_{\text{lex}} last[c, x, a]$ and $\tau[x] = a$ is computed at line 8 (τ may also be nil) by calling Algorithm 17. For GAC2001, when a new support is found, this support (or its identity) is recorded in the structure $last$ (see line 11).

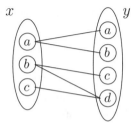

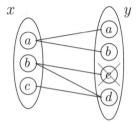

(a) First call: eight constraint checks for both AC3 and AC2001

(b) Second call: seven constraint checks for AC3 but only one constraint check for AC2001

Figure 4.3. *Binary constraint used to illustrate the effort required to perform* revise(c_{xy}, x)

EXAMPLE.– With the binary constraint c_{xy} in Figure 4.3 we can illustrate the difference of behavior between (G)AC3 and (G)AC2001. When revise(c_{xy}, x) is called for the first time by AC3 (Figure 4.3(a)), the following operations are performed.

– For (x, a): (y, a) is successfully checked, i.e. the valid tuple (a, a) is found to belong to rel(c_{xy}).

– For (x, b): (y, a) and (y, b) are unsuccessfully checked, but (y, c) is successfully checked.

– For (x, c): (y, a), (y, b) and (y, c) are unsuccessfully checked, but (y, d) is successfully checked.

Exactly eight constraint checks are needed to find that all values in dom(x) have at least one support in c_{xy}. Now consider the first revision of (c_{xy}, x) by AC2001. Because this is the first revision, all elements of the array $last$ have been initialized to nil. In this case AC2001, like AC3, requires eight constraint checks. But after the first revision by AC2001, we have:

– $last[c_{xy}, x, a] = a$;

$- last[c_{xy}, x, b] = c$;

$- last[c_{xy}, x, c] = d$.

Here, adopting a simplification that is usual for the binary case, we only show strict supports, i.e. single values instead of pairs of values. Without this simplification, $last[c_{xy}, x, a]$ designates (a, a) or $((x, a), (y, a))$ in extended notation, which is easily seen to be equivalent.

Suppose now that the v-value (y, c) has been deleted elsewhere (by another revision involving y and a constraint other than c_{xy}) and that revise(c_{xy}, x) is called again. In Figure 4.3(b), AC3 needs $1 + 3 + 3 = 7$ constraint checks, whereas AC2001 only needs one constraint check (plus three validity checks) because:

$- last[c_{xy}, x, a] = a$, which remains valid;

$- last[c_{xy}, x, b] = c$, which is not valid; but as (y, d) is successfully checked, we obtain $last[c_{xy}, x, b] = d$;

$- last[c_{xy}, x, c] = d$, which remains valid.

Comparison of the worst-case time complexities of GAC3 and GAC2001 confirms the theoretical interest of GAC2001. We now consider versions of these algorithms that use variable-oriented propagation. For GAC3, the worst-case time complexity is as stated in [BES 06], but the worst-case space complexity is different since the propagation schemes are different. Here, GAC3 corresponds to Algorithm 9 which calls Algorithm 18 indirectly.

PROPOSITION 4.2.– *GAC3 admits a worst-case time complexity in $O(er^3 d^{r+1})$ and a worst-case space complexity in $O(n + e)$.*

Proof. First, note that the space complexity of introducing time-stamps (for the variable-oriented scheme) is $\Theta(n + e)$ while the time complexity of managing them has no impact on the overall worst-case time complexity of the algorithm. If we consider the total[5] worst-case time complexity of revise for a given c-value (c, x, a) with r being the arity of c, we know that it can be called at most $(r - 1)d$ (each time a value is removed from the domain of a variable which is different from x and in the scope of c), and that for each call, at most d^{r-1} tuples will be checked. Assuming that a constraint check is $O(r)$, we obtain a total worst-case time complexity of revise for a given c-value (c, x, a) in $O(r^2 d^r)$. Assuming that r is the largest constraint arity, as the number of c-values is $O(erd)$, we obtain a total worst-case time complexity of revise in $O(er^3 d^{r+1})$. We can show that the rest (i.e. when ignoring the calls to revise) of Algorithm enforceGAC^{var} is $O(n + der^2)$. As n is $O(er)$, the worst-case

---

5. Total means considering the cost of all successive calls to the mentioned procedure or algorithm.

time complexity of enforceGAC^{var} is $O(er^3d^{r+1})$. In terms of space, Q is $O(n)$ and time-stamps are $\Theta(n + e)$. So, we obtain an overall worst-case space complexity in $O(n + e)$. $\square$

COROLLARY 4.3.– *On a binary constraint network, GAC3, which is classically called AC3, admits a worst-case time complexity in $O(ed^3)$ and a worst-case space complexity in $O(e)$.*

For GAC2001, we obtain the following complexities; proofs can be found in [BES 05c]. Here GAC2001 is Algorithm 7 or Algorithm 9 calling Algorithm 19 indirectly.

PROPOSITION 4.4.– *GAC2001 admits a worst-case time complexity in $O(er^2d^r)$ and a worst-case space complexity in $O(erd)$.*

COROLLARY 4.5.– *On a binary constraint network, GAC2001, which is classically called AC2001, admits a worst-case time complexity in $O(ed^2)$ and a worst-case space complexity in $O(ed)$.*

Interestingly enough, for binary networks, AC2001 has optimal worst-case time complexity.

4.4. More about general-purpose GAC algorithms

Incrementality, *multi-directionality* and *substitutability* are important properties of GAC algorithms. These properties allow better characterization of general-purpose GAC algorithms. After an introduction to these properties, this section provides an overview of classical generic GAC algorithms, including fine-grained ones. Various recent developments are postponed to the next section.

4.4.1. *Important properties*

4.4.1.1. *Incrementality*

GAC3, GAC2001 and other known generic GAC algorithms, are incremental, as defined below. This property is used in the development of further efficient algorithms based on (generalized) arc consistency (e.g. see SAC-Opt and SAC3 described later in Chapter 6).

The general meaning of incrementality is as follows. Many algorithms repeatedly compute a new value from an old one after a small modification to the computation context. An algorithm is incremental if it does not compute the new value from scratch but exploits both the old value and the modifications made to the environment. For example, if f is a function that computes the sum of a set of integers, f is incremental if after including a further integer in the set, the new sum is computed from the old one simply by adding this new integer. Inside MAC, when a search decision (variable assignment or value refutation) is made, there is a transition from a search node to a new one after enforcing GAC. Here GAC is enforced on the current network (not the initial one) with a modification of the domain of the variable involved in the search decision. In this respect, GAC algorithms are incremental. Incrementality of GAC algorithms is more specifically understood in terms of worst-case time complexity as follows:

DEFINITION 4.6.– *[Incrementality] A GAC algorithm is said to be incremental iff its worst-case time complexity is the same when it is applied once on a given network P and when it is applied up to nd times on P where, between any two consecutive executions, at least one value has been deleted.*

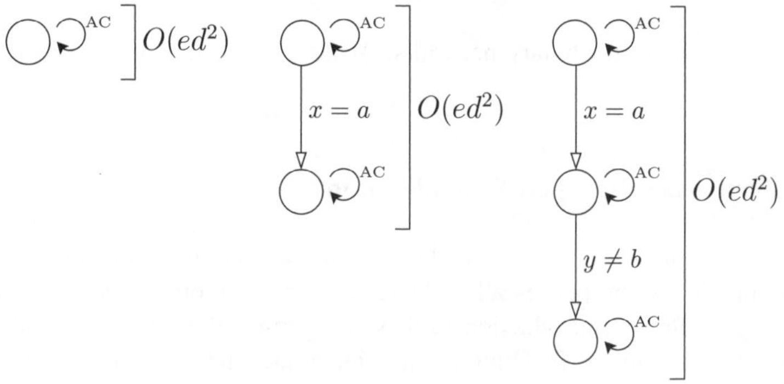

Figure 4.4. *Consequence of the incrementality of GAC algorithms: the worst-case time complexity of enforcing GAC on a node is the same as enforcing GAC all along a branch. This is illustrated here with an optimal AC algorithm*

For example, on the left of Figure 4.4 (G)AC is enforced on a binary constraint network. Assuming an optimal AC algorithm, the worst-case time complexity is then $O(ed^2)$. At the center, the search decision $x = a$ is taken and AC is maintained. The (total) worst-case time complexity of these two AC enforcements remains $O(ed^2)$. After each new decision we remain in $O(ed^2)$, so AC is enforced (maintained) all along a branch of a search tree in $O(ed^2)$.

4.4.1.2. *Multi-directionality*

Multi-directionality is a very general property that enables GAC algorithms to avoid useless work such as unnecessary constraint checks.

DEFINITION 4.7.– *[Multi-directionality] Let c be a constraint and τ be a support on c. The constraint c is said to be* multi-directional *(bi-directional if c is binary) because for each variable $x \in \mathrm{scp}(c)$, τ is a support for $(x, \tau[x])$ on c.*

For example, if c_{xyz} is a ternary constraint and if $\tau = (a, b, c)$ is a support on c_{xyz}, then τ is a support on c_{xyz} for (x, a), (y, b) and (z, c). Although trivial, this general property of constraints is not always exploited by algorithms. Ideally, a GAC algorithm should verify the following related properties. But first, note that in any generic GAC algorithm, a constraint check $\tau \in \mathrm{rel}(c)$ is always performed with respect to a c-value (c, x, a).

DEFINITION 4.8.– *For any given c-value (c, x, a) and for any given tuple τ, a GAC algorithm exploits:*
– positive uni-directionality *iff $\tau \in \mathrm{rel}(c)$ is not checked wrt (c, x, a) if there exists a support τ' for (x, a) on c already successfully checked wrt (c, x, a);*
– negative uni-directionality *iff $\tau \in \mathrm{rel}(c)$ is not checked wrt (c, x, a) if it has already been unsuccessfully checked wrt (c, x, a);*
– positive multi-directionality *iff $\tau \in \mathrm{rel}(c)$ is not checked wrt (c, x, a) if there exists a support τ' for (x, a) on c already successfully checked wrt a c-value (c, y, b) such that $y \neq x$;*
– negative multi-directionality *iff $\tau \in \mathrm{rel}(c)$ is not checked wrt (c, x, a) if $\tau \in \mathrm{rel}(c)$ has already been unsuccessfully checked wrt a c-value (c, y, b) such that $y \neq x$.*

Roughly speaking, these properties correspond to properties 1, 3a, 2 and 3b of [BES 99]. For some values, these properties allow inference of existence or non-existence of a support without requiring any search effort. Before going any further, it is already easy to see that GAC2001/3.1 uses positive and negative uni-directionality.

4.4.1.3. *Substitutability*

Substitutability is defined with respect to all solutions of a constraint network; see Definition 1.62. Neighborhood substitutability [FRE 91] is a restricted form of substitutability defined with respect to all constraints of a constraint network. We now consider a further restricted form of substitutability that is defined independently for each constraint; this is a direct adaptation of neighborhood interchangeability according to one constraint introduced in [HAS 93]. Restricting such a property to a unique constraint may lead to a great number of locally substitutable values, which can be useful in our context. The following definition uses Notation 1.16:

DEFINITION 4.9.– *[Substitutability] Let c be a constraint, $x \in$ scp(c) and $\{a, b\} \subseteq$ dom(x). (x, a) is c-substitutable for (x, b) iff* $\sup(c){\downarrow}_{x=a} \supseteq \sup(c){\downarrow}_{x=b}$.

In the example in Figure 4.5, we have (x, b) c_{xy}-substitutable for (x, a) because $\sup(c_{xy}){\downarrow}_{x=b} = \{a, b, c\} \supseteq \sup(c_{xy}){\downarrow}_{x=a} = \{b, c\}$. Note that this substitutability relation restricted to a constraint is a preorder. The following proposition (the proof of which is trivial) establishes that when (x, a) is c-substitutable for (x, b), the presence of a support for (x, b) on c guarantees the presence of a support for (x, a) on c, and conversely, the absence of supports for (x, a) on c guarantees the absence of supports for (x, b) on c.

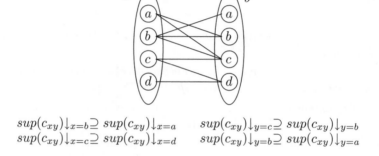

$$sup(c_{xy}){\downarrow}_{x=b} \supseteq sup(c_{xy}){\downarrow}_{x=a} \qquad sup(c_{xy}){\downarrow}_{y=c} \supseteq sup(c_{xy}){\downarrow}_{y=b}$$
$$sup(c_{xy}){\downarrow}_{x=c} \supseteq sup(c_{xy}){\downarrow}_{x=d} \qquad sup(c_{xy}){\downarrow}_{y=b} \supseteq sup(c_{xy}){\downarrow}_{y=a}$$

Figure 4.5. *Presence of c_{xy}-substitutable values*

PROPOSITION 4.10.– *Let c be a constraint, $x \in$ scp(c) and $\{a, b\} \subseteq$ dom(x) such that (x, a) is c-substitutable for (x, b). If* $\sup(c){\downarrow}_{x=b} \neq \emptyset$ *then* $\sup(c){\downarrow}_{x=a} \neq \emptyset$.

EXAMPLE.– Figure 4.6 illustrates how application of Proposition 4.10 can reduce effort of consistency checking. This example assumes that the domain of y has been reduced to the two values a and b, and that the domain of x is to be revised. First, when trying to find a support for (x, a), (y, b) is found. Substitutability information in Figure 4.5 implies directly that (x, b) also admits a support. Second, absence of support for (x, c) implies absence of support for (x, d).

Note finally that two values related by a substitutability relation restricted to a constraint remain in this relation when the domain of some variables in scp(c) are reduced. In other words, the relation is preserved under domain reduction. We can say that a GAC algorithm (partially) exploits substitutability iff it (partially) exploits Proposition 4.10.

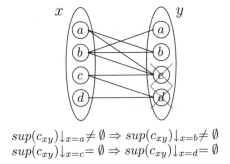

$$sup(c_{xy})\!\downarrow_{x=a}\neq\emptyset \Rightarrow sup(c_{xy})\!\downarrow_{x=b}\neq\emptyset$$
$$sup(c_{xy})\!\downarrow_{x=c}=\emptyset \Rightarrow sup(c_{xy})\!\downarrow_{x=d}=\emptyset$$

Figure 4.6. *Inferences made by exploiting substitutability information from Figure 4.5*

4.4.2. Overview

This section gives a brief account of published generic algorithms that enforce (generalized) arc consistency. We omit AC1 [MAC 77a] which is a brute-force algorithm, AC2 [WAL 72, MAC 77a] which corresponds to a particular case of AC3, and AC5 [HEN 92] which is a parameterized algorithm that can be instantiated to be the same as AC3 or AC4 (or to exploit some properties of constraints). We also omit algorithms GAC3, GAC2001 and GAC3^{rm} because these are described in other sections.

For binary constraint networks, AC4 [MOH 86] is the first published algorithm admitting an optimal worst-case time complexity. By explicitly storing the list of supports for each value, AC4 allows direct identification of values that become unsupported when values are deleted. Unluckily, its initialization phase is expensive because it requires performance of all possible constraint checks on all constraints. This is why AC3 is on average better than AC4 [WAL 93]. Anyway, here is a brief description of AC4 which, when applied to a binary constraint network P, requires the following data structures:

– a propagation queue (set) Q containing values in P that have been deleted but not yet processed;

– for each v-value (x, a) of P, a set $\sup[x, a]$ containing the (initial) supports for (x, a) over all constraints (here $\sup[x, a] = \cup_{c\in\mathrm{cons}(P)|x\in\mathrm{scp}(c)}\sup(c)\!\downarrow_{x=a}$);

– for each c-value (c, x, a) of P, a counter $cnt[c, x, a]$ indicating the number of (current) supports for (x, a) on c, i.e. $cnt[c, x, a] = |\sup(c)\!\downarrow_{x=a}|$.

The structure cnt of counters is updated during the search, permitting the identification of values that no longer have support on a constraint. The structure $\sup$ of supports remains unchanged after its initial computation (during a preprocessing phase). In fine-grained algorithms, constraint propagation is guided by (deleted) values (recorded in Q). AC4, which is the first published fine-grained algorithm, admits a worst-case time complexity in $O(ed^2)$ and a worst-case space complexity in $O(ed^2)$.

The non-binary generalization of AC4 to non-binary constraints also reaches worst-case time optimality; specifically, GAC4 [MOH 88] admits a $O(erd^r)$ time complexity, which is optimal [MOH 88, BES 06]. Its data structures are:

– a propagation queue (set) Q containing values of P that have been deleted but not yet processed;

– for each c-value (c, x, a) of P, a set $\sup[c, x, a]$ containing the current supports for (x, a) on c, i.e. $\sup[c, x, a] = \sup(c)_{x=a}$.

Initialization of GAC4, Algorithm 20, iterates over the set of supports $\sup(c)$ of every constraint c. For an intensional constraint, this set can be obtained by "computing" $\mathrm{val}(c) \cap \mathrm{rel}(c)$: building the three-dimensional array $\sup[]$ is then $O(rd^r)$ per constraint. For an extensional (positive) constraint, we initially have $table[c] = \mathrm{rel}(c) = \sup(c)$: building the three-dimensional array $\sup[]$ is then $O(rt)$ per constraint where $t = table[c].length$. After the initialization phase, all constraints are represented extensionally by means of the structure $\sup[]$. This means that AC4 and GAC4 are essentially filtering algorithms for table constraints. Note that GAC4 applied to binary constraint networks is not exactly equivalent to AC4 (the data structures are slightly different). More information about GAC4 and its implementation will be provided in section 5.5.3.

(G)AC4 suffers both from its space complexity and its time-expensive initialization phase. For the binary case, to reach optimality, it is only necessary to process a single support for each value, instead of collecting and counting all supports. As soon as a support is found for a value, we can simply record this support and consider another value. More precisely, at any moment, if (y, b) is the smallest (strict) support on a binary constraint c_{xy} that has been found for a v-value (x, a), then (x, a) can be recorded in a list $S[y, b]$ associated with (y, b). $S[y, b]$ is a set (list) containing the v-values whose smallest support found most recently is (y, b). AC6 [BES 94] is a fine-grained algorithm that works in this way. In AC6, propagation is guided by (deleted) values as in AC4: when a v-value (y, b) is removed, a new support for each value in $S[y, b]$ is sought. The fine-grained algorithm AC6 admits an optimal worst-case time complexity in $O(ed^2)$ and a worst-case space complexity in $O(ed)$.

The algorithm AC7 [BES 99] can be seen as an optimization of AC6 using bi-directionality of constraints. Whereas AC6 exploits positive and negative uni-directionality, AC7 is additionally able to exploit positive and negative bi-directionality. AC4 also benefits from this nice feature but at the cost of systematically performing all constraint checks at preprocessing time. To complete our comparison, note that the coarse-grained AC3 does not exploit any of these basic properties (this

---

Algorithm 20: GAC4(P: $\mathscr{P}$): Boolean

Output: *true* iff $GAC(P) \neq \perp$

// Initialization of Q; Q contains v-values

1   $Q \leftarrow \emptyset$

2   **foreach** *constraint c of P* **do**

3   **foreach** *pair (x, a) such that $x \in \mathrm{scp}(c) \wedge a \in \mathrm{dom}(x)$* **do**

4         $\sup[c, x, a] \leftarrow \emptyset$

5   **foreach** *support $\tau \in \sup(c)$* **do**

6   **foreach** *variable $x \in \mathrm{scp}(c)$* **do**

7            $\sup[c, x, \tau[x]] \leftarrow \sup[c, x, \tau[x]] \cup \{\tau\}$

8   **foreach** *pair (x, a) such that $x \in \mathrm{scp}(c) \wedge a \in \mathrm{dom}(x)$* **do**

9   **if** $\sup[c, x, a] = \emptyset$ **then**

10   remove a from $\mathrm{dom}(x)$

11            $Q \leftarrow Q \cup \{(x, a)\}$

12   **if** $\mathrm{dom}(x) = \emptyset$ **then**

13   **return** *false*

// Propagation through Q

14 **while** $Q \neq \emptyset$ **do**

15   pick and delete (x, a) from Q

16   **foreach** *constraint c of P such that $x \in \mathrm{scp}(c)$* **do**

17   **foreach** *tuple $\tau \in \sup[c, x, a]$* **do**

18   **foreach** *variable $y \in \mathrm{scp}(c) \mid y \neq x$* **do**

19               $b \leftarrow \tau[y]$

20   **if** $b \in \mathrm{dom}(y)$ **then**

21   remove τ from $\sup[c, y, b]$

22   **if** $\sup[c, y, b] = \emptyset$ **then**

23   remove b from $\mathrm{dom}(y)$

24                      $Q \leftarrow Q \cup \{(y, b)\}$

25   **if** $\mathrm{dom}(y) = \emptyset$ **then**

26   **return** *false*

27 **return** *true*

---

explains its sub-optimality), whereas AC2001 exploits positive and negative uni-directionality, just like AC6. Recall that bi-directionality means that if a v-value (y, b) supports (is compatible with) a v-value (x, a) on a binary constraint c_{xy} then (x, a) symmetrically supports (y, b) on c_{xy}. Hence, if a constraint check $(a, b) \in \text{rel}(c_{xy})$ is performed when looking for a support of (x, a), there is no need to perform the same constraint check when looking for a support of (y, b) provided that the constraint check has been recorded as a success or a failure (positive and negative bi-directionality exploitation). Among all algorithms cited above, AC7 is the only one that fully takes bi-directionality into account

Like AC6, the fine-grained algorithm AC7 admits an optimal worst-case time complexity in $O(ed^2)$ and a worst-case space complexity in $O(ed)$. However, AC7 can save a substantial number of constraint checks due to its refined construction. Unfortunately, although attractive, AC7 is certainly one of the most complex AC algorithms to implement. In particular, management of its data structures upon backtracking in MAC is not trivial; nor is its generalization to non-binary constraints. This is certainly one of the reasons for more recent development of simpler algorithms. One of these is AC3$_d$ [DON 02] which, following AC7, partially exploits bi-directionality. AC3$_d$ is a coarse-grained hybrid of AC3 and dead-end elimination (DEE) [GAS 78]. The main difference between AC3 and AC3$_d$ is that AC3$_d$ sometimes simultaneously revises the domain of two variables involved in the same (binary) constraint. When the revision ordering heuristic of arc-oriented scheme selects an arc (c_{xy}, x) from Q, AC3$_d$ checks whether the arc (c_{xy}, y) is also present in Q. If this is the case, then AC3$_d$ uses a *double-support domain heuristic* to revise the domains of x and y simultaneously. This heuristic checks in priority sequence two values whose status is unknown. The advantage of a double support is that, for price of a single constraint check, it shows that two values are supported. AC3$_{dl}$ and AC3$_{ds}$ [MEH 04] are closely related to AC3$_d$.

In the context of coarse-grained algorithms, constraint multi-directionality has also been considered in [LEC 03a]. By simply grafting residual supports (which easily permit partial exploitation of positive multi-directionality) to GAC2001/3.1, GAC3.2 has produced quite competitive results. GAC3.2 can be defined as GAC2001/3.1 + GAC3^{rm} because it uses the smallest supports of GAC2001/3.1 and the residual supports of GAC3^{rm}. Residual supports, and the algorithm GAC3^{rm}, are introduced in section 4.5.2.

AC3.3 is the only coarse-grained algorithm that takes bi-directionality fully into account. AC3.3 records, for each v-value, the last smallest support that has been found, as in AC2001. AC3.3 also records, for each v-value the number of its current *extern* supports. An extern support for a v-value (x, a) on c_{xy} is a support found for another v-value (y, b) on c_{xy}. The structure *last* in AC2001 is used to benefit from positive and negative uni-directionality and a new structure denoted *ext* is introduced to exploit positive bi-directionality. For every c-value (c, x, a), $ext[c, x, a]$ is the number of current extern supports for (x, a) on c. For a binary constraint c_{xy}, we have: $ext[c_{xy}, x, a] = |\{(y, b) \mid last[c_{xy}, y, b] = (x, a)\}|$.

Algorithm 21: seekSupport-3.3$((c, x, a)$: c-value): Boolean

Require: adapting seekSupport-2001 to deal with v-values as last supports
Output: *true* iff $\sup(c)_{x=a} \neq \emptyset$

1 **if** $ext[c, x, a] > 0$ **then**
2 | **return** *true*

3 $(y, b) \leftarrow last[c, x, a]$ // $last[c, x, a]$ is either a v-value or *nil*
4 **if** $(y, b) \neq nil$ **then**
5 | **if** $b \in \mathrm{dom}(y)$ **then**
6 | **return** *true*
7 | **else**
8 | $ext[c, y, b] \leftarrow ext[c, y, b] - 1$

9 $\tau \leftarrow$ seekSupport-2001$((c, x, a))$ // τ is a v-value or *nil*
10 **if** $\tau = nil$ **then**
11 | remove a from $\mathrm{dom}(x)$
12 | **foreach** *constraint* $c' \in \mathrm{cons}(P) \mid x \in \mathrm{scp}(c') \wedge c' \neq c$ **do**
13 | **if** $last[c', x, a] \neq nil$ **then**
14 | $(z, c) \leftarrow last[c', x, a]$
15 | $ext[c', z, c] \leftarrow ext[c', z, c] - 1$

16 | **return** *false*
17 **else**
18 | $last[c, x, a] \leftarrow \tau$
19 | $(y, b) \leftarrow last[c, x, a]$
20 | $ext[c, y, b] \leftarrow ext[c, y, b] + 1$
21 | **return** *true*

Initialization of AC3.3 sets all *last* elements to *nil* and all *ext* counters to 0. Then AC3.3 uses seekSupport-3.3, Algorithm 21, which is called by revise, Algorithm 8, itself called in Algorithms 7 and 9. For every c-value (c, x, a), $last[c, x, a]$ designates here a v-value (or *nil*). Counters are carefully updated when a support is lost (line 8), or when a support is found (line 20) or when a value is removed (line 15). AC3.3 has a space complexity in $O(ed)$ and an optimal worst-case time complexity in $O(ed^2)$. Indeed, the total worst-case time complexity of updating counters (lines 12 to 15) when values are removed is $O(ed)$ because the total cost of updating counters n times (one value per domain) is $O(e)$. All other operations are performed in constant time, except for seekSupport-2001 (assumed to deal with v-values as last supports without any loss of generality because constraints are binary), which gives a complexity in $O(ed^2)$. Like GAC2001/3.1 and GAC3.2, AC3.3 can exploit negative multi-directionality by focusing the search for supports on so-called candidates [BES 97], which are tuples that have never been checked. A full description can be found in [LEC 03a].

Attempting a synthesis of many related algorithms, Régin [RÉG 05] has devised a general algorithm, called CAC. CAC is claimed to be a configurable, generic and adaptive algorithm for establishing arc consistency on binary constraints. A proposed new nomenclature for different arc consistency algorithms is based on CAC. This nomenclature indicates features of AC algorithms, such as the values that are reconsidered when a domain is modified, or whether bi-directionnality is taken into account, or how a new support is sought. Several new combinations are available. The important concept of residual supports should also be integrated to this general schema.

Another framework [LIK 07] addresses the central issue of enforcing (maintaining) AC during search. New algorithms, called arc consistency during search (ACS), are designed to take advantage of residual data left by previous invocations of the basic AC enforcement procedure, or to employ an adaptive domain re-ordering technique when values are deleted and restored. Some variants of ACS are original and may open some perspectives for existing filtering algorithms, including those that achieve a stronger form of local consistency.

Finally, as shown earlier (following [HAS 93, BOU 04c]), substitutability is a general constraint property allowing inference of support. Substitutability can be integrated into AC-Inference [BES 99] which is an arc consistency algorithm that avoids useless constraint checks by taking account of generic and specific properties of constraints. AC7 is a derivative of AC-Inference that simply uses bi-directionality. It should be possible to derive from AC-Inference a general-purpose fine-grained arc consistency algorithm exploiting both bi-directionaly and substitutability. Although substitutability is promising, its practical value appears to be limited to certain applications, such as job shop scheduling, where the number of substitutable values is substantial.

4.5. Improving the efficiency of generic GAC algorithms

This section presents three simple mechanisms for improving performance of general-purpose GAC algorithms. The first mechanism avoids some useless revisions and constraint checks, which are operations at the heart of generic GAC algorithms. This mechanims uses static information, computed in a preprocessing stage, concerning *cardinality* of conflict sets. Next, *residual supports*, also called *residues*, deal simply and efficiently with supports. Grafted to GAC3, known pathological cases disappear. Furthermore, when residues are used within MAC, no maintenance has to be done upon backtracking, and so there is no overhead; in contrast, other sophisticated (and optimal) GAC algorithms have backtracking overheads. The final idea in this section is to use *bitwise operations* to speed up important computations such as the search of supports.

4.5.1. *Exploiting cardinality of conflict sets*

When a local consistency is maintained during search, this means that a propagation phase is repeated at each elementary step of the search process, i.e. after each search decision. The idea presented here, following [BOU 04c, MEH 05a], is to do substantial computation during a preprocessing stage in order to reduce the cost of the successive propagation phases. More precisely, [BOU 04c] proposes a static analysis of the nature of each constraint in order to extract interesting information about conflict sets, covering sets and substitutability. This knowledge can be used by any backtracking algorithm that alternates between search decisions and constraint propagation enforcing a domain-filtering consistency. In this book, we concentrate on using the cardinality of conflict sets to make some inferences about the presence of supports. We believe that it is well worthwhile to integrate this quite simple idea into any (coarse-grained) GAC algorithm in order to improve its performance.

The following proposition (whose proof is immediate) shows that if P is a network obtained from P^{init} after deleting some values, it is possible to infer directly that a value is supported by a constraint in P from information about the conflict set of this value in P^{init}. Roughly speaking, we can say it allows a partial exploitation of uni-directionality. To distinguish between conflict sets in P and P^{init}, we note $\text{con}^{\text{init}}(c)_{x=a}$ the set of conflicts for (x,a) on c in P^{init}; $\text{sup}(c)_{x=a}$ is the set of supports for (x,a) on c in P. Recall that a conflict on a constraint c is a valid tuple τ on c that is not accepted by c; if a conflict τ on c involves a v-value (x,a), τ is a conflict for (x,a) on c.

PROPOSITION 4.11.– *Let P and P^{init} be two constraint networks such that $P \preceq_d P^{\text{init}}$, and (c,x,a) be a c-value of P. If $|\text{con}^{\text{init}}(c)_{x=a}| < |\prod_{y \in \text{scp}(c) \setminus \{x\}} \text{dom}(y)|$ then $\text{sup}(c)_{x=a} \neq \emptyset$.*

EXAMPLE.– To illustrate Proposition 4.11, consider a binary constraint c_{xy}. In Figure 4.7, (a,b) and (a,e) are two conflicts for (x,a) on c_{xy} (in P^{init}); this is why $|\text{con}^{\text{init}}(c_{xy})_{x=a}| = 2$. For every value $a \in \text{dom}(x)$, when the number of conflicts for (x,a) on c_{xy} in P^{init} is strictly less than the size of $\text{dom}(y)$, this implies the existence of a support for (x,a) on c_{xy} in P. Figures 4.7 and 4.8 provide an example.

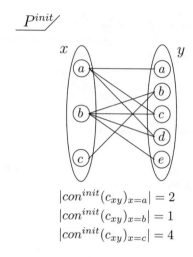

$$|con^{init}(c_{xy})_{x=a}| = 2$$
$$|con^{init}(c_{xy})_{x=b}| = 1$$
$$|con^{init}(c_{xy})_{x=c}| = 4$$

Figure 4.7. *Cardinality of conflict sets for the arc (c_{xy}, x)*

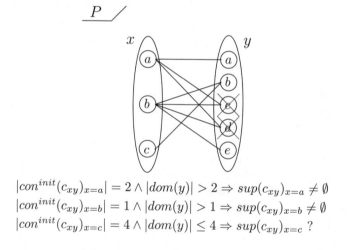

$$|con^{init}(c_{xy})_{x=a}| = 2 \wedge |dom(y)| > 2 \Rightarrow sup(c_{xy})_{x=a} \neq \emptyset$$
$$|con^{init}(c_{xy})_{x=b}| = 1 \wedge |dom(y)| > 1 \Rightarrow sup(c_{xy})_{x=b} \neq \emptyset$$
$$|con^{init}(c_{xy})_{x=c}| = 4 \wedge |dom(y)| \leq 4 \Rightarrow sup(c_{xy})_{x=c} \, ?$$

Figure 4.8. *Inferences made by exploiting cardinality information from Figure 4.7*

Some useless constraint checks can be avoided by an algorithm that exploits this property. Moreover the following corollary allows avoidance of full revision:

COROLLARY 4.12.– *Let P and P^{init} be two constraint networks such that $P \preceq_d P^{init}$, $c \in cons(P)$ and $x \in scp(c)$. If $\max_{a \in dom(x)} |con^{init}(c)_{x=a}| < |\prod_{y \in scp(c) \setminus \{x\}} dom(y)|$ then for every value a in $dom(x)$, we have $sup(c)_{x=a} \neq \emptyset$.*

To use Proposition 4.11 and Corollary 4.12 in practice, we need first to count the initial conflicts for each value. Also, to avoid the overhead of iterating over values in the current domain, it is certainly worth considering $\max_{a \in \mathrm{dom}^{\mathrm{init}}(x)} |\mathrm{con}^{\mathrm{init}}(c)_{x=a}|$ instead of $\max_{a \in \mathrm{dom}(x)} |\mathrm{con}^{\mathrm{init}}(c)_{x=a}|$ in Corollary 4.12. Two data structures are required:

– a three-dimensional array $nbConflicts$ that gives for each c-value (c, x, a) the number of elements in $\mathrm{con}^{\mathrm{init}}(c)_{x=a}$;

– a two-dimensional array $nbMaxConflicts$ that gives for each arc (c, x) the maximum number of conflicts on c for all values in $\mathrm{dom}^{\mathrm{init}}(x)$.

These arrays can be initialized by function $\mathsf{initialize}^{\mathrm{CS}}$, Algorithm 22 (CS stands for Conflict Sets); the formal parameter P is certainly P^{init} in practice (or the constraint network obtained after having preprocessed P^{init} as explained below). The worst-case space complexity of this algorithm is $O(erd)$, and the worst-case time complexity is $O(erd^r)$, assuming, as usual, that a constraint check is $O(r)$.

Algorithm 22: $\mathsf{initialize}^{\mathrm{CS}}(P: \mathscr{P})$

---

1 $\forall c \in \mathrm{cons}(P), \forall x \in \mathrm{scp}(c), \forall a \in \mathrm{dom}(x)$
2      $nbConflicts[c, x, a] \leftarrow 0$
3 $\forall c \in \mathrm{cons}(P), \forall \tau \in \mathrm{val}(c) \setminus \mathrm{rel}(c), \forall x \in \mathrm{scp}(c)$
4      $nbConflicts[c, x, \tau[x]] \leftarrow nbConflicts[c, x, \tau[x]] + 1$
5 $\forall c \in \mathrm{cons}(P), \forall x \in \mathrm{scp}(c)$
6      $nbMaxConflicts[c, x] \leftarrow max\{nbConflicts[c, x, a] \mid a \in \mathrm{dom}(x)\}$

After initialization of the structures, revisions can be made more efficient. It is sufficient to employ Algorithm 23 instead of Algorithm 8. Line 2 avoids some useless revisions simply by testing whether the presence of a support for every value can be inferred from knowledge of the maximum number of conflicts. For each value, line 5 avoids useless constraint (or validity) checks by using the number of conflicts initially computed for this value.

Of course, this variant is not very interesting for establishing GAC stand-alone. The initialization phase is heavy (similar to that of GAC4), and indeed penalizing if no search is performed. Therefore this variant should be used within MAC, which maintains GAC during a backtrack search. Initializing the new data structures before or after preprocessing and using them throughout search balances the initialization cost against the benefit that can be obtained.

Initialization can be achieved with no overhead if the number of conflicts (or an upper approximation) is known in advance. More precisely, for some constraints, the semantics provides this information directly. For example, for an inequation constraint

---

Algorithm 23: revise^{CS}(c: constraint, x: variable): Boolean

---

Output: *true* iff the revision of the arc (c, x) is effective

1   $nbTuples \leftarrow |\prod_{y \in \text{scp}(c) \setminus \{x\}} \text{dom}(y)|$
2   **if** $nbTuples > nbMaxConflicts[c, x]$ **then**
3   $\quad \lfloor$ **return** *false*
4   $nbElements \leftarrow |\text{dom}(x)|$
5   **foreach** *value* $a \in \text{dom}(x) \mid nbTuples \leq nbConflicts[c, x, a]$ **do**
6   $\quad$ **if** $\neg seekSupport(c, x, a)$ **then**
7   $\quad \quad \lfloor$ remove a from $\text{dom}(x)$ $[\text{expl}(x \neq a) \leftarrow getExplanation(c, x, a)]$

8   **return** $nbElements \neq |\text{dom}(x)|$

$x \neq y$, the number of conflicts for each c-value is at most 1. For such a constraint we can use this fact to initialize the data structures in $O(d)$, whereas function initialize^{CS} is $O(d^2)$. In any case, once the counters are initialized there will be no revision concerning an inequation constraint unless a variable becomes fixed. This means that, for some constraints, generic filtering, i.e. the general function revise^{CS}, may become as efficient as specialized filtering procedures.

The idea described here has been generalized in [MEH 05a] by associating a weight with every support and reasoning with weights to avoid useless constraint checks and useless revisions, with so-called *support conditions* and *revision conditions*. Actually finding a weighting function that gives better practical results (in terms of CPU time) than the one given here (the weight of each support being equal to 1) is not easy.

In related work, *probabilistic support conditions* and *probabilistic revision conditions* have been investigated in [MEH 07]. The probabilistic support condition holds for a v-value (x, a) with respect to a constraint c, if the probability of having a support for (x, a) on c exceeds a carefully chosen threshold. The probabilistic revision condition holds for an arc (c, x) if the probability of having some support on c for each value a in $\text{dom}(x)$ is above some threshold. Even if choosing the threshold value seems a little bit tricky, the practical value of these probabilistic conditions has been shown on many problems (with a threshold value set to 0.9).

We develop the idea of probabilistic revision condition below for binary constraints. Similarly to $nbMaxConflicts$, we define $nbMinSupports[c, x]$ to be the minimum number of supports on c for values in $\text{dom}^{\text{init}}(x)$; we have $nbMinSupports[c, x] = \min_{a \in \text{dom}^{\text{init}}(x)} |\sup^{\text{init}}(c)_{x=a}|$. For a binary constraint c_{xy}, if we assume that each value in $\text{dom}^{\text{init}}(y)$ is equally likely to be removed during inference or search processes, the probability $Pr(c_{xy}, x)$ that there exists a support on c_{xy} for each value of x is:

$$Pr(c_{xy}, x) = 1 - \left(\frac{|\operatorname{dom}^{\text{init}}(y) \setminus \operatorname{dom}(y)|}{nbMinSupports[c_{xy}, x]} \right) \Big/ \left(\frac{|\operatorname{dom}^{\text{init}}(y)|}{nbMinSupports[c_{xy}, x]} \right)$$

If $|\operatorname{dom}^{\text{init}}(y) \setminus \operatorname{dom}(y)| < nbMinSupports[c_{xy}, x]$, then $\left(\frac{|\operatorname{dom}^{\text{init}}(y) \setminus \operatorname{dom}(y)|}{nbMinSupports[c_{xy}, x]} \right) = 0$. In that case, we deduce that all values in $\operatorname{dom}(x)$ are arc-consistent, i.e. have a support on c_{xy} because $Pr(c_{xy}, x) = 1$; this deduction is made differently by means of the test at line 2 of Algorithm 23. Concretely, the probabilistic revision condition allows us to generalize the procedure revise^{CS}: considering a threshold value $T \in [0, 1]$, we replace lines 2 and 3 of Algorithm 23 by:

> **if** $Pr(c, x) \geq T$ **then**
> $\lfloor$ **return** $false$

When T is set to 1, we have the guarantee that arc consistency is fully enforced. Otherwise, one may only reach a partial form of arc consistency.

4.5.2. *Exploiting residues*

We now introduce *residual supports*, which are also known as *residues*. A residue for a c-value is a support that has previously been found and stored for future use. The point is that a residue is not required (guaranteed) to represent a lower bound of the smallest current support for a value. *Multi-directional* residues were introduced in [LEC 03a], *uni-directional* residues were introduced in [LIK 04] and *multiple* residues were studied in [LEC 08b].

4.5.2.1. *Algorithm GAC3^{rm}*

The basic algorithm GAC3 can be refined as follows: before searching for a support for a value from scratch, the validity of the residue associated with this value is checked. This development of GAC3 is denoted by GAC3^{rm}. GAC3^{rm} partially exploits positive multi-directionality (and also uni-directionality), by using Algorithm 24 instead of Algorithm 18. Every element of a three-dimensional array *res* is initialized to the special value *nil*. For a c-value (c, x, a), $res[c, x, a]$ stores the residue for (x, a) on c. Whenever a support is required for a c-value (c, x, a), the validity of the residue associated with (c, x, a) is tested first (line 1, Algorithm 24). If this fails, a new support is sought from scratch (lines 3 through 9). If a support τ is found, multi-directionality is exploited to update the residues of all values present in τ (lines 6 and 7), since τ is also a support for $(y, \tau[y])$ on c for each $y \in scp(c)$. Thus $r - 1$ residues (where r is the arity of c) are obtained for the other values of the tuple without any effort.

To derive the variant GAC3^r that partially exploits positive uni-directionality, we replace lines 6 and 7 of Algorithm 24 with:

$$res[c, x, a] \leftarrow \tau$$

For establishing GAC stand-alone on a given constraint network, GAC3^r (which is a derivative of GAC3 exploiting uni-directional residues) can be replaced advantageously by GAC2001. However, when GAC has to be maintained during search, MAC3^r which corresponds to mac3.1residue in [LIK 04] becomes quite competitive. GAC3^{rm} is interesting in its own right because it exploits multi-directional residues just like GAC3.2 [LEC 03a].

Algorithm 24: seekSupport-3^{rm}((c, x, a): c-value): Boolean

Output: *true* iff $\sup(c)_{x=a} \neq \emptyset$

1 **if** *isValidTuple*$(c, res[c, x, a])$ **then**
2   **return** *true*
3 $\tau \leftarrow$ getFirstValidTuple$((c, x, a))$
4 **while** $\tau \neq nil$ **do**
5   **if** $\tau \in \mathrm{rel}(c)$ **then**
6   **foreach** *variable* $y \in \mathrm{scp}(c)$ **do**
7            $res[c, y, \tau[y]] \leftarrow \tau$
8   **return** *true*
9      $\tau \leftarrow$ getNextValidTuple$((c, x, a), \tau)$
10 **return** *false*

EXAMPLE.– Figure 4.3 on page 203 provides an example illustrating the new algorithm GAC3^{rm}. When revise(c_{xy}, x) is called for the first time by AC3^{rm}, Figure 4.3(a), all elements of the array *res* have been initialized to *nil* (assuming that revise(c_{xy}, y) has not yet been called). At this time AC3^{rm} requires eight constraint checks, but after the revision we have:

– $res[c_{xy}, x, a] = a$;
– $res[c_{xy}, x, b] = c$;
– $res[c_{xy}, x, c] = d$.

Here we record strict supports. Suppose now that the v-value (y, c) has been deleted elsewhere, that residues have not changed, and that revise(c_{xy}, x) is called again; see Figure 4.3(b). At this time AC3^{rm} requires three constraint checks (plus three validity checks) since:

– $res[c_{xy}, x, a] = a$, which remains valid;

$- res[c_{xy}, x, b] = c$, which is no longer valid $((y, a)$ and (y, b) are unsuccessfully checked, but (y, d) is successfully checked yielding $res[c_{xy}, x, b] = d)$;

$- res[c_{xy}, x, c] = d$ which remains valid.

Remember that here seven constraint checks were required by AC3 but only one by AC2001. However, as will be explained, GAC3^{rm} has some nice features that make it a good candidate for service as a general-purpose GAC algorithm in constraint solvers.

For the binary case, theory proves that AC3^{rm}, unlike AC3, behaves optimally when constraints are tight. Consider, for example, the Domino problem introduced in [BES 05c] and briefly described in section 2.2.5. In this, all constraints except one are equality constraints. Table 4.1 shows experimental results obtained with AC2001, AC3 and the new algorithm AC3^{rm} on some instances of this problem. The time in seconds (CPU) and the number of constraint checks (#ccks) are given for each instance. In an instance named domino-n-d, n is the number of variables and d the number of values in each domain. These results show that the Domino problem is a pathological case for AC3 but not for AC3^{rm}.

Instance		AC2001	AC3	AC3^{rm}
domino-100-100	CPU	0.23	1.81	0.16
	#ccks	1.5 M	18 M	0.9 M
domino-300-300	CPU	6.01	134	3.40
	#ccks	40 M	1,377 M	27 M
domino-500-500	CPU	21.4	951	15.0
	#ccks	187 M	10,542 M	125 M
domino-800-800	CPU	87	6,144	60
	#ccks	767 M	68,778 M	511 M

Table 4.1. *Establishing arc consistency on Domino instances*

4.5.2.2. *Complexity issues*

To understand why residues work, we present some theoretical results for binary instances. In particular, we study the complexity of AC3^{rm} when used stand-alone and when embedded in MAC. Without any loss of generality, we assume that each domain contains exactly d values.

PROPOSITION 4.13.– *AC3^{rm} admits a worst-case time complexity in $O(ed^3)$ and a worst-case space complexity in $O(ed)$.*

Proof. The space complexity of AC3^{rm} is $O(ed)$ since the space for Q (the propagation queue when using a variable-oriented propagation scheme) is $O(n)$

and the space for *res* is $O(e * 2 * d) = O(ed)$. Like the optimality proof of AC2001 [BES 05c], the number of validity checks performed by AC3^{rm} cannot exceed the number of constraint checks performed by AC3. As AC3 is in $O(ed^3)$ in the worst case, so is AC3^{rm}.   □

AC3^{rm} is clearly not optimal. However, it is possible to refine the previous result by taking into account the tightness of constraints.

PROPOSITION 4.14.– *In AC3^{rm}, the total worst-case time complexity of seekSupport-3^{rm} for any c-value (c, x, a) is $O(cs + d)$ where $c = |con(c)_{x=a}|$ and $s = |sup(c)_{x=a}|$.*

Proof. Let P be the constraint network that must be enforced AC, and let c_{xy} be a binary constraint of P. After observing that $c + s = d$, we can show that the worst case (in terms of constraint checks with respect to a c-value (c_{xy}, x, a)) occurs when:

– only one value is removed from $dom(y)$ between two successive calls to revise(c_{xy}, x);

– initial values of $dom(y)$ are ordered in such a way that the c first values correspond to values that do not support a and the s last values correspond to values that do support a;

– the first s values removed from $dom(y)$ systematically correspond to the residual supports successively recorded by AC3^{rm} (until a domain wipe-out is encountered).

Figure 4.9 provides an illustration. For these $s + 1$ calls (note the initial call) to seekSupport-3^{rm}(c_{xy}, x, a), there are $s \times (c + 1) + c$ constraint checks. The number of other operations (validity checks and updates of the *res* structure) in Algorithm 24 performed with respect to (c_{xy}, x, a) is $O(d)$. Hence we have a total worst-case complexity in $O(sc + s + c + d) = O(cs + d)$.   □

We can directly exploit this result for *tightness-bounded* constraints:

DEFINITION 4.15.– *[Tightness-bounded Constraint] A constraint c is tightness-bounded iff for every v-value (x, a) such that $x \in scp(c)$, either the number of supports for (x, a) on c is $O(1)$ or the number of conflicts for (x, a) on c is $O(1)$ when the greatest domain size $d \to \infty$.*

Many common constraints are tightness-bounded; for example, an equality constraint $x = y$ or an inequation constraint $x \neq y$. For equations, each value is supported at most once, whereas for inequations, each value allows at most one conflict. A less-than constraint $x \leq y$ is also tightness-bounded. More precisely, if we consider that $dom(x) = 1..d$ and $dom(y) = 1..d$ then, when $d \to \infty$, the number of

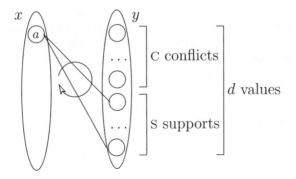

Figure 4.9. *Worst-case configuration for a c-value* (c_{xy}, x, a) *in AC3*^{rm}*: conflicts precede supports, and between two successive calls to* **seekSupport-3**^{rm}(c_{xy}, x, a)*, only the value in* $\mathrm{dom}(y)$ *that corresponds to res*$[c_{xy}, x, a]$ *is removed*

conflicts for any value i of $\mathrm{dom}(x)$ is bounded by i while the number of supports for any value j of $\mathrm{dom}(y)$ is bounded by j.

We can now show that AC3^{rm} behaves in an optimal way (for a general-purpose AC algorithm) when it is applied to constraints of small or high tightness, or more precisely to tightness-bounded constraints.

PROPOSITION 4.16.– *Applied to a binary constraint network only involving tightness-bounded constraints, AC3*^{rm} *admits a worst-case time complexity in* $O(ed^2)$*, which is optimal.*

Proof. From Proposition 4.14 the total worst-case time complexity of seekSupport-3^{rm} for every c-value (c, x, a) is $O(\text{C}\text{S} + d)$ where C is the number of conflicts for (x, a) on c and S the number of supports for (x, a) on c. If the binary constraint c is tightness-bounded, then either C $= O(1)$ and S $= O(d)$, or C $= O(d)$ and S $= 0(1)$ since C+S $= d$. This implies that the total worst-case time complexity of seekSupport-3^{rm} for a c-value (c, x, a) is $O(d + d) = O(d)$. The overall complexity of AC3^{rm} is therefore $O(ed^2)$. □

Proposition 4.16 shows that AC3^{rm} behaves optimally when constraints are tightness-bounded. The (non-optimal) worst-case is when the tightness of the constraints is medium, i.e. equal to 0.5.

4.5.2.3. *Residues within MAC*

The previous results are confirmed when the state-of-the-art complete search algorithm MAC (presented in Chapter 8) is considered. The following results are directly obtained from previous propositions, the fact that AC3^{rm} is an incremental algorithm, and the fact that residues are backtrack-stable structures. This last observation means that no maintenance of data structures is necessary when backtracking, as illustrated in Figure 4.10. MAC3^{rm} is MAC maintaining arc consistency using algorithm AC3^{rm}.

PROPOSITION 4.17.– *MAC3*^{rm} *admits a worst-case time complexity in* $O(ed^3)$ *for any given branch of the search tree.*

PROPOSITION 4.18.– *Applied to a binary constraint network only involving tightness-bounded constraints, MAC3*^{rm} *admits a worst-case time complexity in* $O(ed^2)$ *for any given branch of the search tree, which is optimal.*

Proof. AC3^{rm} is easily shown to be incremental. The only difference, for the worst-case scenario, between a single execution of AC3^{rm} and all successive executions along a branch of the search tree is that residues may be modified when exploring a subtree. More precisely, imagine that at a given node v of the search tree, we have a residue τ for a c-value (c, x, a). Next, assume that a positive decision $y = b$ is taken, and the corresponding subtree is proved to be unsatisfiable. During exploration of this subtree, a new residue τ' may be associated with (c, x, a). The point is that τ' is also a valid residue for (c, x, a) at node v. Hence, if the branch (considered in the proposition) contains the node v followed by the negative decision $y \neq b$, even if the residue τ associated with (c, x, a) at node v is replaced by τ' due to the exploration of the left subtree, this will have no impact, concerning (c, x, a), in the worst-case scenario of AC3^{rm}. $\qquad\qquad\qquad\Box$

These theoretical results justify the data in [LIK 04, LEC 07c]. Besides, it is easy to embed GAC3^{rm} in MAC and SAC algorithms because GAC3^{rm} does not require any maintenance of data structures during MAC search and SAC inference. On the other hand, embedding an optimal algorithm such as GAC2001 entails an extra development effort, with an additional overhead during execution. For MAC2001, on binary constraint networks this overhead is $O(\mu ed)$ per branch of the binary tree built by MAC, as we have to take into account the reinitialization of the structure *last*. Here, μ denotes the number of refutations (negative decisions) of the branch.

4.5.3. *Exploiting bitwise operations*

Bitwise parallel operations can improve the practical performance of arc consistency operations. To enforce arc consistency within a MAC framework, Ullmann [ULL 76] gave a detailed description of bitwise parallel operations on bit vectors representing domains and sets of supports. Using this mechanism in a more general context within MAC and also within FC, McGregor [MCG 79] enhanced

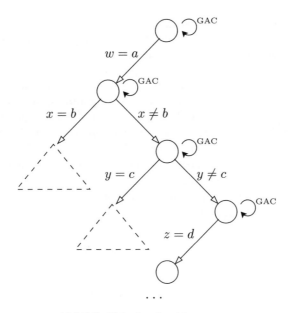

(a) MAC with backtrack-stable structures

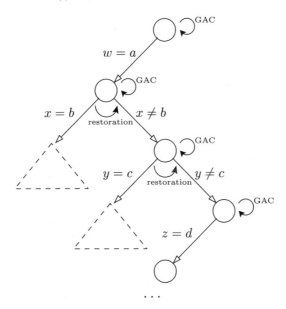

(b) MAC with non-backtrack-stable structures

Figure 4.10. *MAC embedding optimal generic GAC algorithms such as GAC2001 requires a restoration effort before each negative decision along a branch of the search tree. Optimal GAC algorithms employ non-backtrack-stable data structures, unlike GAC3^{rm}*

speed by using bitwise parallel operations. Bit parallel FC was used subsequently in [HAR 80, NUD 83]. Following [BLI 96, LEC 08c] we now provide a precise description of bitwise parallel operations in the enforcement of arc consistency.

It is usual to employ the O notation when presenting results of asymptotic analysis of time (and space) complexities of algorithms; see Appendix A.2.1. Asymptotic analysis is relevant to the assessment of algorithms provided that terms and coefficients ignored from the raw complexity expression are not too large. Consider, for example, a constraint network having n variables, their domains comprising d values, and suppose that this network has e binary max-support constraints. A max-support constraint involving the variables x and y is defined as follows: the greatest value in the domain of x supports all values in the domain of y, and vice versa. An example is shown in Figure 4.11.

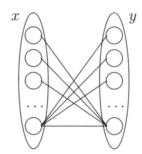

Figure 4.11. *A max-support constraint. As usual, an edge represents an allowed tuple*

If we enforce AC on this network using AC3 or AC2001, exactly $2e.(d^2 - d + 1)$ constraint checks are necessary to prove that the network is arc-consistent. Suppose now (without any loss of generality) that the current state of a domain is represented by a bit vector, in which a bit is associated with each value. A bit is 1 or 0 according as the associated value is currently present in, or absent from, the domain. Assume that constraints are represented similarly, so a bit vector represents all allowed and forbidden values for each c-value (c, x, a). When seeking a support for (x, a) on c, we can simply apply the bitwise operator AND to two vectors: if the result is not $ZERO$ (a vector whose each bit is 0), then a support exists.

When each bit vector is implemented as an array of words (natural data units of the computer architecture), each bitwise operation on two complete bit-vectors requires a sequence of elementary bitwise operations on pairs of constituent words. If p is the word size (which is the number of bits per word, usually 32 or 64), then a bitwise parallel operation on two operand words does p operations on pairs of bits. Returning to our example, a bitwise parallel operation on two words accomplishes p constraint checks, so we need up to p times fewer operations when enforcing AC using this mechanism (which we call AC3^{bit}) instead of classical AC3, AC2001 and AC3^{rm} algorithms. Table 4.2 shows experimental results that we have obtained for instances of this problem on a 64-bit processor. Here instances are denoted by n-d-e, and #ops is the number of bitwise operations performed by AC3^{bit} or the number of constraint checks performed by AC3, AC3^{rm} and AC2001. As expected, AC3^{bit} is about 60 times more efficient although AC3^{bit} and AC3 both are $O(ed^3)$.

Instance		AC2001	AC3	AC3^{rm}	AC3^{bit}
250-50-5000	CPU	1.61	1.58	1.56	0.05
	#ops	24.5 M	24.5 M	24.3 M	0.5 M
250-100-5000	CPU	6.26	6.17	6.15	0.10
	#ops	99.0 M	99.0 M	98.5 M	2.0 M
500-50-10000	CPU	3.21	3.11	3.11	0.11
	#ops	49.0 M	49.0 M	48.5 M	1.0 M
500-100-10000	CPU	12.48	12.29	12.27	0.19
	#ops	198.0 M	198.0 M	197.0 M	4.0 M

Table 4.2. *Establishing arc consistency on* **max-support** *instances*

4.5.3.1. *Binary representation*

This section provides some details of binary representation of domains and constraints, assuming that each bit vector is implemented as an array of words (natural data units of the computer architecture). Some programming languages do not include bit vector syntax and semantics that hide the packing of bit vectors into words. However, we show that for some bitwise computations, explicit use of arrays of words allows greater efficiency than can be achieved with monolithic bit vectors.

Without any loss of generality, we assume the use of a 64-bit processor. This means for example that the declaration of arrays in the Java language would be *long*[] since one *long* corresponds to 64 bits. In this section, we also assume that indices of arrays start at 0 rather than at 1.

4.5.3.1.1. Representing domains

When a copying mechanism [SCH 99] is used to manage domains during a backtrack search, a single bit can be associated with each value of each domain. More precisely, a bit can be associated with the index (starting at 0) of each value of a domain. When this bit is 1 (resp. 0), this means that the corresponding value is present in (resp. absent from) the domain. We will call arrays of words, constituting a compact bit vector representation, the *binary representation* of domains. For any variable x, the space complexity is $\Theta(|\operatorname{dom}(x)|)$, which is optimal.

Another mechanism used in many current CP systems is called trailing. Section 1.5.1 precisely describes a possible representation of domains using trailing. The space complexity of this representation is also $\Theta(|\operatorname{dom}(x)|)$ for any variable x, and the time complexity of all elementary operations (determining if a value is present, removing a value, adding a value, etc.) is $O(1)$. In this context, including and maintaining the structures for the binary representation of domains does not modify worst-case space and time complexities as shown below.

In addition to structures proposed in section 1.5.1, we now introduce a two-dimensional array called $bitDom$ that associates with the domain of each variable x the binary representation $bitDom[x]$ of $\operatorname{dom}(x)$, and:

– when adding (or restoring) the ith value in $\operatorname{dom}(x)$, the only operation required on the structure $bitDom$ is the following:

$$bitDom[x][i \text{ div } 64] \leftarrow bitDom[x][i \text{ div } 64] \text{ OR } masks1[i \text{ mod } 64];$$

– when removing the ith value from $\operatorname{dom}(x)$, the only operation required on the structure $bitDom$ is the following:

$$bitDom[x][i \text{ div } 64] \leftarrow bitDom[x][i \text{ div } 64] \text{ AND } masks0[i \text{ mod } 64].$$

Here, div denotes integer division, mod the remainder operator, OR the bitwise operator that performs a logical OR operation on each pair of corresponding bits and AND the bitwise operator that performs a logical AND operation on each pair of corresponding bits. The structure $masks1$ (resp. $masks0$) is a predefined array of 64 words that contains in its ith word a value that represents a sequence of 64 bits that are all set to 0 (resp. 1) except for the ith one. Figures 4.12 and 4.13 illustrate this, using 16-bit words because 64-bit words would be too big for these figures.

4.5.3.1.2. Representing constraints

We shall only consider binary constraints (although this mechanism could be extended to non-binary constraints of small arity). Recall that a binary constraint can be represented in extension using a two-dimensional array of Booleans (called a $(0, 1)$-matrix) or a list of tuples (called a table), or in intension using a predicate expression.

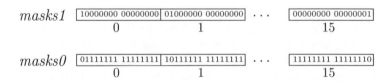

Figure 4.12. *Masks used for elementary bitwise operations, considering here words of size* 16

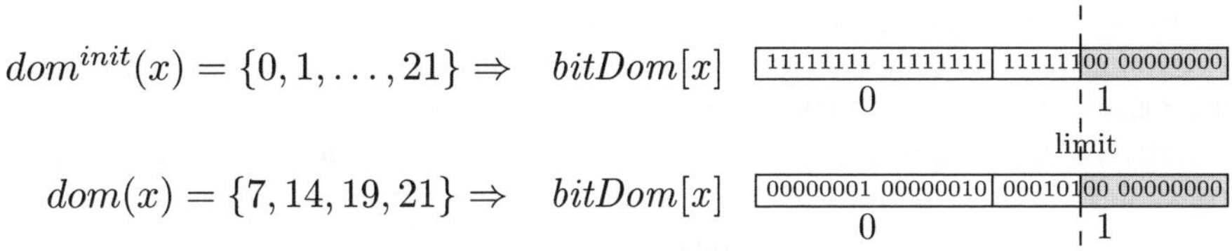

$$dom^{init}(x) = \{0, 1, \ldots, 21\} \Rightarrow \quad bitDom[x]$$

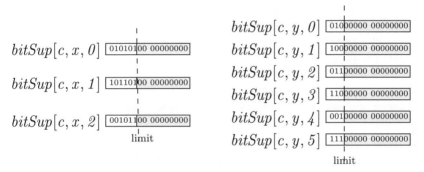

$$dom(x) = \{7, 14, 19, 21\} \Rightarrow \quad bitDom[x]$$

Figure 4.13. *Binary representation of a domain, considering here words of size* 16

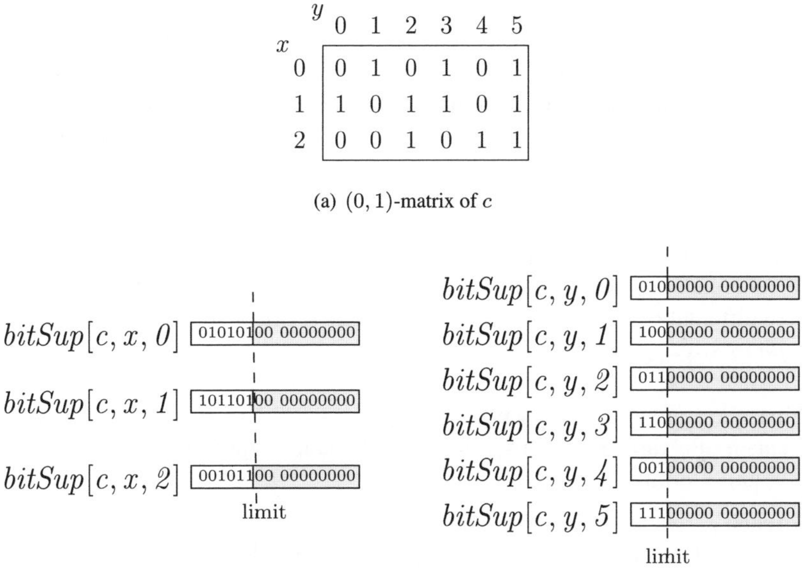

(a) (0, 1)-matrix of c

(b) Binary representation of c

Figure 4.14. *Binary representation of a constraint* c, *considering here words of size* 16. *We have* scp(c) = $\{x, y\}$ *with* dom(x) = $\{0, 1, 2\}$ *and* dom(y) = $\{0, 1, 2, 3, 4, 5\}$

We propose to use a multi-dimensional array called $bitSup$ to obtain a *binary representation* of constraints. More precisely, for each c-value (c, x, a), $bitSup[c, x, a]$ represents the binary representation of the (initial) supports for (x, a) on c. To simplify the presentation and without any loss of generality, we can assume that each (initial) domain contains all positive integer values strictly smaller than a given value: a domain whose size is d is $\{0, 1, \ldots, d-1\}$. If c is such that scp(c) = $\{x, y\}$, then $(a, b) \in$ rel(c) iff the bit at index b in $bitSup[c, x, a]$ is set to 1 and the bit at index a in $bitSup[c, y, b]$ is set to 1. An illustration is given in Figure 4.14, again using 16-bit words.

Building the *bitSup* array does not present any particular difficulty if the constraints are initially given to the solver in extensional form. On the other hand, if the constraints are given in intension, then all constraints checks have to be performed initially (by evaluating a predicate) in order to build *bitSup*. Assuming that each constraint check is performed in constant time, this incurs an initial overhead of $\Theta(ed^2)$. However, for similar predicates and similar signatures of constraints (i.e. similar Cartesian products built from the domains associated with the variables involved in the constraints), sub-arrays of *bitSup* can be shared, potentially saving a large amount of space and initial constraint checks.

The worst-case space complexity of the binary representation of constraints is $\Theta(ed^2)$, while the best-case space complexity is $\Theta(e + d^2)$, which corresponds to sharing the same binary representation between all constraints. The worst-case is associated with unstructured (random) instances, while the best-case corresponds to structured (academic or real-world) instances that usually involve similar constraints.

4.5.3.1.3. Exploiting binary representations

We can now use binary representations of domains and constraints to implement some computations efficiently by using bitwise operators. We illustrate our purpose in three different contexts. Note that for any array t, $t[0]$ denotes its first element and $t.length$ its size.

First, the following sequence of instructions can be used to determine whether the domain of a variable x is a subset of the domain of another variable y (such that $\mathrm{dom}^{\mathrm{init}}(x) = \mathrm{dom}^{\mathrm{init}}(y)$):

foreach i *from* 0 *to* $bitDom[x].length - 1$ **do**
    if $(bitDom[x][i]$ OR $bitDom[y][i]) \neq bitDom[y][i]$ **then**
        └ **return** *false*
return *true*

This kind of computation may be useful, for example, when implementing a symmetry-breaking method by dominance detection; see Chapter 12. In that case, we can compare the current domain of a variable with one that was recorded earlier, perhaps from the same variable. This computation can determine efficiently whether one state is dominated by another.

Second, the following sequence of instructions checks whether, for a binary constraint c involving a variable x, a v-value (x, a) is c-substitutable for a v-value (x, b) (see Definition 4.9):

foreach i *from* 0 *to* $bitSup[c, x, a].length - 1$ **do**
    if $(bitSup[c, x, a][i]$ OR $bitSup[c, x, b][i]) \neq bitSup[c, x, a][i]$ **then**
        └ **return** *false*
return *true*

Neighborhood substitutability has been introduced in [FRE 91] and is defined as follows: given a variable x and two values $\{a, b\} \subseteq \text{dom}(x)$, (x, a) is neighborhood-substitutable for (x, b) iff for every constraint $c \mid x \in \text{scp}(c)$, (x, a) is c-substitutable for (x, b). The code presented above can be useful in practice to reduce the search space by eliminating neighborhood-substitutable values (e.g. see [BEL 94, COO 97]).

Finally, the following sequence of instructions can be used to check whether there exists at least one support for a v-value (x, a) on a constraint c (involving x and a second variable y):

> **foreach** i *from* 0 *to* $bitDom[y].length - 1$ **do**
> $\quad$ **if** $(bitSup[c, x, a][i]\ AND\ bitDom[y][i]) \neq ZERO$ **then**
> $\quad\quad$ **return** *true*
> **return** *false*

Note that $ZERO$ denotes a word defined as a sequence of bits all set to 0. This way of seeking a support was described and used in [ULL 76, MCG 79]. We now provide a detailed modern formulation of this approach.

For all operations described above, a Boolean answer may be obtained before all the words have been iterated over. For example, for all three operations, it is possible to obtain a result after a bitwise operation on the first pair of words (i.e. where $i = 0$). However, performing a bitwise operation on bit vectors, and then comparing the result with another bit vector, can be much more expensive.

4.5.3.2. *Algorithms AC3^{bit} and AC3$^{\text{bit}+\text{rm}}$*

Algorithm AC3^{bit} [LEC 08c] is a derivative of AC3 in which revision is performed by the function revise, Algorithm 8 or the function revise^{CS}, Algorithm 23. In AC3^{bit} the function used to seek supports is seekSupport-3^{bit}, Algorithm 25. Given the binary representation $bitDom[y]$ of $\text{dom}(y)$ and the binary representation $bitSup[c_{xy}, x, a]$ of the (initial) supports for (x, a) on c_{xy}, AC3^{bit} executes the code presented earlier.

Algorithm 25: seekSupport-3^{bit}((c_{xy}, x, a): c-value): Boolean

---

Require: c_{xy} is binary with $\text{scp}(c_{xy}) = \{x, y\}$
Output: *true* iff $\sup(c_{xy})_{x=a} \neq \emptyset$

1 **foreach** i *from* 0 *to* $bitDom[y].length - 1$ **do**
2 $\quad$ **if** $(bitSup[c_{xy}, x, a][i]\ AND\ bitDom[y][i]) \neq ZERO$ **then**
3 $\quad\quad$ **return** *true*

4 **return** *false*

PROPOSITION 4.19.– *The worst-case time complexity of AC3^{bit} is $O(ed^3)$.*

The proof is immediate. The following observation indicates that in practice, AC3^{bit} can be far more efficient than the other AC3-based variants. This was illustrated in the introduction to this section.

OBSERVATION 4.20.– *The number of bitwise operations performed by AC3^{bit} can be up to p times less than the number of constraint checks performed by AC3, AC2001 and AC3^{rm}, where p is the word size of the computer.*

At this point, one can wonder if there is still an interest of exploiting residues for binary instances. For domains having up to 300 values, checking whether a c-value has a support requires not more than five operations (on a 64-bit architecture). However, when domains become larger, the cost of simple bitwise operations can become penalizing. This is why bit vectors are combined with residues in Algorithm 26, which uses a three-dimensional array *res* of integers (all set to 0 initially). We obtain a new AC3 variant called AC3$^{\mathrm{bit+rm}}$. Whenever a support is detected, its position in the binary representation of the constraint is recorded. When seeking a support in Algorithm 26, the residual position is first checked (line 2), and when a support is found, its position is recorded (line 6).

Algorithm 26: seekSupport-3$^{\mathrm{bit+rm}}((c_{xy}, x, a)$: c-value): Boolean

---

Require: c_{xy} is binary with $\mathrm{scp}(c_{xy}) = \{x, y\}$
Output: *true* iff $\sup(c_{xy})_{x=a} \neq \emptyset$

1 $i \leftarrow res[c_{xy}, x, a]$
2 **if** $(bitSup[c_{xy}, x, a][i]$ AND $bitDom[y][i]) \neq ZERO$ **then**
3 $\quad$ | **return** *true*

4 **foreach** i *from* 0 *to* $bitDom[y].length - 1$ **do**
5 $\quad$ | **if** $(bitSup[c_{xy}, x, a][i]$ AND $bitDom[y][i]) \neq ZERO$ **then**
6 $\quad$ | $\quad$ | $res[c_{xy}, x, a] \leftarrow i$
7 $\quad$ | $\quad$ | **return** *true*

8 **return** *false*

To illustrate the importance of combining bitwise operations with residues when domains are large, Table 4.3 shows results obtained on instances of the Domino problem. Remember that this problem was introduced to emphasize the sub-optimality of AC3. For the most difficult instance, where domains contain 3000 values, AC3$^{\mathrm{bit+rm}}$ is about 5 times more efficient than AC3^{bit} and AC3^{rm}, and is 9 times more efficient than AC2001.

Instance		AC2001	AC3	AC3^{rm}	AC3^{bit}	AC3$^{\text{bit+rm}}$
domino-	CPU	12.7	403	9.4	4.3	3.7
500-500	mem	27	23	27	23	23
domino-	CPU	89.5	5,911	62.4	25.1	14.3
1000-1000	mem	66	42	54	42	46
domino-	CPU	678	> 5 hours	443	289	91
2000-2000	mem	210		156	117	132
domino-	CPU	2,349	> 5 hours	1,564	1,274	278
3000-3000	mem	454		322	240	275

Table 4.3. *Establishing arc consistency on* Domino *instances*

4.6. Experimental results

This section reports a few experimental results, starting with binary networks. These are experiments with different AC algorithms embedded in MAC which is the algorithm that maintains arc consistency during the search for a solution; MAC is presented in Chapter 8. MAC is used here because this is the usual way of solving constraint networks (when a complete approach is employed), so the behavior of arc consistency algorithms in this context is particularly important. During the search, these experiments use the variable ordering heuristic *dom/wdeg* and the value ordering heuristic *min-conflicts*: these heuristics are presented in Chapter 9. These experiments do not use any restart policy. The general algorithm used is enforceGAC^{var}, Algorithm 9, calling the function revise^{CS}, Algorithm 23. Within this framework, we report experimental results obtained with arc consistency algorithms AC3, AC2001, AC3^{rm} and AC3^{bit} running on our platform Abscon using a computer equipped with a 2.4 GHz i686 Intel CPU, 512MB of RAM and Sun JRE 5.0 for Linux. We report results for random, academic and real-world problems. Performance[6] is measured in terms of the CPU time in seconds and the amount of memory (mem) in megabytes.

We have experimented with seven classes of binary random instances generated by Model D. For each class $\langle n, d, e, t \rangle$, the number of variables n has been set to 40, the domain size d set between 8 and 180, the number of constraints e set between 753 and 84 (so the density between 0.1 and 0.96) and the tightness t, which here denotes the probability that a relation forbids a pair of values, set between 0.1 and 0.9. In Table 4.4, even for small domains (e.g. $d = 8$), MAC3^{bit} is the fastest algorithm on binary random instances; it is from two to four times faster than MAC2001 and from 1.5 to

---

6. In these experiments, all constraint checks are performed in constant time and are as cheap as possible since constraints are represented in extension.

Instance		MAC embedding			
		AC2001	AC3	AC3^{rm}	AC3^{bit}

Random instances (100 instances per series)

Instance		AC2001	AC3	AC3^{rm}	AC3^{bit}
$\langle 40, 8, 753, 0.1 \rangle$	CPU	13.8	9.8	10.4	7.7
	mem	11	9.5	10	9.5
$\langle 40, 11, 414, 0.2 \rangle$	CPU	19.6	15.0	14.5	10.0
	mem	8.8	8.0	8.4	8.0
$\langle 40, 16, 250, 0.35 \rangle$	CPU	21.6	18.5	16.1	9.7
	mem	8.5	7.9	8.2	7.9
$\langle 40, 25, 180, 0.5 \rangle$	CPU	28.9	27.8	21.2	11.5
	mem	8.4	7.9	8.2	7.9
$\langle 40, 40, 135, 0.65 \rangle$	CPU	21.1	22.0	15.4	7.8
	mem	8.5	8.0	8.2	8.1
$\langle 40, 80, 103, 0.8 \rangle$	CPU	16.6	19.5	12.2	5.0
	mem	10	9.5	9.8	9.6
$\langle 40, 180, 84, 0.9 \rangle$	CPU	24.3	36.6	18.4	6.7
	mem	15	14	14	14

Structured instances

Instance		AC2001	AC3	AC3^{rm}	AC3^{bit}
blackHole-4-4	CPU	1.46	1.37	1.35	0.91
(10 instances)	mem	8.6	7.9	8.7	7.9
driver	CPU	3.89	2.99	3.14	2.75
(7 instances)	mem	35	24	56	24
ehi-85	CPU	1.75	0.92	1.12	0.71
(100 instances)	mem	30	19	38	19
ehi-90	CPU	1.73	0.91	1.11	0.72
(100 instances)	mem	31	20	39	20
enddr1	CPU	1,616	1,694	1,218	453
(10 instances)	mem	14	13	14	13
enddr2	CPU	1,734	2,818	1,491	568
(6 instances)	mem	15	14	15	14
geom	CPU	12.4	10.8	8.9	5.8
(100 instances)	mem	11	10	11	10
hanoi	CPU	1.00	1.16	1.11	0.50
(5 instances)	mem	13	11	12	12
qwh-20	CPU	266	183	242	153
(10 instances)	mem	33	21	44	21

Table 4.4. *Mean results of MAC, embedding various AC algorithms, on series of binary random and structured instances*

Instance		MAC embedding				
		GAC3	GAC3^{r}	GAC3^{rm}	GAC2001	GAC3.2

Random instances (mean results for 10 instances)

Instance		GAC3	GAC3^{r}	GAC3^{rm}	GAC2001	GAC3.2
$\langle 6, 20, 6, 32, 0.55 \rangle$	CPU	0.75	0.50	0.46	0.58	0.49
	#ccks	676 K	357 K	278 K	364 K	235 K
$\langle 6, 20, 6, 36, 0.55 \rangle$	CPU	13.1	8.7	8.0	10.2	8.5
	#ccks	12 M	6,481 K	4,997 K	6,825 K	4,324 K
$\langle 6, 20, 8, 22, 0.75 \rangle$	CPU	2.5	1.5	1.3	1.6	1.3
	#ccks	2,313 K	1,240 K	971 K	1,232 K	804 K
$\langle 6, 20, 8, 24, 0.75 \rangle$	CPU	51.7	31.8	27.7	34.6	26.8
	#ccks	48 M	26 M	20 M	26 M	17 M
$\langle 6, 20, 10, 13, 0.95 \rangle$	CPU	35.2	20.7	15.8	20.8	13.9
	#ccks	40 M	23 M	17 M	22 M	14 M
$\langle 6, 20, 10, 14, 0.95 \rangle$	CPU	220	135	102	135	89
	#ccks	249 M	151 M	108 M	149 M	91 M
$\langle 6, 20, 20, 10, 0.99 \rangle$	CPU	659	392	267	254	177
	#ccks	1,653 M	1,037 M	647 M	662 M	462 M
$\langle 6, 20, 20, 15, 0.99 \rangle$	CPU	869	489	301	351	220
	#ccks	2255 M	1,289 M	785 M	887 M	583 M

Structured instances

Instance		GAC3	GAC3^{r}	GAC3^{rm}	GAC2001	GAC3.2
tsp-20-366	CPU	387	242	243	266	235
	#ccks	607 M	370	364 M	387 M	333 M
gr-44-9-a3	CPU	73.1	37.2	38.4	56.3	43.6
	#ccks	166 M	44 M	41 M	74 M	33 M
gr-44-10-a3	CPU	2,945	1,401	1,465	2,129	1,631
	#ccks	6,819 M	1,513 M	1,527 M	2,914 M	1,224 M
series-14	CPU	233	218	217	312	285
	#ccks	1,135 M	531 M	490 M	618 M	422 M
renault	CPU	25.0	25.4	16.2	25.2	15.2
	#ccks	68 M	66 M	42 M	66 M	42 M

Table 4.5. *Results of MAC, embedding various GAC algorithms, on non-binary random and structured instances*

3 times more efficient than MAC3^{rm}. The behavior of MAC3^{bit} on different series of binary structured instances is also good: MAC3^{bit} outperforms the other algorithms in Table 4.4. This is particularly true for the job-shop series enddr1 and enddr2 in which the average domain size is about 120 values, so only two main operations are required when seeking a support on a 64-bit processor.

When applied to non-binary instances, the behavior of an algorithm that exploits residues is of particular interest. In this section, c-value complexity means the total worst-case time complexity of seeking a support for a given c-value. Note first that seeking a support for a c-value from scratch requires iterating over $O(d^{r-1})$ tuples in the worst-case for a constraint of arity r. Thus the c-value complexity is $O(r^2 d^r)$ for GAC3 and $O(rd^{r-1})$ for GAC2001 [BES 05c], assuming that a constraint check is $O(r)$ and remembering that there are possibly $O(rd)$ calls to the implemented seekSupport function. We conclude that the difference is a factor rd, so the difference between the two algorithms grows linearly with r (if d is invariant). On the other hand, if $\text{c} > 0$ and $\text{s} > 0$ denote the number of conflicts and supports, respectively, for a given c-value, then the c-value complexity can be shown to be $O(\text{c}\text{s}r)$ for GAC3^{rm}; this complexity is also $O(r^2 d^r)$. If $\text{c} = O(1)$ or $\text{s} = O(1)$, the c-value complexity becomes $O(rd^{r-1})$ for GAC3^{rm} because $\text{c} + \text{s} = d^{r-1}$; this is the same complexity as GAC2001. But in practice we are unlikely to have small (bounded) values of c or s when dealing with non-binary constraints.

On series of non-binary random instances, we have performed experiments with algorithms that maintain GAC during search. These instances belong to classes of the form $\langle k, n, d, e, t \rangle$ where k denotes the arity of the constraints and all other parameters are defined as usual. In these experiments the arity is six and the tightness $t \in \{0.55, 0, 75, 0.95, 0.99\}$. For small values of t, we find (as in the binary case) that the difference between all algorithms is slight. In Table 4.5, GAC3^{rm} and GAC3.2 are the most efficient embedded algorithms. Of course, when the tightness is high, GAC3 is penalized and GAC3^{r} is less efficient than GAC3^{rm} because exploitation of multi-directionality pays off. GAC3^{r} and GAC3^{rm} showed good behavior on non-binary structured instances within the 2005 constraint solver competition.

4.7. Discussion

The lessons I have learned over the years, partly from my experience with the constraint solver Abscon, are the following. For binary constraints, generic AC algorithms can be quite competitive, compared to specialized filtering procedures, provided that the size of the domains is not too large and/or the cardinality of conflict sets is exploited. An algorithm such as AC3$^{\text{bit+rm}}$ is appropriate up to a few hundred values per domain. This is the fastest generic AC algorithm when binary constraints are extensional. For binary intensional constraints (that cannot be translated efficiently into extension), AC3^{rm} seems the best option since this algorithm benefits from complexity results on the theoretical side, and backtrack-stable data structures on the practical side. For non-binary constraints, the situation is a little bit more complex. If the constraints are defined in extension, then specialized table constraint algorithms are appropriate; such algorithms are introduced in the next chapter. If the constraints are defined in intension, using an algorithm such as $GAC3^{rm}$ may be the right solution if the semantic of the constraints is not known to be exploitable or if the number of valid tuples (that will be iterated over) is not too large. For global constraints, except where a decomposition can be handled efficiently using a general-purpose filtering algorithm, a specialized filtering procedure is certainly a good choice.

Chapter 5

Generalized Arc Consistency for Table Constraints

This chapter is concerned with efficient filtering procedures for table constraints. Here the word *table* means the same thing as *extensional* except that table constraints are usually non-binary. A table constraint is defined by explicitly listing the tuples that are either allowed or disallowed for the variables of its scope. In the former case, the table constraint is said to be *positive*, while in the latter case, it is said *negative*. Table constraints are also sometimes referred to as *ad-hoc* (non-binary) constraints [CHE 06].

Table constraints arise naturally in configuration problems, where they represent available combinations of options. For some applications, compatibilities (or incompatibilities) between resources, e.g. people or machines, can be expressed in tables. For example, for use in the selection of k people to form a working group, a table may enumerate possible associations according to certain abilities while taking into account a (subjective) agreement criterion. Another example is that in some puzzles, e.g. crosswords, non-binary constraints can only be expressed extensionally. Tabular data may also come from databases: the results of database queries are sometimes expressed as tables that have large arity. It is well known (e.g. see [GYS 94]) that there are strong theoretical connections between relational database theory and constraint satisfaction.

Table constraints are important in constraint programming because they are easily handled by end-users of constraint systems. For simplicity reasons, an inexperienced user sometimes specifies extensional constraints although some of these should preferably be intensional. It is crucial to handle such extensional constraints as efficiently as possible, ideally as though their semantics were known (or, why not, even better). Furthermore, because any constraint can theoretically be expressed in tabular form (although this may lead to a time and space explosion), tables provide a universal way of representing constraints.

Some recent research articles have focused on theoretical and practical aspects of table constraints. As a result, there are many new ways to enforce generalized arc consistency (GAC) on table constraints and/or to compress their representation. It is likely that several of these new techniques will soon be combined to achieve further improvements in propagation speed. This chapter therefore attempts a substantial overview of these approaches.

This chapter is predominantly concerned with positive table constraints. Section 5.1 introduces two classical schemes, which iterate over valid tuples and allowed tuples, respectively. Section 5.2 introduces auxiliary indexing structures for tables. Next, section 5.3 compares approaches that use memory-efficient graph-like structures to represent tables. Section 5.4 explains how the two basic classical schemes can be combined, and section 5.5 introduces an original approach based on reduction of tables. Finally, we deal with negative table constraints in section 5.6.

5.1. Classical schemes

The general-purpose algorithms presented in sections 4.3 and 4.5 can be used to establish GAC on (positive) table constraints. There are two different ways in which these algorithms can seek a support. The support-seeking scheme called *GAC-valid* iterates over valid tuples until an allowed one is found; basic functions to realize this scheme were presented in section 4.2. The other natural support-seeking scheme, which is called *GAC-allowed*, iterates over allowed tuples until a valid one is found. Roughly speaking, GAC-valid and GAC-allowed correspond to GAC-scheme-predicate and GAC-scheme-allowed, respectively, in [BES 97].

After some further preparatory work on positive table constraints, the following sections present these two classical schemes. For simplicity, we present these schemes within GAC3, but they can directly and easily be adapted to other coarse-grained generalized arc consistency algorithms such as e.g. GAC2001 and GAC3^{rm}.

5.1.1. *Positive table constraints*

A positive table constraint is a constraint given in extension and defined by a set of allowed tuples. As in Chapter 1, the set of allowed tuples associated with a positive table constraint c is denoted by $table[c]$. This set is represented here by an array of tuples indexed from 1 to $table[c].length$ which denotes the size of the table (i.e. the number of allowed tuples). To record this set, the worst-case space complexity is $O(tr)$ where $t = table[c].length$ and r is the arity of c.

We are often interested in the list of allowed tuples that include a v-value (x, a). For every c-value (c, x, a), we can consider the *sub-table* $table[c, x, a]$ of allowed tuples involving (x, a), from $table[c]$. This is an array whose indices ranges from 1 to $table[c, x, a].length$, such that any element $table[c, x, a][i]$ gives the position (index) in $table[c]$ of the ith allowed tuple involving (x, a). Thus sub-tables are indexing structures, as illustrated in Figure 5.1.

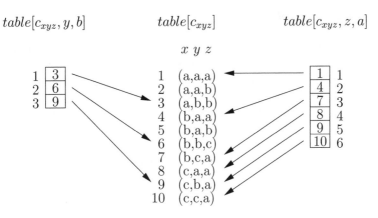

$$table[c_{xyz}, y, b] \qquad table[c_{xyz}] \qquad table[c_{xyz}, z, a]$$

Figure 5.1. c_{xyz} *is a positive table constraint for which* $table[c_{xyz}]$ *contains* 10 *allowed tuples. We have* $\mathrm{dom}(x) = \mathrm{dom}(y) = \mathrm{dom}(z) = \{a, b, c\}$. *The sub-tables* $table[c_{xyz}, y, b]$ *and* $table[c_{xyz}, z, a]$ *are shown*

The total space complexity of sub-tables is $O(tr)$ because each tuple in $table[c]$ is referenced exactly r times. Consequently, overall worst-case space complexity remains $O(tr)$. Assuming that each sub-table is in the lexicographic order of referenced tuples, the worst-case time complexity of checking (using a binary search) whether a tuple τ involving (x, a) is allowed by c is $O(\log(t_{c,x,a})r)$ where $t_{c,x,a} = table[c, x, a].length$.

Instead of providing indexes, an alternative is a hash map giving "direct" access to allowed tuples. This has been proposed in [BES 97] for negative table constraints. The worst-case space complexity remains $O(tr)$. If the hash function is $O(r)$ and if it randomizes properly, the worst-case time complexity of performing a constraint check is only $O(r)$. This hashing approach will not be considered in this chapter.

5.1.2. *GAC-valid scheme*

As explained in section 4.2, GAC-valid iterates over valid tuples until an allowed one is found. We now describe a GAC-valid implementation of a constraint check in GAC3 for a positive table constraint. The test $\tau \in \mathrm{rel}(c)$ at line 3 of

Algorithm 18 corresponds to the test $\tau \in table[c, x, a]$, which is $O(\log(t_{c,x,a})r)$ with $t_{c,x,a} = table[c, x, a].length$ since one can use a binary search (i.e. a dichotomic divide and conquer search algorithm), as mentioned above. Assuming that the function binarySearch handles the indirection (so as to compare a tuple τ with the element of $table[c]$ at index $table[c, x, a][i]$, i being the position of the element of $table[c, x, a]$ to be checked) and returns τ when τ is present, the test $\tau \in \mathrm{rel}(c)$ corresponds to:

$$\mathsf{binarySearch}(table[c, x, a], \tau) = \tau$$

We use seekSupport-v as an alias for seekSupport-3 when the GAC-valid scheme is employed; this function is called in Algorithm 8. The number of valid tuples built from c and involving (x, a) is $v_{c,x,a} = |\mathrm{val}(c)_{x=a}|$, so we have:

PROPOSITION 5.1.– *For an r-ary positive table constraint c, the worst-case time complexity of* seekSupport-v, *with input* (c, x, a), *is* $O(v_{c,x,a} \log(t_{c,x,a})r)$.

COROLLARY 5.2.– *Using a hash map with a hash function in* $O(r)$ *achieving ideal randomization, the worst-case time complexity of function* seekSupport-v *is* $O(v_{c,x,a}r)$.

5.1.3. *GAC-allowed scheme*

GAC-allowed iterates over allowed tuples in the table until a valid one is found. As already mentioned, for simplicity we now describe a GAC-allowed implementation of GAC3; we do not handle last supports as in GAC2001, or residual supports as in GAC3^{rm}.

Algorithm 27: seekSupport-a$((c, x, a)$: c-value): Boolean

// Implementation of GAC-allowed
1   $i \leftarrow 1$
2   **while** $i \leq table[c, x, a].length$ **do**
3      $index \leftarrow table[c, x, a][i]$
4      $\tau \leftarrow table[c][index]$
5   **if** *isValidTuple*(c, τ) **then**
6   **return** *true*
7      $i \leftarrow i + 1$
8   **return** *false*

The function seekSupport-a, Algorithm 27, to be called at line 3 of Algorithm 8, checks the validity of each allowed tuple until a support is found. The function isValidTuple checks whether all values in the given tuple belong to corresponding current domains. The time complexity of isValidTuple is $O(r)$: see Algorithm 15.

PROPOSITION 5.3.– *For an r-ary positive table constraint c, the worst-case time complexity of* **seekSupport-a**, *with input (c, x, a), is $O(t_{c,x,a}r)$.*

5.1.4. *Illustration*

Unfortunately, there are considerable penalties associated with visiting only lists of valid or allowed tuples. This is why many alternatives have been developed, and these are presented in the following sections. In the following example, which illustrates potential drawbacks of both classical schemes, a constraint c involves r variables $x_1, \ldots, x_r$ such that the domain of each variable is initially $\{0, 1, 2\}$. Suppose that exactly 2^{r-1} tuples are allowed by c: these correspond to the binary representation of all values between 0 and $2^{r-1} - 2$ together with the tuple $(2, 2, ..., 2, 2)$, as illustrated in Figure 5.2(a) with $r = 5$. Suppose also that, due to propagation caused by other

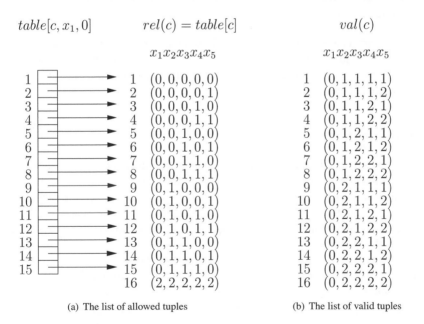

(a) The list of allowed tuples   (b) The list of valid tuples

Figure 5.2. *Constraint c is such that $\mathrm{scp}(c) = \{x_1, x_2, x_3, x_4, x_5\}$ and $\mathrm{rel}(c) = table[c]$ contains 2^4 (allowed) tuples, as shown. Currently, $\mathrm{dom}(x_1) = \{0\}$ and $\forall i \in 2..5, \mathrm{dom}(x_i) = \{1, 2\}$, so $\mathrm{val}(c)$ contains 2^4 (valid) tuples*

constraints, the domains of all variables have been reduced to $\{1, 2\}$ except for the variable x_1 whose domain has been reduced to $\{0\}$. After this propagation, there are exactly 2^{r-1} valid tuples that can be built for c, as illustrated in Figure 5.2(b) with $r = 5$.

Now consider checking whether there is a support for $(x_1, 0)$ on c. Using GAC-valid, the time complexity of determining that $(x_1, 0)$ has no support on c is $\Omega(2^{r-1})$ because 2^{r-1} valid tuples are processed. GAC-allowed has also time complexity $\Omega(2^{r-1})$ because it reviews $2^{r-1} - 1$ allowed tuples to prove that $(x_1, 0)$ has no support on c. The behavior of both schemes is unsatisfactory because it is immediate that $(x_1, 0)$ is generalized arc-inconsistent.

5.2. Indexing-based approaches

This section presents two approaches that associate auxiliary functions/structures with tables. The idea is to associate with each tuple of each table some pointers to next tuples involving particular values. This is an index structure for use in seeking supports. We shall elucidate the relationship between these two approaches to indexing.

We do not classify the GAC-allowed as an indexing-based approach because indexing from sub-tables does not worsen space complexity. Furthermore, sub-tables introduced mainly for GAC-allowed are not strictly necessary (although this point is not exhaustively covered in this book).

5.2.1. NextIn indexing

The first approach [LHO 05b] combines both the concept of "acceptability" (the fact that a tuple is accepted by a constraint) and the concept of validity (the fact that each value in a tuple is valid). A function, called nextIn, indicates for each c-value (c, x, a) and each tuple τ in $table[c]$, the smallest tuple in $table[c]$ that is greater than or equal to τ (according to the lexicographic order) and that contains (x, a). More precisely, this function is defined as follows:

DEFINITION 5.4.– [nextIn] Let c be a positive table constraint. For every c-value (c, x, a) and every tuple $\tau \in table[c]$, we have:

– nextIn$((c, x, a), \tau) = nil$ if $\forall \tau' \in table[c], \tau' \geq_{\text{lex}} \tau \Rightarrow \tau'[x] \neq a$;

– nextIn$((c, x, a), \tau) = \tau'$; otherwise where $\tau' \in table[c], \tau'[x] = a, \tau' \geq_{\text{lex}} \tau$ and $\forall \tau'' \in table[c], \tau' >_{\text{lex}} \tau'' \geq_{\text{lex}} \tau \Rightarrow \tau''[x] \neq a$.

We implement nextIn using a multi-dimensional array, also denoted by $nextIn$, such that for each c-value (c, x, a) and each tuple τ at index i in $table[c]$, we have nextIn$((c, x, a), \tau) = table[c][nextIn[c, x, a][i]]$. Observe that $nextIn[c, x, a][i]$

gives the index i' in $table[c]$ of tuple nextIn$((c, x, a), \tau)$. We have $i' \geq i$, and $i' = table[c].length + 1$ signifies nextIn$((c, x, a), \tau) = nil$. The space complexity required for each constraint c is $O(trd)$. A different implementation uses a data structure called a hologram [LHO 04] to save space.

EXAMPLE.– In Figure 5.3(a), which provides an illustration, the first row of the two-dimensional array under the first tuple (a, a, a) of $table[c_{xyz}]$ corresponds to $nextIn[c_{xyz}, x, a][1]$, $nextIn[c_{xyz}, y, a][1]$ and $nextIn[c_{xyz}, z, a][1]$. The second row correspond to $nextIn[c_{xyz}, x, b][1]$, $nextIn[c_{xyz}, y, b][1]$ and $nextIn[c_{xyz}, z, b][1]$, etc. In these arrays the special value 11 is the position of "the tuple" nil, meaning that the last tuple has been reached.

Note that for every c-value (c, x, a) $nextIn$ is powerful enough to be used in searching over the tuples (indexed) in $table[c, x, a]$. If $nextIn$ is provided then there is no need to associate sub-tables with the c-values.

EXAMPLE.– To iterate over the (indices of the) three first tuples of $table[c]$ that involve (x, a) (i.e. the three first tuples that would be indexed in $table[c, x, a]$), we can write:

$$i \leftarrow nextIn[c, x, a][1]$$
$$j \leftarrow nextIn[c, x, a][i + 1]$$
$$k \leftarrow nextIn[c, x, a][j + 1]$$

In Figure 5.3(a), we obtain $i = 1$, $j = 2$ and $k = 3$ for the c-value (c_{xyz}, x, a), and $i = 1, j = 4$ and $k = 7$ for the c-value (c_{xyz}, z, a). Notice that $nextIn[c_{xyz}, x, a][1]$ and $nextIn[c_{xyz}, z, a][1]$ are equal to 1, because the first tuple in $table[c_{xyz}]$ contains both (x, a) and (z, a).

To enforce GAC using this approach, denoted by GAC-nextIn, the function seekSupport-ni, Algorithm 28, is called at line 3 of Algorithm 8. This basically corresponds to the code used in Algorithm 5 of [LHO 05b]. However, in the present section, we do not manage lower bounds of supports, but instead focus on the main aspects of the algorithm. To simplify the presentation, we assume that for every c-value (c, x, a), $nextIn[c, x, a][i] = table[c].length + 1$ if $i = table[c].length + 1$; this avoids the insertion of three additional tests in the algorithm. The index of the first tuple involving (x, a) in $table[c]$ is obtained at line 1. Then, so long as the current tuple is not valid, we find the index of another one (lines 6 to 15), by using current domains to accelerate traversal of the table. The new index obtained at line 15 gives the position of a tuple involving (x, a) that is a lower bound of the smallest support for (c, x, a). Initially, the index i' of the next tuple of $table[c]$ after i involving (x, a) is considered (note that we have $i + 1$ at line 6). For each variable y involved in c, the index min of the first tuple (after i') involving a valid value for y is computed (see lines 10 to 12). By taking the maximum value over all min indices, we safely skip some tuples that cannot be supports for (x, a) on c. Finally, the index of the next tuple of $table[c]$ involving (x, a) is obtained at line 15.

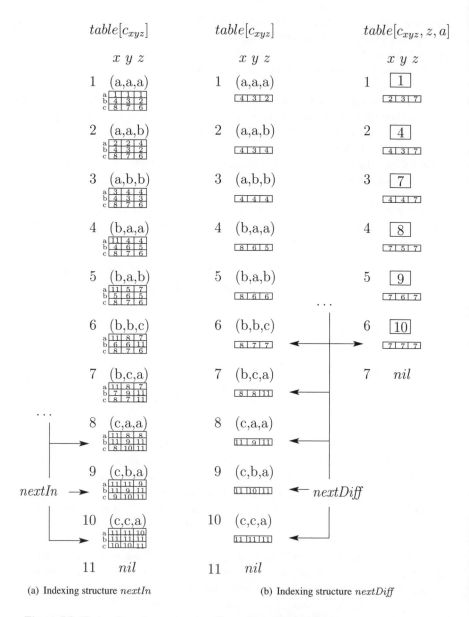

Figure 5.3. *Illustration of structures nextIn and nextDiff with a ternary constraint c_{xyz} defined by a positive table composed of 10 tuples. We have*
$$\text{dom}(x) = \text{dom}(y) = \text{dom}(z) = \{a, b, c\}$$

Algorithm 28: seekSupport-ni((c, x, a): c-value): Boolean

// Implementation of GAC-nextIn

1 $i \leftarrow nextIn[c, x, a][1]$

2 **while** $i \leq table[c].length$ **do**

3       $\tau \leftarrow table[c][i]$

4   **if** *isValidTuple*(c, τ) **then**

5   **return** *true*

6       $i' \leftarrow nextIn[c, x, a][i + 1]$ // $i' = i + 1$ if $i = table[c].length$

7       $max \leftarrow i'$

8   **foreach** *variable* $y \in scp(c) \mid y \neq x$ **do**

9           $min \leftarrow table[c].length + 1$

10   **foreach** *value* $b \in dom(y)$ **do**

11   **if** $nextIn[c, y, b][i'] < min$ **then**

12                   $min \leftarrow nextIn[c, y, b][i']$

13   **if** $min > max$ **then**

14               $max \leftarrow min$

15       $i \leftarrow nextIn[c, x, a][max]$ // $i = max$ if $max = table[c].length + 1$

16 **return** *false*

A variant, introduced in this book and denoted by GAC-nextIn[b], is implemented by function seekSupport-ni[b], Algorithm 29, and only considers the first variable (the leftmost one in the scope) identified by function getFirstInvalidPosition, Algorithm 16, whose value is not valid. The advantage is that we concentrate our effort on the most significant variable, which may provide us with the biggest skip.

EXAMPLE.– Figure 5.4 provides an illustration of both algorithms. Another example is that of Figure 5.2, where the behavior of GAC-nextIn and GAC-nextIn[b] is similar when searching for a support for $(x_1, 0)$ on c. More precisely, both algorithms have the following successive values of the variable i.

– $i = 1$: we have $\tau = (0, 0, 0, 0, 0)$.

– $i = 2^3 = 8$: since the best safe skip comes from $(x_2, 1)$, we have $\tau = (0, 1, 0, 0, 0)$;

– $i = 2^3 + 2^2 = 12$: since the best safe skip comes from $(x_3, 1)$, we have $\tau = (0, 1, 1, 0, 0)$;

– $i = 2^4 - 1$: since the best safe skip comes from $(x_4, 1)$, we have $\tau = (0, 1, 1, 1, 0)$;

– $i = 17$: since there is no further tuple involving $(x_1, 0)$, we have $\tau = nil$.

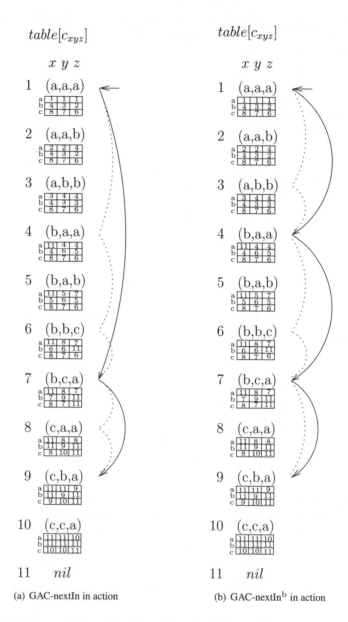

$table[c_{xyz}]$ $table[c_{xyz}]$

(a) GAC-nextIn in action   (b) GAC-nextIn^b in action

Figure 5.4. *Effort required by GAC-nextIn and GAC-nextIn^b to find $\tau = (c, b, a)$ as smallest support of (c_{xyz}, z, a) after the removal of a and c from $\mathrm{dom}(y)$. We have $\mathrm{dom}(x) = \mathrm{dom}(z) = \{a, b, c\}$ and $\mathrm{dom}(y) = \{b\}$. Solid arcs correspond to successive values of i*

Algorithm 29: seekSupport-ni^b((c, x, a): c-value): Boolean

// Implementation of GAC-nextIn^b

1    $i \leftarrow nextIn[c, x, a][1]$

2   **while** $i \leq table[c].length$ **do**

3      $\tau \leftarrow table[c][i]$

4      $j \leftarrow$ getFirstInvalidPosition(c, τ)

5   **if** $j = -1$ **then**

6        $\llcorner$ **return** *true*

7      $y \leftarrow scp(c)[j]$ // y is the jth variable of $scp(c)$

8      $min \leftarrow table[c].length + 1$

9   **foreach** *value* $b \in$ dom(y) **do**

10   **if** $nextIn[c, y, b][i] < min$ **then**

11          $\llcorner$ $min \leftarrow nextIn[c, y, b][i]$

12      $\llcorner$ $i \leftarrow nextIn[c, x, a][min]$ // $i = min$ if $min = table[c].length + 1$

13 **return** *false*

For this example, when one uses GAC-nextIn or GAC-nextIn^b the time complexity of determining that $(x_1, 0)$ has no support on c is $O(r^2)$ (but in practice, GAC-nextIn^b will be faster here since it only deals with a unique variable when a next position has to be computed). This has to be compared with $\Omega(2^{r-1})$ for GAC-valid and GAC-allowed. By using knowledge about current domains, these algorithms skip over a number of allowed tuples that is exponential in the arity of the constraints [LHO 05b].

5.2.2. *NextDiff indexing*

A data structure in a second indexing-based approach [GEN 07] allows us to find for each positive table constraint c, for each tuple τ in $table[c]$ and for each variable $y \in scp(c)$, the next tuple in $table[c]$ with a value for y different from $\tau[y]$. The sub-tables in section 5.1.1 can be refined in order to find for each c-value (c, x, a), for each tuple τ (indexed) in $table[c, x, a]$ and for each variable y the next tuple in $table[c, x, a]$ involving a different value for y.

For homogeneity reasons, we introduce first two functions as follows:

DEFINITION 5.5.– *[nextDiff on global tables] Let c be a positive table constraint. For every tuple $\tau \in table[c]$ and every variable $y \in$ scp(c), we have:*

    – *nextDiff$(c, \tau, y) = nil$ if $\forall \tau' \in table[c], \tau' >_{\text{lex}} \tau \Rightarrow \tau'[y] = \tau[y]$;*

    – *nextDiff$(c, \tau, y) = \tau'$; otherwise where $\tau' \in table[c]$, $\tau' >_{\text{lex}} \tau$, $\tau'[y] \neq \tau[y]$ and $\forall \tau'' \in table[c], \tau' >_{\text{lex}} \tau'' >_{\text{lex}} \tau \Rightarrow \tau''[y] = \tau[y]$.*

DEFINITION 5.6.– *[nextDiff on sub-tables] Let c be a positive table constraint. For every c-value (c, x, a), every tuple $\tau \in table[c, x, a]$ and every variable $y \in \text{scp}(c)$, we have:*

- *$\text{nextDiff}((c, x, a), \tau, y) = nil$ if $\forall \tau' \in table[c, x, a], \tau' >_{\text{lex}} \tau \Rightarrow \tau'[y] = \tau[y];$*
- *$\text{nextDiff}((c, x, a), \tau, y) = \tau';$ otherwise where $\tau' \in table[c, x, a], \tau' >_{\text{lex}} \tau,$ $\tau'[y] \neq \tau[y]$ and $\forall \tau'' \in table[c, x, a], \tau' >_{\text{lex}} \tau'' >_{\text{lex}} \tau \Rightarrow \tau''[y] = \tau[y].$*

Unlike the function nextIn, the function nextDiff always returns a tuple that is strictly greater than the input one. The function nextDiff is naturally implemented using a multi-dimensional array, also denoted $nextDiff$ (ND in [GEN 07]), such that for every constraint c, every tuple τ at position i in $table[c]$ and every variable y at position j in $\text{scp}(c)$, we have $\text{nextDiff}(c, \tau, y) = table[c][nextDiff[c][i][j]]$. Observe that $nextDiff[c][i][j]$ gives the index i' in $table[c]$ of $\text{nextDiff}(c, \tau, y)$ We have $i' > i$, and again $i' = table[c].length + 1$ means $\text{nextDiff}(c, \tau, y) = nil$. Figure 5.3(b) provides an illustration in which the one-dimensional array placed under the first tuple of $table[c_{xyz}]$ corresponds to $nextDiff[c_{xyz}][1][1]$, $nextDiff[c_{xyz}][1][2]$ and $nextDiff[c_{xyz}][1][3]$, where 1, 2 and 3 successively represent positions of x, y and z in $\text{scp}(c_{xyz})$. The space complexity required for each constraint with this solution is $O(tr)$.

With the refined version, the function nextDiff is such that for every c-value (c, x, a), for every tuple $\tau = table[c][k]$ with $k = table[c, x, a][i]$ (k is the index of the ith tuple of $table[c]$ involving (x, a)) and for every variable y at position j in $\text{scp}(c)$, we have $\text{nextDiff}((c, x, a), \tau, y) = table[c][k']$ with $k' = table[c, x, a][i']$ where $i' = nextDiff[c, x, a][i][j]$. We have $i' > i$, and again $\text{nextDiff}((c, x, a), \tau, y) = nil$ implies $i' = table[c, x, a].length + 1$. In Figure 5.3(b) the one-dimensional array placed under the first tuple of $table[c_{xyz}, z, a]$ respectively corresponds to $nextDiff[c_{xyz}, z, a][1][1]$, $nextDiff[c_{xyz}, z, a][1][2]$ and $nextDiff[c_{xyz}, z, a][1][3]$. The space complexity required for each constraint with this solution is $O(tr^2)$.

We denote the first version, which uniquely handles the global table, by GAC-nextDiff and the second version by GAC-nextDiff^b. These two versions are respectively implemented by functions seekSupport-nd and seekSupport-nd^b, Algorithms 30 and 31, called at line 3 of Algorithm 8. The algorithms are quite simple: as long as the (sub-)table is not fully traversed and the current tuple invalid, we skip to the next tuple involving a value different for the first variable whose value is invalid. For GAC-nextDiff, we have to manage the possibility of finding a tuple that does not involve (x, a). As usual, this introduction is minimally complicated and therefore, unlike [GEN 07], we do not handle residual supports and circular domains [LIK 04].

Algorithm 30: seekSupport-nd$((c, x, a)$: c-value): Boolean

// Implementation of GAC-nextDiff

1 $i \leftarrow 1$
2 **while** $i \le table[c].length$ **do**
3 $\quad$ $\tau \leftarrow table[c][i]$
4 $\quad$ $j \leftarrow$ getFirstInvalidPosition(c, τ)
5 $\quad$ **if** $j = -1$ **then**
6 $\quad\quad$ **if** $\tau[x] = a$ **then**
7 $\quad\quad\quad$ **return** $true$
8 $\quad\quad$ **else**
9 $\quad\quad\quad$ $j \leftarrow scp(c)[x]$ $\qquad\qquad$ // x is the jth variable of $scp(c)$
10 $\quad$ $i \leftarrow nextDiff[c][i][j]$
11 **return** $false$

Algorithm 31: seekSupport-nd$^b((c, x, a)$: c-value): Boolean

---

// Implementation of GAC-nextDiff^b

1 $i \leftarrow 1$
2 **while** $i \le table[c, x, a].length$ **do**
3 $\quad$ $index \leftarrow table[c, x, a][i]$
4 $\quad$ $\tau \leftarrow table[c][index]$
5 $\quad$ $j \leftarrow$ getFirstInvalidPosition(c, τ)
6 $\quad$ **if** $j = -1$ **then**
7 $\quad\quad$ **return** $true$
8 $\quad$ $i \leftarrow nextDiff[c, x, a][i][j]$
9 **return** $false$

EXAMPLE.– The behavior of both algorithms is illustrated in Figure 5.5. For the example in Figure 5.2, GAC-nextDiff and GAC-nextDiff^b have exactly the same behavior (in terms of skips) as GAC-nextIn and GAC-nextIn^b. However, there are situations where the nextIn approach is exponentially better than the nextDiff approach [CHE 08a].

We can now see the similarity between nextIn and nextDiff indexing, and especially between GAC-nextIn^b and GAC-nextDiff^b. The former has the advantage of only considering valid values, whereas the latter performs each skip in constant time. For similar values of parameters, lines 7 to 12 of Algorithm 29 always allow skipping at least the same number of tuples as line 7 of Algorithm 31. If y denotes the

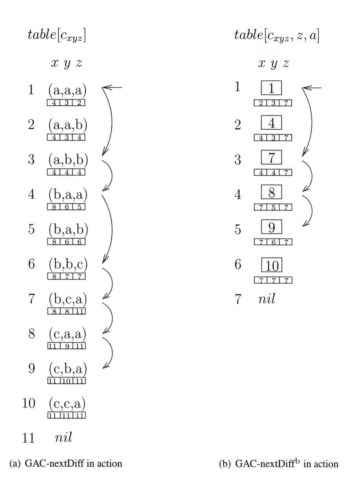

(a) GAC-nextDiff in action   (b) GAC-nextDiff^b in action

Figure 5.5. *Effort required by GAC-nextDiff and GAC-nextDiff^b to find $\tau = (c, b, a)$ as smallest support of (c_{xyz}, z, a) after the removal of a and c from $\text{dom}(y)$. We have $\text{dom}(x) = \text{dom}(z) = \{a, b, c\}$ and $\text{dom}(y) = \{b\}$. Solid arcs correspond to successive values of i*

first variable (from the left) whose value b is invalid in the current tuple, the former skips to the next tuple involving a valid value of y different from b, whereas the latter skips to the next tuple involving any value of y different from b. The two approaches admit different worst-case space complexities: $O(trd)$ for GAC3-nextIn^b against $O(tr^2)$ for GAC-nextDiff^b.

It remains for us to experimentally validate the new variant GAC-nextIn^b, and to investigate its behavior when residues and/or holograms are used.

5.3. Compression-based approaches

This section presents four different approaches to the reduction of space required by tables. Roughly speaking, significant reduction of space turns out to reduce running time for enforcing generalized arc consistency. The key success factor is basically the compression ratio achieved when tables are represented by sophisticated data structures such as tries, multi-valued decision diagrams, compressed tables or deterministic finite automata.

5.3.1. *Tries*

In addition to the nextDiff indexing approach presented earlier in this chapter, Gent *et al.* [GEN 07] have used tries to represent and propagate table constraints. A *trie* [FRE 60] is a rooted tree used to store and retrieve strings over an alphabet. A trie can represent a large dictionary because a trie has only one node for each common prefix. The term *trie* comes from "retrieval": a trie allows retrieval of a word of length r in $O(r)$. Within a trie, each directed edge (also called arc) is labeled with a symbol of the alphabet. To access a word in a dictionary that is represented by a trie, we start at the root and traverse a path leading to a leaf that provides access to the word (and/or to associated information). The first letter in the word selects the first edge along this path, then the second letter selects the second edge, and so on. Along this path, successive nodes are said to be at successive levels or depths.

The table of an r-ary constraint c can be represented by a trie in which successive levels are associated with successive variables in the scope of c. At each level, the alphabet is the domain of the associated variable. At the leaf level we have a special terminal node $\boxed{\top}$. All root-to-leaf paths are of uniform length since all tuples are composed of exactly r elements.

In [GEN 07], the authors propose to specifically exploit tries to look for supports. To enable supports to be found quickly, r separate tries are associated with each r-ary positive table constraint. In fact a separate trie is associated with each variable in the scope of each constraint. For a constraint c involving a variable x, the trie associated with x on c is searched when a support for a c-value (c, x, a) is sought. The first level of this trie concerns x, and for each c-value (c, x, a), the root, denoted by $\mathrm{trie}(c, x)$, of this trie has a child node[1] denoted by $\mathrm{trie}(c, x, a)$. This child node $\mathrm{trie}(c, x, a)$ is connected to $\mathrm{trie}(c, x)$ by an edge labeled with a.

EXAMPLE.– For example, Figure 5.7 shows the trie for the first variable x of the ternary constraint c_{xyz} that has served as an illustration in previous sections; the trie

---

1. For simplicity we assume here that each value is initially supported. If this is not the case, one can easily manage such a situation at construction time.

is directly built from the table depicted in Figure 5.6(a). In this trie, which is used for finding supports for values in the domain of x, the first, second and third levels are associated with the variables x, y and z. Figure 5.8 shows a second example of a trie, this time for the third variable, z, in the scope of c_{xyz}. In this trie, which is used for finding supports for values in the domain of z, the first, second and third levels are associated with the variables z, x and y. Note how the table has been reordered in Figure 5.6(b) before building this second trie.

<table>
<tr><td colspan="2">$table[c_{xyz}]$</td><td colspan="2">$table[c_{xyz}]$</td></tr>
<tr><td></td><td>x y z</td><td></td><td>z x y</td></tr>
<tr><td>1</td><td>(a,a,a)</td><td>1</td><td>(a,a,a)</td></tr>
<tr><td>2</td><td>(a,a,b)</td><td>2</td><td>(a,b,a)</td></tr>
<tr><td>3</td><td>(a,b,b)</td><td>3</td><td>(a,b,c)</td></tr>
<tr><td>4</td><td>(b,a,a)</td><td>4</td><td>(a,c,a)</td></tr>
<tr><td>5</td><td>(b,a,b)</td><td>5</td><td>(a,c,b)</td></tr>
<tr><td>6</td><td>(b,b,c)</td><td>6</td><td>(a,c,c)</td></tr>
<tr><td>7</td><td>(b,c,a)</td><td>7</td><td>(b,a,a)</td></tr>
<tr><td>8</td><td>(c,a,a)</td><td>8</td><td>(b,a,b)</td></tr>
<tr><td>9</td><td>(c,b,a)</td><td>9</td><td>(b,b,a)</td></tr>
<tr><td>10</td><td>(c,c,a)</td><td>10</td><td>(c,b,b)</td></tr>
<tr><td colspan="2">(a) Initial table.</td><td colspan="2">(b) Reordered table.</td></tr>
</table>

Figure 5.6. *Tables used to build tries*

To represent and traverse tries, we need the following structures.

The *Node* structure or type is composed of the following fields:

– *variable*: identifies the associated variable;

– *outs*: an array of outgoing arcs, indexed from 1 to *outs.length*.

The *Arc* structure or type is composed of the following fields:

– *value*: identifies the associated value (label);

– *destination*: identifies the head of the arc. When it corresponds to a leaf node, it is set to ⏊.

Without any loss of generality, we assume that outgoing arcs are ordered in sequence of increasing values (which are totally ordered) of the labels. The field *variable* is introduced here for convenience and could be advantageously (in terms of space) replaced by some global arrays, one per trie. These structures are illustrated in Figure 5.9, which shows part of the trie rooted at $\mathrm{trie}(c_{xyz}, x)$.

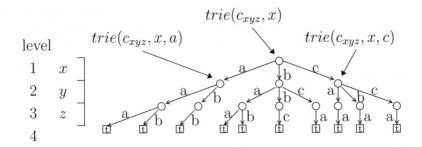

Figure 5.7. *Trie built for x from table in Figure 5.6(a)*

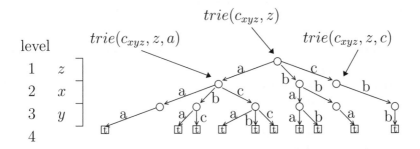

Figure 5.8. *Trie built for z from table in Figure 5.6(b)*

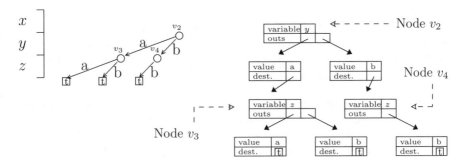

Figure 5.9. *Illustration of the structures introduced to represent tries. v_2 is the node corresponding to* trie(c_{xyz}, x, a) *from Figure 5.7*

Using tries, generalized arc consistency enforcement is denoted by GAC-trie. In this case the function seekSupport-trie, Algorithm 32, is called at line 3 of Algorithm 8. The recursive function extendSupport performs a depth-first search,

---

Algorithm 32: seekSupport-trie((c, x, a): c-value): Boolean

// Implementation of GAC-trie
// let τ be an array of size $|\operatorname{scp}(c)|$
1 $\tau[x] \leftarrow a$
2 **return** *extendSupport*$(\operatorname{trie}(c, x, a), \tau) \neq nil$

Algorithm 33: extendSupport($node$: Node, τ: tuple): tuple

Output: the smallest $\tau' \in \operatorname{val}(c)_{x=a}$ extending τ accessible from $node$, or nil

1 **if** $node = \boxed{\perp}$ **then**
2 $\quad \mid$ **return** τ // since we have reached a leaf node
3 $x \leftarrow node.variable$
4 **foreach** $arc \in node.outs$ **do**
5 $\quad \mid$ **if** $arc.value \in \operatorname{dom}(x)$ **then**
6 $\quad \mid \quad \mid$ $\tau[x] \leftarrow arc.value$
7 $\quad \mid \quad \mid$ $\tau' \leftarrow$ extendSupport($arc.destination, \tau$)
8 $\quad \mid \quad \mid$ **if** $\tau' \neq nil$ **then**
9 $\quad \mid \quad \mid \quad \mid$ **return** τ'
10 **return** nil

---

collecting[2] valid values in τ and backtracking whenever a dead-end occurs. If nil is returned by the initial call to extendSupport at line 2 of Algorithm 32, no support for (x, a) exists on c. Otherwise, the support that has been found for (x, a) on c is returned from lines 2 and 9 of Algorithm 33. For simplicity, we omit consideration of residual supports and circularity (used in [GEN 07]); we have therefore omitted fields that enable bottom-up traversal of tries.

EXAMPLE.– Suppose that when $\operatorname{dom}(y)$ has been reduced to $\{b\}$, seekSupport-trie is called for the c-value (c_{xyz}, x, a). The initial call to extendSupport has parameters v_2 for trie(c_{xyz}, x, a), and τ such that $\tau[x] = a$: see Figures 5.7 and 5.9. The variable y is the current variable and the value of the first outgoing arc is a. The test at line 5 of

---

2. Collecting values in τ is not strictly necessary here, but this shows how found supports can be recorded.

Algorithm 33 returns *false* because $a \notin \mathrm{dom}(y)$ in this example. In the next iteration of the loop at lines 4 through 9, the test at line 5 is successful because b, the value of the second outgoing arc, is valid. So extendSupport is called recursively with parameters v_4 and τ such that $\tau[x] = a$ and $\tau[y] = b$. The first and only child of v_4 completes τ with $\tau[z] = b$, thus finding a support.

Tries allow many validity operations to be shared, especially at the first levels. In the extreme case, a single validity operation may prevent fruitless access to an exponential number of allowed tuples. The effectiveness of this approach depends strongly on the order of variables within tries. For the example in Figure 5.2, GAC-trie only needs to visit r nodes (and $2r - 3$ arcs) before concluding that there is no support for $(x_1, 0)$ on c. On the other hand, the worst-case space complexity of an individual trie is $O(tr)$ since in the worst-case, we need r nodes and r edges per allowed tuple. The worst-case space complexity for a table constraint c is then $O(tr^2)$ since we need one trie per variable. In practice, memory usage is normally better than this because in many cases the first few nodes along a path from the root node are shared by many tuples.

PROPOSITION 5.7.– *For a positive table constraint c, the worst-case time complexity of seekSupport-trie, with input (c, x, a), is $O(e_{\mathrm{trie}(c,x,a)})$ where $e_{\mathrm{trie}(c,x,a)}$ is the number of edges in the (sub)-trie rooted at* trie(c, x, a).

5.3.2. *Multi-valued decision diagrams*

Starting with a trie, which is an arc-labeled rooted tree that eliminates prefix redundancy, we can eliminate shared suffixes [CAR 06, CHE 08a] to obtain a *multi-valued decision diagram* (MDD), which is an arc-labeled *directed acyclic graph* (DAG). In the special case where all domains are binary we obtain a *binary decision diagram* (BDD) instead of an MDD. An MDD has at least one root node, which is known in this context as a *source*. Moreover an MDD has exactly two terminal nodes, known as *sink* nodes. One of these is $\boxed{\mathrm{t}}$, which means the same as in the previous section. The other sink node is $\boxed{\mathrm{f}}$ which corresponds to the state reached for disallowed tuples; for simplicity we omit $\boxed{\mathrm{f}}$ from diagrams. In the example in Figure 5.10 there is only one source (which is a node with no incoming arcs) and we denote this by $mdd(c_{xyz})$.

Although there is a clear advantage of using MDDs in terms of space complexity, enforcing generalized arc consistency requires new filtering procedures that must be shown to be effective. Available algorithms [CAR 06, CHE 08a] that enforce generalized arc consistency using MDDs are not revision-based. This means that instead of seeking a support for each value in turn, GAC is enforced globally on each constraint. A depth-first exploration of the MDD identifies all values that must be removed from domains in order to enforce GAC. We say that a node v is *supported*

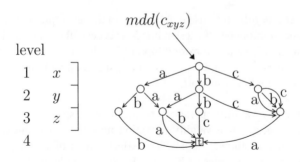

Figure 5.10. *MDD built from the trie in Figure 5.7*

(resp. *unsupported*) iff there exists a (resp. no) path from v to a leaf such that all values labeling the arcs along this path are valid. Leaf nodes are trivially supported (considering the empty path).

Our implementation of MDDs retains the structures introduced for tries. Following [CHE 08a], Σ^{true} will be the set of supported nodes, and Σ^{false} will be the set of unsupported nodes encountered during the search (an alternative implementation includes an additional field in the structure associated with each node [CAR 06]). Also, corresponding to each variable x we provide a set $gacValues[x]$ that will contain all values in $\mathrm{dom}(x)$ which are proved to have a support during the search that enforces GAC on a constraint c. It is sufficient to collect values for uninstantiated variables. This is why variables in $\mathrm{past}(P)$ are not considered in the algorithms below.

Algorithm 9 calls a non-revision-based filtering procedure, Algorithm 34, to enforce GAC on a (positive table) constraint c using an MDD: enforceGAC-type in Algorithm 9 corresponds here to enforceGAC-mdd. Initially, sets Σ^{true}, Σ^{false} and $gacValues$ are emptied at lines 1 through 4. Then exploration of the diagram starts from the root.

The function exploreMDD, Algorithm 35, explores the sub-DAG rooted at a given node. If this node corresponds to a leaf or has already been explored, the algorithm can decide directly whether or not it is supported. Otherwise, the algorithm explores each child (i.e. node reached from an outgoing edge) such that the value labeling the linking arc is still present in its domain. When a supported child node is found, both the parent node and the value labeling the arc are supported. Finally, Algorithm 35 updates one of the sets Σ^{true} and Σ^{false}.

After exploration of the MDD, unsupported values are removed at lines 7 through 12 of Algorithm 34: these are the values in $\mathrm{dom}(x) \setminus gacValues[x]$. The test $gacValues[x] \subset \mathrm{dom}(x)$ at line 8 is (in our context) equivalent to $|gacValues[x]| \neq |\mathrm{dom}(x)|$, which is performed in constant time provided that the size of sets are managed. If the domain of a variable x becomes empty then $\{x\}$ is returned at line 11 and the inconsistency will be caught in Algorithm 9.

Algorithm 34: enforceGAC-mdd(P: $\mathscr{P}$, c: constraint): set of variables

Output: the set of variables in $\mathrm{scp}(c)$ with reduced domain

1   $\Sigma^{true} \leftarrow \emptyset$

2   $\Sigma^{false} \leftarrow \emptyset$

3   **foreach** *variable* $x \in \mathrm{scp}(c) \mid x \notin \mathrm{past}(P)$ **do**

4     $\lfloor$ $gacValues[x] \leftarrow \emptyset$

5   exploreMDD($mdd(c)$)   // $gacValues$ is updated during exploration

    // domains are now updated and X_{evt} computed

6   $X_{\mathrm{evt}} \leftarrow \emptyset$

7   **foreach** *variable* $x \in \mathrm{scp}(c) \mid x \notin \mathrm{past}(P)$ **do**

8   **if** $gacValues[x] \subset \mathrm{dom}(x)$ **then**

9        $\mathrm{dom}(x) \leftarrow gacValues[x]$

10   **if** $\mathrm{dom}(x) = \emptyset$ **then**

11          $\lfloor$ **return** $\{x\}$

12       $X_{\mathrm{evt}} \leftarrow X_{\mathrm{evt}} \cup \{x\}$

13 **return** X_{evt}

PROPOSITION 5.8.– *For a positive table constraint c, the worst-case time complexity of enforceGAC-mdd is $O(e_{mdd(c)} + \lambda)$ where $e_{mdd(c)}$ is the number of edges in the MDD used to represent c and λ the number of values detected GAC-inconsistent.*

This GAC algorithm has been formulated without any optimization. First, it is possible to deal with intervals (of values) instead of values as for the case constraint [CAR 06]. Next, the loop iterating over arcs (starting at line 9 of Algorithm 35) can terminate as soon as all values have been collected in $gacValues$ arrays because it means that the constraint is generalized arc-consistent. Certainly the most important optimization is the management of the incrementality/decrementality of Σ^{false} when GAC is maintained during search. Basically, we can avoid resetting (i.e. emptying) this set as long as no backtracking occurs. A node that is unsupported at time t is always unsupported at time t' if between t and t' no value is restored (and potentially new values are deleted). To manage decrementality, one has to keep track of Σ^{false} at the different levels of search. Time-stamping is one solution but, unluckily this is not compatible with early cutoff [CHE 08a]. Other decremental solutions are the use of bit vectors [CHE 06] and sparse sets. In particular, the sparse set data structure [BRI 93] is shown [CHE 08a] to be a very competitive choice when solving both structured and random instances.

Algorithm 35: exploreMDD(*node*: Node): Boolean

    Output: *true* iff *node* is supported

1 **if** $node = \boxed{\tau}$ **then**
2 | **return** *true*   // since we are at a leaf
3 **if** $node \in \Sigma^{true}$ **then**
4 | **return** *true*   // since already proved to be supported
5 **if** $node \in \Sigma^{false}$ **then**
6 | **return** *false*   // since already proved to be unsupported
7 $x \leftarrow node.variable$
8 $supported \leftarrow false$
9 **foreach** $arc \in node.outs$ **do**
10 | **if** $arc.value \in \mathrm{dom}(x)$ **then**
11 | | **if** *exploreMDD*($arc.destination$) **then**
12 | | | $supported \leftarrow true$
13 | | | $gacValues[x] \leftarrow gacValues[x] \cup \{arc.value\}$
14 **if** $supported = true$ **then**
15 | $\Sigma^{true} \leftarrow \Sigma^{true} \cup \{node\}$
16 **else**
17 | $\Sigma^{false} \leftarrow \Sigma^{false} \cup \{node\}$
18 **return** *supported*

Whereas there were r tries per constraint in the previous section, the MDD approach requires only one MDD per constraint, which immediately improves space complexity by a factor r, not counting space saving from node sharing. An MDD representing a constraint relation should be small or preferably minimal. In [CHE 08a] a procedure to build an MDD from a trie is in $O(tr)$, which is optimal; but nothing is said about the variable ordering in the trie and in the MDD. An (ordered) BDD is a type of (ordered) MDD, and it is known that the size of an (O)BDD is determined by the Boolean function it represents as well as the chosen variable ordering. Depending on the variable ordering, at one extreme the number of nodes in an OBDD is linear (in the number of variables), and at the other extreme this number is exponential. Actually, the problem of finding the best variable ordering is NP-hard and this is why the variable ordering is usually determined heuristically.

5.3.3. *Compressed tables*

The use of so-called *compressed tuples* [KAT 07] can reduce the amount of memory required for tables. A compressed tuple can be defined as follows:

DEFINITION 5.9.– *[Compressed Tuple] A compressed tuple* Γ *for an r-ary constraint c is an r-tuple* $(D_1, \ldots, D_r)$ *such that* $D_1 \times \cdots \times D_r \subseteq \prod_{x \in \mathrm{scp}(c)} \mathrm{dom}^{\mathrm{init}}(x)$.

If $\mathrm{scp}(c) = \{x_1, \ldots, x_r\}$ and $\Gamma = (D_1, \ldots, D_r)$ is a compressed tuple for c, then $\Gamma[x_i]$ denotes D_i. Any (uncompressed) tuple in $D_1 \times \cdots \times D_r$ is said to be *covered* by Γ. We are particularly interested in *allowed* compressed tuples:

DEFINITION 5.10.– *[Allowed Compressed Tuple] A compressed tuple* $\Gamma = (D_1, \ldots, D_r)$ *for an r-ary constraint c is* allowed *by c iff* $D_1 \times \cdots \times D_r \subseteq \mathrm{rel}(c)$.

A *compressed table* can be defined in terms of allowed compressed tuples:

DEFINITION 5.11.– *[Compressed Table] A (positive)* compressed table *for a constraint c is a set of allowed compressed tuples for c such that every tuple in* $\mathrm{rel}(c)$ *is covered by at least one of these compressed tuples. A compressed table is* disjoint *iff no tuple of* $\mathrm{rel}(c)$ *is covered by two distinct compressed tuples of the table.*

Informally, a compressed table is *minimal* iff it is not possible to merge two compressed tuples from the table. Minimal disjoint compressed tables can be generated by a method [KAT 07] based on constructing decision trees. Because the problem of constructing a decision tree with minimum average branch length is NP-hard, Katsirelos and Walsh have heuristically selected at each construction step a decision used to expand the tree.

A compressed table, ctable for short, contains compressed tuples, ctuples for short, that can be built from an MDD by collecting all values along each path from the root to a leaf; the reverse is also true.

EXAMPLE.– Figure 5.11 provides a first illustration. As another example, the compressed table for the (uncompressed) table in Figure 5.2 contains only five compressed tuples:

$$(\{0\}, \{0\}, \{0, 1\}, \{0, 1\}, \{0, 1\})$$
$$(\{0\}, \{1\}, \{0\}, \{0, 1\}, \{0, 1\})$$
$$(\{0\}, \{1\}, \{1\}, \{0\}, \{0, 1\})$$
$$(\{0\}, \{1\}, \{1\}, \{1\}, \{0\})$$
$$(\{2\}, \{2\}, \{2\}, \{2\}, \{2\})$$

For this example, in the general case where the constraint is r-ary, we can show that r compressed tuples are sufficient to represent the uncompressed table.

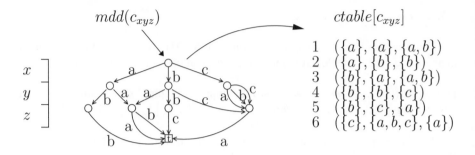

$$mdd(c_{xyz}) \qquad\qquad ctable[c_{xyz}]$$

$$
\begin{array}{cl}
1 & (\{a\}, \{a\}, \{a, b\}) \\
2 & (\{a\}, \{b\}, \{b\}) \\
3 & (\{b\}, \{a\}, \{a, b\}) \\
4 & (\{b\}, \{b\}, \{c\}) \\
5 & (\{b\}, \{c\}, \{a\}) \\
6 & (\{c\}, \{a, b, c\}, \{a\})
\end{array}
$$

Figure 5.11. *Compressed tables can be built from decision trees (not shown here) or MDDs*

Consider that constraints are represented by compressed tables; the compressed table for constraint c is denoted by $ctable[c]$. We provide indexes which, for each c-value (c, x, a), give access to all all compressed tuples Γ of $ctable[c]$ such that $a \in \Gamma[x]$. The index structure for (c, x, a) is denoted by $ctable[c, x, a]$ and is similar to the concept of sub-table introduced in section 5.1.1. When GAC is enforced within the coarse-grained GAC-allowed scheme described in section 5.1.3, supports are sought by the function seekSupport-a, Algorithm 27. The new support-seeking scheme, called GAC-allowed-compressed and adapted to compressed tables, is implemented by function seekSupport-a-c, Algorithm 36. The function seekInCompressedTuple, Algorithm 37, simply searches for a valid tuple covered by a compressed tuple supporting (x, a). If there is not support for (x, a) in Γ, *nil* is returned by function seekInCompressedTuple. Otherwise, an (uncompressed) tuple is built up and returned: it may be recorded as a last support or as a residual support (not shown here) in seekSupport-a-c.

Algorithm 36: seekSupport-a-c$((c, x, a)$: c-value): Boolean

// Implementation of GAC-allowed-compressed

1 $i \leftarrow 1$

2 **while** $i \leq ctable[c, x, a].length$ **do**

3      $index \leftarrow ctable[c, x, a][i]$

4      $\Gamma \leftarrow ctable[c][index]$ // necessarily, $a \in \Gamma[x]$

5   **if** *seekInCompressedTuple*$((c, x, a), \Gamma) \neq nil$ **then**

6          $\lfloor$ **return** *true*

7      $i \leftarrow i + 1$

8 **return** *false*

Algorithm 37: seekInCompressedTuple((c, x, a): c-value, Γ: ctuple): tuple

---

Output: a tuple $\tau \in \mathrm{val}(c)_{x=a}$ covered by Γ, or *nil*

// let τ be an array of size $|\mathrm{scp}(c)|$

1 $\tau[x] \leftarrow a$

2 **foreach** *variable* $y \in \mathrm{scp}(c) \mid y \neq x$ **do**

3     $found \leftarrow false$

4   **foreach** *value* $b \in \Gamma[y]$ **do**

5   **if** $b \in \mathrm{dom}(y)$ **then**

6         $\tau[y] \leftarrow b$

7         $found \leftarrow true$

8   break

9   **if** $\neg found$ **then**

10   **return** *nil*

11 **return** τ

We have described here a coarse-grained implementation for use with compressed tables. A fine-grained implementation is proposed in [KAT 07].

5.3.4. *Deterministic finite automata*

A *deterministic finite automaton* (DFA) is defined by a 5-tuple $(Q, \Sigma, \delta, q_0, F)$ where:

– Q is a finite set of states;

– Σ is a finite set of symbols called the alphabet;

– $\delta : Q \times \Sigma \to Q$ is a transition function;

– $q_0 \in Q$ is the initial state;

– $F \subseteq Q$ is the set of final states.

Given an input string (a finite sequence of symbols taken from the alphabet Σ), the automaton starts in the initial state q_0, and for each symbol in sequence of the string, applies the transition function to update the current state. If the last state reached is a final state then the input string is accepted by the automaton. The set of strings that the automaton accepts constitutes a language, which is technically a regular language.

In [PES 04], a global constraint, called regular, is introduced: the sequence of values taken by the successive variables in the scope of this constraint must belong to a given regular language. For such constraints, a deterministic finite automaton can be used to determine whether or not a given tuple is accepted. This can be an attractive approach when constraint relations can be naturally represented by regular expressions in a known regular language. For example, in rostering problems, regular expressions can represent valid patterns of activities.

EXAMPLE.– For the example in Figure 5.2, the regular expression $01^*0(0 + 1)^* + 2^*$ represents a superset of $table[c]$. Within the language defined by this expression, the set of strings of length five is exactly $table[c]$. This seems to be the ultimate way of compressing tables as shown in Figure 5.12.

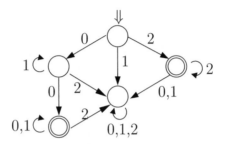

Figure 5.12. *DFA built from the table depicted in Figure 5.2. The initial state is pointed by an arrow and final states are double circled*

Working with constraints defined by a DFA, Pesant's filtering algorithm [PES 04] enforces GAC by means of a two-stage forward–backward exploration, which is not described here in detail. This two-stage process constructs a layered directed multi-graph and collects the set of states that support each v-value (x, a). The worst-case time and space complexities of this bounded incremental algorithm are both $O(nd|Q|)$.

There are (global) constraints that can be directly expressed using regular languages. An example is the stretch constraint [PES 01] which puts restrictions on maximal subsequences of identical values. On the other hand, when the allDifferent constraint is represented by a regular expression, the DFA suffers exponential growth. Finally, it is worth noting that there is a direct correspondence between MDDs and DFAs. An acyclic and minimized deterministic finite automaton is equivalent to a merged MDD [HAD 08]. This means that the structures employed in [VEM 92, AMI 02] for compiling CSP instances are basically multi-valued decision diagrams.

5.4. GAC-valid+allowed scheme

In section 5.1, the classical scheme GAC-valid iterates over valid tuples seeking supports, whereas the scheme GAC-allowed iterates over allowed tuples. Subsequent sections have introduced various developments that rely on sophisticated data structures. We now introduce a refinement that combines GAC-valid and GAC-allowed without any additional data structure. Following [LEC 06d], visits to lists of valid and allowed tuples are alternated. The idea is to jump over sequences of valid tuples containing no allowed tuple and to jump over sequences of allowed tuples containing no valid tuple.

For example, when seeking a support for $(x_1, 0)$ on the constraint c in Figure 5.2, this refined scheme starts by finding, in $O(r)$, the first valid tuple $\tau = (0, 1, ..., 1, 1)$. Next, the first allowed tuple τ' greater than or equal to τ is sought. When dichotomic search is used here, this involves $\log_2(2^{r-1})$ comparisons of tuples, which is $O(r^2)$ because comparing two tuples is $O(r)$. As no such tuple exists for $(x_1, 0)$, $(x_1, 0)$ is proven to be generalized arc-inconsistent. Note that this refined scheme, which is called GAC-valid+allowed, is able to skip a number of tuples that grows exponentially with the arity of the constraints, but in a manner different to that of approaches presented previously. GAC-valid+allowed can be implemented using binary search or instead using tries.

5.4.1. *Using binary search*

Algorithm 38: seekSupport-v+a$((c, x, a)$: c-value): Boolean

// Implementation of GAC-valid+allowed

1 $\tau \leftarrow$ getFirstValidTuple$((c, x, a))$
2 **while** $\tau \neq nil$ **do**
3       $\tau' \leftarrow$ binarySearch$(table[c, x, a], \tau)$
4   **if** $\tau' = nil$ **then**
5           $\lfloor$ **return** *false*
6       $j \leftarrow$ getFirstInvalidPosition(c, τ')
7   **if** $j = -1$ **then**
8           $\lfloor$ **return** *true*
9       $\tau \leftarrow$ getNextValidTuple$((c, x, a), \tau', j)$
10 **return** *false*

When binary search is used, line 3 of Algorithm 8 calls function seekSupport-v+a, Algorithm 38. Each execution of the while loop body processes a valid tuple (initially, the first one). At line 3 the function binarySearch performs a dichotomic search which returns the smallest tuple τ' of $table[c] = \text{rel}(c)$ such that $\tau' \geq_{lex} \tau$ and $\tau'[x] = a$ (or nil if it does not exist). If $\tau' = nil$, no support has been found (lines 4 and 5). Otherwise, τ' corresponds to an allowed tuple whose validity must be checked (line 6). If getFirstInvalidPosition(c, τ') returns -1 this means that τ' is valid too, so it is a support and *true* is returned at line 8. If τ' is not valid then getNextValidTuple (line 9) finds the smallest valid tuple τ built from c such that $\tau >_{\text{lex}} \tau'$ and $\tau[x] = a$ (or *nil* if it does not exist). Auxiliary functions used here are described in section 4.2.

EXAMPLE.– Figure 5.13 provides overall illustration of GAC-valid+allowed using a ternary constraint. The first valid tuple is (a, b, a). Then, the first allowed tuple greater than or equal to (a, b, a) is found: this is (b, a, a). Next, the first valid tuple greater than or equal to (b, a, a) is computed: this is (b, b, a). And so on.

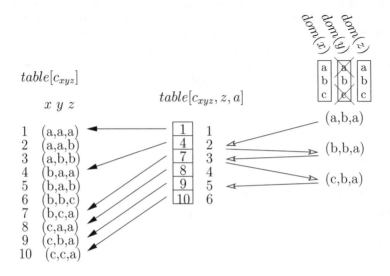

Figure 5.13. *Effort required by GAC-valid+allowed to find* $\tau = (c, b, a)$ *as smallest support of* (c_{xyz}, z, a) *after the removal of a and c from* dom(y)

We call a *sequence of valid tuples* for a c-value (c, x, a) a pair $(\tau_{\text{min}}, \tau_{\text{max}})$ with $\tau_{\text{min}} \in \text{val}(c)_{x=a}$, $\tau_{\text{max}} \in \text{val}(c)_{x=a}$ and $\tau_{\text{min}} \leq_{\text{lex}} \tau_{\text{max}}$. A sequence $(\tau_{\text{min}}, \tau_{\text{max}})$ of valid tuples for a c-value (c, x, a) *contains* an allowed tuple $\tau' \in \text{rel}(c)_{x=a}$ iff $\tau_{\text{min}} \leq_{\text{lex}} \tau' \leq_{\text{lex}} \tau_{\text{max}}$; τ' is not necessarily valid. A sequence $(\tau_{\text{min}}, \tau_{\text{max}})$ of valid tuples containing no allowed tuple is *maximal* if it is not possible to enlarge it (decreasing τ_{min} or increasing τ_{max}) without obtaining a sequence of valid tuples that contains an allowed tuple.

PROPOSITION 5.12.– *For an r-ary positive table constraint c, the worst-case time complexity of seekSupport-v+a (using a binary search), with input* (c, x, a), *is* $O(N(d + \log(t_{c,x,a})r))$ *where N is the number of maximal sequences of valid tuples for* (c, x, a) *containing no allowed tuple.*

Proof. The worst-case time complexity of binarySearch is $O(\log(t_{c,x,a})r)$. The worst-case time complexity of getFirstInvalidPosition is $O(r)$. The overall worst-case time complexity of getNextValidTuple is $O(r + d)$. The overall worst-case time complexity for one execution of loop body is then $O(d + \log(t_{c,x,a})r)$. The number of turns of the main loop is bounded by N because each computed intermediate allowed tuple allows us to skip from a maximal sequence of valid tuples to the next one.   □

Returning again to the example from Figure 5.2, when seekSupport-v+a is called with $(c, x_1, 0)$, we have $N = 1$.

5.4.2. *Using tries*

Following [GEN 07], a trie can be used instead of binary search to find the first allowed tuple greater than or equal to a valid one. We exploit this idea to provide a description of a variant of GAC-valid+allowed below.

As in section 5.3.1, there is a separate trie associated with each variable x in the scope of a table constraint c: x corresponds to the first level of its associated trie. We now need to be able to retrieve a tuple from a trie. This is why we include an additional field in the structure *Node* (introduced in section 5.3.1). More precisely, for each node, we have a new field which is an array *access* that provides for each value a in the domain of the associated variable, the reference to the outgoing arc that is labeled with the smallest value $b \geq a$, or *nil* if there is none. We also include an additional field *next*, in the structure *Arc*. The field *next* provides the reference to the next arc outgoing from the parent node, or *nil* if the current arc is the the last one. Remember that outgoing arcs are ordered according to increasing values of the labels.

To implement GAC-valid+allowed scheme with tries, we just replace line 3 of Algorithm 38 with:.

$\tau' \leftarrow$ trieSearch$(\text{trie}(c, x, a), \tau)$

where trieSearch is Algorithm 39, which makes a top-down traversal of the trie dedicated to x from the node trie(c, x, a). Recursive calls at line 6 continue so long as the trie contains successive values within the given tuple. If the given tuple is found in the trie it is returned at lines 2 and 8. If the given tuple does not belong to the trie, this means that at a certain level, we can't satisfy *arc.value* $= \tau[y]$ where y is the variable associated with the current parent node. In this case, from there, so long as there is no node at successive backtracked levels with a value strictly greater than $\tau[y]$ (i.e. as long as *arc* $=$ *nil*), we climb up the trie (see lines 10 and 12). If such a level can be found, we build the smallest allowed tuple that is strictly greater than the given one by following the leftmost branch of the trie from the current level (lines 13 to 20).

Algorithm 39: trieSearch(*node*: Node, τ: tuple): tuple

Output: the smallest $\tau' \in \mathrm{rel}(c)_{x=a}$ accessible from *node* | $\tau' \geq_{\mathrm{lex}} \tau$, or *nil*

// First part: τ can still be found

1 **if** $node = \boxed{\bot}$ **then**
2 | **return** τ // since we have reached a leaf node

3 $y \leftarrow node.variable$
4 $arc \leftarrow node.access[\tau[y]]$ // arc with the smallest value $b \geq \tau[y]$
5 **if** $arc \neq nil \wedge arc.value = \tau[y]$ **then**
6 | $\tau' \leftarrow$ trieSearch($arc.destination, \tau$)
7 | **if** $\tau' \neq nil$ **then**
8 | | **return** τ'
9 | **else**
10 | | $arc \leftarrow arc.next$

// Second part: τ cannot be found yet

11 **if** $arc = nil$ **then**
12 | **return** *nil*

13 $\tau' \leftarrow \tau$
14 $\tau'[y] \leftarrow arc.value$
15 $node \leftarrow arc.destination$
16 **while** $node \neq \boxed{\bot}$ **do**
17 | $y \leftarrow node.variable$
18 | $arc \leftarrow node.outs[1]$ // the leftmost arc
19 | $\tau'[y] \leftarrow arc.value$
20 | $node \leftarrow arc.destination$
21 **return** τ'

PROPOSITION 5.13.– *For an r-ary positive table constraint c, the worst-case time complexity of **seekSupport-v+a** (using a trie search), with input (c, x, a) is $O(N(d + r))$, where N is the number of maximal sequences of valid tuples for (c, x, a) containing no allowed tuple.*

Unfortunately the worst-case space complexity is now $O(trd)$ per trie. Note that it is possible to trade off time for space by abandoning the field access and "simulating" a random access by replacing line 4 of Algorithm 39 with:

$arc \leftarrow node.outs[1]$
while $arc \neq nil \wedge arc.value < \tau[y]$ **do**
    $arc \leftarrow arc.next$

A dichotomic search can also be employed.

5.5. Simple tabular reduction

To enforce GAC on positive table constraints, *simple tabular reduction* (STR) is another approach introduced by Ullmann [ULL 07] which significantly differs from previous methods in that it dynamically maintains the tables of allowed tuples. More precisely, whenever a value is removed from the domain of a variable, all tuples that have become invalid are removed from tables. This facilitates identification and removal of values that are no longer GAC-consistent. GAC is enforced while removing invalid tuples; only supports are kept in tables. This work is related to the AC algorithm [SAM 05] for the hidden variable encoding.

5.5.1. *Original algorithm*

Although STR can be applied stand-alone, we now present it in the more general context of a backtrack search algorithm. Indeed, an important feature of STR is the cheap restoration of its structures when backtracking occurs. The principle of STR is to split each table into different sets such that each tuple is a member of exactly one set. One of these sets contains all tuples that are currently valid (and are therefore supports): tuples in this set constitute the content of the *current table*. Any tuple of the current table of a constraint c is called a *current tuple* of c. Other sets contain tuples removed at different levels of search.

The following arrays provide access to the disjoint sets within $table[c]$.

– $position[c]$ is an array of size $t = table[c].length$ that provides indirect access to the tuples of $table[c]$. At any given time the values in $position[c]$ are a permutation of $\{1, 2, \ldots, t\}$. The ith tuple of c is $table[c][position[c][i]]$.

– $currentLimit[c]$ is the position of the last current tuple in $table[c]$. The current table of c is composed of exactly $currentLimit[c]$ tuples. The values in $position[c]$ at indices ranging from 1 to $currentLimit[c]$ are positions of the current tuples of c.

– $levelLimits[c]$ is an array of size $n + 1$ such that $levelLimits[c][p]$ is the position of the first invalid tuple of $table[c]$ removed when the search was at level p (the level corresponds to the number of instantiated or past variables). $levelLimits[c][p] = -1$ if none was removed at level p. If p is the current search level and $levelLimits[c][p] \neq -1$, all tuples removed at level p can be accessed using indices at locations in array $position[c]$ ranging from $currentLimit[c] + 1$ to $levelLimits[c][p]$.

Note that the array $levelLimits[c]$ is indexed from 0 to n (although we usually have array indexing from 1). If the search is preceded by preprocessing then we find at level 0 the tuples removed after the initial call to STR during preprocessing (i.e. before search). The structure $levelLimits$ is not required if there is no search. The structures introduced here[3], following [BRI 93], are simpler than those presented in [ULL 07, LEC 08a] but the complexities remain the same.

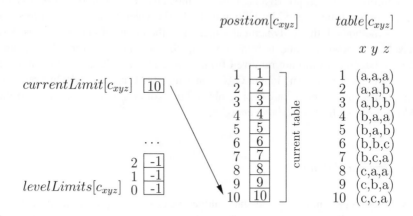

Figure 5.14. *Initialization of STR data structures for a ternary positive table constraint c_{xyz}*

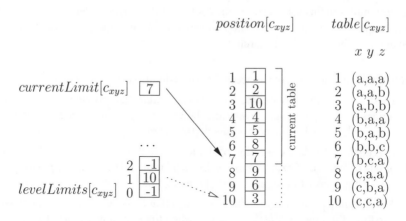

Figure 5.15. *STR applied after the removal of (y, b) at level 1. (z, c) no longer has support and will therefore be deleted*

EXAMPLE.– To illustrate their use, the following example has a positive table constraint c_{xyz} such that:

– $\text{scp}(c_{xyz}) = \{x, y, z\}$;

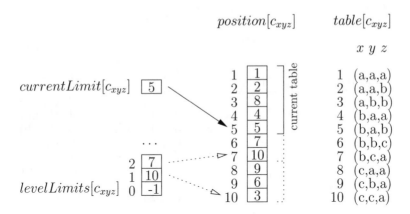

Figure 5.16. *STR applied after the removal of (y, c) at level 2. No value will be deleted*

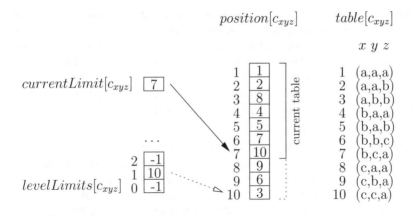

Figure 5.17. *Structures obtained after the restoration performed at level 1*

– $\mathrm{rel}(c_{xyz}) = \{(a, a, a), (a, a, b), (a, b, b), (b, a, a), (b, a, b),$
  $(b, b, c), (b, c, a), (c, a, a), (c, b, a), (c, c, a)\}.$

Figure 5.14 shows the initialized STR data structures for c_{xyz}. Now suppose that at level 1 (that is to say, after a first variable assignment), (y, b) is deleted by propagation (using other constraints) and STR is applied on c_{xyz}. Tuples at position 3, 6 and 9 in $table[c_{xyz}]$ are no longer valid: their locations in array $position$ are swapped with locations of three valid tuples. Locations of tuples that are not valid are now at the end of the array $position$. $levelLimits[c_{xyz}][1]$ is initialized with the old value of $currentLimits[c]$, namely 10, as shown in Figure 5.15. Moreover, (z, c) is deleted because it is no longer supported by any current tuple of c_{xyz}. After a second variable

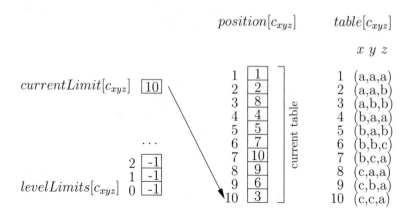

Figure 5.18. *Structures obtained after the restoration performed at level* 0

assignment, the removal of (y, c) by propagation and the application of STR, the situation is as shown in Figure 5.16. Suppose now that the search backtracks to level 1. By modifying two pointers (in constant time), we can restore the structures so that tuples removed at level 2 are now included in the current table, as shown in Figure 5.17. Finally, if the search algorithm backtracks to level 0, we obtain the situation shown in Figure 5.18. Tuples in the current table in Figure 5.18 are not ordered as initially in Figure 5.14, but for STR this is not a problem.

Corresponding to each variable x, we provide a set $gacValues[x]$ [ULL 77] that will contain all values in $\text{dom}(x)$ which are proved to have a support when GAC is enforced on a constraint c; this is the same structure as the one introduced in section 5.3.2. To enforce GAC on a given constraint network P, Algorithm 9 can be used and, as for enforceGAC-mdd, a non-revision-based filtering procedure establishes generalized arc consistency on positive table constraints. For STR, this is Algorithm 40: enforceGAC-type in Algorithm 9 corresponds to enforceGAC-str. The loops at lines 1, 8 and 15 only iterate over uninstantiated variables because it is only possible (and it is sufficient) to remove values from domains of these variables. The sets $gacValues$ are emptied at lines 1 and 2 of Algorithm 40 because no value is initially guaranteed to be GAC-consistent. Then the loop at lines $4 - 13$ successively processes all current tuples of the table of c. When a tuple τ is proved to be valid (see Algorithm 15), we know that it is necessarily a support since it is (by definition) allowed; values that have been proved to be GAC-consistent are collected at lines 8 to 10. In constant time at line 13 an invalid tuple τ is removed (see Algorithm 41), from the current table: actually it is located at the end of the current table before the value of $currentLimit[c]$ is decremented. If this tuple is the first removed at the current level p, then the current limit is recorded in $levelLimits[c][p]$. Note that τ is effectively removed without actually being moved in memory. After all current tuples have been considered, unsupported values are removed (lines 14 to 21): these are the values in $\mathrm{dom}(x) \setminus gacValues[x]$. The test at line 16 can be performed in constant time, as discussed in section 5.3.2. If the domain of a variable x becomes empty, then $\{x\}$ is returned at line 19, and the inconsistency will be caught in Algorithm 9.

Algorithm 40: enforceGAC-str(P: $\mathscr{P}$, c: constraint): set of variables

Output: the set of variables in $\mathrm{scp}(c)$ with reduced domain

1 **foreach** *variable* $x \in \mathrm{scp}(c) \mid x \notin \mathrm{past}(P)$ **do**
2     $gacValues[x] \leftarrow \emptyset$

3 $i \leftarrow 1$
4 **while** $i \leq currentLimit[c]$ **do**
5     $index \leftarrow position[c][i]$
6     $\tau \leftarrow table[c][index]$
7   **if** *isValidTuple*(c, τ) **then**
8   **foreach** *variable* $x \in \mathrm{scp}(c) \mid x \notin \mathrm{past}(P)$ **do**
9   **if** $\tau[x] \notin gacValues[x]$ **then**
10                 $gacValues[x] \leftarrow gacValues[x] \cup \{\tau[x]\}$
11         $i \leftarrow i + 1$
12   **else**
13   removeTuple($c, i, |\mathrm{past}(P)|$)   // *currentLimit*[c] is decremented

   // domains are now updated and X_{evt} computed
14 $X_{\mathrm{evt}} \leftarrow \emptyset$
15 **foreach** *variable* $x \in \mathrm{scp}(c) \mid x \notin \mathrm{past}(P)$ **do**
16   **if** $gacValues[x] \subset \mathrm{dom}(x)$ **then**
17         $\mathrm{dom}(x) \leftarrow gacValues[x]$
18   **if** $\mathrm{dom}(x) = \emptyset$ **then**
19   **return** $\{x\}$
20         $X_{\mathrm{evt}} \leftarrow X_{\mathrm{evt}} \cup \{x\}$

21 **return** X_{evt}

The worst-case time complexity of enforceGAC-str, Algorithm 40, is $O(r'd + rt')$ where, for a given constraint c, $r' = |\mathrm{scp}(c) \setminus \mathrm{past}(P)|$ denotes the number of uninstantiated variables in c and t' the size of the current table of c. The loops at lines 1, 4 and 15 are $O(r')$, $O(rt')$ and $O(r'd)$, respectively. The worst-case space complexity of enforceGAC-str is $O(n + rt)$ per constraint since *levelLimits* is $O(n)$, *table* is $O(rt)$ and *position* is $O(t)$.

It is well known that values must be restored to domains when backtracking occurs. After this restoration, tuples that were invalid may now be valid. If a tuple τ was

---

Algorithm 41: removeTuple(c: constraint, i, p: integers)

// i is the position of the tuple to be removed

// p is the current level (number of past variables)

1 **if** $levelLimits[c][p] = -1$ **then**

2 | $levelLimits[c][p] \leftarrow currentLimit[c]$

3 $tmp \leftarrow position[c][i]$

4 $position[c][i] \leftarrow position[c][currentLimit[c]]$

5 $position[c][currentLimit[c]] \leftarrow tmp$

6 $currentLimits[c] \leftarrow currentLimit[c] - 1$

---

removed from the current table of c at level p, then τ must be restored to the current table of c when the search backtracks to level $p - 1$. In our implementation, tuples are restored by calling Algorithm 42 which puts the set of invalid tuples removed at the given level into the current table, at the tail end. Restoration is achieved in constant time (for each constraint) without traversing either set and without moving any tuple in memory [ULL 07].

Algorithm 42: restoreTuples(c: constraint, p: integer)

// p is the level at which tuples must be restored

1 **if** $levelLimits[c][p] \neq -1$ **then**

2 | $currentLimit[c] \leftarrow levelLimits[c][p]$

3 | $levelLimits[c][p] \leftarrow -1$

5.5.2. *Optimizing STR*

It is possible to improve STR in two directions [LEC 08a]. First, as soon as all values in the domain of a variable have been detected GAC-consistent, it is futile to continue to seek supports for values of this variable. We therefore introduce a set, S^{sup}, of uninstantiated variables in $\text{scp}(c)$ whose domain contains at least one value for which a support has not yet been found. In enforceGAC-str2, Algorithm 43, which is an optimized version of enforceGAC-str, lines 1, 5 and 7 initialize S^{sup} to be the same as $\text{scp}(c) \setminus \text{past}(P)$. If $|gacValues[x]| = |\text{dom}(x)|$ at line 19 then all values of $\text{dom}(x)$ are supported, so line 20 removes x from S^{sup}. Efficiency is gained by iterating only over variables in S^{sup} at lines 16 and 25.

The second direction of improvement avoids unnecessary validity operations. At the end of an invocation of STR for constraint c, we know that for every variable $x \in \text{scp}(c)$, every tuple τ such that $\tau[x] \notin \text{dom}(x)$ has been removed from the current table of c. If there is no backtrack and $\mathrm{dom}(x)$ does not change between this invocation and the next invocation, then at the time of the next invocation it is certainly true that $\tau[x] \in \mathrm{dom}(x)$ for every tuple τ in the current table of c. In this case, there is no need to check whether $\tau[x] \in \mathrm{dom}(x)$; efficiency is gained by omitting this check. We implement this optimization by means of a set S^{val}, which is the set of uninstantiated variables whose domain has been reduced since the previous invocation of enforceGAC-str2. Initially, this set also contains the last assigned variable, denoted by $lastPast(P)$ here, if it belongs to the scope of the constraint c. After any variable assignment $x = a$, some tuples may become invalid due to the removal of values from $\mathrm{dom}(x)$. The last assigned variable is the only instantiated variable for which validity operations must be performed. Algorithm 44 checks validity only for variables in S^{val}. The set S^{val} is initialized at lines 2 through 4 of Algorithm 43. At line 8 of this algorithm, $\mathrm{dom}(x).tailAbsent$ is the value that was most recently removed from the (initial) domain of x while processing this or any other constraint, as presented in section 1.5.1; $\mathrm{dom}(x).tailAbsent$ has the special value -1 when no value has been removed from the domain of x. $lastRemoved[c][x]$ is the value that was most recently removed from the domain of x while processing the specific constraint c (see lines 10 and 30); initially we have $lastRemoved[c][x] = -1$ for every arc (c, x). If these two values differ at line 8 then $\mathrm{dom}(x)$ has changed since the previous invocation of Algorithm 43 for the specific constraint c. In this case, x is included in S^{val} at line 9. This is how the membership of S^{val} is determined.

The worst-case time complexity of enforceGAC-str2 is $O(r'(d + t'))$. Performing a validity check is now $O(r')$ instead of $O(r)$, as can be seen in Algorithm 44. Moreover, the loop starting at line 12 is $O(r't')$. Like enforceGAC-str, the worst-case space complexity of enforceGAC-str2 is $O(n + rt)$ per constraint since data structures inherited from enforceGAC-str are $O(n + rt)$, $lastRemoved$ is $O(r)$; S^{sup} and S^{val} are also $O(r)$ but may be shared by all constraints.

The worst case scenarios used to develop the worst-case time complexities of both enforceGAC-str and enforceGAC-str2 do not entirely characterize the difference in behavior that may occur, in practice, between the two algorithms. Let us consider a positive table constraint c such that $\mathrm{scp}(c) = \{x_1, ..., x_r\}$ and the table initially includes:

```
(0,0,...,0)
(1,1,...,1)
...
(d-2,d-2,...,d-2)
(d-2,d-1,...,d-1)
(d-1,0,...,0)
...
```

Algorithm 43: enforceGAC-str2(P: $\mathscr{P}$, c: constraint): set of variables

---

Output: the set of variables in $\mathrm{scp}(c)$ with reduced domain

1 $S^{\mathrm{sup}} \leftarrow \emptyset$
2 $S^{\mathrm{val}} \leftarrow \emptyset$
3 **if** $lastPast(P) \in \mathrm{scp}(c)$ **then**
4 $\quad\lfloor\ S^{\mathrm{val}} \leftarrow S^{\mathrm{val}} \cup \{lastPast(P)\}$
5 **foreach** *variable* $x \in \mathrm{scp}(c) \mid x \notin \mathrm{past}(P)$ **do**
6 $\quad$ $gacValues[x] \leftarrow \emptyset$
7 $\quad$ $S^{\mathrm{sup}} \leftarrow S^{\mathrm{sup}} \cup \{x\}$
8 $\quad$ **if** $\mathrm{dom}(x).tailAbsent \neq lastRemoved[c][x]$ **then**
9 $\quad\quad$ $S^{\mathrm{val}} \leftarrow S^{\mathrm{val}} \cup \{x\}$
10 $\quad\quad\lfloor$ $lastRemoved[c][x] \leftarrow \mathrm{dom}(x).tailAbsent$

11 $i \leftarrow 1$
12 **while** $i \leq currentLimit[c]$ **do**
13 $\quad$ $index \leftarrow position[c][i]$
14 $\quad$ $\tau \leftarrow table[c][index]$
15 $\quad$ **if** $isValidTuple(c, S^{\mathrm{val}}, \tau)$ **then**
16 $\quad\quad$ **foreach** *variable* $x \in S^{\mathrm{sup}}$ **do**
17 $\quad\quad\quad$ **if** $\tau[x] \notin gacValues[x]$ **then**
18 $\quad\quad\quad\quad$ $gacValues[x] \leftarrow gacValues[x] \cup \{\tau[x]\}$
19 $\quad\quad\quad\quad$ **if** $|gacValues[x]| = |\mathrm{dom}(x)|$ **then**
20 $\quad\quad\quad\quad\lfloor$ $S^{\mathrm{sup}} \leftarrow S^{\mathrm{sup}} \setminus \{x\}$

21 $\quad\quad$ $i \leftarrow i + 1$
22 $\quad$ **else**
23 $\quad\quad\lfloor$ removeTuple($c, i, |\mathrm{past}(P)|$)   // $currentLimit[c]$ is decremented

// domains are now updated and X_{evt} computed
24 $X_{\mathrm{evt}} \leftarrow \emptyset$
25 **foreach** *variable* $x \in S^{\mathrm{sup}}$ **do**
26 $\quad$ $\mathrm{dom}(x) \leftarrow gacValues[x]$
27 $\quad$ **if** $\mathrm{dom}(x) = \emptyset$ **then**
28 $\quad\quad\lfloor$ **return** $\{x\}$
29 $\quad$ $X_{\mathrm{evt}} \leftarrow X_{\mathrm{evt}} \cup \{x\}$
30 $\quad$ $lastRemoved[c][x] \leftarrow \mathrm{dom}(x).tailAbsent$
31 **return** X_{evt}

Algorithm 44: isValidTuple(c: constraint, S^{val}: variables, τ: tuple): Boolean

---

1 **foreach** *variable* $x \in S^{\mathrm{val}}$ **do**
2   **if** $\tau[x] \notin \mathrm{dom}(x)$ **then**
3       $\lfloor$ **return** *false*

4 **return** *true*

In this example, the domain of each variable involved in c comprises all digits from 0 to $d - 1$. In the table, the each of the first $d - 1$ tuples is a sequence that repeats the same digit (from 0 to $d - 2$). The dth tuple consists of the digit $d - 2$ followed by a sequence of $d - 1$. The $(d + 1)$th tuple consists of the digit $d - 1$ followed by a sequence of 0. Assume that $\mathrm{past}(P) = \emptyset$ (no variable has been assigned) and that STR (either of the two algorithms) is applied to this constraint. No value is removed because all values are present in domains, and there exists a support for each value. Now, imagine that $(x_1, d - 1)$ is deleted while propagating some other constraints, whereas all other values remain valid. If STR is applied again to this constraint, no value will be removed (since the constraint is still GAC-consistent as any remaining value has still a support), but some tuples (at least the $(d + 1)$th one) will be eliminated. Interestingly, calling enforceGAC-str requires $O(r)$ constant-time operations to deal with *gacValues* structures (loops starting at lines 1 and 15), $O(rt)$ operations to perform validity checks, $O(rt)$ operations to check GAC values, and $O(rd)$ operations to collect GAC values. On the other hand, calling enforceGAC-str2 requires $O(r)$ operations to deal with *gacValues* structures, $O(t)$ operations to perform validity checks (since $S^{\mathrm{val}} = \{x_1\}$), $O(rd)$ operations to check GAC values (since $S^{\mathrm{sup}} = \emptyset$ after the treatment of the first d tuples) and $O(rd)$ operations to collect GAC values. This leads to:

OBSERVATION 5.14.– *There exist situations where applying* enforceGAC-str *to an r-ary constraint is* $O(rt + rd)$, *whereas applying* enforceGAC-str2 *is* $O(t + rd)$.

Most of the time, $d \ll t$ since $t \in O(d^r)$. In this case, Observation 5.14 shows that enforceGAC-str2 is potentially r times faster than enforceGAC-str. The higher the arity, the greater the possible benefit of using enforceGAC-str2. Finally, there are two possible ways to cope with backtracking. One way is to to reinitialize all arrays *lastRemoved*, filling them with the special value -1. The other way is to record the content of such arrays at each depth of search, so that the original state of the arrays can be restored upon backtracking. This approach, which requires an additional structure that is $O(nr)$ per constraint, is denoted by enforceGAC-str2+.

5.5.3. Relationship with GAC4

Section 4.4.2 includes an outline of the algorithm GAC4 which is a filtering algorithm for table constraints. The worst-case time complexity of GAC4 is $O(rt)$ per constraint, which is optimal. To show optimality, it is necessary to describe how tuples are discarded when they become invalid (lines 17 to 21 of Algorithm 20). Mohr and Masini show [MOH 88] that an r-tuple can be removed in $O(r)$. As usual, an array $table[c]$ contains the set of tuples allowed by c. For each c-value (c, x, a), a double linked list indicates the position in $table[c]$ of each tuple involving (x, a). Double linked list organization allows removal of an element in constant time. This list, whose head is denoted by $\sup[c, x, a]$, replaces the sub-table $table[c, x, a]$ introduced for some algorithms. Finally, we need an array $ptr[c]$ of the same size as $table[c]$. Whereas $table[c][i]$ denotes the ith tuple τ allowed by c, $ptr[c][i]$ denotes an array tab of size r such that $\forall j \in 1..r$, if $\tau[j] = (x, a)$ then $tab[j]$ is the reference (pointer) of the node in $\sup[c, x, a]$ whose value is i. This is illustrated in Figure 5.19.

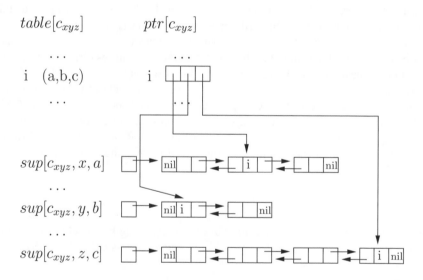

Figure 5.19. *Data structures of GAC4*

GAC4 and STR are related in that they both dynamically maintain the set of supports of each constraint. A major difference is that GAC4 is guided by (deleted) values, whereas STR globally enforces generalized arc consistency. The application of GAC4 during search remains to be studied; a practical comparison of these algorithms would be interesting.

5.6. GAC for negative table constraints

For negative table constraints, we present three approaches. The first is simply GAC-valid, the second is an adaptation of GAC-valid+allowed, and the third is based on converting sets of forbidden tuples into positive compressed tables or MDDs.

5.6.1. *Negative table constraints*

A negative table constraint is a constraint given in extension and defined by a set of forbidden tuples. The set of forbidden tuples associated with a negative table constraint c is denoted by $\overline{table}[c]$ and represented here by an array indexed from 1 to $\overline{table}[c].length$. The space complexity to record this set is $O(tr)$ where $t = \overline{table}[c].length$ is the size of the table (i.e. the number of forbidden tuples) and r is the arity of c.

For negative constraints, we introduce index structures similar to those proposed for positive table constraints in section 5.1.1. For each c-value (c, x, a) the sub-table $\overline{table}[c, x, a]$ provides access to forbidden tuples involving (x, a) in $\overline{table}[c]$. This sub-table (index) is an array whose indices ranges from 1 to $\overline{table}[c, x, a].length$ such that element $\overline{table}[c, x, a][i]$ gives the index in $\overline{table}[c]$ of the ith disallowed tuple involving (x, a). With these sub-table index structures, the space complexity remains $O(tr)$ per constraint.

Assuming that each sub-table is ordered (according to the lexicographic order of referenced tuples), the worst-case time complexity of checking (using a binary search) that a tuple τ involving (x, a) is allowed is $O(\log(t_{c,x,a})r)$ where $t_{c,x,a} = \overline{table}[c, x, a].length$.

5.6.2. *GAC-valid scheme*

GAC-valid is easily adapted to negative table constraints. Once again, considering the general approach presented in first sections of Chapter 4, we just have to describe the way a constraint check is performed (by GAC3). We simply replace the test $\tau \in rel(c)$ at line 3 of Algorithm 18 by $\tau \notin \overline{table}[c, x, a]$. As mentioned above, it is $O(\log(t_{c,x,a})r)$ with $t_{c,x,a} = \overline{table}[c, x, a].length$.

Remember that in the context of table constraints, we use seekSupport-v as alias for seekSupport-3. Also, recall that the number of valid tuples built from c and involving (x, a) is $v_{c,x,a} = |\,\text{val}(c)_{x=a}|$. Thus:

PROPOSITION 5.15.– *For an r-ary negative table constraint c, the worst-case time complexity of seekSupport-v, with input (c, x, a), is $O(v_{c,x,a} \log(t_{c,x,a})r)$.*

COROLLARY 5.16.– *Using a hash map with a hash function in $O(r)$ that properly disperses disallowed tuples, the worst-case time complexity of the function seekSupport-v is $O(v_{c,x,a}r)$.*

When a constraint is specified by a list of disallowed tuples, this means that the constraint tightness is greater than 0.5 (otherwise, to save space, we can just transform the negative table constraint into a positive table constraint). Then, on average, we can expect to find a support for a value quickly. More than a valid tuple on two valid tuples built from the initial domains is allowed and GAC-valid iterates over valid tuples until an allowed one is found.

5.6.3. *GAC-valid+forbidden scheme*

When a negative table constraint is highly structured (long sequences of forbidden tuples), it may still be quite expensive to find a support for some values with GAC-valid. This is why an adaptation of GAC-valid+allowed, called GAC-valid+forbidden, is now proposed.

To skip in constant time sequences of valid tuples containing no allowed tuples, we introduce an additional array of pointers for each c-value (c, x, a). Specifically, if τ is a tuple of $\overline{table}[c, x, a]$, then $lastSequ(\tau)$ denotes the greatest tuple τ' in $\overline{table}[c, x, a]$ such that $\tau' \geq_{\text{lex}} \tau$ and any tuple τ'' such that $\tau' >_{\text{lex}} \tau'' \geq_{\text{lex}} \tau$ also belongs to $\overline{table}[c, x, a]$. In other words, $lastSequ(\tau)$ denotes the last forbidden tuple of a convex sequence containing τ and serves as an auxiliary index. Note, however, that the overall worst-case space complexity remains $O(tr)$.

The function seekSupport-v+f, Algorithm 45, is designed to be called at line 3 of Algorithm 8. Each execution of the while loop in seekSupport-v+f processes a valid tuple (initially, the first is computed). At line 3, binarySearch performs a dichotomic search that returns the smallest disallowed tuple τ' of c such that $\tau' \geq_{\text{lex}} \tau$ and $\tau'[x] = a$. If $\tau' \neq \tau$ (including the case $\tau' = nil$), this means that τ is allowed and is therefore a support, so *true* is returned at line 5. Otherwise, $lastSequ(\tau)$ skips a convex sequence of forbidden tuples before getFirstInvalidPosition(c, τ') is called. If -1 is returned, we still have to find the next valid tuple strictly greater than τ' (since τ' cannot be a support). Otherwise, we compute the next valid tuple strictly greater than τ' (using the position of the first invalid position). The function getFirstInvalidPosition is described in Algorithm 16, the first overloaded function getNextValidTuple is described in Algorithm 14 and the second one is described in Algorithm 17.

Algorithm 45: seekSupport-v+f((c, x, a): c-value): Boolean

// Implementation of GAC-valid+forbidden
1 $\tau \leftarrow$ getFirstValidTuple$((c, x, a))$
2 **while** $\tau \neq nil$ **do**
3 | $\tau' \leftarrow$ binarySearch$(\overline{table}[c, x, a], \tau)$
4 | **if** $\tau' \neq \tau$ **then**
5 | | **return** $true$
6 | $\tau' \leftarrow lastSequ(\tau)$
7 | $j \leftarrow$ getFirstInvalidPosition(c, τ')
8 | **if** $j = -1$ **then**
9 | | $\tau \leftarrow$ getNextValidTuple$((c, x, a), \tau')$
10 | **else**
11 | | $\tau \leftarrow$ getNextValidTuple$((c, x, a), \tau', j)$
12 **return** $false$

PROPOSITION 5.17.– *For an r-ary negative table constraint c, the worst-case time complexity of seekSupport-v-f (using a binary search), with input (c, x, a), is $O(N(d + \log(t_{c,x,a})r))$ where N is the number of maximal sequences of valid tuples for (c, x, a) containing no allowed tuple.*

5.6.4. *Compressed tuples and MDDs*

A set of disallowed tuples can be converted efficiently into a set of allowed compressed tuples [KAT 07]. For a negative table constraint c, a compressed table is built from $\prod_{x \in \text{scp}(c)} \text{dom}^{\text{init}}(x) \setminus \overline{table}[c]$. When the number of allowed tuples is exponentially greater than the number of disallowed ones, this is not true of the number of allowed compressed tuples. [KAT 07] uses decision trees and shows that the number of compressed tuples obtained from a decision tree F is $O(nd|F|)$ where $|F|$ denotes the number of nodes in the decision tree.

A set of tuples can be represented by a multi-valued decision diagram (MDD), as in section 5.3.2. For disallowed tuples, the terminal node is denoted by $\boxed{f}$. In this case, it is easy to generate a set of allowed compressed tuples. Let us consider a node v at level $i \in 1..r$ of the graph (where $v \neq \boxed{f}$). Let $\Delta(v)$ be the set of values present in the domain of the variable associated with v but not present in any label (of the arcs) outgoing from v. If $\Delta(v) = \emptyset$, we say that v is *covered* in the diagram. If

$\Delta(v) \neq \emptyset$, we can add a path to the diagram composed of a first arc labeled with $\Delta(v)$ and $r - i$ intermediate successive arcs leading finally to $\boxed{t}$. Each intermediate arc is labeled with the values present in the domain of the variable associated with its parent node. We proceed analogously with every (old) node of the diagram and we merge similar subgraphs. From the resulting completed MDD it is easy to extract allowed compressed tuples.

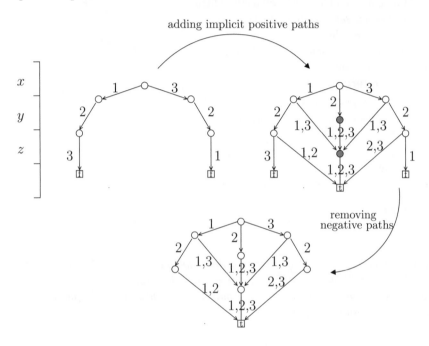

Figure 5.20. *Translating a "negative" MDD into a "positive" one*

EXAMPLE.– Let us consider as in [KAT 07] a constraint c_{xyz} with $\text{dom}(x) = \text{dom}(y) = \text{dom}(z) = \{1, 2, 3\}$ and $\overline{table}[c_{xyz}] = \{(1, 2, 3), (3, 2, 1)\}$. Here there are two disallowed tuples and $3^3 - 2 = 25$ allowed tuples. Figure 5.20 shows how the initial MDD representing these two forbidden tuples can be completed to include the entire set of allowed tuples. Discarding negative paths, i.e. paths leading to $\boxed{f}$, we obtain a "positive" MDD. The set of allowed compressed tuples can then be easily collected by following every path leading to node $\boxed{t}$. For our example, we obtain:

$(\{1\}, \{1, 3\}, \{1, 2, 3\})$
$(\{1\}, \{2\}, \{1, 2\})$
$(\{2\}, \{1, 2, 3\}, \{1, 2, 3\})$
$(\{3\}, \{1, 3\}, \{1, 2, 3\})$
$(\{3\}, \{2\}, \{2, 3\})$

If we use the order y, x, z to build the MDD, we obtain a different compressed table containing only four elements as in [KAT 07]. More generally, the number of allowed compressed tuples obtained from an MDD G representing the set of forbidden tuples is exactly the number of nodes in G that are not covered.

Of course, once a (positive) compressed table has been built from a negative table constraint, we can use the approach described in section 5.3.3. We can also use the MDD approach in section 5.3.2 by translating negative MDDs into positive ones, or by slightly modifying the filtering procedure [CHE 08b].

5.7. Experimental results

An experimental comparison of all approaches mentioned in this chapter would be very difficult and is beyond the scope of this book. Published results, e.g. [LHO 05b, LEC 06d, GEN 07, KAT 07, LEC 08a, CHE 08a], give some impression of the relative efficiency of various approaches. This section provides a few tables showing dramatic differences of behavior between some selected approaches, always with table constraints.

Our experiments have used a cluster of Xeon 3.0 GHz with 1 GB of RAM under Linux, employing MAC with *dom/ddeg* and *lexico* as variable[4] and value ordering heuristics, respectively; MAC and heuristics are described in Chapters 8 and 9. We have compared STR with classical schemes that enforce GAC on (positive) table constraints. More specifically, on the one hand we have implemented GAC-valid (GAC-v for short), GAC-allowed (GAC-a for short) and GAC-valid+allowed (GAC-v+a for short) schemes, while on the other hand we have implemented the original STR algorithm (GAC-str), the optimized version of this algorithm (GAC-str2) and this last one made incremental (GAC-str2+). As mentioned earlier, the three classical schemes can be easily instantiated from different general-purpose coarse-grained GAC algorithms; our experiments have used GAC3^{rm}. Performance has been measured in terms of the CPU time in seconds.

First, we have experimented on various series of (random and structured) CSP instances. These series represent a large spectrum of instances, and importantly, allow anyone to reproduce this experimentation "easily". The first two series [CHE 06] bdd-21-2713-15 and bdd-21-133-18 (bdd-15 and bdd-18 in Table 5.1) contain 35 instances each, with 21 Boolean variables and large and small BDD constraints of arity 15 and 18, respectively. The series renault-mod contains 45 real-world instances (we were unable to solve 5 of them with the selected heuristics within a reasonable amount of

---

4. In our implementation, using *dom/wdeg* does not guarantee exploring the same search tree with classical and STR schemes. This is why we didn't choose it.

Series	#Inst	Classical GAC schemes			Simple tabular reduction		
		GAC-v	GAC-a	GAC-v+a	GAC-str	GAC-str2	GAC-str2+
bdd-15	35	69.3	386	58.8	164	94.5	52.1
bdd-18	35	37.3	(23 out)	36.0	66.1	38.3	26.2
renault-mod	45	83.8	45.7	48.0	61.6	54.9	45.4
tsp-20	15	28.4	23.3	14.9	8.80	8.95	8.35
tsp-25	15	254	273	196	119	122	118
rand-8	20	107	(16 out)	119	108	81.2	65.6
rand-10	20	(20 out)	4.49	5.61	1.00	0.77	0.53

Table 5.1. *Mean CPU time to solve instances of different series with MAC (a time-out of* 1,200 *seconds was set per instance). For classical algorithms, GAC3^{rm} was embedded in MAC*

time) involving domains containing up to 42 values and constraints of various arity defined by large tables (the greatest one contains about 50,000 6-tuples). The two series tsp-20 and tsp-25 contain 15 instances of the traveling salesperson problem with domains containing up to 1,000 values and ternary constraints defined by large tables (about 20,000 3-tuples). Finally, the two series rand-8-20-5-18 and rand-10-20-10-5 (rand-8 and rand-10 in Table 5.1) contain 20 random instances each with 20 variables. Each instance of the series rand-8-20-5-18 (resp. rand-10-20-10-5) involves domains containing 5 (resp. 10) values and 18 (resp. 5) constraints of arity 8 (resp. 10); tables contain about 78,000 and 10,000 tuples, respectively.

Table 5.1 shows the mean CPU time required to solve the instances of these different series with MAC. Overall, GAC-str2+ is always the most efficient approach; it is three times faster than GAC-str on the bdd-21-2713-15 series and ten times faster than GAC-v+a on the rand-10-20-10-5 series. Memory consumption (not shown here) of all these algorithms differs at most by a factor of two. The additional structure in GAC-str2+ is in $O(nd)$ and has a very limited practical impact in all these series of experiments.

We have also experimented with some series of crossword puzzles. For each white square within each grid, there is one variable that can be assigned any of the 26 letters of the Latin alphabet. For each sequence of white squares where a word should be placed on the grid, the word is constrained to belong to a given dictionary. Each such constraint is defined by a table that contains all words of the right length. The series prefixed by cw-m1c (omitted in the table) are defined from blank grids and only contain positive table constraints (unlike model m1 in [BEA 01] where no two identical words can be put in the grid, which is a constraint expressed in intension). The arity of the constraints is given by the size of the grids: for example, cw-m1c-lex-vg5-6 involves table constraints of arity 5 and 6 (the grid being 5 by 6). Our results (see Table 5.2) with respect to four dictionaries (lex, words, uk, ogd) of different length

		Classical GAC schemes			Simple tabular reduction		
		GAC-v	GAC-a	GAC-v+a	GAC-str	GAC-str2	GAC-str2+
Crossword puzzles with dictionary lex (24,974 words)							
lex-vg5-6	CPU	> 1,200	38.8	54.2	14.3	12.4	10.7
#nodes=26,679	mem		2.821	2.859	2.863	2.866	2.898
lex-vg5-7	CPU	> 1,200	357	875	134	114	96.3
#nodes=171 K	mem		4.037	4.075	7.817	7.866	7.870
lex-vg6-6	CPU	> 1,200	2.98	4.29	1.28	1.05	0.91
#nodes=1,602	mem		4.318	4.242	4.127	4.104	4.195
lex-vg6-7	CPU	> 1,200	436	1,174	176	143	118
#nodes=152 K	mem		5.749	5.559	9.236	9.216	9.331
Crossword puzzles with dictionary words (45,371 words)							
words-vg5-5	CPU	> 1,200	0.04	0.05	0.05	0.05	0.04
#nodes=38	mem		4.852	4.870	4.710	4.678	4.696
words-vg5-6	CPU	> 1,200	1.19	1.46	0.48	0.37	0.33
#nodes=718	mem		6.355	6.373	6.199	6.126	6.199
words-vg5-7	CPU	> 1,200	18.6	36.0	6.61	5.21	4.03
#nodes=6,957	mem		8.271	8.290	8.082	7.954	8.044
words-vg5-8	CPU	> 1,200	866	> 1,200	273	229	187
#nodes=256 K	mem		4.496		10	10	10
Crossword puzzles with dictionary uk (225,349 words)							
uk-vg5-5	CPU	> 1,200	0.05	0.05	0.1	0.07	0.07
#nodes=28	mem		12	12	12	12	12
uk-vg5-6	CPU	> 1,200	0.55	0.5	0.21	0.17	0.17
#nodes=145	mem		17	17	16	16	16
uk-vg5-7	CPU	> 1,200	2.97	5.18	0.51	0.37	0.34
#nodes=408	mem		22	22	22	22	22
uk-vg5-8	CPU	> 1,200	82.5	71.9	7.08	5.71	4.78
#nodes=8,148	mem		12	12	11	11	11
Crossword puzzles with dictionary ogd (435,705 words)							
ogd-vg6-6	CPU	> 1,200	0.37	0.31	0.23	0.17	0.15
#nodes=98	mem		46	47	46	46	48
ogd-vg6-7	CPU	> 1,200	95.3	56.1	12.0	8.01	6.81
#nodes=9,522	mem		11	11	11	11	11
ogd-vg6-8	CPU	> 1,200	53.0	6.44	2.91	2.0	1.72
#nodes=2,806	mem		24	23	22	22	24
ogd-vg6-9	CPU	> 1,200	727	214	35.1	25.1	19.1
#nodes=23,283	mem		42	41	39	37	40

Table 5.2. *Representative results obtained on series of crossword puzzles using dictionaries of different length. The number of nodes (#nodes) explored by MAC is given below the name of each instance*

confirm our previous results. On the most difficult instances, GAC-str2+ is about twice as fast as GAC-str and is one order of magnitude faster than GAC-v+a. We do not report mean timings for these series because many instances cannot be solved within 1,200 seconds.

5.8. Conclusion

Table constraints have received much attention over the last few years, partially because they play a central role in the development of robust generic constraint solvers. This chapter has attempted to provide a substantial overview of general approaches that deal with such constraints. Of course, we did not introduce all subtleties of all of them. For example, we did not describe the hologram structure that can be used with the nextIn approach, nor how for the MDD approach incrementality can be managed by using a sparse set data structure.

We are convinced that several ideas, techniques and data structures involved in these different proposals could advantageously be extended and combined to obtain further improvements in the speed of propagation of table constraints. A related development explores the possibility of reformulating table constraints of large arity as conjunctions of lower arity constraints. In [CAM 08] such decomposition is based on functional dependencies and is shown to be complementary to compression-based approaches.

Chapter 6

Singleton Arc Consistency

Maintaining arc consistency (MAC), which is the subject of Chapter 8, is certainly the most popular systematic search algorithm for solving instances of the constraint satisfaction problem. At each step of backtrack search, MAC enforces generalized arc consistency (GAC) to reduce domains inferentially. Thus MAC interleaves inference with search. This chapter reviews proposals for enforcing stronger consistencies, instead of arc consistency, before and/or during the search. Examples of stronger consistencies are max-restricted path consistency (Max-RPC), path-inverse consistency (PIC) and singleton arc consistency (SAC).

Singleton consistencies, and more particularly singleton arc consistency, have recently received much attention; see for example [DEB 97b, PRO 00, BAR 04, BES 04b, BES 04a, LEC 05, BES 08a]. A constraint network is singleton arc-consistent[1] if no value is singleton arc-inconsistent, i.e. if after instantiating any variable, enforcement of generalized arc consistency does not empty any domain. Singleton arc consistency is quite easy to define and understand as it is based straightforwardly on instantiation and on enforcement of generalized arc consistency. This makes it all the more attractive since it is substantially stronger than generalized arc consistency: it looks one step in advance in all "directions". Strong inferences during a preprocessing stage or during the early stages of a backtrack search can dramatically reduce the search space. It is therefore possible that singleton arc consistency may be important in the development of a new generation of robust constraint solvers.

---

1. A formal definition can be found in section 3.3.

A *SAC algorithm* is an algorithm that enforces singleton arc consistency: given a constraint network P, a SAC algorithm computes the SAC-closure of P, denoted by $SAC(P)$. The efficiency of an algorithm that enforces singleton arc consistency depends mainly on its ability to avoid useless singleton checks and on its incrementality level, which is the extent to which the incrementality of the underlying GAC algorithm is exploited. Compared to the basic algorithm SAC1, SAC2 avoids many singleton checks. Going further, SAC-Opt is made incremental (and consequently worst-case time optimal) by associating a constraint network with each v-value. Unfortunately, SAC-Opt requires substantial memory for these duplicated constraint networks and for data structures that permit incrementality. SAC-SDS is derived from SAC-Opt by trading optimal time complexity for a better space complexity. SAC3 exploits incrementality by performing greedy runs of an algorithm that maintains generalized arc consistency. The variant SAC3+ stores the result of each run, for subsequent advantageous reuse.

Experience suggests that maintaining singleton arc consistency during search may not be cost-effective because of the high risk that many singleton checks are fruitless. In particular, the complexity of systematically checking all values in all domains obviously grows with the size of the domains. To mitigate complexity, *bound SAC* and *existential SAC* [LEC 06a] are partial forms of SAC that restrict the inference effort to one value per domain, ensuring that there exists at least one possibility of instantiating each variable, while applying GAC. When SAC is only enforced during a preprocessing stage before search, stronger forms of SAC may be appropriate. A promising example is weak k-SAC [DON 06], which finds for each value at least one "consistent" instantiation of $k - 1$ variables.

This chapter is organized as follows. Section 6.1 presents SAC1 and SAC2, which are historically the first algorithms for enforcing singleton arc consistency. Section 6.2 introduces SAC-Opt which enforces SAC with optimal worst-case time complexity; this section also includes a brief discussion of SAC-SDS. Sections 6.3 and 6.4 introduce SAC3 and SAC3+ which perform greedy runs to achieve SAC. The behavior of these different algorithms is compared in section 6.5. Finally, section 6.6 shows how algorithms for existential SAC and weak k-SAC are natural developments, also using a greedy approach.

Important In accordance with well-established usage, this chapter uses the acronym SAC instead of SGAC even in the general case, i.e. for singleton GAC on networks involving constraints of arbitrary arity. However, complexities will only be given for binary constraint networks. On the other hand, an instruction of the form $GAC(P, X_{evt})$ must always be understood as a call to the function enforceGAC^{var}, Algorithm 9, which takes P and X_{evt} as parameters, and returns *false* when a domain wipe-out is identified, denoted here by $GAC(P, X_{evt}) = \bot$. Instead of returning a Boolean value, $GAC(P, X_{evt})$ is assumed to return the constraint network obtained after enforcing GAC on P from events in X_{evt}.

6.1. SAC1 and SAC2

SAC1 [DEB 97b] is the first algorithm that establishes singleton arc consistency. SAC1, Algorithm 46, starts by enforcing generalized arc consistency and then checks each v-value (x, a) in turn. The test $GAC(P|_{x=a}, \{x\}) = \perp$ at line 7 corresponds to a *singleton check* on (x, a). Because GAC is maintained on P (at lines 1 and 8), the instruction $GAC(P|_{x=a}, \{x\})$ is guaranteed to return the constraint network $GAC(P|_{x=a})$. If a value is detected to be SAC-inconsistent, it is removed from its domain and the effect is propagated by enforcing GAC at line 8. If P is proved to be SAC-inconsistent (i.e. if $SAC(P) = \perp$), then *false* is returned at line 10 (or at line 3). Otherwise, the repeat loop terminates at the end of the first iteration in which no domain has been modified.

SAC1 has no additional data structure, so its space complexity is the same as that of the underlying GAC algorithm. The lack of additional data structure means that SAC1 must systematically recheck all (remaining) values whenever a value is deleted. This brute-force algorithm can be regarded as an extension of the basic algorithm AC1 [MAC 77a].

Algorithm 46: SAC1(P: $\mathscr{P}$): Boolean

Output: *true* iff $SAC(P) \neq \perp$

1   $P \leftarrow GAC(P, \text{vars}(P))$ // GAC is initially enforced
2   **if** $P = \perp$ **then**
3 | **return** *false*

4 **repeat**
5 | *modified* $\leftarrow$ *false*
6 | **foreach** *v-value* (x, a) of P **do**
7 | | **if** $GAC(P|_{x=a}, \{x\}) = \perp$ **then**
8 | | | $P \leftarrow GAC(P|_{x \neq a}, \{x\})$ // a is removed from $\text{dom}(x)$ and GAC enforced
9 | | | **if** $P = \perp$ **then**
10 | | | | **return** *false*
11 | | | *modified* $\leftarrow$ *true*

12 **until** $\neg$*modified*
13 **return** *true*

PROPOSITION 6.1.– *On binary constraint networks, SAC1 embedding an optimal arc consistency algorithm such as AC2001, admits a worst-case space complexity in $O(ed)$ and a worst-case time complexity in $O(en^2d^4)$.*

The *SAC support* for a v-value (x, a) on P is the complete set of v-values of $GAC(P|_{x=a})$, resulting from a singleton check on (x, a). The second algorithm, SAC2 [BAR 04], avoids some useless singleton checks by recording, for each v-value, the entire set of v-values that supported it. SAC2 uses the fact that if $GAC(P|_{x=a}) \neq \bot$ then (x, a) remains SAC-consistent so long as its support remains unchanged, i.e. so long as each v-value present in $GAC(P|_{x=a})$ is not deleted elsewhere. Consequently, a v-value (x, a) has to be singleton checked (again) after the removal of a v-value (y, b) if and only if (y, b) belongs to the SAC support for (x, a) on P. As expected, the practical performance of SAC2 is an improvement [BAR 04] on SAC1. But the worst-case time complexity of SAC2 is the same as for SAC1 because consistency has to be enforced on $P|_{x=a}$ from scratch every time (x, a) is singleton checked. In SAC2 the extra data structures that manage SAC supports are in $O(n^2 d^2)$.

6.2. SAC-Opt and SAC-SDS

To enforce singleton arc consistency, GAC may be enforced on $P|_{x=a}$ at worst nd times for each v-value (x, a). SAC-Opt avoids enforcing GAC on $P|_{x=a}$ from scratch each time (x, a) is singleton checked. For each v-value (x, a), SAC-Opt has a separate dedicated constraint network P_{x_a} representing the subproblem $P|_{x=a}$ where the domain of x only contains the value a. Every time (x, a) is singleton checked, SAC-Opt uses the network P_{x_a} that has been dedicated to (x, a). This enables SAC-Opt, unlike SAC1 and SAC2, to benefit from the incrementality of the underlying GAC algorithm and thereby to enforce singleton arc consistency with optimal[2] worst-case time complexity [BES 04b, BES 08a].

For each of the separate subproblem networks P_{x_a}, the domains and the data structures used specifically for (x, a) by the underlying GAC algorithm are represented. A single representation of all constraints is shared by all of the subproblem networks and is not duplicated. Each subproblem network has its own dedicated propagation queue of variables: the propagation queue for P_{x_a} is Q_{x_a}. SAC-Opt, Algorithm 47, also has a single set Q_{sac} of v-values whose singleton arc consistency must be checked. At line 14, the instruction of the form $GAC^+(P, X_{\text{evt}})$ returns a pair $(P', deleted)$ where $P' = GAC(P, X_{\text{evt}})$ and $deleted = \{(x, a) \mid x \in \text{vars}(P) \land a \in \text{dom}^P(x) \setminus \text{dom}^{P'}(x)\}$. Algorithms presented in Chapter 4 can easily be adapted to additionally return $deleted$, which is the set of v-values removed after enforcing GAC.

At line 1 in Algorithm 47, SAC-Opt enforces generalized arc consistency on the given network. Then all subproblem networks are initialized and all v-values are put into Q_{sac}. For each v-value (x, a) picked in Q_{sac}, SAC-Opt enforces GAC on the

---

2. Optimality is proved for binary constraint networks and conjectured for non-binary networks.

appropriate subproblem at line 10. If (x, a) is proven to be SAC-consistent, then Q_{x_a} is emptied since all events (deleted values) have been treated. Otherwise, (x, a) has to be removed from the original network P, and GAC has to be enforced again (the original algorithm does not include this slight modification). Q_{sac} is updated at line 9 to discard the v-value singleton checked, and at line 17 to discard the v-values deleted while enforcing GAC. The function updateSubproblems, Algorithm 48, updates every subproblem network that involves any deleted v-value, including (x, a). Specifically, for each v-value (x, a) that has just been removed and that belongs to a subproblem P_{y_b}, the function updateSubproblems updates P_{y_b}, Q_{y_b} and also Q_{sac}. Iteration continues until a fixed point is reached, or *false* is returned at line 16 because P is proved to be SAC-inconsistent.

Algorithm 47: SAC-Opt($P: \mathscr{P}$): Boolean

Output: *true* iff $SAC(P) \neq \bot$

1 $P \leftarrow GAC(P, \text{vars}(P))$ // GAC is initially enforced
2 **if** $P = \bot$ **then**
3 $\quad\lfloor$ **return** *false*

4 **foreach** *v-value* (x, a) *of* P **do**
5 $\quad\lvert \quad P_{x_a} \leftarrow P|_{x=a}$ // we have $\text{dom}^{P_{x_a}}(x) = \{a\}$
6 $\quad\lfloor \quad Q_{x_a} \leftarrow \{x\}$

7 $Q_{\text{sac}} \leftarrow \{(x, a) \mid x \in \text{vars}(P) \wedge a \in \text{dom}(x)\}$
8 **while** $Q_{\text{sac}} \neq \emptyset$ **do**
9 $\quad\lvert \quad$ pick and delete (x, a) from Q_{sac}
10 $\quad\lvert \quad P_{x_a} \leftarrow GAC(P_{x_a}, Q_{x_a})$
11 $\quad\lvert \quad$ **if** $P_{x_a} \neq \bot$ **then**
12 $\quad\lvert \quad\lvert \quad Q_{x_a} \leftarrow \emptyset$
13 $\quad\lvert \quad$ **else**
14 $\quad\lvert \quad\lvert \quad (P, deleted) \leftarrow GAC^+(P|_{x \neq a}, \{x\})$ // a is removed from $\text{dom}(x)$ and
   $\quad\quad\quad\quad$ GAC enforced - deleted values are returned
15 $\quad\lvert \quad\lvert \quad$ **if** $P = \bot$ **then**
16 $\quad\lvert \quad\lvert \quad\lfloor$ **return** *false*
17 $\quad\lvert \quad\lvert \quad Q_{\text{sac}} \leftarrow Q_{\text{sac}} \setminus deleted$
18 $\quad\lfloor \quad\lfloor$ updateSubproblems($P, deleted \cup \{(x, a)\}$)

19 **return** *true*

What is interesting about SAC-Opt is that the total worst-case time complexity of successively enforcing GAC on each subproblem is the same as a single call to the GAC enforcement procedure. Exploitation of incrementality of the underlying (general-purpose) GAC algorithm allows SAC-Opt to enforce SAC on binary

---

Algorithm 48: updateSubproblems(P: $\mathscr{P}$, *deleted*: set of v-values)

1 **foreach** *v-value* $(x, a) \in$ *deleted* **do**
2   **foreach** *v-value* (y, b) *of* P **do**
3   **if** $a \in \mathrm{dom}^{P_{yb}}(x)$ **then**
4   remove a from $\mathrm{dom}^{P_{yb}}(x)$
5              $Q_{yb} \leftarrow Q_{yb} \cup \{x\}$
6              $Q_{\mathrm{sac}} \leftarrow Q_{\mathrm{sac}} \cup \{(y, b)\}$

---

constraint networks in $O(end^3)$, which is the lowest time complexity that can be expected [BES 04b, BES 08a].

PROPOSITION 6.2.– *On binary constraint networks, SAC-Opt embedding an optimal arc consistency algorithm such as AC2001, admits a worst-case space complexity in $O(end^2)$ and an optimal worst-case time complexity in $O(end^3)$.*

Unfortunately, SAC-Opt cannot be used on large constraint networks because its worst-case space complexity is in $O(end^2)$. This is why Bessiere and Debruyne [BES 05b] have proposed another algorithm called SAC-SDS, which incorporates a trade-off between time and space. Space requirements are reduced by sharing, instead of duplicating, data structures required for establishing (generalized) arc consistency on different subproblems. Worst-case space and time complexities of SAC-SDS are respectively $O(n^2 d^2)$ and $O(end^4)$. SAC-SDS has performed well in experiments with random instances.

6.3. SAC3

All the SAC algorithms mentioned previously perform a kind of breadth-first search with depth equal to 1. Each "branch" of this search corresponds to a singleton check on a value that is removed if an inconsistency is found. An alternative [LEC 05] is to check a value in the continuity of previous checks. The idea is to build fewer branches of greater length using *greedy runs*, maintaining GAC at each step. The current branch is extended until a dead-end (or the impossibility of making further variable assignments) is reached. In this context the current run is stopped when the first assigned value is SAC-inconsistent, or when all assigned values, except the last one, are SAC-consistent. This last statement relies on Proposition 6.3.

PROPOSITION 6.3.– *Let P be a constraint network, I a valid instantiation on P and $P' = GAC(P|_I)$. If $P' \neq \bot$, then every v-value (x, a) of P such that $\mathrm{dom}^{P'}(x) = \{a\}$ is SAC-consistent on P.*

Proof. We know that every v-value (x, a) of P' such that $\mathrm{dom}^{P'}(x) = \{a\}$ is SAC-consistent on P' because $GAC(P'|_{x=a}) = P'$ (P' is GAC-consistent and a is the unique value in $\mathrm{dom}^{P'}(x)$). On the other hand, as SAC is stable (see Definition 3.13) for $(\mathscr{P}, \preceq_d)$ and $P' \preceq_d P$, every v-value SAC-consistent on P' is necessarily SAC-consistent on P. We deduce that v-values (x, a) of P such that $\mathrm{dom}^{P'}(x) = \{a\}$ are SAC-consistent on P. $\square$

This means that all v-values in I are SAC-consistent, but there may be also some v-values (y, b) of P such that $(y, b) \notin I$ and $\mathrm{dom}^{P'}(y) = \{b\}$. These values are detected SAC-consistent while others (those in I) are checked. Proposition 6.3, which can be seen as a generalization of Property 2 in [CHM 00], is also related to the exploitation of singleton-valued variables in [SAB 97].

Algorithm 49: SAC3(P: $\mathscr{P}$): Boolean

Output: *true* iff $SAC(P) \neq \bot$

1   $P \leftarrow GAC(P, \mathrm{vars}(P))$ // GAC is initially enforced
2   **if** $P = \bot$ **then**
3    $\lfloor$ **return** *false*

4 **repeat**
5    $modified \leftarrow false$
6    $Q_{\mathrm{sac}} \leftarrow \{(x, a) \mid x \in \mathrm{vars}(P) \land a \in \mathrm{dom}(x)\}$
7   **while** $Q_{\mathrm{sac}} \neq \emptyset$ **do**
8      $(x, a) \leftarrow$ buildBranch(P)
9   **if** $(x, a) \neq nil$ **then**
10       $(P, deleted) \leftarrow GAC^+(P|_{x \neq a}, \{x\})$ // a is removed from $\mathrm{dom}(x)$
          and GAC enforced - del. values are returned
11   **if** $P = \bot$ **then**
12        $\lfloor$ **return** *false*
13       $Q_{\mathrm{sac}} \leftarrow Q_{\mathrm{sac}} \setminus deleted$
14       $modified \leftarrow true$

15 **until** $\neg modified$
16 **return** *true*

SAC3 is the first algorithm using a greedy search mechanism to establish singleton arc consistency. As in SAC-Opt, Q_{sac} is the set of v-values whose singleton arc consistency must be checked, and *deleted* is the set of v-values removed during enforcement of GAC. After initially enforcing generalized arc consistency on the given network, SAC3, Algorithm 49, puts all v-values into Q_{sac}, and then successive branches are built in order to check these v-values. Branches are built by function

---

Algorithm 50: buildBranch(**in** P: $\mathscr{P}$): v-value

Output: a SAC-inconsistent v-value, or nil

1 $length \leftarrow 0$
2 **repeat**
3 $\quad$ pick and delete (x, a) from $Q_{\text{sac}} \mid a \in \text{dom}^P(x)$
4 $\quad P \leftarrow GAC(P|_{x=a}, \{x\})$
5 $\quad$ **if** $P \neq \bot$ **then**
6 $\quad\quad \mid length \leftarrow length + 1$
7 $\quad$ **else if** $length > 0$ **then**
8 $\quad\quad \lfloor Q_{\text{sac}} \leftarrow Q_{\text{sac}} \cup \{(x, a)\}$
9 **until** $P = \bot \vee \nexists (x, a) \in Q_{\text{sac}} \mid a \in \text{dom}^P(x)$
10 **if** $length = 0$ **then**
11 $\quad \mid$ **return** (x, a) $\qquad\qquad$ // (x, a) is SAC-inconsistent
12 **else**
13 $\quad \lfloor$ **return** nil

---

buildBranch, Algorithm 50 where P is an input parameter[3], which returns either the first v-value that has been assigned if this has led directly to failure, or otherwise returns nil. In the first case, the SAC-inconsistent value is removed, GAC is re-established and, in order to guarantee SAC enforcement, the flag $modified$ is set to $true$. Q_{sac} is updated at line 3 in Algorithm 50 to discard the v-values proved to be SAC-consistent when building a branch (see also line 8), and at line 13 in Algorithm 49 to discard the v-values deleted while enforcing GAC. When the set Q_{sac} is eventually empty, a new pass is started if the flag $modified$ indicates that at least one value was removed during the previous pass. This process continues until a fixed point is reached, or $false$ is returned at line 12.

When a value is detected SAC-inconsistent in the function buildBranch, this inference is necessarily associated with the first variable assignment: we have $length = 0$. The repeat loop in Algorithm 50 may terminate when no dead-end has been encountered (i.e. even if $P \neq \bot$): a solution may have been found (this is not shown here), or it may be impossible to extend the current branch using v-values currently in Q_{sac}. Note also that when buildBranch is called, we know that Q_{sac} is not empty and that every v-value in Q_{sac} belongs to the current problem since after any modification (value removal), Q_{sac} is maintained at line 13 of Algorithm 49.

At line 3 of Algorithm 50, it is best to select first those v-values, if any, that are guaranteed to be SAC-consistent because they already belong to singleton domains

---

3. Consequently, all modifications made to P are localized to buildBranch.

(see Proposition 6.3). This direct identification of SAC-consistent values comes for free, since no GAC propagation effort has to be done when a variable with a singleton domain is instantiated on a network that is already GAC-consistent. At line 3 of Algorithm 50, it is also important to use a heuristic that succeeds in making branches as long as possible, in order to benefit maximally from the incrementality of the underlying GAC algorithm.

A nice feature of SAC3 is that, like SAC1, its space complexity is that of the underlying GAC algorithm. It is important to note that greedy runs that maintain GAC benefit naturally from incrementality. Iteratively establishing GAC on a progressively reduced search space is less penalizing than repeatedly establishing GAC on the original search space. Besides, it becomes possible to learn relevant information from conflicts (recording no-goods or weighting failure culprits as in subsequent chapters). Furthermore, some (lucky) solutions may be found fortuitously while enforcing SAC.

PROPOSITION 6.4.– *On binary constraint networks, SAC3 embedding an optimal arc consistency algorithm such as AC2001, admits a worst-case space complexity in* $O(ed)$ *and a worst-case time complexity in* $O(bed^2)$, *where* b *denotes the number of branches built by the algorithm.*

Proof. If SAC3 embeds an optimal coarse-grained arc consistency algorithm such as AC2001, then the overall space complexity is $O(ed)$ since the space complexity of AC2001 is $O(ed)$ and the data structure Q_{sac} is $O(nd)$; recall that we reasonably assume that n is $O(e)$ for binary constraint networks. The overall time complexity is $O(bed^2)$ since, due to incrementality, each branch built by the algorithm is $O(ed^2)$. To guarantee this complexity, the structure $last$ of AC2001 must be saved before building a new branch and restored when the construction of the branch is finished.   □

Note that b includes the number of "empty" branches associated with SAC-inconsistent values. In the worst case, we have $b = \frac{n^2d^2+nd}{2}$ because up to nd branches may be built before the first value is removed, up to $nd - 1$ additional branches may be built before the second value is removed, and so on. Hence we obtain a worst-case time complexity (with AC2001 embedded) in $O(en^2d^4)$, which is the same as for SAC1. However, when a binary constraint network is already singleton arc-consistent, we can make the following observation:

REMARK 6.5.– *On a binary constraint network that is singleton arc-consistent, SAC3 builds between* d *and* nd *branches.*

The best and worst cases correspond respectively to branches of maximum length n and length 1 (one consistent variable assignment followed by an inconsistent one). We have then respectively $b = d$ (all branches delivering a solution) and $b = nd$ branches.

As a consequence of this observation, on a binary constraint network that is already singleton arc-consistent, SAC3 embedding an optimal arc consistency algorithm, such as AC2001, has a time complexity in $O(end^3)$ because it explores at most $b = nd$ branches. This suggests that SAC3 may be quite competitive on structured (not necessarily singleton arc-consistent) instances which contain large under-constrained parts, as can be expected in many real-world applications.

6.4. SAC3+

Algorithm 51: SAC3+(P: $\mathscr{P}$): Boolean

Output: *true* iff $SAC(P) \neq \bot$

1 $P \leftarrow GAC(P, \text{vars}(P))$ // GAC is initially enforced
2 **if** $P = \bot$ **then**
3 $\quad \lfloor$ **return** *false*

4 $brs \leftarrow \emptyset$
5 $Q_{\text{sac}} \leftarrow \{(x, a) \mid x \in \text{vars}(P) \land a \in \text{dom}(x)\}$
6 **repeat**
7 $\quad$ **while** $Q_{\text{sac}} \neq \emptyset$ **do**
8 $\quad\quad$ $(x, a) \leftarrow$ buildBranch+(P)
9 $\quad\quad$ **if** $(x, a) \neq nil$ **then**
10 $\quad\quad\quad$ $(P, deleted) \leftarrow GAC^+(P|_{x \neq a}, \{x\})$ // a is removed from $\text{dom}(x)$
   $\quad\quad\quad\quad$ and GAC enforced - del. values are returned
11 $\quad\quad\quad$ **if** $P = \bot$ **then**
12 $\quad\quad\quad\quad \lfloor$ **return** *false*

13 $\quad\quad\quad$ $Q_{\text{sac}} \leftarrow Q_{\text{sac}} \setminus deleted$
14 $\quad\quad\quad$ updateBranches($deleted \cup \{(x, a)\}$)

15 $\quad$ checkBranches()
16 **until** $Q_{\text{sac}} = \emptyset$
17 **return** *true*

It is possible to improve the behavior of the algorithm SAC3 by recording the *domain*, i.e. the full set of v-values, of the constraint network obtained after each greedy run, that is to say, for each branch. We record the domain of (the constraint network associated with) each branch built by the algorithm, discarding the last variable assignment and its propagation if it leads to failure. When a value is removed, it is then possible to determine which previously built branches must be reconsidered. If a removed value does not support a branch br, i.e. does not belong to the domain associated with the branch br, every value that has been assigned to a variable along the branch remains SAC-consistent. On the other hand, if a

---

Algorithm 52: buildBranch+(**in** P: $\mathscr{P}$): v-value

Output: a SAC-inconsistent v-value, or nil

1 $br \leftarrow \emptyset$
2 **repeat**
3   pick and delete (x, a) from $Q_{\mathrm{sac}} \mid a \in \mathrm{dom}^P(x)$
4    $P' \leftarrow GAC(P|_{x=a}, \{x\})$
5   **if** $P' \neq \perp$ **then**
6     $br \leftarrow br \cup \{(x, a)\}$
7     $P \leftarrow P'$
8   **else if** $br \neq \emptyset$ **then**
9     $Q_{\mathrm{sac}} \leftarrow Q_{\mathrm{sac}} \cup \{(x, a)\}$
10 **until** $P' = \perp \vee \nexists (x, a) \in Q_{\mathrm{sac}} \mid a \in \mathrm{dom}^P(x)$
11 **if** $br = \emptyset$ **then**
12   **return** (x, a) // (x, a) is SAC-inconsistent
13 **else**
14   $P[br] \leftarrow P$
15   $Q[br] \leftarrow \emptyset$
16   $brs \leftarrow brs \cup \{br\}$
17   **return** nil

Algorithm 53: updateBranches($deleted$: set of v-values)

---

1 **foreach** *v-value* $(x, a) \in deleted$ **do**
2   **foreach** *branch* $br \in brs$ **do**
3   **if** $a \in \mathrm{dom}^{P[br]}(x)$ **then**
4   remove a from $\mathrm{dom}^{P[br]}(x)$
5      $Q[br] \leftarrow Q[br] \cup \{x\}$

Algorithm 54: checkBranches()

---

1 **foreach** *branch* $br \in brs \mid Q[br] \neq \emptyset$ **do**
2    $P[br] \leftarrow GAC(P[br], Q[br])$
3    $Q[br] \leftarrow \emptyset$
4   **if** $P[br] = \perp$ **then**
5     $Q_{\mathrm{sac}} \leftarrow Q_{\mathrm{sac}} \cup br$
6     $brs \leftarrow brs \setminus \{br\}$

removed value does support a branch, we have to verify that the branch still remains consistent by re-establishing GAC from the recorded domain. A branch that is no longer consistent is deleted. In summary, SAC3+ (partially) exploits incrementality as SAC3 does and also as SAC-Opt and SAC-SDS do.

All branches built by SAC3+ are recorded in a set called brs; a branch corresponds to an instantiation. Arrays denoted $P[]$ and $Q[]$ are used to manage domain and propagation in constraint networks that correspond to branches. For each branch br, $P[br]$ corresponds to the constraint network associated with br, while $Q[br]$ corresponds to the events that must be propagated on $P[br]$. For the constraint network associated with br, $P[br]$ records only the domain; $P[br]$ does not record the constraints because these are shared naturally by the constraint networks for all branches. Thus $P[br]$ and $Q[br]$ play the same role as P_{x_a} and Q_{x_a} in SAC-Opt and SAC-SDS. In this book, we consider that for binary constraint networks, AC2001 is the underlying optimal AC algorithm for SAC3+. The data structures of AC2001 are assumed to be shared between the main problem (i.e. P) and the subproblems (i.e. the branches).

After enforcing generalized arc consistency on the given network, Algorithm 51 builds successive branches by calling the function buildBranch+ (note that P is an input parameter). The while loop starting at line 7 tests the singleton arc consistency of all v-values of Q_{sac} and may delete values after a branch has been built. As in SAC3, when a value is detected SAC-inconsistent, it is removed and GAC is re-established. The state of all recorded branches is updated to take account of deleted values: function updateBranches, Algorithm 53, removes deleted values and updates the propagation queues. The function checkBranches, Algorithm 54, checks later (i.e. when Q_{sac} is empty) the validity of the branches that have been built and recorded in brs. For each branch br, the function checkBranches re-establishes generalized arc consistency on $P[br]$ if necessary, and, if there is a domain wipe-out, deletes this branch and updates Q_{sac}.

Algorithm 52 differs from Algorithm 50 in two respects. First, all values (those successively assigned with success) of the current branch are recorded at line 6. Second, the (domain of the) constraint network corresponding to the new branch is recorded at line 14 and this branch is added to brs. If the last variable assignment entails a domain wipe-out, the local variable P is not updated (see lines 4 and 7). For the implementation, $P[br]$ can be directly set (backtracking one step if necessary) without any duplication of domain.

PROPOSITION 6.6.– *On binary constraint networks SAC3+, embedding the optimal arc consistency algorithm AC2001, admits a worst-case space complexity in $O(ed + b_{\max}nd)$ and a worst-case time complexity in $O(b^+ed^2)$, where $b_{\max}$ denotes the maximum number of branches recorded at the same time by the algorithm, and b^+ denotes the total number of times a branch is built or checked by the algorithm.*

Proof. The data structures of AC2001, shared between the main problem and the subproblems (i.e. branches), are in $O(ed)$. For each branch, we need to include the domain of the associated constraint network in $O(nd)$ and the propagation queue in $O(n)$. Thus we obtain $O(ed + b_{\max}nd)$. We consider that the structure *last* of AC2001 is saved before building or checking a branch, and restored when such an operation is finished. Saving and restoring last supports is $O(ed)$. So the worst-case time complexity is $O(b^+ed^2)$. $\qquad\Box$

The correctness of SAC3+ follows from Proposition 6.3 and from the fact that after all v-values have been singleton checked and some branches have been recorded, checkBranches verifies that the property still holds. Overall, one can be optimistic about the practical behavior of this algorithm since it avoids building unnecessary new branches. In practice, using GAC3^{rm} as underlying (non-optimal) GAC algorithm for SAC3+ has the advantage that the data structures of GAC3^{rm} are naturally shared between the main problem and the subproblems without any overhead. For binary constraint networks, the worst-case time complexity becomes $O(bed^3)$ where b is the number of branches built by the algorithm. If constraints are tightness-bounded, we obtain $O(bed^2)$. Note that the number of branches built by SAC3+ is expected to be less than the number of branches built by SAC3.

6.5. Illustration

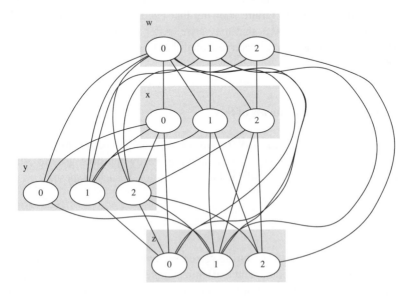

Figure 6.1. *A binary constraint network P before enforcing singleton arc consistency*

Figure 6.1 shows the compatibility graph of a simple binary constraint network that is used in the following illustration of behavior of different SAC algorithms. This constraint network P has $\text{vars}(P) = \{w, x, y, z\}$, three values per domain, and $\text{cons}(P) = \{c_{wx}, c_{wy}, c_{wz}, c_{xy}, c_{xz}, c_{yz}\}$ such that:

- $\text{rel}(c_{wx}) = \text{rel}(c_{wy}) = \text{rel}(c_{xy}) = \{(0,0), (0,1), (0,2), (1,1), (2,2)\}$;
- $\text{rel}(c_{wz}) = \{(0,0), (0,1), (1,0), (1,1), (2,2)\}$;
- $\text{rel}(c_{xz}) = \{(0,0), (1,1), (1,2), (2,1), (2,2)\}$;
- $\text{rel}(c_{yz}) = \{(0,1), (1,0), (2,0), (2,1), (2,2)\}$.

Figures 6.2, 6.3, 6.4 and 6.5 show the result of checking the singleton arc consistency of some v-values. For SAC1, these are exactly the first eight steps performed by the algorithm during a first pass. When the v-values $(w,1)$, $(x,1)$ and $(y,0)$ are detected SAC-inconsistent, they are removed and a second pass is necessary, as in Figure 6.6, where nine additional singleton checks are performed. SAC2 differs in that only v-values supported by deleted values must be reconsidered. Looking at domains obtained after each singleton check, the reader can verify that $(w,0)$ is the only one in that case. Consequently, only one singleton check is performed after the "initial" pass, as shown in Figure 6.7. For SAC-Opt and SAC-SDS, instead of checking from scratch the singleton arc consistency of $(w,0)$ for the second time, Figure 6.8 shows the benefit from using the subproblem P_{w_0} obtained after the first check. Figure 6.9 shows several branches built by SAC3. The first leads to a solution and to the inference that $(w,0)$, $(x,0)$, $(y,1)$ and $(z,0)$ are SAC-consistent. The second directly leads to failure showing that $(w,1)$ is SAC-inconsistent. These represent the two extreme cases that may arise. After the first pass, some branches must be built because none have been recorded; but this is not the case with SAC3+: see Figure 6.10.

6.6. Weaker and stronger forms of SAC

Existential SAC and *weak k-SAC* are weaker and stronger forms of SAC, respectively. The following section shows that the greedy approach used to establish singleton arc consistency can be adapted naturally to forms such as these.

6.6.1. *Existential SAC*

The cost of maintaining SAC during search seems to be prohibitive. This is why some partial forms such as bound and existential singleton arc consistency [LEC 06a] have been studied. A constraint network is *bound SAC* iff every value corresponding to the bound (minimum or maximum value) of a domain is SAC-consistent. In a related field, namely operations research, this is a classical form of *shaving*. Existential SAC

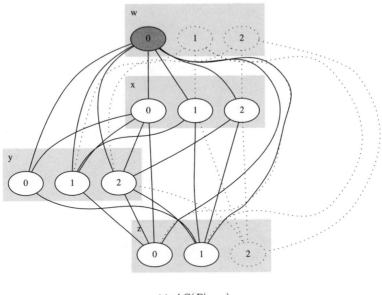

(a) $AC(P|_{w=0})$

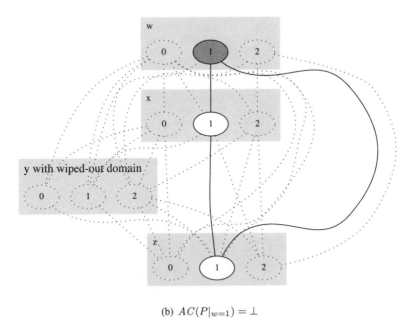

(b) $AC(P|_{w=1}) = \bot$

Figure 6.2. *Constraint networks obtained when checking the singleton arc consistency of* $(w, 0)$ *and* $(w, 1)$

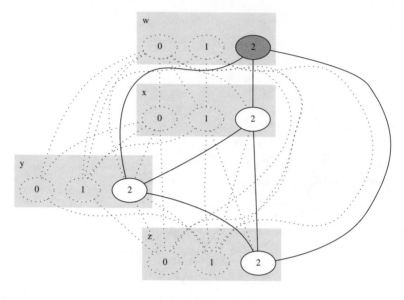

(a) $AC(P|_{w=2})$

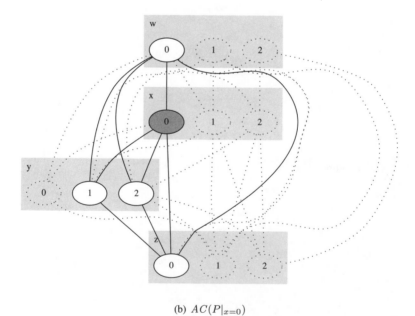

(b) $AC(P|_{x=0})$

Figure 6.3. *Constraint networks obtained when checking the singleton arc consistency of* $(w, 2)$ *and* $(x, 0)$

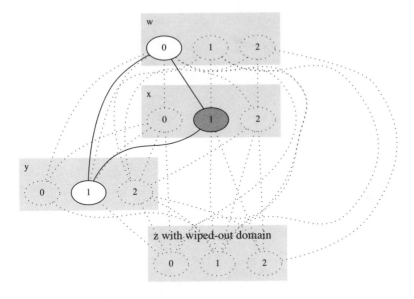

(a) $AC(P|_{x=1}) = \bot$

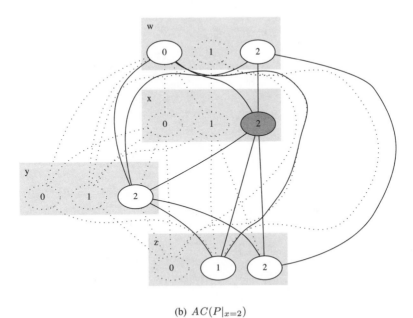

(b) $AC(P|_{x=2})$

Figure 6.4. *Constraint networks obtained when checking the singleton arc consistency of*
$(x, 1)$ *and* $(x, 2)$

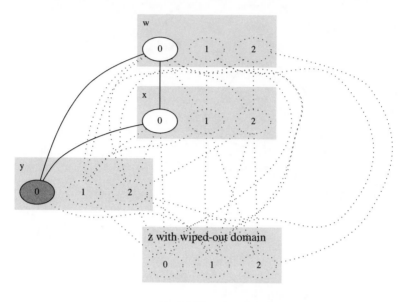

w

x

y

z with wiped-out domain

(a) $AC(P|_{y=0}) = \bot$

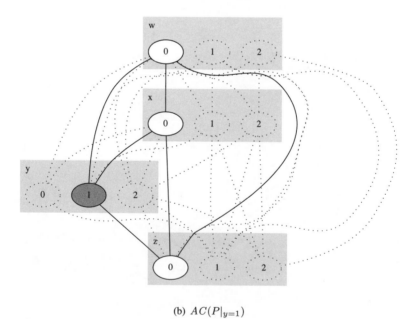

w

x

y

z

(b) $AC(P|_{y=1})$

Figure 6.5. *Constraint networks obtained when checking the singleton arc consistency of* $(y, 0)$ *and* $(y, 1)$

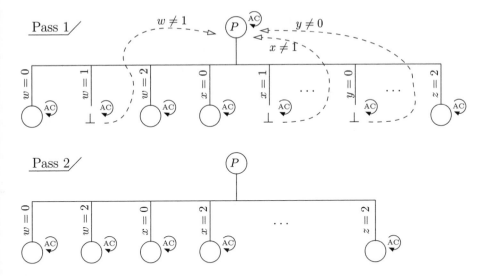

Figure 6.6. *Singleton checks performed by SAC1 for the constraint network P of Figure 6.1*

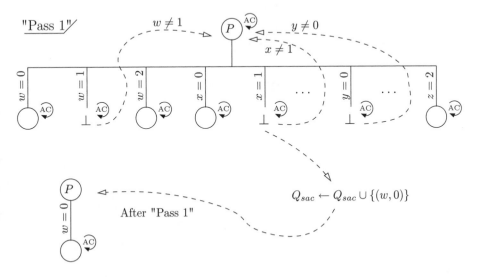

Figure 6.7. *Singleton checks performed by SAC2 for the constraint network P of Figure 6.1.*
Q_{sac} *is the queue used by SAC2*

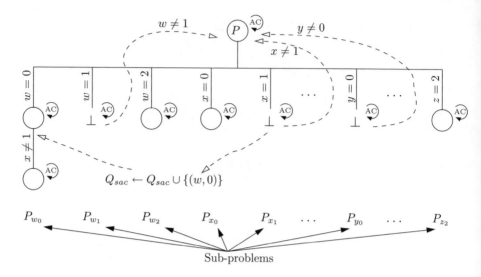

Figure 6.8. *Singleton checks performed by SAC-Opt and SAC-SDS for the constraint network P of Figure 6.1*

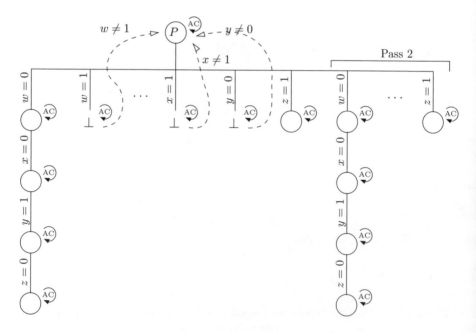

Figure 6.9. *Branches built by SAC3 for the constraint network P of Figure 6.1*

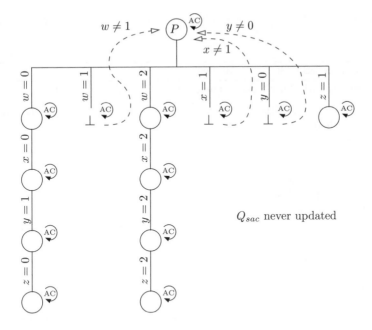

Figure 6.10. *Branches built (and recorded) by SAC3+ for the constraint network P of Figure 6.1*

just stipulates that at least one value in each domain is SAC-consistent, and is therefore weaker than Bound SAC:

DEFINITION 6.7.– *[Existential SAC] Let P be a constraint network.*

– *A variable x of P is* existentially SAC-consistent, *iff x is GAC-consistent and* $\exists a \in \mathrm{dom}(x)$ *such that* (x, a) *is SAC-consistent.*

– *P is* existentially SAC-consistent *iff every variable of P is existentially SAC-consistent.*

Existential SAC is defined on variables (and by extension on constraint networks) but not on values. This makes it quite different from consistencies introduced in Chapter 3. Surprisingly, enforcing existential SAC on a constraint network is meaningless. Either the network is (already) existentially SAC-consistent, or the network is SAC-inconsistent, so it is better to talk about checking existential SAC. An algorithm to check existential SAC seeks a SAC-consistent value in each domain. As a side-effect, SAC-inconsistent values that are identified can be removed. The non-deterministic nature of the inference process implies that we have absolutely no guarantee about the network obtained after checking existential SAC. This is because existential SAC is not precisely a nogood-identifying consistency as defined in Chapter 3.

Algorithm 55: ESAC3(P: $\mathscr{P}$): Boolean

Output: *true* iff P is checked to be existentially SAC-consistent

1   $P \leftarrow GAC(P, \text{vars}(P))$ // GAC is initially enforced
2   **if** $P = \bot$ **then**
3 | **return** *false*

4   $Q_{esac} \leftarrow \text{vars}(P)$
5   **while** $Q_{esac} \neq \emptyset$ **do**
6 | $(x, a) \leftarrow$ buildBranchE(P)
7 | **if** $(x, a) \neq nil$ **then**
8 | | $P \leftarrow GAC(P|_{x \neq a}, \{x\})$ // a is removed and GAC enforced
9 | | **if** $P = \bot$ **then**
10 | | | **return** *false*
11 | | $Q_{esac} \leftarrow \text{vars}(P)$

12 **return** *true*

Algorithm 56: buildBranchE(**in** P: $\mathscr{P}$): v-value

Output: a SAC-inconsistent v-value, or *nil*

1   $length \leftarrow 0$
2   **repeat**
3 | pick and delete x from Q_{esac}
4 | select a value $a \in \text{dom}^P(x)$
5 | $P \leftarrow GAC(P|_{x=a}, \{x\})$
6 | **if** $P \neq \bot$ **then**
7 | | $length \leftarrow length + 1$
8 | **else**
9 | | $Q_{esac} \leftarrow Q_{esac} \cup \{x\}$
10 **until** $P = \bot \vee Q_{esac} = \emptyset$
11 **if** $length = 0$ **then**
12 | **return** (x, a) // (x, a) is SAC-inconsistent
13 **else**
14 | **return** *nil*

The nice thing is that using a greedy approach to check existential SAC seems to be quite appropriate. In particular, the algorithm SAC3 can be adapted straightforwardly to guarantee existential SAC. As mentioned above, such an algorithm can generate different constraint networks depending on the order in which variables and values are considered, i.e. there may be multiple fixed points.

In the following brief description of this new algorithm, ESAC3, Q_{esac} is the set of variables for which existential SAC must be checked. Algorithm 55 starts by enforcing GAC on the given network. Next, all variables are put into Q_{esac} and, to check existential SAC, successive branches are built. If a value is found to be SAC-inconsistent while building a new branch, this value is removed, GAC is re-established and the process of checking existential SAC is re-started from scratch. Iteration continues until existential SAC has been checked, or the constraint network has been detected as SAC-inconsistent. Algorithm 56 allows a branch to be built by performing successive variable assignments on P (it is important that P is an input parameter) while maintaining GAC. When a dead-end is encountered or the set Q_{esac} becomes empty, the greedy run is stopped; if the branch is of length 0, the inconsistent v-value is returned.

Figure 6.11 illustrates the non-deterministic nature of ESAC3. In Figure 6.11(a), only one branch is built by ESAC3 (because this corresponds to a solution that has been found, and so all variables are proved to be existentially SAC-consistent), whereas in Figure 6.11(b), using a different search heuristic, $(w, 1)$ is first selected and found to be SAC-inconsistent before checking that P is existentially SAC-consistent. Figure 6.11(c) illustrates the extreme case where existentially checking SAC enforces SAC: the three SAC-inconsistent values have been selected first by the search heuristic.

The space required specifically by ESAC3 is $O(n)$ since the only extra structure is Q_{esac} which is $O(n)$. The time complexity of ESAC3 is that of SAC3, that is to say, $O(bed^2)$ where b denotes the number of branches built by the algorithm; using an optimal AC algorithm such as AC2001, each branch built is $O(ed^2)$ due to the incrementality of AC2001. In the best case, only one branch is built (leading directly to a solution), and then we obtain $O(ed^2)$. In the worst-case, before detecting a SAC-inconsistent value, $n - 1$ branches of length 1 are built (one consistent variable assignment followed by an inconsistent one); the number of values that can be removed is $O(nd)$, so we obtain $O(en^2d^3)$. Finally, when no inconsistent value is detected, the worst-case time complexity of ESAC3 is $O(end^2)$.

Greedy runs have some practical advantages, including a chance to find solutions by luck. Moreover, different search heuristics can be tried because usually several branches have to be built: for each new branch, a search heuristic can be selected from a portfolio. Existential SAC seems to be a good compromise between the computational cost of enforcing SAC and the benefits that can be obtained. In the second and third constraint solver competitions, the solver Abscon checked existential SAC during preprocessing.

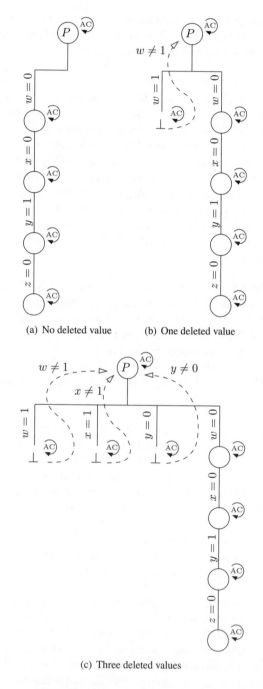

(a) No deleted value   (b) One deleted value

(c) Three deleted values

Figure 6.11. *Illustration of the non-deterministic nature of checking existential SAC with the constraint network P of Figure 6.1*

6.6.2. *Weak k-singleton arc consistency*

Weak k-singleton arc consistency [DON 06] (variants are introduced in [BES 05a]) is equal to SAC when $k = 1$ and is stronger when $k > 1$. A v-value (x, a) is weakly k-SAC iff after initially assigning the value a to x it is possible to reach a node at level k within the MAC search tree.

DEFINITION 6.8.– *[Weak k-SAC] Let P be a constraint network and $1 \leq k \leq n$ be an integer.*

– *A v-value (x, a) of P is* weakly k-SAC-consistent, *or* WSAC$_k$-consistent, *iff there exists a set Y of $k - 1$ variables of P, with $x \notin Y$, and a valid instantiation I of Y on P such that $GAC(P|_{\{(x,a)\} \cup I}) \neq \bot$.*

– *A variable x of P is* weakly k-SAC-consistent *iff every v-value (x, a), with $a \in$* dom(x), *is weakly k-SAC-consistent.*

– *P is* weakly k-SAC-consistent *iff every variable of P is weakly k-SAC-consistent.*

Weak k-SAC is a stable domain-filtering consistency, so its enforcement is meaningful. Algorithm 57 enforces weak k-SAC on the given constraint network P; the constraint network obtained by enforcing weak k-SAC on P is denoted by $WSAC_k(P)$. For each v-value, this algorithm systematically explores a MAC search tree until a node at level k is reached (in which case the run is greedy until a dead-end occurs or a solution is found). Algorithm 57 starts by enforcing GAC on the given network. Next, all v-values are put in the structure Q_{wsac}, which is the set of v-values for which weak k-SAC must be checked. For each v-value in Q_{wsac}, the function extendable performs a limited exploration of the MAC search tree. If a v-value (x, a) is found to be WSAC$_k$-inconsistent, $extendable(P|_{x=a}, x)$ returns *false*, this value is removed, GAC is re-established, and the process of checking weak k-SAC starts again from scratch. Iteration continues until a fixed point is reached.

The function extendable, described in Algorithm 58, is called just after a (positive or negative) decision is taken. For example, the value for which weak k-SAC must be checked is assigned initially at line 7 of Algorithm 57: this is a positive decision. If GAC enforcement at line 1 of Algorithm 58 results in failure, *false* is returned at line 3. Next, the number of fixed variables is obtained at line 4. Although not shown here, this number can be obtained cheaply by using an incremental/decremental mechanism. When all variables are fixed, we know that a solution has been found since GAC has just been enforced (lines 5 to 7). Because $n \geq k$, we learn that the initial value for which the exploration has been conducted is WSAC$_k$-consistent but also that all the other values in the solution are WSAC$_k$-consistent. This is why Q_{wsac} is updated at line 6. Otherwise, we select a new v-value and try to extend the current branch. If this extension is successful, *true* is returned at line 10. If a failure has been detected at the next level, so *false* has been returned by extendable at line 9, we verify that we were not trying to extend a branch while we were at a level already greater than or equal to k, and if this is the case we update Q_{wsac} at line 12. To continue the exploration we refute the last assigned value.

Algorithm 57: WSAC(P: $\mathscr{P}$, k: integer): Boolean

Output: *true* iff $WSAC_k(P) \neq \emptyset$

1   $P \leftarrow GAC(P, \text{vars}(P))$ // GAC is initially enforced
2   **if** $P = \bot$ **then**
3     $\lfloor$ **return** *false*
4   $Q_{wsac} \leftarrow \{(x, a) \mid x \in \text{vars}(P) \wedge a \in \text{dom}(x)\}$
5   **while** $Q_{wsac} \neq \emptyset$ **do**
6   pick and delete (x, a) from Q_{wsac}
7   **if** $\neg$*extendable*($P|_{x=a}, x$) **then**
8        $P \leftarrow GAC(P|_{x \neq a}, \{x\})$ // a is removed and GAC enforced
9   **if** $P = \bot$ **then**
10          $\lfloor$ **return** *false*
11        $Q_{wsac} \leftarrow \{(x, a) \mid x \in \text{vars}(P) \wedge a \in \text{dom}(x)\}$

12 **return** *true*

Algorithm 58: extendable(**in** P: $\mathscr{P}$, y: variable): Boolean

Output: *true* iff at least k variables of P can be fixed by MAC

1   $P \leftarrow GAC(P, \{y\})$ // a decision has just been taken on y
2   **if** $P = \bot$ **then**
3     $\lfloor$ **return** *false*
4   $nbFixed \leftarrow |\{x \in \text{vars}(P) \text{ s.t. } |\text{dom}(x)| = 1\}|$
5   **if** $nbFixed = n$ **then**
6     $Q_{wsac} \leftarrow Q_{wsac} \setminus \{(x, a) \mid x \in \text{vars}(P) \wedge \text{dom}(x) = \{a\}\}$
7   **return** *true*   // a solution has been found
8   select a v-value (x, a) of P such that $|\text{dom}(x)| > 1$
9   **if** $extendable(P|_{x=a}, x)$ **then**
10    $\lfloor$ **return** *true*
11 **if** $nbFixed \geq k$ **then**
12    $Q_{wsac} \leftarrow Q_{wsac} \setminus \{(x, a) \mid x \in \text{vars}(P) \wedge \text{dom}(x) = \{a\}\}$
13   **return** *true*   // weak k-SAC is guaranteed for assigned values
14 **return** $extendable(P|_{x \neq a}, x)$

Note that the algorithm described here differs slightly from that given by van Dongen [DON 06] in that a binary branching scheme is used. Moreover, "computing" all fixed variables allows us to discard from Q_{wsac} not only the values for variables that have been instantiated explicitly during search but also those that have indirectly become fixed. The benefit of these modifications remains to be proved empirically.

This approach can be related to the greedy approach for SAC and existential SAC because the construction of a branch leading to a node at depth k does not stop when the initial value is proved to be weakly k-SAC-consistent but instead continues greedily to obtain the maximum number of $WSAC_k$-consistent values. And some lucky solutions may be found opportunistically.

Experimental results in [DON 06] show that weak k-SAC is a promising consistency. Enforcement of weak k-SAC in preprocessing improves the subsequent performance of MAC for structured problems. Furthermore, for many published problems the algorithm discovers lucky solutions. Surprisingly, for some instances, inverse consistency, i.e. $(1, n)$-consistency, is proved because each (remaining) value participates in at least one solution found during the inference process. Weak k-SAC was enforced during preprocessing by the solver Buggy in the second constraint solver competition.

6.7. Experimental results

This section briefly reports practical behavior of algorithms presented in this chapter, including those in section 6.6.

For SAC algorithms, some results of experiments with random instances can be found in [BES 04a, LEC 05]. In summary, SAC3 and SAC3+ behave well before the beginning of the phase transition but are clearly outperformed by SAC-SDS at the peak of difficulty. This is not really surprising since the generated instances have no structure, and this corresponds to the worst-case for SAC3 and SAC3+ because the average length of the branches (at the critical point) is very small. However, Table 6.1 shows that SAC3, and especially SAC3+, perform well on certain structured instances. Performance has been measured by the number of singleton checks (#scks) and the CPU time in seconds. The number (#×) of values removed by SAC algorithms is also given: when #×=0, this means that the instance is initially singleton arc-consistent. As expected, a significant improvement is obtained on instances (cc-20-2, cc-20-3, scen2) that are already SAC-consistent. This is also true for the other instances that contain large under-constrained parts. Note that SAC-SDS runs out of memory on the instance graph10. It is also worth noting that on some instances, some solutions (the number of found solutions is enclosed in brackets near CPU time) have been found during the inference process. For example, 16 solutions have been found on scen02 by SAC3 and SAC3+.

Instance		SAC Algorithm			
		SAC1	SAC-SDS	SAC3	SAC3+
cc-20-2	CPU	14.4	14.4	3.46	3.48
(#× = 0)	#scks	800	800	819	819
cc-20-3	CPU	22.6	22.7	7.01	7.02
(#× = 0)	#scks	1,200	1,200	1,200	1,200
gr-34-8	CPU	66.0	17.4	38.2	18.6
(#× = 351)	#scks	6,335	3,340	5,299	1,558
gr-34-9	CPU	111	31.2	91.5	32.0
(#× = 513)	#scks	8,474	4,720	11,017	2,013
qa-5	CPU	2.47	2.50	0.93	0.96
(#× = 9)	#scks	622	622	732	732
qa-6	CPU	27.5	14.3	8.23	4.38
(#× = 48)	#scks	2,523	1,702	2,855	1,448
scen2	CPU	20.9	20.7	4.09 (16)	4.08 (16)
(#× = 0)	#scks	8,004	8,004	8,005	8,005
scen5	CPU	11.7	20.0	1.55 (1)	1.87
(#× = 13,814)	#scks	6,513	4,865	4,241	2,389
graph3	CPU	215	136	74.9	39.1
(#× = 1,274)	#scks	20,075	17,069	22,279	8,406
graph10	CPU	1,389	–	675	349
(#× = 2,572)	#scks	74,321	–	82,503	29,398

Table 6.1. *Results obtained when enforcing SAC on some structured instances*

Instance	FC	MAC	Maintaining		
			SAC1	SAC3	ESAC3
100-queens	0.5 (194)	4.2 (118)	–	17.4 (0)	18.9 (2)
110-queens	–	–	–	37.9 (0)	22.7 (1)
120-queens	–	1,636 (323 K)	–	16.7 (0)	47.3 (2)
scen11-f12	69.1 (18 K)	3.6 (695)	1,072 (41)	418 (5)	48.3 (30)
scen11-f10	131 (34 K)	4.4 (862)	1,732 (52)	814 (8)	38.3 (25)
scen11-f8	260 (66 K)	67.8 (14 K)	–	–	290 (213)

Table 6.2. *CPU time (and number of visited nodes) for instances of the queens and RLFAP problems, given 30 minutes*

We have also explored the effect of maintaining existential SAC on satisfiable instances using ESAC3: due to greedy runs, solutions may be found at any step of the search. Table 6.2 illustrates this with some instances of the n-queens problem. Table 6.2 also shows results for FC, MAC and SAC maintained during search with SAC1 and SAC3. It is interesting to note that for all these satisfiable instances, SAC3 and ESAC3 explore not more than two nodes. However, one should expect to find less impressive results with unsatisfiable instances. To check this, we have tested some difficult (modified) unsatisfiable RLFAP instances. The results show that maintaining SAC3 or ESAC3 really limits the number of nodes that have to be visited. This can be explained by the fact that both algorithms learn from failures (of greedy runs) via use of the *dom/wdeg* heuristic (presented in Chapter 9).

| | SAC1 | | $k = 2$ | | $k = 8$ | | $k = 16$ | |
	del	CPU	del	CPU	del	CPU	del	CPU
frb30-15-1 (30-450)	0	0.04	0	0.10	i 410	6.55	i 410	0.54
frb35-17-1 (35-595)	0	0.05	0	0.14	0	1.72	i 559	3.19
frb40-19-1 (40-760)	0	0.08	0	0.21	0	0.51	i 701	15.0
scen-11 (680-26,856)	0	15.1	0	4.89	0	4.78	76	4,803
scen11-f1 (680-26,524)	332	13.9	332	4.39	26,524	3,097		–
scen1-f8 (916-29,496)	6,704	6.29	6,704	2.55	6,704	2.55	6,704	2.58
scen1-f9 (916-28,596)	7,628	5.24	7,628	2.47	28,596	2.46	28,596	2.89
qa-5 (26-631)	9	0.16	9	0.10	12	0.45	i 386	24.0
qa-6 (37-1,302)	48	2.19	48	0.80	67	1.86	127	1,923
enddr1-10 (50-5,760)	0	16.0	0	5.83		–		–
enddr2-2 (50-6,315)	0	25.9	0	10.7		–		–

(The table above is headed by a spanning header $WSAC_k$ over the $k=2$, $k=8$, and $k=16$ columns.)

Table 6.3. *Excerpt from results obtained by Marc van Dongen [DON 06] for* $WSAC_k$

Finally, Table 6.3 is an excerpt from experimental results obtained by van Dongen [DON 06] with an algorithm for weak k-SAC. Table 6.3 lists for each instance the number of deleted values (del) and the CPU time for SAC1 and $WSAC_k$ for $k \in \{2, 8, 16\}$. Also, between brackets, this table shows the number of variables and the number of values over all domains. An "i" in the column del indicates that the instance has been made and proved inverse consistent. RLFAP instances scen1-f9 and scen11-f1 are proved unsatisfiable by WSAC, whereas SAC1 fails to prove this. Although the instance scen11-f1 is very difficult in that MAC alone cannot solve it within days of search, it has been proved unsatisfiable within one hour by enforcing $WSAC_8$. Interestingly, the instances from the classes frb-30-15, frb-35-17, and frb40-19 are made and proved inverse consistent by making them $WSAC_{16}$.

6.8. Conclusion

Singleton arc consistency should play a more and more important role in the future: the general trend is clearly to extend the level of local reasoning in constraint solvers. In the mid-1990s there was a transition from FC (which enforces a partial form of arc consistency) to MAC (which enforces full arc consistency). Analogously, the next generation of solvers should less restrictively enforce consistencies which are stronger than GAC. This is already the case for some solvers that enforce derived forms of SAC such as existential SAC and weak k-SAC. Nevertheless, we have to admit that practical progress has been mainly confined to preprocessing.

Singleton consistencies can be combined naturally with some (impact-based) search heuristics. For example, SAC can be restricted to a subset of variables, those that are more likely to be chosen by the variable ordering heuristic [COR 07]. Here the consistency enforcing procedure is to some extent adaptive since it is guided by the heuristic(s). This illustrates the idea [STE 08] of dynamically adapting the level of local consistency applied during search. Information about domain wipe-outs and value deletions during search can be used not only to select variables for instantiation, but also to adapt automatically the level of constraint propagation. Several procedures (heuristics) to switch dynamically between enforcing a weak, and cheap local consistency, and a strong but more expensive one, have been proposed; these procedures depend on the activity of individual constraints. Although not investigated experimentally in [STE 08], SAC, or one of its derived forms, seems a good candidate to play the role of the strong consistency.

Finally, for interval-based solvers that solve numeric (or continuous) constraint problems, tentative attempts to find SAC-inconsistent values are limited to the bounds of variable domains in order to tighten them. This leads to a consistency called 3B-consistency [LHO 93] for which an optimal algorithm has been developed [BOR 01]. Deleted values are sometimes said to be shaved: a shavable value is a value which, when assigned and propagated, yields an inconsistency. Shaving (which is a term introduced in the context of scheduling [CAR 94, MAR 96b]) means attempting to identify and remove some shavable values. For discrete domains, different mechanisms of guiding the shaving process have recently been studied. For example, in [LHO 05a], values are selected for shaving according to the failures that occur during search, whereas in [SZY 08], (global) constraints are invoked to suggest values to be used in the shaving procedure.

Table 6.4 summarizes time and space complexities of SAC algorithms presented in this chapter.

Algorithm	Time complexity	Space complexity	Reference
SAC1	$O(en^2d^4)$	$O(ed)$	[DEB 97b]
SAC2	$O(en^2d^4)$	$O(n^2d^2)$	[BAR 04]
SAC-Opt	$O(end^3)$	$O(end^2)$	[BES 04b]
SAC-SDS	$O(end^4)$	$O(n^2d^2)$	[BES 05b]
SAC3	$O(bed^2)$	$O(ed)$	[LEC 05]
SAC3+	$O(b^+ed^2)$	$O(ed + b_{max}nd)$	[LEC 05]

Table 6.4. *Worst-case complexities of SAC algorithms for binary constraint networks, assuming that AC2001 is the underlying AC algorithm. b is the number of branches built by SAC3, b_{max} the maximum number of branches recorded at the same time by SAC3+, and b^+ the total number of times a branch is built or checked by SAC3+*

Chapter 7

Path and Dual Consistency

We have hitherto been interested primarily in domain-filtering consistencies that identify individual values which are (globally) inconsistent: such values correspond to nogoods of size one. This chapter is concerned with second-order consistencies that locally identify globally inconsistent pairs of values, which correspond to nogoods of size 2. The most studied second-order consistency is certainly *path consistency* (PC): a constraint network P is path-consistent iff every locally consistent instantiation of two variables on P can be extended consistently to each third variable of P.

Nowadays, path consistency, and more generally higher-order consistencies, are rather neglected by designers and developers of general constraint solvers. This is somewhat surprising because strong path consistency (which is equivalent to strong 3-consistency when no ternary constraint is present) is a sufficient condition for global consistency for many tractable classes. Perhaps neglect of higher-order consistencies is due partly to the limited scope of these classes since exciting progress in this area has only been very recent (e.g. see [GRE 08]). Path consistency has, however, continued to play an important role in temporal reasoning. Indeed, for some classes of interval algebra, path consistency (adapted to temporal constraint networks [ALL 83]) is enough to decide satisfiability.

Another possible reason for low practical interest for path consistency, in the discrete constraint satisfaction field, is that path consistency enforcement modifies constraint relations, and more importantly, modifies the structure of the constraint graph. When a pair of v-values $\{(x, a), (y, b)\}$ is found to be path-inconsistent, this information is recorded in the constraint network; if there is no constraint binding x with y, a new one is inserted, thus changing the constraint graph. For example, the instance scen-11 of the radio link frequency assignment problem (RLFAP) involves 680 variables and 4,103 constraints. Enforcing a second-order consistency on this network could at worst create $\binom{680}{2} - 4{,}103 = 226{,}757$ new constraints, which would be really counter-productive both in time and in space.

The main apparent drawback of path consistency can be avoided by adopting a relation-filtering or *conservative* approach, in which the search for inconsistent pairs of values is restricted to existing constraints. As seen in section 3.4.1, this is called conservative path consistency (CPC) [DEB 99] when restricted to 2-length graph-paths, and partial path consistency (PPC) [BLI 99] when restricted to graph-paths of arbitrary length. CPC and PPC are equivalent [BLI 99] when the constraint graph is triangulated, but this is not generally true.

In section 7.1 we introduce a recent second-order consistency, called *dual consistency* (DC), which uses the outcome of GAC enforcement, and we compare this with various forms of path consistency. On binary constraint networks, DC is equivalent to PC although this could have been predicted since McGregor had already proposed an algorithm built on top of AC to establish (strong) path consistency [MCG 79]. On the other hand, PC is strictly stronger than *conservative dual consistency* (CDC) which itself is strictly stronger than PPC and CPC – CDC can then filter out conservatively more inconsistent pairs of values than PPC or CPC. Before proposing algorithms to enforce (conservative) dual consistency, we present in section 7.2 some classical algorithms to enforce path consistency. We restrict our attention to coarse-grained path consistency algorithms, and in particular to PC8 and PC2001, and to conservative variants of those two algorithms. PC8 has been shown to be quite efficient in practice, whereas PC2001 is time-optimal.

Section 7.3 introduces sCDC1 and sDC2, which enforce strong conservative dual consistency and strong dual consistency, respectively. These algorithms require no specific data structure, except for those of the underlying GAC algorithm and a time-stamping structure in $O(n)$ for sDC2. While sCDC1 can be seen as a conservative adaptation of McGregor's algorithm, sDC2 is more sophisticated in that it is partially incremental. (Strong) path consistency can be enforced by these two algorithms (after completing, if necessary, the constraint network with missing binary constraints), and also by a third one, sDC3 (not described here), which totally exploits the incrementality of the underlying GAC algorithm. A few experimental results in section 7.4 illustrate the practical interest of (conservative) dual consistency.

Important In this chapter, space analysis only takes account of data structures required specifically by second-order consistency algorithms. This analysis never includes the space complexity of representation of a binary constraint network; this is $O(ed^2)$ for a conservative consistency, and $O(n^2d^2)$ for a non-conservative one since the constraint graph has to be assumed to be complete.

7.1. Qualitative study

This section qualitatively studies path consistency and its partial forms, together with a related consistency called dual consistency (DC). Dual consistency, whose idea has initially been used by McGregor [MCG 79], records inconsistent pairs of values identified by successive singleton checks. Just like singleton arc consistency, dual consistency is built on top of generalized arc consistency. When applied to all constraints of a binary instance (including the implicit universal ones), DC is equivalent to PC, but when it is applied conservatively (i.e. only on explicit constraints of the binary network), conservative DC (CDC) is strictly stronger than conservative PC (CPC) and partial PC (PPC).

Let us first introduce dual consistency. Informally, a network is dual-consistent iff each pair of values that is locally consistent is not detected inconsistent after assigning either of those two values and enforcing GAC. To simplify, we write $(x, a) \in P$ iff $(x, a) \in$ v-vals(P), i.e. iff $x \in$ vars$(P) \land a \in \text{dom}^P(x)$; when $P = \bot$, for every v-value (x, a), we have $(x, a) \notin P$. Below, we assume that locally consistent instantiations $\{(x, a), (y, b)\}$ are such that $x \neq y$.

DEFINITION 7.1.– *[Dual Consistency] Let P be a constraint network.*

– A locally consistent instantiation $\{(x, a), (y, b)\}$ on P is dual-consistent, *or* DC-consistent, *iff* $(y, b) \in GAC(P|_{x=a})$ *and* $(x, a) \in GAC(P|_{y=b})$.

– P is dual-consistent *iff every locally consistent instantiation $\{(x, a), (y, b)\}$ on P is dual-consistent.*

Dual consistency is a second-order consistency, whence a relation-filtering consistency can be derived as follows.

DEFINITION 7.2.– *[Conservative Dual Consistency] Let P be a constraint network.*

– A locally consistent instantiation $\{(x, a), (y, b)\}$ on P is conservative dual-consistent, *or* CDC-consistent, *iff either* $\nexists c \in \text{cons}(P) \mid \text{scp}(c) = \{x, y\}$ *or* $\{(x, a), (y, b)\}$ *is dual-consistent.*

– P is conservative dual-consistent *iff every locally consistent instantiation $\{(x, a), (y, b)\}$ on P is conservative dual-consistent.*

To illustrate the difference between DC and CDC, let us consider a constraint network P such that vars$(P) = \{w, x, y, z\}$ and cons$(P) = \{c_{wx}, c_{wz}, c_{xyz}\}$, where subscripts indicate constraint scopes. DC reviews (locally consistent instantiations of) all of the six possible distinct pairs of variables, whereas CDC reviews only the two pairs (w, x) and (w, z).

We shall also be interested in strong variants of (second-order) consistencies that additionally guarantee generalized arc consistency. For example, a binary constraint network is *strong path-consistent*, or *sPC-consistent*, iff it is both arc-consistent and path-consistent. A constraint network is *strong dual-consistent*, or *sDC-consistent* iff it is both GAC-consistent and DC-consistent. sPPC, sCPC and sCDC are defined similarly. For binary (normalized) constraint networks, strong path consistency and strong 3-consistency are equivalent.

DEFINITION 7.3.– *[Strong Consistency] Let ϕ be a second-order consistency. A constraint network P is* strong ϕ-consistent, *or* $s\phi$-consistent, *iff P is GAC+ϕ-consistent, i.e. both GAC-consistent and ϕ-consistent.*

A strong second-order consistency ϕ identifies both ϕ-inconsistent values (nogoods of size one) and ϕ-inconsistent pairs of values (nogoods of size two). It is important that the closure of a constraint network can be computed for all second-order consistencies mentioned so far. All such consistencies can be proved to be stable and therefore well-behaved; see Theorem 3.14.

PROPOSITION 7.4.– *PC and DC are second-order consistencies which are stable for $(\mathscr{P}, \preceq)$. CDC, PPC and CPC are second-order relation-filtering consistencies which are stable for $(\mathscr{P}, \preceq_r)$.*

Canonical nogood representations are required for strong consistencies because nogoods of various sizes may be identified. These strong versions are stable on the partial order built from $\preceq$ on the quotient set of $\mathscr{P}$ by the nogood-equivalence relation; see section 1.4.1.

When studying the relationships existing between all these consistencies, the first surprise is that, on binary constraint networks, DC is equivalent to PC although this could be predicted since McGregor had already proposed an AC-based algorithm to establish sPC [MCG 79]. We first show that DC is strictly stronger than PC in the general case.

PROPOSITION 7.5.– *DC is strictly stronger than PC.*

Proof. Let P be a constraint network and $I = \{(x, a), (y, b)\}$ be a locally consistent instantiation on P. If I is path-inconsistent then $\exists z \in \text{vars}(P) \mid \forall c \in \text{dom}(z)$, $\{(x, a), (z, c)\}$ or $\{(y, b), (z, c)\}$ is not locally consistent (see Definition 3.43). In this case, we know that $(y, b) \notin GAC(P_{|x=a})$ since after enforcing GAC on $P_{|x=a}$, every value c remaining in $\text{dom}(z)$ is such that $\{(x, a), (z, c)\}$ is consistent. Necessarily, by hypothesis, all these remaining values are incompatible with (y, b), so b is removed from $\text{dom}(y)$ when enforcing GAC. Hence I is dual-inconsistent. Consequently every locally consistent instantiation on P that is identified as path-inconsistent and therefore in $\widetilde{P'}$ with $P' = PC(P)$ is also identified as dual-inconsistent and therefore in $\widetilde{P''}$ with $P'' = DC(P)$. We deduce that $DC(P) \preceq PC(P)$ and also that DC is stronger than PC; see Theorem 3.25. To show strictness, we simply consider a constraint network P involving a single non-binary constraint that is not generalized arc-consistent. Whereas $PC(P) = P$, $DC(P)$ necessarily involves some new binary constraints. So we have a constraint network that is PC-consistent but not DC-consistent.   □

PROPOSITION 7.6.– *On binary constraint networks, DC is equivalent to PC.*

Proof. We know from the previous proposition that DC is stronger than PC. We now show that, on binary constraint networks, PC is stronger than DC, whence we can conclude that DC and PC are equivalent. Let P be a binary constraint network and $I = \{(x,a),(y,b)\}$ be a locally consistent instantiation on P. If I is dual-inconsistent then $(y,b) \notin AC(P_{|x=a})$, or symmetrically $(x,a) \notin AC(P_{|y=b})$. We consider the first case. Let $H(n)$ be the following induction hypothesis: if the number of fruitful revisions performed in (a coarse-grained AC algorithm such as) AC3 to remove a v-value (z,c) when enforcing AC on $P_{|x=a}$ is less than or equal to n then $\{(x,a),(z,c)\} \in \widetilde{P'}$ with $P' = PC(P)$, i.e. $\{(x,a),(z,c)\}$ is either initially locally inconsistent or identified as path-inconsistent. We show first that $H(1)$ holds. If (z,c) is a v-value removed during the first fruitful revision, this means that (z,c) has no support on a binary constraint involving z and a second variable w. If $\{(x,a),(z,c)\}$ is locally inconsistent, then H(1) holds trivially. Otherwise, necessarily $w \neq x$ (because this would mean that (z,c) is not compatible with (x,a) since a has been assigned to x, so $\{(x,a),(z,c)\}$ is initially locally inconsistent). Therefore $\{(x,a),(z,c)\}$ clearly has no support on the path $\langle x, w, z \rangle$ and is thus path-inconsistent. We now assume that $H(n)$ is true and show that $H(n+1)$ holds. If (z,c) is a v-value removed during the $(n+1)$th fruitful revision while enforcing AC on $P_{|x=a}$, this means that this last fruitful revision involves a constraint binding z with another variable w. The value (z,c) has no support on this constraint, so every value in $\mathrm{dom}(w)$ initially supporting (z,c), if any, has been removed after at most n fruitful revisions. By hypothesis this means that for any such value b, $\{(x,a),(w,b)\} \in \widetilde{P'}$ with $P' = PC(P)$. In any case, we can now deduce that $\{(x,a),(z,c)\} \in \widetilde{P'}$ and, as a special case, we can identifiy I as path-inconsistent. Consequently, every locally consistent instantiation on P that is identified as dual-inconsistent and is thus in $\widetilde{P''}$ with $P'' = DC(P)$ is also identified as path-inconsistent and is thus in $\widetilde{P'}$ with $P' = PC(P)$. We deduce that $PC(P) \preceq DC(P)$ and also that PC is stronger than DC on binary networks.   □

We can show that PC and CDC are incomparable in general, but on binary constraint networks, PC is strictly stronger than CDC.

PROPOSITION 7.7.– *On binary constraint networks, PC is strictly stronger than CDC.*

Proof. By definition, DC is stronger than CDC, so it follows from Proposition 7.6 that PC is stronger than CDC. Moreover, Figure 7.1 shows a network (more precisely, its compatibility graph) that is CDC-consistent but not PC-consistent.   □

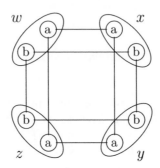

Figure 7.1. *A network (no constraint binds w with y and x with z) that is CDC-consistent and sCDC-consistent but neither sPC-consistent nor PC-consistent. For example, $\{(x, a), (z, b)\}$ is not path-consistent*

The remainder of the section is focused on the relationships between, on the one hand, the conservative variant of DC, namely CDC, and, on the other hand DC, PPC and CPC.

PROPOSITION 7.8.– *DC is strictly stronger than CDC.*

Proof. By definition, DC is stronger than CDC. Besides, we know that for some binary constraint networks (see Figure 7.1), CDC holds, whereas $DC = PC$ does not hold.   □

PROPOSITION 7.9.– *CDC is strictly stronger than PPC.*

Proof. Assume that a constraint network P is CDC-consistent and consider a closed graph-path $\langle x_1, \ldots, x_p \rangle$ of P. For every locally consistent instantiation $\{(x_1, a_1), (x_p, a_p)\}$ on P, $(x_p, a_p) \in P'$ with $P' = GAC(P|_{x_1=a_1})$ since P is CDC-consistent. It also implies $P' \neq \bot$. Therefore, in the context of P', there exists at least one value in each domain and since P' is generalized arc-consistent, there is clearly a v-value (x_{p-1}, a_{p-1}) of P' compatible with (x_p, a_p), a v-value (x_{p-2}, a_{p-2}) of P' compatible with (x_{p-1}, a_{p-1}), $\ldots$, and a v-value (x_1, a'_1) of P' compatible with (x_2, a_2). Because $\mathrm{dom}^{P'}(x_1) = \{a_1\}$, we have $a'_1 = a_1$, so the locally consistent instantiation $\{(x_1, a_1), (x_p, a_p)\}$ is consistent on the closed graph-path $\langle x_1, \ldots, x_p \rangle$ of P. Hence P is PPC-consistent, so CDC is stronger than

PPC. The fact that CDC is strictly stronger than PPC is illustrated in Figures 7.2, 7.3 and 7.4, which represent the same constraint network P. In Figure 7.3, P is shown to be not CDC-consistent because the locally consistent instantiation $\{(x, a), (y, b)\}$ is dual-inconsistent. Indeed, $(y, b) \notin AC(P|_{x=a})$. In Figure 7.4, P is shown to be CPC-consistent because, for example, the locally consistent instantiation $\{(x, a), (y, b)\}$ is consistent on all 2-length graph-paths linking x to y, namely, $\langle x, z, y \rangle$ and $\langle x, w, y \rangle$. Here, the constraint graph is triangulated, which means that CPC is equivalent to PPC. Hence we can deduce our result. ☐

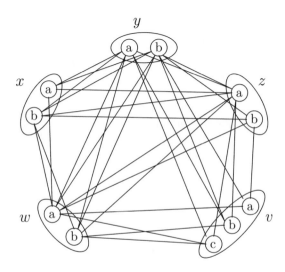

Figure 7.2. *A binary constraint network P (no constraint binds x with v)*

PROPOSITION 7.10.– *PPC is strictly stronger than CPC.*

Proof. PPC is stronger than CPC by definition. Moreover, the binary constraint network in Figure 7.5 is CPC-consistent but not PPC-consistent. Because there is no 3-clique in its constraint graph, this network is trivially CPC-consistent. ☐

Before studying the relationships existing between strong variants of second-order consistencies, we observe that, in the binary case, enforcing AC (only once) on a path-consistent network is sufficient to obtain a strong path-consistent network. This well-known fact is also true in the general case for DC and CDC. We define $\phi \circ \psi(P)$ as being $\phi(\psi(P))$ and $(\phi \circ \psi)^{n+1}(P)$ as being $\phi \circ \psi \circ (\phi \circ \psi)^n(P)$.

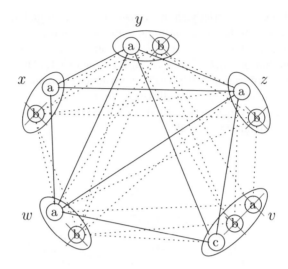

Figure 7.3. *The constraint network P from Figure 7.2 is not CDC-consistent. We can see that $(y, b) \notin AC(P|_{x=a})$. So the locally consistent instantiation $\{(x, a), (y, b)\}$ is dual-inconsistent*

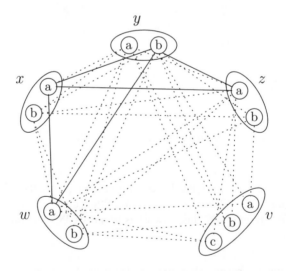

Figure 7.4. *The constraint network P from Figure 7.2 is CPC-consistent and sCPC-consistent (and hence, PPC-consistent and sPPC-consistent since P is triangulated). Any (closed) 2-length graph-path of P linking x to y is consistent. This is shown here for $\{(x, a), (y, b)\}$*

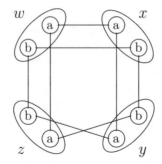

Figure 7.5. *A network (no constraint binds x with z and y with w) that is CPC-consistent and sCPC-consistent but is neither sPPC-consistent nor PPC-consistent. For example,* $\{(x, a), (w, a)\}$ *is not PPC-consistent*

PROPOSITION 7.11.– *For any binary constraint network P, we have* $AC \circ PC(P) = sPC(P)$.

Proof. If a v-value (x, a) is arc-inconsistent while enforcing PC, every tuple involving this value is detected as path-inconsistent (and then removed). When (x, a) is subsequently removed while enforcing AC, this cannot possibly have any impact on path consistency because this v-value is completely isolated. In other words, we have: $PC \circ AC \circ PC(P) = AC \circ PC(P)$. □

PROPOSITION 7.12.– *For any constraint network P, we have:*
  – $GAC \circ DC(P) = sDC(P)$;
  – $GAC \circ CDC(P) = sCDC(P)$.

Proof. If a value is GAC-inconsistent on P, then this value is removed whenever a singleton check is performed. Discarding it before performing a singleton check has clearly no impact. We deduce our result. □

It is interesting that the schema of previous propositions does not hold for CPC and PPC.

PROPOSITION 7.13.– *For some binary constraint networks P, we have:*
  – $AC \circ CPC(P) \neq sCPC(P)$;
  – $AC \circ PPC(P) \neq sPPC(P)$.

Proof. Consider the example in Figures 7.6, 7.7 and 7.8. Initially, enforcing AC implies the removal of (w, b). Enforcing CPC removes all tuples corresponding to dotted edges[1]. Next, if AC is enforced again, (z, b) and (w', b) are removed. We can imagine the same pattern (w, x, y, z) occurring an arbitrary number of times (here, it occurs twice). So for any integer n we can build a network P such that $(AC \circ CPC)^{n+1}(P) = sCPC(P)$ while $(AC \circ CPC)^n(P) \neq sCPC(P)$ (and such that the size of P grows polynomially with n). The constraint graph is triangulated in our example. Hence, the result also holds for PPC.   □

PROPOSITION 7.14.– *Let ϕ and ψ two second-order consistencies. If ϕ is stronger than ψ then $s\phi$ is stronger than $s\psi$.*

Proof. If a network is both GAC-consistent and ϕ-consistent, it is necessarily both GAC-consistent and ψ-consistent since ϕ is stronger than ψ. Consequently, $s\phi$ is stronger than $s\psi$.   □

PROPOSITION 7.15.– *On binary constraint networks, sPC is strictly stronger than sCDC.*

Proof. From Propositions 7.7 and 7.14 we know that sPC is stronger than sCDC. Figure 7.1 proves strictness by showing a network that is sCDC-consistent but not sPC-consistent.   □

PROPOSITION 7.16.– *sDC is strictly stronger than sCDC.*

Proof. From Propositions 7.8 and 7.14 we know that sDC is stronger than sCDC. Figure 7.1 proves strictness by showing a network that is sCDC-consistent but not sDC-consistent (because PC = DC on binary constraint networks).   □

PROPOSITION 7.17.– *sCDC is strictly stronger than sPPC.*

Proof. From Propositions 7.9 and 7.14 we know that sCDC is stronger than sPPC. Figures 7.2, 7.3 and 7.4 prove strictness by showing a network that is sPPC-consistent but not sCDC-consistent.   □

---

1. Strictly speaking, the tuples $(a, b) \in \text{rel}(c_{xw})$ and $(a, b) \in \text{rel}(c_{yw})$ are not deleted because they correspond to invalid instantiations (and consequently to instantiations that are not locally consistent).

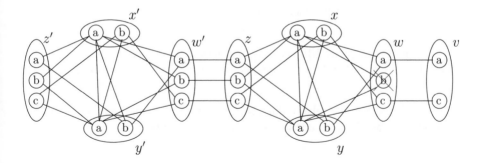

Figure 7.6. *A binary constraint network P made arc-consistent*

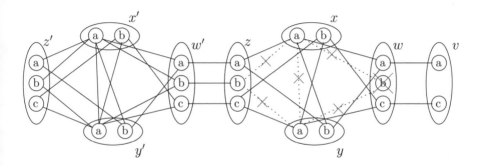

Figure 7.7. *The constraint network P′ obtained after enforcing CPC on the constraint network P from Figure 7.6*

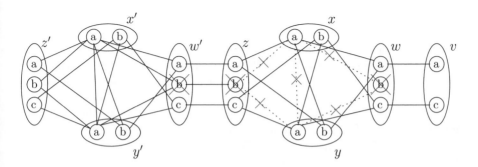

Figure 7.8. *The constraint network P″ obtained after enforcing AC on the constraint network P′ from Figure 7.7*

PROPOSITION 7.18.– *sPPC is strictly stronger than sCPC.*

Proof. From Propositions 7.10 and 7.14 we know that sPPC is stronger than sCPC. Figure 7.5 shows a network that is sPPC-consistent but not sCPC-consistent.   □

Figure 7.9 shows the relationships between (strong) second-order consistencies introduced so far. We conclude this section by establishing some connections with SAC.

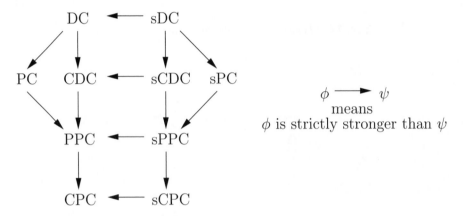

Figure 7.9. *Summary of the relationships between consistencies that have been studied. On binary constraint networks, PC = DC*

PROPOSITION 7.19.– *On binary constraint networks, sCDC is strictly stronger than SAC.*

Proof. Let P be a sCDC-consistent binary constraint network. Assume that a v-value (x, a) of P is SAC-inconsistent. This means that $AC(P|_{x=a}) = \perp$. As P is AC-consistent (since P is sCDC-consistent), necessarily x is involved in (at least) a binary constraint c (otherwise no propagation is possible to deduce $AC(P|_{x=a}) = \perp$). Consequently, there is no tuple allowed by c involving (x, a) since P is CDC-consistent (because when $P = \perp$, for every v-value (y, b), we consider $(y, b) \notin P$). We deduce that (x, a) is AC-inconsistent. This contradiction shows that sCDC is stronger than SAC. To prove strictness, it suffices to observe that sCDC reasons both with inconsistent values and inconsistent pairs of values.   □

PROPOSITION 7.20.– *On binary constraint networks, sCDC is equivalent to SAC+CDC.*

Proof. Clearly, SAC+CDC is stronger than sCDC since SAC is stronger than AC (and sCDC is AC+CDC on binary constraint networks). On the other hand, sCDC is trivially stronger than CDC and we know from Proposition 7.19 that sCDC is stronger than SAC. We deduce that sCDC is stronger than SAC+CDC, and that SAC+CDC is equivalent to sCDC. □

PROPOSITION 7.21.– *SAC+CDC is strictly stronger than sCDC.*

Proof. Clearly, SAC+CDC is stronger than sCDC since SAC is stronger than GAC (and sCDC is GAC+CDC). To show strictness, it suffices to build a constraint network P which is GAC-consistent, trivially CDC-consistent because involving no binary constraint, and not SAC-consistent. □

7.2. Enforcing (conservative) path consistency

There are many published algorithms that enforce path consistency; a *PC algorithm* computes the PC-closure $PC(P)$ of every constraint network P. PC1, which is called algorithm C in [MON 74], is a brute-force path consistency algorithm. PC2 [MAC 77a] is the first algorithm to use a queue to manage 2-length paths that have to be revised. PC_{MG} [MCG 79], which is a path consistency algorithm built on top of arc consistency, was ignored for a long time, but has been "resurrected" via its derivatives in this chapter. PC3 [MOH 86] is based on the use of counters and lists of supports, as in AC4. Some errors in PC3 required a correction called PC4 [HAN 88]. PC3/4 is the first path consistency algorithm proved to be optimal: its worst-case time complexity is $O(n^3d^3)$, but its space complexity is $O(n^3d^3)$ which is rather prohibitive. PC5 [SIN 96] and PC6 [CHM 96] are based on the idea of recording smallest supports (analogous to AC6). These two algorithms are equivalent but were developed independently. PC5/6 is time optimal and reduces the space complexity to $O(n^3d^2)$. PC8 [CHM 98], which is inspired by PC5/6, searches for the smallest supports without recording them. PC8 is suboptimal because its worst-case time complexity is $O(n^3d^4)$, but it is applicable to many problems because its space complexity is $O(n^2d)$. Furthermore, PC8 has been shown experimentally to outperform algorithms devised previously. Finally, PC2001 uses the same idea as AC2001 and is time-optimal while being rather simple to implement.

We henceforth restrict our attention to coarse-grained path consistency algorithms. Specifically, we describe PC8 and PC2001 and their conservative variants.

7.2.1. *Algorithms PC8 and PC2001*

We consider enforcement of path consistency on a binary constraint network P that must belong to $\mathscr{P}_{2^*}$, which means that there must be a binary constraint between

---

Algorithm 59: enforcePC(P: $\mathscr{P}_{2*}$): Boolean

Output: *true* iff $PC(P) \neq \perp$

// Initialization phase

1 $Q_{pc} \leftarrow \emptyset$
2 **foreach** *variable* $x \in \mathrm{vars}(P)$ **do**
3 $\quad$ **foreach** *variable* $y \in \mathrm{vars}(P) \mid y \neq x$ **do**
4 $\quad\quad$ **foreach** *variable* $z \in \mathrm{vars}(P) \mid z \neq x \wedge z \neq y$ **do**
5 $\quad\quad\quad$ **foreach** *tuple* $(a,b) \in \mathrm{rel}(c_{xy})$ **do**
6 $\quad\quad\quad\quad$ **if** $\neg$*isPathConsistent*$((x,a),(y,b),z)$ **then**
7 $\quad\quad\quad\quad\quad$ remove (a,b) from $\mathrm{rel}(c_{xy})$
8 $\quad\quad\quad\quad\quad$ **if** $\mathrm{rel}(c_{xy}) = \emptyset$ **then**
9 $\quad\quad\quad\quad\quad\quad$ **return** *false*
10 $\quad\quad\quad\quad$ $Q_{pc} \leftarrow Q_{pc} \cup \{(c_{xy}, x, a), (c_{xy}, y, b)\}$

// Propagation phase

11 **while** $Q_{pc} \neq \emptyset$ **do**
12 $\quad$ pick and delete (c_{xy}, x, a) from Q_{pc} $\qquad$ // (x,a) lost a support on c_{xy}
13 $\quad$ **foreach** *variable* $z \in \mathrm{vars}(P) \mid z \neq x \wedge z \neq y$ **do**
14 $\quad\quad$ **foreach** *value* $c \in \mathrm{dom}(z) \mid (a,c) \in \mathrm{rel}(c_{xz})$ **do**
15 $\quad\quad\quad$ **if** $\neg$*isPathConsistent*$((x,a),(z,c),y)$ **then**
16 $\quad\quad\quad\quad$ remove (a,c) from $\mathrm{rel}(c_{xz})$
17 $\quad\quad\quad\quad$ **if** $\mathrm{rel}(c_{xz}) = \emptyset$ **then**
18 $\quad\quad\quad\quad\quad$ **return** *false*
19 $\quad\quad\quad$ $Q_{pc} \leftarrow Q_{pc} \cup \{(c_{xz}, x, a), (c_{xz}, z, c)\}$

20 **return** *true*

---

each pair of variables (there might also be some non-binary constraints which would be simply ignored). Without any loss of generality, we consider that each constraint c of P is tailored, i.e. each tuple allowed by c is a support on c; we have $\mathrm{rel}(c) = \sup(c)$. The idea of the coarse-grained path consistency scheme is to record in a propagation queue, denoted by Q_{pc} all c-values of P that have recently lost a support. If (c_{xy}, x, a) is in Q_{pc} then (at least) one tuple τ such that $\tau[x] = a$ has been removed from $\mathrm{rel}(c_{xy})$. This tuple was a support for (x,a) on c_{xy} and has been discarded in one of the two phases of Algorithm 59. The function enforcePC returns the Boolean value *false* iff the constraint network P given as parameter is path-inconsistent, i.e. iff $PC(P) = \perp$. In the first phase (lines 1 to 10), the global structure Q_{pc} is initially empty. For every locally consistent instantiation $\{(x,a),(y,b)\}$ on P and for every third variable z, the algorithm checks whether there is a consistent 2-length path that includes z. The function isPathConsistent determines whether or not there is a support for $\{(x, a), (y, b)\}$ on the path $\langle x, z, y\rangle$; different implementations of this function are described below. If there is no support for $\{(x, a), (y, b)\}$, the tuple (a, b) is removed from $\mathrm{rel}(c_{xy})$ and the set Q_{pc} is updated. A relation wipe-out shows that the constraint network is path-inconsistent, so *false* is returned at line 9. At lines 11 to 19 each c-value (c_{xy}, x, a) in Q_{pc} is "propagated" by checking that for every variable z and for every value c in $\mathrm{dom}(z)$ such that $(a, c) \in \mathrm{rel}(c_{xz})$, there is still a consistent 2-length path that includes y.

To enforce strong path consistency on a binary constraint network P, it is sufficient to insert:

$$P \leftarrow AC(P, \mathrm{vars}(P))$$

at the end of Algorithm 59 (before line 20). From Proposition 7.11 we know that enforcing arc consistency on a path-consistent network results in a strong path-consistent network. Moreover, efficiency may also be enhanced by enforcing (generalized) arc consistency at the beginning of Algorithm 59.

Different implementations of the function isPathConsistent yield different instantiations of Algorithm 59. PC8 is an instantiation in which Algorithm 59 calls the function isPathConsistent-8, Algorithm 60. A support for $\{(x, a), (y, b)\}$ on $\langle x, z, y\rangle$ is sought simply by iterating over all values of z.

Algorithm 60: isPathConsistent-8($(x, a), (y, b)$: v-values, z: variable): Boolean

---

Output: *true* iff there is a support for $\{(x, a), (y, b)\}$ on $\langle x, z, y\rangle$

1 **foreach** *value* $c \in \mathrm{dom}(z)$ **do**
2   **if** $(a, c) \in \mathrm{rel}(c_{xz}) \wedge (b, c) \in \mathrm{rel}(c_{yz})$ **then**
3   **return** *true*

4 **return** *false*

PROPOSITION 7.22.– *[CHM 98] PC8 admits a worst-case time complexity in $O(n^3 d^4)$ and a worst-case space complexity in $O(n^2 d)$.*

PC2001 is an instantiation of Algorithm 59 that calls the function isPathConsistent-2001, Algorithm 61, using a structure *last* to store the last supports found. More precisely, $last[c_{xy}, (a, b), z]$ indicates the last support found[2] for $\{(x, a), (y, b)\}$ on $\langle x, z, y\rangle$. Initially, the first value in $\mathrm{dom}(z)$ is assigned to $last[c_{xy}, (a, b), z]$. Like

---

2. Of course, instead of recording a triplet of values (a, c, b), we can only record the value c.

334   Constraint Networks

GAC2001, the function isPathConsistent-2001 avoids starting from scratch each time it seeks a support for $\{(x,a),(y,b)\}$, perhaps finding a new one.

Algorithm 61: isPathConsistent-2001$((x,a),(y,b)$: v-values, z: variable): Bool

---

Output: *true* iff there is a support for $\{(x,a),(y,b)\}$ on $\langle x,z,y \rangle$

1 **foreach** *value* $c \in \text{dom}(z) \mid c \geq last[c_{xy},(a,b),z]$ **do**
2   **if** $(a,c) \in \text{rel}(c_{xz}) \wedge (b,c) \in \text{rel}(c_{yz})$ **then**
3        $last[c_{xy},(a,b),z] \leftarrow c$
4   **return** *true*

5 **return** *false*

PROPOSITION 7.23.– *[BES 05c] PC2001 admits a worst-case time complexity in $O(n^3 d^3)$ and a worst-case space complexity in $O(n^3 d^2)$.*

7.2.2. Algorithms CPC8 and CPC2001

Algorithm 62 enforces conservative path consistency on a binary constraint network P by processing 3-cliques, without processing other sets of three variables. Here, a 3-clique is a set of three variables with a binary constraint between every pair of these. For each 3-clique, three closed graph-paths are initially processed at line 2 because there are three constraints between the three variables. The condition $x \lhd y$ precludes useless symmetric treatments. Whenever a constraint c_{xy} is picked (via a c-value) at line 10, line 11 finds every variable z that is connected to both x and y. The rest of the algorithm is similar to Algorithm 59. Note that the constraint network P that must be enforced conservative path-consistent belongs to $\mathscr{P}_2$ (the constraint graph of P is not necessarily complete), whereas $P \in \mathscr{P}_{2^*}$ for PC.

In the following analysis, K denotes the number of 3-cliques of P; K is equal to the number of closed 2-length graph-paths of P divided by six. CPC8 denotes Algorithm 62 calling the function isPathConsistent-8, Algorithm 60.

PROPOSITION 7.24.– *CPC8 admits a worst-case time complexity in $O(Kd^4)$ and a worst-case space complexity in $O(ed + K)$.*

Proof. In P, there are initially 3 K closed graph-paths $\langle x,z,y \rangle$ of P such that $x \lhd y$, so the time complexity of the initialization phase is $O(Kd^3)$. For the propagation phase, for any connected pair (x,y) of variables, i.e. any two variables involved in the same binary constraint, we iterate over the closed graph-paths $\langle x,y,z \rangle$ of P. Thus the total number of iterated closed graph-paths is 6 K when each connected pair of

---

Algorithm 62: enforceCPC(P: $\mathscr{P}_2$): Boolean

Output: *true* iff $CPC(P) \neq \bot$

// Initialization phase

1   $Q_{pc} \leftarrow \emptyset$

2   **foreach** *closed graph-path* $\langle x, z, y \rangle$ *of P such that* $x \lhd y$ **do**

3   **foreach** *tuple* $(a, b) \in \mathrm{rel}(c_{xy})$ **do**

4   **if** $\neg isPathConsistent((x, a), (y, b), z)$ **then**

5   remove (a, b) from $\mathrm{rel}(c_{xy})$

6   **if** $\mathrm{rel}(c_{xy}) = \emptyset$ **then**

7   **return** *false*

8         $Q_{pc} \leftarrow Q_{pc} \cup \{(c_{xy}, x, a), (c_{xy}, y, b)\}$

// Propagation phase

9   **while** $Q_{pc} \neq \emptyset$ **do**

10   pick and delete (c_{xy}, x, a) from Q_{pc} // (x, a) lost a support on c_{xy}

11   **foreach** *closed graph-path* $\langle x, y, z \rangle$ *of P* **do**

12   **foreach** *value* $c \in \mathrm{dom}(z) \mid (a, c) \in \mathrm{rel}(c_{xz})$ **do**

13   **if** $\neg isPathConsistent((x, a), (z, c), y)$ **then**

14   remove (a, c) from $\mathrm{rel}(c_{xz})$

15   **if** $\mathrm{rel}(c_{xz}) = \emptyset$ **then**

16   **return** *false*

17          $Q_{pc} \leftarrow Q_{pc} \cup \{(c_{xz}, x, a), (c_{xz}, z, c)\}$

18 **return** *true*

---

variables is processed only once. Each connected pair (x, y) can be processed up to d^2 times (because a c-value involving the arc (c_{xy}, x) can be picked d^2 times). The cost of lines 12 to 17 is $O(d^2)$, so the time complexity of the propagation phase is $O(Kd^4)$, which is the overall worst-case time complexity of CPC8. The space complexity of Q_{pc} is $O(ed)$; efficient implementation of lines 2 and 11 requires data structures in $O(K)$. So, the overall space-complexity is $O(ed + K)$. $\square$

CPC2001 denotes Algorithm 62 calling the function isPathConsistent-2001, Algorithm 61.

PROPOSITION 7.25.– *CPC2001 admits a worst-case time complexity in $O(Kd^3)$ and a worst-case space complexity in $O(ed + Kd^2)$.*

Proof. Following [BES 05c] we can prove that the cost of lines 12 to 17 is $O(2d)$ instead of $O(d^2)$. Hence CPC2001 has a worst-case time complexity in $O(Kd^3)$. The space complexity of Q_{pc} is $O(ed)$ and the space complexity of the *last* structure is $3Kd^2 = O(Kd^2)$; so the overall space-complexity is $O(ed + Kd^2)$. □

Unfortunately, as indicated in Proposition 7.13, enforcing arc consistency on a conservative path-consistent binary network does not necessarily yield a sCPC-consistent network, although apparently this is often the case in practice. Several passes may be needed, enforcing CPC then AC then CPC then AC, and so on.

7.3. Enforcing strong (conservative) dual consistency

We now introduce sCDC1 [LEC 07a], which establishes strong conservative dual consistency on binary constraint networks (and SAC+CDC on non-binary constraint networks), and sDC2 [LEC 07b], which enforces strong dual (path) consistency[3] on binary networks. For binary networks, when the constraint graph is (made) complete, both algorithms enforce strong path consistency, and here sDC2 has the advantage of being partially incremental. Recall that any instruction of the form $GAC(P, X)$ must be seen as a call to the function enforceGAC^{var} depicted in Algorithm 9, which takes P and X as parameters, and returns *false* when $GAC(P, X) = \bot$.

7.3.1. *Algorithm sCDC1*

sCDC1, Algorithm 63, which establishes strong conservative dual consistency on binary constraint networks, performs successive singleton checks until a fixed point is reached. This algorithm returns *false* iff P given as a parameter (and assumed first to be binary) is sCDC-inconsistent, i.e. iff $sCDC(P) = \bot$. (G)AC is enforced at line 1, and then a variable is considered at each turn of the main loop to establish the consistency. For any set X of variables (totally ordered by $\lhd$), first(X) is the smallest variable of X and nextCircular(x, X) is the smallest variable of X strictly greater than x if any, or first(X) otherwise. These two functions allow circular (and potentially infinite) iteration over the variables of P. For example, if vars$(P) = \{w, x, y, z\}$, then the iteration has the form $w, x, y, z, w, x, y, z, w, \ldots$.

The function reviseStrongCDC, Algorithm 64, revises the given variable x by means of strong conservative dual consistency, i.e. it explores all possible inferences with respect to x by performing singleton checks on values of x. The sCDC revision of a variable x means removing from dom(x) all values that are SAC-inconsistent and from every relation rel(c_{xy}), associated with a binary constraint involving x, all tuples that are CDC-inconsistent. To achieve this, GAC is enforced on $P|_{x=a}$ for each value

---

3. Enforcing the strong form of (conservative) dual consistency comes for free. For this reason we do not present any algorithm that enforces DC or CDC alone.

Algorithm 63: sCDC1(P: $\mathscr{P}$): Boolean

Output: *true* iff $sCDC(P) \neq \perp$

1   $P \leftarrow GAC(P, \text{vars}(P))$ // GAC is initially enforced
2   **if** $P = \perp$ **then**
3 | **return** *false*

4   $x \leftarrow \text{first}(\text{vars}(P))$
5   $marker \leftarrow x$
6   **repeat**
7 | **if** $|\text{dom}(x)| > 1$ **then**
8 | **if** *reviseStrongCDC*(P, x) **then**
9 | | $P \leftarrow GAC(P, \{x\})$ // GAC is maintained
10 | **if** $P = \perp$ **then**
11 | | **return** *false*

12 | $marker \leftarrow x$

13 | $x \leftarrow \text{nextCircular}(x, \text{vars}(P))$
14 **until** $x = marker$
15 **return** *true*

Algorithm 64: reviseStrongCDC(P: $\mathscr{P}$, x: variable): Boolean

---

Output: *true* iff the sCDC revision of x is effective

1   $modified \leftarrow false$
2   **foreach** *value* $a \in \text{dom}^P(x)$ **do**
3 | $P' \leftarrow GAC(P|_{x=a}, \{x\})$ // singleton check on (x, a)
4 | **if** $P' = \perp$ **then**
5 | remove a from $\text{dom}^P(x)$ // SAC-inconsistent value
6 | $modified \leftarrow true$
7 | **else**
8 | **foreach** *binary constraint* $c_{xy} \in \text{cons}(P)$ **do**
9 | **foreach** *value* $b \in \text{dom}^P(y) \mid (a, b) \in \text{rel}^P(c_{xy})$ **do**
10 | **if** $b \notin \text{dom}^{P'}(y)$ **then**
11 | | remove (a, b) from $\text{rel}^P(c_{xy})$ // CDC-inconsistent pair of values
12 | | $modified \leftarrow true$

13 **return** $modified$

a in the domain of x. If a is SAC-inconsistent, then a is removed from the domain of x (line 5). Otherwise (lines 8 to 12), for every variable y such that there is a binary constraint between x and y and for every v-value (y, b) present in P but not in P', the tuple (a, b) is removed from $\text{rel}(c_{xy})$, because this tuple is CDC-inconsistent. The sCDC revision is effective for x if a value or a tuple is deleted.

At line 8 of Algorithm 63, reviseStrongCDC may make changes relating to the variable x. When the sCDC revision of x is effective, i.e. when there is at least one inference (removal of a value or a tuple), reviseStrongCDC returns *true* and (generalized) arc consistency is re-established (line 9). Any domain or relation wipe-out is detected at line 10 (in constant time if we use an additional flag in reviseStrongCDC). A marker, initialized with the first variable of $\text{vars}(P)$ (line 4) and updated whenever there are inferences (line 12), manages termination. There can be no inferential deletion of values or tuples when the currently selected variable is fixed, because the network is always maintained (generalized) arc-consistent. This is the reason of the test at line 7.

There is a strong connection between the algorithm sCDC1 and the algorithm proposed in [MCG 79] to establish strong path consistency. sCDC1 enforces (strong) conservative dual consistency and can therefore be regarded as a refinement of McGregor's algorithm. sCDC1 incorporates two improvements. First, GAC is maintained during execution so as to start singleton checks with a propagation queue limited to a single variable (thus avoiding many useless revisions, particularly on sparse constraint graphs). Second, a simple but enhanced mechanism handles termination. Coarse grain reasoning about termination is appropriate because for every variable x and for every pair of values a and b in $\text{dom}(x)$, any inference concerning (x, a) (the removal of (x, a) or the removal of a tuple linking (x, a) to another value) has no effect on $P|_{x=b}$, and vice-versa.

PROPOSITION 7.26.– *The algorithm sCDC1 enforces strong conservative dual consistency on binary constraint networks.*

Proof. First, it is immediately clear that any inference performed by sCDC1 is correct. Completeness, i.e. the fact that all possible inferences are performed, is guaranteed by the following invariant: when $P' \leftarrow GAC(P|_{x=a}, \{x\})$ is performed at line 3 of Algorithm 64, we obtain a network P' that is exactly $GAC(P|_{x=a})$, or equivalently from an operational point of view, P' is the constraint network returned by $GAC(P|_{x=a}, \text{vars}(P))$. The reasons are a) that the network is maintained GAC-consistent whenever a modification is performed (line 9 of Algorithm 63) and b) that any inference performed with respect to a v-value (x, a) has no effect on $P|_{x=b}$, where b is any other value in the domain of the variable x. □

One *pass* of sCDC1 means calling reviseStrongCDC exactly once per variable. We first analyze one pass.

PROPOSITION 7.27.– *On binary constraint networks, one pass of sCDC1 admits a worst-case time complexity in $O(end^3)$, and a worst-case space complexity in $O(ed)$.*

Proof. Consider first the total worst-case time complexity of reviseStrongCDC when sCDC1 is executed. For one pass of sCDC1, the total complexity of executing line 3 of Algorithm 64 is clearly $O(nded^2) = O(end^3)$ when using an optimal $O(ed^2)$ arc consistency algorithm such as AC2001. The "if" part (lines 5 and 6) is negligible, whereas the total worst-case time complexity of executing the "else" part (lines 8 to 12) is $O(d2ed) = O(ed^2)$. Thus the total worst-case time complexity of reviseStrongCDC is in $O(end^3)$. The total worst-case time complexity of line 9 of Algorithm 63 is $O(ned^2)$ since there are exactly n turns of the main loop. Since other instructions are negligible, the overall complexity is $O(end^3)$. In terms of space, the only data structures used by sCDC1 are those employed by the underlying AC algorithm. For AC2001 or $AC3^{rm}$, this is $O(ed)$, which is therefore the worst-case space complexity of sCDC1.   □

If $\lambda = \sum_{c \in \text{cons}(P)} |\sup(c)|$ is the number of supports over all relations of the network, then the number of passes of sCDC1 is bounded by $nd + \lambda$ since between two successive calls, at least one value is removed from a domain or a support is removed from a relation. Because λ is in $O(ed^2)$, sCDC1 is in $O(e^2nd^5)$. This seems to be rather high, but our opinion is that sCDC1 quickly reaches a fixed point (i.e. the number of passes is very small in practice) because inferences about inconsistent values and inconsistent pairs of values are immediately taken into account. The following corollary also indicates that the time wasted by applying sCDC1 to a binary network which is already strongly conservative dual-consistent is quite limited provided that domain cardinalities are not too high.

COROLLARY 7.28.– *Applied to a binary network that is sCDC-consistent, the worst-case time complexity of sCDC1 is $O(end^3)$.*

The proof is immediate since there is only one pass before a fixed point is reached.

On non-binary constraint networks, Algorithm 63 enforces SAC+CDC; in this context, a better name for this algorithm is certainly SAC/CDC1.

7.3.2. *Algorithm sDC2*

The algorithm sCDC1 can enforce strong path (dual) consistency on binary constraint networks that have a constraint between every two variables, i.e. networks in $\mathscr{P}_{2^*}$. Algorithm sDC2 [LEC 07b] is a refinement of sCDC1 for networks in $\mathscr{P}_{2^*}$ that limits the cost of enforcing AC at each singleton check. For binary networks, sCDC1 systematically applies $AC(P|_{x=a}, \{x\})$ at line 3 of Algorithm 64 even when there has been a previous singleton check on (x, a). In the case where $P \in \mathscr{P}_{2^*}$, the entire domain of $P' = AC(P|_{x=a}, \{x\})$ is "recorded" in the network P itself since there is a constraint between x and every other variable of P. When P is modified by removing all DC-inconsistent tuples involving (x, a) from constraint relations (as identified in P'), we can easily and cheaply recover the domain of P'. Specifically, we have $P' = FC(P|_{x=a}, x)$ where FC is limited to making arc-consistent every constraint involving x. An instruction of the form $FC(P, x)$ must be understood as a call to the function applyFC depicted in Algorithm 11, which takes P and x as parameters. However, instead of returning a Boolean value, $FC(P, x)$ is assumed now to return the constraint network obtained after applying FC on P from the event variable x.

When a coarse-grained AC algorithm with a variable-oriented propagation scheme is used, we know that $AC(P|_{x=a}, \{x\})$ is equivalent to $AC(FC(P|_{x=a}, x), X_{\text{evt}})$, where X_{evt} denotes the set of variables of P whose domain has been reduced by $FC(P|_{x=a}, x)$. Indeed, execution of $AC(P|_{x=a}, \{x\})$ starts by revising each arc (c_{xy}, y) of P, such that $x \in \text{scp}(c_{xy})$, and putting y in the propagation queue if $\text{dom}(y)$ has been reduced. Here the first pass of AC enforcement is equivalent to forward checking. Except for the first singleton check on each v-value (x, a), in sDC2, we apply $AC(FC(P|_{x=a}, x), Y_{\text{evt}})$ where Y_{evt} is a set of variables built up during propagation. The point is that necessarily $Y_{\text{evt}} \subseteq X_{\text{evt}}$ and $AC(FC(P|_{x=a}, x), Y_{\text{evt}}) = AC(FC(P|_{x=a}, x), X_{\text{evt}})$. So, sDC2 is less expensive than sCDC1 (since some useless revisions may be avoided, and, as we will show, the cost of managing the additional information is negligible). Roughly speaking, sDC2 partially exploits the incrementality of the underlying arc consistency algorithm.

Algorithm 65, which enforces strong path (dual) consistency on a given binary network P, differs from sCDC1 in that it uses time-stamping. A global counter $time$ counts the number of turns of the main loop (see lines 6 and 8), and a time-stamp is associated with each variable: $stamp[x]$ indicates the time (turn number) of the most recent occurrence of an inference concerning the variable x. In this context, inference means removal of a value from $\text{dom}(x)$ or removal of a tuple from the relation associated with a constraint involving x. When the function reviseStrongDC returns $true$, this means that at least one inference concerning x has been performed, so $stamp[x]$ is updated (line 11). Then AC is maintained, and deleted values are collected; see a description of $(G)AC^+$ on page 290. For every variable y whose domain has been reduced, i.e. $y \in \text{vars}(deleted)$, $stamp[y]$ is updated at line 16.

All inferences, if any, concerning a given variable x, are implemented by the function reviseStrongDC, Algorithm 66; this function revises x by means of strong dual consistency, as previously explained with sCDC. If $time \leq n$, this is the first time

---

Algorithm 65: sDC2(P: $\mathscr{P}_{2*}$): Boolean

Output: *true* iff $sPC(P) \neq \bot$

1 $P \leftarrow AC(P, \text{vars}(P))$ // AC is initially enforced
2 **if** $P = \bot$ **then**
3 $\quad \lfloor$ **return** *false*
4 $x \leftarrow \text{first}(\text{vars}(P))$
5 $marker \leftarrow x$
6 $time \leftarrow 0$
7 **repeat**
8 $\quad time \leftarrow time + 1$
9 $\quad$ **if** $|\text{dom}(x)| > 1$ **then**
10 $\quad\quad$ **if** *reviseStrongDC*(P, x) **then**
11 $\quad\quad\quad stamp[x] \leftarrow time$
12 $\quad\quad\quad (P, deleted) \leftarrow AC^+(P, \{x\})$ // AC is maintained – values deleted
   $\quad\quad\quad$ by AC are returned
13 $\quad\quad\quad$ **if** $P = \bot$ **then**
14 $\quad\quad\quad\quad \lfloor$ **return** *false*
15 $\quad\quad\quad$ **foreach** *variable* $y \in \text{vars}(deleted)$ **do**
16 $\quad\quad\quad\quad \lfloor stamp[y] \leftarrow time$
17 $\quad\quad\quad marker \leftarrow x$
18 $\quad x \leftarrow \text{nextCircular}(x, \text{vars}(P))$
19 **until** $x = marker$
20 **return** *true*

---

reviseStrongDC has been called with the variable x as a parameter; in this case, each value a in $\text{dom}(x)$ is processed as usual. Otherwise, an "event" set X'_{evt} comprising all variables that were subject to at least one inference during the last $n - 1$ calls to reviseStrongDC is first computed at line 3. Note that events in X'_{evt} have already been propagated in the main problem since AC is maintained at each step at line 12 of Algorithm 65. Then, if $time > n$, for each value a in $\text{dom}(x)$ $FC^+(P|_{x=a}, x)$ returns at line 8 a pair (P', X_{evt}) where $P' = FC(P|_{x=a}, x)$ and $X_{\text{evt}} = \{y \in \text{vars}(P) \mid \text{dom}^{P'}(y) \subset \text{dom}^{P|_{x=a}}(y)\}$. The algorithm presented in section 4.1.3 can easily be adapted to additionally return X_{evt}, which is the set of variables whose domain has been reduced by FC. Importantly, FC initially removes (at least) all the values that were removed by the last AC enforcement on (x, a). AC is then applied at line 9 from $X_{\text{evt}} \cap X'_{\text{evt}}$ because no new event concerns variables in $X_{\text{evt}} \setminus X'_{\text{evt}}$, and so it is useless to revise against these variables; this is where incrementality is partially exploited. Note also that new inferences performed when checking a v-value (x, a) has no impact on the singleton check on any other v-value (x, b) for the same variable

---

Algorithm 66: reviseStrongDC(P: $\mathscr{P}_{2^*}$, x: variable): Boolean

---

Output: *true* iff the sDC revision of x is effective

1   $modified \leftarrow false$
2   **if** $time > n$ **then**
3     $\lfloor \; X'_{\text{evt}} \leftarrow \{y \in \text{vars}(P) \mid time - stamp[y] < n\}$ // new events for x
4   **foreach** *value* $a \in \text{dom}^P(x)$ **do**
5   **if** $time \leq n$ **then**
6       $\mid \; P' \leftarrow AC(P|_{x=a}, \{x\})$ // first singleton check on (x, a)
7   **else**
8       $(P', X_{\text{evt}}) \leftarrow FC^+(P|_{x=a}, x)$ // FC is applied and variables with reduced domains returned
9       $\lfloor \; P' \leftarrow AC(P', X_{\text{evt}} \cap X'_{\text{evt}})$
10   **if** $P' = \perp$ **then**
11   remove a from $\text{dom}^P(x)$ // SAC-inconsistent value
12       $modified \leftarrow true$
13   **else**
14   **foreach** *binary constraint* $c_{xy} \in \text{cons}(P)$ **do**
15   **foreach** *value* $b \in \text{dom}^P(y) \mid (a, b) \in \text{rel}^P(c_{xy})$ **do**
16   **if** $b \notin \text{dom}^{P'}(y)$ **then**
17   remove (a, b) from $\text{rel}^P(c_{xy})$ // DC-inconsistent pair of values
18             $stamp[y] \leftarrow time$
19             $\lfloor \; modified \leftarrow true$

20 **return** $modified$

---

x; this is why X'_{evt} can be initially computed and is never updated. The remainder of the function is identical to reviseStrongCDC, except for the update of some time-stamps (line 18) whenever a tuple is removed. Note that $stamp[x]$ is not immediately updated because this is done at line 11 in Algorithm 65.

PROPOSITION 7.29.– *The algorithm sDC2 enforces strong path consistency.*

Proof. (sketch) First, it is immediate that any inference performed by sDC2 is correct. Completeness is guaranteed by the following invariant: when P' is computed at line 9 of Algorithm 66, P' is exactly the constraint network $AC(P|_{x=a})$, or equivalently from an operational point of view P' is the constraint network returned by $AC(P|_{x=a}, \text{vars}(P))$. The invariant holds because every occurrence of an inference is recorded via time-stamps. $\square$

One pass of sDC2 means calling reviseStrongDC exactly once per variable.

PROPOSITION 7.30.– *One pass of sDC2 admits a worst-case time complexity in* $O(n^3 d^3)$, *and a worst-case space complexity in* $O(n^2 d)$.

7.3.3. *Illustration*

Figure 7.10 shows the compatibility graph of a simple binary constraint network that is used in the following illustration of sCDC1. This constraint network P has $\text{vars}(P) = \{v, w, x, y, z\}$, three values per domain, and $\text{cons}(P) = \{c_{vx}, c_{vy}, c_{wx}, c_{wz}, c_{xy}, c_{xz}, c_{yz}\}$ such that:

- $\text{rel}(c_{vx}) = \{(0,0), (1,0), (1,2), (2,0), (2,1), (2,2)\}$;
- $\text{rel}(c_{vy}) = \{(0,0), (0,1), (1,0), (1,2), (2,0), (2,2)\}$;
- $\text{rel}(c_{wx}) = \{(0,0), (0,1), (0,2), (1,0), (1,2), (2,2)\}$;
- $\text{rel}(c_{wz}) = \{(0,1), (0,2), (1,1), (1,2), (2,0), (2,2)\}$;
- $\text{rel}(c_{xy}) = \{(0,1), (0,2), (1,0), (1,1), (1,2), (2,2)\}$;
- $\text{rel}(c_{xz}) = \{(0,2), (1,0), (1,2), (2,0), (2,1), (2,2)\}$;
- $\text{rel}(c_{yz}) = \{(0,0), (0,1), (0,2), (1,0), (1,1), (2,0)\}$.

For this binary constraint network P, Figures 7.11, 7.12, 7.13, 7.14, 7.15 and 7.16 show the first general steps performed by sCDC1. Figure 7.17 shows the sCDC-closure of P. In each figure, dotted vertices indicate invalid values and dotted edges indicate invalid tuples, when performing singleton checks. Dashed vertices and edges indicate values and tuples found to be globally inconsistent by sCDC.

7.3.4. *Discussion*

7.3.4.1. *Comparison with CPC*

It is interesting to compare sCDC1 with algorithms that enforce sCPC. Recall that CPC8 admits a worst-case time complexity in $O(Kd^4)$ and a worst-case space complexity in $O(ed + K)$, whereas CPC2001 admits a worst-case time complexity in $O(Kd^3)$ and a worst-case space complexity in $O(ed + Kd^2)$. The number, K, of 3-cliques is important here. Typically, the less dense the network, the smaller the number of 3-cliques, which means that CPC algorithms require less the space and time. Intuitively, for sparse networks, sCDC1 is expected to be slower than sCPC8 and sCPC2001, but for dense (or highly structured) networks, sCDC1, due to its ability to make and use inferences quickly, is expected to be faster. This is confirmed in [LEC 07a].

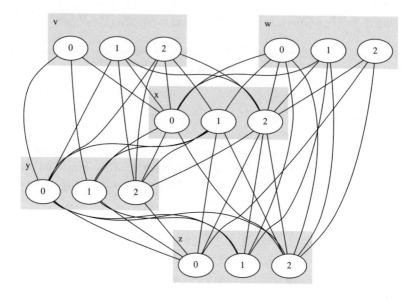

Figure 7.10. *A binary constraint network P before enforcing sCDC*

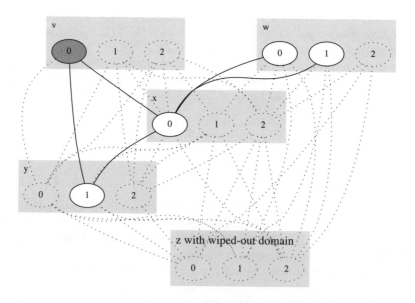

Figure 7.11. *First singleton check performed by sCDC1. We have $AC(P|_{v=0}) = \bot$ since we have a domain wipe-out for z*

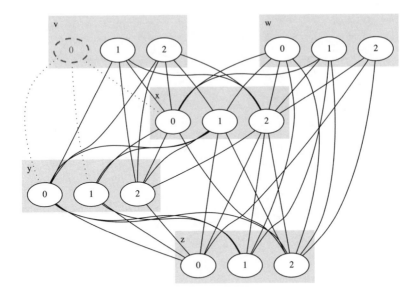

Figure 7.12. *The new state of P: the v-value $(v, 0)$ is removed since it has been detected SAC-inconsistent; see Figure 7.11*

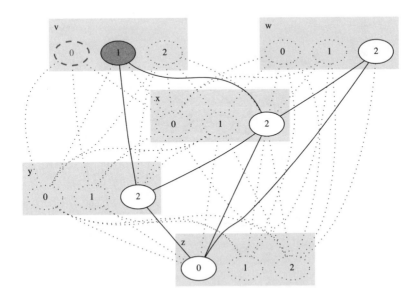

Figure 7.13. *Second singleton check performed by sCDC1. We have $AC(P|_{v=1}) \neq \bot$, but note that $\{(v, 1), (x, 0)\}$ and $\{(v, 1), (y, 0)\}$ are DC-inconsistent*

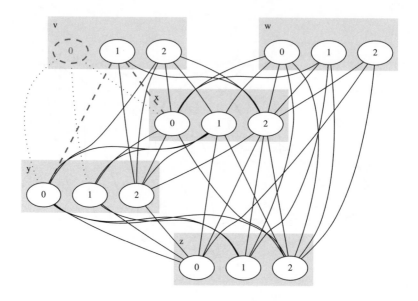

Figure 7.14. *The tuple* $(1,0)$ *is removed from both* $\mathrm{rel}(c_{vx})$ *and* $\mathrm{rel}(c_{vy})$ *since these two occurrences correspond to DC-inconsistent instantiations; see Figure 7.13*

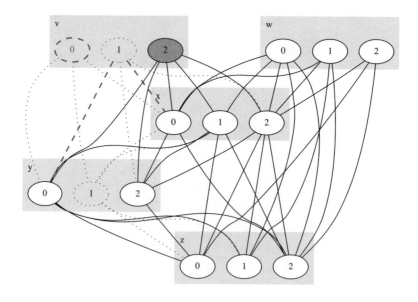

Figure 7.15. *Third singleton check performed by sCDC1. No inference is possible*

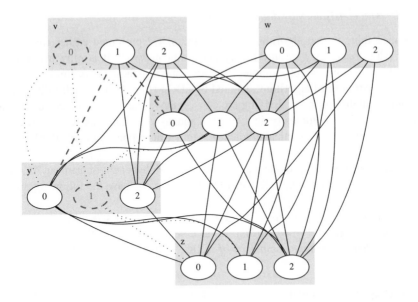

Figure 7.16. *The new state of P obtained after enforcing arc consistency since checking values of v is finished (and the sDC revision of v was effective). The v-value (y, 1) is detected arc-inconsistent*

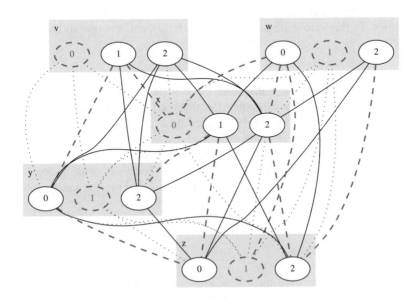

Figure 7.17. *The sCDC-closure sCDC(P) of the network P from Figure 7.10*

7.3.4.2. *Path consistency by dual consistency*

A nice thing is that algorithms sCDC1 and sDC2 presented earlier can enforce strong path consistency on any binary constraint network. It is only necessary to make the constraint graph complete before applying these algorithms. It is also possible to use a third algorithm, denoted by sDC3 [LEC 07b], which fully exploits the incrementality of the underlying arc consistency algorithm, and therefore admits a worst-case time complexity in $O(n^3 d^4)$ and a worst-case space complexity in $O(n^2 d^2)$. However, its practical efficiency is rather disappointing [LEC 07b].

Some **extreme** cases provide clues about the possible benefit of using an AC-based approach to enforce (strong) path consistency. Indeed, we have the following result.

PROPOSITION 7.31.– *Applied to a binary constraint network involving a universal constraint between every two variables, the time complexity of PC8 and PC2001 is* $\Theta(n^3 d^2)$, *whereas the time complexity of sCDC1 and sDC2 is* $\Theta(n^2 d^2)$.

Proof. Consider the initialization phase of Algorithm 59, used for both PC8 and PC2001. The cost of a call to the function isPathConsistent is $O(1)$, because all constraints are universal, and so the time complexity of the initialization phase is $\Theta(n^3 d^2)$. Because Q_{pc} remains empty, the overall time complexity is $\Theta(n^3 d^2)$. When all constraints are universal, FC can enforce AC after a variable assignment, since we just need to check that each value of every variable is compatible with the current assignment. In this case a singleton check is $\Theta(nd)$, and the overall complexity is $\Theta(n^2 d^2)$.   □

Another interesting case is that after the first pass of AC (actually, FC), many revisions can be avoided by exploiting Corollary 4.12. If a network is strong path-consistent and if all revisions can be avoided by using this revision condition, the worst-case time complexity becomes $O(nd.(nd+n^2)) = O(n^2 d. \max(n, d))$ because for each singleton check the number of revisions after FC is $O(n^2)$, each being $O(1)$ since the revision effort is avoided. This has to be compared with the cost of the initialization phase of PC8 and PC2001 which is $O(n^3 d^2)$ in the same context, so there may be an improvement by a factor $O(\min(n, d))$.

7.4. Experimental results

This section reports experiments on binary constraint networks using an i686 2.4 GHz processor equipped with 1024 MB RAM. For the algorithms sCDC and sDC the underlying arc consistency algorithm was AC3$^{\text{bit+rm}}$, with revisions performed by function revise^{CS} (see Algorithm 23).

7.4.1. *With CDC algorithms*

Our first series of experiments compares the CPU time (expressed in seconds) and filtering strength of algorithms AC3$^{\text{bit+rm}}$, SAC-SDS, sCPC8, sCPC2001 and sCDC1. We use the λ value to assess the filtering level achieved by enforcing first- and/or second-order consistencies. Recall that λ denotes the total number of supports over all constraints of a constraint network P, i.e. $\lambda = \sum_{c \in \text{cons}(P)} |\sup(c)|$. These experiments used $AC \circ CPC$ as an approximation to establish strong conservative path consistency because we found that that one pass was usually sufficient to enforce sCPC.

We have tested the selected algorithms against problems enumerated in Table 7.1; intensional constraints were converted to be extensional. As theory predicts, sCDC1 filters more than the other algorithms: the smaller λ the greater the reduction of the search space. Although sCDC1 is almost one order of magnitude faster than sCPC8 and sCPC2001 on some series, it is almost one order of magnitude slower on series $\langle 40, 180, 84, 0.9 \rangle$. The binary random instances of class $\langle 40, 180, 84, 0.9 \rangle$ contain on average only twelve 3-cliques, so for these it is cheap to enforce strong conservative path consistency.

We have also compared the performance of the complete search algorithm MAC (presented in Chapter 8) with and without CDC enforcement during preprocessing. This assessment has addressed some difficult real-world instances of the radio link frequency assignment problem (RLFAP). To observe the real impact (on search) of enforcing sCDC (using sCDC1) during preprocessing, these experiments do not employ efficiency enhancing techniques such as restarts, nogood recording, symmetry breaking, etc. Table 7.2 shows that for the hardest instances, sCDC at preprocessing pays off: without sCDC, MAC is about 40% slower than sCDC-MAC and visits almost twice as many nodes.

7.4.2. *With DC algorithms*

Our second series of experiments has compared the CPU time required to enforce strong path consistency with algorithms sPC8, sCDC1 and sDC2[4]. We have first tested these algorithms against random instances. We have obtained results for classes of the form $\langle 50, 90, 1225, t \rangle$ and $\langle 50, 90, 612, t \rangle$ with t ranging from 0.01 to 0.99. For the second of these classes, 50% of constraints are universal and 50% are of tightness t. Constraint graphs being (considered) complete, sCDC1 do enforce strong path consistency. Figure 7.18 shows the average CPU time required to enforce strong

---

4. The implementation of sDC2 used for the experiments is not optimized as proposed in this book.

	AC3$^{\text{bit+rm}}$	SAC-SDS	sCPC8	sCPC2001	sCDC1
langford (4 instances)					
CPU	0.22	0.46	4.0	4.9	0.52
λ	105,854	105,769	75,727	75,727	75,727
blackhole-4-13 (7 instances) $(K = 92,769)$					
CPU	1.2	19.3	140	−	46.9
λ	8,206,320	8,206,320	8,206,320		7,702,906
$\langle 40, 180, 84, 0.9 \rangle$ (20 instances) $(K = 12)$					
CPU	0.71	10.5	2.2	2.0	17.4
λ	272,253	244,887	244,272	244,272	210,874
$\langle 40, 8, 753, 0.1 \rangle$ (20 instances) $(K = 8,860)$					
CPU	0.16	0.21	0.62	0.69	0.20
λ	43,320	43,320	43,318	43,318	43,318
job-shop enddr1 (10 instances) $(K = 600)$					
CPU	1.5	4.0	7.9	10.5	4.6
λ	2,937,697	2,937,697	2,937,697	2,937,697	2,930,391
RLFAP scens (11 instances)					
CPU	0.86	−	25.9	−	3.4
λ	1,674,286		1,471,132		1,469,286

Table 7.1. *Mean results obtained with various filtering algorithms, including sCDC1, on some series of binary instances. The symbol − indicates that the algorithm runs out of memory*

Instance		MAC	sCDC1-MAC
scen11-f8	CPU	8.0	14.3
	#nodes	14,068	4,946
scen11-f6	CPU	68.4	58.2
	#nodes	302 K	145 K
scen11-f4	CPU	582	559
	#nodes	2,826 K	1,834 K
scen11-f3	CPU	2,338	1,725
	#nodes	12 M	5,863 K
scen11-f2	CPU	7,521	5,872
	#nodes	37 M	21 M
scen11-f1	CPU	17,409	13,136
	#nodes	93 M	55 M

Table 7.2. *Impact of enforcing sCDC at preprocessing on MAC*

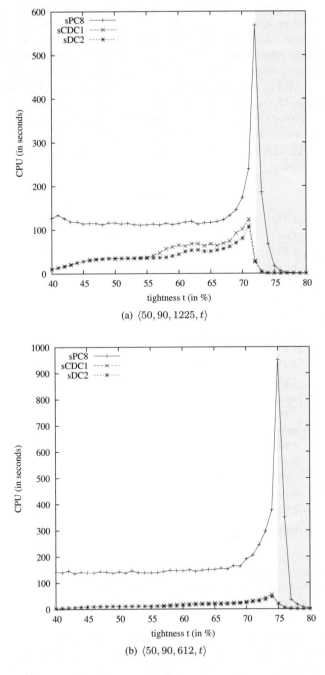

(a) $\langle 50, 90, 1225, t\rangle$

(b) $\langle 50, 90, 612, t\rangle$

Figure 7.18. *Mean results obtained with PC algorithms on classes of* 100 *random binary instances*

path consistency on these classes. The shaded area on each figure indicates tightnesses for which more than 50% of the generated instances were proved to be inconsistent. The main experimental result here is that sDC2, although slightly more efficient than sCDC1, is far more efficient than sPC8. For small tightnesses, there is a significant gap (up to two orders of magnitude) between sDC2 and sPC8, which is partly due to the fact that many revisions can be avoided, as discussed in section 7.3.4. For tightnesses around the threshold, the gap is still very important (about one order of magnitude). We can also see that the gap increases when the density (number of non-universal constraints) decreases, which is not surprising since the number of allowed tuples increases with the number of universal constraints; classical PC algorithms mainly handle allowed tuples.

Instance		sPC8	sPC2001	sCDC1	sDC2
queens-20	CPU	1.86	1.89	1.65	1.62
	mem	17	25	17	17
queens-30	CPU	5.0	5.3	2.2	2.2
	mem	17	76	17	17
queens-50	CPU	50	–	4.6	4.5
	mem	30		22	22
queens-80	CPU	557	–	26	24
	mem	97		44	44
queens-100	CPU	1,549	–	62	58
	mem	197		73	73
langford-3-15	CPU	34	46	4.29	4.25
	mem	25	456	21	21
langford-3-16	CPU	45	66	4.9	4.4
	mem	27	612	21	21
langford-3-17	CPU	63	–	6.0	6.0
	mem	34		22	22
langford-3-20	CPU	140	–	11	9.7
	mem	43		26	26
langford-3-30	CPU	1,247	–	60	50
	mem	138		56	56

Table 7.3. *Results obtained with algorithms enforcing strong path consistency on academic queens and Langford instances. The symbol − indicates that the algorithm runs out of memory*

Table 7.3, which shows results on two series of academic instances, confirms the results obtained for random instances. On these structured instances (whose constraint graph is complete), sDC2 is about 20 times more efficient than sPC8 for large instances, regardless of the number of inferences performed. The queens instances are already strongly path-consistent, which is not the case for the Langford instances.

7.5. Conclusion

For binary constraint networks, it is known that strong path consistency is equivalent to strong 3-consistency. There are several theoretical results that relate global consistency to strong 3-consistency, e.g. Corollaries 3.56 and 3.70. In the next generation of robust constraint solvers, tractable classes of CSP instances will certainly have to be identified and exploited during search. This will increase the importance of strong path consistency in constraint solvers.

Obviously, algorithms that enforce strong (conservative) dual consistency via singleton checks are closely related to algorithms that enforce singleton arc consistency. Compared to the time-optimal SAC-Opt and sub-optimal SAC-SDS algorithms, sCDC1 and sDC2 have the advantage of pruning the search space more efficiently, since on binary networks sCDC is strictly stronger than SAC (while limiting space complexity for sCDC1 to the existing extensional representation of the constraint network). We should also mention bidirectional singleton arc consistency (BiSAC) [BES 08a], called SPAC in [BES 04b], which is strictly stronger than singleton arc consistency and strictly weaker than strong path consistency, while being incomparable with strong conservative dual consistency. This domain-filtering consistency exploits the nogoods of size 2 that are identified when performing singleton checks but does not record them in the network.

Algorithm	Time complexity	Space complexity	Reference
PC1	$O(n^5 d^5)$	$O(n^3 d^2)$	[MON 74]
PC2	$O(n^3 d^5)$	$O(n^3)$	[MAC 77a]
PC3/4	$O(n^3 d^3)$	$O(n^3 d^3)$	[MOH 86, HAN 88]
PC5/6	$O(n^3 d^3)$	$O(n^3 d^2)$	[SIN 96, CHM 95]
PC8	$O(n^3 d^4)$	$O(n^2 d)$	[CHM 98]
PC2001	$O(n^3 d^3)$	$O(n^3 d^2)$	[BES 05c]
sCDC1	$O(pn^3 d^3)$	$O(n^2 d)$	[MCG 79, LEC 07a]
sDC2	$O(pn^3 d^3)$	$O(n^2 d)$	[LEC 07b]
sDC3	$O(n^3 d^4)$	$O(n^2 d^2)$	[LEC 07b]

Table 7.4. *Worst-case time and space complexities for (strong) path consistency algorithms on binary constraint networks. p is the number of passes of algorithms sCDC1 and sDC2*

Finally, note that the idea of restricting inferences to a specific variable ordering can be applied to path consistency. Under certain conditions, directional path consistency is equivalent to path consistency, but is cheaper to enforce; several algorithms have been proposed [TSA 93, DEC 03].

Table 7.4 summarizes the time and space complexity of the (strong) path consistency algorithms presented in this chapter. p is the number of passes (the last one potentially incomplete) of algorithms sCDC1 and sDC2. In the worst-case, p is $O(n^2 d^2)$ but informal arguments and experimental results suggest that p is a small integer in practice.

PART TWO

Search

Global inconsistency may be identified by reasoning locally. There are also special cases where some form of local consistency implies global consistency. However, in the general case, neither the *search problem* (i.e. finding a solution, if any) nor the *decision problem* (i.e. deciding global consistency) can be solved by (consistency-based) inference methods without search. These methods can be regarded as incomplete methods for detecting satisfiability or unsatisfiability. Their main value lies in their ability to simplify constraint networks, making subsequent solution easier.

An attempt to solve a constraint satisfaction problem instance generally requires search. A search for solutions, within the space of possibilities, may or may not be exhaustive. Exaustive search takes account, perhaps implicitly, of every complete instantiation of the variables of the instance to be solved; an exhaustive search algorithm is said to be *complete* or *systematic*. *Incomplete* search algorithms cannot always find a solution, even if one exists, and generally cannot prove unsatisfiability. Typically, incomplete search algorithms proceed by checking complete instantiations in sequence, the first instantiation being randomly or heuristically generated, successors being derived from predecessors by simple minor modification. Within the category of incomplete search algorithms, local search methods (see e.g. [HOO 06]), which are not described in this book, have been found valuable for solving large (satisfiable) problem instances, in particular when an optimization criterion has to be satisfied.

Within the category of complete search algorithms there are several paradigms: depth-first search, best-first search, breadth-first search, iterative deepening depth-first search [KOR 85], limited discrepancy search [HAR 95b], etc. *Backtrack search* explores the search space depth-first and backtracks when a dead-end is encountered. To solve CSP instances, backtrack search has become the standard approach, mainly because it requires only a polynomial amount of space. Backtrack search only needs to store the current search path being explored, because it seeks one solution at a time. Backtrack search systems have four major components: *branching*, *propagation*, *backtracking* and *learning*.

All the efforts made by researchers to devise sophisticated search strategies are related to *thrashing*. Within the tree that represents the progress of depth-first search, thrashing means repeated exploration of similar subtrees that contain no solution, i.e. repeated exploration of subproblems whose unsatisfiability has a similar origin. Thrashing is sometimes the result of bad choices earlier during search. Thrashing can be mitigated by the use of an appropriate search heuristic and/or by substantially filtering variable domains and/or by learning useful information before and especially during the search. In the following chapters, various forms of learning will be illustrated by non-intrusive techniques such as constraint weighting and last-conflict reasoning, controllable nogood recording and state-based search.

Chapter 8

Backtrack Search

Practical solution of constraint satisfaction problem instances usually involves *backtrack search*. This is a *complete* approach in which systematic exploration of the search space of a CSP instance finds the full set of solutions or proves that no solution exists. By contrast, *incomplete* approaches, such as those based on local search, are not guaranteed to find a solution (when solutions exist) or to prove unsatisfiability. Unfortunately, backtrack search is not guaranteed to terminate within polynomial time. We are unaware of any general polynomial algorithm for CSP; unless $P = NP$, none exists. This is why there have been considerable efforts during the past three decades to maximize the practical efficiency of backtrack search.

Within backtrack search [GOL 65], depth-first exploration instantiates variables and a backtracking mechanism deals with dead-ends. The depth-first search considers a different variable at each level and tries to extend (in turn) different complementary branching decisions concerning this variable. In its simplest form, each branching decision is an assignment of a value to a variable: this is followed by checking that every constraint covered by the current instantiation is satisfied. A more sophisticated strategy applies a filtering procedure after each assignment of a value to a variable: this procedure is intended to simplify the subsequent search or to show that a dead-end has been reached, which means that the current set of decisions cannot be extended to a solution. When a dead-end is encountered, one or more decisions must be retracted before continuing the quest for a solution. The process of undoing decisions in order to escape from a dead-end is called *backtracking*.

Backtrack search systems have four main components: *branching* (how and which decisions to take to go forward to a solution), *propagation* (how and which level of filtering to apply to reduce the search space at each step), *backtracking* (how to go backward when a dead-end is encountered) and *learning* (what information to collect during search so as to facilitate subsequent parts of the search). Each of these components has many possible implementations: there has been much effort to identify the right combinations of implementations. In particular, the interplay between propagation and backtracking techniques has been debated for a long time.

After each branching decision, enforcement of some kind of local consistency prunes some parts of the search space that contain no solution. For example, maintaining arc consistency (MAC) is the backtrack search algorithm that enforces generalized arc consistency (GAC) after each decision taken; when the domain of a variable becomes empty (so-called *domain wipe-out*), a dead-end has been reached. And when a dead-end is reached, conflicting decisions can be reviewed via *eliminating explanations*, which are recorded during the search. Instead of backtracking to the most recent previous decision, so-called *chronological backtracking*, it may be helpful to jump back to the most recent decision among those that could possibly have caused the failure. This backward jump is a form of *intelligent backtracking* and can be managed so as to guarantee that no solution will be missed.

The relationship between *look-back* (efficient escape from dead ends) and *look-ahead* (simplification of subsequent search), has been the subject of much investigation. MAC was used in the 1970s [GAS 74, ULL 76, ULL 77] with non-binary branching, without backjumping and without dynamic variable ordering. Non-chronological backtracking was initiated with dependency-directed backtracking [STA 77, DOY 79, KLE 86] and Prolog intelligent backtracking [BRU 81, BRU 84]. Early in the 1990s, the forward checking (FC) algorithm (introduced ten years before [MCG 79, HAR 80]) associated with the variable ordering heuristic *dom* [HAR 80] and the conflict-directed backjumping (CBJ) technique [PRO 93] was considered to be the most efficient generic approach to solve CSP instances. In 1994, Sabin and Freuder [SAB 94] reintroduced MAC using binary branching and simple chronological backtracking. This algorithm was shown to be more efficient than FC and FC-CBJ; CBJ was considered to be useless to MAC, especially when MAC had a good variable ordering heuristic [BES 96].

The situation subsequently became more confused. First, [BAY 97] showed that many large propositional satisfiability instances derived from real-world problems are easy when CSP look-back techniques are combined with the "Davis–Putnam" procedure. Second, although theoretical results [CHE 01] showed that the backward phase is less useful when the forward phase is more advanced, some experiments on hard structured problems showed that combining CBJ with MAC can still produce significant improvements. Third, look-back techniques appeared to be improved by associating an eliminating explanation (or conflict set) with any value rather than with any variable. Indeed, refined eliminating explanations allows a stronger form of backjumping [BAC 00] and the possibility of saving much search effort with the principle of dynamic backtracking (DBT) [GIN 93]. Experimental results [BAC 00, JUS 00b] showed that MAC can be outperformed by algorithms embedding such advanced look-back techniques. Later chapters will show that some form of learning, perhaps limited to a statistical form, is essential to the efficient guidance of search.

This chapter presents backtrack search together with very classical anti-thrashing schemes, which are basically those mentioned above. Section 8.1 introduces various concepts related to backtrack search and presents a general model called BPBL. Section 8.2 provides a detailed description of MAC, and section 8.3 introduces a parameterized algorithm that gives a uniform view of FC, MAC, CBJ, DBT and combinations thereof. Examples in section 8.4 illustrate different techniques introduced in this chapter, which concludes in section 8.5 with a brief discussion of the role of explanations.

8.1. General description

Backtrack search algorithms develop *search trees*. A search tree is basically a rooted tree (see Appendix A.1) that allows us to visualize successive decisions performed by a backtrack search algorithm. In the context of search trees, we prefer to use the term *node* to mean the same thing as a vertex. Starting at the root node with the initial constraint network that must be solved, each step in the search derives a new constraint network. Each node in the search tree is associated with one such constraint network and each (directed) edge is associated with a search decision. The search tree grows during the search. More specifically, if the search has currently reached node v, then after taking a new (branching) decision δ, we insert into the search tree a new node v', representing the new step of the search, and a new edge $\{v, v'\}$ labeled with δ. The new edge $\{v, v'\}$ is directed from v to v': v is called the *parent* of v' and v' a *child* of v. $\mathrm{dn}(v)$ is the set of decisions that label successive edges in the path from the root to node v. The constraint network associated with node v is $\mathrm{cn}(v) = \phi(P^{\mathrm{init}}|_{\mathrm{dn}(v)})$, where P^{init} is the initial constraint network and ϕ is the consistency enforced during search. Hence the constraint network associated with the root of the search tree is simply $\phi(P^{\mathrm{init}})$.

Figure 8.1 provides an example of a search tree. Every node in a search tree is either a *leaf* node or an *internal node*. A leaf node differs from an internal node in that a leaf node has no children. When an inconsistency is detected at node v during search, this means that $\mathrm{cn}(v) = \perp$ and also that node v is a leaf node which is called a *dead-end* (node). The search backtracks when a dead-end is reached.

Any node v in the search tree is the root of a subtree obtained by retaining only v and its descendants (with all related edges). A node v is fully explored when the search space of the constraint network $\mathrm{cn}(v)$ has been fully explored. If v is a fully explored internal node such that $\mathrm{cn}(v)$ is unsatisfiable, v is called an *internal dead-end*, and the subtree rooted at v is called a *refutation tree* of $\mathrm{cn}(v)$. If v' is an internal dead-end, and is a child of node v such that $\mathrm{cn}(v)$ is satisfiable, then v' is a *mistake*

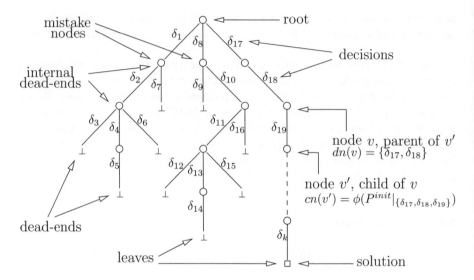

mistake nodes

internal dead-ends

root

decisions

node v, parent of v'
$dn(v) = \{\delta_{17}, \delta_{18}\}$

node v', child of v
$cn(v') = \phi(P^{init}|_{\{\delta_{17},\delta_{18},\delta_{19}\}})$

dead-ends

leaves

solution

Figure 8.1. *A search tree built by a backtrack search algorithm. Note that decisions are taken depth-first. P^{init} is the instance to be solved initially and ϕ is the consistency enforced during search*

node. A (sub)tree containing no solution is said to be *fruitless*. Finally, during search (i.e. when the tree is being built), we distinguish between an *opened node*, for which at least one case (branch) has not been considered, and a *closed node*, for which all cases (branches) have been considered (i.e. explored).

Branching decisions, also called *branching constraints*, split a constraint network $P = cn(v)$ associated with an internal node v of the search tree into two or more constraint networks, the union of which is equivalent to P in term of solutions. Classical branching schemes impose positive and negative decisions during search under a strategy of *enumeration* or *labeling* (see e.g. [APT 03]). The idea of enumeration is to select a v-value (x, a), and to branch on $x = a$ and then on $x \neq a$. The idea of labeling is to select a variable x, and to successively branch on $x = a$ for each value a present in $\text{dom}(x)$. Enumeration and labeling correspond to *binary branching* (or *2-way branching*) and *non-binary branching* (or *d-way branching*), respectively. More specifically, with non-binary branching, at each search step, an unfixed variable x (i.e. a variable whose domain is not singleton) is selected, and then for each value a in $\text{dom}(x)$, the assignment $x = a$ is considered, so there are d branches altogether, where d is the size of $\text{dom}(x)$. With binary branching, at each search step, a pair (x, a) is selected, where x is an unfixed variable, and a is a value in $\text{dom}(x)$, and two cases are considered: the assignment $x = a$ and the refutation $x \neq a$. So there are exactly two branches. Both of these two schemes guarantee complete exploration of the search space. For binary branching, we know for example that any solution S satisfies either $S[x] = a$ or $S[x] \neq a$.

When mentioning a backtrack search algorithm, it is important to indicate whether binary branching or non-binary branching is employed. These two schemes are not equivalent: it has been shown that binary branching is more powerful (to refute unsatisfiable instances) than non-binary branching [HWA 05]. Using the resolution proof system, Hwang and Mitchell show that there exist instances which require exponential search trees for backtracking with d-way branching, but have polynomial search trees for backtracking with 2-way branching. Although various other kinds of decision (e.g. membership decisions when splitting domains or non-binary branching constraints) are possible, these are not commonly used in the solution of discrete CSP instances. Recent exceptions are effective use of *partitioning* and *bundling*. Partitioning is a technique that partitions the domain of a variable and branches on the resulting sub-domains. Roughly speaking, partitioning corresponds to a non-binary branching scheme with membership decisions instead of positive decisions. For example, in [HOE 04], values regarded as equivalent by the heuristic employed during search are grouped together to advantageously postpone positive branching decisions. On the other hand, full interchangeability defines a form of equivalence between values that is stronger than heuristic equivalence. Bundling [HAS 93] partitions domains according to interchangeability and allows us to derive a compact representation of the solution space. Bundling may be static, dynamic [BEC 01, CHO 02] and adapted to non-binary constraints [LAL 05]. In this book, we restrict our study to positive and negative decisions during search; in other words, we concentrate on variable assignments and value refutations, see section 1.4.2.

Algorithm 67: nonBinary-ϕ-search(**in** P: $\mathscr{P}$): Boolean

   Output: *true* iff P is satisfiable

1 $P \leftarrow \phi(P)$
2 **if** $P = \bot$ **then**
3 | **return** *false*
4 **if** $\forall x \in \text{vars}(P), |\text{dom}(x)| = 1$ **then**
    | // display the solution
5 | **return** *true*
6 select a variable x of P such that $|\text{dom}(x)| > 1$
7 **foreach** *value* $a \in \text{dom}(x)$ **do**
8 | **if** *nonBinary-ϕ-search*($P|_{x=a}$) **then**
9 | | **return** *true*
10 **return** *false*

A (backtrack) ϕ-*search* algorithm is a backtrack search algorithm that enforces a consistency ϕ after each decision taken. Algorithm 67 is a general formulation of any backtrack ϕ-search algorithm that employs non-binary branching. This quite reasonably assumes that ϕ is a consistency which (at least) allows detection of any unsatisfied constraint whose variables are all fixed. Algorithm 67 determines satisfiability and does not enumerate all solutions (if any). This algorithm starts by enforcing ϕ on the given constraint network P (which is an input parameter), returning *false* if an inconsistency is detected. If all domains are single valued at line 4 then because of our assumption about ϕ, all constraints are necessarily satisfied, so a solution has been found, and *true* is returned. At line 7, non-binary branching means recursively calling the function nonBinary-ϕ-search for each value in the domain of the variable x that was selected at line 6.

Because a consistency ϕ is enforced at each step, domain sizes d, d', d'', etc., are generally not the same at every node in the example in Figure 8.2. Once a variable has been selected, all values in its domain are explored. At each node, successive values may be selected in a particular order, perhaps determined heuristically. It is important that the order of selection of variables may vary during search. In the example in Figure 8.2, y and z are different variables selected after having taken decisions $x = a_{x,1}$ and $x = a_{x,d}$ respectively at the first level.

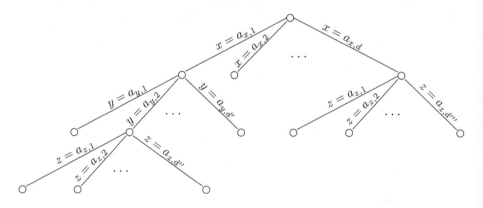

Figure 8.2. *A non-binary search tree built by a backtracking algorithm. The ith value in the current domain of a variable x is denoted by $a_{x,i}$*

Algorithm 68 is a general formulation of any backtrack ϕ-search algorithm that employs binary branching, assuming that ϕ at least detects trivially unsatisfied constraints. Each step of the binary branching algorithm selects a v-value (x, a) of P and recursively calls the function binary-ϕ-search with decisions $x = a$ and $x \neq a$. Depending on implementation of the logical operator $\vee$ at line 7, the algorithm finds a single solution (if $\vee$ is managed in short-circuit) or finds all solutions (if any).

Algorithm 68: binary-ϕ-search(**in** P: $\mathscr{P}$): Boolean

---

Output: *true* iff P is satisfiable

1 $P \leftarrow \phi(P)$
2 **if** $P = \perp$ **then**
3 $\quad \lfloor$ **return** *false*
4 **if** $\forall x \in \text{vars}(P), |\text{dom}(x)| = 1$ **then**
   $\quad \mid$ // display the solution
5 $\quad \lfloor$ **return** *true*
6 select a v-value (x, a) of P such that $|\text{dom}(x)| > 1$
7 **return** *binary-ϕ-search*$(P|_{x=a}) \vee$ *binary-ϕ-search*$(P|_{x \neq a})$

Figure 8.3 illustrates the binary branching process and shows the systematic exploration of two branches for each selected v-value (x, a). Classically, binary branching algorithms select left branches, which assign values, before right branches, which refute values, as in Figure 8.3. The main advantage of binary branching over non-binary branching is the possibility of selecting, after each negative decision, a variable different from the one involved in the last decision. For this reason, heuristics that control the search may be more reactive.

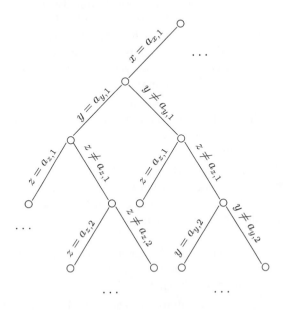

Figure 8.3. *A binary search tree built by a backtracking algorithm. The ith value in the current domain of a variable x is denoted by $a_{x,i}$*

The example in Figure 8.3 assumes that an unsatisfiable subtree is explored after positive decisions $x = a_{x,1}$, $y = a_{y,1}$ and $z = a_{z,1}$. After the negative decision $z \neq a_{z,1}$, the next selected variable is again z, making this portion of the search tree rather similar to one that could be built with non-binary branching. However, along the path labeled with $x = a_{x,1}$ and $y \neq a_{y,1}$, the next branching decisions involve the variable z which is different from y. Here the search heuristic, perhaps learning from previous explorations of subtrees, has decided to branch on a different variable rather than insisting on y.

Having introduced some of the main ideas about backtrack search, we now emphasize that all backtrack search algorithms can be derived from a general model, denoted by BPBL. BPBL comprises four main components and is related to the model introduced in [JUS 02] to characterize both complete and incomplete search algorithms. Components of the model BPBL are:

– Branching: this component is concerned with the branching scheme (how and which kinds of decisions are taken) and the *heuristic(s)* used to select decisions. As explained above, the branching scheme can be binary, non-binary, split-based, etc. Classically (at least for binary and non-binary branching schemes), each decision involves a variable and a value. Selection of variables and values, induced by a variable ordering and a value ordering, is usually determined heuristically. The role of these heuristics, which are presented in the next chapter, is certainly important.

– Propagation: this component is concerned with the level of control and/or filtering after each decision that is taken. The level of control and/or filtering may possibly, but unusually, be different for different (kinds of) decisions. As in Algorithms 67 and 68 filtering usually means enforcing a given local consistency ϕ which is typically generalized arc consistency. Of course, any consistency presented in the first part of this book can be employed instead.

– Backtracking: this component is concerned with the way the algorithm backtracks after reaching a dead-end. Backtracking may be chronological or instead may be made more sophisticated by identifying, for each dead-end, a culprit decision preceding the previous decision.

– Learning: this component is concerned with the information recorded during search, especially when a value is deleted (e.g. when propagating constraints) and when a dead-end is encountered. We shall explain how this component may have connections with all three of the other components.

Figure 8.4 shows model BPBL diagrammatically, and shows learning as an auxiliary mechanism serving to improve the performance of the other components. Information collected during search can be used:

– by heuristics (e.g. statistical information can be used by some search heuristics);

– to filter the search space (e.g. nogoods can be propagated as new constraints by means of watched "literals");

– in non-chronological backtracking (e.g. eliminating explanations for conflict-directed backjumping).

Of course, in some configurations, learning may be used very little or not at all.

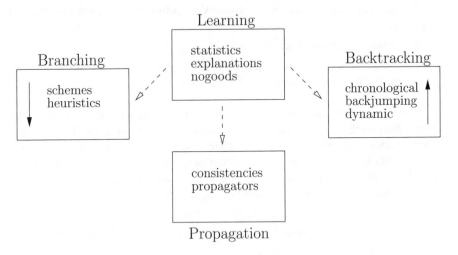

Figure 8.4. *Model BPBL for backtrack search*

Finally, note that constraint networks are usually processed during a so-called *preprocessing* stage initiated before search. Preprocessing may be limited to enforcing a consistency ϕ, but it may also refer to more sophisticated methods such as those based on structural decomposition. During the preprocessing stage, some data structures may also have to be initialized so as to be used later during search by some algorithms. Sometimes, preprocessing alone is sufficient to solve a CSP instance.

8.2. Maintaining (generalized) arc consistency

MAC [SAB 94], which is the backtrack search algorithm that maintains generalized arc consistency during search, is currently considered to be the most efficient complete approach to solving CSP instances. A high-level picture of MAC can be obtained by setting $\phi = GAC$ in Algorithm 68. MAC, as clearly described in [SAB 97], employs binary branching, and (classically) starts by assigning variables before refuting values. The *really full look-ahead* algorithm in [GAS 74, NAD 88] is a non-binary branching variant of MAC. Note also that MAC working with non-binary constraints is sometimes called MGAC since it maintains GAC. However, for simplicity, we shall always refer to this algorithm as MAC, whatever the arity of the constraints.

In terms of the general model BPBL introduced in the previous section, MAC is defined as follows:

– Branching: binary branching is used (so, branching decisions are positive and negative decisions); any variable and value ordering heuristics can be chosen.

– Propagation: generalized arc consistency is enforced after each positive and negative decision.

– Backtracking: chronological backtracking is used.

– Learning: no learning technique is used by MAC itself (but some form of learning may be required by some search heuristics).

Because of the importance of MAC, we now provide an implementation that is more detailed than the simple recursive function in Algorithm 68. This iterative implementation attempts to build a complete instantiation that is a solution. Each variable *explicitly* assigned by the algorithm is put (with its assigned value) into a last-in/first-out structure denoted here by I. This structure represents the current instantiation and, as expected, has the following features:

– $I.push(x, a)$ adds the v-value (x, a) at the top of I;

– $I.pop()$ returns and deletes the v-value which is present at the top of I;

– $I.top()$ returns the v-value which is present at the top of I.

$|I|$ and $\text{vars}(I)$ denote the size (number of v-values) of I and the set of variables in I, respectively. At any moment, every variable in $\text{vars}(I)$ is an instantiated variable, sometimes called a *past* variable; in Chapters 4 and 5, $\text{past}(P)$ is exactly $\text{vars}(I)$. Recall that an uninstantiated variable may be incidentally fixed (i.e. have a singleton domain) if for example, its domain has been reduced by constraint propagation.

The iterative version of MAC, Algorithm 69, uses the representation of domains introduced in section 1.5.1, with a trailing mechanism to deal with backtracking. Unlike the algorithms given in the previous section, Algorithm 69 finds (and displays) all solutions of the constraint network P given as parameter. At each step, a v-value (x, a) of the current problem is selected with the important restriction that x must be an uninstantiated variable. Note that a is necessarily in the current domain of x since (x, a) must be a v-value of the current problem P. The current instantiation is extended and the domain of x reduced to a. GAC is enforced at line 10 by calling the function enforceGAC – which can be either Algorithm 7 or Algorithm 9. This call may modify P which is a parameter passed in input/output mode[1]. If the network is not detected GAC-inconsistent and if all variables have been instantiated, this means that a solution has been found. In order to keep on seeking solutions, the Boolean variable *consistent* is reset to *false* at line 13. So long as the current network is not consistent,

---

1. Recall that unless **in** is used, all parameters are assumed to be passed in input/output mode.

Algorithm 69: MAC($P: \mathscr{P}$)

---

1   $consistent \leftarrow$ enforceGAC(P, vars(P))   // GAC initially enforced
2   **if** $\neg consistent$ **then**
3     $\lfloor$ **return**
4   $I \leftarrow \emptyset$ // I represents the current instantiation
5   $finished \leftarrow false$
6   **while** $\neg finished$ **do**
7   select a v-value (x, a) of P such that $x \notin$ vars(I)
8     $I.push(x, a)$
9   dom(x).reduceTo($a, |I|$)   // x is assigned the value a
10     $consistent \leftarrow$ enforceGAC($P, \{x\}$)
11   **if** $consistent \wedge |I| = n$ **then**
12       $\lfloor$ $print(I)$ // a solution has been found and is printed
13         $consistent \leftarrow false$ // inserted to keep searching for solutions
14   **while** $\neg consistent \wedge I \neq \emptyset$ **do**
15       $(x, a) \leftarrow I.pop()$
16   **foreach** *variable* $y \in$ vars(P) \ vars(I) **do**
17         $\lfloor$ dom(y).restoreUpto($|I| + 1$)   // domains are restored
18   dom(x).removeValue($a, |I|$)   // a is removed from dom(x)
19       $consistent \leftarrow$ dom(x) $\neq \emptyset \wedge$ enforceGAC($P, \{x\}$)
20   **if** $\neg consistent$ **then**
21       $\lfloor$ $finished \leftarrow true$

---

the algorithm discards the most recent positive decision, restores the domains, refutes the last discarded positive decision and enforces GAC (provided that dom(x) $\neq \emptyset$). Finally, when backtracking reaches the root of the search tree, this means that the exploration of the search tree is finished. To obtain forward checking (FC), it is only necessary to remove the preprocessing step (the first 3 lines), replace the second call (line 10) to enforceGAC by applyFC (see Algorithm 12), and remove the third call (line 19) to enforceGAC.

Unlike the general binary search algorithm presented in the previous section, Algorithm 69 distinguishes between instantiated variables (i.e. explicitly assigned variables) and uninstantiated variables (i.e. unfixed variables and incidentally fixed variables). For example, a solution can be found only when all variables have been explicitly assigned values. This simplifies presentation of the algorithm. Of course, when a v-value (x, a) such that dom(x) $= \{a\}$ is selected, i.e. when an incidentally fixed variable is selected, there is no need to call enforceGAC. In practice, useless calls can be avoided by identifying such situations or by detecting at each step all incidentally fixed variables and putting them directly into I.

8.3. Classical look-ahead and look-back schemes

As explained previously, backtrack search combines depth-first exploration, which instantiates variables, with a backtracking mechanism, which deals with dead-ends. There has been much work on improving forward and backward phases by developing look-ahead and look-back schemes [DEC 02, DEC 03]. This section provides a brief overview of some well-known schemes.

Within the propagation component of the general model BPBL, different look-ahead schemes apply different levels of filtering after each decision. We obtain different schemes according to which consistency is enforced. Three usual schemes are *backward checking* (BC), *forward checking* (FC) and *maintaining arc consistency* (MAC). BC is the simplest look-ahead algorithm, excluding the *generate and test* approach which checks every possible complete instantiation in turn. After each variable assignment, BC simply checks that no constraint covered by the current instantiation is violated (this is a kind of trivial consistency). After each decision, both FC and MAC achieve some amount of domain filtering, which detects and removes some locally inconsistent values. More precisely, in the binary case, FC guarantees the arc consistency of every constraint involving the *current variable*, i.e. the last assigned variable, and exactly one uninstantiated variable, whereas MAC, as described earlier, guarantees the arc consistency of all constraints of the current network. If a domain wipe-out occurs, i.e. if a domain becomes empty, then a dead-end has been encountered.

Published look-back schemes differently identify the level of backtracking to which it is safe to jump back. Look-back schemes belong primarily to the backtracking component of the general model BPBL, but they also require learning. Three representative look-back algorithms are *standard backtracking* (SBT), *conflict-directed backjumping* (CBJ) and *dynamic backtracking* (DBT). The essential characteristic of these schemes is that they jump back to a decision suspected of being a cause of the current failure (dead-end). SBT, which is the same thing as *chronological backtracking*, is the simplest look-back algorithm because it jumps back to the most recently instantiated variable. Decisions concerning this variable may not have caused the dead-end, so SBT may cause thrashing. CBJ and DBT introduce eliminating explanations (a form of learning) which provide reasons for the removal of any value. When a domain wipe-out occurs, CBJ and DBT use eliminating explanations to identify an earlier decision, perhaps earlier than the most recent decision, that may be a cause of the dead-end. Unlike CBJ, DBT simply discards the identified culprit decision while preserving subsequent decisions. In other words, DBT jumps back to the (expected) source of conflict without undoing the intermediate decisions. DBT is particularly useful for problems that are highly structured such as those that contain several more-or-less independent components.

There are nine different combinations of these look-ahead and look-back techniques:

- BC-SBT (usually called BT);
- BC-CBJ (usually called CBJ);
- BC-DBT (usually called DBT);
- FC-SBT (usually called FC);
- FC-CBJ;
- FC-DBT;
- MAC-SBT (usually called MAC);
- MAC-CBJ;
- MAC-DBT.

BT, CBJ [PRO 93], DBT [GIN 93], FC [HAR 80] and MAC [SAB 94] are well-known algorithms. Non-trivial combinations are FC-CBJ [PRO 93], MAC-CBJ [PRO 95], FC-DBT [VER 94] and MAC-DBT [JUS 00b].

8.3.1. *A general backtracking algorithm*

We now present an algorithm that provides a uniform view of different algorithms mentioned in the previous section. This general unifying algorithm may be helpful because it facilitates understanding of relationships between techniques (look-back and look-ahead) that are involved. To simplify the presentation we introduce, instead of CBJ, a related look-back algorithm, denoted here by IBT. IBT is a direct variant of DBT and corresponds to the "Conflict Based" technique introduced in [BAC 00], where it was observed that IBT, when combined with FC or MAC, can be seen as a refinement of CBJ because it has a more powerful backjumping capability. Thus, although BC-IBT corresponds to CBJ, FC-IBT and MAC-IBT can be seen as refinements of FC-CBJ and MAC-CBJ, respectively. These refinements roughly correspond to the CFFC and CFMAC algorithms of [BAC 00]. Note also that when constraints are non-binary, FC as presented here[2] corresponds to nFC2 [BES 02].

As in section 8.2, we use a last-in/first-out structure denoted by I to represent the current instantiation. For dynamic backtracking, we additionally require a non-standard function $I.delete(x, a)$ which removes the v-value (x, a) from I even when this v-value is not at the top of I. After (x, a) has been removed, $I.delete(x, a)$ reorganizes I as if (x, a) had never been pushed.

---

2. It is important to note that different non-binary generalizations of FC exist.

Eliminating explanations [GIN 93] are used in the management of domains. When a v-value (x, a) is deleted, i.e. when we have $a \in \mathrm{dom}^{\mathrm{init}}(x) \setminus \mathrm{dom}(x)$, this can be given an eliminating explanation, denoted by $\mathrm{expl}(x \neq a)$, which is a subset, I', of the current instantiation I, such that $I' \cup \{(x, a)\}$ is globally inconsistent, i.e. is a (standard) nogood. If we have the instantiation $I' = \mathrm{expl}(x \neq a)$ then certainly $x \neq a$:

$$\bigwedge_{(y,b)\in\mathrm{expl}(x\neq a)} y = b \Rightarrow x \neq a$$

Thus an eliminating explanation can be regarded as the left-hand side of an implication which rules out a value. This is just another way to represent a nogood.

EXAMPLE.– If $I = \{(v, a), (w, b), (x, b), (y, c)\}$ is the current instantiation, if consistency enforcement deletes (z, b) and if $\{(v, a), (x, b), (z, b)\}$ is an instantiation proved to be a nogood (techniques to realize this are presented below) then a possible eliminating explanation for (z, b) is $I' = \mathrm{expl}(z \neq b) = \{(v, a), (x, b)\}$. In logical directed form, we obtain:

$$v = a \wedge x = b \Rightarrow z \neq b$$

Of course, the current instantiation I is also an eliminating explanation for (z, b) but this is trivial, and is subsumed by I' and is less useful.

Note that $\mathrm{expl}(x \neq a) = \emptyset$ means that the value (x, a) has been proved to be globally inconsistent. This may arise, for example, when a value is removed by an inference process (such as enforcing a domain-filtering consistency) at preprocessing time.

In this context, *nil* requires special definition. The proposition $\mathrm{expl}(x \neq a) = nil$ means that a is still present in the current domain of x: we have $a \in \mathrm{dom}(x)$. Similarly, if a function returns *nil* when a nogood is expected (see Algorithms 7, 9 and 12), this means that no inconsistency has been detected, so no nogood has been identified.

Eliminating explanations can be used for two complementary purposes. Basically, they are introduced to compute nogoods serving to jump back to relevant culprit decisions. But they can also be used to represent domains (as briefly shown above) and especially to manage restoration of domains upon backtracking; this is a "form" of trailing (combined with limited recomputation) that is based on explanations. Indeed, by means of eliminating explanations, it is always possible to identify values that must be restored when a backtrack occurs. In the following algorithms, we shall use this facility instead of employing the trailing mechanism described in section 1.5.1. Consequently, the functions reduceTo, restoreUpto and removeValue will not be used in this section.

For recording eliminating explanations, the space complexity is $O(n^2 d)$ since it is $O(n)$ per eliminating explanation and the number of eliminating explanations is

$O(nd)$. Note, however, that eliminating explanations can be generalized to take into account any kind of constraints (not only decision constraints) and to justify different kinds of action by the constraint solver (value removal, bound update, contradiction, etc.). Note also that in the context of assumption-based CSP instances, an explanation is defined as being globally consistent [AMI 02]. This is not the case here.

8.3.2. The kernel of the algorithm

The parameters of generalSearch, Algorithm 70, are the constraint network to be solved and the user's choice of look-back and look-ahead techniques. After data structures have been initialized, the outermost while loop seeks a solution by successively instantiating variables. After an assignment $x = a$, all values, except a, in the current domain of x are logically removed by setting $\{(x, a)\}$ as their eliminating explanation (see e.g. [PRO 95]). The function checkConsistencyAfterAssignment (described later) checks/enforces the selected consistency and returns a (standard) nogood if a dead-end is identified. Otherwise this function returns nil. If $nogood \neq nil$, so a contradiction has to be handled, then the most recent culprit variable assignment in $nogood$ is selected and will be undone (together with all subsequent assignments in the case of IBT). SBT always takes the most recently assigned variable to be the most recent culprit variable. The value that was assigned can now be removed, i.e. given an eliminating explanation, because the corresponding portion of the search space has just been explored. The eliminating explanation is built directly from the nogood. Finally, checkConsistencyAfterRefutation (described later) checks/enforces the chosen consistency. The search terminates when an empty nogood is found.

When a variable assignment is undone, Algorithm 71, it is necessary to remove this from all eliminating explanations that contain the corresponding v-value. For values occurring in the domain of instantiated variables, this immediately yields a new (self) eliminating explanation. For values occurring in the domain of uninstantiated variables, it is necessary to determine whether some other eliminating explanations exist; this search for new explanations is postponed until the function checkConsistencyAfterRefutation is called.

Note that if MAC is chosen, then the constraint network is initially made GAC-consistent by a preprocessing step. Line 4 of Algorithm 70 is replaced by:

$$finished \leftarrow \mathsf{enforceGAC}(P, \mathrm{vars}(P)) \neq nil$$

8.3.3. Dealing with constraint propagation

After each variable assignment, Algorithm 72 checks whether the resulting instantiation is consistent. BC simply checks the satisfaction of all constraints covered

---

Algorithm 70: generalSearch(P: $\mathscr{P}$)

Input: *lookBack* is a value among SBT, IBT and DBT
Input: *lookAhead* is a value among BC, FC and MAC

1 **foreach** *v-value* (x, a) *of* P **do**
2 $\quad \lfloor$ expl$(x \neq a) \leftarrow nil$ $\qquad\qquad$ // each value (x, a) is initially present
3 $I \leftarrow \emptyset$ $\qquad\qquad\qquad\qquad\qquad$ // I represents the current instantiation
4 *finished* $\leftarrow$ *false*
5 **while** $\neg$*finished* **do**
6 $\quad\mid$ select a v-value (x, a) of P such that $x \notin$ vars(I)
7 $\quad\mid$ $I.push(x, a)$
8 $\quad\mid$ **foreach** *value* $b \in$ dom(x) *such that* $b \neq a$ **do**
9 $\quad\mid \quad \lfloor$ expl$(x \neq b) \leftarrow \{(x, a)\}$
10 $\quad\mid$ $nogood \leftarrow$ checkConsistencyAfterAssignment(P, x)
11 $\quad\mid$ **if** $nogood = nil \wedge |I| = n$ **then**
12 $\quad\mid \quad\mid$ $print(I)$ $\qquad\qquad$ // a solution has been found and is printed
13 $\quad\mid \quad \lfloor$ $nogood \leftarrow I$ $\qquad\qquad$ // inserted to keep searching for solutions
14 $\quad\mid$ **while** $nogood \neq nil \wedge nogood \neq \emptyset$ **do**
15 $\quad\mid \quad\mid$ $(x, a) \leftarrow$ last v-value pushed in I and present in $nogood$
16 $\quad\mid \quad\mid$ **if** $lookBack = IBT$ **then**
17 $\quad\mid \quad\mid \quad\mid$ **while** $I.top() \neq (x, a)$ **do**
18 $\quad\mid \quad\mid \quad \lfloor$ undoAssignment$(I.top())$
19 $\quad\mid \quad\mid$ undoAssignment(x, a)
20 $\quad\mid \quad\mid$ expl$(x \neq a) \leftarrow nogood \setminus \{(x, a)\}$ $\qquad$ // a is removed from dom(x)
21 $\quad\mid \quad \lfloor$ $nogood \leftarrow$ checkConsistencyAfterRefutation(P, x)
22 $\quad\mid$ **if** $nogood = \emptyset$ **then**
23 $\quad \lfloor \quad \lfloor$ *finished* $\leftarrow$ *true*

Algorithm 71: undoAssignment $((x, a)$: v-value)

---

1 $I.delete(x, a)$ $\qquad\qquad$ // corresponds to $I.pop()$ except for DBT
$\quad$ // domains are restored using explanations
2 **foreach** *v-value* (y, b) *of* P^{init} *such that* $(x, a) \in$ expl$(y \neq b)$ **do**
3 $\quad\mid$ **if** $y \in$ vars(I) **then**
4 $\quad\mid \quad\mid$ expl$(y \neq b) \leftarrow \{(y, c)\}$ where $(y, c) \in I$
5 $\quad\mid$ **else**
6 $\quad \lfloor \quad \lfloor$ expl$(y \neq b) \leftarrow nil$

Algorithm 72: checkConsistencyAfterAssignment(P: $\mathscr{P}$, x: variable): nogood

---

Require: x has just been instantiated; $x \in \text{vars}(I)$
Output: a nogood if an inconsistency is detected, or *nil*

1   **switch** *lookAhead* **do**
2   **case** *BC:*
3   **foreach** *constraint* $c \in \text{cons}(P) \mid x \in \text{scp}(c) \wedge \text{scp}(c) \subseteq \text{vars}(I)$ **do**
4   **if** *I does not satisfy c* **then**
5   **if** *lookBack* $= SBT$ **then**
6   **return** I
7   **else**
8   **return** $\{(y, b) \in I \mid y \in \text{scp}(c)\}$

9   **return** *nil*

10   **case** *FC:*
11   **return** applyFC(P, x)

12   **case** *MAC:*
13   **return** enforceGAC($P, \{x\}$)

Algorithm 73: checkConsistencyAfterRefutation(P: $\mathscr{P}$, x: variable): nogood

---

Require: x has just been refuted a value; $x \notin \text{vars}(I)$
Output: a nogood if an inconsistency is detected, or *nil*

1   **if** $\text{dom}(x) = \emptyset$ **then**
2   **return** handleEmptyDomain(x)

3   **switch** *lookAhead* **do**
4   **case** *BC:*
5   **return** *nil*

6   **case** *FC:*
7   **if** *lookBack* $= DBT$ **then**
8   **return** applyFC($P, \text{vars}(I)$)
9   **else**
10   **return** *nil*

11   **case** *MAC:*
12   **if** *lookBack* $= SBT$ **then**
13   **return** enforceGAC($P, \{x\}$)
14   **else**
15   **return** enforceGAC($P, \text{vars}(P)$)

by the current instantiation: BC determines if the current instantiation is locally consistent. If there is an unsatisfied constraint c (preferably the earliest unsatisfied constraint [DEC 03]), the set of culprit variables is exactly $\mathrm{scp}(c)$. For SBT the current instantiation is regarded as the conflict set; the algorithm backtracks chronologically. Look-ahead techniques such as FC and MAC require some constraint propagation, which is accomplished by applyFC and enforceGAC, Algorithms 12 and 7,9, with alternative instructions between square brackets.

When, a value a of a variable x is refuted at line 20 of Algorithm 70, Algorithm 73 checks whether the instance is still consistent. The function handleEmptyDomain, which is described later, handles the situation where $\mathrm{dom}(x)$ becomes empty after removing the value a. Otherwise, the removal of a must be taken into account, although for BC nothing needs to be done. For FC combined with SBT or IBT, there is also nothing to do, since a value has just been removed from the domain of an uninstantiated variable. However, when FC is combined with DBT, the algorithm verifies that all values (put back into domains) do not have eliminating explanations (since dynamic backtracking performs jumps without erasing intermediate decisions). Calling applyFC with the set of all instantiated variables ensures that the network is "forward checked". An optimization is possible here (by considering only the variables that have been assigned after x and/or by keeping track of restored values) to save some constraint checks. When MAC-SBT is used, arc consistency is maintained from x, as usual, whereas when MAC-IBT or MAC-DBT is used, it is necessary to verify that all restored values have no eliminating explanations. This is necessary for MAC-IBT because successive backjumps may occur and arc consistency is not necessarily fully established when a domain wipe-out occurs. Again, several optimizations can be introduced to save some constraint checks: for MAC-IBT, call $enforceGAC(P, \{x\})$ if only one backjump has occurred and in the general case, only consider the variables that have been assigned after x. These optimizations do have no effect on the backjumping capability of the algorithms.

Algorithm 74: handleEmptyDomain(x: variable): nogood

Require: $\mathrm{dom}(x) = \emptyset$
Output: a nogood

1 **if** $lookBack = SBT$ **then**
2 $\quad\mid\quad$ **return** I
3 $nogood \leftarrow \emptyset$
4 **foreach** $value\ a \in \mathrm{dom}^{\mathrm{init}}(x)$ **do**
5 $\quad\mid\quad nogood \leftarrow nogood \cup \mathrm{expl}(x \neq a)$
6 **return** $nogood$

Algorithm 75: getExplanation$((c, x, a)$: c-value): explanation

---

Require: (x, a) has been removed because of the absence of support on c
Output: an explanation $\text{expl}(x \neq a)$

1 **if** $lookBack = SBT$ **then**
2 $\quad$ **return** I

3 $explanation \leftarrow \emptyset$
4 **foreach** *variable* $y \in \text{scp}(c) \mid y \neq x$ **do**
5 $\quad$ **foreach** *value* $b \in \text{dom}^{\text{init}}(y) \mid \text{expl}(y \neq b) \neq nil \wedge \text{expl}(y \neq b) \neq \emptyset$ **do**
6 $\quad\quad$ **if** $\exists \tau \in \text{rel}(c) \mid \tau[x] = a \wedge \tau[y] = b$ **then**
7 $\quad\quad\quad$ $explanation \leftarrow explanation \cup \text{expl}(y \neq b)$

8 **return** $explanation$

The function handleEmptyDomain is called when a domain wipe-out occurs, either during propagation (see Algorithms 12, 7 and 9) or after refuting the last value of a domain (see line 2 of Algorithm 73). The function handleEmptyDomain gathers the eliminating explanations of all (removed) values, except in the case of SBT, for which the current instantiation I represents the conflict set. During propagation, revision is performed by the function revise (Algorithm 8). The function getExplanation, Algorithm 75, provides an eliminating explanation for each value that is removed. For SBT, as usual, the current instantiation is the conflict set. For IBT and DBT, eliminating explanations for values supporting (x, a) on c are collected; note that $b \in \text{dom}^{\text{init}}(y) \mid \text{expl}(y \neq b) \neq nil$ is equivalent to $b \in \text{dom}^{\text{init}}(y) \setminus \text{dom}(y)$.

8.3.4. *Closely related algorithms*

For instances involving constraints of arbitrary arity, the parameterized function generalSearch, Algorithm 70, encompasses several important look-ahead and look-back techniques and is affiliated with some works.

First, [JUS 00b] describes MAC-DBT and reports that this outperforms MAC on some randomly generated structured instances (when using classical variable ordering heuristics). This differs from our presentation mainly in that a fine-grained arc consistency algorithm (AC4) is used in [JUS 00b]. In fact coarse-grained algorithms are simpler to implement and have been found to be quite competitive. However, obtaining a precise eliminating explanation with a coarse-grained algorithm requires effort that is visible between lines 4 and 7 of Algorithm 75. This effort can be reduced as shown below, but perhaps at the expense of reduced quality of the explanations obtained in practice.

Bacchus proposes [BAC 00] a general template for extending forward checking. The main algorithm (FC+Prune) is based on non-binary branching, whereas the parameterized Algorithm 70 uses binary branching (as in [JUS 00b]). The algorithm CFFC proposed by Bacchus is in some respects similar to FC-IBT. A variant, denoted by CFFC⁻, allows many constraint checks to be avoided (especially, when non-binary constraints are involved). This is similar to computing less expensive but also less precise eliminating explanations by replacing lines 4 to 7 of Algorithm 75 with:

> **foreach** *variable* $y \in \mathrm{scp}(c) \mid y \neq x$ **do**
> > **if** $y \in \mathrm{vars}(I)$ **then**
> > > $\mid$ *explanation* $\leftarrow$ *explanation* $\cup \{(y, b)\}$ with $(y, b) \in I$
> >
> > **else**
> > > **foreach** *value* $b \in \mathrm{dom}^{\mathrm{init}}(y) \mid \mathrm{expl}(y \neq b) \neq nil$ **do**
> > > > $\lfloor$ *explanation* $\leftarrow$ *explanation* $\cup \mathrm{expl}(y \neq b)$

8.4. Illustrations

The 4-queens instance from the queens problem (see the second model in section 1.3.1) provides a first illustration of backtrack search. Figures 8.5, 8.6 and 8.7 show the search steps performed by BT, FC and MAC, respectively, to solve this instance using standard backtracking (i.e. SBT). Queens (variables) are put (instantiated) in columns from left to right and values are assigned in a bottom-up manner. For FC and MAC, hatched squares represent values removed from variable domains due to constraint propagation. For example, the square at column b and row 1 and the square at column b and row 2 are hatched in Figure 8.6(a) because x_a has just been assigned the value 1 and there is a constraint between the variables x_a and x_b associated with the first two columns defined as: $x_a \neq x_b \wedge |x_a - x_b| \neq 1$. For FC and MAC, both positive and negative decisions are shown. For example, after FC puts the second queen onto the square of the chessboard at column b and row 3, a dead-end is reached, so this square must then be discarded. These two actions correspond to the positive and negative decisions that can be seen in Figures 8.6(b) and 8.6(c), respectively. Similarly, after MAC puts the first queen onto the square of the chessboard at column a and row 1, Figure 8.7(a), a dead-end is reached and this square is then discarded as shown in Figure 8.7(b). Whereas BT requires a large number of steps to find a solution (the six final steps are not shown), FC and especially MAC are far more efficient because they prune some useless portions of the search space.

As a first illustration of look-back schemes, let us consider a constraint network involving the variables $\{x_1, x_2, x_3, x_4, x_5, x_6\}$ with $\mathrm{dom}(x_i) = \{1, 2\}, \forall i \in 1..6$, and constraints $\{x_1 = x_2, x_2 = x_3, x_2 = x_4, x_3 = x_4, x_1 \neq x_5, x_1 \neq x_6, x_5 \neq$

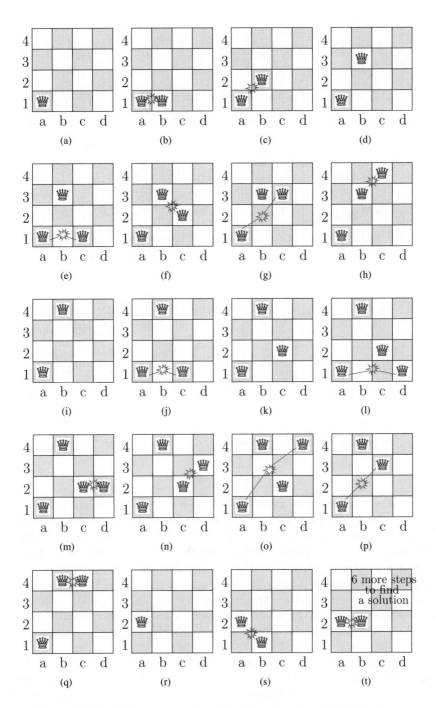

Figure 8.5. *The 20 first steps performed by BT to solve the **4-queens** instance*

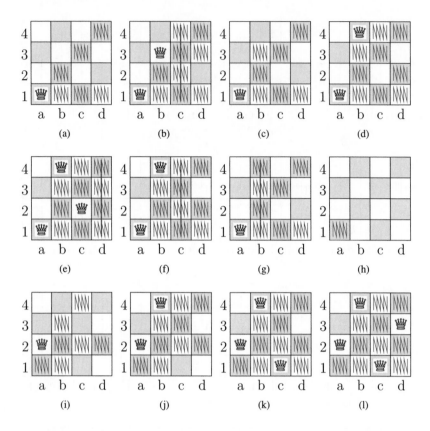

Figure 8.6. *The 12 steps performed by FC to solve the* **4-queens** *instance*

x_6}. This network is clearly unsatisfiable since it is impossible to instantiate x_1, x_5 and x_6 without violating a constraint. Figure 8.8 shows the first search steps of CBJ (i.e. BC-IBT) on this instance, to prove that $(x_1, 1)$ is globally inconsistent. Variables and values are selected in lexicographic order; the first four variables are instantiated without any problem. When 1 is assigned to x_5, the constraint $x_1 \neq x_5$ covered by the current instantiation $\{(x_1, 1), (x_2, 2), (x_3, 1), (x_4, 1), (x_5, 1)\}$ is violated, so we obtain $\text{expl}(x_5 \neq 1) = \{(x_1, 1)\}$; see Figure 8.8(f) and 8.8(g). Here eliminating explanations are depicted by small labeled arrows and only refer to variables (here, x_1). With BC this is no problem because these variables are always assigned (so, e.g. from x_1, we retrieve $(x_1, 1)$). Figure 8.9 shows the next steps: there are new conflicts. As $x_1 = 1$ and $x_6 = 1$ are incompatible, we have $\text{expl}(x_6 \neq 1) = \{(x_1, 1)\}$; see Figures 8.9(a) and 8.9(b). Then, as $x_5 = 2$ and $x_6 = 2$ are incompatible, we have $\text{expl}(x_6 \neq 2) = \{(x_5, 2)\}$, Figures 8.9(c) and 8.9(d), and a domain wipe-out for

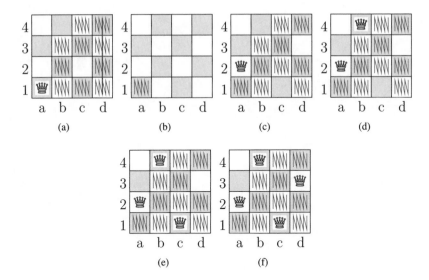

Figure 8.7. *The 6 steps performed by MAC to solve the* **4-queens** *instance*

x_6. The nogood identified by handleEmptyDomain is $\text{expl}(x_6 \neq 1) \cup \text{expl}(x_6 \neq 2) = \{(x_1,1),(x_5,2)\}$. This is used as explanation for $(x_5,2)$: $\text{expl}(x_5 \neq 2) = \{(x_1,1),(x_5,2)\} \setminus \{(x_5,2)\} = \{(x_1,1)\}$, Figure 8.9(e). This time there is a domain wipe-out for x_5. The nogood identified by handleEmptyDomain is $\text{expl}(x_5 \neq 1) \cup \text{expl}(x_5 \neq 2) = \{(x_1,1)\}$. This allows us to backtrack up to $x_1 = 1$ and refute it globally: we have $\text{expl}(x_1 \neq 1) = \emptyset$, Figure 8.9(f). This simple example illustrates the value of managing explanations to perform intelligent backtracking. With standard backtracking, we would have wasted time by performing additional useless decisions. More generally, there are some situations where CBJ can be exponentially better (in terms of taken decisions) than backtracking.

Figure 8.10 serves to illustrate non-chronological backtracking combined with constraint propagation. Here, the search algorithm has reached a dead-end after a few decisions have been taken. This example assumes that the domain of each variable initially contains three values $\{a,b,c\}$, that a consistency ϕ is enforced at each step of search, and that $y = c$ has previously been refuted (and explained). For this example, we prefer to use sets of positive decisions instead of sets of v-values. At the dead-end associated with the domain wipe-out of z the nogood is $\text{expl}(z \neq a) \cup \text{expl}(z \neq b) \cup \text{expl}(z \neq c) = \{v = a, w = b, y = b\}$. Thus the eliminating explanation for $y \neq b$ is $\text{expl}(y \neq b) = \{v = a, w = b, y = b\} \setminus \{y = b\} = \{v = a, w = b\}$ as shown in Figure 8.11. After assigning a to y, a new dead-end is associated with a domain wipe-out for variable u, Figure 8.12. The eliminating explanation for $y \neq a$ is

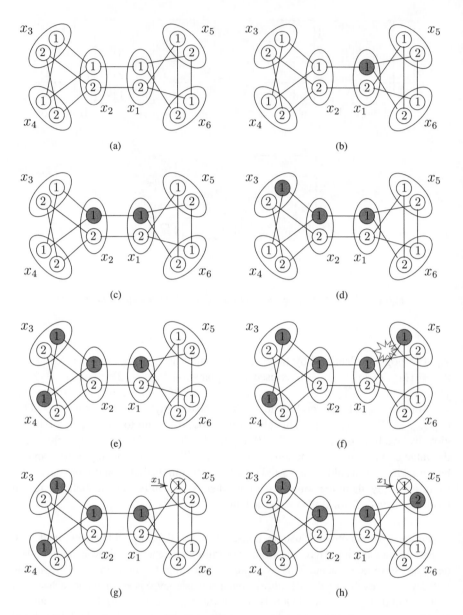

Figure 8.8. *The first steps performed by CBJ to prove that* $(x_1, 1)$ *is globally inconsistent*

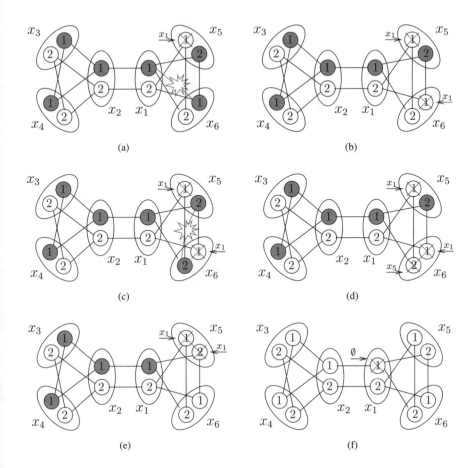

Figure 8.9. *The next steps performed by CBJ to prove that* $(x_1, 1)$ *is globally inconsistent*

then computed, and Figure 8.13 shows that we have to backtrack since a was the last value in $\mathrm{dom}(y)$. The nogood computed is $\mathrm{expl}(y \neq a) \cup \mathrm{expl}(y \neq b) \cup \mathrm{expl}(y \neq c) = \{v = a, w = b\}$. This allows backtrack up to decision $w = b$, refuting this with an explanation, Figure 8.14. Dynamic backtracking would have not discarded intermediate decisions: this is shown in Figure 8.15.

8.5. The role of explanations

Managing explanations, or more generally nogoods, is an elegant approach that can be very useful in many fields of constraint programming. Based on a formal

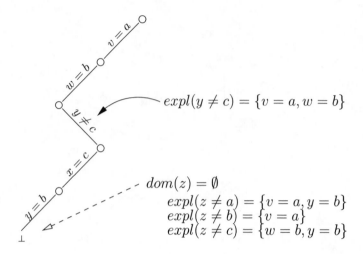

Figure 8.10. *Dead-end encountered after assigning b to y and enforcing a given consistency φ. We have a domain wipe-out for z and explanations given for each value removed from the initial domain of z*

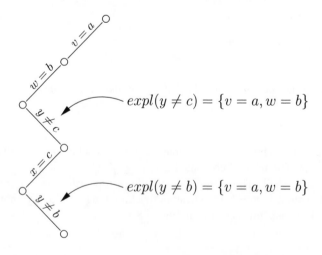

Figure 8.11. *Eliminating explanation computed for y ≠ b from situation of Figure 8.10*

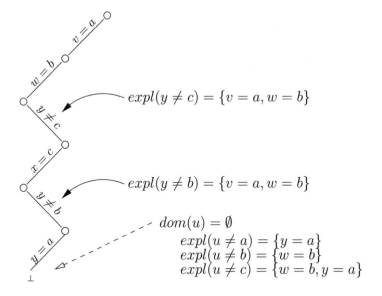

$$expl(y \neq c) = \{v = a, w = b\}$$

$$expl(y \neq b) = \{v = a, w = b\}$$

$$dom(u) = \emptyset$$
$$expl(u \neq a) = \{y = a\}$$
$$expl(u \neq b) = \{w = b\}$$
$$expl(u \neq c) = \{w = b, y = a\}$$

Figure 8.12. *Dead-end after assigning a to y: there is a domain wipe-out for u*

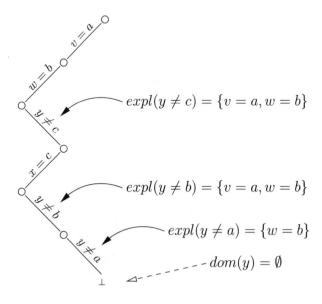

$$expl(y \neq c) = \{v = a, w = b\}$$

$$expl(y \neq b) = \{v = a, w = b\}$$

$$expl(y \neq a) = \{w = b\}$$

$$dom(y) = \emptyset$$

Figure 8.13. *Eliminating explanation computed for $y \neq a$ from situation of Figure 8.12. As both branches $y = a$ and $y \neq a$ (a was the last value in $\mathrm{dom}(y)$) have been explored, we have to backtrack*

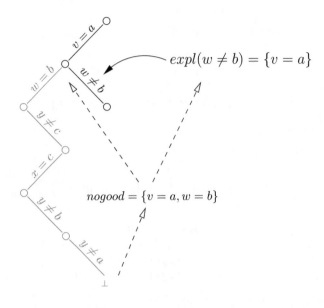

Figure 8.14. *Backtrack guided by the nogood extracted from situation of Figure 8.13*

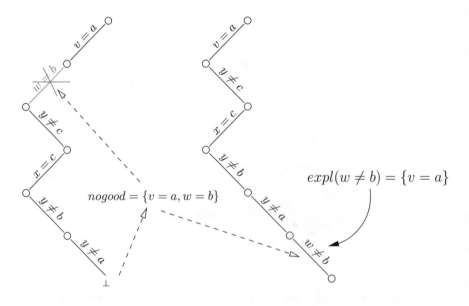

Figure 8.15. *Dynamic backtracking in action from situation of Figure 8.13*

foundation, nogoods can be used to provide an uniform view of many existing approaches and also to support proofs of correctness. Explanations can be used to explain inconsistencies of constraint networks and can be exploited advantageously in a dynamic context. Furthermore, explanations can reduce thrashing by showing how to jump back to the origin of failures. Here we have given a number of reasons for the success of explanations.

Classically, and as explained in section 8.3, an eliminating explanation indicates why a value has been removed from the domain of a variable. There may be several eliminating explanations for the removal of a value, but it is usual to record only the first explanation that is encountered, because taking all of them into account would lead to exponential space complexity [STA 77, JUS 00b]. Unfortunately, the recorded eliminating explanations are not always the most appropriate for guiding non-chronological backtracking. We illustrate this below.

Let us consider again the well-known n-queens problem which is to put n queens on a chessboard of size $n \times n$ so that no two queens can attack each other. Classically, each queen is represented by a variable (here, called queen variable) whose domain contains exactly n values; see section 1.3.1. The number of solutions of this easy problem increases with n. A second academic problem, called the knights problem, is to put k knights on a chessboard of size $n \times n$ such that all knights form a cycle (when considering knight moves). This problem does not admit any solution when the value of k is odd. In a CSP model of this problem, each knight is represented by a variable (here, called knight variable) whose domain contains exactly $n \times n$ values corresponding to all squares of the chessboard; a constraint between each knight variable and the variable that comes next (modulo k) ensures that one can pass from a knight to the next with a single knight move. Besides, for every pair of variables, there is a constraint ensuring that two knights cannot be placed on the same square.

By simply merging the two (sub)problems without any interaction (that is to say, there is no constraint involving both a queen variable and a knight variable), we obtain a new problem. We denote each instance of this new problem by qk-n-k-add where n represents the number of queens and k the number of knights (the chessboard is of size $n \times n$). For this problem there is thrashing if the number of knights is odd and if MAC (i.e. MAC-SBT) is used with a classical variable ordering heuristic such as *dom* that selects at each search step the variable with the smallest domain; this heuristic is presented in the next chapter. The k-knights subproblem is unsatisfiable but, because *dom* first selects queen variables (due to their small domain sizes), the unsatisfiable k-knights subproblem is rediscovered for each new solution of the n-queens subproblem. There is no thrashing if explanations (i.e. MAC-IBT or MAC-DBT) are used to perform non-chronological backtracking, as can be seen in Figure 8.16(a). For MAC-SBT, MAC-IBT and MAC-DBT, Figure 8.16(a) shows the CPU time required to solve qk-n-5-add instances for n ranging from 5 to 38; when an instance has not been solved within 600 seconds, the corresponding point is missing. In fact, MAC (whatever the look-back technique) first finds a solution to the n-queens subproblem and then proves that the k-knights subproblem is unsatisfiable. Chronological backtracking backtracks to the last assigned queen variable (suspected of being the culprit of the failure) but if non-chronological backtracking is used instead, the problem is directly proved to be unsatisfiable. More specifically, with MAC using *dom*, after traversing the n-queens subproblem, we focus on a knight variable x_k and, with IBT or DBT, we successively prove that every value i in $\mathrm{dom}(x_k)$ is globally inconsistent, i.e. is such that $\mathrm{expl}(x_k \neq i) = \emptyset$. The function handleEmptyDomain is then called for x_k at line 2 of Algorithm 73, itself called at line 21 of Algorithm 70. As $\emptyset$ is returned by the functions handleEmptyDomain and checkConsistencyAfterRefutation, the loop starting at line 14 of Algorithm 70 terminates, and the overall search is finished (see lines 22 and 23).

Let us now combine the two (sub)problems differently, such that queens and knights cannot share the same square: for each pair composed of a queen variable and a knight variable, there is a kind of inequation constraint[3]. We denote each instance of this new problem by qk-n-k-mul where n is the number of queens and k is the number of knights (the chessboard is of size $n \times n$). This time, MAC-SBT, MAC-IBT and MAC-DBT all thrash, as can be seen in Figure 8.16(b). The reason why MAC-IBT and MAC-DBT cannot now prevent thrashing is as follows. Whenever a queen variable x_c is assigned a value r, this means that the associated queen is put on the square at the intersection of column c and row r. Assuming that this square is the ith square of the chessboard (i is computed from both c and r), then this value i is removed from the domain of each knight variable x_k, by propagation, so $\mathrm{expl}(x_k \neq i) = \{(x_c, r)\}$. In this case, when handleEmptyDomain is called for a knight variable x_k, a conflict set representing the current instantiation is returned. There is therefore no more difference in the behavior of these look-back techniques.

To summarize, in some cases, no pertinent culprit variable(s) can be identified by a backjumping technique although predictable thrashing occurs. The problem is that if there are several different eliminating explanations for a removed value, only the first of these is recorded. It may be possible to improve existing non-chronological backtracking techniques by updating eliminating explanations, computing new ones [JUN 04] or managing several k-relevant explanations [OUI 02]; this certainly deserves further study. On the other hand, it has been shown [LEC 04] that for many structured problems there are adaptive heuristics (presented in the next chapter) which make non-chronological techniques useless. This may appear disconcerting since look-back techniques are currently very popular in the SAT community. There are two main reasons for this success. Firstly, recording explanations in SAT is a very natural and light mechanism (basically, recording new clauses). Secondly, the explanations

---

3. This is not exactly an inequation constraint since the nature of the domains on which queen variables and knight variables are defined are different.

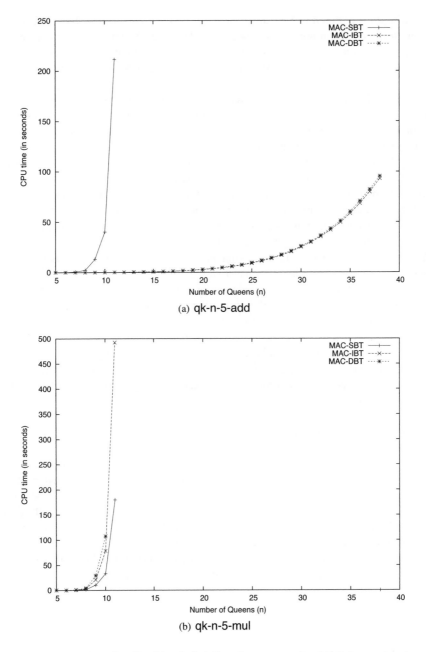

(a) qk-n-5-add

(b) qk-n-5-mul

Figure 8.16. *Solving* qk-n-5-add *and* qk-n-5-mul *instances using MAC-dom and various backtracking techniques. A missing point indicates that the corresponding instance has not been solved within 600 seconds*

that arise during search in SAT are kept and used for a longer time than is necessary purely for purposes of non-chronological backtracking. Retention of new clauses can be perceived as a form of learning (nogood recording) oriented toward propagation; in Chapter 10, we shall investigate nogood recording for CSP in another context.

Finally, let us return again to dynamic backtracking, which is an appealing approach because it allows much search effort to be avoided when a dead-end is encountered. After identifying a culprit decision δ, the algorithm discards only δ while preserving all decisions made at later times than δ. This approach is valuable mainly for problems that can be decomposed into independent parts (perhaps during search), as in many real-world applications. Unfortunately, dynamic backtracking suffers from two main drawbacks. The first is the complexity of managing non-backtrack-stable structures (i.e. structures that need some form of restoration when backtracking occurs). It is usually rather difficult to update data structures, such as those of incremental propagators, at the time of a DBT backjump. The second drawback is that dynamic backtracking may conflict with principles that underlly search heuristics. The problem is that a variable whose assignment has been erased at a certain level may need to be assigned later at a far deeper level. If this variable is "sensitive", the efficiency of the search algorithm may be reduced. As shown in [BAK 94], if there is no logical reason to discard subsequent decisions, there may be good heuristic reasons for doing so. However, extensions of DBT have been devised in order to overcome partially this last drawback. Partial order dynamic backtracking (PDB) [GIN 94] provides greater flexibility than DBT in terms of exploration of the search space. General partial order dynamic backtracking [BLI 98] generalizes both DBT and PDB.

For SAT, a lightweight alternative to DBT, which mitigates inefficiency arising from far-backjumping, has been proposed in [PIP 07]. This alternative can be viewed as a partial component caching scheme that helps SAT solvers to avoid re-solving subproblems multiple times. This technique, which is called *progress saving*, simply requires management of an additional array. Every time the solver backtracks and erases some assignments, each erased assignment is saved in the array. If the solver subsequently has to branch on a variable, it first tries the saved value, if one exists. Otherwise, the solver resorts to the default value ordering heuristic. Substantial improvements in practical performance [PIP 07] indicate that progress saving deserves to be tested (and compared with DBT) in constraint solvers.

Chapter 9

Guiding Search toward Conflicts

As explained in the previous chapter, there are some (structured) problems for which non-chronological backtracking techniques may appear not to prevent thrashing effectively. This chapter enquires whether looking-ahead techniques may compensate such a deficiency on some of these problems. For such structured problems, can we find generic search-guiding heuristics and combine these with classical consistency enforcement (maintaining generalized arc consistency) to achieve more efficient exploration of the search space?

The answer is affirmative if we use recently introduced *adaptive heuristics* based on *variable impacts* and *constraint weighting*. These (variable-ordering) heuristics learn and use information from every node explored in the search tree, whereas traditional static and dynamic heuristics only use information about the initial and current nodes. By taking account of the impact of each value (i.e. each variable assignment) on the search space, the search can be made to explore the most conflicting variables first. It is important that this information can be regularly and easily updated after each positive branching decision, i.e. each variable assignment. A further technique associates a weight with each constraint and systematically increments weights of constraints violated during search. A simple conflict-directed heuristic (and some variants) selects and assigns first the variables involved in constraints that have the greatest weight. As search progresses, the weight of constraints located in the hard parts of the network become higher and higher, so the heuristic focuses search effort on variables involved in these constraints.

This chapter also shows how a very basic learning approach enables guidance of backtrack search toward sources of conflicts obtaining, as a side effect, behavior similar to backjumping. The idea is that after each conflict, the last instantiated variable is selected in priority, so long as the constraint network cannot be made consistent. This allows us to find, by traversing the current partial instantiation from the leaf toward the root of the search tree, the most recent culprit decision that prevents the last variable from being instantiated. In other words, the variable ordering heuristic is violated until the culprit decision is reached by backtrack and a compatible value is found for the priority variable. This tactic can easily be grafted onto many variants of backtracking algorithms and represents an original way to avoid thrashing.

Guiding search toward conflicts by reasoning from past (permanently adjusting impacts or weights, or simply recording the variable involved in the last failure) is found to outperform classical heuristics significantly. This chapter is organized as follows. After a review of static and dynamic search-guiding heuristics, recently introduced adaptive variable ordering heuristics are presented. We emphasize the value of constraint weighting for boosting systematic search and extracting small unsatisfiable cores. Finally, before concluding, this chapter explains the principle of reasoning from last conflicts.

9.1. Search-guiding heuristics

Two choices are made at each step within backtrack search. First, before branching, the search algorithm selects the variable that is most constrained. Second, the most promising value for this variable is chosen. Thus the search algorithm imposes an ordering on variables and on their values. However, finding an optimal ordering is at least as difficult as solving a constraint satisfaction problem instance. This is why, in practice, ordering is determined by *heuristics*. A heuristic is a general guideline rule that is expected to lead to good results, such as good selections of variables and values. Heuristics are derived from experience, intuition and common sense, but are not claimed to give optimal outcomes in every situation.

For backtrack search, a first general principle is that it is better to start by assigning variables that belong to the most difficult part(s) of the problem instance. This principle is derived from recognition that there is no point in traversing the easy part(s) of an instance and then backtracking repeatedly when it turns out that the first choices are incompatible with the remaining difficult part(s). Here the underlying *fail-first* principle is [HAR 80]:"To succeed, try first where you are most likely to fail". Roughly speaking, a variable ordering heuristic conforming to the fail-first principle tries initially to focus the search effort on a small strong backdoor (see section 2.2.1).

Value selection can be based on the *succeed-first* or *promise* principle, which comes from the simple observation that to find a solution quickly, it is better to move at each step to the most promising subtree, primarily by selecting a value that is most likely to participate in a solution. It is preferable to avoid branching on a value that is globally inconsistent, because this implies exploration of a fruitless subtree, which is clearly a waste of time if there is a solution elsewhere.

Although these two principles may seem to be somewhat contradictory, variable ordering can to some extent comply with both of them [BEC 04, WAL 06a, HUL 06a]. Various different measures of promise of variable ordering heuristics try to assess the ability of the heuristics to avoid making mistakes, i.e. to keep the search on the path to a solution regardless of the value ordering. There appears to be quite a complex relationship between promise and fail-firstness. For value ordering, the extent of adherence to both heuristics can also be assessed; first elements related to this can be found in [SZY 06, LEC 06c].

When starting to build the search tree, the initial variable/value choices are particularly important. Bad choices near the root of the search tree may turn out to be disastrous because they lead to exploration of very large fruitless subtrees. To make good initial choices, one strategy is to select the first branching decisions with special care, perhaps calling sophisticated and expensive procedures for this purpose. Another strategy is to restart search several times, ideally learning some information each time in order to refine search guidance.

This section introduces some well-known classical variable and value ordering heuristics, without claiming to be exhaustive. More information about heuristics can be found e.g. in [BEE 06]. Adaptive (variable) ordering heuristics, which have been introduced more recently, are presented in the next section.

9.1.1. *Classical variable ordering heuristics*

The order in which variables are assigned by a backtrack search algorithm has been recognized as a key issue for a long time. Using different variable ordering heuristics can drastically effect the efficiency of algorithms solving CSP instances. Introducing some form of randomization into a given variable ordering heuristic can cause great variability in performance. An ideal variable ordering selects first a small strong backdoor, i.e. a set of variables which, once assigned, make the remaining problem easy to solve.

Static, or fixed, variable ordering heuristics (SVOs) keep the same ordering throughout the search, using only (structural) information about the initial state of search. The simplest such heuristic is *lexico* which orders variables lexicographically. When variables are indexed by integers, *lexico* is usually implemented so as to order the variables according to the value of their index. If $\text{vars}(P) = \{x_1, x_2, \ldots, x_n\}$, then *lexico* will select first x_1, then $x_2, \ldots$ and finally x_n (except that some variables may never be reached if the instance is unsatisfiable). The heuristic *deg*, which is also known as *max-deg*, orders variables in sequence of decreasing degree, so variables with the highest degree are selected first [ULL 76, DEC 89a]. The dynamic variant of *deg*, which is called *ddeg*, orders variables in sequence of decreasing dynamic degree – see Definition 1.25. Note that *ddeg* is classified as a static heuristic because its ordering is fixed throughout search (and besides, it can be computed cheaply). Further static heuristics are *width* and *bandwidth* where variables are increasingly ordered in order to minimize the width [FRE 82] and bandwidth [ZAB 90] of the constraint graph, respectively.

Dynamic variable ordering heuristics (DVOs) take account of the current state of the instance being solved. These heuristics are dynamic because their ordering generally varies during the search. The well-known dynamic heuristic *dom*, or *min-dom*, [BIT 75, HAR 80] orders variables in sequence of increasing size of domain, so a variable that has the smallest domain size is selected at each step. The heuristics *dom/deg* and *dom/ddeg* take account of degrees of variables, as well as sizes of domains. At each step, these heuristics select a variable with the smallest ratio "current domain size" to "(dynamic) degree". Here division combines the minimization of *dom* with the maximization of *deg*. Various theory-based dynamic heuristics proposed in [GEN 96a, HOR 00] are conceptually elegant, but they require additional computation and they have not been tested on structured problems.

A variable ordering heuristic (usually) computes a score for each variable. A *tie* is a set of variables that have the same score. Ties occur quite frequently at the beginning of search; for example *deg* cannot distinguish between variables that have the same degree, and *dom* cannot distinguish between variables that have the same domain size. For example, when the only remaining uninstantiated variables are w, x, y and z such that $|\mathrm{dom}(x)| = |\mathrm{dom}(z)| = 2$ and $|\mathrm{dom}(w)| = |\mathrm{dom}(y)| = 4$, then for the *dom* heuristic, $\{x, z\}$ is a tie that needs to be broken. Breaking a tie means finally selecting one of the tied variables. Where a tie-breaker is not specified explicitly, *lexico* is usually understood to be specified implicitly as the tie breaker. For example, *dom* implicitly means *dom+lexico* which selects the first variable lexicographically in the tie of variables that have the smallest current domain size. In this notation, the criterion or heuristic specified after the "+" breaks ties for the heuristic specified before the "+". Some other composite heuristics are *dom+deg* [FRO 95] and *bz* which corresponds to *dom+ddeg* [BRE 79, SMI 99]. The heuristic *bz* can be seen as a refinement of *dom* since the main criterion is the current domain size of variables; *bz* uses dynamic degree only to break ties. Another possibility is to break ties by selecting one tied variable at random. Randomly breaking ties of variable ordering heuristics is one way to randomize a backtrack search algorithm.

The 3-queens instance from the n-queens problem provides a very simple illustration of the merit of the fail-first principle. The 3-queens instance is unsatisfiable, but the ordering of variables used to explore the search space effects the size of the refutation tree. Figure 9.1 shows the search steps that solve this instance with FC as search algorithm and *dom* as variable ordering heuristic. Ties are broken

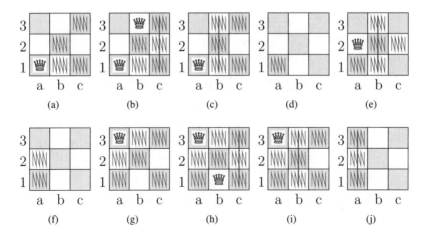

Figure 9.1. *Proving the unsatisfiability of instance 3-queens with FC-dom, i.e. forward checking and (variable ordering) heuristic dom*

by selecting the variable associated with the leftmost column, and the first value in the domain of the selected variable is always chosen. For the same instance, Figure 9.2 shows the search steps when using the anti-heuristic *max-dom*, which selects the variable that has the largest domain. Figure 9.2 illustrates the penalizing cost of diversifying exploration instead of focusing on the difficult part of the problem. The behavior of these two heuristics differs for the first time in Figures 9.1(e) and 9.2(e). We can see that in Figure 9.1(d) *dom*, unlike *max-dom*, selects the first variable which is clearly the most constrained because only two values remain in its domain.

Any heuristic can be generalized by taking into account the neighborhood of the variables [BES 01a]. For instance, if an heuristic h employs a function α_h to give a score to each variable, then it is possible to use an operator $\odot$ to define a generalization $h_1^\odot$ of the heuristic h at a neighborhood distance equal to 1. The generalized heuristic employs a function $\alpha_{h,1}^\odot$ that gives a score to each variable x as follows:

$$\alpha_{h,1}^\odot(x) = \frac{\sum_{y\in\Gamma(x)} \alpha_h(x) \odot \alpha_h(y)}{|\Gamma(x)|^2}$$

$\Gamma(x)$ denotes the neighbors of variable x, i.e. the set of variables involved with x in at least one constraint, and for example, we could have $\odot \in \{+, \times\}$. Such kinds of generalization enable us to compute various constrainedness measures of variables by means of simple syntactical properties.

When comparing algorithms or heuristics, it may be interesting to use an heuristic that randomly selects variables. The heuristic *random* can be defined statically (the

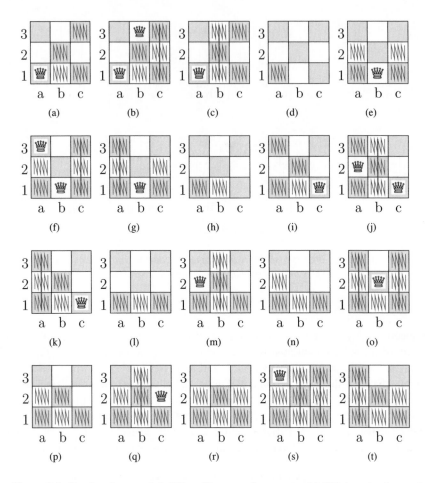

Figure 9.2. *Proving the unsatisfiability of instance* 3-queens *with FC-dom, i.e. forward checking and anti-heuristic max-dom*

same ordering along all branches) or dynamically (a new choice at each branching point). Randomly selecting variables may serve as a baseline.

It is rather difficult to rank classical general-purpose variable ordering heuristics according to their relative efficiency. Dynamic heuristics such as *dom*, *bz* and *dom/ddeg* are usually considered to be the most effective (although neighborhood generalizations may turn out to be a little bit more robust). However, the variable ordering heuristics introduced in this section are clearly outperformed by adaptive heuristics presented in section 9.2.

9.1.2. *Value ordering heuristics*

Value ordering, which is classically a second selection step at a branching point, has for a long time been thought to have marginal effect on search efficiency. The main reason why value ordering was acknowledged not very useful is that, when facing unsatisfiable instances or when searching for all solutions, all values must be considered. Smith and Sturdy [SMI 05] have shown that this reason holds when search is based on d-way branching but not for 2-way branching. And even for d-way branching, when an adaptive variable ordering heuristic is used, value ordering heuristics may have an impact [MEH 09].

Following the promise principle, much work supports the idea that a value should be chosen after estimating the number of solutions (or conflicts) involving each value. Some proposed heuristics select the value that maximizes the estimated number of solutions in the constraint network obtained after assigning this value [DEC 88, GEE 92, HOR 00, PRC 02, KAS 04]. Here, we will only describe the well-known *min-conflicts* heuristic [MIN 92, FRO 95], which selects a value that minimizes the number of conflicts with variables in the neighborhood [FRO 95, MEH 05b].

Recall that $\mathrm{con}(c)_{x=a}$ is the set of conflicts for (x, a) on c, i.e. $\mathrm{val}(c)_{x=a} \setminus \mathrm{sup}(c)_{x=a}$, or $\{\tau \in \prod_{y \in \mathrm{scp}(c)} \mathrm{dom}(y) \mid \tau[x] = a \land \tau \notin \mathrm{rel}(c)\}$. For a binary constraint c_{xy}, when considering strict supports $\mathrm{con}(c_{xy})_{x=a}$ is equivalent to $\{b \in \mathrm{dom}(y) \mid (a, b) \notin \mathrm{rel}(c_{xy})\}$, that is to say, the set of values in $\mathrm{dom}(y)$ that are incompatible with (x, a). For each v-value (x, a) the *min-conflicts* heuristic evaluates the conflict count:

$$cc(x, a) = \sum_{c \in \mathrm{cons}(P) \mid x \in \mathrm{scp}(c)} |\mathrm{con}(c)_{x=a}|$$

This heuristic selects a v-value (x, a) for which the conflict count $cc(x, a)$ is a minimum.

EXAMPLE.– Figure 9.3 shows an example in which the variable w is only involved in three binary constraints c_{wx}, c_{wy} and c_{wz}; lines indicate supports, i.e. compatibilities between w and its neighbors. By counting the number of values in the neighborhood of w that are incompatible with each value of $\mathrm{dom}(w)$, we obtain the order given by *min-conflicts*, namely b, c and a. If w is the variable selected by the variable ordering heuristic, then the v-value used for branching is (w, b).

The foregoing definition of the conflict count $cc(x, a)$ has been formulated for the general case, i.e. for constraints of any arity. Of course, other formulations can be imagined for the non-binary case (e.g. taking into account the arity of the constraints). Importantly, our formulation is correct as it simplifies into the one given classically

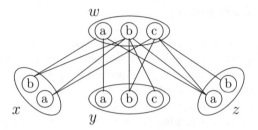

Figure 9.3. *A variable w involved in three binary constraints. We have*
$cc(w, a) = 1 + 2 + 1 = 4$, $cc(w, b) = 0 + 1 + 1 = 2$ *and* $cc(w, c) = 1 + 2 + 0 = 3$. *The*
order given by min-conflicts for w is then b, c and a

for binary constraints. Conflict counts can be computed dynamically for each variable each time a value must be assigned, or instead can be obtained during preprocessing initialization and then be used statically [MEH 05b]. Whereas *min-conflicts* selects a value with the smallest conflict count (perhaps after breaking ties), the anti-heuristic *max-conflicts* contrarily selects a value with the highest conflict count, thus complying with the fail-first principle.

The heuristics *lexico* and *random* can select variables, just as they can select values. In practice *lexico*, which selects the first value in the current domain of the selected variable, is often employed (e.g. in the version of Mistral in the 2008 constraint solver competition).

Finally, we may wonder whether it would be worthwhile to select v-values (x, a) globally during search because this would be appropriate for the basic mechanism of 2-way branching. Global selection would replace the separate selection of a variable and its value. Finding heuristics and efficient implementations of global selection remains an open challenge.

9.2. Adaptive heuristics

A search-guiding heuristic is said to be *adaptive* when it makes choices that depend on the current state of the problem instance as well as previous states. Thus an adaptive heuristic learns, in the sense that it takes account of information concerning the subtree already been explored. Figure 9.4 illustrates the fact that an adaptive heuristic may behave differently when two similar nodes (i.e. two nodes such that their associated constraint networks are identical) are reached after exploring different subtrees.

Static and non-adaptive dynamic (variable) ordering heuristics are relatively poor general-purpose heuristics. This section presents two adaptive heuristics that

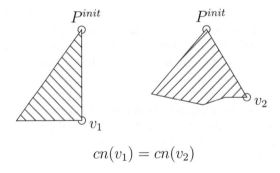

$$cn(v_1) = cn(v_2)$$

Figure 9.4. *Two partial search trees built from the same instance* P^{init}. *We have* v_1 *and* v_2 *representing similar nodes, i.e. nodes such that their associated constraint networks are identical. Unlike a static or dynamic variable ordering heuristic, an adaptive variable ordering heuristic can make a different selection at nodes* v_1 *and* v_2

can reasonably be considered to be state-of-the-art. The first is based on constraint weighting and the second uses the concept of impacts.

9.2.1. *Using constraint weighting*

This section starts by outlining some work related to *constraint weighting*, mainly in the context of local search and/or SAT solving. Then we show the importance of using information about constraint violations to demarcate inconsistent or hard parts of CSP instances. Finally, we introduce adaptive conflict-directed heuristics for complete backtrack search algorithms.

Dynamic weighting is an efficient adaptive mechanism for identifying hard parts of combinatorial problems. It was first introduced to improve the performance of local search methods. The breakout method [MOR 93] simply increases the weights of all current nogoods (tuples corresponding to unsatisfied constraints) whenever a local minimum is encountered, and then uses these weights to escape from local minima. Another method, devised independently [SEL 93], increments the weight of all clauses (of a propositional formula in conjunctive normal form) not satisfied by the current assignment. This weighting strategy (combined with two other strategies: random walk and averaging-in) has been shown to enhance dramatically the applicability of a randomized greedy local search procedure (GSAT) for propositional satisfiability testing. Thornton [THO 00] has studied constraint weighting in the context of applying local search to solve CSP instances, and has shown this weighting to be effective on structured problems, particularly when connections between constraints that are simultaneously violated are weighted.

A hybrid search technique in [MAZ 98] combines a GSAT-like procedure with the well known DP procedure. The branching strategy of the logically complete DP procedure is based on the dynamic constraint weighting managed by GSAT in order to direct search toward an inconsistent kernel. Similarly, a hybrid algorithm in [EID 03] solves CSP instances by combining the breakout method with a systematic backtrack search. When the local search is stopped (without finding any solution), all variables are sorted according to the constraint weights. We can then expect to prove efficiently the unsatisfiability of an instance (and to identify a minimal unsatisfiable subproblem). Clause weighting is also used in [BRU 00] to detect minimally unsatisfiable sub-formulae in SAT instances.

We now give an example that provides some insight into the main motivation of the approach presented in what follows. This example is based on the queens-knights problem that was introduced in section 8.5. To attempt identifying the inconsistent part of the qk-8-5-add instance, a counter is first associated with each constraint. Then the search algorithm MAC is run with *dom/ddeg* as variable ordering heuristic (and *lexico* as value ordering heuristic), and whenever the constraint propagation process finds that a constraint is not satisfied, the counter attached to this constraint is incremented by 1. We observe the maximum value of counters attached to queen constraints (i.e. constraints involving queens) and the maximum value of counters attached to knight constraints (i.e. constraints involving knights). Figure 9.5 shows the growth of these two values with respect to the number of assignments performed by MAC when proving the unsatisfiability of the instance involving eight queens

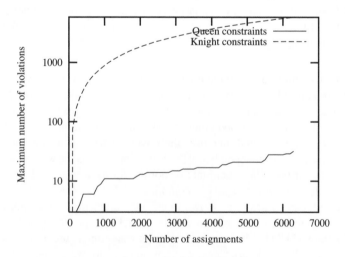

Figure 9.5. *Evolution of constraint violations when running MAC on the instance* qk-8-5-add *with dom/ddeg as variable ordering heuristic*

and five knights.[1] It is clear that some knight constraints are violated far more often than any queen constraint. In other words, these counters emphasize the inconsistent knights subproblem. This example illustrates and confirms that the number of times a constraint is violated during search is important information that can help to locate hard, or even inconsistent, part(s) of CSP instances.

Another illustration is provided by the instance composed-25-1-2-0 which comprises a main under-constrained sub-network and a small auxiliary unsatisfiable one. The auxiliary sub-network has eight variables, whose indices range from 25 to 32, and is connected to the main fragment by only one variable, as shown in Figure 9.6. Of course, intelligent backtracking and decomposition techniques would exploit such a structure efficiently, but in this section we are interested in a much simpler approach. Specifically, we show that weighting constraints provides a lazy way of discovering the small unsatisfiable core. As will be explained below, weighted degrees of variables are defined in terms of weights that are associated with constraints. After 100 variable assignments performed by MAC-*dom/ddeg* in our example, the weighted degrees of variables are as follows:

Variable	Weighted Degree
V31	40
V30	37
V29	36
V32	29
V6	19
V25	19
V20	17
...	

The four best ranked variables belong to the unsatisfiable auxiliary fragment.

As stated earlier, classical dynamic variable ordering heuristics use information about the current state of the instance being solved such as current domain sizes and dynamic degrees of variables. One limitation of these heuristics is that they do not use information about previous states of the search. Such information can be easily captured by associating a counter, denoted by $weight[c]$, with each constraint c. Whenever a dead-end (domain wipe-out) occurs, these counters are updated as follows.

---

1. A similar behavior can be observed when using *dom* or *bz* as variable ordering heuristic.

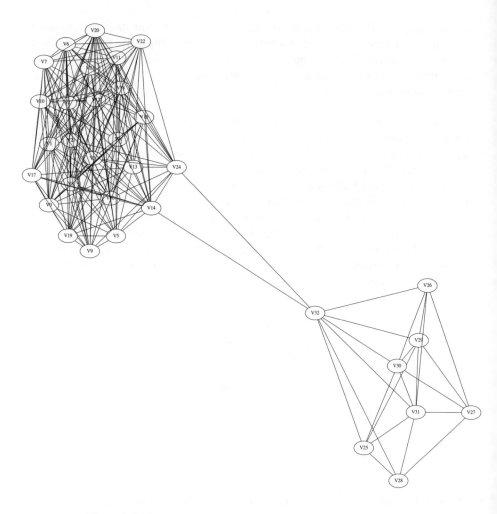

Figure 9.6. *The constraint graph of the instance* **composed-25-1-2-0**

For BC, lines 4 to 8 of Algorithm 72 are replaced with:

if *I does not satisfy c* **then**
  $weight[c] \leftarrow weight[c] + 1$
  if *lookback* $= SBT$ **then**
  | **return** *I*
  else
  | **return** $\{(y, b) \in I \mid y \in \mathrm{scp}(c)\}$

For FC and MAC, lines 4-5 of Algorithm 12 and lines 10-11 of Algorithm 9 are replaced with:

if $\text{dom}(y) = \emptyset$ **then**
$\quad$ $weight[c] \leftarrow weight[c] + 1$
$\quad$ **return** *false*

Using these counters, we define a new variable ordering heuristic, denoted by *wdeg*, which selects variables in sequence of decreasing $\alpha_{wdeg}(x)$. $\alpha_{wdeg}(x)$, which is called the *weighted degree* of an uninstantiated variable x (of a constraint network P) is defined as follows:

$$\alpha_{wdeg}(x) = \sum_{\substack{c \in \text{cons}(P) | x \in \text{scp}(c) \\ \wedge \, \text{scp}(c) \backslash \text{past}(P) \neq \{x\}}} weight[c]$$

Thus the weighted degree of a variable x is the sum of weights of constraints that involve x and at least another uninstantiated variable; recall that $\text{past}(P)$ denotes the set of instantiated (or past) variables of P, and is given by $\text{vars}(I)$ in Algorithm 70. The practical effect of selecting first the variables with greatest weighted degrees is to examine first the locally inconsistent or hard parts of networks, in conformity with the fail-first principle.

The *wdeg* heuristic is somewhat related to *ddeg* in that it only takes account of constraints that involve two uninstantiated variables. The reason of this limitation is that a constraint with only one uninstantiated variable is very likely to be entailed: at least, this will be the case for search algorithms FC and MAC. Entailed constraints are discarded because they no longer have any role to play (until a backtrack breaks entailment). Setting all *weight* counters to 1 makes *wdeg* the same as *ddeg*. Thus at the beginning of the search, to take account of degrees of variables, it is best to initialize all *weight* counters to 1. This initialization makes *wdeg* be initially the same as *ddeg*.

The next development combines weighted degrees and domain sizes to obtain the *dom/wdeg* heuristic, which selects first the variable having the smallest ratio of current domain size to current weighted degree. Both of the heuristics *wdeg* and *dom/wdeg* can be classified as *conflict-directed* (variable ordering) heuristics.

Amongst published heuristics that are related to the conflict-directed heuristics, those proposed in [SAD 96] are adapted to job-shop scheduling and are intended to focus the search toward critical variables, i.e. variables that are most likely to be involved in a conflict. For such problems the use of conflicting sets of operations [SAD 95] or measures of resource contention [SAD 96] is found experimentally to yield significant improvements.

9.2.2. *Using impacts*

Another family of adaptive heuristics is based on the concept of *impacts*. An impact is a measure of the effect of an assignment. More specifically, an impact is a measure of the relative amount of search space reduction that an assignment is expected to achieve. The impact of a variable is the "sum" of impacts of possible assignments to this variable. Impacts can be used in the heuristic selection of variables and values. The variable with highest impact is typically selected first. For this variable, the value with lowest impact is selected. It is important that impacts can be refined during search, allowing learning from experience. The use of impacts was studied initially in [GEE 92] and has been revisited in [REF 04] inspired by pseudo-costs that are widely used in integer programming.

Let σ denote a function that provides for any constraint network P a measure of the search space of P. The most precise measure is given by $\sigma_{mul}(P) = \prod_{x \in \text{vars}(P)} |\text{dom}(x)|$, which is the size of the Cartesian product of the domains of variables of the constraint network P. Another measure, which is less expensive to compute and does not involve big integers, is simply the total number of values in the constraint network: $\sigma_{add}(P) = \sum_{x \in \text{vars}(P)} |\text{dom}(x)|$.

The *impact of an assignment* $x = a$ on P with respect to a consistency ϕ is defined by:

$$Imp(x = a) = \frac{\sigma(P) - \sigma(\phi(P|_{x=a}))}{\sigma(P)}$$

This simply compares the size of the search space of P before and after assigning x to a and enforcing ϕ. Higher impact generally means greater reduction of the search space. At one extreme, if $\text{dom}(x) = \{a\}$ and P is already ϕ-consistent, then $Imp(x = a) = 0$. At the other extreme, if $\phi(P|_{x=a}) = \bot$, then $Imp(x = a) = 1$ assuming that $\sigma(\bot) = 0$ whatever the implementation of σ.

The *impact of a variable* x can be directly derived by summing, for example, impacts of assignments as follows:

$$Imp(x) = \sum_{a \in \text{dom}(x)} Imp(x = a)$$

If impact-based heuristics are used, the impact of an assignment $x = a$ may be assessed many times before reaching the current state of the search. Let $H_{x=a}$ be the multi-set of impacts successively measured for the assignment $x = a$ before reaching the current node in the search tree. An algorithm can compute for (almost) free an *average impact* [REF 04] of an assignment as follows:

$$Imp^{avg}(x = a) = \frac{\sum_{Imp \in H_{x=a}} Imp}{|H_{x=a}|}$$

Complying with the classical precept that the variable that most constrains the search space should be selected first, we can decide to select the variable with the highest average impact:

$$Imp^{\text{avg}}(x) = \sum_{a \in \text{dom}(x)} Imp^{\text{avg}}(x = a)$$

After a variable x has been selected, we can decide to select the value of $\text{dom}(x)$ that minimally constrains the search space. This is the value a in $\text{dom}(x)$ such that $Imp^{\text{avg}}(x = a)$ is a minimum. This process of selecting a v-value (x, a) for branching is not global since we have first the selection of the variable x and then the selection of the value a. These two consecutive tasks can be regarded as employing a variable ordering heuristic *var-impact* followed by a value ordering heuristic *val-impact*.

Impact-based search heuristics have many variants; heuristics can use different operators (e.g. sum, product, max, etc.) at different levels when computing impacts of variables. Although enumeration of all of these alternatives is beyond the scope of this book, some recent proposals deserve mention. Impacts defined in terms of recorded explanations [CAM 06] can measure the real effects of every decision taken during search. Moreover, the natural resonance between singleton consistencies and impact-based variable and value ordering heuristics has been investigated in [COR 07].

9.3. Strength of constraint weighting

Although adaptive heuristics seem to be quite attractive at first sight, their practical value remains to be proved. This section focuses on constraint weighting and shows that this can be quite useful to boost systematic search and to identify unsatisfiable CSP cores. We also explore kinds of policy that value ordering heuristics should follow. Finally, we introduce some recent new extensions and analysis.

9.3.1. *Boosting systematic search*

Again using the queens-knights problem, we now illustrate the use of constraint weighting to reduce thrashing and thereby boost the efficiency of (systematic) search. Figure 9.7 shows the CPU time required to solve some instances of this problem using dom/wdeg. Although IBT or DBT are more efficient than dom/wdeg on qk-n-5-add instances, the introduction of dom/wdeg makes thrashing far less prominent on the more realistic qk-n-5-mul instances: compare Figures 8.16(b) and 9.7(b).

Going further, Table 9.1 shows results obtained for two different chessboard sizes ($n = 8$ and $n = 12$) and for three different unsatisfiable problems. For each instance and each heuristic, the CPU time (in seconds), the number of constraint checks (ccks)

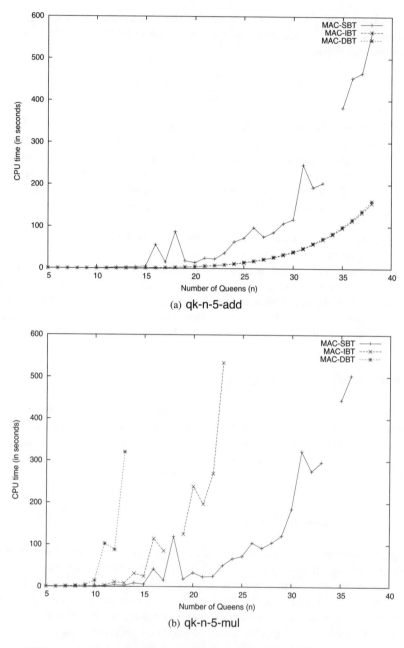

(a) qk-n-5-add

(b) qk-n-5-mul

Figure 9.7. *Solving qk-n-5-add and qk-n-5-mul instances using MAC-dom/wdeg and various backtracking techniques. A missing point indicates that the corresponding instance has not been solved within 600 seconds*

Instance		Heuristics			
		dom	*bz*	*ddeg/dom*	*wdeg/dom*
knights-8-5	CPU	0.08	0.08	0.09	0.09
	#ccks	70,432	70,432	70,432	75,828
	#nodes	63	63	63	93
qk-8-5-add	CPU	1.55	1.56	1.56	0.18
	#ccks	5,342 K	5,342 K	5,342 K	310 K
	#nodes	6,465	6,465	6,373	381
qk-8-5-mul	CPU	1.43	1.44	1.43	0.32
	#ccks	4,039 K	4,039 K	4,039 K	629 K
	#nodes	5,721	5,721	5,721	789
knights-12-5	CPU	0.17	0.16	0.16	0.19
	#ccks	352 K	352 K	352 K	382 K
	#nodes	143	143	143	213
qk-12-5-add	CPU	1,026	1,021	1,045	1.64
	#ccks	3,907 M	3,907 M	3,907 M	5,637 K
	#nodes	2,188 K	2,188 K	2,174 K	3,263
qk-12-5-mul	CPU	988	1,026	987	3.30
	#ccks	3,296 M	3,296 M	3,296 M	9,846 K
	#nodes	2,017 K	2,017 K	2,017 K	5,557

Table 9.1. *Comparison of heuristics using MAC on* **queens-knights** *instances*

and the number of assignments (nodes) are given. Here, knights-n-5 is an instance of the knights problem involving five knights to be put on a chessboard of size $n \times n$. It is clear that *dom/wdeg* drastically improves the performances of MAC compared to other heuristics. These results clearly show the occurrence of thrashing when using *dom*, *bz* or *dom/ddeg*: the number of assignments (and constraint checks) to solve a qk-n-5-add or a qk-n-5-mul instance is roughly equal to the product of the number of assignments (and constraint checks) to solve knights-n-5 and the number of solutions of the n-queens instance (92 for $n = 8$, and 14,200 for $n = 12$). This behavior is not observed when the conflict-directed heuristic *dom/wdeg* is used. In this case, after finding a limited number of solutions to the queens subproblem, the knight variables are selected first since the weight of the knight constraints become large enough, thereby preventing thrashing.

Binary branching allows search to adapt to evolving contexts more rapidly than non-binary branching, particularly when a conflict-directed heuristic is employed. This means that binary branching allows the search algorithm to push up hard parts of constraint networks faster than non-binary branching: decisions concerning these

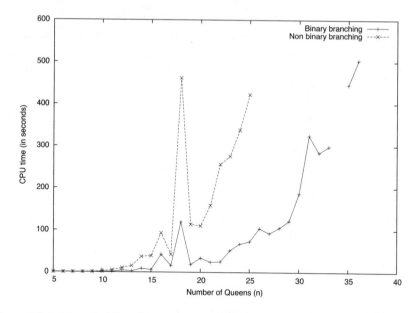

Figure 9.8. *Solving* qk-n-5-mul *instances using MAC-dom/wdeg while considering binary and non-binary branching*

parts are located faster near the root of the search tree. Figure 9.8 illustrates this for the queens-knights problem.

The robustness of heuristic *dom/wdeg* is best demonstrated by comparing it with classical heuristics on a wide range of problems. Figure 9.9 shows the results obtained on a large set of instances, including various series of random and structured instances, when using MAC with the adaptive heuristic *dom/wdeg* and with the classical heuristics *bz* and *dom/ddeg*. In these scatter plots, each dot represents an instance and each axis represents the CPU time required to solve the instances with MAC using the heuristic labeling the axis. Many dots are located on the right side of the plots, which means that *dom/wdeg* solves far more instances than *bz* and *dom/ddeg* within the allotted time.

9.3.2. *Identifying small unsatisfiable cores*

When a search algorithm (such as FC or MAC) that interleaves branching and propagation proves that a CSP instance is unsatisfiable, an unsatisfiable core (see section 2.2.2) can be extracted automatically. This can be done by keeping track of all constraints which, during propagation, have served to remove at least one value from

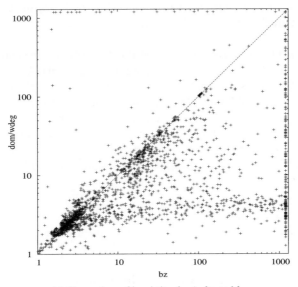

(a) Comparison of heuristics *dom/wdeg* and *bz*

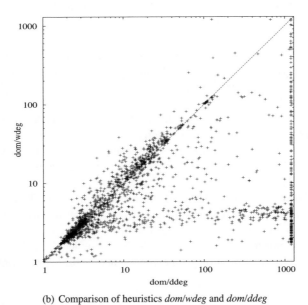

(b) Comparison of heuristics *dom/wdeg* and *dom/ddeg*

Figure 9.9. *Pairwise comparison (CPU time) of heuristics when used by MAC to solve the instances used as benchmarks (first round) of the 2006 constraint solver competition (time out set to 1000 seconds per instance)*

the domain of a variable. This idea was mentioned in [BAK 93] and can be related to the implication graph in SAT (e.g. see [MAR 96a, ZHA 03a]).

We now explain how to keep track of constraints involved in the removal of at least one value when, for instance, a general-purpose coarse-grained GAC algorithm is used within MAC. In this case, Algorithm 8 removes unsupported values from domains. We now introduce an additional data structure, denoted *active*, which associates a Boolean variable with each constraint. Before commencement of the search, all of these Booleans are initialized to *false*. During the search, whenever a constraint is involved in an effective revision, the Boolean associated with that constraint is set to *true*. This is achieved by replacing lines 2 to 4 of Algorithm 8 with:

> **foreach** *value* $a \in \text{dom}(x)$ **do**
> > **if** $\neg seekSupport(c, x, a)$ **then**
> > > remove a from $\text{dom}(x)$
> > > $active[c] \leftarrow true$ // c is involved in an effective revision

After the initial constraint network P^{init} has been proved unsatisfiable by MAC, it is only necessary to return the sub-network P^{sub} obtained by removing from P^{init} every constraint c such that $active[c]$ is *false*. Although the core P^{sub} is guaranteed to be unsatisfiable, it is not necessarily minimal; see Definition 2.13.

We have seen that using *dom/wdeg* leads to efficient proof of unsatisfiability of many instances. However, in order to obtain a proof of unsatisfiability of moderate size, we need to restart search several times to perform successive complete runs.

EXAMPLE.– Consider the queens-knights problem. The unsatisfiable instance qk-6-3-mul with six queens and three knights involves nine variables and 36 constraints. Actually we know that the 3-knights subproblem, involving three variables and three constraints, is unsatisfiable. In a first phase, solving this instance with MAC-*dom/wdeg* (i.e. MAC using *dom/wdeg* as variable ordering heuristic) yields a proof of unsatisfiability integrating all constraints of the instance (that is to say, all Boolean *active* have been set to *true*). However, solving the same instance again after reinitializing all Boolean *active* to *false*, and this time starting with current weighting of the constraints obtained after the first complete run, yields a new proof of unsatisfiability referring to only nine constraints. A further run yields the same result.

Figure 9.10 illustrates the developments of such proofs of unsatisfiability. Constraint networks are represented by constraint graphs; vertices correspond to variables and edges to binary constraints. Constraints irrelevant to unsatisfiability after a run are represented by gray-colored edges. This example shows that it is possible to refine the extraction of an unsatisfiable core by removing all the constraints that are not involved in it. The second phase starts with the unsatisfiable core identified during the first phase, and yields a new unsatisfiable core that corresponds to the 3-knights subproblem. The third phase cannot make any further reduction.

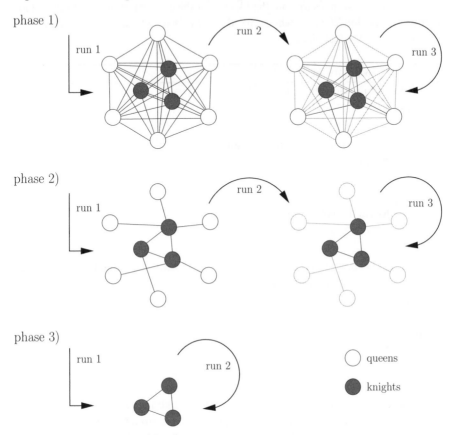

Figure 9.10. *Evolution of the proof of unsatisfiability*

As illustrated above, several runs of a MAC solver may be required to demarcate an unsatisfiable core provided that a conflict-directed heuristic such as *dom/wdeg* is used. In Algorithm 76, the outer loop performs several extraction phases as mentioned in the illustration. When a phase starts, all weights are first initialized to be 1. During each iteration of the inner loop, MAC-*dom/wdeg* is run at line 10 and line 11 obtains the number of constraints found in the unsatisfiable core detected by the current run. The *weight* counters are preserved from one iteration (i.e. run) to the next, which potentially concentrates the search into a smaller and smaller unsatisfiable core. Two iterations of the inner loop are guaranteed by initializing n^{aft} to $+\infty$; MAC is given the opportunity to benefit from a good initialization of constraint weights. The inner loop stops when the size of the current unsatisfiable core is greater than or equal to the size of the previous one. At line 13, an unsatisfiable core is identified, but if $n^{\text{aft}} > n^{\text{bef}}$, we will certainly prefer to obtain the last but one identified core; although not shown here, it suffices to store the identity of the constraints active at the previous iteration. Algorithm 76 stops when a fixed point is reached, i.e. when no reduction is achieved during the last phase.

Algorithm 76: wcore(**in** P: $\mathscr{P}$): $\mathscr{P}$

    Output: an unsatisfiable core of P

1 **repeat**
2      $n^{\text{cur}} \leftarrow |\operatorname{vars}(P)|$
3   **foreach** *constraint* $c \in \operatorname{cons}(P)$ **do**
4          $\lfloor$ *weight*$[c] \leftarrow 1$
5      $n^{\text{aft}} \leftarrow +\infty$
6   **repeat**
7   **foreach** *constraint* $c \in \operatorname{cons}(P)$ **do**
8              $\lfloor$ *active*$[c] \leftarrow$ *false*
9          $n^{\text{bef}} \leftarrow n^{\text{aft}}$
10   MAC-*dom/wdeg*(P) // active constraints are identified
11          $n^{\text{aft}} \leftarrow |\{c \in \operatorname{cons}(P) \mid active[c]\}|$
12   **until** $n^{\text{aft}} \geq n^{\text{bef}}$
13      $P \leftarrow (\operatorname{vars}(P), \{c \in \operatorname{cons}(P) \mid active[c]\})$
14 **until** $n^{\text{aft}} = n^{\text{cur}}$
15 **return** P

Performing successive runs of a complete backtrack search, with constraint weighting, to demarcate an inconsistent part of a constraint network turns out to be quite efficient in practice [HEM 06]. This has also been found for propositional satisfiability (SAT), where Bruni and Sassano [BRU 00] have proposed an "adaptive core search" to recover a small unsatisfiable sub-formula.

9.3.3. *Questioning heuristic policies*

Much work supports selection of values in accordance with the promise policy, which selects first the value that has the highest probability (estimated in various ways) of being part of a solution. In this section we challenge the practical value of this policy, which has previously been supported mainly by experimental results with non-binary branching and/or non-adaptive variable heuristics (such as *dom*, *bz* and *dom/ddeg*). We now report experimental results using MAC, testing both branching schemes and also testing dynamic and adaptive variable ordering heuristics. These were experiments on seven classes of random binary instances located at the phase transition, which is where about half of the instances are satisfiable. Section 2.1.4.1 provides a description of these classes.

Tables 9.2 and 9.3 show results obtained with the classical value ordering heuristic *min-conflicts* and the anti-heuristic *max-conflicts*. These experiments have used static value ordering heuristics [MEH 05b], which means that the order of values is computed in a preprocessing step. Tables 9.2 and 9.3 show average CPU time (in seconds), average number of constraint checks (ccks) and the average number of nodes explored in the search tree. What is interesting to note is that while the performance ratio of *max-conflicts* to *min-conflicts* usually lies between 1.1 and 1.3 with non-binary branching or with *dom/ddeg*, it falls to around 1 when binary branching and *dom/wdeg* are used. The class $\langle 40,80,103,0.8 \rangle$ is a notable exception. Note also that the proportion of constraint checks per visited node is smaller when *max-conflicts* is used. This is natural because when conflicting values are selected first, the size of the search space is reduced faster.

These results show that, on these random instances, the anti-promise heuristic *max-conflicts* is often as efficient as the standard promise *min-conflicts* heuristic when binary branching and *dom/wdeg* are used. Our understanding of this phenomenon is that, since *dom/wdeg* efficiently refutes unsatisfiable subtrees, the overhead of refuting more unsatisfiable subtrees (since, more often than not, we guide search toward unsatisfiable subtrees) is compensated by the benefit of rapidly reducing the search space. Although *max-conflicts* may be helpful to *dom/wdeg* for quickly refuting unsatisfiable subtrees, it is certainly unhelpful when solution(s) can still be reached. Should we try to develop hybrid procedures able to switch between *min-conflicts* and *max-conflicts* during search?

9.3.4. *Statistical analysis and extensions*

Hulubei and O'Sullivan [HUL 06b] study the effect of variable and value ordering heuristics on the heavy-tailedness of runtime distributions of backtrack search algorithms; see section 10.1.1 for more information about heavy-tailedness. This work shows that heavy-tailed behavior can be eliminated from particular classes of problems by carefully selecting the search heuristics. Statistical arguments conclude that the combination of *dom/wdeg* with *min-conflicts* is the best (tested) combination for some random and quasi-group problems. The heuristic *dom/wdeg* is also found to be the best among those tested in [HUL 06a], "not because it makes the smallest number of mistakes or because it refutes them with less effort but because it strikes a good balance between these two properties".

Whereas *dom/wdeg* collects information in the course of search, another idea [GRI 07] is to learn similar information during an initial phase in which variables are chosen at random and the search is repeatedly run to a fixed cutoff. This *random*

Class		dom/ddeg			dom/wdeg		
		min-conflicts	max-conflicts	ratio	min-conflicts	max-conflicts	ratio
⟨40-8-753-0.1⟩	CPU	42.0	51.4	1.22	34.5	41.6	1.20
	ccks	22 M	27 M	1.22	20 M	24 M	1.20
	nodes	43,269	55,558	1.28	38,104	48,158	1.59
⟨40-11-414-0.2⟩	CPU	30.9	35.0	1.13	29.4	32.7	1.11
	ccks	26 M	29 M	1.11	26 M	29 M	1.11
	nodes	58,955	70,007	1.18	58,055	67,905	1.17
⟨40-16-250-0.35⟩	CPU	22.1	28.9	1.30	21.0	26.6	1.26
	ccks	30 M	40 M	1.33	30 M	37 M	1.23
	nodes	59,669	83,445	1.39	56,036	75,025	1.33
⟨40-25-180-0.5⟩	CPU	33.1	37.1	1.12	28.6	30.0	1.04
	ccks	62 M	67 M	1.08	55 M	57 M	1.03
	nodes	85,122	98,519	1.15	69,805	78,005	1.11
⟨40-40-135-0.65⟩	CPU	25.9	34.6	1.33	20.0	25.1	1.25
	ccks	68 M	89 M	1.30	53 M	66 M	1.24
	nodes	52,622	74,592	1.41	36,571	49,211	1.34
⟨40-80-103-0.8⟩	CPU	25.8	52.8	2.04	15.3	36.3	2.37
	ccks	98 M	193 M	1.96	59 M	133 M	2.25
	nodes	29,989	72,841	2.42	16,163	45,177	2.79
⟨40-180-84-0.9⟩	CPU	113.1	121.3	1.07	40.6	44.6	1.09
	ccks	554 M	587 M	1.05	217 M	231 M	1.06
	nodes	76,788	85,482	1.11	20,077	22,557	1.12

Table 9.2. *MAC with non-binary branching, dom/ddeg and dom/wdeg*

Class		dom/ddeg			dom/wdeg		
		min-conflicts	max-conflicts	ratio	min-conflicts	max-conflicts	ratio
⟨40-8-753-0.1⟩	CPU	29.3	35.8	1.22	28.9	28.4	0.98
	ccks	22 M	27 M	1.22	24 M	23 M	0.95
	nodes	43,268	55,557	1.28	45,650	46,645	1.02
⟨40-11-414-0.2⟩	CPU	23.0	25.9	1.12	26.1	27.3	1.04
	ccks	26 M	29 M	1.11	32 M	33 M	1.03
	nodes	59,002	70,026	1.18	69,111	76,941	1.11
⟨40-16-250-0.35⟩	CPU	18.5	24.5	1.32	23.0	24.4	1.06
	ccks	30 M	40 M	1.33	39 M	41 M	1.05
	nodes	59,773	83,531	1.18	72,555	82,459	1.13
⟨40-25-180-0.5⟩	CPU	28.8	31.9	1.33	28.5	30.7	1.07
	ccks	62 M	67 M	1.08	65 M	68 M	1.04
	nodes	85,187	98,548	1.15	80,017	91,464	1.14
⟨40-40-135-0.65⟩	CPU	21.4	28.6	1.33	19.8	19.6	0.98
	ccks	68 M	89 M	1.30	65 M	64 M	0.98
	nodes	52,569	74,544	1.41	44,120	46,573	1.05
⟨40-80-103-0.8⟩	CPU	20.4	42.3	2.07	12.6	18.6	1.47
	ccks	98 M	193 M	1.96	64 M	89 M	1.39
	nodes	29,931	72,747	1.41	16,168	28,087	1.73
⟨40-180-84-0.9⟩	CPU	85.0	92.0	1.08	26.4	27.1	1.02
	ccks	553 M	587 M	1.06	192 M	193 M	1.00
	nodes	76,489	85,255	1.11	15,835	16,566	1.04

Table 9.3. *MAC with binary branching, dom/ddeg and dom/wdeg*

probing method is intended to start the "real" search better informed after gathering information from different parts of the search space. Besides, this method allows more efficient identification of sources of global contention, i.e. contention that holds across the entire search space, as opposed to contention localized in some parts of the search space. To characterize weighted degree heuristics the *contention* principle [WAL 08] states: "If a constraint is identified as a source of contention, then a variable associated with that constraint is more likely to cause failure after instantiation than variables not associated with such a constraint". By instantiating at the beginning of search the variables associated with global contention, we are most likely to reduce the overall search effort.

Some variants are also studied in [BAL 08b]. By noting the constraint responsible of each value deletion (a kind of explanation), it is possible to implement different weighting strategies. For example, whenever there is a domain wipe-out on a variable x while propagating constraint c, the weight of every constraint responsible for the removal of a value of x is incremented. Another variant uses an aging mechanism, as in some SAT solvers, which periodically divides the value of all weights by a constant, thereby giving greater importance to conflicts discovered recently. Surprisingly, the "basic" *dom/wdeg* heuristic is still competitive with such attractive variants. The same authors show that constraint weighting can also be used to select the order of the different revisions performed when enforcing/maintaining arc consistency using a generic coarse-grained GAC algorithm. New revision ordering heuristics based on weighted degrees can improve the resolution of some hard instances [BAL 08a]. Note that any new revision ordering, combined with constraint weighting, may have a different search tree.

Finally, to show the importance of adaptive heuristics, simply note that all of the best ranked CSP solvers in the 2008 constraint solver competition have as their variable ordering heuristic either *dom/wdeg*, or a variant of it, or a combination of it with *impact*.

9.4. Guiding search to culprit decisions

As shown in the previous section, the conflict-directed heuristic *dom/wdeg* is effective for reducing thrashing. This heuristic complies with the fail-first precept: "To succeed, try first where you are most likely to fail". But finding the ideal ordering of variables is generally intractable. Even when efficient heuristics are used, we may sometimes be able to do better by seeking the reason for a dead-end. A dead-end is due to (at least) a conflict between a subset of previous decisions. To prevent thrashing, it is helpful to identify such a conflict set and to consider the most recent decision participating in it, called here *culprit decision*. Once the culprit has been identified, the search can safely jump back to it, as in look-back techniques such as CBJ and DBT.

This section presents a general scheme [LEC 06b] for identifying a culprit decision in any sequence of decisions leading to a dead-end. This is made possible by introducing a specific set of variables, called a *testing-set*. The idea is to determine the largest prefix of the sequence of decisions such that there exists an instantiation of all variables in the testing-set that does not yield domain wipe-out when a given consistency is enforced. In a simple embodiment of this general scheme the testing-set consists of the single variable involved in the last decision taken at a dead-end; this is what is called *last-conflict based reasoning*, or LC for short.

LC is an original approach that allows the search to backtrack (indirectly) to a culprit decision that caused the most recent dead-end. To achieve this, the last assigned variable before reaching a dead-end is always the next variable to be selected, so long as its successive assignments make the network inconsistent. More precisely, LC checks the singleton ϕ-consistency of this variable from the dead-end toward the root of the search tree until a value is found to be singleton ϕ-consistent, where ϕ denotes the consistency maintained during search. Here the usual variable ordering heuristic is over-ridden until the search has backtracked to the culprit decision and has found a singleton ϕ-consistent value for the variable involved in the culprit decision. In fact LC can be generalized by successively adding to the current testing-set the variable involved in the last detected culprit decision. The intention is to build a testing-set that may improve backtracking higher, i.e. nearer the root of the search tree. This mechanism hopefully identifies a (small) set of incompatible variables involved in decisions of the current branch, despite many interleaved decisions that are irrelevant. The practical effect is to avoid useless exploration of many subtrees.

The section is organized as follows. After introducing the principle of nogood identification through testing-sets, we present last-conflict based reasoning and its generalization. Finally, we provide some experimental results to show the value of the approach.

9.4.1. *Nogood identification through testing-sets*

We first present a general approach that uses a testing-set, which is a pre-established set of variables, to identify a nogood from a so-called *dead-end sequence* of decisions. By carefully selecting the testing-set, we aim to identify a nogood that is smaller than the dead-end sequence itself.

DEFINITION 9.1.– *[Dead-end Sequence] Let P be a constraint network, and let $\Sigma = \langle \delta_1, \ldots, \delta_i \rangle$ be a sequence of decisions on P. Σ is said to be a* dead-end sequence *of P iff $\{\delta_1, \ldots, \delta_i\}$ is a nogood of P.*

We can now introduce the notions of *culprit decision* and *culprit subsequence*. The culprit decision of a dead-end sequence $\Sigma = \langle \delta_1, \ldots, \delta_i \rangle$ with respect to a testing-set

X of variables and a consistency ϕ is the rightmost decision δ_j in Σ such that there is no instantiation of X with which decisions of $\langle \delta_1, \ldots, \delta_j \rangle$ can be extended without ϕ detecting an inconsistency. More formally:

DEFINITION 9.2.– *[Pivot, Culprit Decision, Testing-set] Let P be a constraint network, with $\Sigma = \langle \delta_1, \ldots, \delta_i \rangle$ a sequence of decisions on P. Let ϕ be a consistency, and let $X = \{x_1, \ldots, x_k\}$ be a non-empty set of variables of P.*

– A pivot *of Σ wrt ϕ and X is a decision $\delta_j \in \Sigma$ such that $\exists a_1 \in \mathrm{dom}(x_1),$ $\ldots, \exists a_k \in \mathrm{dom}(x_k) \mid \phi(P|_{\{\delta_1,\ldots,\delta_{j-1}\}\cup\{\neg\delta_j\}\cup\{x_1=a_1,\ldots,x_k=a_k\}}) \neq \bot.$*

– The rightmost pivot subsequence *of Σ wrt ϕ and X is either the empty sequence $\langle \rangle$ if there is no pivot of Σ wrt ϕ and X, or the sequence $\langle \delta_1, \ldots, \delta_j \rangle$, where δ_j is the rightmost pivot of Σ wrt ϕ and X.*

If Σ is a dead-end sequence then the rightmost pivot (if it exists) of Σ wrt ϕ and X is called the culprit decision *of Σ wrt ϕ and X, and the rightmost pivot subsequence of Σ wrt ϕ and X is called the* culprit subsequence *of Σ wrt ϕ and X. The set of variables X is called a* testing-set.

In the definition of pivots there are three subsets of decisions: the first $j - 1$ decisions of Σ are taken as they are, the jth decision of Σ is taken negated, and the third subset is an instantiation of the testing-set.

EXAMPLE.– Suppose that $\Sigma = \langle x = a, y \neq b, z = c, y \neq c, y = a \rangle$, $\phi = AC$ and $X = \{v, w\}$. Suppose also that $x = a$ and $z = c$ are the only pivots of Σ wrt AC and X. This means that for the pivot $x = a$ there is at least one instantiation I of X such that $AC(P|_{\{x\neq a\}\cup I}) \neq \bot$. For the pivot $z = c$ there is another instantiation I' of X such that $AC(P|_{\{x=a,y\neq b\}\cup\{z\neq c\}\cup I'}) \neq \bot$. In this case $z = c$ is the culprit decision of Σ wrt AC and X, and $\langle x = a, y \neq b, z = c \rangle$ is the culprit subsequence of Σ wrt AC and X.

As expected intuitively, a culprit subsequence of a dead-end sequence is a nogood.

PROPOSITION 9.3.– *Let P be a constraint network, with $\Sigma = \langle \delta_1, \ldots, \delta_i \rangle$ a dead-end sequence of P. Let ϕ be a consistency, and let $X \subseteq \mathrm{vars}(P)$ be a testing-set. The set of decisions contained in the culprit subsequence of Σ wrt ϕ and X is a nogood of P.*

It is important that the newly identified nogood may be the same as the original one. This is the case when the culprit decision of a sequence $\Sigma = \langle \delta_1, \ldots, \delta_i \rangle$ is δ_i. Note also that P is unsatisfiable if the culprit subsequence of Σ is empty.

To see how Proposition 9.3 can be useful in practice, recall that the complete set of decisions leading to a dead-end in a search tree is a nogood. Proposition 9.3 enables detection of smaller nogoods for use in backjumping. In fact there are as many ways to achieve this task as there are different testing-sets. Backjumping capability will depend upon the policy adopted for defining the testing-sets. Different policies can be introduced to identify the source of conflicts and so to reduce thrashing, as discussed in next section.

9.4.2. *Reasoning from the last conflict*

The rest of this chapter works with a binary branching backtrack search algorithm (e.g. MAC) enforcing a consistency ϕ at each node of the search tree. A simple embodiment of the general scheme presented in the previous section has a testing-set that consists of the single variable involved in the last decision taken at a dead-end. This embodiment is called *last-conflict based reasoning* (LC).

An *LC-subsequence* is a culprit subsequence identified by last-conflict based reasoning. For any decision δ, var(δ) denotes the variable involved in δ.

DEFINITION 9.4.– *[LC-testing-set, LC-subsequence] Let P be a constraint network, let $\Sigma = \langle \delta_1, \ldots, \delta_i \rangle$ be a dead-end sequence of P with $x_i = var(\delta_i)$, and let ϕ be a consistency.*

– *The* LC-testing-set *of Σ is the set $\{x_i\}$.*

– *The* LC-subsequence *of Σ wrt ϕ is the culprit subsequence of Σ wrt ϕ and $\{x_i\}$.*

Thus the LC-subsequence of a dead-end sequence Σ ends with the most recent decision such that, when this is negated, there exists a singleton ϕ-consistent value in the domain of the variable involved in the last decision in Σ. The culprit decision δ_j of Σ may possibly be a negative decision and/or may be the last decision in Σ. In the second case, $j = i$, and we can find a value for x_i (the variable involved in the last decision of Σ) that is compatible with all other decisions of Σ. Specifically, if $j = i$ and δ_i is a culprit negative decision $x_i \neq a_i$, then $\phi(P|_{\{\delta_1,\ldots,\delta_{i-1},x_i=a_i\}}) \neq \bot$. On the other hand, if $j = i$ and δ_i is a culprit positive decision $x_i = a_i$, then there exists a value $a_i' \neq a_i$ in dom(x_i) such that $\phi(P|_{\{\delta_1,\ldots,\delta_{i-1},x_i\neq a_i,x_i=a_i'\}}) = \phi(P|_{\{\delta_1,\ldots,\delta_{i-1},x_i=a_i'\}}) \neq \bot$.

LC allows identification of nogoods as shown by the following proposition. Note that the set of decisions contained in an LC-subsequence is not necessarily a minimal nogood.

PROPOSITION 9.5.– *Let P be a constraint network, with Σ a dead-end sequence of P, and let ϕ be a consistency. The set of decisions contained in the LC-subsequence of Σ wrt ϕ is a nogood of P.*

Proof. Let δ_i be the last decision of Σ and $x_i = var(\delta_i)$. From Definition 9.4, the LC-subsequence of Σ wrt ϕ is the culprit subsequence of Σ wrt ϕ and $\{x_i\}$. We deduce our result from Proposition 9.3 with $X = \{x_i\}$. □

It is important that after each conflict encountered during search it is possible to identify an LC-subsequence and "backjump"[2] safely to the last decision therein. The identification and exploitation of such a sequence (which basically represents a nogood) can be easily incorporated into the backtrack search algorithm by making a simple modification to the variable ordering heuristic. In practice, we propose to use last-conflict based reasoning only when an opened node, that is to say, a positive decision, lies at a dead-end. In other words, LC will be used only if δ_i (the last decision of the sequence mentioned in Definition 9.4) is a positive decision. To implement LC in this case, it is sufficient (i) to register the variable whose assignment to a given value directly leads to an inconsistency, and (ii) always select this variable first in subsequent decisions (so long as it cannot be instantiated), over-riding the selection made by the underlying heuristic – whichever heuristic is used. Note that LC does not require any additional data structures.

With this implementation, note that only positive decisions are "checked" as pivots by the search algorithm. When a negative decision is refuted (i.e. when the right subtree of a node has been entirely explored), backtracking occurs immediately. This means that LC within a backtrack search algorithm may indirectly identify a shorter dead-end subsequence. More precisely, the longest prefix of the LC-subsequence ending with a positive decision will be "computed".

Figure 9.11 illustrates last-conflict based reasoning. The leftmost branch on the figure has positive decisions $x_1 = a_1, \ldots, x_i = a_i$, such that $x_i = a_i$ leads to a conflict. With ϕ denoting the consistency maintained during search, we have: $\phi(P|_{\{x_1=a_1,\ldots,x_i=a_i\}}) = \bot$. At this point, x_i is registered by LC for future use, i.e. the LC-testing-set is $\{x_i\}$. As a consequence, a_i is removed from $\mathrm{dom}(x_i)$, i.e. $x_i \neq a_i$. Then, instead of consulting the usual variable ordering heuristic to select a new variable, a new value is directly assigned to x_i. In Figure 9.11 this leads once again to a conflict, the value is removed from $\mathrm{dom}(x_i)$, and the process loops until all values are removed from $\mathrm{dom}(x_i)$, leading to a domain wipe-out (symbolized by a triangle labeled with x_i whose base is drawn using a solid line). The algorithm then backtracks to the assignment $x_{i-1} = a_{i-1}$, going to the right branch $x_{i-1} \neq a_{i-1}$. Because x_i is still recorded by LC, it is now selected first, and all values of $\mathrm{dom}(x_i)$ are excluded due to the same process as above. The algorithm finally backtracks to the decision $x_j = a_j$, going to the right branch $x_j \neq a_j$. Then, as $\{x_i\}$ is still an active LC-testing-set, x_i is preferred again and the values of $\mathrm{dom}(x_i)$ are tested. This time one value does not lead to a conflict (symbolized by a triangle labeled with x_i whose base is drawn using a dotted line), so the search can continue with a new assignment for x_i. The variable x_i is then unregistered (the testing-set becomes empty), and the choice of subsequent decisions is left to the underlying heuristic, until the next conflict occurs.

---

2. We propose a lazy form of backjumping, obtained after a controlled search effort.

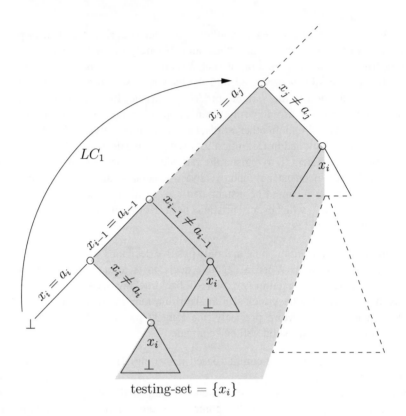

testing-set $= \{x_i\}$

Figure 9.11. *Last-conflict based reasoning illustrated with a partial search tree. A consistency φ is maintained at each node. A triangle labeled with a variable x_i and drawn using a solid base line (resp. a dotted base line) represents the fact that no (resp. a) singleton φ-consistent value exists for x_i*

EXAMPLE.– In a more concrete example, a constraint network has six variables $\{x_1, \ldots, x_6\}$, an entailed binary constraint on variables $\{x_2, x_3\}$, the domain of each of these being $\{1, 2\}$, and a clique of inequation constraints on variables $\{x_1, x_4, x_5, x_6\}$, the domain of each of these being $\{0, 1, 2\}$. Figure 9.12 shows the compatibility graph of this constraint network. Although the introduction of entailed constraints seems weird, it can really happen during search after some decisions have been taken. This phenomenon, as well as the presence of several connected components, frequently occurs when solving structured instances (e.g. RLFAP instances). Figure 9.13 shows the MAC search tree where variables and values are selected in lexicographic order, which is used here to facilitate understanding of the example; other heuristics yield similar examples. In Figure 9.13, each branch that has no child shown represents direct failure when arc consistency is enforced. Here, MAC explores 33 nodes to prove that this problem instance is unsatisfiable. Figure 9.14

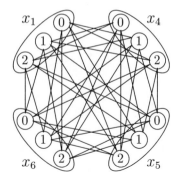

Figure 9.12. *The compatibility graph of a constraint network involving an entailed constraint and a clique of inequation constraints*

depicts the MAC-LC search tree using the same lexicographic order, where MAC-LC denotes MAC equipped with last-conflict based reasoning. This time, MAC-LC only explores nine nodes because reasoning from the last conflict allows search to focus on the difficult part of the network (i.e. the clique of inequation constraints). For example, the first failure occurs (leftmost branch), just after assigning the variable x_4. The reason of this failure is x_1 since it is impossible to assign both variables without detecting inconsistency when enforcing arc consistency. Reasoning from explanations would justify a direct backjump to x_1. To some extent, LC behaves similarly since it backtracks up to x_1 after a controlled search effort.

Reasoning from last conflict can be implemented by a slight modification of a classical tree search algorithm; see Algorithm 77. The recursive function binary-ϕ-search-LC must be called with a ϕ-consistent constraint network. Thus the initial call must be binary-ϕ-search-LC($\phi(P^{\text{init}})$) where P^{init} is the initial constraint network that needs to be solved. Remember that even if $P = \bot$, P is considered to be ϕ-consistent. To implement LC, we only need to introduce a variable *priority*. When its value is *nil*, this means that the LC-testing-set is empty. Otherwise this identifies the single variable in the LC-testing-set.

By using an operator that enforces ϕ to identify LC-subsequences as described above, we obtain the following complexity result:

PROPOSITION 9.6.– *Let P be a constraint network, let ϕ be a consistency, and let $\Sigma = \langle \delta_1, \ldots, \delta_i \rangle$ be a dead-end sequence of P. The worst-case time complexity of computing the LC-subsequence of Σ wrt ϕ is $O(id\gamma)$ where γ is the worst-case time complexity of enforcing ϕ.*

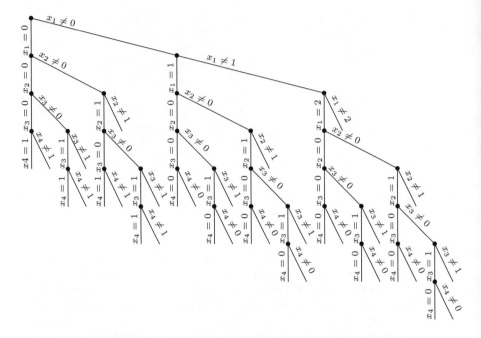

Figure 9.13. *Search tree built by MAC (33 explored nodes)*

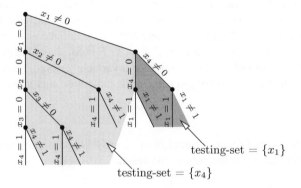

Figure 9.14. *Search tree built by MAC-LC (9 explored nodes)*

Algorithm 77: binary-ϕ-search-LC(P: $\mathscr{P}$): Boolean

Require: P is ϕ-consistent
Output: *true* iff P is satisfiable

1   **if** $P = \bot$ **then**
2 | **return** *false*
3   **if** $\forall x \in \mathrm{vars}(P), |\,\mathrm{dom}(x)| = 1$ **then**
      | // display the solution
4 | **return** *true*
5   **if** *priority* $\neq$ *nil* **then**
6 | $x \leftarrow priority$
7   **else**
8 | $x \leftarrow variableOrderingHeuristic.selectVariable()$
9   $a \leftarrow valueOrderingHeuristic.selectValueFor(x)$
10   **if** $\phi(P|_{x=a}) = \bot$ **then**
11 | $priority \leftarrow x$
12   **else**
13 | $priority \leftarrow nil$
14   **return** *binary-ϕ-search-LC($\phi(P|_{x=a})$) $\vee$ binary-ϕ-search-LC($\phi(P|_{x\neq a})$)*

Proof. The worst case is when the computed LC-subsequence of Σ is empty. In this case for each decision we check the singleton ϕ-consistency of x_i, which is the variable involved in δ_i. Because checking the singleton ϕ-consistency of a variable corresponds to at most d calls to a ϕ-enforcing algorithm, the worst-case time complexity is id times the complexity of the ϕ algorithm, denoted by γ here. Hence the overall time complexity $O(id\gamma)$. $\square$

When LC is embedded in MAC, we obtain:

COROLLARY 9.7.– *Let P be a binary constraint network and $\Sigma = \langle \delta_1, \ldots, \delta_i \rangle$ be a dead-end sequence of decisions that corresponds to a branch built by MAC-LC. Assuming that the current LC-testing-set is $\{var(\delta_i)\}$, the worst-case time complexity, for MAC-LC, to backtrack up to the last decision of the LC-subsequence of Σ wrt AC is $O(end^3)$.*

Proof. Because MAC makes positive decisions first, the number of opened nodes in a branch of the search tree is at most n. Moreover, for each closed node, we do not check the singleton arc consistency of $x_i = var(\delta_i)$ since instead we backtrack directly. So, using an optimal AC algorithm in $O(ed^2)$, the overall complexity is $O(end^3)$. $\square$

To summarize, reasoning from the last conflict is a way of reducing thrashing by considering culprit decisions taken in the past, while still being a look-ahead technique (combined with a very limited form of learning, namely recording variables in testing-sets). Guiding search to the last decision of a culprit subsequence is like using a form of backjumping to that decision. For example, when a backjump to a culprit decision occurs with Gaschnig's technique [GAS 79], then LC, in the same context, also reaches this decision in polynomial time. Table 9.4 shows the behavior of LC on two instances of the queens-knights problem. With bz as variable ordering heuristic, MAC, MAC-IBT and MAC-DBT cannot prevent thrashing for the qk-25-5-mul instance which remains unsolved after 2 hours. This is also the case when other classical variable ordering heuristics are used, but not for the adaptive $dom/wdeg$. However, MAC-LC can in about one minute prove the unsatisfiability of this instance. The reason is that all values of all knight variables are SAC-inconsistent. When any such variable is reached, LC guides search up to the root of the search tree.

Instance		MAC	MAC-IBT	MAC-DBT	MAC-LC
qk-25-5-add	CPU	> 2 hours	11.7	12.5	58.9
	#nodes	–	703	691	10,053
qk-25-5-mul	CPU	> 2 hours	> 2 hours	> 2h hours	66.6
	#nodes	–	–	–	9,922

Table 9.4. *Cost of running variants of MAC with bz as variable ordering heuristic (time-out set to 2 hours)*

We have explained that in the last-conflict based approach, the variable ordering heuristic is over-ridden until a backtrack to the culprit variable has been completed and a singleton consistent value has been found. There is an alternative approach that does not select the singleton consistent value, which has been found, to be the next value assigned. This approach is a pure inference technique that (partially) maintains a singleton consistency (SAC, for example) on the variable involved in the last conflict. This is related to the "quick shaving" technique [LHO 05a].

9.4.3. Generalized reasoning from the last conflict

To define testing-sets, the policy previously introduced can be generalized as follows. At each dead-end the testing-set initially consists, as before, of the variable x_i involved in the most recent decision δ_i. When the culprit decision δ_j is identified, the variable x_j involved in δ_j is included in the testing-set. The new testing-set $\{x_i, x_j\}$ may help backtracking nearer the root of the search tree. Of course, this form of reasoning can be extended recursively. This mechanism is intended to identify a (small) set of incompatible variables involved in decisions of the current branch, although these may be interleaved with many irrelevant decisions. We now formalize this approach before illustrating it.

DEFINITION 9.8.– *[LC$_k$-testing-set, LC$_k$-subsequence] Let P be a constraint network, Σ be a dead-end sequence of P and ϕ be a consistency. We recursively define the kth LC-testing-set and kth LC-subsequence of Σ wrt ϕ, which are respectively called the LC$_k$-testing-set (X_k) and the LC$_k$-subsequence (Σ_k), as follows.*

    – For $k = 1$, X_1 and Σ_1 correspond to the LC-testing-set of Σ and the LC-subsequence of Σ wrt ϕ, respectively.

    – For $k > 1$, if $\Sigma_{k-1} = \langle\rangle$, then $X_k = X_{k-1}$ and $\Sigma_k = \Sigma_{k-1}$. Otherwise, $X_k = X_{k-1} \cup \{x_{k-1}\}$ where x_{k-1} is the variable involved in the last decision of Σ_{k-1}, and Σ_k is the rightmost pivot subsequence of Σ_{k-1} wrt ϕ and X_k.

The following proposition, which is a generalization of Proposition 9.5, can be proved by induction on k.

PROPOSITION 9.9.– *Let P be a constraint network, Σ be a dead-end sequence of P and ϕ be a consistency. For any $k \geq 1$, the set of decisions contained in Σ_k, which is the LC$_k$-subsequence of Σ wrt ϕ, is a nogood of P.*

For any $k > 1$ and any given dead-end sequence Σ, LC_k will denote the process that consists of computing the LC_k-subsequence Σ_k of Σ. When computing Σ_k, we may have $\Sigma_k \neq \Sigma_{k-1}$ meaning that the original nogood has been reduced k times (and X_k is composed of k distinct variables). However, a fixed point may be reached at a level $1 \leq j < k$, meaning that $\Sigma_j = \Sigma_{j+1}$ and either $j = 1$ or $\Sigma_j \neq \Sigma_{j-1}$. The fixed point is reached when the current testing set is composed of $j + 1$ variables: no new variable can be added to the testing set because the identified culprit decision is the last decision of the current dead-end sequence.

In practice, the generalized version of LC can be applied in the context of a binary branching backtrack search. If a fixed point is reached at a level $j < k$, the process of last-conflict based reasoning is stopped and the choice of subsequent decisions is left to the underlying heuristic until the next conflict occurs. On the other hand, we will restrict pivots to be positive decisions, only. Indeed, it is not relevant to consider a negative decision $x \neq a$ as a pivot because it would consist of building a third branch within the MAC search tree identical to the first one. The subtree under the opposite decision $x = a$ has already been refuted, since positive decisions are taken first.

EXAMPLE.– We consider an illustration with LC_3, i.e. the size of the testing-sets is limited to three variables. In Figure 9.15, which shows a partial view of a search tree, the leftmost branch is a dead-end sequence of decisions Σ. By definition, the LC_1-testing-set of Σ consists of the single variable x_i (which is involved in the last decision of Σ). So the algorithm first assigns values to x_i in order to identify the culprit

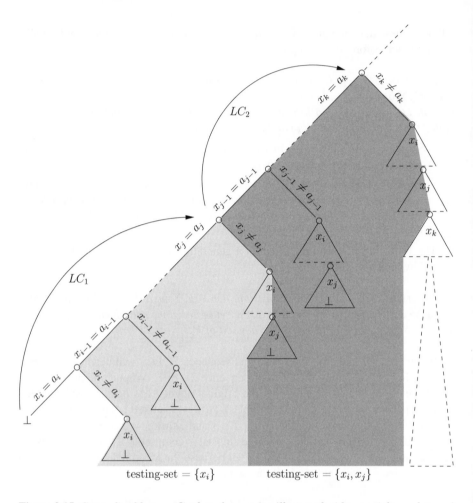

Figure 9.15. *Generalized last-conflict based reasoning illustrated with a partial search tree. A consistency ϕ is maintained at each node. A triangle labeled with a variable x and drawn using a solid base line (resp. a dotted base line) represents the fact that no (resp. a) singleton ϕ-consistent value exists for x*

decision of Σ (and the LC_1-subsequence). In this example, no value in $\mathrm{dom}(x_i)$ is found to be singleton ϕ-consistent until the algorithm backtracks up to the positive decision $x_j = a_j$. This is identified as the culprit decision of Σ, so the LC_2-testing-set is $\{x_i, x_j\}$, which means that values will be assigned first to x_i and x_j. With this the LC_2-subsequence is identified when backtracking to the decision $x_k = a_k$. In fact when $x_k \neq a_k$ it is possible to instantiate both variables in the LC_2-testing-set. The variable x_k is now included in the testing-set, but because all of the variables in this new testing-set can now be instantiated together, last-conflict reasoning stops because a fixed point is reached (at level 2) and the search continues as usual. Note that with LC_2 instead of LC_3, x_k would not have been included in the current testing-set, as last-conflict based reasoning would have been stopped after a successful instantiation of the two variables in the LC_2-testing-set. A variable other than x_k might have been chosen after x_i and x_j had been instantiated.

9.4.4. *Experimental results*

To demonstrate the practical value of last-conflict based reasoning, we now present some experimental results obtained on a PC Pentium IV 2.4 GHz 512 MB under Linux, with MAC (using chronological backtracking). The effect of LC has been investigated using the representative classical heuristic *dom/ddeg* (very similar results are obtained with *dom* and *bz*) and also the adaptive heuristic *dom/wdeg*.

On the suite of instances selected for the second constraint solver competition, Figure 9.16 shows overall results with a scatter plot for each heuristic. Each dot represents an instance and its coordinates are, on the horizontal axis, the CPU time required to solve the instance with MAC, and on the vertical axis, the CPU time required to solve the instance with MAC-LC (LC without any subscript means LC_1). LC greatly improves the efficiency of MAC when *dom/ddeg* is used, but with the conflict-directed heuristic *dom/wdeg* LC sometimes makes the search more efficient, sometimes less efficient. The interaction between these two adaptive mechanisms certainly deserves an in-depth study. Notice that, on pure random instances, last-conflict based reasoning is usually unhelpful (although not shown here) because there is no structure to exploit.

Finally, on very hard structured instances of series scens11, it is interesting that with *dom/ddeg*, Figure 9.17(a), the best results are obtained with a high level, i.e. high value of k, of the generalized reasoning. This is less obvious with *dom/wdeg*, Figure 9.17(b), but note that the y-axis scale is logarithmic. Here the time-out has been set to 48 hours per instance. MAC-LC_0 is MAC alone (i.e. without using last-conflict based reasoning).

9.5. Conclusion

It is well known that non-chronological backtracking techniques such as conflict-directed backjumping and dynamic backtracking can in some cases mitigate thrashing that may otherwise occur during backtrack search. These techniques are conceptually elegant, admit a $O(n^2d)$ space complexity and have been proved effective on many problems, but they require substantial development effort.

This chapter has focused on simple and adaptive approaches that guide search toward conflicts so as to reduce thrashing. Adaptive variable ordering heuristics based

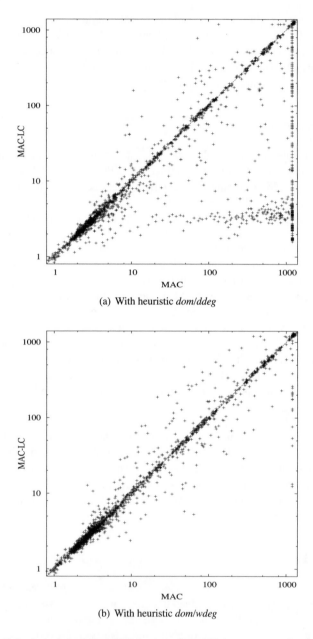

(a) With heuristic *dom/ddeg*

(b) With heuristic *dom/wdeg*

Figure 9.16. *Pairwise comparison (CPU time) on the 3,293 instances used as benchmarks of the 2006 CSP Solver Competition. The time-out to solve an instance is set to 20 minutes*

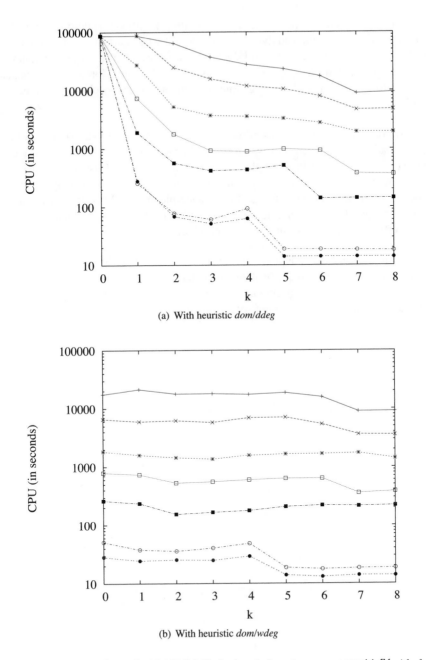

(a) With heuristic *dom/ddeg*

(b) With heuristic *dom/wdeg*

Figure 9.17. *Results obtained with MAC-LC$_k$ for $k \in 0..8$ on instances* **scen11-fX** *with, from top to bottom, $X \in 1..7$*

Constraint Networks

on impacts and weights are, at the time of writing this book, state-of-the-art: they outperform classical static and dynamic variable ordering heuristics. In particular, the conflict-directed heuristics *wdeg* and *dom/wdeg* are conceptually very simple, have a space complexity[3] in $O(e)$ and are quite easy to implement. Moreover, they appear to outperform (in terms of solving time) current intelligent backtracking methods [LEC 04].

Last conflict (LC) techniques allow lazy detection of culprit decisions that have lead to dead-ends. The idea is to assign first to the variable involved in the most recent conflict (i.e. the last assignment that failed) until the network is made consistent. LC has achieved quite interesting results in two related domains, namely constraint satisfaction and automated Artificial Intelligence planning [LEC 09b]. Furthermore, LC has been implemented in a state-of-the-art WCSP (Weighted CSP) solver and has proved effective on some bio-informatics problems [SAN 08].

To summarize, the adaptive approaches presented in this chapter are all characterized by a limited form of learning that improves guidance of the search. Other nice features are conceptual simplicity and ease of implementation. These approaches help to make constraint solvers more robust.

---

3. In fact, by associating a weight with every variable rather than with every constraint, it can only be $O(n)$.

Chapter 10

Restarts and Nogood Recording

This chapter investigates the interrelated techniques of recording nogoods and regularly restarting search. *Restarts* are important in modern SAT and CSP solvers because they can take account of the erratic behavior of (backtrack) search algorithms on many combinatorial problems. Introduction of restarts requires *diversification* of exploration of the search space, which means being sure to take different paths each time a new run is started. One way to achieve this is by randomization and another way is by learning. A search algorithm can usually be diversified by randomizing the variable and/or value ordering heuristics (for example breaking ties at random). Learning effects search ordering when nogoods are identified and recorded to make further inferences.

Nogood recording is a kind of learning that has been initially introduced for constraint-based problem-solving systems [STA 77, STE 80] and assumption-based truth maintenance systems (ATMS) [KLE 86, KLE 89]. Nogood recording was proposed to enhance CSP solving in [DEC 90]. The idea is to record a nogood whenever a conflict occurs during backtrack search. Such nogoods subsequently serve to prevent exploration of useless parts of the search tree. The first experiments with nogood recording for constraint satisfaction were reported in the early 1990s [DEC 90, FRO 94, SCH 94a, SCH 94b].

The recent impressive progress in SAT, unlike CSP, has been achieved using nogood recording (clause learning) under a randomization and restart policy enhanced by a very efficient lazy data structure [MOS 01]. The value of clause learning has risen with the availability of large instances (encoding practical applications) that include some structure and show heavy-tailed phenomena. Learning in SAT is an example of a successful technique derived from cross-fertilization between CSP and SAT: nogood recording [DEC 90] and conflict-directed backjumping [PRO 93] were originally introduced for CSP and were later imported into SAT solvers [BAY 97, MAR 96a]. At the time of writing, progress within the SAT framework has certainly stimulated renewed interest of the CSP community in nogood recording [KAT 05, BOU 06, RIC 06, LEC 07e].

Because the number of recorded nogoods may be exponential, restrictions have to be considered. For example, when the size of the recorded nogoods is limited (to i decisions), one obtains *ith-order learning*. In SAT, the size of learned nogoods can be limited by using the idea of a first unique implication point (first UIP). Different variants (e.g. relevance bounded learning [BAY 97]) attempt to find the best trade-off between the overhead of learning and the improvement of performances. Because of this trade-off, the recording of nogoods cannot completely eliminate redundancy in developed search trees. An original alternative to combining search scattering with redundancy avoidance performs random jumps [ZHA 02a] in the search space. This is particularly relevant when a limited amount of time has been allotted.

One simple learning approach [BAP 01, FUK 03, LEC 07f] identifies and records nogoods from the last branch of the search tree before each restart, ensuring that subsequent runs do not explore parts of the the search tree that have been explored previously. Nogoods can be used for propagation by posting them as new constraints and introducing an efficient filtering algorithm using *watched literals* [MOS 01]. This algorithm enforces generalized arc consistency on nogood constraints and can easily be integrated to any constraint propagation engine. The good worst-case time complexity, namely $O(n|\mathscr{B}|)$ where $|\mathscr{B}|$ denotes the number of recorded nogoods, renders this approach attractive. As the number of nogoods recorded before each new restart run is bounded by the length of the last branch of the search tree, the total number of recorded nogoods is polynomial in n, d and the number of restarts.

This chapter is organized as follows. Section 10.1 introduces restarts; sections 10.2 and 10.3 describe nogood recording from restarts. Section 10.4 addresses minimization of identified nogoods. Finally, a few experimental results are presented.

10.1. Restarting search

On random instances, a plot of mean or median behavior of (backtrack) search algorithms against constraint tightness shows a characteristic "easy-hard-easy" pattern. For many structured problems (e.g. quasi-group completion problems) the pattern is similar. The hard instances are located in the phase transition region around the crossover point where 50% of the instances are satisfiable; further away from the crossover point, under-constrained and over-constrained instances are usually easy to solve, as explained in section 2.1. Nevertheless, exceptionally hard instances sometimes occur in the easily soluble region (see e.g. [HOG 94, GEN 94, SMI 95]).

This is usually attributed to a few bad choices near the root of the search tree, leading to unsatisfiable subproblems that take a long time to explore.

These exceptionally hard instances are not inherently difficult to solve; if several different search processes are applied, some will certainly solve these instances quickly. Ideally these would be parallel processes, but in practice they usually run in turn, each being given a short time to solve the instance. There are several ways to ensure that these trial processes differ sufficiently from each other. One way is to use the same algorithm for each trial, but with randomized search ordering, leading to different search space explorations. Harvey reports [HAR 95a] that "restarting depth-first search periodically with random value orders yields a dramatic improvement in overall performance with only a small change to the original algorithm... periodically restarting depth-first search with different variable orders virtually eliminated its problem with early mistakes."

10.1.1. *Heavy-tailed behavior*

Gomes *et al.* [GOM 97, GOM 98, GOM 00] have contributed an in-depth study of runtime variability of search methods. Experience shows that for many combinatorial problems, including structured ones, two distinct search methods can behave quite differently on the very same instance: the first may conclude in a few seconds, whereas the second may require days of computing. For a single given instance, analysis of the *distribution of run times*, or *runtime distribution*, of different search methods can be quite informative. When the variance of this distribution is very large, this instance (and probably also other instances of the same problem) may best be solved using the restart strategy mentioned earlier: each of a set of different search methods is run for a limited amount of time.

The *survival function* $S(x) = P[X > x]$ is the probability that the random variable X is larger than a given value x. For backtrack search, it is instructive to plot $P[X > x]$ against x when x is the number of backtracks[1] required to solve the instance. We have $P[X > x] = 1 - F(x)$ where $F(x) = P[X \leq x]$ is the *cumulative distribution function* (CDF) of X. A runtime distribution is *heavy-tailed* if

$$P[X > x] \sim cx^{-\alpha} \qquad (x > 0),$$

where $\alpha > 0$ and $c > 0$ are constants. In this case, a log–log plot of $S(x) = P[X > x]$ versus x is linear, with slope determined by the tail index α, as illustrated in Figure 10.1. Hence, a near-straight line in a log-log plot for $P[X > x]$ is a clear sign of a heavy-tailed behavior. This means that the tail of the distribution decays

---

1. Of course, we can consider other criteria such as the CPU time or the number of wrong decisions.

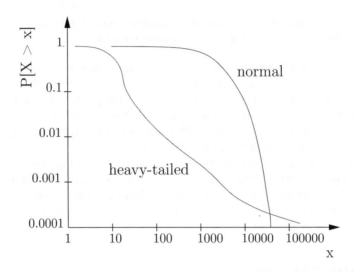

Figure 10.1. *Comparison between a normal and a heavy-tailed runtime distribution*

polynomially. Such a distribution has infinite variance and finite mean when $1 < \alpha < 2$; its mean and variance are both infinite when $0 < \alpha \leq 1$.

Analysis of the runtime distribution of a randomized search algorithm may elucidate the difficulty of a given instance. An instance for which this distribution is heavy-tailed can be solved efficiently and is therefore not difficult. An instance for which this distribution is normal is such that the different search methods behave similarly, which may suggest that this instance is inherently difficult [GOM 04]. To confirm this experimentally we have obtained the runtime distribution for a randomized search algorithm on distinct random instances generated near crossover by Model RB (see section 2.1.2). These instances include forced satisfiable instances wherein a solution is imposed as described in [XU 07]. Figure 10.2 shows the survival function of a randomized MAC algorithm for 5,000 independent runs on each of four representative instances generated at $p_{cr} \approx 0.41$ for $k = 2$, $\alpha = 0.8$, $r = 1.5$ and $n \in \{40, 45\}$. With a log-log scale, Figure 10.2 shows that the distribution is not heavy-tailed, and this suggests that these instances are inherently hard.

10.1.2. *Restart strategies*

A *restart strategy* is defined by an infinite sequence $\langle (A_1, t_1), (A_2, t_2), \dots (A_i, t_i), \dots \rangle$ or by a finite sequence $\langle (A_1, t_1), (A_2, t_2), \dots (A_{i-1}, t_{i-1}), (A_i, \infty) \rangle$ of *runs*, also called *restart runs*. For each run, the A_i term identifies the algorithm and the t_i term is the number of steps that algorithm A_i is allowed to execute. Thus to

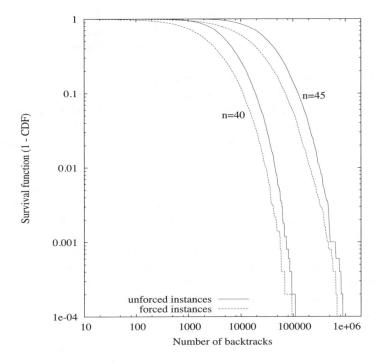

Figure 10.2. *Non heavy-tailed regime for instances in RB(2,{40, 45},0.8,1.5,p_{cr} ≈ 0.41)*

solve a given instance, algorithm A_1 is run for t_1 steps, algorithm A_2 for t_2 steps, and so on. When the sequence of runs is finite, the last algorithm A_i is allowed to execute an unlimited number of steps (symbolized by ∞). The *cutoff*, which is the number of allowed steps, may be the number of backtracks, the number of wrong decisions, the number of seconds or any other relevant measure.

A first solution to perform different search space explorations with a unique algorithm (the usual case) is to use *randomization*. If the search space is to be explored with different randomizations of a single algorithm, there are several ways to randomize. Random variable ordering and/or value ordering heuristics can be used, as mentioned previously. This may seem appropriate for tackling random instances, but for structured instances there may be appreciable loss of efficiency if non-random ordering heuristics are not used. With structured instances it may be better to use non-random heuristics except that ties are broken randomly. Another idea is to make the first few decisions (near the root of the search tree) purely randomly, and use non-random ordering heuristics thereafter. Clearly, randomization must be balanced against heuristic guidance.

We now assume the use of a randomized search algorithm. In a *fixed* cutoff restart strategy the t_i are all equal. When the runtime distribution is fully known, a fixed cutoff restart strategy is optimal [LUB 93]. However, the runtime distribution is usually unknown in practice. In this case, Luby *et al.* have shown that there is a universal strategy which has the best performance, up to a constant factor, achievable by any universal strategy. In practice, a fixed cutoff restart strategy eliminates heavy-tailed behavior [GOM 98], but a good cutoff value has to be found by trial and error. By increasing the cutoff geometrically [WAL 99] we can get close to the optimal value in a few runs (with the hope of being then successful). Besides, this guarantees completeness.

Learning provides another way of managing successive restarts of a single algorithm. Nogoods that are recorded, and kept until the instance is solved, can serve to influence the search in subsequent restart runs. However, to guarantee both completeness and systematicity (which ensures that no node in the search tree is visited more than once [FUK 03]), a nogood must systematically be extracted and recorded for each dead-end that is reached. The number of recorded nogoods may grow exponentially, but there is a simple approach that permits control of the number of nogoods required to guarantee completeness and systematicity. Learning can be limited to nogoods "present" in the last branch of the search tree before each restart; subsequent runs omit parts of the search tree that have already been explored. This idea is called *search signature* in [BAP 01], *path recording* in [FUK 03] and *restart nogoods* in [LEC 07e, LEC 07f]. Further information about restarts (and randomization) can be found in [BEE 06, GOM 06].

10.2. Nogood recording from restarts

This chapter henceforth considers a backtrack search algorithm (e.g. MAC) using binary branching, taking positive decisions first, maintaining a consistency at each step, and using a restart strategy. For any branch of the search tree (built during a run of the backtrack search algorithm), a set of relevant standard nogoods (instantiations that cannot lead to a solution) can be identified directly. *Nogood recording from restarts* means recording these nogoods but only for the last (rightmost) branch of the search tree just before the restart.

10.2.1. *Reduced nld-nogoods*

Each branch of the search tree is a sequence of positive and negative decisions. For each branch starting from the root, a generalized nogood can be extracted from each negative decision [PUG 05b, LEC 07f], as follows:

DEFINITION 10.1.– *[nld-subsequence] Let $\Sigma = \langle \delta_1, \ldots, \delta_m \rangle$ be a sequence of decisions. If δ_i is a negative decision, with $1 \leq i \leq m$, then the subsequence*

$\langle \delta_1, \ldots, \delta_i \rangle$ *of* Σ *comprising the* i *first decisions of* Σ *is called a* nld-subsequence *(negative last decision subsequence) of* Σ*. The sets of positive and negative decisions of* Σ *are denoted by* $pos(\Sigma)$ *and* $neg(\Sigma)$*, respectively.*

PROPOSITION 10.2.– *[nld-nogood] Let* P *be a a constraint network and* Σ *be the sequence of decisions taken along a branch (starting from the root) of the search tree built for* P*. For any nld-subsequence* $\langle \delta_1, \ldots, \delta_i \rangle$ *of* Σ*, the set* $\Delta = \{\delta_j \in \Sigma \mid 1 \leq j < i\} \cup \{\neg\delta_i\}$ *is a generalized nogood of* P*, called* nld-nogood.

Proof. As positive decisions are taken first, when the negative decision δ_i is encountered, the subtree corresponding to the opposite decision $\neg\delta_i$ has been refuted. □

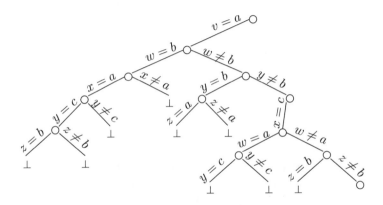

Figure 10.3. *A partial search tree built by a backtrack search algorithm*

EXAMPLE.– The sequence of decisions taken along the rightmost branch in Figure 10.3 is $\langle v = a, w \neq b, y \neq b, x = c, w \neq a, z \neq b \rangle$. The nld-subsequences and nld-nogoods that can be extracted from this branch are as follows:

nld-subsequences	nld-nogoods
$\langle v = a, w \neq b \rangle$	$\{v = a, w = b\}$
$\langle v = a, w \neq b, y \neq b \rangle$	$\{v = a, w \neq b, y = b\}$
$\langle v = a, w \neq b, y \neq b, x = c, w \neq a \rangle$	$\{v = a, w \neq b, y \neq b, x = c, w = a\}$
$\langle v = a, w \neq b, y \neq b, x = c, w \neq a, z \neq b \rangle$	$\{v = a, w \neq b, y \neq b, x = c, w \neq a, z = b\}$

Although Σ is a sequence, we use set notation ($\delta_j \in \Sigma$) because there is no ambiguity; no decision occurs more than once in Σ. Nogoods identified by proposition 10.2 are generalized nogoods because they can contain both positive and negative decisions. However, in our particular context, nld-nogoods can be systematically reduced in size by omitting negative decisions, thus reducing space requirements and improving pruning capability. Besides, as shown later, (standard) nogoods can easily be handled to make inferences, in a not too intrusive way.

PROPOSITION 10.3.– *[Reduced nld-nogood] Let P be a constraint network and Σ be the sequence of decisions taken along a branch of the search tree (starting from the root). For any nld-subsequence $\Sigma' = \langle \delta_1, \ldots, \delta_i \rangle$ of Σ, the set $\Delta = pos(\Sigma') \cup \{\neg\delta_i\}$ is a (standard) nogood of P, called a* reduced nld-nogood.

EXAMPLE.– For the rightmost branch in Figure 10.3 the nld-nogoods and reduced nld-nogoods are:

nld-nogoods	reduced nld-nogoods
$\{v = a, w = b\}$	$\{v = a, w = b\}$
$\{v = a, w \neq b, y = b\}$	$\{v = a, y = b\}$
$\{v = a, w \neq b, y \neq b, x = c, w = a\}$	$\{v = a, x = c, w = a\}$
$\{v = a, w \neq b, y \neq b, x = c, w \neq a, z = b\}$	$\{v = a, x = c, z = b\}$

The proof of Proposition 10.3, which can be found in [LEC 07f], is based on a certain form of *resolution*. When decisions are regarded as literals (see e.g. constraint resolution [MIT 03]), propositional resolution can be applied directly.

DEFINITION 10.4.– *[Resolvent] Let P be a constraint network, (x, a) be a v-value of P, Γ and Λ be two sets of decisions on P that do not involve (x, a). If $\Delta_1 = \Gamma \cup \{x = a\}$ and $\Delta_2 = \Lambda \cup \{x \neq a\}$ then the* resolvent *of Δ_1 and Δ_2 on (x, a) is $\Gamma \cup \Lambda$.*

If Δ_1 and Δ_2 are generalized nogoods then clearly the resolvent of Δ_1 and Δ_2 on (x, a) is also a generalized nogood of P. For example, the resolvent of $\{x = b, z \neq a\}$ and $\{w = c, y \neq b, z = a\}$ on (z, a) is $\{x = b, w = c, y \neq b\}$. Imagine that $\{x = b, w = c, y \neq b\}$ is not a nogood, whereas $\{x = b, z \neq a\}$ and $\{w = c, y \neq b, z = a\}$ are nogoods. This would mean that $\{x = b, w = c, y \neq b\}$ could be extended to a solution S with either $S[z] = a$ or $S[z] \neq a$; but each of these extensions would violate a nogood, thus contradicting our assumption. For our example, the reduced nld-nogoods can be obtained by resolution as shown in Figure 10.4.

The space required to store the standard nogoods that can be extracted from any branch of the search tree is polynomial with respect to the number of variables and the greatest domain size:

PROPOSITION 10.5.– *Let P be a constraint network and Σ be the sequence of decisions taken along a branch of the search tree. The worst-case space complexity to record all reduced nld-nogoods of Σ is $O(n^2d)$.*

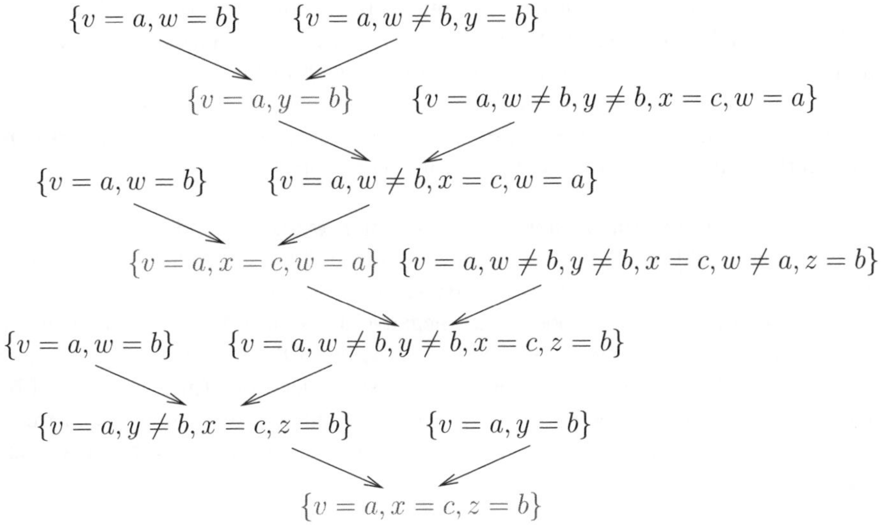

$$\{v = a, w = b\} \qquad \{v = a, w \neq b, y = b\}$$

$$\{v = a, y = b\} \qquad \{v = a, w \neq b, y \neq b, x = c, w = a\}$$

$$\{v = a, w = b\} \qquad \{v = a, w \neq b, x = c, w = a\}$$

$$\{v = a, x = c, w = a\} \quad \{v = a, w \neq b, y \neq b, x = c, w \neq a, z = b\}$$

$$\{v = a, w = b\} \qquad \{v = a, w \neq b, y \neq b, x = c, z = b\}$$

$$\{v = a, y \neq b, x = c, z = b\} \qquad \{v = a, y = b\}$$

$$\{v = a, x = c, z = b\}$$

Figure 10.4. *Derivation of reduced nld-nogoods using resolution*

Proof. First, the number of negative decisions in any branch is $O(nd)$. For each negative decision, we can extract a reduced nld-nogood. A reduced nld-nogood contains only positive decisions, so its size is $O(n)$. Hence the overall space complexity is $O(n^2 d)$. □

Each nld-nogood is subsumed by its reduced nld-nogood, which has greater pruning capability. Besides, reduced nld-nogoods are easier to manage because they are standard nogoods.

10.2.2. *Extracting nogoods*

As mentioned earlier, the runtime distribution of a randomized search algorithm is sometimes characterized by an extremely long tail with some infinite moment. For some instances, it has been found worthwhile to employ restarts with a randomized search heuristic. However, if restarts are employed without learning (as it is currently the case for most of the academic and commercial constraint solvers), the average performance of the solver can be damaged on some instances because the same parts of the search space may be explored several times. On the other hand, nogood recording without restarts has not yet been shown to be entirely convincing for constraint satisfaction; when uncontrolled, nogood recording can lead to exponential space complexity. Although restarts without nogood recording, and also nogood recording without restarts, may be of limited use, a combination of both of these techniques can be more useful. Reduced nld-nogoods can be extracted (to be recorded in a nogood base) from the current (rightmost) branch of the search tree at the end of each run. These nogoods can be used to prevent parts of the search space from being explored more than once. Thus we can then benefit from restarts and learning capabilities without sacrificing solver performance or space complexity.

When the current run is stopped, the function extractNogoods, Algorithm 78, derives reduced nld-nogoods from the current branch of the search tree. This function admits as parameter the sequence of decisions along the current rightmost branch and returns a set of standard nogoods. Each negative decision in this sequence yields a standard nogood, as explained in section 10.2.1. From the root to the last decision of the current branch, we record successive positive decisions (in a set denoted by *positiveDecisions*). For each negative decision encountered, Algorithm 78 constructs a nogood Δ from the negation of this decision and all previous positive decisions recorded (line 7).

Algorithm 78: extractNogoods(Σ: sequence of decisions): set of nogoods

---

Input: $\Sigma = \langle \delta_1, \ldots, \delta_m \rangle$
Output: the set of reduced nld-nogoods extracted from Σ

1   $nogoods \leftarrow \emptyset$
2   $positiveDecisions \leftarrow \emptyset$
3   **for** i *ranging from 1 to* m **do**
4   **if** δ_i *is a positive decision* **then**
5         $positiveDecisions \leftarrow positiveDecisions \cup \{\delta_i\}$
6   **else**
7         $\Delta \leftarrow positiveDecisions \cup \{\neg \delta_i\}$
8         $nogoods \leftarrow nogoods \cup \{\Delta\}$

9   **return** $nogoods$

Recorded nogoods are used to prevent repeated exploration of the same parts of the search space during subsequent runs. This is accomplished by ensuring that the set of decisions along the current branch is not subsumed by any recorded nogood. Moreover, nogoods can be used to make inferences, as described in the next section. For example, when the decision $v = a$ becomes true during search, $w \neq b$ can be inferred from the nogood $\{v = a, w = b\}$.

Finally, note that reduced nld-nogoods extracted from the last branch subsume all reduced nld-nogoods that could be extracted from any branch previously explored during the current run. This is true because each subtree that is completely explored (and, thus, all nld-nogoods that could be derived from all branches of this subtree) is prefixed by at least one nld-nogood of the last branch. However, this is not true when nogoods are minimized; see section 10.4.

10.3. Managing standard nogoods

This section explains how to make efficient use of standard nogoods (and therefore also reduced nld-nogoods recorded during restart runs) in the domain of constraint satisfaction. Standard nogoods, which are sets (conjunctions) of positive decisions, are now recorded in an equivalent form as sets (disjunctions) of negative decisions. Using this representation, an efficient propagation algorithm can enforce generalized arc consistency on *nogood constraints* by means of the SAT technique of watched literals [MOS 01, ZHA 02b, EÉN 03].

10.3.1. *Nogood constraints*

A problem that entails a nogood has no solution. Standard nogoods can be used to prune the search tree by ensuring that no nogood is entailed by the current problem. Entailment of decisions was the subject of Definition 1.60, which we now develop as follows:

DEFINITION 10.6.– *[Almost Entailment] Let P be a constraint network and Δ be a set of positive decisions on P.*

– *P entails Δ iff $P|_\Delta = P$, i.e. $\forall x = a \in \Delta, \mathrm{dom}^P(x) = \{a\}$.*

– *P almost entails Δ iff there exists a positive decision $x = a$ in Δ such that $\mathrm{dom}^P(x) \neq \{a\}$, $a \in \mathrm{dom}^P(x)$ and P entails $\Delta \setminus \{x = a\}$.*

Every time a backtrack search algorithm generates a new node v, we can check whether $\mathrm{cn}(v)$, the constraint network associated with v, entails a nogood recorded earlier. Actually, there are two main flavors of pruning: either v is directly rejected because it entails a nogood, or some domains of variables in $\mathrm{cn}(v)$ are filtered to ensure that almost entailed nogoods will not be entailed later.

Each standard nogood can be represented by a *nogood constraint*. More precisely, if Δ is a standard nogood, then the scope of the nogood constraint c_Δ is $\mathrm{vars}(\Delta)$ and the relation of this constraint forbids only the singe tuple found in Δ. For example, if $\Delta = \{x = a, y = b, z = c\}$ is a nogood, then we have a ternary nogood constraint c_Δ such that $\mathrm{scp}(c_\Delta) = \{x, y, z\}$ and $\mathrm{rel}(c_\Delta) = \mathrm{dom}^{\mathrm{init}}(x) \times \mathrm{dom}^{\mathrm{init}}(y) \times \mathrm{dom}^{\mathrm{init}}(z) \setminus \{(a, b, c)\}$. A nogood constraint can be represented in intensional form simply by applying De Morgan's law to nogoods viewed as logical conjunctions of positive decisions. The intensional representation is a disjunction of negative decisions. For example, from the nogood $\Delta = \{x = a, y = b, z = c\}$, we can derive the nogood constraint c_Δ : $x \neq a \vee y \neq b \vee z \neq c$. For each decision $x = a$ in Δ, the complementary decision $x \neq a$ is included in the intensional predicate expression of the nogood constraint c_Δ. We shall refer to these negative decisions as decisions of the constraint c_Δ.

We now present a direct translation in CSP of the mechanism of SAT unit propagation based on watched literals. A negative decision may be in three different states with respect to the current problem. A negative decision $x \neq a$ is said to be *satisfied* (i.e. inevitably true) iff $a \notin \mathrm{dom}(x)$. A negative decision $x \neq a$ is said to be *falsified* (i.e. inevitably false) iff $\mathrm{dom}(x) = \{a\}$. A negative decision which is neither satisfied nor falsified is said to be *free* (undetermined); in this case $a \in \mathrm{dom}(x) \wedge |\mathrm{dom}(x)| > 1$. For example, if $\mathrm{dom}(x) = \{b,c\}$, $\mathrm{dom}(y) = \{b\}$ and $\mathrm{dom}(z) = \{a,b,c\}$, then $x \neq a \vee y \neq b \vee z \neq c$ is (the predicate expression of) a nogood constraint such that the first decision is satisfied, the second one is falsified and the third one is free.

A nogood Δ, viewed as a constraint c_Δ, simply states that at least one decision (occurring in the predicate expression) of c_Δ must be evaluated to true. Four cases are possible when dealing with a nogood constraint c_Δ:

1) c_Δ is entailed because one decision of c_Δ is satisfied: the current problem does not entail the nogood Δ.

2) c_Δ is disentailed because all decisions of c_Δ are falsified: the current problem entails the nogood Δ (so backtrack is necessary).

3) c_Δ contains no satisfied decisions and exactly one free decision: the current problem almost entails the nogood Δ (this free decision can be forced to be satisfied).

4) c_Δ contains no satisfied decisions and (at least) two free decisions: the nogood Δ is neither entailed nor almost entailed by the current problem.

It is easy to see that as long as there are (at least) two free decisions in c_Δ, the constraint c_Δ is GAC-consistent. Conversely, c_Δ is not GAC-consistent when the current problem entails or almost entails the nogood Δ. If the current problem entails the nogood Δ, then the constraint c_Δ is violated, so the search must backtrack (if possible). If the current problem almost entails the nogood Δ, then forcing the unique free decision (to be satisfied) means enforcing generalized arc consistency by removing a GAC-inconsistent value from the domain of the variable involved in this decision. For example, if $\mathrm{dom}(x) = \{a\}$, $\mathrm{dom}(y) = \{b\}$ and $\mathrm{dom}(z) = \{a,b,c\}$, then c_Δ : $x \neq a \vee y \neq b \vee z \neq c$ is a nogood constraint that almost entails $\Delta = \{x = a, y = b, z = c\}$. Forcing $z \neq c$ to true means removing c from $\mathrm{dom}(z)$; this is safe because there is no support for (z, c) on c_Δ.

A search algorithm can simply insist that no nogood is entailed, or can go further by forcing some decisions when necessary. This is exactly the difference between backward checking and enforcing generalized arc consistency. Enforcing generalized arc consistency seems a better solution because it can be implemented cheaply (lazily) by using watched literals, and also because it can prune the search space by looking ahead.

10.3.2. *Watched decisions*

Standard nogoods that are identified (e.g. extracted from the rightmost branch after each new restart run) can be recorded in the form of nogood constraints in a *base* denoted here by $\mathscr{B}$. Each time a positive decision is (explicitly or implicitly) taken during search, the search algorithm checks whether the current set of decisions is compatible with all the nogood constraints in $\mathscr{B}$.

The watched literals [MOS 01, ZHA 02b, EÉN 03] lazy data structure provides efficient access to nogood constraints in $\mathscr{B}$. In the present context, a nogood constraint is a disjunction of decisions instead of literals, so we shall refer to *watched decisions* instead of watched literals. The idea is to mark two decisions in each nogood constraint. These allow identification of the moment when a nogood is entailed or almost entailed by the current problem. Suppose, for example, that two standard nogoods $\Delta_1 = \{x = a, y = b, z = c\}$ and $\Delta_2 = \{x = a, w = b\}$, have been recorded as constraints $c_{\Delta_1} : x \neq a \vee y \neq b \vee z \neq c$ and $c_{\Delta_2} : x \neq a \vee w \neq b$. Figure 10.5 shows the nogood constraint base, with decisions $x \neq a$ and $z \neq c$ watched in the first nogood constraint and decisions $x \neq a$ and $w \neq b$ watched in the second one. Watched decisions are designated by markers w_1 and w_2. We also have an array of nd entries such that each entry corresponds to a v-value (x, a) of the (initial) problem and represents the head of a linked list allowing the access to the nogood constraints of $\mathscr{B}$ that contain the watched decision $x \neq a$. We can access to such a list, denoted by $\mathscr{B}_{(x,a)}$, in constant time. For example, in Figure 10.5, $\mathscr{B}_{(x,a)}$ is a linked list providing access to c_{Δ_1} and c_{Δ_2} because in both constraints, $x \neq a$ is watched, whereas $\mathscr{B}_{(z,c)}$ is a linked list providing access only to c_{Δ_1} because $z \neq c$ is only watched decision in c_{Δ_1}.

So long as both watched decisions in a nogood constraint are free or satisfied, inference is not possible because the constraint is generalized arc-consistent. Propagation is guided by *fix(x)* events [SCH 06]: the nogood constraint base is woken up when a variable becomes fixed, or in other words, when a positive decision is (explicitly or implicitly) taken. Whenever a positive decision $x = a$ is taken, the list $\mathscr{B}_{(x,a)}$ is visited. For each nogood constraint c_Δ of this list, $x \neq a$ is a watched decision and we have first to check if the other watched decision of c_Δ is satisfied. If this is the case, c_Δ is entailed (so, we can abandon c_Δ). Otherwise, another *watchable decision*, i.e. a decision that is free or satisfied, must be sought. Either this search is successful[2] and this decision becomes the new watched one (replacing $x \neq a$),

---

2. If the second watched decision is falsified, it will be necessarily woken up later.

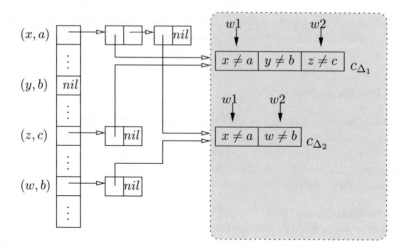

Figure 10.5. *A nogood constraint base $\mathcal{B}$ including two nogoods constraints*
$c_{\Delta_1} : x \neq a \vee y \neq b \vee z \neq c$ *and* $c_{\Delta_2} : x \neq a \vee w \neq b$

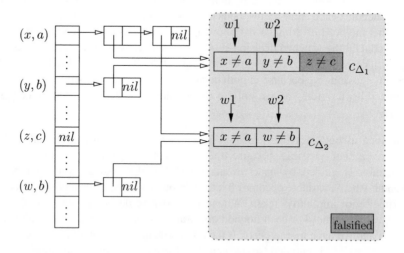

Figure 10.6. *The nogood constraint base $\mathcal{B}$ of Figure 10.5 after taking the decision $z = c$. A new decision is watched in the nogood constraint c_{Δ_1} since $z \neq c$ is now falsified*

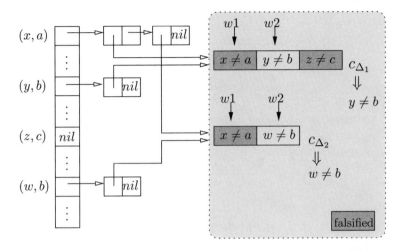

Figure 10.7. *The nogood constraint base $\mathscr{B}$ of Figure 10.6 after taking the decision $x = a$. The decisions $y \neq b$ and $w \neq b$ are inferred since $z \neq c$ and now $x \neq a$ are falsified*

or instead we have to force the second watched decision of c_Δ in order to make c_Δ generalized arc-consistent (potentially generating a domain wipe-out).

For example, the nogood constraint base in Figure 10.6 is obtained from Figure 10.5 after the decision $z = c$ has been taken, assuming that $x \neq a$ is not satisfied and $y \neq b$ watchable. Consequently, the decision $y \neq b$ is now watched instead of $z \neq c$ in the nogood constraint c_{Δ_1}. When the decision $x = a$ is made, the two nogood constraints are visited. But for each of these two constraints, since there is no other watchable decision, the second watched decision is forced by inference, as shown in Figure 10.7.

The following *watched decision invariant* is important. At each node v of the search tree such that $cn(v) \neq \bot$ (recall that $cn(v)$ is obtained after enforcing ϕ), the state obtained after having propagated all *fix(x)* events on the base $\mathscr{B}$ is consistent: every nogood constraint is guaranteed to be either entailed (and thus generalized arc-consistent) because at least one of its watched decisions is satisfied, or generalized arc-consistent (and possibly entailed[3]) because its two watched decisions are free.

Another nice feature of watched decisions (or literals) is that they are backtrack-stable, i.e. they remain valid upon backtracking. This means that when the search algorithm backtracks, even if the watched decisions have been changed in the subtree that has just been explored, the watched decision invariant still holds. Consequently,

---

3. A non-watched decision may be satisfied.

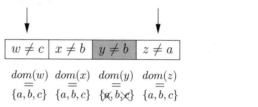

$$\boxed{\; w \neq c \;\vert\; x \neq b \;\vert\; y \neq b \;\vert\; z \neq a \;}$$

$$\begin{array}{cccc} dom(w) & dom(x) & dom(y) & dom(z) \\ \{a,\overline{b},c\} & \{a,\overline{b},c\} & \{a,\overline{b},c\} & \{a,\overline{b},c\} \end{array}$$

(a) Initially (level 0), the first and last decision of the nogood constraint are watched

$$\boxed{\; w \neq c \;\vert\; x \neq b \;\vert\; y \neq b \;\vert\; z \neq a \;} \qquad \fbox{falsified}$$

$$\begin{array}{cccc} dom(w) & dom(x) & dom(y) & dom(z) \\ \{a,\overline{b},c\} & \{a,\overline{b},c\} & \{\not a,b,\not c\} & \{a,\overline{b},c\} \end{array}$$

(b) After setting $y = b$ (level 1). As $y \neq b$ is not watched, the nogood constraint is not handled

$$\boxed{\; w \neq c \;\vert\; x \neq b \;\vert\; y \neq b \;\vert\; z \neq a \;} \qquad \fbox{falsified}$$

$$\begin{array}{cccc} dom(w) & dom(x) & dom(y) & dom(z) \\ \{a,\overline{b},c\} & \{a,\overline{b},c\} & \{\not a,b,\not c\} & \{a,\not b,\not c\} \end{array}$$

(c) After setting $z = a$ (level 2). As $z \neq a$ is watched and is now falsified, a watchable decision is sought: $x \neq b$ is found

$$\boxed{\; w \neq c \;\vert\; x \neq b \;\vert\; y \neq b \;\vert\; z \neq a \;} \qquad \fbox{falsified}$$

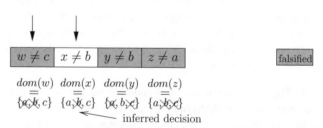

(d) After setting $w = c$ (level 3). As $w \neq c$ is watched and is now falsified, a watchable decision (different from $x \neq b$) is sought: none can be found and consequently, $x \neq b$ is inferred. The watched decisions remain the same (one is falsified and the other satisfied)

$$\boxed{\; w \neq c \;\vert\; x \neq b \;\vert\; y \neq b \;\vert\; z \neq a \;}$$

$$\begin{array}{cccc} dom(w) & dom(x) & dom(y) & dom(z) \\ \{a,\overline{b},c\} & \{a,\overline{b},c\} & \{a,\overline{b},c\} & \{a,\overline{b},c\} \end{array}$$

(e) After backtracking to level 0. There is no need to modify watched decisions as found at (d) before backtracking

Figure 10.8. *Evolution of watched decisions during search*

no data-structures need to be restored when backtracking. When an inference is made, the constraint nogood becomes entailed with a watched decision satisfied and a watched decision falsified. However, the falsified watched decision will again be watchable after a backtrack. This is why the structures remain unchanged in Figure 10.7 even when the watched decision $x \neq a$ is falsified. Figure 10.8 provides another detailed illustration.

Finally, we provide some details of the initial recording of nogoods (as constraints) in $\mathcal{B}$ and of the initialization of watched decisions. First, any nogood of size one (i.e. involving only one decision) returned by function extractNogoods can be discarded after definitively removing the corresponding value (i.e. for all subsequent runs). For example, if $\Delta = \{x = a\}$ is a nogood, then a can be permanently removed from $\mathrm{dom}(x)$. Consequently, all nogood constraints in $\mathcal{B}$ have arity not less than two. Second, two decisions must be watched each time a nogood is recorded, but any decision in the nogood can be watched since the search algorithm is about to restart. For each decision $x \neq a$ that is selected to be watched, a new link (for the new nogood constraint) is inserted into the list $\mathcal{B}_{(x,a)}$. Third, at the beginning of each new restart run, entailed nogood constraints may be removed from the base $\mathcal{B}$ and falsified decisions may be removed from nogood constraints.

10.3.3. *Making inferences*

An algorithm can use standard nogoods to make inferences while establishing (maintaining) generalized arc consistency on the full set of constraints. We now show this with the coarse-grained GAC algorithm presented in section 4.1. More precisely, to take account of constraint nogoods in the base $\mathcal{B}$, we simply include the following instructions between lines 5 and 6 of enforceGAC^{var}, Algorithm 9:

```
// These instructions must be put between lines 5 and 6 of function
  enforceGAC^var described in Algorithm 9
if | dom(x) | = 1 then
    let a be the unique value in dom(x)
    foreach decision y ≠ b ∈ makeInferences(x = a) do
        // By construction, we know that b ∈ dom(y)
        remove b from dom(y)
        if dom(y) = ∅ then
            return false
        insert(Q, y)
```

Remember that variables are picked iteratively from the queue Q during propagation. If a variable x has just been picked and if $\mathrm{dom}(x)$ is a singleton $\{a\}$, we may benefit from some nogood constraints recorded in the base $\mathcal{B}$. In this case the function makeInferences (described below) iterates over all nogood constraints containing $x \neq a$ as watched decision and returns a set of inferences (negative decisions) made from these constraints. Each of these inferred negative decisions allows a value to be removed from a domain, possibly causing an inconsistency or an update of Q.

Algorithm 79: makeInferences($x = a$: decision): set of decisions

Output: a set of negative decisions inferred from $x = a$

1 $\Gamma \leftarrow \emptyset$
2 **foreach** *nogood constraint* $c_\Delta \in \mathscr{B}_{(x,a)}$ **do**
      // $x \neq a$ is a decision watched in c_Δ that is now falsified
3   Let $(y \neq b)$ be the second decision watched in c_Δ
      // c_Δ is entailed if $b \notin \text{dom}(y)$
4   **if** $b \in \text{dom}(y)$ **then**
5         $\delta \leftarrow$ findWatchableDecision(c_Δ)
6   **if** $\delta = nil$ **then**
7            $\Gamma \leftarrow \Gamma \cup \{y \neq b\}$
8   **else**
9   watch δ instead of $x \neq a$ in c_Δ
10   remove c_Δ from $\mathscr{B}_{(x,a)}$
11   add c_Δ to $\mathscr{B}_{(z,c)}$ where δ is $z \neq c$

12 **return** Γ

Algorithm 80: findWatchableDecision(c_Δ: nogood constraint): decision

Output: a watchable decision in c_Δ, or nil

1 **foreach** *decision* $(z \neq c) \in c_\Delta$ **do**
2   **if** $z \neq c$ *is not watched in* c_Δ **then**
         // we are searching for a satisfied or free decision
3   **if** $c \notin \text{dom}(z)$ *or* $|\text{dom}(z)| > 1$ **then**
4   **return** $z \neq c$

5 **return** nil

Algorithm 79 iterates over the list of nogood constraints that have a watched decision which is the negation of the decision given as parameter. Each turn of the main loop processes a nogood constraint c_Δ. If the second watched decision in c_Δ is not satisfied because b is in $\text{dom}(y)$ (line 4), the function findWatchableDecision, Algorithm 80, examines all decisions (not currently watched) in c_Δ, seeking the next decision to watch. A watchable decision is either satisfied or free. If no new watchable decision is found (symbolized by nil), then the second decision currently watched ($y \neq b$) is collected (and will be forced a little bit later in the propagation process). Otherwise, a new decision is watched instead of $x \neq a$. We omit details about updating lists $\mathscr{B}_{x \neq a}$ and $\mathscr{B}_\delta$.

10.3.4. *Complexity analysis*

In the following analysis of complexity of algorithms that extract and use nogoods, $\mathscr{B}$ denotes the nogood constraint base and $|\mathscr{B}|$ denotes the number of nogood constraints in $\mathscr{B}$.

PROPOSITION 10.7.– *The worst-case time complexity of extracting reduced nld-nogoods from restarts, i.e. the worst-case time complexity of* extractNogoods, *is* $O(n^2 d)$.

Proof. First, each nogood Δ extracted (line 8 of Algorithm 78) is composed of at most $|pos(\Sigma)|$ decisions, and at most $|neg(\Sigma)|$ nogoods can be extracted from Σ. Thus the worst-case time complexity of extractNogoods is $O(|pos(\Sigma)|.|neg(\Sigma)|)$. Because $|pos(\Sigma)|$ is $O(n)$ and $|neg(\Sigma)|$ is $O(nd)$, we obtain $O(n^2 d)$. $\qquad\square$

PROPOSITION 10.8.– *The worst-case time complexity of exploiting reduced nld-nogoods at each node of the search tree, i.e. the total worst-case time complexity of* makeInferences *for a single call to* propagateGAC^{var} *is* $O(n|\mathscr{B}|)$.

The proof requires a small modification of the algorithm to guarantee that each decision is checked to be watchable only once. Basically, Proposition 10.8 says that enforcing GAC on a nogood constraint c_Δ is $O(n)$, and even more precisely $O(r)$ where r is the arity of c_Δ. Note that for each branch of the search tree the total worst-case time complexity of using reduced nld-nogoods is also $O(n|\mathscr{B}|)$ since each variable x can be fixed only once per branch.

COROLLARY 10.9.– *Combined with nogood recording from restarts, the worst-case time complexity of* propagateGAC^{var} *is* $O(er^2 d^r + n|\mathscr{B}|)$ *where r is the greatest constraint arity.*

Proof. The cost of establishing GAC is $O(er^2 d^r)$ when a generic algorithm such as GAC2001 is used (GAC4 is $O(erd^r)$ but requires an extensional representation). Moreover, the cost of exploiting nogoods has just been shown to be $O(n|\mathscr{B}|)$. $\qquad\square$

PROPOSITION 10.10.– *The worst-case space complexity of storing reduced nld-nogoods is* $O(nd + n|\mathscr{B}|)$.

Proof. We know that $|\mathcal{B}|$ nogoods of size at most n are recorded. Further, the number of cells introduced to access nogoods is $O(|\mathcal{B}|)$ and the size of the introduced array (with one pointer per negative decision) is $O(nd)$. Thus we obtain $O(nd+n|\mathcal{B}|)$.   □

10.4. Minimizing nogoods

In section 10.2.1, nld-nogoods were reduced in size by considering positive decisions only. To obtain more powerful nogoods, we now introduce reduced nld-nogoods minimized with respect to a consistency ϕ.

10.4.1. *Minimal ϕ-nogoods*

In the context of a backtrack ϕ-search algorithm, ϕ is a consistency that is enforced at each step of search. Whenever a dead-end is reached, a ϕ-nogood is identified (see Definition 3.26). ϕ-nogoods can easily be *minimized* by a polynomial algorithm such as QuickXplain or one of its variants [JUN 01]. At the end of each restart run, reduced nld-nogoods extracted from the current branch can then be attempted to be minimized. One interesting thing is that nld-nogoods which are not ϕ-nogoods can be directly discarded: attempting to minimize them is useless. This is the case when the last decision δ_m of the nld-subsequence from which a nld-nogood Δ has been extracted, does not directly lead to a failure when applying ϕ. This means that the decision δ_m has led to exploration of a non-trivial subtree. On the other hand, when δ_m leads directly to a dead-end, then δ_m inevitably belongs to a minimal ϕ-nogood included in Δ. Consequently δ_m can be selected directly as the first *transition decision* of the minimization algorithm defined in the next section.

Figure 10.9 shows part of the search tree for a run stopped after the decision $z \neq b$; a consistency ϕ is maintained at each node. Among the four nld-nogoods that can be extracted, only two yield a direct dead-end: $\Delta_1 = \{v = a, w \neq b, y = b\}$ and $\Delta_2 = \{v = a, w \neq b, y \neq b, x = c, w \neq a, z = b\}$. Δ_1 and Δ_2 are clearly ϕ-nogoods, since the application of ϕ after the decisions $y = b$ and $z = b$ (shown by an arrow) directly leads to an inconsistency. So the reduced nld-nogoods that will be considered for minimization are $\Delta_1' = \{v = a, y = b\}$ and $\Delta_2' = \{v = a, x = c, z = b\}$. Note, however, that a reduced nld-nogood obtained from a nld-nogood which is a ϕ-nogood is not itself inevitably a ϕ-nogood. Indeed, some negative decisions removed when reducing a nld-nogood may actively participate in the conflict. An alternative is to minimize nld-nogoods, and not minimizing reduced nld-nogoods, but generalized nogoods may have to be handled subsequently (this is the topic of the next chapter).

When reduced nld-nogoods are highly minimized, the effect on subsequent runs may be important. In the best case, minimization yields some ϕ-nogoods of size 1: these are singleton ϕ-inconsistent values. For example, for $\phi = AC$ and

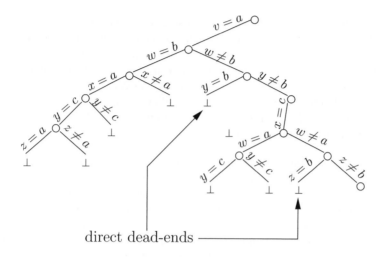

direct dead-ends

Figure 10.9. *Identification of (reduced) nld-nogoods susceptible to be minimized*

for instances of the queens-knights problem involving five knights, we know that each knight variable is singleton arc-inconsistent. If a knight variable is involved in the last decision of a reduced nld-nogood, the minimization algorithm necessarily detects a singleton arc-inconsistent value. Some experimental results in Table 10.2 of section 10.5 confirm this observation.

10.4.2. *Minimization techniques*

There are several techniques for identification of minimal ϕ-nogoods (also called conflict-sets) [JUN 01, PET 03b]. Because extracting a minimal ϕ-nogood is an activity limited to a single branch in a search tree, the proposed algorithms involve (at least, partially) a constructive scheme in order to retain some of the incrementality of the propagation process. Although the most recent version of QuickXplain [JUN 04] applies divide and conquer (as in [MAU 02]), it is defined in a more general context. For example, it can extract minimal unsatisfiable cores from constraint networks.

To summarize, in order to find a minimal ϕ-nogood, its constituent decisions must be identified iteratively. Given a ϕ-nogood $\Delta = \{\delta_1, \delta_2, \ldots, \delta_m\}$ of a constraint network P and a total ordering on the decisions (assuming for simplicity that the order is given by the indices of decisions), there exists a decision δ_i such that $\phi(P|_{\{\delta_1,\ldots,\delta_{i-1}\}}) \neq \perp$ and $\phi(P|_{\{\delta_1,\ldots,\delta_i\}}) = \perp$. This decision δ_i necessarily belongs to a minimal ϕ-nogood and is called the *transition decision* of Δ (according to the given ordering). Note also that each decision δ_j with $j > i$ can be safely removed. A transition decision is analogous to a *transition constraint* in [HEM 06].

A transition decision is identified by using a *minimization scheme* which can be constructive, destructive or dichotomic. The *constructive* minimization scheme successively includes the decisions of Δ (according to the given ordering) in the constraint network until an inconsistency is detected when applying ϕ. The *destructive* minimization scheme initially includes all decisions of Δ in the network and successively removes them one by one until no further inconsistency is detected when ϕ is applied. The *dichotomic* minimization scheme identifies the transition decision by means of a binary search.

Any one of these three approaches can extract a minimal ϕ-nogood. After finding a first transition decision δ_i in Δ, a second can be sought after removing from Δ all decisions δ_j with $j > i$ (since unsatisfiability is preserved) and re-ordering the decisions such that found transition decisions are the smallest ones in the order (the background of [JUN 04]). This process can be repeated until all decisions of the current nogood correspond to transition decisions that have been successively found. The idea of this iterative process has been described in [SIQ 88, JUN 01, PET 03b, HEM 06].

EXAMPLE.– Figure 10.10 illustrates the constructive approach, assuming that $\Delta = \{\delta_1, \delta_2, \ldots, \delta_m\}$ is a ϕ-nogood. The first transition decision that is found by successively including the decisions of Δ is δ_i. When a new ϕ-nogood $\Delta' = \{\delta_i, \delta_1, \ldots, \delta_{i-1}\}$ is identified, δ_i becomes the first decision in the underlying order. The second transition decision that is found is δ_j; $\Delta'' = \{\delta_i, \delta_j, \delta_1, \ldots, \delta_{j-1}\}$ is a new ϕ-nogood. Finally, if we assume that $\phi(P|_{\{\delta_i, \delta_j\}}) = \bot$, then $\Delta^m = \{\delta_i, \delta_j\}$ is a minimal ϕ-nogood. Recall here that the last decision of a nld-subsequence plays the role of the first transition decision, and is then initially the first decision in the underlying order.

In the context of identifying a minimal nogood, the constructive, destructive and dichotomic approaches outlined above can be related to the algorithms called RobustXplain, ReplayXplain and QuickXplain [JUN 01]. In the present context, the inference operator that enforces ϕ is assumed to be incremental. This simply means that the worst-case time complexities of applying ϕ on a given constraint network from two respective sets of decisions Δ and Δ' such that $\Delta \subset \Delta'$ are the same. For example, all (known) generic algorithms that enforce $\phi = (G)AC$ are incremental. Consequently, constructive identification of a transition decision is appropriate for our purpose and has been used in our experiments. Its complexity is the subject of the next section.

10.4.3. *Complexity analysis*

PROPOSITION 10.11.– *The worst-case time complexity of extracting a minimal GAC-nogood from a GAC-nogood is $O(enr^2d^r)$.*

Proof. A generic algorithm such as GAC2001 that enforces GAC on a constraint network is incremental. Consequently, using a constructive approach to identify

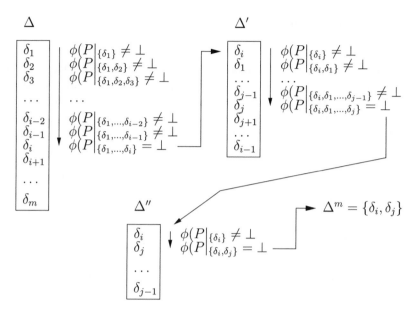

Figure 10.10. *Identifying a minimal ϕ-nogood Δ^m from a ϕ-nogood Δ using a constructive approach*

a transition decision is $O(er^2d^r)$, which is the worst-case time complexity of establishing GAC only once. If the extracted nogood is composed of k decisions, then we obtain an overall complexity in $O(ker^2d^r)$. Since k is $O(n)$, we obtain $O(enr^2d^r)$. □

COROLLARY 10.12.– *In the binary case (i.e. for $r = 2$), the worst-case time complexity of extracting a minimal AC-nogood from an AC-nogood is $O(end^2)$.*

PROPOSITION 10.13.– *The worst-case time complexity of extracting minimal reduced GAC-nld-nogoods (at the end of each run) is $O(en^2r^2d^{r+1})$.*

Proof. Extracting reduced nld-nogoods from restarts is $O(n^2d)$. Here, we obtain reduced GAC-nld-nogoods. Extracting a minimal GAC-nogood from a GAC-nogood is $O(enr^2d^r)$ and we know that there are at most $O(nd)$ reduced nld-nogoods that are GAC-nogoods to be minimized. □

COROLLARY 10.14.– *In the binary case (i.e. for $r = 2$), the worst-case time complexity of extracting minimal reduced AC-nld-nogoods (at the end of each run) is $O(en^2d^3)$.*

10.5. Experimental results

Results of experiments on a Xeon processor clocked at 3 GHz and with 1 GB RAM demonstrate the practical value of nogood recording from restarts. We have run MAC embedding GAC3^{rm} and have studied the impact of exploiting restarts (denoted by MAC+RST), nogood recording from restarts (denoted by MAC+RST+NG) and the same technique with minimization (denoted by MAC+RST+NG^m). We have employed a restart policy in which the number of backtracks allowed for the first run is ten, and at each new run the number of allowed backtracks is increased by a factor equal to 1.5. This is a geometric restart policy as in [WAL 99]. For search, we have used three different variable ordering heuristics: the classical bz and $dom/ddeg$ as well as the adaptive $dom/wdeg$. It is important to note that when restarts have been performed, ties have been broken randomly in bz and $dom/ddeg$ because these heuristics do not learn. For $dom/wdeg$, the weights of constraints are preserved from each run to the next, which makes randomization useless (weights discriminate sufficiently). We have tested the different combinations on the full set of 3,621 instances used as benchmarks for the first round of the 2006 constraint solver competition. The time limit to solve an instance was 20 minutes.

For MAC, MAC+RST, MAC+RST+NG and MAC+RST+NG^m, Table 10.1 summarizes the number of instances unsolved within the time limit (#timeouts) and the average CPU time in seconds. On random instances, for all the heuristics, restarting search appears to be unhelpful, which is not surprising since there is no structure to exploit from one run to the next. However, on random instances, recording (minimized) nogoods from restarts yields approximately the same results as MAC without restarts. On structured instances, as expected, recording nogoods from restarts is beneficial. Also, minimizing nogoods has a significant effect, particularly when classical heuristics are used. In an overall analysis, while restarting without learning somewhat improves results, nogood recording from restarts significantly improves the robustness of the solver. Nogood recording reduces the number of unsolved instances and also the average CPU time. This is because with restarts the solver never explores the same portion of the search space more than once. Figures 10.11, 10.12 and 10.13 are scatter plots displaying pairwise comparisons for MAC, MAC+RST and MAC+RST+NG^m when the heuristic $dom/ddeg$ is used. Note the presence of many dots on the right-hand side of these figures, which represent instances unsolved (within 20 minutes) by the methods whose name labels the x-axis.

Table 10.2 shows results obtained for some instances of the queens-knights problem. As indicated in section 10.4, minimizing nogoods is quite relevant on such instances since singleton arc-inconsistent values can be detected. Note that results are less impressive with the heuristic $dom/wdeg$, which helps to reducing thrashing here.

		MAC		
		+RST	+RST+NG	+RST+NG^m
Random instances (1,390 instances)				
dom/ddeg	#time-outs	270	301	276	273
	CPU	40.4	57.6	41.9	42.0
bz	#time-outs	305	330	311	311
	CPU	73.2	103.2	70.5	71.1
dom/wdeg	#time-outs	266	278	274	268
	CPU	36.4	45.8	38.1	41.2
Structured instances (2,231 instances)				
dom/ddeg	#time-outs	873	863	825	772
	CPU	87.5	97.8	79.7	72.4
bz	#time-outs	789	788	757	738
	CPU	79.0	92.4	74.8	71.5
dom/wdeg	#time-outs	623	554	551	551
	CPU	50.5	51.3	51.4	50.8
Random and structured instances (3,621 instances)				
dom/ddeg	#time-outs	1,143	1,164	1,101	1,045
	CPU	66.1	79.6	62.6	58.6
bz	#time-outs	1,094	1,118	1,068	1,049
	CPU	76.4	97.3	72.8	71.3
dom/wdeg	#time-outs	889	832	825	819
	CPU	44.1	48.8	45.4	46.5

Table 10.1. *Number of unsolved instances and average CPU time on the benchmarks of the 2006 constraint solver competition (first round), given 20 minutes*

		MAC		
		+RST	+RST+NG	+RST+NG^m
qk-12-5-mul	dom/ddeg	265.1	408.9	256.2	2.1
	bz	255.7	377.9	250.8	2.1
	dom/wdeg	3.1	1.8	2.6	1.6
qk-25-5-mul	dom/ddeg	time-out	time-out	time-out	4.9
	bz	time-out	time-out	time-out	5.1
	dom/wdeg	time-out	4.2	4.8	4.3
qk-50-5-mul	dom/ddeg	time-out	time-out	time-out	67.3
	bz	time-out	time-out	time-out	65.3
	dom/wdeg	time-out	59.5	44.6	43.9

Table 10.2. *CPU time to solve some instances of the queens-knights problem, given 20 minutes*

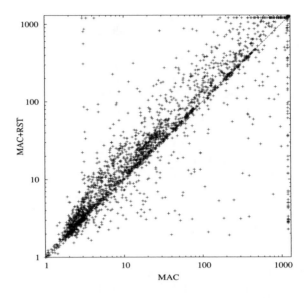

Figure 10.11. *Pairwise comparison (CPU time) between MAC and MAC-RST on the* 3,621 *instances used as benchmarks of the 2006 constraint solver competition (first round). The variable ordering heuristic is dom/ddeg*

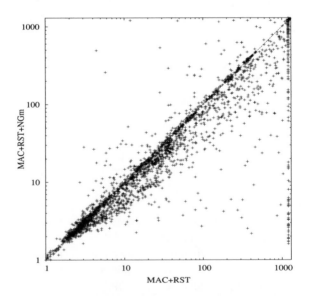

Figure 10.12. *Pairwise comparison (CPU time) between MAC-RST and MAC-RST-NG^{m} on the* 3,621 *instances used as benchmarks of the 2006 constraint solver competition (first round). The variable ordering heuristic is dom/ddeg*

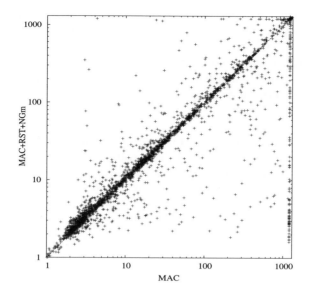

Figure 10.13. *Pairwise comparison (CPU time) between MAC and MAC-RST-NG^{m} on the 3,621 instances used as benchmarks of the 2006 constraint solver competition (first round). The variable ordering heuristic is dom/ddeg*

10.6. Conclusion

This chapter has explored the recording of nogoods in conjunction with a restart strategy. Restarting search can help to avoid the heavy-tailed phenomenon that has been observed on some structured instances. The drawback of restarting without recording nogoods is that parts of the search tree may be explored more than once. Recording nogoods prevents re-exploration and renders randomization unnecessary, especially when an adaptive heuristic is used.

Nogoods are recorded in the form of new constraints which can be propagated efficiently by means of the 2-literal watching technique introduced for SAT. For propagation, the only event we need to intercept is when a variable becomes fixed so that its domain becomes a singleton. This technique does not require maintenance of data structures upon backtracking, so nogood constraints can be easily integrated in constraint solvers.

It is important to note that nogood constraints may share similar scopes and that this directly affects filtering. For example, assume that we have two variables x and y such that $\mathrm{dom}(x) = \mathrm{dom}(y) = \{a, b\}$ and two nogood constraints $c_1 : x \neq a \vee y \neq a$ and $c_2 : x \neq a \vee y \neq b$. There is no possible inference from c_1 and c_2 because the two constraints each involve two free decisions. Normalization of the constraint network would yield a single constraint $c_3 : x \neq a \lor (y \neq a \land y \neq b)$. For $\text{dom}(x) = \text{dom}(y) = \{a, b\}$, it is easy to see that (x, a) has no support on c_3. Merging nogood constraints that have similar scopes strengthens propagation but may produce constraints that have arbitrary constraint relations. This may not be helpful because dynamically integrating and merging arbitrary constraints is complex, and the complexity of enforcing GAC is no longer linear in the arity of the constraints. Nevertheless, this certainly deserves to be studied.

Other uses of watched literals in constraint satisfaction [GEN 06b] include an efficient implementation for the global sum constraint (on Boolean variables), for the global element constraint and also for table constraints. For table constraints the extent to which a watched literal approach can compete with recent techniques (introduced in Chapter 5) is not yet clear.

Chapter 11

State-based Reasoning

In classical heuristic search algorithms (e.g. A* [HAR 68, HAR 72]) or game search algorithms (e.g. Minimax [NEU 28]), nodes in the search tree represent world states, and transitions represent moves. Many states may be encountered several times at possibly different depths because different sequences of moves from the initial state of the problem instance can yield identical situations in the world. Moreover, a state s for a node at depth i of the search tree cannot lead to a better solution than a node containing the same state s previously encountered at a depth $j < i$. As a consequence, some portions of the search space may be unnecessarily evaluated and explored several times, which may be costly.

The phenomenon of revisiting identical states reached from different sequences of transitions, better known as *transpositions*, was identified very early in the context of chess software [GRE 67, SLA 77, MAR 92]. One solution to this problem is to store the encountered nodes, plus some related information (e.g. depth, heuristic evaluation), in a so-called *transposition table*. A direct use of transposition tables in backtrack search algorithms is clearly useless because the state of a constraint network (the current domains of variables) associated with a node of the search tree cannot be encountered twice. Indeed, with a binary branching scheme for example, once it has been proven that a positive decision $x = a$ cannot lead to a solution, the opposite decision $x \neq a$ is taken in the second branch. In other words, in the first branch the domain of x is reduced to the singleton $\{a\}$, while in the second branch a is removed from the domain of x. Obviously, no state where $x = a$ has been asserted can be identical to a state where $x \neq a$ is true.

Fortunately, *partial states* can be extracted from constraint networks when analyzing the role played by variables and constraints. More precisely, at each (leaf or internal) dead-end of the search tree developed by the backtrack search algorithm, a partial snapshot of the current state (roughly speaking, a set of meaningful variables and their domains) can be recorded. In order to avoid explorations of similar subtrees occurring later during search, these *inconsistent* partial states are exploited to prune the search tree. They may be used to detect equivalence [LEC 07g] by means of a transposition table, or to detect dominance [LEC 07d] by posting new constraints. Equivalence and dominance detection by means of partial states is what we call *state-based reasoning*.

A partial state is formally defined as a set of membership decisions, which is equivalent to a generalized nogood. Consequently, the approach proposed in [KAT 03, KAT 05] that learns generalized nogoods by means of explanations can be cast in this general state-based paradigm. Approaches that learn from inconsistent values [FRE 93, RAZ 07] can also be related to state-based reasoning, since they implicitly exploit hidden partial states. Finally, reasoning from states is known to be at the heart of symmetry-breaking methods via dominance detection, see e.g. [FAH 01, FOC 01, PUG 05b, SEL 05]. These methods, presented in the next chapter, remove symmetric states and can be perceived as an additional and complementary mechanism to reinforce state-based pruning.

Section 11.1 introduces (inconsistent) partial states as well as dominance detection. In section 11.2, we present two approaches to identify inconsistent partial states during search by means of eliminating explanations and inconsistent values. Section 11.3 describes several combinable extraction operators that directly process the current states. Equivalence detection using transposition tables is described in section 11.4. Finally, a few experimental results are presented in section 11.5.

11.1. Inconsistent partial states

This section introduces the concept of an (inconsistent) partial state, and shows how it can be used to prune the search tree.

11.1.1. *Definitions*

A *partial state* corresponds to a set of variables that have non-empty domains. Equivalently, a partial state corresponds to a (well-formed) set of membership decisions; see Definition 1.58.

DEFINITION 11.1.– *[Partial State] A partial state* Δ *is a well-formed set of membership decisions;* Δ *is strict iff each membership decision of* Δ *is strict. A partial state* Δ *on a constraint network* P *is a well-formed set of valid membership decisions on* P; Δ *is strict on* P *iff each membership decision of* Δ *is strict on* P.

In a strict partial state, every membership decision constitutes a real restriction. Recall that a set Δ of membership decisions is well-formed when each variable occurs at most once in Δ; we denote by $\mathrm{vars}(\Delta)$ the set of variables occurring in membership decisions of Δ. If Δ is a partial state and if $x \in D_x$ is a membership decision that belongs to Δ, we denote D_x by $\mathrm{dom}^{\Delta}(x)$. It is important that if P is a constraint network involving x and is such that $\mathrm{dom}^{\Delta}(x) \not\subseteq \mathrm{dom}^{P}(x)$, then Δ cannot be a partial state on P; each membership decision of a partial state on P must be valid on P.

There is an immediate partial state on any constraint network P. This partial state is built by taking into account of all variables of P.

DEFINITION 11.2.– *[Current State] The* current state *of a constraint network P is the partial state* $\{(x \in \mathrm{dom}^{P}(x)) \mid x \in \mathrm{vars}(P)\}$ *on P.*

EXAMPLE.– Figure 11.1 shows the current state of a constraint network P, together with three partial states Δ_1, Δ_2 and Δ_3 on P. Δ_1 and Δ_2 are strict on P, but Δ_3 is not strict on P because $\mathrm{dom}^{P}(v) = \mathrm{dom}^{\Delta_3}(v)$. We have $\mathrm{vars}(\Delta_1) = \{w, z\}$, $\mathrm{dom}^{\Delta_1}(w) = \{b, c\}$ and $\mathrm{dom}^{\Delta_1}(z) = \{a, b, d\}$.

P	Δ_1	Δ_2	Δ_3
$v \in \{a, b, c, d\}$	$w \in \{b, c\}$	$v \in \{b, d\}$	$v \in \{a, b, c, d\}$
$w \in \{a, b, c, d\}$	$z \in \{a, b, d\}$	$x \in \{c\}$	$w \in \{b, c\}$
$x \in \{a, b, c, d\}$		$z \in \{a, b\}$	$z \in \{a, b, d\}$
$y \in \{a, b, c, d\}$			
$z \in \{a, b, c, d\}$			

Figure 11.1. *The current state of a constraint network P and three partial states on P. Unlike Δ_3, Δ_1 and Δ_2 are strict on P*

A constraint network can be restricted over one of its partial states as defined in section 1.4.2 (a partial state is a set of decisions). We now provide a definition in the context of this chapter.

DEFINITION 11.3.– *[$P|_\Delta$] Let P be a constraint network and Δ be a partial state on P. The* restriction $P|_\Delta$ *of P over Δ is the constraint network obtained from P by restricting the domain of each variable $x \in \mathrm{vars}(\Delta)$ to $\mathrm{dom}^{\Delta}(x)$; for each $x \in \mathrm{vars}(\Delta)$, we have $\mathrm{dom}^{P|_\Delta}(x) = \mathrm{dom}^{\Delta}(x)$ and for each $x \notin \mathrm{vars}(\Delta)$, we have $\mathrm{dom}^{P|_\Delta}(x) = \mathrm{dom}^{P}(x)$.*

The restricted network $P|_\Delta$ is smaller ($\preceq_d$) than P. More precisely, if $\Delta = \emptyset$, we have $P|_\Delta = P$ and if Δ is not empty and strict on P, we have $P|_\Delta \prec_d P$. Figure 11.2 illustrates restriction over a partial state.

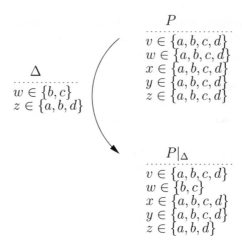

$$\Delta$$
$$w \in \{b, c\}$$
$$z \in \{a, b, d\}$$

$$P$$
$$v \in \{a, b, c, d\}$$
$$w \in \{a, b, c, d\}$$
$$x \in \{a, b, c, d\}$$
$$y \in \{a, b, c, d\}$$
$$z \in \{a, b, c, d\}$$

$$P|_{\Delta}$$
$$v \in \{a, b, c, d\}$$
$$w \in \{b, c\}$$
$$x \in \{a, b, c, d\}$$
$$y \in \{a, b, c, d\}$$
$$z \in \{a, b, d\}$$

Figure 11.2. *The restriction* $P|_{\Delta}$ *of a constraint network* P *over a (strict) partial state* Δ *on* P. *Current states are given for* P *and* $P|_{\Delta}$

When a variable x does not belong to a partial state Δ (more precisely, when $x \notin \text{vars}(\Delta)$), this implicitly means that the domain of x remains unchanged by Δ. Thus, in practice, it is sufficient to handle strict partial states, which have the advantage of being shorter. A strict partial state can be derived readily from any partial state.

DEFINITION 11.4.– *[$\Delta^{s(P)}$] Let P be a constraint network and Δ be a partial state on P. $\Delta^{s(P)}$ denotes the set of membership decisions of Δ that are strict on P.*

For example in Figure 11.1, Δ_1 is $\Delta_3^{s(P)}$. It is important to note that Δ and $\Delta^{s(P)}$ are effectively equivalent because $P|_{\Delta} = P|_{\Delta^{s(P)}}$.

A partial state Δ on a constraint network P is said to be *inconsistent* if the network defined as the restriction of P over Δ is unsatisfiable.

DEFINITION 11.5.– *[Inconsistent Partial State] Let P be a constraint network and Δ be a partial state on P. Δ is an inconsistent partial state on P, IPS for short, iff $P|_{\Delta}$ is unsatisfiable.*

We obtain a strict inconsistent partial state by discarding membership decisions that are not strict.

PROPOSITION 11.6.– *Let P be a constraint network and Δ be an inconsistent partial state on P. $\Delta^{s(P)}$ is an inconsistent partial state on P.*

A partial state Δ is said to *dominate* a constraint network if each variable involved in Δ occurs in this network with a smaller domain.

DEFINITION 11.7.– *[Dominance] Let P be a constraint network and Δ be a partial state such that* $\text{vars}(\Delta) \subseteq \text{vars}(P)$. *$\Delta$ dominates P iff* $\forall x \in \text{vars}(\Delta)$, $\text{dom}^P(x) \subseteq \text{dom}^\Delta(x)$.

When a partial state Δ dominates a constraint network P, P entails[1] Δ, i.e. $P|_\Delta = P$; see Definition 1.60. By definition, a strict (non-empty) partial state Δ on a constraint network P cannot dominate P. So this notion of dominance (by a partial state on P) is useful only for constraint networks strictly smaller than P as shown in Figure 11.3.

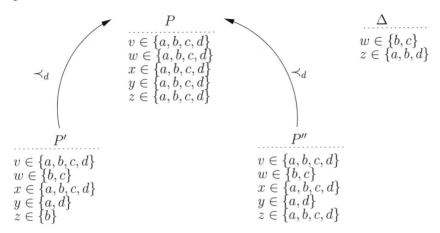

Figure 11.3. *Two constraint networks P' and P'' (strictly) smaller than P and a partial state Δ on P. P' is dominated by Δ*

The following proposition is at the heart of state-based reasoning by dominance detection.

PROPOSITION 11.8.– *Let P and P' be two constraint networks such that $P' \prec_d P$, and Δ be an inconsistent partial state on P. If Δ dominates P' then P' is unsatisfiable.*

Proof. If $P' \prec_d P$, we have by monotony $P'|_\Delta \preceq_d P|_\Delta$. Since P' is dominated by Δ, $P'|_\Delta = P'$. Hence $P' \preceq_d P|_\Delta$. Δ is an IPS on P, which means that $P|_\Delta$ is unsatisfiable. We conclude that P' is unsatisfiable. $\square$

---

1. We prefer the term of dominance in the context of this chapter.

It is important to relate the notion of (inconsistent) partial state with notions of global cut seed (GCS) [FOC 01] and pattern [FAH 01]. The main difference is that a partial state can be defined on a subset of variables of a constraint network, whereas GCSs and patterns, introduced to break global symmetries, systematically contain all variables. However, since the absence of a variable x from a partial state Δ on a constraint network P implicitly means that $x \in \text{dom}^P(x)$, all these notions are fundamentally equivalent. Compared to inconsistent partial states, global cut seeds and patterns are slightly more general in their use: each complete instantiation covered by a global cut seed or a pattern may correspond to a solution that has already been found. Although such a generalization is also possible for partial states, we shall focus on inconsistent partial states because, to simplify, we restrict our presentation to the search of a unique solution.

Partial states are said to be *global* when they are defined on the initial problem P^{init}; otherwise, they are said to be *local*. Global inconsistent partial states are valid for the entire search space, whereas local inconsistent partial states only apply to some search subtrees. Unless otherwise stated, inconsistent partial states will be assumed to be global. Note that a global IPS can always be extracted from an internal dead-end of the search tree built by a backtrack search algorithm: if v is an internal dead-end and $P = \text{cn}(v)$ is the constraint network associated with v, the current state of P is an IPS itself. However, this IPS cannot be exploited later during search, unless restarts are performed or symmetries are exploited. In sections 11.2 and 11.3, we present several approaches to building relevant inconsistent partial states.

11.1.2. *Pruning the search tree*

In the context of backtrack search, Proposition 11.8 can be used to prune nodes dominated by previously identified IPSs. More precisely, every time the search algorithm generates a new node v, one can check whether $\text{cn}(v)$, the constraint network associated with v, is dominated by an IPS recorded earlier. Actually, there are two main flavors of pruning: either v is directly rejected because it is dominated, or instead some domains of variables in $\text{cn}(v)$ are filtered to ensure that dominance cannot happen later. To clarify this, we introduce the following weak version of dominance:

DEFINITION 11.9.– *[Almost Dominance] Let P be a constraint network and Δ be a partial state such that* $\text{vars}(\Delta) \subseteq \text{vars}(P)$. *$\Delta$ almost dominates P iff there exists a membership decision $x \in D_x$ in Δ such that* $\text{dom}^P(x) \not\subseteq \text{dom}^\Delta(x)$, $\text{dom}^P(x) \cap \text{dom}^\Delta(x) \neq \emptyset$ *and $\Delta \setminus \{x \in D_x\}$ dominates P.*

The interesting cases are where dominance or almost dominance involves inconsistent partial states. If a constraint network P is dominated by an inconsistent partial state then P is necessarily unsatisfiable; this follows from Proposition 11.8.

Moreover, a constraint network P that is almost dominated by an IPS Δ can be simplified by removing every value which would make the network dominated. Indeed, if x is the only variable of P such that $\text{dom}^P(x) \not\subseteq \text{dom}^\Delta(x)$, we can safely infer that each value in $\text{dom}^P(x) \cap \text{dom}^\Delta(x)$ is inconsistent; by definition, $\text{dom}^P(x) \cap \text{dom}^\Delta(x) \neq \emptyset$, so we know that at least one inconsistent value is identified. This is called enforcing 1-dominance consistency in [RAZ 03]. For example, the constraint network P'' in Figure 11.3 is almost dominated by Δ. If Δ is an IPS on P, the values a, b and d in the domain of z are inconsistent and can be removed without loosing any solution.

Strictly speaking, as shown below, 1-dominance consistency is not exactly a new consistency if we consider that each inconsistent partial state is represented by a *dominance constraint*. If Δ is an IPS, then a dominance constraint c_Δ can be built such that its scope is $\text{vars}(\Delta)$ and its relation forbids any tuple that simultaneously satisfies the membership decisions in Δ.

EXAMPLE.– Let x, y and z be three variables such that $\text{dom}^{\text{init}}(x) = \text{dom}^{\text{init}}(y) = \text{dom}^{\text{init}}(z) = \{a, b, c\}$ and $\Delta = \{x \in \{a, b\}, y \in \{c\}, z \in \{b, c\}\}$ be an IPS. The ternary dominance constraint c_Δ is such that $\text{scp}(c_\Delta) = \{x, y, z\}$ and $\text{rel}(c_\Delta) = \text{dom}^{\text{init}}(x) \times \text{dom}^{\text{init}}(y) \times \text{dom}^{\text{init}}(z) \setminus \{a, b\} \times \{c\} \times \{b, c\}$. Equivalently, $\text{rel}(c_\Delta) = \{c\} \times \{a, b, c\} \times \{a, b, c\} \cup \{a, b, c\} \times \{a, b\} \times \{a, b, c\} \cup \{a, b, c\} \times \{a, b, c\} \times \{a\}$.

Like nogood constraints (see section 10.3.1), dominance constraints can be represented in intensional form simply by applying De Morgan's law on inconsistent partial states viewed as logical conjunctions of membership decisions. For example, from the IPS $\Delta = \{x \in \{a, b\}, y \in \{c\}, z \in \{b, c\}\}$, we can formulate the dominance constraint $c_\Delta : x \notin \{a, b\} \vee y \notin \{c\} \vee z \notin \{b, c\}$, or equivalently $c_\Delta : x \in \{c\} \vee y \in \{a, b\} \vee z \in \{a\}$ if $\text{dom}^{\text{init}}(x) = \text{dom}^{\text{init}}(y) = \text{dom}^{\text{init}}(z) = \{a, b, c\}$. Generally speaking, for each decision $x \in D_x$ occurring in Δ, the complementary decision $x \in \text{dom}^{\text{init}}(x) \setminus D_x$ occurs in (the predicate expression of) the dominance constraint c_Δ. We shall refer to these complementary decisions as decisions of the constraint c_Δ, which will sometimes be considered to be a set.

Membership decisions may be in three different states with respect to the current problem. A membership decision $x \in D_x$ is said to be *satisfied* (i.e. inevitably true) iff $\text{dom}(x) \subseteq D_x$. A membership decision $x \in D_x$ is said to be *falsified* (i.e. inevitably false) iff $\text{dom}(x) \cap D_x = \emptyset$. A membership decision which is neither satisfied nor falsified is said to be *free* (undetermined); here we have $\emptyset \subset \text{dom}(x) \setminus D_x \subset \text{dom}(x)$. For example, if $\text{dom}(x) = \{a, b\}$, $\text{dom}(y) = \{b\}$ and $\text{dom}(z) = \{a, c\}$, then $x \in \{c\} \vee y \in \{a, b\} \vee z \in \{a\}$ is (the predicate expression of) a dominance constraint such that the first decision is falsified, the second is satisfied and the third is free.

An IPS Δ, viewed as a dominance constraint c_Δ, simply states that at least one decision occurring in the predicate expression of c_Δ must be evaluated to true. Similarly to nogood constraints, four cases are possible when dealing with a dominance constraint c_Δ:

1) c_Δ is entailed because one decision of c_Δ is satisfied: the current problem cannot be dominated by Δ.

2) c_Δ is disentailed because all decisions of c_Δ are falsified: the current problem is dominated by Δ (so backtrack is necessary).

3) c_Δ contains no satisfied decisions and exactly one free decision: the current problem is almost dominated by Δ (this free decision can be forced to be satisfied).

4) c_Δ contains no satisfied decisions and (at least) two free decisions: the current problem is neither dominated nor almost dominated by Δ.

It is easy to see that so long as there are (at least) two free decisions in c_Δ, the constraint c_Δ is generalized arc-consistent. In other words, it is only when Δ dominates or almost dominates the current network that the constraint c_Δ is not generalized arc-consistent. If the current problem is dominated by the IPS Δ, this means that the constraint c_Δ is violated and consequently one has to backtrack (if possible). If the current problem is almost dominated by the IPS Δ, then forcing the unique free decision (to be satisfied) means enforcing generalized arc consistency by removing some value(s) from the domain of the variable involved in this decision. Consequently, checking dominance and enforcing 1-dominance consistency [RAZ 03] from an IPS Δ is equivalent to enforcing generalized arc consistency on c_Δ.

Algorithm 81: enforceGAC-ips(P: $\mathscr{P}$, c_Δ: dominance constraint): set of vars

Output: the set of variables in $\mathrm{scp}(c_\Delta)$ with reduced domain

1   $X \leftarrow \{x \in \mathrm{scp}(c_\Delta) \mid \mathrm{dom}(x) \not\subseteq \mathrm{dom}^\Delta(x)\}$
2   **if** $|X| = 0$ **then**
3     $\lfloor$ throw INCONSISTENT   // P is dominated by the IPS Δ
4   **if** $|X| = 1$ **then**
5   let x be the variable in X
6   **if** $\mathrm{dom}(x) \cap \mathrm{dom}^\Delta(x) \neq \emptyset$ **then**
        // P is almost dominated by the IPS Δ
7       $\mathrm{dom}(x) \leftarrow \mathrm{dom}(x) \setminus \mathrm{dom}^\Delta(x)$
8   **return** $\{x\}$ // potentially, $\mathrm{dom}(x) = \emptyset$
9   **return** $\emptyset$

Algorithm 81 is a non-revision-based filtering procedure that enforces GAC on a dominance constraint. This algorithm [RAZ 03] can be called by Algorithm 9: enforceGAC-type in Algorithm 9 corresponds here to enforceGAC-ips. Algorithm 81 is not optimized but clearly shows how GAC can be enforced. However, in the same way as for nogood constraints, the lazy data structure of watched literals [MOS 01, ZHA 02b, EÉN 03] can be used to enforce GAC efficiently on dominance constraints. In our context, we shall refer to *watched values* (or *watched v-values*), instead of watched literals. The idea is to mark two values in two distinct membership decisions of each dominance constraint: these allow identification of the moment where an IPS dominates or almost dominates the current problem.

EXAMPLE.– Assume that we have found two inconsistent partial states (on P^{init}) $\Delta_1 = \{x \in \{c\}, y \in \{a\}, z \in \{a, b\}\}$ and $\Delta_2 = \{x \in \{b, c\}, w \in \{a, c\}\}$, and recorded them as dominance constraints $c_{\Delta_1} : x \in \{a, b\} \vee y \in \{b, c\} \vee z \in \{c\}$ and $c_{\Delta_2} : x \in \{a\} \vee w \in \{b\}$; the initial domain of each variable is $\{a, b, c\}$. Figure 11.4 shows the dominance constraint base, with v-values (x, a) and (z, c) watched in the first dominance constraint and v-values (x, a) and (w, b) watched in the second one. Watched values are designated by markers w_1 and w_2. We also have an array of nd entries such that each entry corresponds to a v-value (x, a) of the (initial) problem and represents the head of a linked list allowing the access to the dominance constraints of $\mathscr{B}$ that contain the watched v-value (x, a). We can access such a list, denoted by $\mathscr{B}_{(x,a)}$, in constant time.

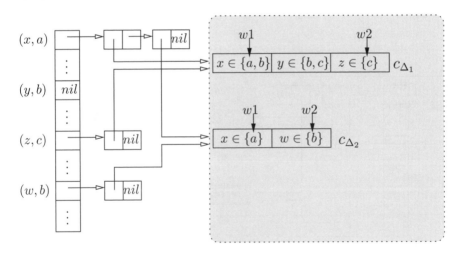

Figure 11.4. *A dominance constraint base $\mathscr{B}$ including two dominance constraints* $c_{\Delta_1} : x \in \{a, b\} \vee y \in \{b, c\} \vee z \in \{c\}$ *and* $c_{\Delta_2} : x \in \{a\} \vee w \in \{b\}$

So long as both watched values in a dominance constraint are present, the membership decisions in which they appear are free (or satisfied), and consequently the constraint is generalized arc-consistent. Propagation is guided by deleted values. Whenever a v-value (x, a) is deleted, the list $\mathscr{B}_{(x,a)}$ is visited. For each dominance constraint c of this list, a *watchable value*, i.e. a value present in the current problem,

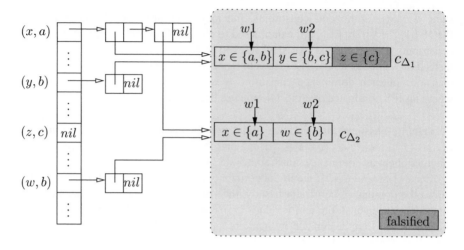

Figure 11.5. *The dominance constraint base $\mathscr{B}$ of Figure 11.4 after deleting the value c from* $\operatorname{dom}(z)$. (y, b) *is the new watched v-value in* c_{Δ_1}

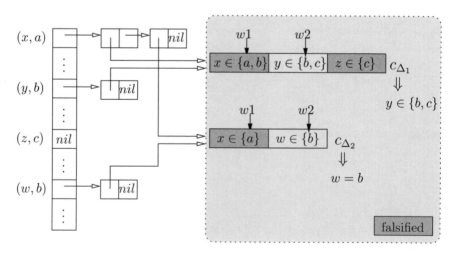

Figure 11.6. *The dominance constraint base $\mathscr{B}$ of Figure 11.5 after assigning the value c to x. The decisions $y \in \{b, c\}$ and $w = b$ are inferred because no other value is watchable in both constraints*

must be sought (but not in the domain containing the second watched value). Either this search is successful and this value becomes the new watched one (replacing (x, a)), or we have to force the decision involving the second watched value of c_Δ in order to make c_Δ generalized arc-consistent (possibly generating a domain wipe-out).

EXAMPLE.– The dominance constraint base in Figure 11.5 is obtained from Figure 11.4 when the v-value (z, c) is removed. Consequently, the v-value (y, b) is now watched instead of (z, c) in c_{Δ_1}. Imagine that the variable x is later assigned the value c; the v-values (x, a) and (x, b) are then deleted. The two dominance constraints in $\mathcal{B}_{(x,a)}$ allow some inferences to be made (because there is no longer a watchable value). This is shown in Figure 11.6.

Using watched values in dominance constraints has two main advantages. First, the worst-case time complexity of enforcing GAC on a dominance constraint c_Δ is linear in the size of c_Δ. More precisely, if k is the total number of values occurring in membership decisions of c_Δ, i.e. $k = \sum_{(x \in D_x) \in c_\Delta} |D_x|$, then c_Δ can be made generalized arc-consistent in $O(k)$; this is bounded by $O(nd)$. It is sufficient to check only once whether a value is watchable. For example, w_1 can traverse the list of values occurring in c from left to right while w_2 can traverse the same list in reversed order. The search for a watchable value is stopped when w_1 and w_2 refer to the same membership decision. The second advantage of using watched values is that, as expected, no restoration work is required upon backtracking. This saves time and furthermore the integration of this technique into constraint solvers is made easy[2] Whenever a v-value (x, a) is deleted, the dominance constraint base $\mathcal{B}$ is woken up, and more precisely, dominance constraints accessed by $\mathcal{B}_{(x,a)}$ are reviewed. When values are restored, no maintenance is required.

Use of the structure of watched literals has been suggested in [KAT 03, RIC 06] to propagate generalized nogoods. And as seen in the next section, generalized nogoods are basically equivalent to inconsistent partial states. For generalized nogoods, inferences may be conducted by using watched decisions, possibly positive or negative, generalizing the approach described in Chapter 10 and developed for nogood constraints. However, this reveals to be strictly weaker than enforcing GAC. For example, let $x = a \vee x = b \vee y \neq c$ be a generalized nogood, seen here as a constraint after applying De Morgan's law. We have $\mathrm{dom}^{\mathrm{init}}(x) = \mathrm{dom}^{\mathrm{init}}(y) = \{a, b, c\}$, $\mathrm{dom}(x) = \{a, b, c\}$ and $\mathrm{dom}(y) = \{c\}$. In this nogood constraint, the two decisions $x = a$ and $x = b$ are free, and so can be watched without producing any inference. The dominance constraint equivalent to this generalized nogood constraint is $x \in \{a, b\} \vee y \in \{a, b\}$. When GAC is enforced on this dominance

---

2. Nevertheless, this requires intercepting each deletion of a value as an elementary event, which makes propagation of dominance constraints a little bit more intrusive than propagation of nogood constraints.

constraint, $x \neq c$ is inferred (this is guaranteed in practice by the fact of selecting two watched values in two different domains).

In [RIC 06], a different approach to store and enforce GAC on (generalized) nogoods is proposed. Nogoods are compactly represented by an automaton but the dynamic compilation of nogoods seems difficult to achieve in practice.

11.2. Learning from explanations and failed values

This section presents two approaches to the identification of inconsistent partial states during search. The first approach allows global IPSs (or equivalently, generalized nogoods) to be identified through the management of eliminating explanations. The second approach allows IPSs to be identified from inconsistent values called *failed values*. The implementation of each of these two approaches can be regarded as an operator ρ that extracts inconsistent partial states from certain nodes of the search tree, or (IPS) *extraction operator*.

11.2.1. *Learning generalized nogoods*

It is worth mentioning that inconsistent partial states are basically equivalent to generalized nogoods. From any inconsistent partial state, it is possible to build an equivalent generalized nogood that only contains negative decisions. Conversely, for any generalized nogood there exists a unique equivalent strict inconsistent partial state; see Proposition 1.59. In fact, strict partial states represent a useful kind of canonical form for equivalent generalized nogoods.

EXAMPLE.– Consider three variables x, y and z such that $\text{dom}^{\text{init}}(x) = \text{dom}^{\text{init}}(y) = \text{dom}^{\text{init}}(z) = \{a, b, c\}$. The sets $\{x = a, y \neq b, y \neq c, z \neq b\}$ and $\{x = a, y = a, z \neq b\}$, regarded as generalized nogoods, are equivalent. They are also equivalent to the strict inconsistent partial state $\{x \in \{a\}, y \in \{a\}, z \in \{a, c\}\}$. A generalized nogood only involving negative decisions and equivalent to previous nogoods is $\{x \neq b, x \neq c, y \neq b, y \neq c, z \neq b\}$.

To derive generalized nogoods (or equivalently inconsistent partial states) the initial observation made in [KAT 03] is the following: if x is a variable of the problem, then to find a solution x must necessarily be assigned a value from its domain. This means that we cannot have: $x \neq a_1 \wedge x \neq a_2 \wedge \cdots \wedge x \neq a_d$ where $\text{dom}^{\text{init}}(x) = \{a_1, a_2, \ldots, a_d\}$. The set $\{x \neq a_1, x \neq a_2, \ldots, x \neq a_d\}$ is thus a "must have a value" generalized nogood[3]. If during search, we obtain a

---

3. Strictly speaking, according to our definitions, this is not a generalized nogood since the set is not well-formed.

domain wipe-out for x, and if we have an eliminating explanation $\text{expl}(x \neq a_i)$ for each value $a_i \in \text{dom}^{\text{init}}(x)$, then a nogood can be computed automatically: this is $\cup_{a_i \in \text{dom}^{\text{init}}(x)} \text{expl}(x \neq a_i)$. However, when classical eliminating explanations are collected, this nogood is standard (i.e. not generalized) because it only contains positive decisions.

To discover generalized nogoods, it is only necessary to keep track of the order in which decisions are made. The *depth* of a positive decision (i.e. variable assignment) taken during search is $(p, 0)$ where p denotes the number of instantiated variables. The *depth* of the negative decisions (i.e. value removals[4]) inferred (directly from the positive decision that have just been taken, or indirectly from propagation) in sequence after this assignment is (p, i) where i is the order in which they occur. A decision δ' at depth (p', i') is deeper than a decision δ at depth (p, i) iff $p' > p$ or $p' = p$ and $i' > i$. A scheme, called a *first-decision scheme*, for learning generalized nogoods is proposed in [KAT 05]. After each conflict, Algorithm 82 iteratively replaces the deepest negative decisions in the implicit "must have a value" nogood with their eliminating explanations until a positive decision becomes the deepest decision.

Algorithm 82: computeGeneralizedNogood(P: $\mathscr{P}$, x: variable): nogood

---

Require: x is a variable whose domain has been wiped-out
Output: a generalized nogood

1   $\Delta \leftarrow \{x \neq a_i \mid a_i \in \text{dom}^{\text{init}}(x)\}$
2   **while** *the deepest decision in Δ is not positive* **do**
3   pick and delete the deepest negative decision $y \neq b$ in Δ ;   // y may be x
4      $\Delta \leftarrow \Delta \cup \text{expl}(y \neq b)$
5   **return** Δ

EXAMPLE.– In the following illustration of the first-decision scheme, Figure 11.7 shows the way some decisions are taken and inferred during depth-first search. Solid and dotted lines are respectively labeled with positive and negative decisions. Here, we have four variables w, x, y and z whose domains are $\{a, b, c\}$. The first positive decision $w = a$ taken by search immediately entails $w \neq b$ and $w \neq c$. Here, by propagation, $x \neq a$ is assumed to be inferred, and an eliminating explanation is computed. The respective depths of $w = a$, $w \neq b$, $w \neq c$ and $x \neq a$ are $(1, 0)$, $(1, 1)$, $(1, 2)$ and $(1, 3)$. Two additional positive decisions are taken by search ($y = a$ and $z = a$), and a few negative decisions are inferred.

Instantiation (and propagation) of the three variables w, y and z leads to a conflict where every value has been removed from $\text{dom}(x)$. A standard nogood computed

---

4. Without any loss of generality, we assume that each inference corresponds to the removal of a value.

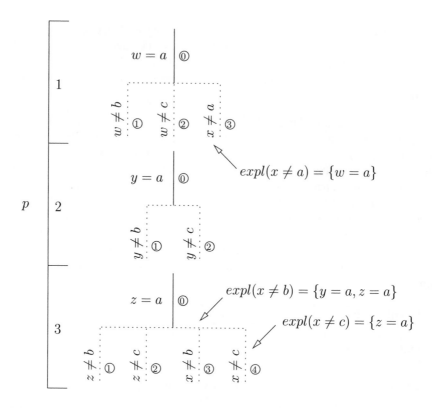

Figure 11.7. *Illustration of decisions taken and inferred during search. p is the number of instantiated variables; the values inside circles indicate the order in which decisions occur at each level. Eliminating explanations are arbitrarily given for values removed from $\mathrm{dom}(x)$*

$$expl(x \neq c) = \{z = a\}$$
$$\mathop{|||}$$

$$\{x \neq a, x \neq b, x \neq c\} \qquad \{x = c, z = a\}$$

$$expl(x \neq b) = \{y = a, z = a\}$$
$$\mathop{|||}$$

$$\{x \neq a, x \neq b, z = a\} \qquad \{x = b, y = a, z = a\}$$

$$\{x \neq a, y = a, z = a\}$$

Figure 11.8. *Generalized nogood computed following the first-decision scheme*

from this conflict using eliminating explanations is $\{w = a, y = a, z = a\}$. However, by running Algorithm 82, we obtain $\{x \neq a, y = a, z = a\}$, which is a generalized nogood, as shown in Figure 11.8. Initially, $x \neq c$ is the deepest decision in the "must have a value" nogood $\{x \neq a, x \neq b, x \neq c\}$; this is why it is replaced by $\text{expl}(x \neq c)$. Then $x \neq b$ becomes the deepest decision; this is why it is replaced by $\text{expl}(x \neq b)$. Finally, the algorithm stops, and the negative decision $x \neq a$ is not replaced, because its depth is $(1, 3)$, whereas the depth of $z = a$ is $(3, 0)$.

Note that the generalized nogood $\{x \neq a, y = a, z = a\}$ is more interesting (powerful) than the standard nogood $\{w = a, y = a, z = a\}$. Indeed, we deduce from the standard nogood that if $w = a$ and $y = a$ then necessarily $z \neq a$. But we can also make the same deduction from the generalized nogood if we simultaneously consider the nogood $\{w = a, x = a\}$, i.e. the eliminating explanation $\text{expl}(x \neq a)$. Besides, there are other situations where only the generalized nogood can be applied: for example, if $a \notin \text{dom}(x)$ and $y = a$ then necessarily $z \neq a$. For more information, see the extended version of [KAT 03].

When MAC is the backtrack search algorithm, the method can profitably be refined as follows. With each value pruned within MAC, we can associate an eliminating explanation that only contains negative decisions. More specifically, when a value is detected GAC-inconsistent because it has no support on a constraint c, it is sufficient to collect all pruned values among the domains of the variables in the scope of the constraint c. For example, if x, y and z are three variables such that $\text{dom}^{\text{init}}(x) = \text{dom}^{\text{init}}(y) = \text{dom}^{\text{init}}(z) = \{0, 1, 2\}$, if the v-values $(x, 2)$ and $(y, 2)$ have been removed, and if the constraint $c_{xyz} : x + y > z$ is enforced to be GAC-consistent, then $(z, 2)$ is removed and a possible explanation is $\text{expl}(z \neq 2) = \{x \neq 2, y \neq 2\}$. More sophisticated methods can be conceived to provide smaller sets of pruned values that cover the supports of the pruned value [KAT 05]. What is particularly interesting is that storing *generalized explanations* permits retention of the logical chain of inferences made during search. From this implicit implication graph, various schemes corresponding to different strategies of learning generalized nogoods can be conceived [ZHA 01a, RIC 06]. Note that the 1-UIP scheme that is popular in SAT solving has been found experimentally to be less effective for constraint satisfaction than the first-decision scheme [KAT 05].

11.2.2. *Reasoning from failed values*

During search some values, which we call *failed values*, are proved to be inconsistent, i.e. not to participate to any solution. It is known [FRE 93] that failed values "convey" some information: given a binary constraint network P and a v-value (x, a) of P, if there is no solution of P containing (x, a) then every solution of P contains a value for a variable $y \neq x$ which is not compatible with (x, a). Thus problem instances can be decomposed dynamically and iteratively

[FRE 93, BEN 08]. This condition concerning failed values is also used as a pruning technique in [RAZ 07].

We now show that each failed value identifies a local inconsistent partial state. A failed value [LEC 09a] is defined as follows:

DEFINITION 11.10.– *[Failed Value] Let P and P' be two constraint networks such that $P' \prec_d P$.*

– *A failed value of P' with respect to P is a v-value (x, a) of P such that $P|_{x=a}$ is unsatisfiable and $a \notin \mathrm{dom}^{P'}(x)$.*

– *A failed value of P' is a failed value of P' with respect to a constraint network strictly greater than P.*

In practice, a failed value is a value pruned from a constraint network because it has been proved to be globally inconsistent. A failed value can be identified by inference and/or search methods. For example, if $P^{\mathrm{init}}|_{x=a}$ is shown to be unsatisfiable, clearly, (x, a) can be removed from $\mathrm{dom}^{\mathrm{init}}(x)$. We then obtain a smaller constraint network $P = P^{\mathrm{init}} \setminus \{(x, a)\}$ with (x, a) being a failed value of P (with respect to P^{init}). In propositions stated in [RAZ 07], values removed during backtracking correspond to failed values.

We need to define *conflict sets* of constraint networks in terms of instantiations.

DEFINITION 11.11.– *[Conflict Set] Let P be a constraint network, x be a variable of P and $a \in \mathrm{dom}^{\mathrm{init}}(x)$.*

– *The conflict set of (x, a) on a constraint c of P involving x, denoted by $\kappa_P(c, x, a)$, is the set of valid instantiations I of $\mathrm{scp}(c) \setminus \{x\}$ on P such that $I \cup \{(x, a)\}$ does not satisfy c.*

– *The conflict set of (x, a) on P is $\kappa_P(x, a) = \cup_{c \in \mathrm{cons}(P)|x \in \mathrm{scp}(c)} \kappa_P(c, x, a)$.*

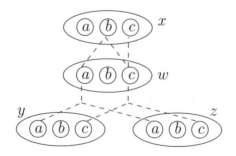

Figure 11.9. *Illustration of conflict sets*

For every conflict set κ, $\text{vars}(\kappa) = \cup_{I \in \kappa} \text{vars}(I)$. Figure 11.9 shows a simple constraint network P with a binary constraint between w and x and a ternary constraint between w, y and z; dashed edges represent forbidden tuples. Here $\kappa_P(w, a) = \{\{(x, b)\}, \{(y, a), (z, a)\}\}$ and $\kappa_P(w, c) = \{\{(x, b)\}, \{(x, c)\}, \{(y, c), (z, c)\}\}$; $\{(x, b)\}$ and $\{(y, a), (z, a)\}$ are two instantiations in $\kappa_P(w, a)$ of size 1 and 2.

Failed values and instantiations can be connected as follows:

DEFINITION 11.12.– *[Covering and Satisfaction] Let P be a constraint network, (x, a) be a failed value of P and I be a valid instantiation on P.*

- *(x, a) is* covered *by I iff $\text{vars}(\kappa_P(x, a)) \subseteq \text{vars}(I)$.*
- *(x, a) is* satisfied *by I iff $\exists J \in \kappa_P(x, a) \mid J \subseteq I$.*

Note that a failed value satisfied by an instantiation is not necessarily covered by it. However, it is shown below that when a failed value is covered by an instantiation but cannot be satisfied, a nogood is identified.

DEFINITION 11.13.– *[Failure Consistency] Let P be a constraint network.*

– *A valid instantiation I on P is* failure-consistent *for a failed value (x, a) of P iff either (x, a) is not covered by I or (x, a) is satisfied by I.*

– *A valid instantiation I on P is* failure-consistent *iff it is failure-consistent for every failed value of P; otherwise, I is said to be* failure-inconsistent.

PROPOSITION 11.14.– *Any failure-inconsistent instantiation is globally inconsistent.*

Proof. Without any loss of generality, we consider here that I is a valid instantiation on a constraint network P that is failure-inconsistent for a failed value (x, a) of P with respect to P^{init}; we have $P \prec_d P^{\text{init}}$. We know that there is no solution of P^{init} involving (x, a) because (x, a) is a failed value of P wrt P^{init}. We can even say more: for every solution S of P^{init}, the complete instantiation, denoted by $S[x/a]$, obtained from S by replacing the value assigned to x in S by a is not a solution because at least one constraint involving x is violated [FRE 93]. Because I is failure-inconsistent for (x, a), we know that I covers $\text{vars}(\kappa_P(x, a))$ while (x, a) being not satisfied by I. This means that it is not possible to extend I into a complete instantiation I' on P such that $I'[x/a]$ violates at least one constraint involving x. Every solution of P is a solution of P^{init} (since $P \prec_d P^{\text{init}}$) and every solution S of P^{init} is such that $S[x/a]$ violates at least one constraint involving x. We can deduce that I is a nogood of P. $\qquad\square$

Otherwise stated, some nogoods can be identified via deleted values (that are themselves nogoods). These nogoods are not necessarily of size 1. For example, in

Figure 11.10 there is a failed value (w, a) and three binary constraints involving w. Any valid instantiation of $\{x, y, z\}$ is globally inconsistent if it only contains values compatible with (w, a), i.e. values that correspond to strict supports for (w, a). In other words, every tuple in $C_x \times C_y \times C_z$ is a nogood (of size 3).

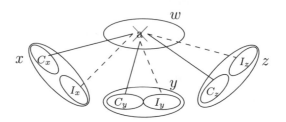

Figure 11.10. *A failed value (w, a), its compatible values in C_x, C_y and C_z and its incompatible values in I_x, I_y and I_z*

For binary constraint networks, each failed value identifies an inconsistent partial state. In Figure 11.10, this is $\{x \in C_x, y \in C_y, z \in C_z\}$. When a failed value corresponds to a globally inconsistent value of the initial problem P^{init} then the identified inconsistent partial state is global. Otherwise, this only holds in the subtree rooted by the constraint network on which the failed value is defined.

Finally, note that the kernel of a failed value (x, a) of a constraint network P, as defined in [RAZ 07], is basically $\text{vars}(\kappa_P(x, a))$. However, by using so-called responsibility sets (a kind of unsatisfiable cores), kernels can be reduced in size. By means of responsibility sets and kernels, the dominance of the current node by "recorded" inconsistent partial states can be checked. This is illustrated with FC and MAC [RAZ 07]. Interestingly, it is shown that FC-CBJ can be simulated by means of responsibility sets and kernels.

11.3. Reducing elementary inconsistent partial states

As briefly described in section 11.2, generalized nogoods can be learned during search, by analyzing conflicts before backtracking. Typically, generalized nogoods involve some instantiated variables as well as some deleted values. Each of them is built from the variable whose domain has been wiped-out, using the implicit "must have a value" nogood. Inconsistent partial states generated this way are constructed by using eliminating explanations.

An alternative approach works directly with states of internal dead-ends encountered during search. Internal dead-ends are nodes that are roots of fruitless subtrees. As already mentioned, the current state of each internal dead-end is a global inconsistent partial state. More precisely, if v is an internal dead-end and $P = \mathrm{cn}(v)$ is the constraint network associated with v, then the current state of P is an IPS on P^{init}. Such inconsistent partial states built from internal dead-ends are *elementary*.

Storing an elementary IPS in a transposition table or representing it by a dominance constraint is not relevant, because this partial state cannot dominate any node developed later by the backtrack search algorithm. In this section, we present several *reduction operators*, a special form of extraction operators, that discard variables (strictly speaking, membership decisions) from elementary IPSs. Partial states obtained by means of these operators are subsets of elementary IPSs and are said to be *simple*.

DEFINITION 11.15.– *[Simple Partial State] A partial state Δ on a constraint network P is simple iff* $\forall x \in \mathrm{vars}(\Delta)$, $\mathrm{dom}^{\Delta}(x) = \mathrm{dom}^{P}(x)$.

EXAMPLE.– Consider a constraint network P such that $\mathrm{vars}(P) = \{x, y, z\}$ with $\mathrm{dom}^{P}(x) = \mathrm{dom}^{P}(y) = \mathrm{dom}^{P}(z) = \{a, b, c\}$. $\Delta = \{x \in \{a, b, c\}, z \in \{a, b, c\}\}$ is a simple partial state on P, whereas $\Delta' = \{x \in \{a, b, c\}, z \in \{a, b\}\}$ is a partial state on P that is not simple because $\mathrm{dom}^{\Delta'}(z) \neq \mathrm{dom}^{P}(z)$.

The simple partial states obtained after reduction (as proposed in this section) are global inconsistent partial states that can be exploited later during search. Intuitively, the fewer the number of variables involved in a simple inconsistent partial state, the higher its pruning capability, and the lower its memory consumption.

We now consider a binary branching backtrack search algorithm that enforces a domain-filtering consistency ϕ at each step of the search. We assume here that ϕ at least performs backward checking, ensuring satisfaction of every constraint that only involves instantiated variables. We also assume that ϕ at most enforces generalized arc consistency. For example, the ϕ-search algorithm could be BT, FC or MAC. Consequently, any inference is performed locally, i.e. at the level of a single constraint, during constraint propagation. The consistency ϕ can be enforced by using a collection of local propagators associated with each constraint, called ϕ-propagators. These propagators may correspond either to a generic coarse-grained revision procedure, or to a specialized filtering procedure (e.g. for global constraints).

11.3.1. *E-eliminable variables*

We present first a reduction operator that removes *e-eliminable* variables. E-eliminable variables are variables that can no longer play a role because they are involved only in entailed constraints. It is rather easy to show that an e-eliminable variable is an eliminable variable; see Definition 1.70 on page 86.

DEFINITION 11.16.– *[e-eliminable Variable] A variable x of a constraint network P is e-eliminable from P iff $\forall c \in \mathrm{cons}(P) \mid x \in \mathrm{scp}(c)$, c is entailed.*

ρ^{ent} is a reduction operator that eliminates e-eliminable variables and returns a simple partial state. In $\rho^{\mathrm{ent}}(P)$, we only keep non-e-eliminable variables.

DEFINITION 11.17.– *[ρ^{ent}] For any constraint network P, $\rho^{\mathrm{ent}}(P)$ denotes the simple partial state $\{(x \in \mathrm{dom}^P(x)) \mid x \in \mathrm{vars}(P) \wedge x$ not e-eliminable from $P\}$ on P.*

The following proposition establishes that ρ^{ent} is an operator that permits extraction of an inconsistent partial state from an unsatisfiable constraint network.

PROPOSITION 11.18.– *If P is an unsatisfiable constraint network then $\rho^{\mathrm{ent}}(P)$ is an inconsistent partial state on every constraint network $P' \succeq_d P$.*

Proof. (Sketch) Let $\Delta = \rho^{\mathrm{ent}}(P)$ and let P' be a constraint network such that $P' \succeq_d P$. In $P'' = P'|_\Delta$, for each $x \in \mathrm{vars}(\Delta)$, we have $\mathrm{dom}^{P''}(x) = \mathrm{dom}^\Delta(x) = \mathrm{dom}^P(x)$ and for each $x \notin \mathrm{vars}(\Delta)$, we have $\mathrm{dom}^{P''}(x) = \mathrm{dom}^{P'}(x)$. What distinguishes P from P'' is that some values are present in P'' but not in P. But those values necessarily belong to the domain of e-eliminable variables from P. Consequently, the satisfiability of P'' is equivalent to the satisfiability of $P = P|_\Delta$, and so Δ is an IPS on P'.   □

This means that for each internal dead-end v encountered during search, ρ^{ent} extracts from $\mathrm{cn}(v)$ an IPS on P^{init}; this is a global IPS.

COROLLARY 11.19.– *If P is an unsatisfiable constraint network derived from P^{init}, i.e. $P \leq_d P^{\mathrm{init}}$, then $\rho^{\mathrm{ent}}(P)$ is a global IPS, i.e. an IPS on P^{init}.*

EXAMPLE.– To illustrate the value of the operator ρ^{ent}, consider an instance of the classical pigeonhole problem; here, we have five pigeons. This instance involves five variables $x_0, \ldots, x_4$ that represent the pigeons, and each initial variable domain is $\{0, \ldots, 3\}$ that represents the holes. The constraints state that two pigeons cannot be in the same hole, making this problem unsatisfiable since there are five pigeons for only four holes. This can be represented by a clique of binary inequation constraints: $x_0 \neq x_1, x_0 \neq x_2, \ldots, x_1 \neq x_2, \ldots$ Figure 11.11 shows a partial view of the search tree built by MAC for this instance, together with the state at each node.

In Figure 11.11(b), we first notice that the constraint networks associated with the nodes $v_1, \ldots, v_6$ are all different, since domains of variables differ by at least one value. At nodes v_3 and v_6 the only difference lies in the domains of x_0 and x_1, which

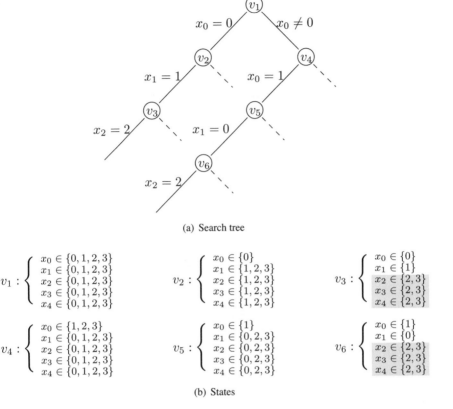

(a) Search tree

$$v_1 : \begin{cases} x_0 \in \{0,1,2,3\} \\ x_1 \in \{0,1,2,3\} \\ x_2 \in \{0,1,2,3\} \\ x_3 \in \{0,1,2,3\} \\ x_4 \in \{0,1,2,3\} \end{cases} \quad v_2 : \begin{cases} x_0 \in \{0\} \\ x_1 \in \{1,2,3\} \\ x_2 \in \{1,2,3\} \\ x_3 \in \{1,2,3\} \\ x_4 \in \{1,2,3\} \end{cases} \quad v_3 : \begin{cases} x_0 \in \{0\} \\ x_1 \in \{1\} \\ x_2 \in \{2,3\} \\ x_3 \in \{2,3\} \\ x_4 \in \{2,3\} \end{cases}$$

$$v_4 : \begin{cases} x_0 \in \{1,2,3\} \\ x_1 \in \{0,1,2,3\} \\ x_2 \in \{0,1,2,3\} \\ x_3 \in \{0,1,2,3\} \\ x_4 \in \{0,1,2,3\} \end{cases} \quad v_5 : \begin{cases} x_0 \in \{1\} \\ x_1 \in \{0,2,3\} \\ x_2 \in \{0,2,3\} \\ x_3 \in \{0,2,3\} \\ x_4 \in \{0,2,3\} \end{cases} \quad v_6 : \begin{cases} x_0 \in \{1\} \\ x_1 \in \{0\} \\ x_2 \in \{2,3\} \\ x_3 \in \{2,3\} \\ x_4 \in \{2,3\} \end{cases}$$

(b) States

Figure 11.11. *Pigeonholes: partial states identified at different nodes of the search tree*

are respectively reduced to the singletons $\{0\}$ and $\{1\}$ in v_3, and $\{1\}$ and $\{0\}$ in v_6. The domains of the other variables x_2, x_3 and x_4 are all equal to $\{2,3\}$. Figure 11.12 represents the networks, $\text{cn}(v_3)$ and $\text{cn}(v_6)$ associated with nodes v_3 and v_6 by their compatibility graphs. The structure of these two networks is very similar, the only difference being the inversion of the values 0 and 1 between x_0 and x_1.

Two crucial points about v_3 and v_6 are: (1) neither x_0 nor x_1 will subsequently play a role, and (2) checking the satisfiability of $\text{cn}(v_3)$ is equivalent to checking the satisfiability of $\text{cn}(v_6)$. Point (1) is easy to see: since arc consistency is maintained, all constraints involving x_0 and x_1 are entailed: whatever the assignment of values to the other variables, these constraints will be satisfied. Variables x_0 and x_1 are e-eliminable and can therefore be disconnected from the constraint networks in v_3 and v_6. Consequently we can immediately see that point (2) is true: the constraint sub-networks $\text{cn}(v_3) \ominus \{x_0, x_1\}$ and $\text{cn}(v_6) \ominus \{x_0, x_1\}$ consisting of the remaining

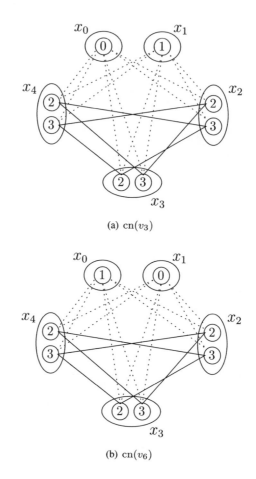

(a) $\mathrm{cn}(v_3)$

(b) $\mathrm{cn}(v_6)$

Figure 11.12. *Pigeonholes: the structure of the constraint networks* $\mathrm{cn}(v_3)$ *and* $\mathrm{cn}(v_6)$, *associated with nodes* v_3 *and* v_6, *is similar. Differently,* $\mathrm{cn}(v_6)$ *is dominated by* $\rho^{\mathrm{ent}}(\mathrm{cn}(v_3)) = \{x_2 \in \{2,3\}, x_3 \in \{2,3\}, x_4 \in \{2,3\}\}$

variables x_2, x_3 and x_4 and of the constraints involving them are identical, so $\mathrm{cn}(v_3)$ is satisfiable if and only if $\mathrm{cn}(v_6)$ is satisfiable.

If we apply the operator ρ^{ent} on node v_3, we obtain $\rho^{\mathrm{ent}}(\mathrm{cn}(v_3)) = \{x_2 \in \{2,3\}, x_3 \in \{2,3\}, x_4 \in \{2,3\}\}$. After proving that v_3 is an internal dead-end, we can record $\rho^{\mathrm{ent}}(\mathrm{cn}(v_3))$ as an inconsistent partial state. By using this IPS, MAC can avoid expanding node v_6, because it is dominated by $\rho^{\mathrm{ent}}(\mathrm{cn}(v_3))$.

11.3.2. *Proof-based extraction*

Not all constraints of an unsatisfiable constraint network are necessary to prove its unsatisfiability. Some of them form (minimal) unsatisfiable cores (see Definition 2.12 on page 112), and different methods have been proposed to extract these. Constraints of an unsatisfiable core can be identified iteratively by means of a constructive [SIQ 88], a destructive [BAK 93] or a dichotomic approach [JUN 04, HEM 06].

The following proposition states that an inconsistent partial state can be extracted from any unsatisfiable core.

PROPOSITION 11.20.– *If K is an unsatisfiable core of a constraint network P then $\Delta = \{(x \in \mathrm{dom}^P(x)) \mid x \in \mathrm{vars}(K)\}$ is an inconsistent partial state on every constraint network $P' \succeq_d P$.*

Proof. We reason by contradiction. If Δ is not an IPS on P', i.e. if $P'' = P'|_\Delta$ is satisfiable, there exists a complete instantiation I of $\mathrm{vars}(P'') = \mathrm{vars}(P') = \mathrm{vars}(P)$ such that $P|_I$ entails Δ (by construction of P'') and such that every constraint $c \in \mathrm{cons}(P'') = \mathrm{cons}(P)$ is satisfied. Since each constraint of K is included in P, and so in P'', this contradicts our hypothesis that K is an unsatisfiable core. Hence Δ is an IPS on P'.   □

From each unsatisfiable core identified during search, a global IPS can be extracted.

COROLLARY 11.21.– *If K is an unsatisfiable core of a constraint network P then $\Delta = \{(x \in \mathrm{dom}^P(x)) \mid x \in \mathrm{vars}(K)\}$ is a global IPS, i.e. an IPS on P^{init}.*

We may wish to extract such cores at internal dead-ends. Computing *a posteriori* (minimal) unsatisfiable cores from scratch using one of the approaches mentioned above seems very expensive, since even for the dichotomic approach the worst-case number of calls to the ϕ-search algorithm is $O(\log(e).k_e)$ [HEM 06], where k_e is the number of constraints of the extracted core. However, it is possible to identify an unsatisfiable core efficiently by keeping track of all constraints involved in a proof of unsatisfiability [BAK 93]. Such constraints are those used during search to remove, through their propagators, at least one value in the domain of one variable. This "proof-based" approach can be adapted to extract an unsatisfiable core from any dead-end by collecting relevant information in the fruitless subtree that has been explored.

Algorithm 83 implements this method within a backtrack ϕ-search algorithm. This is an adaptation of Algorithm 68. The recursive function binary-ϕ-search^{prf} determines the satisfiability of the given network P and returns a set of variables which is either empty if P is satisfiable or represents a proof of unsatisfiability (non-empty set of variables). A proof is composed of the variables involved in the scope of the constraints that triggered at least one removal during ϕ-propagation.

At each node, a proof is built from all inferences produced when enforcing ϕ (line 2) and also from the proofs (lines 8 and 11) associated with the left and right subtrees (once a v-value (x, a) has been selected). Note that when an IPS Δ allows some inference(s) when enforcing ϕ, this participates in the proof of unsatisfiability. Since Δ can be seen as an additional (dominance) constraint included in the initial network, each variable in $\text{vars}(\Delta)$ must be taken into account in the proof. When a node is proved to be an internal dead-end after having considered the two branches (one labeled with $x = a$ and the other with $x \neq a$), a proof of unsatisfiability is obtained by simply merging the proofs associated with the left and right branches; here, this is for P'. Note that the worst-case space complexity of managing the different local proofs of the search tree is in $O(n^2 d)$ since storing a proof is $O(n)$ and there are at most $O(nd)$ nodes per branch.

Using Algorithm 83, we can introduce a second reduction operator that only retains variables involved in a proof of unsatisfiability. This operator can be used incrementally at any internal dead-end of a search tree.

Algorithm 83: binary-ϕ-search^{prf}(P: $\mathscr{P}$): set of variables

Output: a proof of unsatisfiability of P, or $\emptyset$ if P is satisfiable

1 $localProof \leftarrow \emptyset$
2 $P' \leftarrow \phi(P)$ // $localProof$ is updated according to ϕ
3 **if** $P' = \bot$ **then**
4   **return** $localProof$
5 **if** $\forall x \in \text{vars}(P'), |\text{dom}(x)| = 1$ **then**
     // Display the solution
6   **return** $\emptyset$
7 select a v-value (x, a) of P' such that $|\text{dom}(x)| > 1$
8 $leftProof \leftarrow$ binary-ϕ-search^{prf}($P'|_{x=a}$)
9 **if** $leftProof = \emptyset$ **then**
10   **return** $\emptyset$ // since P is satisfiable
11 $rightProof \leftarrow$ binary-ϕ-search^{prf}($P'|_{x \neq a}$)
12 **if** $rightProof = \emptyset$ **then**
13   **return** $\emptyset$ // since P is satisfiable
    // $leftProof \cup rightProof$ is an unsat proof for P'
    // $localProof \cup leftProof \cup rightProof$ is an unsat proof for P
14 **return** $localProof \cup leftProof \cup rightProof$

DEFINITION 11.22.– *[ρ^{prf}] Let P be a constraint network. $\rho^{\mathrm{prf}}(P)$ denotes the simple partial state* $\{(x \in \mathrm{dom}^P(x)) \mid x \in$ *binary-ϕ-search$^{\mathrm{prf}}(P)\}$ on P.*

The following proposition establishes that ρ^{prf} is an operator which permits extraction of an inconsistent partial state from an unsatisfiable constraint network.

PROPOSITION 11.23.– *If P is an unsatisfiable constraint network then $\rho^{\mathrm{prf}}(P)$ is an inconsistent partial state on every constraint network $P' \succeq_d P$.*

Proof. Let $X =$ binary-ϕ-search$^{\mathrm{prf}}(P)$. We can show that $K = (X, \{c \in \mathrm{cons}(P) \mid \mathrm{scp}(c) \subseteq X\})$ is an unsatisfiable core of P. We deduce the result from both the definition of ρ^{prf} and Proposition 11.20. □

COROLLARY 11.24.– *If P is an unsatisfiable constraint network derived from P^{init} then $\rho^{\mathrm{prf}}(P)$ is a global IPS, i.e. an IPS on P^{init}.*

In practice, in Algorithm 83, the operator ρ^{prf} can extract an IPS between lines 13 and 14. Interestingly enough, the following proposition establishes that ρ^{prf} is stronger than ρ^{ent} (i.e. allows extraction of inconsistent partial states representing larger portions of the search space).

PROPOSITION 11.25.– *If P is an unsatisfiable constraint network then $\rho^{\mathrm{prf}}(P) \subseteq \rho^{\mathrm{ent}}(P)$.*

Proof. An entailed constraint cannot occur in any unsatisfiability proof computed by binary-ϕ-search^{prf}. An e-eliminable variable only occurs in entailed constraints, so is necessarily discarded by ρ^{prf} (from assumptions given at the beginning of this section). □

Note that, unlike ρ^{ent}, an inconsistent partial state can be extracted using ρ^{prf} only when the fruitless subtree has been explored completely. Consequently, this operator cannot be used for pruning equivalent states using a transposition table whose keys correspond to partial states, as presented in section 11.4. Nevertheless, ρ^{prf} can be fully exploited in the context of dominance detection.

11.3.3. *Justification-based extraction*

The idea of the reduction operator presented in this section is to build a simple partial state by eliminating the variables whose current domains can be inferred from the others. This is made possible by keeping track of the constraints at the origin of value removals. When a propagator associated with a constraint c deletes a v-value

(x, a), the constraint c is recorded as the *justification* of (x, a) being eliminated, denoted by $\text{just}(x \neq a) = c$. This is a form of eliminating explanation although eliminating explanations are classically decision-based (i.e. formed of positive and negative decisions). To some extent, this corresponds to a basic use of the general definition of nogood proposed in [SCH 94a] that includes a set of constraints playing the role of nogood justification. In the context of achieving arc consistency for dynamic CSP instances [BES 91], such justifications are also used to put values back into domains when constraints are retracted.

Explanations can be represented collectively by an implication graph. Given a set of decisions (the current partial instantiation), the inference process can be modeled using a fine-grained implication graph. More precisely, for each removed value, one can record positive and negative decisions implying this removal (through eliminating explanations in CSP and through clauses in SAT). For our purpose, we simply need to reason with a coarse-grained implication graph, called a *dependency graph* here, built from justifications. When a positive decision $x = a$ is taken (by the search algorithm), $\text{just}(x \neq b)$ is set to *nil* for all values $b \in \text{dom}(x)$ such that $b \neq a$, and when a negative decision $x \neq a$ is taken, $\text{just}(x \neq a)$ is also set to *nil*. On the other hand, whenever a value (x, a) is removed by a propagator associated with a constraint c, the justification of $x \neq a$ is simply given by c: we have $\text{just}(x \neq a) = c$. Since we aim to circumscribe a simple partial state (subset of the current state), we only need to know for each removed v-value (x, a), the variables responsible for its removal; these are the ones involved in $\text{just}(x \neq a)$. From this information, it is possible to build a directed graph G where vertices correspond to variables and arcs (directed edges) to dependencies between variables. More precisely, there is an arc in G from a variable x to a variable y if there is a removed v-value (y, b) whose justification is a constraint involving x. A special node denoted by *nil* is employed; there is an arc from *nil* to a variable x if x is involved in a (positive or negative) decision taken by the search algorithm, i.e. if there is a removed v-value (x, a) whose justification is *nil*. As shown below, the dependency graph can be used to reduce inconsistent partial states.

EXAMPLE.– In Figure 11.13, there is an initial binary constraint network P^{init}; see Figure 11.13(a). P^{init} involves four variables and three constraints; $\text{vars}(P^{\text{init}}) = \{w, x, y, z\}$ and $\text{cons}(P^{\text{init}}) = \{c_{wx} : w \neq x, c_{xy} : x \geq y, c_{xz} : x \geq z\}$. In Figure 11.13(b), we have the constraint network P obtained from P^{init} after assigning the value 3 to w and enforcing AC ($\phi = AC$). Figure 11.13(c) provides the justifications of values removed in P as well as the dependency graph built from these explanations. Justifications are obtained as follows. When the positive decision $w = 3$ is taken, the justifications of $w \neq 1$ and $w \neq 2$ are set to *nil*. These removals are propagated to x through the constraint $w \neq x$, leading to the removal of 3 from $\text{dom}(x)$, whence $\text{just}(x \neq 3) = c_{wx}$. This new removal is now propagated to y and z: 3 is removed from $\text{dom}(y)$ through the propagation of $x \geq y$ which constitutes its justification, and 3 is removed from $\text{dom}(z)$ through the propagation of $x \geq z$. The dependency graph is built directly from these justifications.

Important In all definitions and propositions given below, it is to be understood that P is a constraint network associated with a node of the ϕ-search tree developed for P^{init}. We obviously have $P \preceq_d P^{\text{init}}$.

DEFINITION 11.26.– *[Justification of Deletion] Let x be a variable of P and $a \in \text{dom}^{\text{init}}(x) \setminus \text{dom}^P(x)$. The justification of the deletion of (x, a), denoted by* $\text{just}(x \neq a)$ *is, if it exists, the constraint c whose associated ϕ-propagator has removed (x, a) along the path leading from the root of the search tree to node v where* $\text{cn}(v) = P$; *otherwise* $\text{just}(x \neq a)$ *is nil.*

Justifications can be used to extract a partial state from a constraint network with respect to a set of variables X. This partial state contains the variables of X that cannot be "explained" by X, called *j-eliminable* variables.

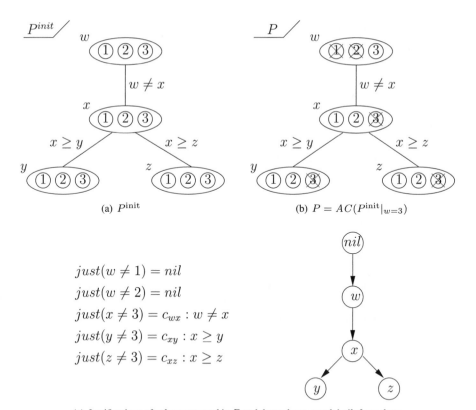

(a) P^{init}

(b) $P = AC(P^{\text{init}}|_{w=3})$

$$just(w \neq 1) = nil$$
$$just(w \neq 2) = nil$$
$$just(x \neq 3) = c_{wx} : w \neq x$$
$$just(y \neq 3) = c_{xy} : x \geq y$$
$$just(z \neq 3) = c_{xz} : x \geq z$$

(c) Justifications of values removed in P and dependency graph built from these justifications

Figure 11.13. *Managing justifications during search*

DEFINITION 11.27.– *[j-eliminable Variable] Let $X \subseteq \text{vars}(P)$ be a set of variables of P. A variable $x \in X$ is* j-eliminable *from P wrt X iff* $\forall a \in \text{dom}^{\text{init}}(x) \setminus \text{dom}^P(x)$, $\text{just}(x \neq a)$ *is a constraint c such that* $c \neq \text{nil}$ *and* $\text{scp}(c) \subseteq X$.

The dependency graph introduced earlier allows direct identification of those variables. We have the following alternative definition.

DEFINITION 11.28.– *[j-eliminable Variable] Let $X \subseteq \text{vars}(P)$ be a set of variables of P and G be the dependency graph associated with P. A variable $x \in X$ is j-eliminable from P wrt X iff $\Gamma^-(x)$, the set of predecessors of x in G, is such that $\Gamma^-(x) \subseteq X$.*

ρ^{jst} can be considered to be a reduction operator that eliminates j-eliminable variables and returns a simple partial state. In $\rho^{\text{jst}}(P)$, we only keep non-j-eliminable variables.

DEFINITION 11.29.– *[ρ^{jst}] Let $X \subseteq \text{vars}(P)$ be a set of variables of P. $\rho_X^{\text{jst}}(P)$ is the simple partial state $\{(x \in \text{dom}^P(x)) \mid x \in X \wedge x \text{ not j-eliminable from P wrt } X\}$ on P.*

The following proposition (whose proof is omitted) shows that reducing simple partial states by discarding j-eliminable variables does not fundamentally lose any information when considering P^{init} and ϕ.

PROPOSITION 11.30.– *Let Δ be a simple partial state on P and $\Delta' = \rho_{\text{vars}(\Delta)}^{\text{jst}}(P)$. We have: $\phi(P^{\text{init}}|_{\Delta'}) = \phi(P^{\text{init}}|_{\Delta})$.*

Using Proposition 11.30, we can show that for any unsatisfiable constraint network $P, \rho_{\text{vars}(P)}^{\text{jst}}(P)$ produces an inconsistent partial state on P^{init}. However, this IPS is not interesting because it is basically equivalent to the current state of P. Indeed, it is a partial state with all variables involved in a decision taken by the search algorithm. Roughly speaking, this IPS is equivalent to the generalized nogood corresponding to the set of decisions labeling the path that leads from the root of the search tree to P. Fortunately, we can safely use the operator ρ^{jst} after any other that produces a simple inconsistent partial state, as shown by the following corollary.

COROLLARY 11.31.– *Let Δ be a simple partial state on P and $\Delta' = \rho_{\text{vars}(\Delta)}^{\text{jst}}(P)$. If Δ is an IPS on P^{init} then Δ' is an IPS on P^{init}.*

Proof. If Δ is an IPS on P^{init} then $P^{\text{init}}|_{\Delta}$ is unsatisfiable (by definition). As ϕ preserves satisfiability (because ϕ is assumed to be a nogood-identifying consistency), and $\phi(P^{\text{init}}|_{\Delta'}) = \phi(P^{\text{init}}|_{\Delta})$ from Proposition 11.30, we deduce that $P^{\text{init}}|_{\Delta'}$ is unsatisfiable. Consequently Δ' is an IPS on P^{init}. □

A direct consequence of Corollary 11.31 is that the next two operators are guaranteed to produce inconsistent partial states from unsatisfiable constraint networks.

DEFINITION 11.32.– $[\rho^{\text{jst}\odot\text{ent}}, \rho^{\text{jst}\odot\text{prf}}]$ *Let P be a constraint network.*

– $\rho^{\text{jst}\odot\text{ent}}(P) = \rho^{\text{jst}}_{\text{vars}(\Delta)}(P)$ *with* $\Delta = \rho^{\text{ent}}(P)$.

– $\rho^{\text{jst}\odot\text{prf}}(P) = \rho^{\text{jst}}_{\text{vars}(\Delta)}(P)$ *with* $\Delta = \rho^{\text{prf}}(P)$.

Figure 11.14 illustrates (here, on consistent partial states) the behavior of ρ^{ent}, ρ^{jst} and their combination $\rho^{\text{jst}\odot\text{ent}}$. Applying ρ^{ent} to P from Figure 11.13 leads to the elimination of w, yielding the simple partial state Δ_1, because w is only involved in entailed constraints. Indeed, the remaining value 3 in dom(w) is compatible with the two remaining values 1 and 2 in dom(x) within the constraint $c_{wx} : w \neq x$. The three other variables are involved in constraints that are not entailed. Applying ρ^{jst} to P wrt $X = \text{vars}(P)$ leads to the elimination of x, y and z, yielding the simple partial state $\Delta_2 = \{w \in \{3\}\}$. Indeed, w is the only variable for which a removal is justified by nil; X being vars(P), this is the only relevant condition for determining variables of interest. This illustrates the fact that applying ρ^{jst} wrt all variables of a constraint network has no value: since we obtain the set of taken decisions (here $w = 3$), the partial state can never be encountered, or dominated, later without restarts. More interesting is the application of $\rho^{\text{jst}\odot\text{ent}}$. Once ρ^{ent} has been applied, yielding the partial state Δ_1 whose variables are $\{x, y, z\}$, ρ^{jst} is applied to determine which variables of Δ_1 have domains that can be determined by other variables of Δ_1. The variable x is the only one for which all removed values cannot be justified by constraints involving variables *inside* Δ_1: just($x \neq 3$) involves a variable *outside* the variables of interest. This is directly visible with the dependency graph in Figure 11.13(c). We thus obtain the simple partial state $\Delta_3 = \{x \in \{1, 2\}\}$.

The space complexity of recording justifications is $O(nd)$ while the time complexity of managing this structure is $O(1)$ whenever a value is removed or restored during search. The worst-case time complexity of ρ^{jst} is $O(ndr)$ where r denotes the greatest constraint arity. Indeed, there are at most $O(nd)$ removed values admitting a justification.

11.4. Equivalence detection

In practice, identified inconsistent partial states can be used to prune dominated nodes of the search tree, as explained in section 11.1.2. An alternative is to identify nodes that are not dominated but are strictly equivalent to IPSs. Although this appears to be a weaker way of using inconsistent partial states, it is appropriate for *transposition tables*. A transposition table is classically implemented as a hash table, which associates keys with values. Keys correspond to precise descriptions of

$$P^{init} : \left\{ \begin{array}{l} w \in \{1,2,3\} \\ x \in \{1,2,3\} \\ y \in \{1,2,3\} \\ z \in \{1,2,3\} \end{array} \right\} \qquad P : \left\{ \begin{array}{l} w \in \{3\} \\ x \in \{1,2\} \\ y \in \{1,2\} \\ z \in \{1,2\} \end{array} \right\}$$

(a) Current state of P^{init} (b) Current state of P

$$\Delta_1 = \rho^{ent}(P) = \left\{ \begin{array}{l} x \in \{1,2\} \\ y \in \{1,2\} \\ z \in \{1,2\} \end{array} \right\}$$

$$\Delta_2 = \rho^{jst}_{vars(P)}(P) = \{\ w \in \{3\}\ \}$$

$$\Delta_3 = \rho^{jst \odot ent}(P) = \rho^{jst}_{vars(\Delta_1)}(P) = \{\ x \in \{1,2\}\ \}$$

(c) Extraction of simple partial states on P

Figure 11.14. *Current states of P^{init} and P from Figure 11.13, and simple partial states on P extracted using ρ^{ent}, ρ^{jst} and $\rho^{jst \odot ent}$*

states: two keys computed from two different states must be different[5]. Values usually correspond to scores obtained after evaluating the states. An example of a hashing function has been proposed in [ZOB 70] for board games such as chess and Go. The transposition table technique has been adapted to heuristic search algorithms such as IDA* [REI 94], and has also been employed successfully in modern automated STRIPS planners such as FF [HOF 01] and YAHSP [VID 04].

In our context, values need not be stored because the only relevant information is that (partial) states are inconsistent. This means that a simple set is sufficient to store IPSs. For efficiency reasons, it is advisable to use a hash set, i.e. a set backed by a hash table. Here this set is perceived as a transposition table. Inconsistent partial states identified during search can be stored in the transposition table and can be checked before expanding each new node. A lookup in the table avoids exploration of a subtree that is equivalent to one already explored. For example, the operators ρ^{ent} and ρ^{jst} can be used to compute a partial state Δ whenever a new node v is created. If Δ belongs to the transposition table, v can be discarded. Otherwise, if v is proved later to be a dead-end, Δ is added to the transposition table. Figure 11.15 provides an illustration. Notice that ρ^{prf} cannot immediately compute a key: this requires complete exploration of the subtree rooted at v.

---

5. This condition may be relaxed for some applications in game playing.

Transposition Table

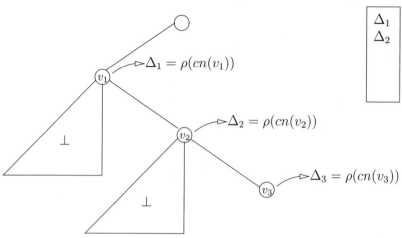

Figure 11.15. *Two inconsistent partial states Δ_1 and Δ_2 extracted using the operator ρ and stored in a transposition table. If the partial state Δ_3 belongs to the table, v_3 can be discarded*

It is important to note that when equivalence is considered, recording strict IPSs is worthwhile. This means that if Δ is an IPS on P^{init} (for example, extracted by ρ^{ent} or ρ^{jst} or learned by the first decision scheme), it is better to record $\Delta^{s(P^{\text{init}})}$ instead of Δ. Indeed, $\Delta^{s(P^{\text{init}})}$ is shorter than Δ, and $\Delta^{s(P^{\text{init}})}$ is also an IPS on P^{init}; see Proposition 11.6. When MAC is used to solve binary instances, strict inconsistent partial states identified by ρ^{ent} during search involve neither fixed variables nor variables with their initial domains.

PROPOSITION 11.33.– *Let v be a node in the search tree developed by MAC to solve a binary constraint network P^{init}, $P = \text{cn}(v)$, $\Delta = \rho^{\text{ent}}(P)$ and $\Delta' = \Delta^{s(P^{\text{init}})}$. Δ' is an IPS on P^{init} such that $\forall x \in \text{vars}(\Delta'), 1 < |\text{dom}^{\Delta'}(x)| < |\text{dom}^{\text{init}}(x)|$.*

Proof. A fixed variable x is necessarily not present in Δ because all constraints involving x are entailed (AC has been enforced). In Δ', a variable x such that $|\text{dom}^{\Delta'}(x)| = |\text{dom}^{\text{init}}(x)|$ is discarded by definition. □

Intuitively, the more variables absent from an IPS Δ, the more future nodes can be pruned by Δ. Indeed, if a node v such that $P = \text{cn}(v)$ is pruned because the partial state extracted from P is equivalent to Δ, this is because the domains of the variables in P that do not appear in Δ are in any of several possible configurations: for example, they can still contain all initial values or they can be reduced so that they only belong to entailed constraints. We can expect that recording strict IPSs is beneficial.

Figures 11.16 and 11.17 illustrate this observation (with consistent partial states). Here an initial network P^{init} involves four binary constraints and four variables whose initial domains are $\{1, 2, 3\}$. A first constraint network P_1 is obtained after assigning the variable y to 1 and enforcing AC on P^{init}. This leaves the domain of w unchanged while eliminating the value 2 from both $\text{dom}(x)$ and $\text{dom}(z)$, as shown in Figure 11.16. A second constraint network P_2 is obtained after assigning the variable w to 1 and enforcing AC on P^{init}. This time the domain of y remains unchanged while the value 2 is eliminated from $\text{dom}(x)$ and from $\text{dom}(z)$, as shown in Figure 11.17. Whereas ρ^{ent} produces two different partial states Δ_1 and Δ_2 from P_1 and P_2, the strict partial states $\Delta_1^{s(P^{\text{init}})}$ and $\Delta_2^{s(P^{\text{init}})}$ derived directly from Δ_1 and Δ_2 are identical. Although the reasons for eliminating the variables w and y in P_1 and P_2 to build partial states are different, we can use the fact that $\Delta_1^{s(P^{\text{init}})} = \Delta_2^{s(P^{\text{init}})}$ to deduce that P_1 is satisfiable iff P_2 is satisfiable.

Algorithm 84: binary-ϕ-search^{tt}(**in** P: $\mathscr{P}$): Boolean

Require: an operator ρ to extract partial states
Output: *true* iff P is satisfiable

1 $P = \phi(P)$
2 **if** $P = \perp$ **then**
3 $\quad\lfloor$ **return** *false*
4 **if** $\forall x \in \text{vars}(P), |\text{dom}(x)| = 1$ **then**
   $\quad$ // Display the solution
5 $\quad\lfloor$ **return** *true*
6 $\Delta \leftarrow \rho(P)^{s(P^{\text{init}})}$ // a strict partial state is extracted
7 **if** $\Delta \in \textit{transposition Table}$ **then**
8 $\quad\lfloor$ **return** *false*
9 select a v-value (x, a) of P such that $|\text{dom}(x)| > 1$
10 **if** *binary-ϕ-search*^{tt}$(P|_{x=a}) \vee$ *binary-ϕ-search*^{tt}$(P|_{x \neq a})$ **then**
11 $\quad\lfloor$ **return** *true*
   // P is unsatisfiable and Δ is an IPS on P^{init}
12 add Δ to *transposition Table*
13 **return** *false*

Algorithm 84, which is an adaptation of Algorithm 68, embeds a transposition table within a backtrack ϕ-search algorithm. The recursive function binary-ϕ-search^{tt} determines the satisfiability of a given network P; it maintains a domain

$$P_1 = AC(P^{init}|_{y=1})$$

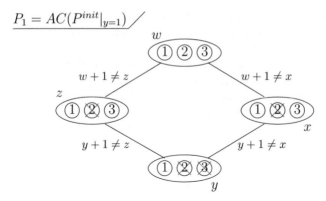

(a) Constraint network

$$\Delta_1 = \rho^{ent}(P_1) = \begin{bmatrix} w \in \{1,2,3\} \\ x \in \{1,3\} \\ z \in \{1,3\} \end{bmatrix} \qquad \Delta_1^{s(P^{init})} = \begin{bmatrix} x \in \{1,3\} \\ z \in \{1,3\} \end{bmatrix}$$

(b) Partial states

Figure 11.16. *Extracting a strict partial state from* $P_1 = AC(P^{init}|_{y=1})$

$$P_2 = AC(P^{init}|_{w=1})$$

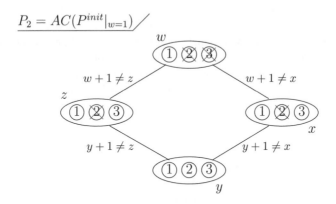

(a) Constraint network

$$\Delta_2 = \rho^{ent}(P_2) = \begin{bmatrix} x \in \{1,3\} \\ y \in \{1,2,3\} \\ z \in \{1,3\} \end{bmatrix} \qquad \Delta_2^{s(P^{init})} = \begin{bmatrix} x \in \{1,3\} \\ z \in \{1,3\} \end{bmatrix}$$

(b) Partial states

Figure 11.17. *Extracting a strict partial state from* $P_2 = AC(P^{init}|_{w=1})$

filtering consistency ϕ (at least, it performs backward checking), and prunes some nodes by means of a transposition table (tt stands for transposition table) and an extraction operator ρ. At any given stage, if the current network (after enforcing ϕ) is unsatisfiable, then *false* is returned, whereas if all variables are fixed, then *true* is returned. Otherwise, we extract a strict partial state Δ by means of the operator ρ. If Δ belongs to the transposition table, this means that Δ is an IPS on P^{init} and that P is dominated by Δ. P is then inferred to be unsatisfiable, so *false* is returned. If search continues, we select a v-value (x, a) and perform binary branching. If a solution is found, *true* is returned. Otherwise, the current network has been proven unsatisfiable and Δ can be added to the transposition table (because it is a global IPS), before returning *false*.

11.5. Experimental results

To demonstrate the potential of state-based backtrack search, we present some promising results obtained using the extraction (reduction) operators introduced in section 11.3. Other promising results are reported in [KAT 05, LEC 07g, LEC 07d, RAZ 07]. Here, our priority is dominance detection. Using a Xeon processor clocked at 3 GHz and 1 GB RAM, we have experimented with benchmarks from the second constraint solver competition including binary and non-binary constraints expressed in extensional and intensional form. We have used MAC with various combinations of extraction operators and variable ordering heuristics. Performance is measured in terms of CPU time in seconds, number of visited nodes (nodes), memory in MB (mem) and average number of variables eliminated when building inconsistent partial states (elim). For ρ^{ent}, we applied the restriction mentioned in [LEC 07g]: only fixed variables involved in constraints whose scope contain at most one unfixed variable are discarded (such variables are necessarily e-eliminable and can be detected with a modest computational effort). We also experimented with equivalence detection (using a transposition table) using the operator ρ^{ent}; the results are shown between brackets in the ρ^{ent} columns.

Table 11.1 shows the results on some series of structured instances. Tested configurations are labeled $\neg\rho$ (MAC without state-based reasoning), ρ^{ent} and $\rho^{\text{jst}\odot\text{prf}}$, each being combined with the two heuristics *dom/ddeg* and *dom/wdeg*. A first observation is that whatever the heuristic, more instances are solved using $\rho^{\text{jst}\odot\text{prf}}$. A second observation is that the performance of dominance detection can be damaged when ρ^{ent} is used: more instances are solved using equivalence detection for *dom/ddeg* (results between brackets). For ρ^{ent}, IPSs can often be quite large, which directly affects dominance checking (even if watched values are used), whereas equivalence detection can be performed in nearly constant time using a hash table.

Table 11.2 shows some results on difficult RLFAP instances. The only heuristic used here is *dom/wdeg*, in combination with all reduction operators mentioned in this

		MAC					
		dom/ddeg			*dom/wdeg*		
Series	#	$\neg\rho$	ρ^{ent}	$\rho^{\text{jst}\odot\text{prf}}$	$\neg\rho$	ρ^{ent}	$\rho^{\text{jst}\odot\text{prf}}$
aim	48	32	25 (29)	38	48	43 (47)	48
dubois	13	4	1 (2)	13	5	13 (3)	11
ii	41	10	9 (10)	16	20	18 (19)	31
os-taillard-10	30	4	4 (4)	4	10	10 (10)	13
pigeons	25	13	17 (19)	13	13	16 (18)	10
pret	8	4	4 (4)	8	4	8 (4)	8
ramsey	16	5	3 (5)	5	6	5 (6)	6
scens-11	12	0	0 (0)	4	9	7 (8)	9
	193	73	63 (73)	105	115	120 (115)	136

Table 11.1. *Number of solved instances per series (1,800 seconds allowed per instance); # is the number of instances per series. Between brackets, results are for equivalence detection*

Instance		MAC-*dom/wdeg*				
		$\neg\rho$	ρ^{ent}	$\rho^{\text{jst}\odot\text{ent}}$	ρ^{prf}	$\rho^{\text{jst}\odot\text{prf}}$
scen11-f7	CPU	26.0	11.1 (9.23)	10.4 (10.06)	5.5	5.6
	mem	29	168 (73)	49 (37)	33	33
	nodes	113 K	13,016 (14,265)	12,988 (13,220)	2,096	1,765
	elim		25.2 (25.4)	584.1 (584.7)	647.5	654.8
scen11-f6	CPU	41.2	15.0 (10.61)	15.5 (10.14)	6.4	6.8
	mem	29	200 (85)	53 (37)	33	33
	nodes	217 K	16,887 (18,938)	16,865 (17,257)	2,903	2,585
	elim		22.7 (22.1)	588.6 (589.3)	648.8	654.8
scen11-f5	CPU	202	− (72.73)	195 (98.16)	31.5	12.2
	mem	29	256	342 (152)	53	41
	nodes	1,147 K	257 K	218 K (244 K)	37,309	14,686
	elim		24.1	592.6 (583.36)	651.6	655.7
scen11-f4	CPU	591	− (−)	555 (261.67)	404	288
	mem	29		639 (196)	113	93
	nodes	3,458 K		365 K (924 K)	148 K	125 K
	elim			586.6 (593.1)	651.7	655.0

Table 11.2. *Results on difficult RLFAP instances (1,800 seconds allowed per instance). Each instance involves 680 variables. Between brackets, results are for equivalence detection*

chapter. Dominance detection with ρ^{ent} clearly suffers from memory consumption: two instances remain unsolved because of the size of the IPSs,. Combining ρ^{ent} with ρ^{jst} (i.e. $\rho^{\mathrm{jst}\odot\mathrm{ent}}$) saves memory. The best performance is obtained by combining justification-based and proof-based reasonings, i.e. with $\rho^{\mathrm{jst}\odot\mathrm{prf}}$. Note that the average size of the inconsistent partial states recorded in the base is very small: these involve about $680 - 655 = 25$ variables.

11.6. Conclusion

State-based reasoning is related to symmetry detection which is a key issue in constraint programming. This form of automated reasoning allows automatic elimination of some forms of symmetry during search. For example, state-based reasoning may discard redundant states arising from interchangeable values. Specifically, if P is a binary constraint network such that values a and b for variable x of P are interchangeable, the partial states obtained from $P|_{x=a}$ and $P|_{x=b}$ are identical after enforcing arc consistency and applying a basic extraction operator such as ρ^{ent}.

Explicit exploitation of symmetries, which is the topic of the next chapter, can dramatically reduce the search effort required to solve a CSP instance. To reach this goal, one has to identify symmetries before making use of them. There are several different ways to make use of symmetries; symmetry breaking via dominance detection (SBDD) [FAH 01, FOC 01, PUG 05b, SEL 05] is one of them and is a form of state-based reasoning. The idea of SBDD is that whenever the search algorithm reaches a new node, it just checks whether this node is equivalent to, or dominated by, a symmetric node that has been expanded previously. This requires (1) storage of information about nodes explored during search (2) using this information by considering some or all of the symmetries in the symmetry group identified initially (i.e. associated with the initial network).

Inconsistent partial states extracted by non-trivial operators or schemes are sufficient alone to break some forms of local[6] symmetry automatically. No symmetry (group) need be identified initially. However, it would be particularly interesting to combine symmetry-breaking methods with methods that extract inconsistent partial states. This would allow the effect of state-based pruning to be reinforced. This is an important perspective.

---

6. [BEN 07] proposes an original strategy to detect and eliminate local symmetries.

Chapter 12

Symmetry Breaking

The use of *symmetries* in search problems is conceptually simple. If two distinct nodes in a search tree are related by a symmetry, there is no need to explore both of them, because symmetries preserve satisfiability. When a node is an internal dead-end, the nodes that are symmetric to it are guaranteed to be internal dead-ends as well. When a node is the root of a fruitful subtree, symmetric solutions can be computed automatically, i.e. without exploring symmetric nodes. Breaking symmetries can facilitate determining the satisfiability of an instance or counting/computing the full set of solutions.

Symmetry breaking involves two distinct issues. First, symmetries must be identified. Either the user is asked to perform this (often difficult) task, or otherwise an automatic procedure identifies symmetries. Much published work does not attempt symmetry detection, but instead assumes that symmetries are given. Second, the symmetries must be exploited. For this, there are two main categories of approaches (apart from reformulation techniques). One approach posts symmetry-breaking constraints during a preprocessing stage, to speed up subsequent search. The other main strategy is to use symmetries dynamically during search to prevent exploration of irrelevant nodes.

Symmetry breaking is an important research topic in constraint programming. Avoidance of symmetric parts of a constraint network may dramatically reduce the search effort required to find a solution or to prove unsatisfiability. For the exploitation of symmetries, published methods include symmetry-breaking constraints [CRA 96, FLE 02, WAL 06b], symmetry-breaking heuristics [MES 01],

Chapter written by Christophe LECOUTRE and Sébastien TABARY.

symmetry breaking during search (SBDS) [BAC 02b, GEN 00, GEN 02b], symmetry breaking via dominance detection (SBDD) [FAH 01, FOC 01, PUG 05b, SEL 05], among others. Whatever technique is used, the construction of robust black-box solvers requires automatic discovery of symmetries.

Automatic detection of symmetries was originally introduced [CRA 92, CRA 96] in the domain of Boolean satisfiability (SAT). The idea is to identify symmetries by identifying graph automorphisms. A graph is constructed from a problem instance such that there is a one-one correspondence between symmetries of the instance and symmetries (automorphisms) of the graph. Graph automorphisms can be found by using software such as Nauty [MCK 81] or Saucy [DAR 04]. This technique has been applied successfully to SAT and CSP [ALO 02, ALO 06, RAM 04, PUG 05a, MEA 09].

This chapter is focused mainly on automatic symmetry detection. Section 12.1 presents basic notions of group theory, and section 12.2 introduces symmetry definitions for constraint networks. An overview of symmetry-breaking methods and automatic detection of symmetries is given in sections 12.3 and 12.4. Lightweight (automatic) detection of variable symmetries is proposed in section 12.5, and an algorithm to enforce GAC on lexicographic ordering constraints (which are usually posted to break symmetries) is described in section 12.6. Section 12.7 reports a few experimental results.

12.1. Group theory

This section provides a brief introduction to *group theory* (partly inspired from [VER 06, GEN 06c]). Group theory (see e.g. [BAB 96]) is the part of the mathematical discipline of abstract algebra that studies the algebraic structures known as groups. Permutation groups were the first to be studied systematically.

DEFINITION 12.1.– *[Group] A group is a pair $(G, \star)$ composed of a set G and a binary operation $\star$ defined on G, such that the following requirements are satisfied.*

 – *Closure:* $\forall f \in G, \forall g \in G, f \star g \in G.$
 – *Identity element:* $\exists e \in G \mid \forall f \in G, e \star f = f \star e = f.$
 – *Inverse element:* $\forall f \in G, \exists g \in G \mid f \star g = g \star f = e; g$ *is notated* $f^{-1}.$
 – *Associativity:* $\forall f \in G, \forall g \in G, \forall h \in G, (f \star g) \star h = f \star (g \star h).$

For example, $(\mathbb{Z}, +)$ is a group, where $\mathbb{Z}$ denotes the set of integers, and $+$ denotes ordinary addition.

A *subgroup* of a group $(G, \star)$ is a group $(H, \star)$ such that $H \subseteq G$. The *order* of a group $(G, \star)$ is the number $|G|$ of elements in G. A group can be represented by means of a subset of its elements, called a *generating set*.

DEFINITION 12.2.– *[Generating Set] A generating set of a group $(G, \star)$ is a subset H of G such that each element of G can be expressed by composition (using $\star$) of elements of H, called* generators, *and their inverses. We write $G = \langle H \rangle$. A generating set is* irredundant *iff no generator can be expressed by composition of the other generators.*

For example, if $f = g \star h$, we say that f is obtained (expressed) by composition of g and h. Generating sets allow compact representations of groups, as stated by the following proposition; an example is given later.

PROPOSITION 12.3.– *For any group $(G, \star)$, there exists a generating set of size $\log_2(|G|)$ or smaller.*

This proposition holds in particular for irredundant sets of generators. This means that groups can be represented by irredundant sets of generators with an exponential compression.

We are interested in permutation groups because we will be concerned with the symmetries that are *permutations*.

DEFINITION 12.4.– *[Permutation] A permutation on a set D is a bijection σ defined from D onto D. The image of an element $a \in D$ by σ is denoted[1] by a^σ.*

For example, let $D = \{1, 2, 3, 4\}$ be a set of four integers. A possible permutation σ on D is: $1^\sigma = 2, 2^\sigma = 3, 3^\sigma = 1$ and $4^\sigma = 4$. A permutation can be represented by a set of *cycles* of the form $(a_1, a_2, \ldots, a_k)$ which means that a_i is mapped to a_{i+1} for $i \in 1..k - 1$ and a_k is mapped to a_1. The set of cycles for our permutation σ is $\{(1, 2, 3), (4)\}$, but in practice, cycles of length 1 can be omitted because such cycles have no effect; therefore we obtain $\{(1, 2, 3)\}$. Considering D as being an ordered list rather than a set, a permutation is a rearrangement of elements in D. A permutation can be naturally applied to tuples, sets, etc. For example:

- $(3, 4, 2, 3)^\sigma = (3^\sigma, 4^\sigma, 2^\sigma, 3^\sigma) = (1, 4, 3, 1)$;
- $\{3, 4\}^\sigma = \{3^\sigma, 4^\sigma\} = \{1, 4\}$;
- $\{(1, 2), (3, 4)\}^\sigma = \{(1, 2)^\sigma, (3, 4)^\sigma\} = \{(1^\sigma, 2^\sigma), (3^\sigma, 4^\sigma)\} = \{(2, 3), (1, 4)\}$.

Henceforth, permutations will be represented by sets of cycles.

---

1. The notation a^σ has the advantage over the notation $\sigma(a)$ that it simplifies reading (mainly by omitting two round brackets).

The number of permutations on a set of n elements is $n!$. Permutations can be composed by applying several of them in sequence. It is easy to show that any composition of permutations is itself a permutation.

DEFINITION 12.5.– *[Composition] Let D be a set and let σ_1, σ_2 be two permutations on D. The composition $\sigma_3 = \sigma_1 \circ \sigma_2$ of σ_1 and σ_2 is defined as follows: $\forall a \in D$, $a^{\sigma_3} = a^{\sigma_1 \circ \sigma_2} = (a^{\sigma_2})^{\sigma_1}$.*

For the previous example, if $\sigma' = \{(2,4),(1,3)\}$ is a second permutation on D, then $\sigma'' = \sigma' \circ \sigma$ is: $1^{\sigma''} = 4, 2^{\sigma''} = 1, 3^{\sigma''} = 3$ and $4^{\sigma''} = 2$, which gives $\{(1,4,2)\}$ in cyclic form.

We can now introduce permutation groups.

DEFINITION 12.6.– *[Permutation Group] A* permutation group *is a group $(\Sigma, \circ)$ where Σ is a set of permutations on an underlying set D.*

In the following general definition of symmetry, a set of subsets of a set D is called a *structure* on D. 2^D is the powerset of D, i.e. the set of all subsets of D.

DEFINITION 12.7.– *[Symmetry] Let D be a set and $R \subseteq 2^D$ be a structure on D. A permutation σ on D is a* symmetry *on D for R iff $R^\sigma = R$.*

A symmetry can be regarded as a permutation that preserves the structure R of a set D; each element of this structure is a subset of D. Equivalently, the pair (D, R) can be regarded as a hypergraph H; a symmetry on D for R is an *automorphism* of the hypergraph H (see Appendix A.1). By considering the full set of symmetries for a structure, we obtain a group.

PROPOSITION 12.8.– *Let D be a set and $R \subseteq 2^D$ be a structure on D. The set of symmetries on D for R constitutes a group.*

Proof. The composition of two symmetries is a symmetry. The identity permutation is a symmetry and plays the role of neutral element for the set of symmetries on D for R. The inverse of a symmetry is a symmetry and the composition of symmetries is associative. □

EXAMPLE.– The symmetries (i.e. rotations and reflections) of a square form a group called a dihedral group. A square can be represented by a set of four vertices $D = \{1, 2, 3, 4\}$ and a set of four edges $R = \{\{1,2\}, \{2,3\}, \{3,4\}, \{4,1\}\}$. Figure 12.1 shows the eight possible symmetries for a square. In cyclic form, these symmetries are:

$$r^0 = \{\}, \; r^{90} = \{(1,4,3,2)\}, \; r^{180} = \{(1,3),(2,4)\}, \; r^{270} = \{(1,2,3,4)\}$$
$$f^v = \{(1,4),(2,3)\}, \; f^h = \{(1,2),(3,4)\}, \; f^d = \{(1,3)\}, \; f^c = \{(2,4)\}$$

Rotations of the square by $0°$ right, $90°$ right, $180°$ right, and $270°$ right are denoted by r^0, r^{90}, r^{180} and r^{270}, respectively. Note that r^0 is the identity permutation leaving the square unchanged. Reflections through the horizontal and vertical middle lines are respectively denoted by f^v and f^h. Reflections through the diagonal and counter-diagonal are respectively denoted by f^d and f^c.

A generating set of the dihedral group is $\{r^{90}, f^d\}$. Here:

$$r^0 = r^{90} \circ r^{90} \circ r^{90} \circ r^{90}, \; r^{90} = r^{90}, \; r^{180} = r^{90} \circ r^{90}, \; r^{270} = r^{90} \circ r^{90} \circ r^{90}$$
$$f^v = f^d \circ r^{90}, \; f^h = r^{90} \circ f^d, \; f^d = f^d, \; f^c = r^{90} \circ r^{90} \circ f^d$$

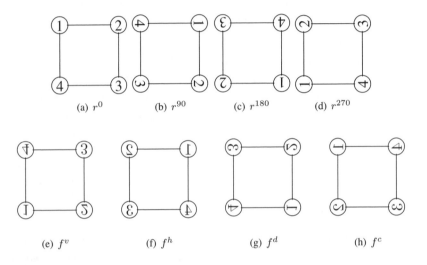

(a) r^0 (b) r^{90} (c) r^{180} (d) r^{270}

(e) f^v (f) f^h (g) f^d (h) f^c

Figure 12.1. *The eight symmetries of the symmetry group of the square. r^0 is the identity permutation*

12.2. Symmetries on constraint networks

For constraint networks, two definitions of symmetries have been recognized [COH 06] as particularly relevant because they are sufficiently general to encompass most of the previous definitions in the literature. Generality comes from the set on which symmetries are defined: this is the set of v-values (variable–value pairs). The first definition, which is used for example in [KEL 04, PUG 05a], introduces *solution symmetries* that only preserve sets of solutions. The second definition introduces *constraint symmetries* (or problem symmetries) that preserve the set of constraints. The second definition is less general than the first but is more applicable in practice. A constraint symmetry is a syntactical symmetry [BEN 94] that is not limited by necessarily choosing values in the same domain.

A simple mechanism to define symmetries, including solution and constraint symmetries, is to refer to instantiations. Sets of valid instantiations play the role of structure:

DEFINITION 12.9.– *[Symmetry on a Constraint Network] Let P be a constraint network and R be a set of valid instantiations on P. A* symmetry *on P for R is a permutation σ of* v-vals(P) *such that $R^\sigma = R$.*

This general definition is basically equivalent to Definition 12.7, but is given here in a form that is specific to constraint networks. Sometimes symmetries are restricted so that only variables or values are permuted. A *variable symmetry* does not change values, whereas a *value symmetry* does not change variables.

DEFINITION 12.10.– *[Variable and Value Symmetries] Let P be a constraint network and R be a set of valid instantiations on P.*

– A variable symmetry *on P for R is a symmetry σ on P for R such that for every $(x, a) \in$ v-vals(P), $(x, a)^\sigma = (x^{\sigma_{\text{vars}}}, a)$ where σ_{vars} is a permutation of* vars(P).

– A value symmetry *on P for R is a symmetry σ on P for R such that for every $(x, a) \in$ v-vals(P), $(x, a)^\sigma = (x, a^{\sigma_x})$ where σ_x is a permutation of* dom(x).

Clearly, a variable symmetry is defined (equivalently) by a permutation on vars(P), and a value symmetry by a permutation on each domain. We shall sometimes use these simpler permutations. The following proposition is related to Proposition 12.8; the proof is omitted.

PROPOSITION 12.11.– *Let P be a constraint network and R be a set of valid instantiations on P. The set of symmetries on P for R is a group, denoted by* Sym(P, R). *The set of variable symmetries on P for R and the set of value symmetries on P for R are two subgroups of* Sym(P, R).

We now define solution and constraint symmetries simply by considering two special structures (sets of instantiations). A solution symmetry is a permutation of the v-values that preserves the set of solutions.

DEFINITION 12.12.– *[Solution Symmetry] A* solution symmetry *on a constraint network P is a symmetry on P for* sols(P), *i.e. a permutation σ of* v-vals(P) *such that* sols$(P)^\sigma =$ sols(P). Hereafter, *symmetry* alone means a solution symmetry.

A constraint symmetry (also called a problem symmetry) is a permutation of the v-values of a constraint network P that preserves its set of constraints, or more precisely, its compatibility hypergraph (or micro-structure) $\mu(P)$; see Definition 1.32.

DEFINITION 12.13.– *[Constraint Symmetry] A* constraint symmetry *on a constraint network P is a symmetry on P for $\mu^E(P)$, i.e. a permutation σ of* v-vals(P) *such that $\mu^E(P)^\sigma = \mu^E(P)$ where $\mu^E(P)$ is the set of hyperedges in the micro-structure of P.*

Note that hyperedges in the set $\mu^E(P)$ are valid instantiations on P; this satisfies Definition 12.9. A constraint symmetry is necessarily a solution symmetry, but the reverse is not true. For example, any permutation of the v-values of an unsatisfiable constraint network is a solution symmetry, irrespective of whether the network has any constraint symmetry. The group $\mathrm{Sym}(P, \mu^E(P))$ is a subgroup [COH 06] of $\mathrm{Sym}(P, \mathrm{sols}(P))$ and is equivalent to the automorphism group of the micro-structure of P.

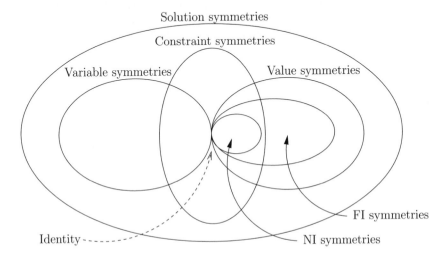

Figure 12.2. *Relationships between groups of symmetries (represented by ovals) on a constraint network. FI and NI symmetries are symmetries built from full interchangeable v-values and neighborhood interchangeable v-values, respectively*

A particular case of solution symmetry is full interchangeability; see Definition 1.62. More precisely, if (x, a) and (x, b) are two interchangeable v-values, then the permutation $\sigma_{(x,a) \leftrightarrow (x,b)}$ that only swaps the two v-values is a solution symmetry; in cyclic form, we have $\sigma_{(x,a) \leftrightarrow (x,b)}$ defined by the unique cycle $((x, a), (x, b))$. This is also a value symmetry. On the other hand, *neighborhood interchangeability* is a weakened form of full interchangeability: neighborhood interchangeability is a sufficient but not a necessary condition for full interchangeability [FRE 91]. Two v-values (x, a) and (x, b) are neighborhood interchangeable iff they admit the same set of strict supports on each constraint. Figure 12.2 shows the relationships between different groups of symmetries. Note that the identity belongs to all groups.

EXAMPLE.– To illustrate symmetries on constraint networks, let us again consider the 4-queens instance (modeled as a normalized binary constraint network). As in section 1.3.1, there is one variable per queen (column) and the values are row numbers. Denoting the variables by x_a, x_b, x_c and x_d, to clarify the correspondence with columns, Figure 12.3 shows the two solutions for this instance. The first is $\{(x_a, 2), (x_b, 4), (x_c, 1), (x_d, 3)\}$ and the second is $\{(x_a, 3), (x_b, 1), (x_c, 4), (x_d, 2)\}$. This instance has exactly eight constraint symmetries, which are the geometrical ones shown for the square in Figure 12.1. For r^{90}, a first cycle is $((x_a, 1), (x_a, 4), (x_d, 4), (x_d, 1))$ a second cycle is $((x_a, 2), (x_b, 4), (x_d, 3), (x_c, 1))$, etc. Among these eight symmetries, if we disregard the identity permutation r^0, only f^h is a variable symmetry and only f^v is a is value symmetry. Using a simplified notation for f^h where only variables are swapped, we obtain in cyclic form $\{(x_a, x_d), (x_b, x_c)\}$, which means that x_a is swapped with x_d and x_b is swapped with x_c. It is interesting to compare the eight constraint symmetries on 4-queens with the 46,448,640 solution symmetries [COH 06].

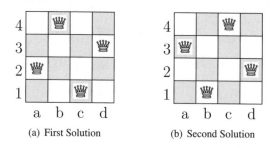

(a) First Solution   (b) Second Solution

Figure 12.3. *The two solutions of the* 4-queens *instance*

Because symmetries preserve the structure of constraint networks, we can reason from solutions and nogoods as will be explained below. We first need to introduce the notion of *admissible instantiations* [WAL 06b].

DEFINITION 12.14.– *[Admissibility] Let P be a constraint network, σ be a symmetry on P and I be a valid instantiation on P. I is* admissible *for σ iff I^σ is an instantiation on P.*

EXAMPLE.– Consider the instantiation $I = \{(x_a, 1), (x_b, 2)\}$ for the 4-queens instance. For the symmetry r^{90}, we obtain $I^{r^{90}} = \{(x_a, 4), (x_b, 3)\}$, which is an instantiation. Thus I is admissible for r^{90}. Now if $I = \{(x_a, 1), (x_b, 1)\}$, by r^{90}, we obtain $I^{r^{90}} = \{(x_a, 4), (x_a, 3)\}$, which is not an instantiation. By definition, an instantiation cannot contain two v-values involving the same variable.

There is no problem of "admissibility" when symmetries only act on variables or only act on values.

REMARK 12.15.– *Valid instantiations are always admissible for variable symmetries and for value symmetries.*

Symmetries preserve solutions. The following proposition is related to Proposition 2.1 in [CRA 96].

PROPOSITION 12.16.– *Let P be a constraint network, σ be a symmetry on P and I be a complete valid instantiation on P. I is a solution of P iff I^σ is a solution of P.*

Proof. If $I \in \mathrm{sols}(P)$ then necessarily $I^\sigma \in \mathrm{sols}(P)$ since $\mathrm{sols}(P)^\sigma = \mathrm{sols}(P)$. The other direction holds because σ^{-1} is also a solution symmetry. □

For example, for the 4-queens instance, $\{(x_a,2),(x_b,4),(x_c,1),(x_d,3)\}^{f^h}$ gives $\{(x_d,2),(x_c,4),(x_b,1),(x_a,3)\}$ which is the second solution. Interestingly, this result can be refined as follows.

PROPOSITION 12.17.– *Let P be a constraint network, σ be a symmetry on P and I be a valid instantiation on P. I is a good (globally consistent instantiation) on P iff I^σ is a good on P.*

Proof. If I is a good, this means that there exists at least a solution I' of P that extends I. We know from Proposition 12.16 that I'^σ is also a solution of P. Necessarily, I'^σ extends I^σ, so I^σ is a good. □

COROLLARY 12.18.– *Let P be a constraint network, σ be a symmetry on P and I be a valid instantiation on P. I is a nogood (globally inconsistent instantiation) on P iff either I is not admissible for σ or I^σ is a nogood on P.*

Proof. From Proposition 12.17, we know that I is a good on P iff I^σ is a good on P. This is equivalent to: I is not a good on P iff I^σ is not a good on P. Because I is by hypothesis a valid instantiation, I is necessarily a nogood. However, nothing can be said precisely about I^σ. I^σ is not a good, which means that either I is not admissible for σ or I^σ is a nogood. □

12.3. Symmetry-breaking methods

To solve a given problem instance, there are three main classical ways to tackle symmetries:

– reformulate the model of the problem to reduce the number of symmetries;

– identify symmetries in the model (or instance) and post symmetry-breaking constraints before starting the solving process;

– use every explored search subtree to avoid exploring symmetric ones.

Different models of the same problem can differ significantly in their number of symmetries. Appropriate reformulation of a problem can help the constraint solver by limiting the number of symmetries. Modeling and reformulation are clearly outside the scope of this book because they are (typically) neither general-purpose nor automatic tasks. More information about modeling can be found in [SMI 06], and [GEN 06c] provides more information about reformulation to deal with symmetries.

12.3.1. Symmetry-breaking constraints

Symmetries (in a given group) induce an equivalence relation on the set of complete instantiations. Two complete instantiations are equivalent iff they are symmetric. Consequently, every equivalence class contains either solutions or non-solutions. For example, if P is a constraint network, S a solution of P and Sym a group of symmetries on P, then the *orbit* of S defined as $\{S^\sigma \mid \sigma \in Sym\}$ forms a class comprising solutions equivalent to S (including S itself since the identity is necessarily a symmetry).

To preserve satisfiability when solving an instance, it "suffices" to retain just one representative from each equivalence class. For groups of variable symmetries, there is a simple approach [CRA 96] (initiated in [PUG 93]) for breaking all symmetries: posting *symmetry-breaking constraints* that can only be satisfied by representatives. The idea is to order all complete instantiations lexicographically and to consider each representative as a canonical element that is the lexicographically smallest instantiation from its class. By means of posted constraints we avoid wasting time with elements that are not canonical. Roughly speaking, the search now visits each equivalence class rather than visiting every complete instantiation. This method is called *lex-leader*.

A lexicographic order $\leq_{\text{lex}}$ on the search space is derived naturally from a total order on domains and a total order on variables; see Definition 1.5. For variable symmetries, *lexicographic ordering constraints* play the role of symmetry-breaking constraints. They are defined on two vectors of variables, and when variables are represented by letters, the two vectors represent words and we obtain the classical order used by dictionaries. A vector of q variables is denoted by $\overrightarrow{x} = \langle x_1, x_2, \ldots, x_q \rangle$. Lexicographic ordering constraints are defined as follows.

DEFINITION 12.19.– *[Lexicographic Ordering Constraint] A lexicographic ordering constraint is a constraint defined on two vectors* $\overrightarrow{x} = \langle x_1, x_2, \ldots, x_q \rangle$ *and* $\overrightarrow{y} = \langle y_1, y_2, \ldots, y_q \rangle$ *of variables. We have:*

- $\overrightarrow{x} <_{\text{lex}} \overrightarrow{y}$ *iff* $\exists i \in 1..q$ *such that* $x_i < y_i$ *and* $\forall j \in 1..i-1, x_j = y_j$;
- $\overrightarrow{x} \leq_{\text{lex}} \overrightarrow{y}$ *iff* $\overrightarrow{x} <_{\text{lex}} \overrightarrow{y}$ *or* $\overrightarrow{x} = \overrightarrow{y}$ *(i.e.* $\forall i \in 1..q, x_i = y_i$).

Here, we assume that the vectors have the same length. The first type of constraint is denoted by Lex. When vectors only contain one variable, we have a binary constraint "less than or equal" of the form $x \leq y$, denoted by Le. Strict lexicographic ordering constraints ($<_{\text{lex}}$) will not be considered in this book. Returning to our example, the vector of ordered variables of the constraint network P is denoted by $\langle x_1, x_2, \ldots, x_n \rangle$. All variables symmetries can be broken by adding the following lexicographic ordering constraints to the constraint network P:

$$\langle x_1, x_2, \ldots, x_n \rangle \leq_{\text{lex}} \langle x_1, x_2, \ldots, x_n \rangle^\sigma, \forall \sigma \in Sym$$

which is equivalent to[2]:

$$\langle x_1, x_2, \ldots, x_n \rangle \leq_{\text{lex}} \langle x_1^\sigma, x_2^\sigma, \ldots, x_n^\sigma \rangle, \forall \sigma \in Sym$$

Such constraints ensure that any solution found is canonical, which means that it is lexicographically less than any symmetric solution obtained by re-ordering the variables. For example, if we consider the variable symmetry f^h on the 4-queens instance, we obtain:

$$\langle x_a, x_b, x_c, x_d \rangle \leq_{\text{lex}} \langle x_a, x_b, x_c, x_d \rangle^{f^h}$$

which gives:

$$\langle x_a, x_b, x_c, x_d \rangle \leq_{\text{lex}} \langle x_d, x_c, x_b, x_a \rangle$$

A portion of the search space is ignored by backtrack search algorithms when this constraint is included. If the instantiation $\{(x_a, 2), (x_b, 4), (x_c, 1), (x_d, 3)\}$ remains a solution of the "reduced" constraint network, this is not the case for $\{(x_a, 3), (x_b, 1), (x_c, 4), (x_d, 2)\}$ because $\langle 3, 1, 4, 2 \rangle \not\leq_{\text{lex}} \langle 2, 4, 1, 3 \rangle$. However, if f^h is applied to the remaining solution, we obtain the second solution of the original network for free.

In theory, posting all possible symmetry-breaking constraints enables the breaking of all variable symmetries. However, in many cases, the size of the group of symmetries is exponential, which renders this technique computationally impracticable. Although symmetries can be organized into a symmetry tree that can be pruned further (potentially obtaining a drastic reduction in size [CRA 96]), there are cases where approximations are really necessary. For example, we can decide to process only symmetries that constitute an irredundant set of generators. This has been studied and shown to be effective in [ALO 02, ALO 06]. This partial form of symmetry breaking captures a reasonable pruning capability "... because an

---

2. We consider here that each variable symmetry on P is defined by a permutation on vars(P), although we do not use the notation σ_{vars} as in Definition 12.10.

irredundant set of generators contains maximally independent symmetries (none of them can be expressed in terms of others)".

The lex-leader method can also be applied to value symmetries [PUG 06, WAL 06b]. Furthermore, it has been extended [WAL 06b] to symmetries acting independently on variables and values by keeping the same variable ordering, and simultaneously on variables and values, by introducing the concept of admissibility (presented in section 12.2). This makes the method quite powerful.

12.3.2. *Dynamic symmetry breaking*

There is an opportunity to learn useful information in order to break symmetries whenever a fruitless[3] search subtree has been fully explored. This information is basically a nogood, but it can also be an inconsistent partial state. By considering symmetric nogoods and inconsistent partial states obtained after applying known symmetries, we can avoid exploring many irrelevant nodes. This can be achieved by posting constraints during search (SBDS for symmetry breaking during search) or by detecting dominance during search (SBDD for symmetry breaking via dominance detection). The difference between SBDS and SBDD (in its basic form) is essentially a matter of implementation [HAR 01].

We first consider the basic use of dynamic symmetry breaking, assuming a constraint network P^{init} to be solved, and a given group[4] Sym of symmetries on P^{init}. We also assume an internal dead-end node v in the search tree developed for P^{init} by a backtracking algorithm (that uses a binary branching scheme) such as MAC. The set of decisions $\text{dn}(v)$ labeling successive edges in the path from the root of the search tree to v is a nogood on P^{init}. We also know that the set Δ of positive decisions in $\text{dn}(v)$ is a nogood of P^{init}, which is called a reduced nld-nogood in section 10.2.1. Then for every symmetry $\sigma \in Sym$, Δ^σ is a nogood on P^{init} that can be exploited after backtracking from v.

SBDS has been introduced in [BAC 99, GEN 00, BAC 02b]. In practical terms, symmetric nogoods are generated when the last decision taken to reach v is a positive decision $x = a$. The right sibling of v is a node v' considered after taking the negative decision $x \neq a$. At node v', for every symmetry σ of Sym we add a nogood constraint c_{Δ^σ}, as in Figure 12.4.

---

3. We restrict our attention to fruitless subtrees, but the idea is directly adaptable to fruitful subtrees.

4. To simplify, we assume that every valid instantiation is admissible for every symmetry in Sym. For example, Sym is a group of variable symmetries or a group of value symmetries.

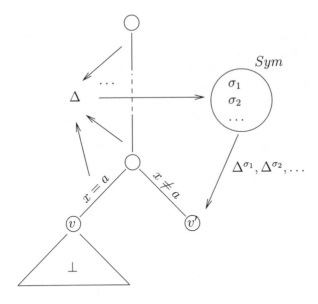

Figure 12.4. *Dynamic symmetry breaking in action. Whenever a nogood Δ is identified from a left subtree, its symmetric variants are considered in the right subtree*

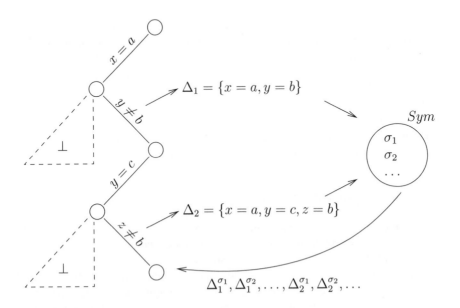

Figure 12.5. *Symmetric nogoods obtained from the current branch are posted*

Although generated symmetric nogoods are global, i.e. valid on P^{init}, they are dynamically included in the constraint network $\text{cn}(v')$ before exploring the subtree rooted at v', and later retracted when backtracking from v'. The reason is that symmetric nogoods identified at the ancestor of v' where the search algorithm backtracks subsume those posted at v'. In other words, only symmetric nogoods obtained from a reduced nld-nogood extracted from the current branch are relevant and must be activated at a given node. Figure 12.5 provides an illustration.

SBDD has been introduced in [BRO 88, FOC 01, FAH 01]. Just before exploring a new node, the search algorithm checks whether the constraint network associated with this node entails (or almost entails) a symmetric nogood obtained from a reduced nld-nogood that can be extracted from the current branch. If this is the case, then a backtrack is forced. The main difference between SBDS and SBDD is that SBDD does not really impose new constraints (in their classical forms), but instead stores separately information about explored node and use (specific) functions to determine whether a node is dominated by a previously explored one under some symmetry. Collected information is called global cut seeds in [FOC 01] and patterns in [FAH 01]. Patterns are partial states that are equivalent to standard nogoods as shown in [PUG 05b]. Nevertheless, the partial states identified in [FOC 01], which are called extended dead end seeds, are more general because they represent generalized nogoods (that are not standard). Automated and efficient procedures for dominance detection have been proposed, e.g. see [GEN 03, SEL 05].

Dynamic symmetry breaking, as implemented by SBDS and SBDD, is known to respect the variable and value ordering heuristics: the first solution found by the search algorithm without symmetry breaking is the same as the first solution found by the search algorithm with symmetry breaking. This is not guaranteed when symmetry-breaking constraints are added to the initial problem. However, even for dynamic symmetry-breaking, this is no longer true if adaptive heuristics are used. Finally, an original dynamic symmetry breaking method, employing heuristics, has been proposed in [MES 01]. The idea is to choose at each step a positive decision that allows the maximum number of symmetries to be broken.

12.4. Automatic symmetry detection

Most methods for breaking symmetries in constraint networks assume that symmetries are given by the user. Some symmetries are well-known, such as the eight symmetries of the geometrical square, and so can be given as input to the constraint solver. However, even when symmetries seem natural, the user may need considerable expertise in order to specify symmetries correctly. A requirement for expertise tends to restrict the use of constraint solvers to experienced users, which is not in accord with our ambition to promote black-box solvers. Furthermore, there is no guarantee that the user will not miss some important symmetries. These considerations have motivated automatic detection of symmetries. We briefly present several recent approaches in this section.

A system called CGRASS [FRI 02b] analyzes CSP instances to identify symmetries and implied constraints automatically. The heart of the system performs a syntactic comparison via computation of normal forms. To detect symmetric variables, the system first groups together pairs of variables with the same domain and with the same number of occurrences in the set of constraints. The set of constraints obtained after swapping each pair of variables is normalized and compared with the original form. Moreover, the transitivity of symmetry serves to minimize the number of pairs of variables that need to be compared. Unfortunately, as mentioned in [FRI 02b], this approach is generally impractical, due to the complexity of computing normal forms over all pairs of variables and over the full set of constraints. A related approach [HEN 05] allows derivation of symmetries in a compositional fashion from symmetries specified for global constraints. These forms of symmetries correspond to value and variable interchangeability.

Quite importantly, the automatic detection and exploitation of symmetries has been addressed using software that computes graph automorphisms. The well-known software of Nauty [MCK 81] and Saucy [DAR 04] has been developed for identifying irredundant generating sets of colored graphs. In practice, from a problem structure that corresponds to a hypergraph, an encoding to a vertex-colored graph is required. This allows symmetry groups to be captured. Symmetries map each vertex into a vertex with the same color; colors do not introduce any computational difficulties and can be formally reduced to plain graph automorphism. Finding the set of automorphisms in a graph is known as the *graph automorphism problem*. The theoretical complexity of this problem is not known precisely: the problem is in NP, but whether or not it is in P is currently unknown.

The first implementation of symmetry detection via graph automorphisms was for SAT. Crawford [CRA 92] has presented a prototype system that takes a propositional theory in clausal form and constructs an approximate symmetry-breaking formula from it. Given a SAT instance in conjunctive normal form, a colored graph is built as follows. Every propositional variable x is represented by two vertices that correspond to the positive literal x and the negative literal $\neg x$. Every clause is represented by a vertex, and there is an edge between a clause c and a literal l if the literal l appears in the clause c. Considering refinements proposed in [CRA 96, ALO 02], literal vertices are painted with a first color, while clause vertices are painted with a second color, vertices of opposite literals are directly linked by an edge, and literals of binary clauses are directly linked by an edge (without creating a vertex for the binary clause). This encoding allows identification of phase-shift symmetries, i.e. symmetries that map a literal x to its opposite $\neg x$, and more generally symmetries that map a positive literal to a negative literal.

EXAMPLE.– Figure 12.6 shows the graph obtained for a SAT instance comprising three variables x, y and z, and three clauses c_1, c_2 and c_3. A non-trivial symmetry on this instance is $\{(x, \neg x), (y, \neg z), (\neg y, z), (c_1, c_2)\}$ [ALO 02].

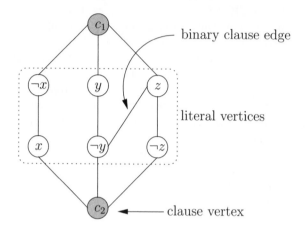

Figure 12.6. *Vertex-colored graph representing a SAT instance (CNF formula) composed of clauses $c_1 = \neg x \vee y \vee z$, $c_2 = x \vee \neg y \vee \neg z$ and $c_3 = \neg y \vee z$*

Ramani and Markov [RAM 04] reduce CSP instances into SAT ones while capturing their symmetric structure (before reduction). They generalize techniques of [CRA 96, ALO 04] to detect symmetries in high-level constraints via reduction to graph automorphism. They use a C-like language to specify constraints and a customized tool to build parse trees. A parse tree (graph) is built from the predicate expressions associated with constraints, and various transformations (e.g. removing brackets, grouping operators) facilitate the detection of symmetries. The authors develop a set of rules for constraints formed from a restricted set of arithmetic and relational operators, but the approach can be extended to additional operators.

EXAMPLE.– Figure 12.7 shows the parse graph for an example in which there are two integer variables x_1 and x_2, two unary constraints $c_1 : x_1 \geq 1$ and $c_2 : x_2 \geq 1$ and one binary constraint $c_3 : x_1 \times x_1 + x_2 \times x_2 = 25$. For this example, the symmetry of variables x_1 and x_2 can be detected.

In this vein, a general automatic symmetry detection method has been proposed in [PUG 05a]. This method allows detection of value and variable symmetries, as well as some non-trivial ones involving both variables and values. Symmetries are computed from different representations of constraints: extension, intension or global constraints. For an extensional constraint, the graph is constructed as follows. There is one vertex per variable and one vertex per value. If a is a value in the domain of a variable x, then there is an edge linking the value vertex a to the variable vertex

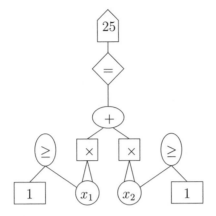

Figure 12.7. *Parse graph built from constraints* $c_1 : x_1 \geq 1, c_2 : x_2 \geq 1$ *and*
$c_3 : x_1 \times x_1 + x_2 \times x_2 = 25$. *Vertices are shaped differently to indicate different colors*

x. There is one vertex per constraint and one vertex per support on the constraint.
If $\tau = (a_1, \ldots, a_r)$ is a support on a constraint c, then there is an edge linking the
constraint vertex c to the support vertex τ which is itself linked to each value vertex
a_i occurring in τ. A unique color is used for all variable vertices, another for all value
vertices[5], another for all support vertices and finally there is one color for all constraint
vertices.

EXAMPLE.– Figure 12.8 shows the colored graph obtained for a binary constraint
c_{xy} such that $\text{dom}(x) = \text{dom}(y) = \{1, 2, 3\}$ and $\text{rel}(c_{xy}) = \{\tau_1 = (1, 2), \tau_2 = (1, 3), \tau_3 = (2, 3)\}$. There is an automorphism in the graph composed of the cycles
$(x, y), (1_x, 3_y), (2_x, 2_y), (3_x, 1_y)$ and (τ_1, τ_3); a_w designates value vertex a linked to
variable vertex w. We can then derive the symmetry $\{((x, 1), (y, 3)), ((x, 2), (y, 2)), ((x, 3), (y, 1))\}$, which is non-trivial.

12.5. Lightweight detection of variable symmetries

This section proposes automatic detection of variable symmetries by partitioning
the scope of each constraint. Each partition shows *locally symmetric variables*. From
this local information, which is computed in time polynomial in the size of the
constraints and their arity, we build a so-called *lsv-graph* whose automorphisms
correspond to variable symmetries. This approach allows us to disregard the
representation of constraints: whatever representation (extension, intension, global)

---

5. To detect variable symmetries only, a distinct color for value vertices must be used per
variable domain.

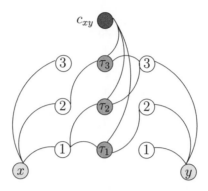

c_{xy}

Figure 12.8. *Colored graph obtained for an extensional constraint using Puget's method. Variable vertices are light gray, value vertices are white, support vertices are mid gray, and the constraint vertex is dark gray*

is used, the same notion (kind of vertices) is implemented in the lsv-graph. Besides, the size of the lsv-graph is only $O(er)$ where r is the greatest constraint arity, making symmetry detection efficient on very large instances with available tools such as Nauty and Saucy. This is what we call *lightweight detection of variable symmetries*.

The proposed approach proceeds in three steps. The first is a local analysis of each constraint in order to identify locally symmetric variables. The second is concerned with the construction of an lsv-graph. In the third step, generators for the symmetry group are classically computed using a graph automorphism algorithm.

12.5.1. *Locally symmetric variables*

We start by introducing locally symmetric variables (related definitions can be found in [PUG 93, ROY 98]). Two variables are locally symmetric for a constraint c, in which they are involved, iff both variables can be permuted without modifying the set of allowed tuples. Note that if τ is a tuple of values built on a set of variables containing x and y then $\tau_{x\leftrightarrow y}$ denotes the tuple obtained from τ by swapping $\tau[x]$ and $\tau[y]$.

DEFINITION 12.20.– *[Locally Symmetric Variables] Two variables x and y are locally symmetric for a constraint c such that $\{x,y\} \subseteq \mathrm{scp}(c)$ iff $\forall \tau \in \mathrm{rel}(c), \tau_{x\leftrightarrow y} \in \mathrm{rel}(c)$.*

For example, the variables x and y are locally symmetric for the constraint c_{xy} : $x \neq y$ iff $\mathrm{dom}(x) = \mathrm{dom}(y)$. Indeed, these variables can be permuted since $\neq$ is commutative. Another example is for the inequality $x + y + z + 1 < v + w$ where the domain of each variable is $\{1, 2, 3\}$. Variables in $\{x, y, z\}$ are pairwise locally symmetric since $+$ is commutative and associative; the same holds for $\{v, w\}$. Here we propose an algorithm that detects locally symmetric variables. This algorithm can be run with intensional constraints using tree representations of predicate expressions as shown in Figure 12.9(a), and also with extensional constraints using tables directly as shown in Figure 12.9(b). Shaded areas in the table emphasize that permutations are possible.

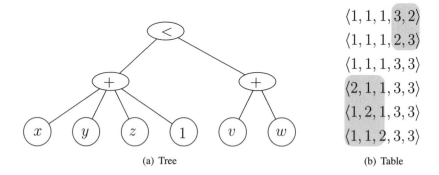

(a) Tree   (b) Table

Figure 12.9. *Representation of the inequality $x + y + z + 1 < v + w$ by a tree (intensional form) and a table (extensional form)*

As symmetry is a transitive property, for each constraint we can compute a partition of its scope, each element of this partition being a set of pairwise locally symmetric variables. This is the role of the function computeSymmetricVariables, Algorithm 85, which identifies locally symmetric variables for any extensional, intensional or global[6] constraint c. A set X is first initialized with all variables involved in c. At each turn of the main loop, the algorithm picks a variable x from X, and computes the set T of variables locally symmetric with x for c. Once, T has been computed, it is added to the partition Γ that is currently being built.

At the heart of Algorithm 85, there is a call to the function isLocallySymmetric, Algorithm 86. For a given constraint c and two variables x and y involved in c, the function isLocallySymmetric simply determines whether x and y are locally symmetric for c. Generally speaking, three cases have to be considered depending on the representation of the constraint c:

1) If the constraint is defined in extension (lines 1 to 5), then the function builds, for each tuple in the (positive or negative) table associated with c, a new tuple by

---

6. We only illustrate our intention with two patterns of global constraints, namely, allDifferent and weightedSum.

Algorithm 85: computeSymmetricVariables(c: constraint): partition

---

Output: a partition of the scope of c

1 $\Gamma \leftarrow \emptyset$
2 $X \leftarrow \text{scp}(c)$
3 **while** $X \neq \emptyset$ **do**
4 $\quad$ pick and delete x from X
5 $\quad T \leftarrow \{x\}$
6 $\quad$ **foreach** *variable* $y \in X \mid y \neq x$ **do**
7 $\quad\quad$ **if** *isLocallySymmetric*(c, x, y) **then**
8 $\quad\quad\quad T \leftarrow T \cup \{y\}$
9 $\quad\quad\quad X \leftarrow X \setminus \{y\}$
$\quad\quad$ // T is a set of pairwise locally symmetric variables for c
10 $\quad \Gamma \leftarrow \Gamma \cup T$
11 **return** Γ

Algorithm 86: isLocallySymmetric(c: constraint, x, y: variables): Boolean

---

Output: *true* iff x and y are locally symmetric for c

1 **if** c *is defined in extension* **then**
$\quad$ // $table[c]$ means indifferently a positive or negative table
2 $\quad$ **foreach** *tuple* $\tau \in table[c]$ **do**
3 $\quad\quad$ **if** $\tau_{x \leftrightarrow y} \notin table[c]$ **then**
4 $\quad\quad\quad$ **return** *false*
5 $\quad$ **return** *true*
6 **if** c *is defined in intension* **then**
7 $\quad \mathcal{G} \leftarrow \text{buildCanonicalTree}(expr[c])$
8 $\quad \mathcal{G}' \leftarrow \text{buildCanonicalTree}(expr[c]_{x \leftrightarrow y})$
9 $\quad$ **return** $\mathcal{G} = \mathcal{G}'$
// necessarily, c is a global constraint
10 **if** *pattern of c is* allDifferent **then**
11 $\quad$ **return** *true*
12 **if** *pattern of c is* weightedSum **then**
13 $\quad$ **return** $\text{coefficient}(c, x) = \text{coefficient}(c, y)$
14 $\ldots$
15 **return** *false*

---

swapping the values of variables x and y, and then checks whether this new tuple also belongs to the table of c.

2) If the constraint is defined in intension (lines 6 to 9), then the algorithm builds at line 7 a canonical tree representation of the predicate expression $expr[c]$ associated with c by a call to function buildCanonicalTree. A detailed description of this approach (but no algorithm) is given in section 12.5.2. A second canonical tree representation is built at line 8 after swapping variables x and y in $expr[c]$, denoted by $expr[c]_{x \leftrightarrow y}$. Both canonical representations are compared, and variables x and y are identified as being locally symmetric for c iff both representations are identical. For example, if $expr[c] = x + y < z$ then $expr[c]_{x \leftrightarrow y} = y + x < z$. Both expressions have the same canonical representation (following the description given in section 12.5.2), so x and y are locally symmetric for c.

3) If the constraint is an instance of a global constraint pattern (lines 10 to 15), this must be treated in a manner that is specific to that constraint. For example, any two variables involved in an allDifferent global constraint are locally symmetric for it. Another example is that two variables involved in a weightedSum global constraint are locally symmetric if they have the same attached coefficient in the constraint. For example, if c is a weightedSum global constraint that represents $3x + 2y + 3z = 5$, then $\text{coefficient}(c, x) = \text{coefficient}(c, z) = 3$, and so x and z are locally symmetric for c.

A partition of the scope of a constraint c (defined in extension or intension) is computed in time polynomial in the arity and the representation size of c. Recall that the representation of an extensional constraint is a table and the representation of an intensional constraint is a predicate expression. The size t of a table corresponds to the number of elements it has, whereas the size of an expression corresponds to the number of tokens (operators, constants and variables) that it contains. We have the two following complexity results:

THEOREM 12.21.– *The worst-case time complexity of computeSymmetricVariables for an extensional constraint c is $O(r^3 t \log(t))$ where r denotes the arity of c and t the size of the table associated with c.*

Proof. The number of calls to isLocallySymmetric is bounded by $O(r^2)$. In the worst case, we have to iterate over all the tuples of the table associated with c and to perform a constraint check whose complexity is $O(\log(t)r)$ (see sections 5.1.1 and 5.6.1). So, we obtain $O(r^3 t \log(t))$. □

THEOREM 12.22.– *The worst-case time complexity of computeSymmetricVariables for an intensional constraint c is $O(r^2 t^2 \log(t))$ where r denotes the arity of c and t the size (number of tokens) of $expr[c]$.*

Proof. The number of calls to isLocallySymmetric (and, so to buildCanonicalTree) is bounded by $O(r^2)$. As shown later by Theorem 12.23 in section 12.5.2, buildCanonicalTree is in $O(t^2 \log(t))$. So, we obtain $O(r^2 t^2 \log(t))$. $\square$

In practice, one may expect better behavior than that predicted in the worst case. First, the number of calls to isLocallySymmetric is only $r - 1$ when the constraint is fully symmetric (i.e. all variables are pairwise locally symmetric), due to the transitivity of symmetry. Second, for an intensional constraint, buildCanonicalTree is reduced to $O(t^2)$ when operators in the predicate expression are binary. Third, when two variables are not locally symmetric for an extensional constraint, we can hope to exit quickly from the foreach loop starting at line 2 of Algorithm 86. Finally, the function computeSymmetricVariables is not necessarily called for each constraint. Indeed, a key (string) can be associated with each constraint, using domain types of variables as prefix. We append to the key the type of the relation for an extensional constraint, and we append a representation of the canonical form of the predicate expression (referring to variables by their position in the scope) for an intensional constraint. Two constraints with the same key admit the same partition. This happens frequently in structured instances.

12.5.2. *Computing normal forms of predicate expressions*

To identify symmetric variables of constraint networks, normal forms [FRI 02b] have been applied globally to the set of constraints, making this approach impracticable (except for small instances). Here, we propose to apply a similar approach to each constraint taken individually. This can be quite efficient, except for some very specific cases where predicate expressions or constraint arities are very large.

To make our presentation concrete, we now consider the grammar [ROU 09], introduced in the context of constraint solver competitions, which can construct predicate expressions. Many of the operators involved are both commutative and associative: add (+), mul (*), min, max, and, or, xor, iff, eq (=), ne ($\neq$). The following indicates simple rewriting rules that can be applied to any expression.

– Group associative operators using n-ary equivalent operators [RAM 04]. For example, replace $\mathsf{add}(x, \mathsf{add}(y, z))$ by $\mathsf{add}(x, y, z)$.

– Put occurrences of not (unary logical negation operator) higher in the expression when possible. For example, replace $\mathsf{and}(\mathsf{not}(e_1), \mathsf{not}(e_2))$ by $\mathsf{not}(\mathsf{or}(e_1, e_2))$, where e_1 and e_2 are sub-expressions.

– Replace all occurrences of ge ($\geq$) and gt ($>$) by le ($\leq$) and lt ($<$) [FRI 02b]. For example, replace $\mathsf{ge}(x, y)$ by $\mathsf{le}(y, x)$.

– Replace the sequence abs sub with a new commutative operator abssub combining both operators. For example, replace $\mathsf{abs}(\mathsf{sub}(x, y))$ by $\mathsf{abssub}(x, y)$.

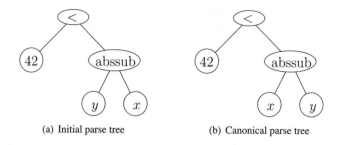

(a) Initial parse tree   (b) Canonical parse tree

Figure 12.10. *Initial and canonical representations of the predicate* $|y - x| > 42$ *built with the function* **buildCanonicalTree**

A parse tree (in which each node is labeled with a token of the expression) can be constructed in one pass while taking all of these rules into account. Although some additional sophisticated rules may be imagined (e.g. specific rules for linear and non-linear equations), this simple set of rules is sufficient to capture locally symmetric variables of many classical constraints. The new operator abssub is important because it occurs in various problems (e.g. frequency assignment problems). Because this new operator is commutative, it allows identification of symmetries that are missed when the (non-commutative) operator sub is used.

To obtain a canonical form from an initial parse tree, it is sufficient to make canonical the root of the tree. A node is made canonical as follows: first, all child nodes (if any) are made canonical and also are sorted if the label associated with the node is a commutative operator. To obtain a normal form, it is necessary to define a total order over the set of operators, integers and variables. This order can be defined rather naturally [FRI 02b].

EXAMPLE.– Figure 12.10(a) shows the initial (i.e. before normalization) parse tree representing the predicate expression $|y - x| > 42$. Since the new operator abssub is commutative, we obtain as the canonical representation the one shown in Figure 12.10(b), assuming that variables are lexicographically ordered by their names.

Except when the size of the predicate expression is large, computing a canonical tree is cheap. Indeed, we have the following complexity result:

THEOREM 12.23.– *The worst-case time complexity of building a tree in canonical form, from a predicate expression* $expr[c]$, *is* $O(t^2 \log(t))$ *where* t *denotes the size of* $expr[c]$.

Proof. In $O(t)$ operations, a tree (containing t nodes) can be built while taking account of all of the rewriting rules mentioned above. In the worst case, the total number of comparisons to sort all nodes is bounded by $O(t \log(t))$, and each comparison involves visiting at most t nodes. So, we obtain $O(t^2 \log(t))$.   □

12.5.3. *Constructing lsv-graphs*

Once locally symmetric variables have been identified for each constraint (through partitioning), we build a colored graph for use in the search of variable symmetries. Each automorphism of this graph identifies a variable symmetry in the constraint network. As mentioned previously, this approach was introduced in [CRA 92, CRA 96] and implemented for example in [ALO 02, RAM 04, PUG 05a]. We now show that the colored graphs that we build are of limited size while capturing many variable symmetries.

Colored graphs, called *lsv-graphs*, are constructed as follows. Each variable of the given constraint network P is represented by a vertex called a variable vertex. For each constraint of arity r, we include a constraint vertex and r binding vertices, one per variable involved in the constraint. Binding vertices connect constraint vertices to variable vertices: if c is a constraint involving x then we have a connection between the constraint vertex representing c and the variable vertex representing x via a binding vertex.

A color is associated with each vertex of the graph (permutations are only allowed between vertices of the same color). Variables with the same domain have the same color (alternatively, we could have used a unique color for all variable vertices by inserting unary constraints to represent domains). Similar constraints (i.e. constraints defined by the same relation or expression) have the same color. For each constraint, binding vertices that correspond to locally symmetric variables have the same color. The same coloring schema of binding vertices is used for similar constraints. In all other cases, colors must be different.

We can show that the above construction is correct: any automorphism in the lsv-graph identifies a variable symmetry in the constraint network. Every element (domain, constraint) constraining the search space of the constraint network is taken into account when constructing the graph and assigning colors.

EXAMPLE.– Consider, for example, a constraint network P that has four variables $\{w, x, y, z\}$ and four intensional constraints $\{c_{wx}, c_{wy}, c_{xz}, c_{yz}\}$. The associated predicate schema of both c_{wx} and c_{wy} is $|\$0 - \$1| = 56$ while it is $|\$0 - \$1| > 42$ for c_{xz} and c_{yz}, where $\$i$ denotes the ith variable (viewed as a formal parameter) of the predicate expression. This means, for example, that $expr[c_{wx}]$ is $|w - x| = 56$ by setting $\$0 = w$ and $\$1 = x$. Figure 12.11 shows the lsv-graph built for P: the four white circles are the variable vertices (assuming that they have the same domain) and the four gray circles are the constraint vertices (mid gray ones for c_{wx} and c_{wy} and dark gray ones for c_{xz} and c_{yz}). Each constraint vertex is linked to two variable vertices through two binding vertices since constraints are binary.

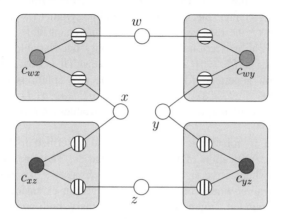

Figure 12.11. *An lsv-graph composed of four variable vertices (white circles), four constraint vertices (middle and dark gray circles) and eight binding vertices (circles with line patterns)*

Running Algorithm 85 on c_{wx}, variables w and x are detected as being locally symmetric for x_{wx}. Consequently, the two binding vertices introduced for c_{wx} receive the same color, which is represented with a horizontal line pattern. In our example, c_{wy} is similar to c_{wx} (the semantics are the same since both constraints are represented by the same predicate schema). This is why the same set of colors is used for c_{wx} and for c_{wy}. A similar observation applies to constraints c_{xz} and c_{yz}: all binding vertices for these two constraints are assigned the same color, represented here by a vertical line pattern. A graph automorphism algorithm (Saucy) identifies a symmetry that maps x into y, and vice-versa, as can be seen in Figure 12.11.

An advantage of lightweight detection of variable symmetries is the controlled size of lsv-graphs.

THEOREM 12.24.– *The number of vertices and edges in the lsv-graph built for a constraint network is $O(er)$ where r denotes the greatest constraint arity.*

Proof. There is a vertex for each variable and each constraint of P. For each variable involved in a constraint, there are a vertex and two edges. Assuming that n is $O(e)$, overall complexity is $O(er)$ for both the number of vertices and the number of edges. $\square$

Some variable symmetries cannot be detected by means of lsv-graphs, but this is not very surprising because finding all variable symmetries of a CSP instance is an intractable task. Although some variable symmetries correspond to interchangeable variables (see Definition 1.68), locally symmetric variables are not necessarily interchangeable. Moreover, variable symmetries identified via lsv-graphs cannot always be expressed in terms of interchangeable variables. For the 4-queens instance, as in section 12.2, there is only one variable symmetry (other than identity). This is $f^h = \{(x_a, x_d), (x_b, x_c)\}$ which is obtained automatically from the lsv-graph generated for 4-queens. The two solutions of 4-queens are $\{(x_a, 2), (x_b, 4), (x_c, 1), (x_d, 3)\}$ and $\{(x_a, 3), (x_b, 1), (x_c, 4), (x_d, 2)\}$. The reader can check that there is no pair of interchangeable variables for this instance.

It is important to relate this approach to that described in [PUG 05a] when restricted to the identification of variable symmetries. The size of generated lsv-graphs is $O(er)$, whereas the size of Puget's graphs grows exponentially with the arity of the constraints when constraints are defined in extension and the size of the tables is not bounded. When constraints are binary, both approaches detect the same groups of variable symmetries, but this is not always true for non-binary constraints. For example, the constraint c such that $\mathrm{scp}(c) = \{w, x, y, z\}$ and $\mathrm{rel}(c) = \{(4, 3, 2, 1), (1, 2, 3, 4)\}$ admits a variable symmetry σ such that $w^\sigma = z$, $x^\sigma = y$, $y^\sigma = x$ and $z^\sigma = w$, but no locally symmetric variables. This is a symmetry composed of two cycles, similar to that found for 4-queens. At the level of a single constraint, an lsv-graph cannot handle this. It would be worthwhile to extend lightweight detection of symmetries to deal with locally symmetric groups of variables (that is, a generalization of locally symmetric variables), while controlling the time complexity of local symmetry detection and the space complexity of generated lsv-graphs.

12.6. A GAC algorithm for lexicographic ordering constraints

Once symmetries have been detected, it remains to make use of them. One approach, introduced in section 12.3.1, employs symmetry-breaking constraints implemented by lexicographic ordering constraints. Classically, a lexicographic ordering constraint is posted for each generator returned by graph automorphism software. Indeed, it has been shown difficult to improve upon symmetry breaking based only on generators [ALO 06]. Symmetries (generators or not) may involve one or several cycles, some of them possibly of length strictly greater than 2. We now illustrate how constraints are posted to break variable symmetries according to different representative scenarios. Consider a constraint network P with four variables w, x, y and z. Imagine that a variable symmetry σ on P is defined by a unique cycle (x, y). In this case we post:

$$\langle w, x, y, z \rangle \leq_{\mathrm{lex}} \langle w, x, y, z \rangle^\sigma$$

which is equivalent to:

$$\langle w, x, y, z \rangle \leq_{\text{lex}} \langle w^\sigma, x^\sigma, y^\sigma, z^\sigma \rangle$$

and also:

$$\langle w, x, y, z \rangle \leq_{\text{lex}} \langle w, y, x, z \rangle$$

Passive variables, which are variables located at the same position in both vectors, can be safely discarded. This gives:

$$\langle x, y \rangle \leq_{\text{lex}} \langle y, x \rangle$$

Swapped variables are pairs of variables occurring together in two different positions of both vectors[7]. The second occurrence of swapped variables can be safely discarded, yielding:

$$\langle x \rangle \leq_{\text{lex}} \langle y \rangle$$

or simply with a usual binary constraint:

$$x \leq y$$

To summarize, vectors can be reduced by discarding passive variables and second occurrences of swapped variables. Imagine now that the symmetry σ on P is defined by a cycle (w, x, y) of length 3. In this case we post:

$$\langle w, x, y, z \rangle \leq_{\text{lex}} \langle x, y, w, z \rangle$$

which simplifies to:

$$\langle w, x, y \rangle \leq_{\text{lex}} \langle x, y, w \rangle$$

This lexicographic ordering constraint, which cannot be reduced further, contains *shared* variables, i.e. variables that occur several times in the combined list (w, x, y, x, y, w) of variables of the two vectors. A lexicographic ordering constraint posted for a variable symmetry involving a cycle of length strictly greater than two generally contains shared variables. Finally, if the symmetry σ is defined by two cycles (w, x) and (y, z) of length 2, we obtain:

$$\langle w, y \rangle \leq_{\text{lex}} \langle x, z \rangle$$

A similar constraint should be posted to break the variable symmetry of the 4-queens instance.

---

7. Naturally, swapped variables correspond to cycles of length 2.

We now present an algorithm that enforces GAC on lexicographic ordering constraints. It is important that this algorithm can be used when shared variables are present. Before this algorithm commences, passive variables must be discarded. This algorithm, derived from one described in [KIZ 04], is quite simple to implement and is well-adapted to generic black-box solvers. We denote by $\min(x)$ and $\max(x)$ the smallest and greatest value in $\text{dom}(x)$. A vector of variables is denoted by $\overrightarrow{x} = \langle x_1, x_2, \ldots, x_q \rangle$, and a subvector $\langle x_i, \ldots, x_j \rangle$ from index $i \geq 1$ to index $j \leq q$ inclusive is denoted by $\overrightarrow{x}_{i..j}$.

To the best of our knowledge, only two algorithms have been described in the literature to enforce GAC on lexicographic ordering constraints. The first, introduced in [FRI 02a, FRI 06], employs two indices denoted by α and β. The index α is the least position of variables in $\overrightarrow{x}$ and $\overrightarrow{y}$ that are not fixed and equal ($q + 1$ if no such position exists). The index β is the least position at which we have the guarantee that $\overrightarrow{x}_{\beta..q} >_{\text{lex}} \overrightarrow{y}_{\beta..q}$ ($q + 2$ if no such position exists).

EXAMPLE.– The expression

$$\overrightarrow{x} = \langle\ x_1,\ x_2,\ x_3,\ x_4\ \rangle$$
$$\{1\}\ \{0\}\ \{0,1\}\ \{1\}$$
$$\{1\}\ \{0\}\ \{0,1\}\ \{0\}$$
$$\overrightarrow{y} = \langle\ y_1,\ y_2,\ y_3,\ y_4\ \rangle$$

represents the constraint $\overrightarrow{x} \leq_{\text{lex}} \overrightarrow{y}$. Domains are located below the name of variables in $\overrightarrow{x}$ and above the name of variables in $\overrightarrow{y}$. Here, we have $\alpha = 3$ because at indices 1 and 2, variables are fixed and equal, and we have $\beta = 4$.

By reasoning from α and β, GAC can be enforced efficiently: the worst-case time complexity of one call is $O(q\lambda)$, where q is the length of the vectors and λ is the complexity of tightening a domain bound. Classically, in solver implementations, we have either λ which is $O(1)$ or λ which is $O(d)$, where d is the greatest domain size. The second algorithm, introduced in [CAR 02], employs a finite automaton operating on a string that captures the relationship between each variable pair of the two vectors. The string (signature) is built from current domains and is given as input to the automaton. Filtering is achieved while making transitions in this automaton. This elegant approach detects entailment and also admits a time complexity in $O(q\lambda)$ plus constant amortized time per propagation event (assuming λ in $O(1)$).

One limitation of the two proposed algorithms is that they are not adapted to the case where there are shared variables. When lexicographic ordering constraints are used to break symmetries, this may happen quite often, as seen above.

EXAMPLE.– The expression

$$\vec{x} = \langle \quad v_0, \quad v_1, \quad v_2, \quad v_3 \quad \rangle$$
$$\{0,1\} \ \{0,1\} \ \{0,1\} \ \{1\}$$
$$\{0,1\} \ \{0,1\} \ \{0,1\} \ \{0\}$$
$$\vec{y} = \langle \quad v_1, \quad v_2, \quad v_0, \quad v_4 \quad \rangle$$

represents the constraint $\vec{x} \leq_{\text{lex}} \vec{y}$ with shared variables v_0, v_1 and v_2. The domain of all variables is $\{0,1\}$, except for v_3 and v_4, whose respective domains are $\{1\}$ and $\{0\}$. If we employ the algorithms mentioned above, we do not filter anything, although $(v_0, 1)$ has no support.

Similarly,

$$\vec{x} = \langle \quad v_0, \quad v_1, \quad v_2, \quad v_3 \quad \rangle$$
$$\{0,1\} \ \{0,1\} \ \{0,1\} \ \{1\}$$
$$\{0,1\} \ \{0,1\} \ \{0,1\} \ \{0\}$$
$$\vec{y} = \langle \quad v_2, \quad v_0, \quad v_1, \quad v_4 \quad \rangle$$

represents another Lex constraint. Once again, if we employ the algorithms mentioned above, we do not filter anything, although $(v_2, 0)$ has no support. To remedy this, Kiziltan has proposed an extension [KIZ 04] to the algorithm in [FRI 02a, FRI 06]. The algorithm presented below is inspired by this.

Algorithm 87 enforces generalized arc consistency on a lexicographic ordering constraint c of the form $\langle x_1, x_2, \ldots, x_q \rangle \leq_{\text{lex}} \langle y_1, y_2, \ldots, y_q \rangle$; recall that GAC enforcement on a constraint c is denoted by $GAC(c)$. This is a non-revision-based (or specific) filtering procedure. For example, enforceGAC-lex can be seen as an implementation (for lexicographic ordering constraints) of enforceGAC-type called in Algorithm 9. To simplify the presentation, enforceGAC-lex simply returns a Boolean value (this can easily be adapted so that a set of variables is returned). So long as x_α and y_α are fixed and equal (the test at line 5 is the opposite condition) after enforcing AC on $x_\alpha \leq y_\alpha$ (line 3), the value of α is incremented. This process is stopped a) when an inconsistency is found while enforcing AC, or b) when $\alpha = q + 1$, or c) when x_α and y_α are no longer fixed and equal. The value of α obtained is similar to that obtained in [FRI 02a, FRI 06], but it is computed in a slightly different manner (besides, at α, we have already enforced $x_\alpha \leq y_\alpha$). If $\alpha = q + 1$, this means that all variables are fixed and equal, so the constraint is GAC-consistent. If $\alpha = q$, only the last (pair of) variables of both vectors are not fixed and equal. However, we know that $x_\alpha \leq y_\alpha$, whence it is not difficult to see that the constraint is GAC-consistent. Both cases are taken into account at line 8. At line 10 we know that only two values are not guaranteed to be GAC-consistent, specifically, $(x_\alpha, \max(x_\alpha))$ and $(y_\alpha, \min(y_\alpha))$. When these values are removed, all other values remain GAC-consistent, as stated by Lemmas 12.25 and 12.26 given below. Note that $\min(y_\alpha)$ may have no support only if $\min(y_\alpha) = \min(x_\alpha)$. In this case, we have to seek a support for $\min(y_\alpha)$ by calling function seekSupportLex, with short-circuit evaluation of the operator $\wedge$. The value $\max(x_\alpha)$ must be treated similarly.

Algorithm 87: enforceGAC-lex($P : \mathscr{P}$, c: constraint): Boolean

---

Require: c is a lexicographic constraint $\langle x_1, x_2, \ldots, x_q \rangle \leq_{\text{lex}} \langle y_1, y_2, \ldots, y_q \rangle$
Output: *true* iff $GAC(c) \neq \bot$

1 $\alpha \leftarrow 1$
2 **while** $\alpha \leq q$ **do**
3   **if** $\neg$*enforceAC*($x_\alpha \leq y_\alpha$) **then**
4   **return** *false*
5   **if** $|\operatorname{dom}(x_\alpha)| \neq 1 \vee \operatorname{dom}(x_\alpha) \neq \operatorname{dom}(y_\alpha)$ **then**
6   break
7      $\alpha \leftarrow \alpha + 1$

8 **if** $\alpha \geq q$ **then**
9   **return** *true*
    // only $(x_\alpha, \max(x_\alpha))$ and $(y_\alpha, \min(y_\alpha))$ may be GAC-inconsistent
10 **if** $\min(x_\alpha) = \min(y_\alpha) \wedge \neg$*seekSupportLex*($\alpha, \min(y_\alpha)$) **then**
11   remove $\min(y_\alpha)$ from $\operatorname{dom}(y_\alpha)$
12 **if** $\max(x_\alpha) = \max(y_\alpha) \wedge \neg$*seekSupportLex*($\alpha, \max(x_\alpha)$) **then**
13   remove $\max(x_\alpha)$ from $\operatorname{dom}(x_\alpha)$

14 **return** *true*

Algorithm 88: enforceAC(c: constraint): Boolean

Require: c is a binary inequation constraint $x_i \leq y_i$
Output: *true* iff $GAC(c) \neq \bot$

1 **if** $\max(x_i) > \max(y_i)$ **then**
2      $\max(x_i) \leftarrow \max(y_i)$ // $a \in \operatorname{dom}(x_i)$ is removed if $a > \max(y_i)$
3   **if** $\operatorname{dom}(x_i) = \emptyset$ **then**
4   **return** *false*

5 **if** $\min(y_i) < \min(x_i)$ **then**
6      $\min(y_i) \leftarrow \min(x_i)$ // $b \in \operatorname{dom}(y_i)$ is removed if $b < \min(x_i)$
7   **if** $\operatorname{dom}(y_i) = \emptyset$ **then**
8   **return** *false*

9 **return** *true*

Algorithm 89: seekSupportLex(α: integer, v: value): Boolean

Output: *true* iff a support is found for value v

1   $I \leftarrow \{(x_\alpha, v), (y_\alpha, v)\}$ // I is a temporary instantiation

2   **for** i *ranging from* $\alpha + 1$ *to* q **do**

3   **if** $x_i \in \text{vars}(I)$ **then**

4         $a \leftarrow I[x_i]$

5   **else**

6         $a \leftarrow \min(x_i)$

       // a is the minimum (or fixed) value of x_i

7   **if** $y_i \in \text{vars}(I)$ **then**

8         $b \leftarrow I[y_i]$

9   **else**

10        $b \leftarrow \max(y_i)$

       // b is the maximum (or fixed) value of y_i

11   **if** $a < b$ **then**

12   **return** *true*

13   **if** $a > b$ **then**

14   **return** *false*

       // $a = b$, which requires fixing x_i and y_i

15     $I \leftarrow I \cup \{(x_i, a), (y_i, b)\}$

16 **return** *true*

The function seekSupportLex, Algorithm 89, finds a support when $\min(x_\alpha) = \min(y_\alpha)$ or $\max(x_\alpha) = \max(y_\alpha)$. The idea is to record in a set I the values that are now fixed: I can be regarded as a temporary instantiation. Recall that $\text{vars}(I)$ denotes the set of variables covered by I, and $I[x]$ is the value a such that $(x, a) \in I$. The set I is initialized with the same value for x_α and y_α. For each position i, we compare the smallest value of x_i with the greatest value of y_i (but when variables are given a fixed value in I, this must be taken into account). The result of this comparison identifies a support, or a failure or the requirement to fix new variables. Roughly speaking, the function seekSupportLex corresponds to the procedure SeekSupport in [KIZ 04].

To prove that the proposed algorithm enforces GAC, we introduce the following lemmas. The set of v-values of P for the variables involved in a constraint c is denoted by v-vals(c): thus v-vals(c) = $\{(x, a) \mid x \in \text{scp}(c) \wedge a \in \text{dom}(x)\}$.

LEMMA 12.25.– *When line 10 of Algorithm 87 is reached, every value that belongs to* v-vals(c) $\setminus \{(x_\alpha, \max(x_\alpha)), (y_\alpha, \min(y_\alpha))\}$ *is GAC-consistent.*

Proof. For any position $i < \alpha$, we know that x_i and y_i are fixed and equal. At position α, we know that $\max(x_\alpha) \leq \max(y_\alpha)$ and $\min(y_\alpha) \geq \min(x_\alpha)$ since enforceAC has been called for position α. We also know that $\min(x_\alpha) < \max(y_\alpha)$ since the main loop has been terminated with a break, and consequently, we know that there is at least one value a in $\mathrm{dom}(x_\alpha)$ and one value b in $\mathrm{dom}(y_\alpha)$ such that $a \neq b$. Hence, every value of every variable $z \in \mathrm{scp}(c)$ different from x_α and y_α admits a support τ such that $\tau[x_\alpha] = \min(x_\alpha)$ and $\tau[y_\alpha] = \max(y_\alpha)$; recall that $x_\alpha \neq y_\alpha$ since passive variables have been discarded. On the other hand, every value $a < \max(x_\alpha)$ in $\mathrm{dom}(x_\alpha)$ has a support τ in c with $\tau[y_\alpha] = \max(y_\alpha)$ since $a < \max(x_\alpha) \leq \max(y_\alpha)$. Similarly, every value $b > \min(y_\alpha)$ in $\mathrm{dom}(y_\alpha)$ has a support τ in c with $\tau[x_\alpha] = \min(x_\alpha)$ since $b > \min(y_\alpha) \geq \min(x_\alpha)$. We therefore have the guarantee that all values in v-vals$(c) \setminus \{(x_\alpha, \max(x_\alpha)), (y_\alpha, \min(y_\alpha))\}$ are GAC-consistent. $\square$

LEMMA 12.26.– *When line* 10 *of Algorithm 87 is reached, if* $|\mathrm{dom}(x_\alpha)| = 1$, *then the unique value in* $\mathrm{dom}(x_\alpha)$ *is GAC-consistent. Similarly, if* $|\mathrm{dom}(y_\alpha)| = 1$, *then the unique value in* $\mathrm{dom}(y_\alpha)$ *is GAC-consistent.*

Proof. If $\mathrm{dom}(x_\alpha)$ is a singleton $\{a\}$, we have to consider two cases. On the one hand, assume that there is only one value b in $\mathrm{dom}(y_\alpha)$. $a > b$ is not possible since we necessarily have $a = \max(x_\alpha) \leq \max(y_\alpha) = b$. Furthermore, $a = b$ is not possible since α would have been increased (both variables being fixed and equal). Necessarily, we have $a < b$, and consequently, a, the unique value in $\mathrm{dom}(x_\alpha)$ is generalized arc-consistent. On the other hand, assume now that there are at least two values in $\mathrm{dom}(y_\alpha)$. We can deduce that $\max(y_\alpha) > a$ since $\max(y_\alpha) > \min(y_\alpha)$ (because there are two values in $\mathrm{dom}(y_\alpha)$) and $\min(y_\alpha) \geq \min(x_\alpha) = a$. Once again, a, the unique value in $\mathrm{dom}(x_\alpha)$ is proved to be generalized arc-consistent. We can reason similarly with $|\mathrm{dom}(y_\alpha)| = 1$. $\square$

THEOREM 12.27.– *Algorithm 87 enforces GAC.*

Proof. When $\alpha \geq q$ at line 8, the constraint is necessarily GAC-consistent. Using Lemmas 12.25 and 12.26, we can prove that when line 14 is reached the constraint is also GAC-consistent. The proof is as follows. If $\min(y_\alpha)$ is removed, this means, by using Lemma 12.26, that there was at least another value in $\mathrm{dom}(y_\alpha)$. Therefore $\max(y_\alpha)$ is still present, even if $\min(y_\alpha)$ is removed. Similarly, we can show that $\min(x_\alpha)$ is still present even if $\max(x_\alpha)$ is removed. This means that supports identified in the proof of Lemma 12.25 are still valid. Hence all values are generalized arc-consistent. $\square$

THEOREM 12.28.– *The worst-case time complexity of Algorithm 87 is* $O(n\lambda)$.

It is worth noting that this algorithm can be made incremental simply by preserving the value of α from one call to the next. The alternative algorithm introduced in [KIZ 04] to deal with shared variables uses a β value, but in the worst-case this value remains equal to $q + 2$. As a consequence, in the worst case, a support will have to be sought at each call by iterating all variables between $\alpha + 1$ and q. Thus both algorithms have a similar worst-case behavior. Note also that while propagation effort can sometimes be reduced by using β, computing such a value may be costly compared to the approach presented here (since Algorithm 87 finishes as soon as enforcement of GAC is guaranteed). Finally, it is important that Algorithm 87 relaxes the condition of a fine-grained management of events. Previous approaches require all bound events to be taken into account individually in order to update values of α and β. In our new approach, events can be aggregated, potentially saving many calls to the algorithm. Finally, note that Algorithm 87 can be easily extended to deal with entailment (i.e. to detect entailed constraints).

12.7. Experimental results

To show the practical value of lightweight detection of variable symmetries, we have experimented extensively using a cluster of Xeon 3.0 GHz with 1 GB of RAM under Linux. We have measured performance in terms of CPU time (in seconds) and the number of nodes visited. We have integrated with MAC several variants of the symmetry breaking approach described in sections 12.5 (automatic identification of variable symmetries) and 12.6 (exploitation of variable symmetries). We have used different variable ordering heuristics (*dom/ddeg*, *bz* and *dom/wdeg*) and the time-out has been set to 20 minutes per instance.

	MAC	MAC_{Le}	MAC_{Lex}	MAC^*_{Le}	MAC^*_{Lex}
dom/wdeg	2,886	2,941	2,921	2,944	2,952
dom/ddeg	2,394	2,424	2,444	2,458	2,486
bz	2,415	2,452	2,469	2,474	2,504

Table 12.1. *Number of solved instances when running MAC and its symmetry-breaking variants on a selection of* 4,003 *instances*

Saucy has been used to identify variable symmetries. For each generator (of the symmetry group) returned by Saucy, we have applied four distinct symmetry breaking procedures. The first, denoted by MAC_{Le}, posts a binary constraint Le (constraint of the form $x \leq y$) whose scope contains the two first variables of the first cycle of the generator. The second, denoted by MAC_{Lex}, posts a lexicographic ordering constraint

		dom/ddeg			dom/wdeg		
		MAC	MAC^*_{Le}	MAC^*_{Lex}	MAC	MAC^*_{Le}	MAC^*_{Lex}
haystack-06	CPU	9.83	0.45	0.46	time-out	0.44	0.44
	nodes	125 K	40	12	−	28	12
haystack-08	CPU	time-out	0.72	0.62	time-out	0.61	0.61
	nodes	−	1,359	595	−	641	501
haystack-10	CPU	time-out	12.2	1.77	time-out	4.42	1.49
	nodes	−	105 K	9,822	−	22,764	4,524
haystack-12	CPU	time-out	738	55.0	time-out	195	8.82
	nodes	−	6,565 K	416 K	−	962 K	38,830
haystack-14	CPU	time-out	time-out	time-out	time-out	time-out	452
	nodes	−	−	−	−	−	2,120 K
fpga-10-8	CPU	time-out	time-out	9.2	12.4	1.66	1.06
	nodes	−	−	66,053	88,611	7,706	4,148
fpga-11-9	CPU	time-out	time-out	18.3	271	19.6	1.14
	nodes	−	−	140 K	1,519 K	116 K	3,228
fpga-12-10	CPU	time-out	time-out	694	time-out	3.28	5.96
	nodes	−	−	3,005 K	−	12,333	35,462
fpga-13-11	CPU	time-out	time-out	417	time-out	566	5.32
	nodes	−	−	1,985 K	−	2,380 K	23,811
fpga-14-12	CPU	time-out	time-out	time-out	time-out	time-out	10.7
	nodes	−	−	−	−	−	41,809
chnl-10-11	CPU	time-out	614	1.06	time-out	377	1.19
	nodes	−	3,301 K	1,827	−	1,617 K	2,572
chnl-10-15	CPU	time-out	time-out	3.14	time-out	time-out	5.32
	nodes	−	−	2,571	−	−	2,706
chnl-10-20	CPU	time-out	time-out	75.3	time-out	time-out	193
	nodes	−	−	3,501	−	−	5,273
chnl-15-20	CPU	time-out	time-out	762	time-out	time-out	time-out
	nodes	−	−	101 K	−	−	−
bibd-6-60-30	CPU	746	703	1.8	477	1,129	2.15
	nodes	2,938 K	2,938 K	2,949	1,832 K	4,330 K	2,876
bibd-6-80-40	CPU	time-out	time-out	3.11	time-out	time-out	3.06
	nodes	−	−	5,423	−	−	3,524
bibd-7-28-12	CPU	108	108	2.67	0.82	2.58	1.59
	nodes	362 K	362 K	5,066	1,052	10,139	3,310
bibd-7-49-21	CPU	time-out	time-out	8.86	1.11	166	time-out
	nodes	−	−	13,587	1,776	681 K	−
bibd-9-36-12	CPU	time-out	time-out	6.88	11.7	49.3	186
	nodes	−	−	8,187	41,568	150 K	554 K
bibd-9-60-20	CPU	time-out	time-out	28.3	186	1,128	6.63
	nodes	−	−	25,919	438 K	3,176 K	8,786

Table 12.2. *Cost of running MAC and its symmetry-breaking variants on some selected instances*

		MAC	MAC_{Le}	MAC_{Lex}	MAC^*_{Le}	MAC^*_{Lex}
scen11-f10	CPU	1.77	1.82	2.08	1.81	1.9
	nodes	468	327	722	109	77
scen11-f9	CPU	2.15	1.96	2.23	1.84	1.97
	nodes	1,064	576	922	109	90
scen11-f8	CPU	2.1	2.09	2.28	2.02	2.0
	nodes	1,354	558	997	112	115
scen11-f7	CPU	4.83	2.28	2.37	1.91	2.05
	nodes	8,369	955	1,247	121	135
scen11-f6	CPU	8.29	2.14	2.37	2.1	2.08
	nodes	17,839	571	1,333	172	157
scen11-f5	CPU	32.0	2.2	3.13	2.19	2.13
	nodes	85,104	988	3,465	253	226
scen11-f4	CPU	112	2.66	3.88	2.36	2.53
	nodes	345 K	1,983	5,007	593	903
scen11-f3	CPU	403	3.41	7.98	2.55	2.45
	nodes	1,300 K	3,926	17,259	946	696
scen11-f2	CPU	time-out	4.32	16.4	2.95	2.92
	nodes	–	6,014	40,615	1,700	1,591
scen11-f1	CPU	time-out	7.56	19.7	3.49	3.4
	nodes	–	14,997	47,318	3,199	2,609

Table 12.3. *Cost of running MAC and its symmetry breaking variants on hard RLFAP instances (38 generators). The variable ordering heuristic is dom/wdeg*

Lex (involving all variables of all cycles of the generator). A Lex constraint is clearly stronger than the corresponding Le constraint: its filtering capability is higher. Note that when the two first variables of the first cycle are contained in the scope of a (non-global) constraint c of the network, c can be merged with a binary constraint Le. In practice, if c is defined in intension, its associated predicate is modified, whereas if c is defined in extension, the set of tuples disallowed by the constraint Le are removed from the table associated with c; see section 1.2.1. The application of such a merging method produces two additional procedures, denoted by MAC^*_{Le} and MAC^*_{Lex}.

Our first series of experiments have tested the four variants (plus MAC alone) on 4,003 instances essentially coming from the 2006 constraint solver competition. Table 12.1 provides an overview of the results in terms of the number of solved instances within the time limit. Whatever variable ordering heuristic is used, the number of solved instances increases with MAC* (merging method). Although, all in all, the use of MAC_{Lex} allows more instances to be solved than MAC_{Le}, this last approach represents an efficient alternative that is easy to implement. Table 12.2 focuses on some representative instances using *dom/ddeg* and *dom/wdeg*. We only present results obtained with MAC^*_{Le} and MAC^*_{Lex} since Table 12.1 shows that, overall, MAC_{Le} and MAC_{Lex} are outperformed by these variants. On some series of instances that have variables with Boolean domains (bibd, chnl, fpga), MAC^*_{Lex} is (unsurprisingly) very efficient. The gap between MAC^*_{Lex} and MAC^*_{Le} is less significant on some other series such as haystack. Table 12.3 shows some results for the hardest RLFAP instances. Clearly, the symmetry breaking methods allow greater efficiency than the classical MAC algorithm. This is partly due to the use of the operator abssub which allows detection of locally symmetric variables. Interestingly enough, on the pigeonhole problem (modeled as a clique of binary inequation constraints), MAC^*_{Le} can prove the unsatisfiability of every instance simply by enforcing arc consistency at preprocessing. Indeed, combining new Le constraints with constraints of the initial clique amounts to imposing a total ordering on the variables of the problem. The results are not presented in tables of this book.

To summarize, the practical value of lightweight detection of variable symmetries has been shown on many series of instances. The number of solved instances has been increased significantly when employing different variable ordering heuristics, showing the robustness of this approach. The best variant identified in this chapter uses lexicographic ordering constraints while merging (when possible) binary Le constraints with original constraints. It is important to note that the time required to determine locally symmetric variables and to compute automorphisms from lsv-graphs was found to be negligible in our experiments. These results confirm that automatically breaking symmetries constitutes a significant breakthrough for black-box constraint solvers.

Appendix A

Mathematical Background

We propose a partial introduction to the basic elements of discrete mathematics. A more detailed description can be found in e.g. [COR 01].

A.1. Sets, relations, graphs and trees

A.1.1. *Sets, relations and functions*

Set, partition, combination A *set* is a collection of distinguishable objects, called its *elements*. A set is *empty* if it contains no element. An empty set is denoted by $\emptyset$. The number of elements in a set D is called the *cardinality* or the *size* of the set, and is denoted by $|D|$. A set whose cardinality is 1 is *singleton*. The *difference* between two sets D_1 and D_2 is $\{a \in D_1 \mid a \notin D_2\}$ and is denoted by $D_1 \setminus D_2$. The set of all subsets of a set D, including the empty set and D itself, is denoted by 2^D and is called the *powerset* of D. For example, $2^{\{a,b\}}$ is $\{\emptyset, \{a\}, \{b\}, \{a, b\}\}$. Two sets D_1 and D_2 are *disjoint* iff $D_1 \cap D_2 = \emptyset$. A set F of subsets of a set D is a *partition* of D iff the elements of F are pairwise disjoint and the union of all elements of F gives D. A *permutation* is an ordered sequence of elements selected without repetition from a given set. The number of possible permutations (of size n) from a set of size n is $n!$ where ! denotes the factorial operator; $n! = n \times (n-1) \times \cdots \times 2 \times 1$. A *combination* of elements of a set D is a subset of D. A *k-combination* of a set D is a subset of D with k elements. The number of k-combinations from a set D which contains n elements is $n!/[k!(n-k)!]$ and is denoted by $\binom{n}{k}$.

Relation, basic properties of relations The Cartesian product of two sets D_1 and D_2 is denoted by $D_1 \times D_2$ and is equal to $\{(a_1, a_2) \mid a_1 \in D_1 \land a_2 \in D_2\}$. A *binary relation* R on two sets D_1 and D_2 is a subset of the Cartesian product $D_1 \times D_2$. A binary relation R on a set D is a subset of $D \times D$. Instead of $(a, b) \in R$, we sometimes use $a \, R \, b$.

A binary relation R on a set D is:

– reflexive iff $\forall a \in D, (a, a) \in R$;

– irreflexive iff $\forall a \in D, (a, a) \notin R$;

– symmetric iff $\forall a, b \in D, (a, b) \in R \Rightarrow (b, a) \in R$;

– antisymmetric iff $\forall a, b \in D, (a, b) \in R \wedge (b, a) \in R \Rightarrow a = b$;

– transitive iff $\forall a, b, c \in D, (a, b) \in R \wedge (b, c) \in R \Rightarrow (a, c) \in R$.

Equivalence relation, preorder, order A relation that is reflexive, symmetric and transitive is an *equivalence relation*. If $\sim$ is an equivalence relation on a set D and a an element of D, then the *equivalence class* of a in D is $\{b \in D \mid a \sim b\}$ and denoted by $[a]$. The equivalence classes of any equivalence relation $\sim$ defined on a set D forms a partition of D; the set of all equivalence classes is denoted by $D/\sim$. A relation that is reflexive and transitive is a *preorder*. A relation that is reflexive, antisymmetric and transitive is a *partial order*; hence a partial order is an antisymmetric preorder. A *partially ordered set*, or *poset*, is a pair $(D, \preceq)$ that consists of a set D together with a partial order $\preceq$ defined on D. Given a poset $(D, \preceq)$, an equivalence relation $\sim$ can be defined on D by $\forall a, b \in D, a \sim b$ iff $a \preceq b$ and $b \preceq a$, and a partial order $\preceq^\sim$ can be defined on $D/\sim$ by $\forall [a], [b] \in D/\sim, [a] \preceq^\sim [b]$ iff $a \preceq b$ where a and b are any representatives (elements) in $[a]$ and $[b]$. A *total* or *linear* order is a partial order $\preceq$ on a set D that additionally verifies: $\forall a, b \in D$, we have $a \preceq b$ or $b \preceq a$. A relation that is irreflexive and transitive is a *strict* order. A strict order $\prec$ on a set D is *total* iff $\forall a, b \in D$, exactly one of $a \prec b, b \prec a$ or $a = b$ holds. For each partial order $\preceq$ defined on a set D there is an associated strict order $\prec$ on D defined by: $\forall a, b \in D$, $a \prec b$ iff $a \preceq b$ and $a \neq b$. If $\preceq$ is total then $\prec$ is total. Similarly, for each strict order $\prec$ defined on a set D there is an associated partial order $\preceq$ on D defined by: $\forall a, b \in D$, $a \preceq b$ iff $a \prec b$ or $a = b$. If $\prec$ is total then $\preceq$ is total.

Function, bijection, permutation A binary relation f defined on two sets D_1 and D_2 is a *mapping* or (total) *function* iff $\forall a \in D_1, \exists! b \in D_2 \mid (a, b) \in f$. We often write $f(a)$ to denote the unique value of D_2 in relation with a by f; $f(a)$ is the *image* of a by f. The set D_1 is called the *domain* of f, D_2 is called the *codomain* of f, and we note $f : D_1 \to D_2$. A function $f : D_1 \to D_2$ is *surjective* or *onto* iff $\forall b \in D_2, \exists a \in D_1 \mid f(a) = b$. A function $f : D_1 \to D_2$ is *injective* or *one-to-one* iff $a \neq b \Rightarrow f(a) \neq f(b)$. A function is a *bijection* iff it is both surjective and injective. A bijection from a set to itself is called a *permutation*.

A.1.2. *Graphs, hypergraphs and trees*

Graph, clique, path, cycle A simple *graph* G is a pair (V, E) where V is a set of elements, called *vertices* or *nodes*, and E is a set of elements, called *edges*, which are subsets of V composed of exactly two vertices. We have $E \subseteq \{\{v, v'\} \mid v \in V \land v' \in V\}$. An edge corresponds to an unordered pair of vertices. In a *simple* graph, the vertices in each edge are distinct, and there is not more than one edge between each pair of distinct vertices. Hereafter, graph alone means a simple graph. A *complete* graph is a graph in which there is an edge between every pair of vertices. A *clique* of a graph $G = (V, E)$ is a set $V' \subseteq V$ of vertices such that there is an edge in G between every pair of vertices in V'. A *k-clique* is a clique that consists of k vertices; a *maximal clique* is a clique that is not contained in any other clique. If $e = \{v, v'\}$ is an edge of a graph G, we say that the vertices v and v' are *adjacent* or *neighbors* in G, and that e is *incident on* or *connects* v and v'. The *degree* of a vertex is the number of vertices adjacent to it. A vertex whose degree is 0 is *isolated*. A path from a vertex v to a vertex v' in a graph $G = (V, E)$ is a sequence $\langle v_0, v_1, \ldots, v_k \rangle$ of vertices of G such that $v = v_0$, $v' = v_k$ and $\{v_i, v_{i+1}\} \in E, \forall i \in 0..k - 1$. The *length* of a path $\langle v_0, v_1, \ldots, v_k \rangle$ is k, i.e. the number of edges in the path. A path is *simple* if all vertices in the path are distinct. A path $\langle v_0, v_1, \ldots, v_k \rangle$ is a *cycle* iff $v_0 = v_k$. A cycle is *simple* iff all edges in the cycle are distinct. Hereafter, cycle alone means a simple cycle. A graph with no cycles is *acyclic*. Figure A.1 provides an illustration of (simple) graph. A graph is *triangulated* or *chordal* if every cycle composed of four or more vertices has a chord, which is an edge joining two vertices that are not adjacent in the cycle.

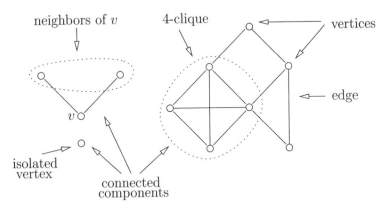

Figure A.1. *A (simple) graph*

Subgraph, connected components Two vertices v and v' of a graph G are *connected* iff there exists a path $\langle v_0, v_1, \ldots, v_k \rangle$ in G such that $v = v_0$ and $v' = v_k$. A graph G is *connected* iff any two vertices of G are connected. A *subgraph* $G' = (V', E')$ of a graph $G = (V, E)$ is a graph such that $V' \subseteq V$ and $E' \subseteq E$. The subgraph of a graph $G = (V, E)$ *vertex-induced* by a set of vertices $V' \subseteq V$ is the graph $G' = (V', E')$ such that $E' = \{e \in E \mid e \subseteq V'\}$. The subgraph of a graph $G = (V, E)$ *edge-induced* by a set of edges $E' \subseteq E$ is the graph $G' = (V', E')$ such that $V' = \{v \in V \mid v \in \cup_{e \in E'} e\}$. A connected subgraph G' of a graph G is *maximal* if G' is not a subgraph of any other connected subgraph of G. The *connected components* of a graph G are the maximal connected subgraphs of G.

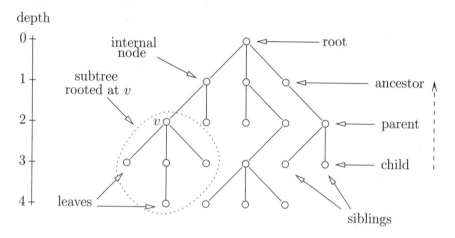

Figure A.2. *A rooted tree*

Forest, rooted tree, parent, child An acyclic graph is called a *forest*. A connected forest is a *(free) tree*. In a tree, any two vertices are connected by a unique simple path, and the number of edges is equal to the number of vertices minus 1. A *rooted tree* is a tree in which one of the vertices, called the *root* of the tree, is distinguished from the others. Vertices in rooted trees are often called *nodes*. If $\langle v_0, v_1, \ldots, v_{k-1}, v_k \rangle$ is a path (with $k \geq 1$) from the root $r = v_0$ of a rooted tree to a node v_k, then v_{k-1} is the *parent* of v_k, and v_k is the *child* of v_{k-1}. Two nodes with the same parent are *siblings*. The root is the only node with no parent. Any node on the (unique) path from the root of a tree to a node v is called an *ancestor* of v. If a node v' is an ancestor of a node v then v is a *descendant* of v'. The *subtree* rooted at a node v is the tree induced by the descendants of v, rooted at v. A node with no children is an *external node* or *leaf*; it is an *internal node* otherwise. The *depth* of a node v is the length of the path from the root to v. A *binary* tree is a tree such that each node has either no children or two children: the *left* child and the *right* child. Figure A.2 provides an illustration of rooted tree.

Graph isomorphism, graph automorphism An *isomorphism* from graph $G = (V, E)$ to graph $G' = (V', E')$ is a bijection $f : V \rightarrow V'$ such that $\{v, v'\} \in E$

iff $\{f(v), f(v')\} \in E'$. Two graphs G and G' are *isomorphic* iff there exists an isomorphism from G to G'; vertices of G can be relabeled to to be vertices of G' while preserving the edges. An *automorphism* of a graph $G = (V, E)$ is an isomorphism from G to itself, i.e. a bijection $f : V \to V$ such that $\{v, v'\} \in E$ iff $\{f(v), f(v')\} \in E$. The set of automorphisms of a graph forms a *group* (defined in section 12.1). Figure A.3 shows a graph automorphism. In the depicted graph G, vertices are identified by numbers from 1 to 4. The bijection f defined by $f(1) = 3$, $f(2) = 2$, $f(3) = 1$ and $f(4) = 4$ is an automorphism.

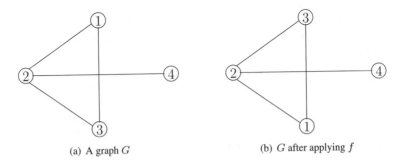

(a) A graph G (b) G after applying f

Figure A.3. *A graph automorphism obtained by swapping vertices labeled 1 and 3 (through a bijection f)*

Hypergraph, primal graph, dual graph A *hypergraph* H is a pair (V, E) where V is a non-empty set of elements, called *vertices* or *nodes*, and E is a set of elements, called *hyperedges*, which are non-empty subsets of V. We have $E \subseteq 2^V \setminus \emptyset$ where 2^V is the powerset of V. A (simple) graph G is a special hypergraph in which each hyperedge links exactly two distinct vertices. The *primal graph* of a hypergraph $H = (V, E)$ is a pair (W, F) where $W = V$ and $F = \{\{v, v'\} \mid \exists e \in E \text{ such that } \{v, v'\} \subseteq e\}$. The *dual graph* of a hypergraph $H = (V, E)$ is a pair (W, F) where $W = E$ and $F = \{\{e, e'\} \mid e \in E \wedge e' \in E \wedge e \cap e' \neq \emptyset\}$.

Directed graph, directed path A *directed graph* is a pair (V, E) where V is a set of vertices and E is a binary relation on V. Each element of E is called a *directed edge* or an *arc*. Self-loops, arcs from an edge to itself, are possible. A *directed path* from a vertex v to a vertex v' in a directed graph $G = (V, E)$ is a sequence $\langle v_0, v_1, \ldots, v_k \rangle$ of vertices of G such that $v = v_0$, $v' = v_k$ and $(v_i, v_{i+1}) \in E$, $\forall i \in 0..k - 1$. A directed path $\langle v_0, v_1, \ldots, v_k \rangle$ is a *directed cycle* iff $v_0 = v_k$. A directed graph is *acyclic* if it has no directed cycle. A directed acyclic graph is often called a DAG.

A.2. Complexity

A.2.1. *Asymptotic notation*

Throughout the book, we analyze the behavior of algorithms by determining their efficiency in terms of running time and consumed memory. Indeed, an algorithm is planned to become a piece of software that makes use of computational resources, which are typically CPU time and memory space. The *complexity* of an algorithm expresses the order of growth of a resource consumption with respect to the size of the input. When resources of interest are time and space, we obtain *time complexity* and *space complexity*, respectively. A common approach to computational complexity is the *worst-case* analysis, i.e. the estimation of the maximal amount of consumed resources to run an algorithm for an input of a certain size. Below, we focus on time complexity.

Complexity analysis is conducted asymptotically. That is, our concern is how the running time $T(n)$ of an algorithm behaves (usually, increases) with respect to the size n of the input, when the size of the input increases without bound. Assuming that $n \in \mathbb{N}^+$, i.e. n is a positive integer, the task is to find an estimation of $T(n)$ for $n \to \infty$. The notation used to describe the asymptotic running time of an algorithm is defined in terms of several sets of functions. We present first the O-notation which is clearly the most employed in practice. For a given function $g(n), n \in \mathbb{N}^+, O(g(n))$ is defined as follows:

$$O(g(n)) = \{f(n) \mid \exists c \in \mathbb{N}^+, \exists n_0 \in \mathbb{N}^+ \text{ s.t. } 0 \leq f(n) \leq cg(n), \forall n \geq n_0\}$$

We use O-notation to give an *asymptotic upper bound* on a function. Intuitively, a function $f(n)$ is in $O(g(n))$ iff for all values of n that are sufficiently large ($n \geq n_0$),

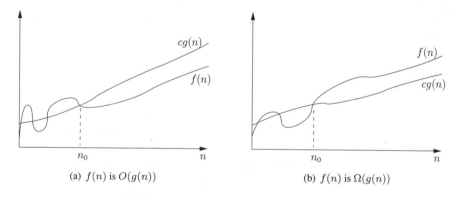

(a) $f(n)$ is $O(g(n))$ (b) $f(n)$ is $\Omega(g(n))$

Figure A.4. *Illustration of O and Ω notation*

the value of $f(n)$ is bounded above by $cg(n)$ for some constant c. Stated otherwise, $f(n)$ does not grow faster than $g(n)$. Figure A.4(a) gives an illustration. For example, if the running time $T(n)$ of an algorithm is in $O(n^2)$, or following the usage $T(n)$ is $O(n^2)$, this means that for large enough inputs, the number of basic steps performed by the algorithm is bounded by cn^2 with c being a constant. Suppose now that a detailed analysis of an algorithm shows that the number of basic operations performed by the algorithm for an input of size n is exactly $4 + n + 2n^2$ in the worst-case (i.e. among all inputs of size n, one requires $4 + n + 2n^2$ operations, which is the highest possible cost). We do not usually need to say that the worst-case time complexity is precisely $4 + n + 2n^2$ because some terms in the expression are negligible. Indeed, when $n \to \infty$, the lower-order terms 4 and n can be ignored; we have for example, $\lim_{n\to\infty} n/n^2 = \lim_{n\to\infty} 1/n = 0$. Besides, the coefficient 2 of the highest-order term $2n^2$ can also be ignored when the O-notation is used. Consequently, we say that the worst-case time complexity of the algorithm is $O(n^2)$, which is usually sufficient for establishing a comparison with other algorithms.

On the other hand, Ω-notation provides *asymptotic lower bounds*. For a given function $g(n), n \in \mathbb{N}^+, \Omega(g(n))$ is defined as follows:

$$\Omega(g(n)) = \{f(n) \mid \exists c \in \mathbb{N}^+, \exists n_0 \in \mathbb{N}^+ \text{ s.t. } 0 \le cg(n) \le f(n), \forall n \ge n_0\}$$

Figure A.4(b) gives a pictorial illustration. Finally, Θ-notation is used for *asymptotic tight bounds*. A function $g(n)$ is an asymptotic tight bound for a function $f(n)$ iff $g(n)$ is both an asymptotic upper bound and an asymptotic lower bound for $f(n)$. Otherwise stated, $f(n)$ is $\Theta(g(n))$ iff $f(n)$ is $O(g(n))$ and $f(n)$ is $\Omega(g(n))$.

It is important to be aware that there is a gap between *polynomial-time* algorithms and *exponential-time* algorithms. Polynomial time refers to the running-time $T(n)$ of an algorithm that is *polynomially bounded*, i.e. $T(n)$ is $O(n^k)$ for some constant k. As the size n of the input increases linearly, the time to run the algorithm is not greater than a polynomial function of n. Exponential time refers to the running-time $T(n)$ of an algorithm that is tightly bounded by an exponential function, i.e. $T(n)$ is $\Theta(k^n)$ for some constant $k > 1$. As the size of the input increases linearly, the time to run the algorithm increases exponentially. Note that there are algorithms that are neither polynomial-time nor exponential-time.

Figure A.5 shows the growth of some representative functions. Whereas the *exponential function* $y = 2^x$ has an extremely fast growth, the *logarithmic function* $y = \log_2(x)$, which is its inverse, has an extremely slow growth. The *linear function* $y = x$ and the *quadratic function* $y = x^2$ are polynomial functions that are negligible with respect to $y = 2^x$. We have for example $\lim_{x\to\infty} x^2/2^x = 0$. Polynomial-time algorithms are considered to be feasible or acceptable computing procedures.

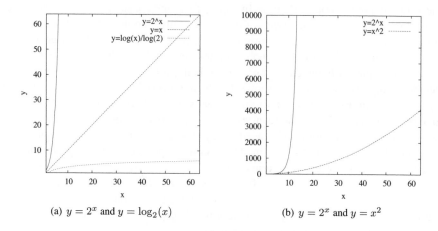

(a) $y = 2^x$ and $y = \log_2(x)$ (b) $y = 2^x$ and $y = x^2$

Figure A.5. *Growth of representative functions*

A.2.2. *Complexity classes*

We now turn to complexity classes that identify problems for which algorithms of certain complexity exist. A *decision problem* is a problem that takes as input a string x and outputs "yes" or "no". Each string given as input defines a problem *instance*; the *size* of the instance is the size, denoted by $|x|$, of the string x that defines it. An instance x of P is positive (resp. negative) when P returns "yes" (resp. "no") for x. P is the class of decision problems that can be solved by an algorithm (more precisely, by a deterministic Turing machine) that runs in polynomial time. This means that if a decision problem P is in P then there exists an algorithm A and integer constants c and k such that A can solve every instance x of P in at most $c|x|^k$ basic steps. P is the complexity class of decision problems which are believed to be "efficiently" solvable or *tractable*.

A *verification* algorithm V for a decision problem P is an algorithm that takes as input two strings and outputs "yes" or "no". P is said to be positively *verified* by V when an instance x of P is positive if and only if there exists a string y, called a *certificate*, such that $V(x, y)$ returns "yes". NP is the complexity class[1] of decision problems that can be positively verified by an algorithm (more precisely, by a deterministic Turing machine) that runs in polynomial time. P is said to be negatively verified by V when an instance x of P is negative if and only if there exists a string y such that $V(x, y)$ returns "yes". co-NP is the class of decision problems that can be

---

1. NP is equivalently defined as the set of decision problems that are solvable in polynomial time by a non-deterministic Turing machine.

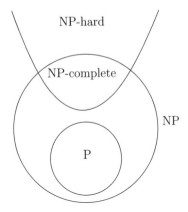

Figure A.6. *Relationships between some complexity classes, under the assumption that*
$$P \neq NP$$

negatively verified by a polynomial time algorithm. In other words, the validity of a certificate can be verified in polynomial time for all problems in NP and also for all problems in co-NP.

We have P ⊆ NP. Indeed, a polynomial-time verification algorithm can be easily built from a polynomial-time algorithm that solves a problem. NP-complete problems form an additional central complexity class. Informally, complete problems of a complexity class are the hardest problems of that class. All other problems in the same class can be reduced to them using polynomial-time transformations (reduction functions). A problem P is NP-hard iff every problem in NP can be reduced in polynomial time to P; P is then at least as hard as any problem in NP. If P is also in NP, P is NP-complete. Several thousands of problems have been identified as NP-complete. However, no polynomial-time algorithm is known for any problem of this class. If a polynomial-time algorithm is ever found to solve an NP-complete problem, then we shall be able to solve all NP problems in polynomial time. It is widely accepted that no such algorithm exists, or equivalently that P ≠ NP. However, no formal proof has been produced so far. Figure A.6 shows relationships among some complexity classes under the hypothesis that P ≠ NP.

Appendix B

XML Representation of Constraint Networks

Before being attacked by a constraint solver, instances of the constraint satisfaction problem must be represented and stored in computer data files[1]. The extensible markup language (XML) [WWW97] offers standardized representation of problem instances. XML is a simple and flexible text format that is increasingly important in the exchange of a wide variety of data on the web. The aim of the XML representation of CSP instances is to facilitate testing and comparison of constraint algorithms by providing a common test-bed. The CSP XML representation format, denoted by XCSP, has been introduced for international constraint solver competitions. Its current specification, XCSP 2.1 [ROU 09], is low-level, although introducing higher level constructs is envisioned. XCSP exhaustively describes domains, variables, relations (if any), predicates (if any) and constraints for each CSP instance.

Interestingly, the proposed XML format offers two variants: a fully tagged representation and an abridged representation. The first is a full, completely structured XML representation that is suitable for use in generic XML tools, but is also relatively verbose. The second is a shorthand notation for the first representation, and is easier for a human to read and write. The two representations are equivalent: automatic translation tools allow us to use the shorthand notation to encode an instance while still being completely able to use available XML tools.

The XML format XCSP is intended to be a good compromise between readability, verbosity and structuring.

---

1. CSP instances can also be directly generated by programming, but this prevents broadcasting them.

Indeed, the representation is:

– Readable: we can easily modify an instance by hand, whereas this would be almost impossible with a tabular format. Only a few constructions require an *a priori* knowledge of the format.

– Concise: with the abridged version which does not systematically use XML tags and attributes, the proposed representation can be comparable in length to one that would be given in tabular format. This is important, for example, in the representation of instances that involve extensional constraints.

– Structured: because the format is based on XML, it is easy to parse instances and it is possible to use XML tools.

It is important that many forms of constraints and constraint networks can be represented:

– extensional constraints;

– intensional constraints;

– global constraints;

– quantified constraint networks;

– weighted constraint networks.

For global constraints, a direct XML translation from the well-known catalog of global constraints [BEL 08] has been proposed. By inserting quantification and cost functions, we obtain instances of the QCSP (Quantified CSP) and WCSP (Weighted CSP) frameworks, but we will not discuss these.

Each CSP instance is represented in the format given in Figure B.1, where q, n, r, p and e respectively denote the number of distinct domains, the number of variables, the number of distinct relations, the number of distinct predicates and the number of constraints. Some attributes have been omitted here. Note that $q \leq n$ because the same domain definition can be used for different variables. Moreover, $r \leq e$ and $p \leq e$ because the same relation or predicate definition can be used for different constraints. Thus, each instance is defined by an XML element, which is <instance> and which contains four, five or six elements. Indeed, an instance may be defined without any reference to a relation and/or to a predicate, in which case the elements <relations> and <predicates> are missing (instead, only global constraints are referenced).

For more information about the format, see [ROU 09]. As illustrations, Figures B.2 and B.3 show the XML representations of the 3-queens instance, by considering two of the models introduced in section 1.3.1. Many series of instances, collected over years, are represented in format XCSP 2.1 and can be downloaded[2].

---

2. See http://www.cril.fr/~lecoutre

```
<instance>
   <presentation  name='the name of the instance' ...
                  format='XCSP 2.1'/>
   <domains  nbDomains='q'>
      <domain     name='the name of the domain'>
         Put here the list of values
      </domain>
      ...
   </domains>
   <variables  nbVariables='n'>
      <variable   name='the name of the variable'
                  domain='the name of the variable domain'/>
      ...
   </variables>
   <relations  nbRelations='r'>
      <relation   name='the name of the relation'
                  semantics='supports or conflicts'>
         Put here the list of tuples
      </relation>
      ...
   </relations>
   <predicates  nbPredicates='p'>
      <predicate  name='the name of the predicate'>
         <parameters>
            Put here a list of formal parameters
         </parameters>
         <expression>
            Put here a representation of the predicate expression
         </expression>
      </predicate>
      ...
   </predicates>
   <constraints  nbConstraints='e'>
      <constraint  name='the name of the constraint'
                   scope='the constraint scope'
                   reference='the name of a relation, a predicate
                              or a global constraint'>
         ...
      </constraint>
      ...
   </constraints>
</instance>
```

Figure B.1. *XML representation of constraint networks*

```
<instance>
    <presentation  name="Queens"  nbSolutions="0"
                   format="XCSP 2.1">
        This is the 3-queens instance represented in intension.
    </presentation>
    <domains  nbDomains="1">
        <domain      name="D0"  nbValues="3">
           1..3
        </domain>
    </domains>
    <variables  nbVariables="3">
        <variable    name="V0"  domain="D0"/>
        <variable    name="V1"  domain="D0"/>
        <variable    name="V2"  domain="D0"/>
    </variables>
    <predicates  nbPredicates="1">
        <predicate  name="P0">
           <parameters> int X0 int X1 int X2 </parameters>
           <expression>
              <functional> ne(abs(sub(X0,X1)),X2) </functional>
           </expression>
        </predicate>
    </predicates>
    <constraints  nbConstraints="4">
        <constraint  name="C0"  arity="3"  scope="V0 V1 V2"
                     reference="global:allDifferent">
        <constraint  name="C1"  arity="2"  scope="V0 V1"
                     reference="P0">
           <parameters> V0 V1 1 </parameters>
        </constraint>
        <constraint  name="C2"  arity="2"  scope="V0 V2"
                     reference="P0">
           <parameters> V0 V2 2 </parameters>
        </constraint>
        <constraint  name="C3"  arity="2"  scope="V1 V2"
                     reference="P0">
           <parameters> V1 V2 1 </parameters>
        </constraint>
    </constraints>
</instance>
```

Figure B.2. *The 3-queens instance represented in intension (abridged version)*

```
<instance>
   <presentation   name="Queens"   nbSolutions="0"
                   format="XCSP 2.1">
      This is the 3-queens instance represented in extension.
   </presentation>
   <domains   nbDomains="1">
      <domain       name="D0"   nbValues="3">
         1..3
      </domain>
   </domains>
   <variables   nbVariables="3">
      <variable    name="V0"   domain="D0"/>
      <variable    name="V1"   domain="D0"/>
      <variable    name="V2"   domain="D0"/>
   </variables>
   <relations   nbRelations="2">
      <relation    name="R0"   arity="2"   nbTuples="2"
                   semantics="supports">
         1 3|3 1
      </relation>
      <relation    name="R1"   arity="2"   nbTuples="4"
                   semantics="supports">
         1 2|2 1|2 3|3 2
      </relation>
   </relations>
   <constraints   nbConstraints="3">
      <constraint  name="C0"   arity="2"   scope="V0 V1"
                   reference="R0"/>
      <constraint  name="C1"   arity="2"   scope="V0 V2"
                   reference="R1"/>
      <constraint  name="C2"   arity="2"   scope="V1 V2"
                   reference="R0"/>
   </constraints>
</instance>
```

Figure B.3. *The 3-queens instance represented in extension (abridged version)*

Bibliography

[ACH 97] ACHLIOPTAS D., KIROUSIS L., KRANAKIS E., KRIZANC D., MOLLOY M., STAMATIOU Y., "Random constraint satisfaction: a more accurate picture", *Proceedings of CP'97*, p. 107–120, 1997.

[ACH 00] ACHLIOPTAS D., GOMES C., KAUTZ H., SELMAN B., "Generating satisfiable problem instances", *Proceedings of AAAI'00*, p. 256–301, 2000.

[ALB 99] ALBERT R., JEONG H., , BARABASI A., "Diameter of the World-Wide Web", *Nature*, vol. 401, p. 130–131, 1999.

[ALB 00] ALBERT R., JEONG H., , BARABASI A., "Error and attack tolerance of complex networks", *Nature*, vol. 406, p. 378–482, 2000.

[ALL 83] ALLEN J., "Maintaining knowledge about temporal intervals", *Communications of the ACM*, vol. 26, num. 11, p. 832–843, 1983.

[ALO 02] ALOUL F., RAMANI A., MARKOV I., SAKALLAH K., "Solving difficult SAT instances in the presence of symmetry", *Proceedings of DAC'02*, p. 731–736, 2002.

[ALO 04] ALOUL F., RAMANI A., MARKOV I., SAKALLAH K., "ShatterPB: symmetry-breaking for pseudo-Boolean formulas", *Proceedings of ASP-DAC'04*, p. 883–886, 2004.

[ALO 06] ALOUL F., SAKALLAH K., MARKOV I., "Efficient symmetry breaking for Boolean satisfiability", *IEEE Transactions on Computers*, vol. 55, num. 5, p. 549–558, 2006.

[AMI 02] AMILHASTRE J., FARGIER H., MARQUIS P., "Consistency restoration and explanations in dynamic CSPs – application to configuration", *Artificial Intelligence*, vol. 135, num. 1–2, p. 199–234, 2002.

[ANB 08] ANBULAGAN, BOTEA A., "Crossword puzzles as a constraint problem", *Proceedings of CP'08*, p. 550–554, 2008.

[ANS 08] ANSOTEGUI C., BÉJAR R., FERNANDEZ C., MATEU C., "Edge matching puzzles as hard SAT/CSP benchmarks", *Proceedings of CP'08*, p. 560–565, 2008.

[APT 03] APT K., *Principles of Constraint Programming*, Cambridge University Press, 2003.

[BAB 96] BABAI L., "Automorphism groups, isomorphism, reconstruction", *Handbook of Combinatorics*, Chapter 27, p. 1447–1551, MIT Press, 1996.

[BAC 99] BACKOFEN R., WILL S., "Excluding symmetries in constraint based search", *Proceedings of CP'99*, p. 73–87, 1999.

[BAC 00] BACCHUS F., "Extending Forward Checking", *Proceedings of CP'00*, p. 35–51, 2000.

[BAC 02a] BACCHUS F., CHEN X., VAN BEEK P., WALSH T., "Binary versus non binary constraints", *Artificial Intelligence*, vol. 140, num. 1–2, p. 1–37, 2002.

[BAC 02b] BACKOFEN R., WILL S., "Excluding symmetries in constraint based search", *Constraints*, vol. 7, num. 3–4, p. 333–349, 2002.

[BAK 93] BAKER R., DIKKER F., F.TEMPELMAN, WOGNUM P., "Diagnosing and solving over-determined constraint satisfaction problems", *Proceedings of IJCAI'93*, p. 276–281, 1993.

[BAK 94] BAKER A., "The hazards of fancy backtracking", *Proceedings of AAAI '94*, p. 288–293, 1994.

[BAL 08a] BALAFOUTIS T., STERGIOU K., "Exploiting constraint weights for revision ordering in arc consistency algorithms", *Proceedings of the ECAI-2008 workshop on Modeling and Solving Problems with Constraints*, 2008.

[BAL 08b] BALAFOUTIS T., STERGIOU K., "On conflict-driven variable ordering heuristics", *Proceedings of CSCLP'08*, 2008.

[BAN 03] DE LA BANDA M. G., STUCKEY P., WAZNY J., "Finding all minimal unsatisfiable subsets", *Proceedings of PPDP'03*, 2003.

[BAP 01] BAPTISTA L., LYNCE I., MARQUES-SILVA J., "Complete search restart strategies for satisfiability", *Proceedings of SSA'01 workshop held with IJCAI'01*, 2001.

[BAR 04] BARTAK R., ERBEN R., "A new algorithm for singleton arc consistency", *Proceedings of FLAIRS'04*, p. 257–262, 2004.

[BAY 97] BAYARDO R., SHRAG R., "Using CSP look-back techniques to solve real-world SAT instances", *Proceedings of AAAI'97*, p. 203–208, 1997.

[BEA 01] BEACHAM A., CHEN X., SILLITO J., VAN BEEK P., "Constraint programming lessons learned from crossword puzzles", *Proceedings of Canadian Conference on AI*, p. 78–87, 2001.

[BEC 01] BECKWITH A., CHOUEIRY B., ZOU H., "How the level of interchangeability embedded in a finite constraint satisfaction problem affects the performance of search", *Proceedings of AI'01*, p. 50–61, 2001.

[BEC 04] BECK J., PROSSER P., WALLACE R., "Variable ordering heuristics show promise", *Proceedings of CP'04*, p. 711–715, 2004.

[BEE 83] BEERI C., FAGIN R., MAIER D., YANNAKAKIS M., "On the desirability of acyclic database schemes", *Journal of the ACM*, vol. 30, num. 3, p. 479–513, 1983.

[BEE 92] VAN BEEK P., "On the minimality and decomposability of constraint networks", *Proceedings of AAAI'92*, p. 447–452, 1992.

[BEE 94a] VAN BEEK P., "On the inherent level of local consistency in constraint networks", *Proceedings of AAAI'94*, p. 368–373, 1994.

[BEE 94b] VAN BEEK P., DECHTER R., "Constraint tightness versus global consistency", *Proceedings of KR'94*, p. 572–582, 1994.

[BEE 95] VAN BEEK P., DECHTER R., "On the minimality and global consistency of row-convex constraint networks", *Journal of the ACM*, vol. 42, num. 3, p. 543–561, 1995.

[BEE 97] VAN BEEK P., DECHTER R., "Constraint tightness and looseness versus local and global consistency", *Journal of the ACM*, vol. 44, num. 4, p. 549–566, 1997.

[BEE 06] VAN BEEK P., "Backtracking search algorithms", *Handbook of Constraint Programming*, Chapter 4, p. 85–134, Elsevier, 2006.

[BEL 94] BELLICHA A., CAPELLE C., HABIB M., KOKÉNY T., VILAREM M., "CSP techniques using partial orders on domain values", *Proceedings of ECAI'94 workshop on constraint satisfaction issues raised by practical applications*, 1994.

[BEL 08] BELDICEANU N., CARLSSON M., RAMPON J., Global constraint catalog, Report num. T2005-08, Swedish Institute of Computer Science, http://www.emn.fr/x-info/sdemasse/gccat/, 2005–2008.

[BEN 92] BENSON B., FREUDER E., "Interchangeability preprocessing can improve forward checking search", *Proceedings of ECAI'92*, p. 28–30, 1992.

[BEN 94] BENHAMOU B., "Study of symmetry in constraint satisfaction problems", *Proceedings of CP'94*, p. 246–254, 1994.

[BEN 01] BEN-SASSON E., WIGDERSON A., "Short proofs are narrow – resolution made simple", *Journal of the ACM*, vol. 48, num. 2, p. 149–169, 2001.

[BEN 07] BENHAMOU B., SAIDI M., "Local symmetry breaking during search in CSPs", *Proceedings of CP'07*, p. 195–209, 2007.

[BEN 08] BENNACEUR H., LECOUTRE C., ROUSSEL O., "A decomposition technique for solving Max-CSP", *Proceedings of ECAI'08*, p. 500–504, 2008.

[BES 91] BESSIERE C., "Arc-consistency in dynamic constraint satisfaction problems.", *Proceedings of AAAI'91*, p. 221–226, 1991.

[BES 94] BESSIERE C., "Arc consistency and arc consistency again", *Artificial Intelligence*, vol. 65, p. 179–190, 1994.

[BES 96] BESSIERE C., RÉGIN J., "MAC and combined heuristics: two reasons to forsake FC (and CBJ?) on hard problems", *Proceedings of CP'96*, p. 61–75, 1996.

[BES 97] BESSIERE C., RÉGIN J., "Arc consistency for general constraint networks: preliminary results", *Proceedings of IJCAI'97*, p. 398–404, 1997.

[BES 99] BESSIERE C., FREUDER E., RÉGIN J., "Using constraint metaknowledge to reduce arc consistency computation", *Artificial Intelligence*, vol. 107, p. 125–148, 1999.

[BES 01a] BESSIERE C., CHMEISS A., SAIS L., "Neighborhood-based variable ordering heuristics for the constraint satisfaction problem", *Proceedings of CP'01*, p. 565–569, 2001.

[BES 01b] BESSIERE C., RÉGIN J., "Refining the basic constraint propagation algorithm", *Proceedings of IJCAI'01*, p. 309–315, 2001.

[BES 02] BESSIERE C., MESEGUER P., FREUDER E., LARROSA J., "On Forward Checking for non-binary constraint satisfaction", *Artificial Intelligence*, vol. 141, p. 205–224, 2002.

[BES 04a] BESSIERE C., DEBRUYNE R., "Optimal and suboptimal singleton arc consistency algorithms",   *Proceedings of CP'04 workshop on constraint propagation and implementation*, p. 17–27, 2004.

[BES 04b] BESSIERE C., DEBRUYNE R., "Theoretical analysis of singleton arc consistency", *Proceedings of ECAI'04 workshop on modelling and solving problems with constraints*, p. 20–29, 2004.

[BES 05a] BESSIERE C., COLETTA R., PETIT T., "Apprentissage de contraintes globales implicites", *Proceedings of JFPC'05*, p. 249–258, 2005.

[BES 05b] BESSIERE C., DEBRUYNE R., "Optimal and suboptimal singleton arc consistency algorithms", *Proceedings of IJCAI'05*, p. 54–59, 2005.

[BES 05c] BESSIERE C., RÉGIN J., YAP R., ZHANG Y., "An optimal coarse-grained arc consistency algorithm", *Artificial Intelligence*, vol. 165, num. 2, p. 165–185, 2005.

[BES 06] BESSIERE C., "Constraint propagation", *Handbook of Constraint Programming*, Chapter 3, Elsevier, 2006.

[BES 08a] BESSIERE C., DEBRUYNE R., "Theoretical analysis of singleton arc consistency and its extensions", *Artificial Intelligence*, vol. 172, num. 1, p. 29–41, 2008.

[BES 08b] BESSIERE C., PETIT T., ZANUTTINI B., "Réordonnancement de domaines dans les réseaux de contraintes", *Proceedings of JFPC'08*, p. 133–142, 2008.

[BES 08c] BESSIERE C., STERGIOU K., WALSH T., "Domain filtering consistencies for non-binary constraints", *Artificial Intelligence*, vol. 72, num. 6–7, p. 800–822, 2008.

[BIT 75] BITNER J., REINGOLD E., "Backtrack programming techniques", *Communications of the ACM*, vol. 18, num. 11, p. 651–656, 1975.

[BLI 96] BLIEK C., Wordwise algorithms and improved heuristics for solving hard constraint satisfaction problems, Report num. 12-96-R045, ERCIM, 1996.

[BLI 98] BLIEK C., SAM-HAROUD D., "Generalizing partial order and dynamic backtracking", *Proceedings of AAAI'98*, p. 319–325, 1998.

[BLI 99] BLIEK C., SAM-HAROUD D., "Path consistency on triangulated constraint graphs", *Proceedings of IJCAI'99*, p. 456–461, 1999.

[BOR 01] BORDEAUX L., MONFROY E., BENHAMOU F., "Improved bounds on the complexity of kB-consistency", *Proceedings of IJCAI'01*, p. 303–308, 2001.

[BOR 04] BORDEAUX L., CADOLI M., MANCINI T., "Exploiting fixable, removable, and implied values in constraint satisfaction problems", *Proceedings of LPAR'04*, p. 270–284, 2004.

[BOR 08] BORDEAUX L., CADOLI M., MANCINI T., "A unifying framework for structural properties of CSPs: definitions, complexity, tractability", *Journal of Artificial Intelligence Research*, vol. 32, p. 607–629, 2008.

[BOU 04a] BOUSSEMART F., HEMERY F., LECOUTRE C., "Revision ordering heuristics for the constraint satisfaction problem", *Proceedings of CPAI'04 workshop held with CP'04*, p. 29–43, 2004.

[BOU 04b] BOUSSEMART F., HEMERY F., LECOUTRE C., SAIS L., "Boosting systematic search by weighting constraints", *Proceedings of ECAI'04*, p. 146–150, 2004.

[BOU 04c] BOUSSEMART F., HEMERY F., LECOUTRE C., SAIS L., "Support inference for generic filtering", *Proceedings of CP'04*, p. 721–725, 2004.

[BOU 06] BOUTALEB K., JÉGOU P., TERRIOUX C., "(no)good recording and ROBDDs for solving structured (V)CSPs.", *Proceedings of ICTAI'06*, p. 297–304, 2006.

[BRE 79] BRELAZ D., "New methods to color the vertices of a graph", *Communications of the ACM*, vol. 22, p. 251–256, 1979.

[BRI 93] BRIGGS P., TORCZON L., "An efficient representation for sparse sets", *ACM Letters on Programming Languages and Systems*, vol. 2, num. 1–4, p. 59–69, 1993.

[BRO 88] BROWN C., L. FINKELSTEIN P. P., "Backtrack searching in the presence of symmetry", *Proceedings of AAECC'88*, p. 99–110, 1988.

[BRU 81] BRUYNOOGHE M., "Solving combinatorial search problems by intelligent backtracking", *Information Processing Letters*, vol. 12, num. 1, p. 36–39, 1981.

[BRU 84] BRUYNOOGHE M., PEREIRA L. M., "Deduction revision by intelligent backtracking", *Implementations of Prolog*, p. 194–215, 1984.

[BRU 00] BRUNI R., SASSANO A., "Detecting minimaly unsatisfiable subformulae in unsatisfiable SAT instances by means of adaptative core search", *Proceedings of SAT'00*, 2000.

[CAB 99] CABON B., DE GIVRY S., LOBJOIS L., SCHIEX T., WARNERS J., "Radio Link Frequency Assignment", *Constraints*, vol. 4, num. 1, p. 79–89, 1999.

[CAM 06] CAMBAZARD H., JUSSIEN N., "Identifying and exploiting problem structures using explanation-based constraint programming", *Constraints*, vol. 11, num. 4, p. 295–313, 2006.

[CAM 08] CAMBAZARD H., O'SULLIVAN B., "Reformulating positive table constraints using functional dependencies", *Proceedings of CP'08*, p. 418–432, 2008.

[CAR 94] CARLIER J., PINSON E., "Adjustments of heads and tails for the job-shop problem", *European Journal of Operational Research*, vol. 78, p. 146–161, 1994.

[CAR 02] CARLSSON M., BELDICEANU N., Revisiting the lexicographic ordering constraint, Report num. T2002-17, Swedish Institute of Computer Science, 2002.

[CAR 06] CARLSSON M., "Filtering for the case constraint", 2006, Talk given at the advanced school on global constraints.

[CHE 91] CHEESEMAN P., KANEFSKY B., TAYLOR W., "Where the really hard problems are", *Proceedings of IJCAI'91*, p. 331–337, 1991.

[CHE 01] CHEN X., VAN BEEK P., "Conflict-directed backjumping revisited", *Journal of Artificial Intelligence Research*, vol. 14, p. 53–81, 2001.

[CHE 06] CHENG K., YAP R., "Maintaining generalized arc consistency on ad hoc n-ary Boolean constraints", *Proceedings of ECAI'06*, p. 78–82, 2006.

[CHE 08a] CHENG K., YAP R., "Maintaining generalized arc consistency on ad hoc r-ary constraints", *Proceedings of CP'08*, p. 509–523, 2008.

[CHE 08b] CHENG K., YAP R., "An overview of mddc-solve", *Proceedings of the third constraint solver competition*, p. 3–7, 2008.

[CHM 95] CHMEISS A., JÉGOU P., Partial and global path consistency revisited, Report num. 120.95, L.I.M., 1995.

[CHM 96] CHMEISS A., "Sur la consistance de chemin et ses formes partielles", *Proceedings of RFIA'96*, p. 212–219, 1996.

[CHM 98] CHMEISS A., JÉGOU P., "Efficient path-consistency propagation", *International Journal on Artificial Intelligence Tools*, vol. 7, num. 2, p. 121–142, 1998.

[CHM 00] CHMEISS A., SAIS L., "About the use of local consistency in solving CSPs", *Proceedings of ICTAI'00*, p. 104–107, 2000.

[CHM 03] CHMEISS A., JÉGOU P., KEDDAR L., "On a generalization of triangulated graphs for domains decomposition of CSPs", *Proceedings of IJCAI'03*, p. 203–208, 2003.

[CHO 95] CHOUEIRY B., FALTINGS B., WEIGEL R., "Abstraction by interchangeability in resource allocation", *Proceedings of IJCAI'95*, p. 1694–1710, 1995.

[CHO 98] CHOUEIRY B., NOUBIR G., "On the computation of local interchangeability in discrete constraint satisfaction problems", *Proceedings of AAAI'98*, p. 326–333, 1998.

[CHO 01] CHOI C., HENZ M., NG K., "Components for state restoration in tree search", *Proceedings of CP'01*, p. 240–255, 2001.

[CHO 02] CHOUEIRY B., DAVIS A., "Dynamic bundling: Less effort for more solutions", *Proceedings of SARA'02*, p. 64–82, 2002.

[COH 03a] COHEN D., "A new class of binary CSPs for which arc-consistency is a decision procedure", *Proceedings of CP'03*, p. 807–811, 2003.

[COH 03b] COHEN D., JEAVONS P., "Tractable constraint languages", *Constraint Processing*, Chapter 11, p. 299–331, Morgan Kaufmann, 2003.

[COH 06] COHEN D., JEAVONS P., JEFFERSON C., PETRIE K., SMITH B., "Symmetry definitions for constraint satisfaction problems", *Constraints*, vol. 11, num. 2–3, p. 115–137, 2006.

[COO 89] COOPER M., "Characterising tractable constraints", *Artificial Intelligence*, vol. 41, num. 1, p. 89–95, 1989.

[COO 94] COOPER M., COHEN D., JEAVONS P., "Characterising tractable constraints", *Artificial Intelligence*, vol. 65, p. 347–361, 1994.

[COO 97] COOPER M., "Fundamental properties of neighbourhood substitution in constraint satisfaction problems", *Artificial Intelligence*, vol. 90, p. 1–24, 1997.

[COO 08] COOPER M., JEAVONS P., SALAMON A., "Hybrid tractable CSPs which generalize tree structure", *Proceedings of ECAI'08*, p. 530–534, 2008.

[COR 01] CORMEN T., LEISERSON C., RIVEST R., STEIN C., *Introduction to Algorithms*, MIT Press, 2001.

[COR 07] CORREIA M., BAROHONA P., "On the integration of singleton consistency and look-ahead heuristics", *Proceedings of CSCLP'07*, p. 62–75, 2007.

[COV 06] COVER T., THOMAS J., *Elements of information theory*, Wiley-Interscience, 2006.

[CRA 92] CRAWFORD J., "A theoretical analysis of reasoning by symmetry in first-order logic", *Proceedings of the workshop on Tractable Reasoning, held with AAAI'92*, p. 17–22, 1992.

[CRA 96] CRAWFORD J., GINSBERG M., LUKS E., ROY A., "Symmetry-breaking predicates for search problems", *Proceedings of KR'96*, p. 148–159, 1996.

[CRU 04] CRUCITTIA P., LATORAB V., MARCHIORIC M., RAPISARDAB A., "Error and attack tolerance of complex networks", *Physica A*, vol. 340, p. 388–394, 2004.

[DAR 04] DARGA P., LIFFITON M., SAKALLAH K., MARKOV I., "Exploiting structure in symmetry generation for CNF", *Proceedings of DAC'04*, p. 530–534, 2004.

[DAV 62] DAVIS M., LOGEMANN G., LOVELAND D., "A machine program for theorem-proving", *Communication of the ACM*, vol. 5, num. 7, p. 394–397, 1962.

[DEB 97a] DEBRUYNE R., BESSIERE C., "From restricted path consistency to max-restricted path consistency", *Proceedings of CP'97*, p. 312–326, 1997.

[DEB 97b] DEBRUYNE R., BESSIERE C., "Some practical filtering techniques for the constraint satisfaction problem", *Proceedings of IJCAI'97*, p. 412–417, 1997.

[DEB 98] DEBRUYNE R., Consistances locales pour les problèmes de satisfaction de contraintes de grande taille, PhD thesis, Universite Montpellier II, 1998.

[DEB 99] DEBRUYNE R., "A strong local consistency for constraint satisfaction", *Proceedings of ICTAI'99*, p. 202–209, 1999.

[DEB 01] DEBRUYNE R., BESSIERE C., "Domain filtering consistencies", *Journal of Artificial Intelligence Research*, vol. 14, p. 205–230, 2001.

[DEC 88] DECHTER R., PEARL J., "Network-based heuristics for constraint satisfaction problems", *Artificial Intelligence*, vol. 34, num. 1, p. 1–38, 1988.

[DEC 89a] DECHTER R., MEIRI I., "Experimental evaluation of preprocessing techniques in constraint satisfaction problems", *Proceedings of IJCAI'89*, p. 271–277, 1989.

[DEC 89b] DECHTER R., PEARL J., "Tree clustering for constraint networks", *Artificial Intelligence*, vol. 38, num. 3, p. 353–366, 1989.

[DEC 90] DECHTER R., "Enhancement schemes for constraint processing: backjumping, learning and cutset decomposition", *Artificial Intelligence*, vol. 41, p. 273–312, 1990.

[DEC 92a] DECHTER R., "Constraint networks", *Encyclopedia of Artificial Intelligence*, p. 276–285, Wiley, 1992.

[DEC 92b] DECHTER R., "From local to global consistency", *Artificial Intelligence*, vol. 55, num. 1, p. 87–108, 1992.

[DEC 97] DECHTER R., VAN BEEK P., "Local and global relational consistency", *Theoretical Computer Science*, vol. 173, num. 1, p. 283–308, 1997.

[DEC 02] DECHTER R., FROST D., "Backjump-based backtracking for constraint satisfaction problems", *Artificial Intelligence*, vol. 136, p. 147–188, 2002.

[DEC 03] DECHTER R., *Constraint Processing*, Morgan Kaufmann, 2003.

[DEC 06] DECHTER R., "Tractable structures for CSPs", *Handbook of Constraint Programming*, Chapter 7, p. 209–244, Elsevier, 2006.

[DEV 99] DEVILLE Y., BARETTE O., VAN HENTENRYCK P., "Constraint satisfaction over connected row-convex constraints", *Artificial Intelligence*, vol. 109, p. 243–271, 1999.

[DON 02] VAN DONGEN M., "AC3$_d$ an efficient arc consistency algorithm with a low space complexity", *Proceedings of CP'02*, p. 755–760, 2002.

[DON 06] VAN DONGEN M., "Beyond singleton arc consistency", *Proceedings of ECAI'06*, p. 163–167, 2006.

[DOY 79] DOYLE J., "A truth maintenance system", *Artificial Intelligence*, vol. 12, num. 3, p. 231–272, 1979.

[EÉN 03] EÉN N., SORENSSON N., "An extensible SAT-solver", *Proceedings of SAT'03*, 2003.

[EID 03] EIDENBERG C., FALTINGS B., "Using the breakout algorithm to identify hard and unsolvable subproblems", *Proceedings of CP'03*, p. 822–826, 2003.

[ERD 59] ERDOS P., RENYI A., "On random graphs", *Publicationes Mathematicae*, vol. 6, p. 290–297, 1959.

[FAH 01] FAHLE T., SCHAMBERGER S., SELLMAN M., "Symmetry breaking", *Proceedings of CP'01*, p. 93–107, 2001.

[FLE 02] FLENER P., FRISCH A., HNICH B., KIZILTAN Z., MIGUEL I., PEARSON J., WALSH T., "Breaking row and column symmetries in matrix models", *Proceedings of CP'02*, p. 462–476, 2002.

[FLE 06] FLENER P., PEARSON J., SELLMANN M., VAN HENTENRYCK P., "Static and dynamic structural symmetry breaking", *Proceedings of CP'06*, p. 695–699, 2006.

[FOC 01] FOCACCI F., MILANO M., "Global cut framework for removing symmetries", *Proceedings of CP'01*, p. 77–92, 2001.

[FRE 60] FREDKIN E., "Trie memory", *Communications of the ACM*, vol. 3, num. 9, p. 490–499, 1960.

[FRE 78] FREUDER E., "Synthesizing constraint expressions", *Communication of the ACM*, vol. 21, num. 11, p. 958–965, 1978.

[FRE 82] FREUDER E., "A sufficient condition for backtrack-free search", *Journal of the ACM*, vol. 29, num. 1, p. 24–32, 1982.

[FRE 85a] FREUDER E., "A sufficient condition for backtrack-bounded search", *Journal of the ACM*, vol. 32, num. 4, p. 755–761, 1985.

[FRE 85b] FREUDER E., QUINN M., "Taking advantage of stable sets of variables in constraint satisfaction problems", *Proceedings of IJCAI'85*, p. 1076–1078, 1985.

[FRE 91] FREUDER E., "Eliminating interchangeable values in constraint satisfaction problems", *Proceedings of AAAI'91*, p. 227–233, 1991.

[FRE 93] FREUDER E., HUBBE P., "Using inferred disjunctive constraints to decompose constraint satisfaction problems", *Proceedings of IJCAI'93*, p. 254–261, 1993.

[FRE 96] FREUDER E., ELFE C., "Neighborhood inverse consistency preprocessing", *Proceedings of AAAI'96*, p. 202–208, 1996.

[FRE 97] FREUDER E., SABIN D., "Interchangeability supports abstraction and reformulation for multi-dimensional constraint satisfaction", *Proceedings of AAAI'97*, p. 191–196, 1997.

[FRE 06] FREUDER E., MACKWORTH A., "Constraint satisfaction: an emerging paradigm", *Handbook of Constraint Programming*, Chapter 2, Elsevier, 2006.

[FRI 02a] FRISCH A., HNICH B., KIZILTAN Z., MIGUEL I., WALSH T., "Global constraints for lexicographic orderings", *Proceedings of CP'02*, p. 93–108, 2002.

[FRI 02b] FRISCH A., MIGUEL I., WALSH T., "CGRASS: A system for transforming constraint satisfaction problems", *Proceedings of CSCLP'02*, p. 23–36, 2002.

[FRI 03] FRIEZE A., MOLLOY M., "The satisfiability threshold for randomly generated binary constraint satisfaction problems", *Proceedings of Random'03*, p. 275–289, 2003.

[FRI 06] FRISCH A., HNICH B., KIZILTAN Z., MIGUEL I., WALSH T., "Propagation algorithms for lexicographic ordering constraints", *Artificial Intelligence*, vol. 170, num. 10, p. 803–834, 2006.

[FRO 94] FROST D., DECHTER R., "Dead-end driven learning", *Proceedings of AAAI'94*, p. 294–300, 1994.

[FRO 95] FROST D., DECHTER R., "Look-ahead value ordering for constraint satisfaction problems", *Proceedings of IJCAI'95*, p. 572–578, 1995.

[FUK 03] FUKUNAGA A., "Complete restart strategies using a compact representation of the explored search space", *Proceedings of SSA'03 workshop held with IJCAI'03*, 2003.

[GAO 04] GAO Y., CULBERSON J., "Consistency and random constraint satisfaction models with a high constraint tightness", *Proceedings of CP'04*, p. 17–31, 2004.

[GAS 74] GASCHNIG J., "A constraint satisfaction method for inference making", *Proceedings of the 12th Annual Allerton Conference on Circuit and System Theory*, p. 866–874, 1974.

[GAS 78] GASCHNIG J., "Experimental case studies of backtrack vs. Waltz-type vs. new algorithms for satisficing assignment problems", *Proceedings of the second Canadian Conference on Artificial Intelligence*, p. 268–277, 1978.

[GAS 79] GASCHNIG J., Performance measurement and analysis of search algorithms, Report num. CMU-CS-79-124, Carnegie Mellon, 1979.

[GAU 97] GAUR D., JACKSON W., HAVENS W., "Detecting unsatisfiable CSPs by coloring the micro-structure", *Proceedings of AAAI'97*, p. 215–220, 1997.

[GEE 92] GEELEN P., "Dual viewpoint heuristics for binary constraint satisfaction problems", *Proceedings of ECAI'92*, p. 31–35, 1992.

[GEN 94] GENT I., WALSH T., "Easy problems are sometimes hard", *Artificial Intelligence*, vol. 70, num. 1–2, p. 335–345, 1994.

[GEN 96a] GENT I., MACINTYRE E., PROSSER P., SMITH B., WALSH T., "An empirical study of dynamic variable ordering heuristics for the constraint satisfaction problem", *Proceedings of CP'96*, p. 179–193, 1996.

[GEN 96b] GENT I., MACINTYRE E., PROSSER P., WALSH T., "The Constrainedness of Search", *Proceedings of AAAI-96*, p. 246–252, 1996.

[GEN 99] GENT I., HOOS H., PROSSER P., WALSH T., "Morphing: Combining structure and randomness", *Proceedings of AAAI'99*, p. 654–660, 1999.

[GEN 00] GENT I., SMITH B., "Symmetry breaking during search", *Proceedings of ECAI'00*, p. 599–603, 2000.

[GEN 01] GENT I., MACINTYRE E., PROSSER P., SMITH B., WALSH T., "Random constraint satisfaction: flaws and structure", *Constraints*, vol. 6, num. 4, p. 345–372, 2001.

[GEN 02a] GENT I., "Arc consistency in SAT", *Proceedings of ECAI'02*, p. 121–125, 2002.

[GEN 02b] GENT I., HARVEY W., KELSEY T., "Groups and constraints: Symmetry breaking during search", *Proceedings of CP'02*, p. 415–430, 2002.

[GEN 03] GENT I., HARVEY W., KELSEY T., LINTON S., "Generic SBDD using computational group theory", *Proceedings of CP'03*, p. 333–347, 2003.

[GEN 06a] GENT I., JEFFERSON C., MIGUEL I., "Minion: A fast, scalable constraint solver", *Proceedings of ECAI'06*, p. 98–102, 2006.

[GEN 06b] GENT I., JEFFERSON C., MIGUEL I., "Watched literals for constraint propagation in minion", *Proceedings of CP'06*, p. 182–197, 2006.

[GEN 06c] GENT I., PETRIE K., PUGET J., "Symmetry in constraint programming", *Handbook of Constraint Programming*, Chapter 10, p. 329–376, Elsevier, 2006.

[GEN 07] GENT I., JEFFERSON C., MIGUEL I., NIGHTINGALE P., "Data structures for generalised arc consistency for extensional constraints", *Proceedings of AAAI'07*, p. 191–197, 2007.

[GIN 90] GINSBERG M., FRANK M., HALPIN M., TORRANCE M., "Search lessons learned from crossword puzzles", *Proceedings of AAAI'90*, p. 210–215, 1990.

[GIN 93] GINSBERG M., "Dynamic backtracking", *Journal of Artificial Intelligence Research*, vol. 1, p. 25–46, 1993.

[GIN 94] GINSBERG M., MCALLESTER D., "GSAT and dynamic backtracking", *Proceedings of KR'94*, p. 226–237, 1994.

[GIV 06] DE GIVRY S., SCHIEX T., VERFAILLIE G., "Exploiting tree decomposition and soft local consistency in weighted CSP", *Proceedings of AAAI'06*, 2006.

[GOL 65] GOLOMB S., BAUMERT L., "Backtrack programming", *Journal of the ACM*, vol. 12, num. 4, p. 516–524, 1965.

[GOM 97] GOMES C., SELMAN B., CRATO N., "Heavy-tailed probability distributions in combinatorial search", *Proceedings of CP'97*, p. 121–135, 1997.

[GOM 98] GOMES C., SELMAN B., KAUTZ H., "Boosting combinatorial search through randomization.", *Proceedings of AAAI'98*, p. 431–437, 1998.

[GOM 00] GOMES C., SELMAN B., CRATO N., KAUTZ H., "Heavy-tailed phenomena in satisfiability and constraint satisfaction problems", *Journal of Automated Reasoning*, vol. 24, p. 67–100, 2000.

[GOM 02] GOMES C., SHMOYS D., "Completing quasigroups or latin squares: a structured graph coloring problem", *Proceedings of Computational Symposium on Graph Coloring and Generalization*, 2002.

[GOM 04] GOMES C., FERNÁNDEZ C., SELMAN B., BESSIERE C., "Statistical regimes across constrainedness regions", *Proceedings of CP'04*, p. 32–46, 2004.

[GOM 06] GOMES C., WALSH T., "Randomness and structure", *Handbook of Constraint Programming*, Chapter 18, p. 639–664, Elsevier, 2006.

[GOO 83] GOODMAN N., SHMUELI O., "Syntactic characterization of tree database schemas", *Journal of the ACM*, vol. 30, num. 4, p. 767–786, 1983.

[GOT 00] GOTTLOB G., LEONE N., SCARCELLO F., "A comparison of structural CSP decomposition methods", *Artificial Intelligence*, vol. 124, p. 243–282, 2000.

[GOT 01] GOTTLOB G., LEONE N., SCARCELLO F., "The complexity of acyclic conjunctive queries", *Journal of the ACM*, vol. 43, num. 3, p. 431–498, 2001.

[GOT 02] GOTTLOB G., LEONE N., SCARCELLO F., "Hypertree decompositions and tractable queries", *Journal of Computer and System Sciences*, vol. 64, num. 3, p. 579–627, 2002.

[GRE 67] GREENBLATT R., EASTLAKE D., CROCKER S., "The Greenblatt chess program", *Proceedings of the Fall Joint Computer Conference*, p. 801–810, 1967.

[GRE 06] GREGOIRE E., MAZURE B., PIETTE C., "Extracting MUSes", *Proceedings of ECAI'06*, p. 387–391, 2006.

[GRE 07] GREGOIRE E., MAZURE B., PIETTE C., "MUST: Provide a finer-grained explanation of unsatisfiability", *Proceedings of CP'07*, p. 317–331, 2007.

[GRE 08] GREEN M., COHEN D., "Domain permutation reduction for constraint satisfaction problems", *Artificial Intelligence*, vol. 172, p. 1094–1118, 2008.

[GRI 07] GRIMES D., WALLACE R., "Learning to identify global bottlenecks in constraint satisfaction search", *Proceedings of FLAIRS'07*, 2007.

[GYS 94] GYSSENS M., JEAVONS P., COHEN D., "Decomposing constraint satisfaction problems using database techniques", *Artificial Intelligence*, vol. 66, num. 1, p. 57–89, 1994.

[HAD 08] HADZIC T., HANSEN E., O'SULLIVAN B., "On automata, MDDs and BDDs in constraint satisfaction", *Proceedings of ECAI'08 Workshop on Inference Methods Based on Graphical Structures of Knowledge*, 2008.

[HAN 88] HAN C., LEE C., "Comments on Mohr and Henderson's path consistency", *Artificial Intelligence*, vol. 36, p. 125–130, 1988.

[HAN 99] HAN B., LEE S.-J., "Deriving minimal conflict sets by cs-trees with mark set in diagnosis from first principles", *IEEE Tansactions on Systems, Man and Cybernetics*, vol. 29, num. 2, p. 281–286, 1999.

[HAR 68] HART P., NILSSON N., RAPHAEL B., "A formal basis for the heuristic determination of minimum cost paths", *IEEE Transactions on Systems Science and Cybernetics*, vol. 4, num. 2, p. 100–107, 1968.

[HAR 72] HART P., NILSSON N., RAPHAEL B., "Correction to "a formal basis for the heuristic determination of minimum cost paths"", *SIGART Newsletter*, vol. 37, p. 28–29, 1972.

[HAR 80] HARALICK R., ELLIOTT G., "Increasing tree search efficiency for constraint satisfaction problems", *Artificial Intelligence*, vol. 14, p. 263–313, 1980.

[HAR 95a] HARVEY W., Nonsystematic backtracking search, PhD thesis, Stanford University, 1995.

[HAR 95b] HARVEY W., GINSBERG M., "Limited discrepancy search", *Proceedings of IJCAI'95*, p. 607–615, 1995.

[HAR 01] HARVEY W., "Symmetry breaking and the social golfer problem", *Proceedings of the workshop on Symmetry in Constraint Satisfaction Problems held with CP'01*, p. 9–16, 2001.

[HAS 93] HASELBOCK A., "Exploiting interchangeabilities in constraint satisfaction problems", *Proceedings of IJCAI'93*, p. 282–287, 1993.

[HEB 08] HEBRARD E., "Implementing a constraint solver: a case study", Slides of the workshop of the third international constraint solver competition, http://www.cril. univ-artois.fr/CPAI08, 2008.

[HEM 06] HEMERY F., LECOUTRE C., SAIS L., BOUSSEMART F., "Extracting MUCs from constraint networks", *Proceedings of ECAI'06*, p. 113–117, 2006.

[HEN 92] VAN HENTENRYCK P., DEVILLE Y., TENG C., "A generic arc-consistency algorithm and its specializations", *Artificial Intelligence*, vol. 57, p. 291–321, 1992.

[HEN 05] VAN HENTENRYCK P., FLENER P., PEARSON J., AGREN M., "Compositional derivation of symmetries for constraint satisfaction", *Proceedings of SARA'05*, p. 234–247, 2005.

[HOE 04] VAN HOEVE W., MILANO M., "Postponing branching decisions", *Proceedings of ECAI'04*, p. 1105–1106, 2004.

[HOE 06] VAN HOEVE W., KATRIEL I., "Global constraints", *Handbook of Constraint Programming*, Chapter 6, p. 169–208, Elsevier, 2006.

[HOF 01] HOFFMANN J., NEBEL B., "The FF planning system: Fast plan generation through heuristic search", *Journal of Artificial Intelligence Research*, vol. 14, p. 253–302, 2001.

[HOG 94] HOGG T., WILLIAMS C., "The hardest constraint problems: A double phase transition", *Artificial Intelligence*, vol. 69, num. 1–2, p. 359–377, 1994.

[HOG 98] HOGG T., "Which search problems are random?", *Proceedings of AAAI'98*, p. 438–443, 1998.

[HOO 06] HOOS H., TSANG E., "Local search methods", *Handbook of Constraint Programming*, Chapter 5, p. 135–167, Elsevier, 2006.

[HOR 00] HORSCH M., HAVENS W., "An empirical study of probabilistic arc consistency as a variable ordering heuristic", *Proceedings of CP'00*, p. 525–530, 2000.

[HUL 06a] HULUBEI T., O'SULLIVAN B., "Failure analysis in backtrack search for constraint satisfaction", *Proceedings of CP'06*, p. 731–735, 2006.

[HUL 06b] HULUBEI T., O'SULLIVAN B., "The impact of search heuristics on heavy-tailed behaviour", *Constraints Journal*, vol. 11, num. 2–3, p. 159–178, 2006.

[HWA 05] HWANG J., MITCHELL D., "2-way vs d-way branching for CSP", *Proceedings of CP'05*, p. 343–357, 2005.

[INT 03] INTERIAN Y., "Backdoor sets for random 3-SAT", *Proceedings of SAT'03*, 2003.

[JAN 89] JANSSEN P., JÉGOU P., NOUGUIER B., VILAREM M., "A filtering process for general constraint-satisfaction problems: achieving pairwise-consistency using an associated binary representation", *Proceedings of IEEE Workshop on Tools for Artificial Intelligence*, p. 420–427, 1989.

[JEA 95a] JEAVONS P., COHEN D., GYSSENS M., "A unifying framework for tractable constraints", *Proceedings of CP'95*, p. 276–291, 1995.

[JEA 95b] JEAVONS P., COOPER M., "Tractable constraints on ordered domains", *Artificial Intelligence*, vol. 79, p. 327–339, 1995.

[JEA 98] JEAVONS P., COHEN D., COOPER M., "Constraints, consistency and closure", *Artificial Intelligence*, vol. 101, p. 251–265, 1998.

[JÉG 91] JÉGOU P., Contribution à l'étude des problèmes de satisfaction de contraintes, PhD thesis, Université Montpellier II, 1991.

[JÉG 93] JÉGOU P., "Decomposition of domains based on the micro-structure of finite constraint-satisfaction problems", *Proceedings of AAAI'93*, p. 731–736, 1993.

[JÉG 03] JÉGOU P., TERRIOUX C., "Hybrid backtracking bounded by tree-decomposition of constraint networks", *Artificial Intelligence*, vol. 146, num. 1, p. 43–75, 2003.

[JÉG 04] JÉGOU P., TERRIOUX C., "Decomposition and Good Recording for Solving Max-CSPs", *Proceedings of ECAI'04*, p. 196–200, 2004.

[JÉG 08] JÉGOU P., NDIAYE S., TERRIOUX C., "A new evaluation of Forward Checking and its consequences on efficiency of tools for decomposition of CSPs", *Proceedings of ICTAI'08*, p. 486–490, 2008.

[JÉG 09] JÉGOU P., NDIAYE S., TERRIOUX C., "Stratégies hybrides pour des décompositions optimales et efficaces", *Proceedings of JFPC'09*, 2009.

[JUN 01] JUNKER U., "QuickXplain: conflict detection for abitrary constraint propagation algorithms", *Proceedings of IJCAI'01 Workshop on Modelling and Solving Problems with Constraints*, p. 75–82, 2001.

[JUN 04] JUNKER U., "QuickXplain: preferred explanations and relaxations for over-constrained problems", *Proceedings of AAAI'04*, p. 167–172, 2004.

[JUS 00a] JUSSIEN N., BARICHARD V., "The PaLM system: explanation-based constraint programming", *Proceedings of TRICS'00 workshop held with CP'00*, p. 118–133, 2000.

[JUS 00b] JUSSIEN N., DEBRUYNE R., BOIZUMAULT P., "Maintaining arc-consistency within dynamic backtracking", *Proceedings of CP'00*, p. 249–261, 2000.

[JUS 02] JUSSIEN N., LHOMME O., Unifying search algorithms for CSP, Report num. 02-3-INFO, Ecole des Mines de Nantes, 2002.

[JUS 07] JUSSIEN N., *A to Z of sudoku*, ISTE, 2007.

[KAS 04] KASK K., DECHTER R., GOGATE V., "Counting-based look-ahead schemes for constraint satisfaction", *Proceedings of CP'04*, p. 317–331, 2004.

[KAT 03] KATSIRELOS G., BACCHUS F., "Unrestricted nogood recording in CSP search", *Proceedings of CP'03*, p. 873–877, 2003.

[KAT 05] KATSIRELOS G., BACCHUS F., "Generalized nogoods in CSPs", *Proceedings of AAAI'05*, p. 390–396, 2005.

[KAT 07] KATSIRELOS G., WALSH T., "A compression algorithm for large arity extensional constraints", *Proceedings of CP'07*, p. 379–393, 2007.

[KEL 04] KELSEY T., LINTON S., RONEY-DOUGAL C., "New developments in symmetry breaking in search using computational group theory", *Proceedings of AISC'04*, p. 199–210, 2004.

[KIL 05] KILBY P., SLANEY J., THIEBAUX S., WALSH T., "Backbones and backdoors in satisfiability", *Proceedings of AAAI'05*, p. 1368–1373, 2005.

[KIR 93] KIROUSIS L., "Fast parallel constraint satisfaction", *Artificial Intelligence*, vol. 64, num. 1, p. 147–160, 1993.

[KIZ 04] KIZILTAN Z., Symmetry breaking ordering constraints, PhD thesis, Uppsala University, 2004.

[KLE 86] DE KLEER J., "An assumption-based TMS", *Artificial Intelligence*, vol. 28, num. 2, p. 127–162, 1986.

[KLE 89] DE KLEER J., "A comparison of ATMS and CSP techniques", *Proceedings of IJCAI'89*, p. 290–296, 1989.

[KNU 00] KNUTH D., "Dancing links", 2000, http://www-cs-faculty.stanford.edu/ knuth/preprints.html.

[KOR 85] KORF R., "Depth-first iterative-deepening: An optimal admissible tree search", *Artificial Intelligence*, vol. 27, num. 1, p. 97–109, 1985.

[LAB 06] LABURTHE F., ROCHART G., JUSSIEN N., "Evaluer la difficulté d'une grille de sudoku à l'aide d'un modèle contraintes", *Proceedings of JFPC'06*, p. 239–248, 2006.

[LAL 05] LAL A., CHOUEIRY B., FREUDER E., "Neighborhood interchangeability and dynamic bundling for non-binary finite CSPs", *Proceedings of AAAI'05*, p. 397–404, 2005.

[LAN 98] LANG J., MARQUIS P., "Complexity results for independence and definability in propositional logic", *Proceedings of KR'98*, p. 356–367, 1998.

[LAW 07] LAW Y., LEE J., WALSH T., YIP J., "Breaking symmetry of interchangeable variables and values", *Proceedings of CP'07*, p. 423–437, 2007.

[LEC 03a] LECOUTRE C., BOUSSEMART F., HEMERY F., "Exploiting multidirectionality in coarse-grained arc consistency algorithms", *Proceedings of CP'03*, p. 480–494, 2003.

[LEC 03b] LECOUTRE C., BOUSSEMART F., HEMERY F., "Implicit random CSPs", *Proceedings of ICTAI'03*, p. 482–486, 2003.

[LEC 04] LECOUTRE C., BOUSSEMART F., HEMERY F., "Backjump-based techniques versus conflict-directed heuristics", *Proceedings of ICTAI'04*, p. 549–557, 2004.

[LEC 05] LECOUTRE C., CARDON S., "A greedy approach to establish singleton arc consistency", *Proceedings of IJCAI'05*, p. 199–204, 2005.

[LEC 06a] LECOUTRE C., PROSSER P., "Maintaining singleton arc consistency", *Proceedings of CPAI'06 workshop held with CP'06*, p. 47–61, 2006.

[LEC 06b] LECOUTRE C., SAIS L., TABARY S., VIDAL V., "Last conflict-based reasoning", *Proceedings of ECAI'06*, p. 133–137, 2006.

[LEC 06c] LECOUTRE C., SAIS L., VION J., "Using SAT encodings to derive CSP value ordering heuristics", *Proceedings of SAT/CP workshop held with CP'06*, p. 33–47, 2006.

[LEC 06d] LECOUTRE C., SZYMANEK R., "Generalized arc consistency for positive table constraints", *Proceedings of CP'06*, p. 284–298, 2006.

[LEC 07a] LECOUTRE C., CARDON S., VION J., "Conservative dual consistency", *Proceedings of AAAI'07*, p. 237–242, 2007.

[LEC 07b] LECOUTRE C., CARDON S., VION J., "Path consistency by dual consistency", *Proceedings of CP'07*, p. 438–452, 2007.

[LEC 07c] LECOUTRE C., HEMERY F., "A study of residual supports in arc consistency", *Proceedings of IJCAI'07*, p. 125–130, 2007.

[LEC 07d] LECOUTRE C., SAIS L., TABARY S., VIDAL V., "Exploiting past and future: Pruning by inconsistent partial state dominance", *Proceedings of CP'07*, p. 453–467, 2007.

[LEC 07e] LECOUTRE C., SAIS L., TABARY S., VIDAL V., "Nogood recording from restarts", *Proceedings of IJCAI'07*, p. 131–136, 2007.

[LEC 07f] LECOUTRE C., SAIS L., TABARY S., VIDAL V., "Recording and minimizing nogoods from restarts", *Journal on Satisfiability, Boolean Modeling and Computation (JSAT)*, vol. 1, p. 147–167, 2007.

[LEC 07g] LECOUTRE C., SAIS L., TABARY S., VIDAL V., "Transposition Tables for Constraint Satisfaction", *Proceedings of AAAI'07*, p. 243–248, 2007.

[LEC 08a] LECOUTRE C., "Optimization of simple tabular reduction for table constraints", *Proceedings of CP'08*, p. 128–143, 2008.

[LEC 08b] LECOUTRE C., LIKITVIVATANAVONG C., SHANNON S., YAP R., ZHANG Y., "Maintaining arc consistency with multiple residues", *Constraint Programming Letters*, vol. 2, p. 3–19, 2008.

[LEC 08c] LECOUTRE C., VION J., "Enforcing arc consistency using bitwise operations", *Constraint Programming Letters*, vol. 2, p. 21–35, 2008.

[LEC 09a] LECOUTRE C., ROUSSEL O., "Failure consistencies for constraint satisfaction", *Submission*, 2009.

[LEC 09b] LECOUTRE C., SAIS L., TABARY S., VIDAL V., "Reasoning from last conflict(s) in constraint programming", *Submitted*, 2009.

[LHO 93] LHOMME O., "Consistency techniques for numeric CSPs", *Proceedings of IJCAI'93*, p. 232–238, 1993.

[LHO 04] LHOMME O., "Arc-consistency filtering algorithms for logical combinations of constraints", *Proceedings of CPAIOR'04*, p. 209–224, 2004.

[LHO 05a] LHOMME O., "Quick shaving", *Proceedings of AAAI'05*, p. 411–415, 2005.

[LHO 05b] LHOMME O., RÉGIN J., "A fast arc consistency algorithm for n-ary constraints", *Proceedings of AAAI'05*, p. 405–410, 2005.

[LI 05] LI L., ALDERSON D., DOYLE J., WILLINGER W., "Towards a theory of scale-free graphs: Definition, properties, and implications", *Internet Mathematics*, vol. 2, num. 4, p. 431–523, 2005.

[LIK 04] LIKITVIVATANAVONG C., ZHANG Y., BOWEN J., FREUDER E., "Arc consistency in MAC: a new perspective", *Proceedings of CPAI'04 workshop held with CP'04*, p. 93–107, 2004.

[LIK 07] LIKITVIVATANAVONG C., ZHANG Y., SHANNON S., BOWEN J., FREUDER E., "Arc consistency during search", *Proceedings of IJCAI'07*, p. 137–142, 2007.

[LUB 93] LUBY M., SINCLAIR A., ZUCKERMAN D., "Optimal speedup of Las Vegas algorithms", *Information Processing Letters*, vol. 47, num. 4, p. 173–180, 1993.

[LYN 04a] LYNCE I., MARQUES-SILVA J., "Hidden structure in unsatisfiable random 3-SAT: An empirical study", *Proceedings of ICTAI'04*, p. 246–251, 2004.

[LYN 04b] LYNCE I., MARQUES-SILVA J., "On computing minimum unsatisfiable cores", *Proceedings of SAT'04*, 2004.

[MAC 77a] MACKWORTH A., "Consistency in networks of relations", *Artificial Intelligence*, vol. 8, num. 1, p. 99–118, 1977.

[MAC 77b] MACKWORTH A., "On reading sketch maps", *Proceedings of IJCAI'77*, p. 598–606, 1977.

[MAI 83] MAIER D., *The theory of relational databases*, Computer Science Press, Rockville, MD, 1983.

[MAN 07] MANCINI T., CADOLI M., "Exploiting functional dependencies in declarative problem specifications", *Artificial Intelligence*, vol. 171, num. 16–17, p. 985–1010, 2007.

[MAR 92] MARSLAND T., "Computer chess and search", *Encyclopedia of Artificial Intelligence*, p. 224–241, J. Wiley & Sons, 1992.

[MAR 96a] MARQUES-SILVA J., SAKALLAH K., Conflict analysis in search algorithms for propositional satisfiability, Report num. RT/4/96, INESC, Lisboa, Portugal, 1996.

[MAR 96b] MARTIN P., SHMOYS D., "A new approach to computing optimal schedules for the job-shop scheduling problem", *Proceedings of IPCO'96*, p. 389–403, 1996.

[MAR 05a] MARINESCU R., DECHTER R., "Advances in AND/OR Branch-and-Bound Search for Constraint Optimization", *Proceedings of the CP'05 Workshop on Preferences and Soft Constraints*, 2005.

[MAR 05b] MARINESCU R., DECHTER R., "AND/OR Branch-and-Bound for Graphical Models", *Proceedings of IJCAI'05*, p. 224–229, 2005.

[MAU 02] MAUSS J., TATAR M., "Computing minimal conflicts for rich constraint languages", *Proceedings of ECAI'02*, p. 151–155, 2002.

[MAZ 98] MAZURE B., SAIS L., GREGOIRE E., "Boosting complete techniques thanks to local search methods", *Annals of Mathematics and Artificial Intelligence*, vol. 22, p. 319–331, 1998.

[MCG 79] MCGREGOR J., "Relational consistency algorithms and their application in finding subgraph and graph isomorphisms", *Information Sciences*, vol. 19, p. 229–250, 1979.

[MCK 81] MCKAY B., "Practical graph isomorphism", *Congressus Numerantium*, vol. 30, p. 45–87, 1981.

[MEA 09] MEARS C., DE LA BANDA M. G., WALLACE M., "On implementing symmetry detection", Forthcoming in *Constraints*, 2009.

[MEH 04] MEHTA D., VAN DONGEN M., "Two new lightweight arc consistency algorithms", *Proceedings of CPAI'04 workshop held with CP'04*, p. 109–123, 2004.

[MEH 05a] MEHTA D., VAN DONGEN M., "Reducing checks and revisions in coarse-grained MAC algorithms", *Proceedings of IJCAI'05*, p. 236–241, 2005.

[MEH 05b] MEHTA D., VAN DONGEN M., "Static value ordering heuristics for constraint satisfaction problems", *Proceedings of CPAI'05 workshop held with CP'05*, p. 49–62, 2005.

[MEH 07] MEHTA D., VAN DONGEN M., "Probabilistic consistency boosts MAC and SAC", *Proceedings of IJCAI'07*, p. 143–148, 2007.

[MEH 09] MEHTA D., Augmenting the efficiency of arc consistency algorithms, PhD thesis, National University of Ireland, Cork, 2009.

[MES 01] MESEGUER P., TORRAS C., "Exploiting symmetries within constraint satisfaction search", *Artificial Intelligence*, vol. 129, num. 1–2, p. 133–163, 2001.

[MIN 92] MINTON S., JOHNSTON M., PHILIPS A., LAIRD P., "Minimizing conflicts: a heuristic repair method for constraint-satisfaction and scheduling problems", *Artificial Intelligence*, vol. 58, num. 1–3, p. 161–205, 1992.

[MIT 00] MITCHELL D., "Some random CSPs are hard for resolution", Submitted, 2000.

[MIT 02] MITCHELL D., "Resolution complexity of random constraints", *Proceedings of CP'02*, p. 295–309, 2002.

[MIT 03] MITCHELL D., "Resolution and constraint satisfaction", *Proceedings of CP'03*, p. 555–569, 2003.

[MOH 86] MOHR R., HENDERSON T., "Arc and path consistency revisited", *Artificial Intelligence*, vol. 28, p. 225–233, 1986.

[MOH 88] MOHR R., MASINI G., "Good old discrete relaxation", *Proceedings of ECAI'88*, p. 651–656, 1988.

[MOL 03] MOLLOY M., "Models for random constraint satisfaction problems", *SIAM Journal of computing*, vol. 32, num. 4, p. 935–949, 2003.

[MON 74] MONTANARI U., "Network of constraints : Fundamental properties and applications to picture processing", *Information Science*, vol. 7, p. 95–132, 1974.

[MON 99] MONASSON R., ZECCHINA R., KIRKPATRICK S., SELMAN B., TROYANSKY L., "Determining computational complexity from characteristic phase transitions", *Nature*, vol. 400, p. 133–137, 1999.

[MOR 93] MORRIS P., "The breakout method for escaping from local minima", *Proceedings of AAAI'93*, p. 40–45, 1993.

[MOS 01] MOSKEWICZ M. W., MADIGAN C. F., ZHAO Y., ZHANG L., MALIK S., "Chaff: Engineering an Efficient SAT Solver", *Proceedings of DAC'01*, p. 530–535, 2001.

[NAD 88] NADEL B., "Tree search and arc consistency in constraint satisfaction algorithms", KANAL L., KUMAR V., Eds., *Search in Artificial Intelligence*, p. 287–342, Springer-Verlag, London, UK, 1988.

[NAG 03] NAGARAJAN S., GOODWIN S., SATTAR A., "Extending dual arc consistency", *International Journal of Pattern Recognition and Artificial Intelligence*, vol. 17, num. 5, p. 781–815, 2003.

[NEU 28] VON NEUMANN J., "Zur theorie der gesellschaftsspiele", *Mathematische Annalen*, vol. 100, p. 295–320, 1928.

[NIS 02] NIST, Secure hash standard, National Institute of Standards and Technology, http://csrc.nist.gov/publications/fips/fips180-2/fips180-2.pdf, 2002, FIPS 180-2.

[NUD 83] NUDEL B., "Consistent-labeling problems and their algorithms: expected-complexities and theory based heuristics", *Artificial Intelligence*, vol. 21, num. 1–2, p. 135–178, 1983.

[OH 04] OH Y., MNEIMNEH M., ANDRAUS Z., SAKALLAH K., MARKOV I., "AMUSE: A minimally-unsatisfiable subformula extractor", *Proceedings of DAC'04*, p. 518–523, 2004.

[OST 02] OSTROWSKI R., GREGOIRE E., MAZURE B., SAIS L., "Recovering and exploiting structural knowledge from CNF formulas", *Proceedings of CP'02*, p. 185–199, 2002.

[OUI 02] OUIS S., JUSSIEN N., BOIZUMAULT P., "k-relevant explanations for constraint programming", *Proceedings of the workshop on User-Interaction in Constraint Satisfaction (UICS'02) held with CP'02*, p. 109–123, 2002.

[PAP 88] PAPADIMITRIOU C., WOLFE D., "The complexity of facets resolved", *Journal of Computer and System Sciences*, vol. 37, p. 2–13, 1988.

[PES 01] PESANT G., "A filtering algorithm for the stretch constraint", *Proceedings of CP'01*, p. 183–195, 2001.

[PES 04] PESANT G., "A regular language membership constraint for finite sequences of variables", *Proceedings of CP'04*, p. 482–495, 2004.

[PET 03a] PETCU A., FALTINGS B., "Applying interchangeability techniques to the distributed breakout algorithm", *Proceedings of CP'03*, p. 925–929, 2003.

[PET 03b] PETIT T., BESSIERE C., RÉGIN J., "A general conflict-set based framework for partial constraint satisfaction", *Proceedings of SOFT'03 workshop held with CP'03*, 2003.

[PHA 07] PHAM D., THORNTON J., SATTAR A., "Building structure into local search for SAT", *Proceedings of IJCAI'07*, p. 2359–2364, 2007.

[PIN 97] PINCUS S., KALMAN R., "Not all (possibly) "random" sequences are created equal", *National Academy of Sciences of the United States of America*, vol. 94, num. 8, p. 3513–3518, 1997.

[PIP 07]   PIPATSRISAWAT K., DARWICHE A., "A lightweight component caching scheme for satisfiability solvers", *Proceedings of SAT'07*, p. 294–299, 2007.

[PRC 02]   PRCOVIC N., NEVEU B., "Progressive focusing search", *Proceedings of ECAI'02*, p. 126–130, 2002.

[PRO 93]   PROSSER P., "Hybrid algorithms for the constraint satisfaction problems", *Computational Intelligence*, vol. 9, num. 3, p. 268–299, 1993.

[PRO 95]   PROSSER P., MAC-CBJ: maintaining arc consistency with conflict-directed backjumping, Report num. 95/177, Department of Computer Science, University of Strathclyde, 1995.

[PRO 96]   PROSSER P., "An empirical study of phase transitions in binary constraint satisfaction problems", *Artificial Intelligence*, vol. 81, p. 81–109, 1996.

[PRO 00]   PROSSER P., STERGIOU K., WALSH T., "Singleton consistencies", *Proceedings of CP'00*, p. 353–368, 2000.

[PUG 93]   PUGET J., "On the satisfiability of symmetrical constrained satisfaction problems", *Proceedings of ISMIS'93*, p. 475–489, 1993.

[PUG 04]   PUGET J., "The next challenge for CP: Ease of use", Invited Talk at CP-2004, 2004.

[PUG 05a]   PUGET J., "Automatic detection of variable and value symmetries", *Proceedings of CP'05*, p. 475–489, 2005.

[PUG 05b]   PUGET J., "Symmetry breaking revisited", *Constraints*, vol. 10, num. 1, p. 23–46, 2005.

[PUG 06]   PUGET J., "An efficient way of breaking value symmetries", *Proceedings of AAAI'06*, p. 117–122, 2006.

[RAM 04]   RAMANI A., MARKOV I., "Automatically exploiting symmetries in constraint programming", *Proceedings of CSCLP'04*, p. 98–112, 2004.

[RAZ 03]   RAZGON I., MEISELS A., "Maintaining dominance consistency", *Proceedings of CP'03*, p. 945–949, 2003.

[RAZ 07]   RAZGON I., MEISELS A., "A CSP search algorithm with responsibility sets and kernels", *Constraints*, vol. 12, num. 2, p. 151–177, 2007.

[REF 04]   REFALO P., "Impact-based search strategies for constraint programming", *Proceedings of CP'04*, p. 557–571, 2004.

[RÉG 05]   RÉGIN J., "AC-*: a configurable, generic and adaptive arc consistency algorithm", *Proceedings of CP'05*, p. 505–519, 2005.

[REI 94]   REINEFELD A., MARSLAND T. A., "Enhanced iterative-deepening search", *IEEE Transactions on Pattern Analysis and Machine Intelligence*, vol. 16, num. 7, p. 701–710, 1994.

[RIC 06]   RICHAUD G., CAMBAZARD H., O'SULLIVAN B., JUSSIEN N., "Automata for nogood recording in constraint satisfaction problems", *Proceedings of SAT/CP workshop held with CP'06*, 2006.

[RIV 92]   RIVEST R., The md5 message-digest algorithm, MIT Laboratory for Computer Science and RSA Data Security, Inc., 1992, Request for Comments 1321.

[ROB 86] ROBERTSON N., SEYMOUR P., "Graph minors II: Algorithmic aspects of tree-width", *Journal of Algorithms*, vol. 7, num. 3, p. 309–322, 1986.

[ROU 09] ROUSSEL O., LECOUTRE C., XML representation of constraint networks: Format XCSP 2.1, Report num. arXiv:0902.2362, CoRR, 2009.

[ROY 98] ROY P., PACHET F., "Using symmetry of global constraints to speed up the resolution of constraint satisfaction problems", *Proceedings of the workshop on non-binary constraints, held with ECAI'98*, 1998.

[RUA 04] RUAN Y., KAUTZ H., HORVITZ E., "The backdoor key: A path to understanding problem hardness", *Proceedings of AAAI'04*, p. 124–130, 2004.

[SAB 94] SABIN D., FREUDER E., "Contradicting conventional wisdom in constraint satisfaction", *Proceedings of CP'94*, p. 10–20, 1994.

[SAB 97] SABIN D., FREUDER E., "Understanding and improving the MAC algorithm", *Proceedings of CP'97*, p. 167–181, 1997.

[SAD 95] SADEH N., SYCARA K., XIONG Y., "Backtracking techniques for the job shop scheduling constraint satisfaction problem", *Artificial Intelligence*, vol. 76, p. 455–480, 1995.

[SAD 96] SADEH N., FOX M., "Variable and value ordering heuristics for the job shop scheduling constraint satisfaction problem", *Artificial Intelligence*, vol. 86, p. 1–41, 1996.

[SAM 05] SAMARAS N., STERGIOU K., "Binary encodings of non-binary constraint satisfaction problems: algorithms and experimental results", *Journal of Artificial Intelligence Research*, vol. 24, p. 641–684, 2005.

[SAM 08] SAMER M., SZEIDER S., "Backdoor trees", *Proceedings of AAAI'08*, p. 363–368, 2008.

[SAN 08] SANCHEZ M., DE GIVRY S., SCHIEX T., "Mendelian error detection in complex pedigrees using weighted constraint satisfaction techniques", *Constraints Journal*, vol. 13, num. 1–2, p. 130–154, 2008.

[SCH 94a] SCHIEX T., VERFAILLIE G., "Nogood recording for static and dynamic constraint satisfaction problems", *International Journal of Artificial Intelligence Tools*, vol. 3, num. 2, p. 187–207, 1994.

[SCH 94b] SCHIEX T., VERFAILLIE G., "Stubborness: a possible enhancement for backjumping and nogood recording", *Proceedings of ECAI'94*, p. 165–172, 1994.

[SCH 96] SCHIEX T., RÉGIN J., GASPIN C., VERFAILLIE G., "Lazy arc consistency", *Proceedings of AAAI'96*, p. 216–221, 1996.

[SCH 99] SCHULTE C., "Comparing trailing and copying for constraint programming", *Proceedings of ICLP'99*, p. 275–289, 1999.

[SCH 06] SCHULTE C., CARLSSON M., "Finite domain constraint programming systems", *Handbook of Constraint Programming*, Chapter 14, p. 495–526, Elsevier, 2006.

[SEL 93] SELMAN B., KAUTZ H., "Domain-independent extensions to GSAT: solving large structured satisfiability problems", *Proceedings of IJCAI'93*, p. 290–295, 1993.

[SEL 05] SELLMANN M., VAN HENTENRYCK P., "Structural symmetry breaking", *Proceedings of IJCAI'05*, p. 298–303, 2005.

[SHA 48] SHANNON C., "A mathematical theory of communication", *Bell System Technical Journal*, vol. 27, p. 379–423, 1948.

[SIM 05] SIMONIS H., "Sudoku as a constraint problem", *Proceedings of the workshop on modelling and reformulating constraint satisfaction problems held with CP'05*, p. 13–27, 2005.

[SIN 96] SINGH M., "Path consistency revisited", *International Journal on Artificial Intelligence Tools*, vol. 5, p. 127–141, 1996.

[SIQ 88] DE SIQUEIRA J., PUGET J., "Explanation-based generalisation of failures", *Proceedings of ECAI'88*, p. 339–344, 1988.

[SLA 77] SLATE D., ATKIN L., "Chess 4.5: The northwestern university chess program", *Chess Skill in Man and Machine*, p. 82–118, Springer-Verlag, 1977.

[SMI 95] SMITH B., GRANT S., "Sparse constraint graphs and exceptionally hard problems", *Proceedings of IJCAI'95*, p. 646–654, 1995.

[SMI 96] SMITH B., DYER M., "Locating the phase transition in binary constraint satisfaction problems", *Artificial Intelligence*, vol. 81, p. 155–181, 1996.

[SMI 99] SMITH B., "The brelaz heuristic and optimal static orderings", *Proceedings of CP'99*, Alexandria, VA, p. 405–418, 1999.

[SMI 01] SMITH B., "Constructing an asymptotic phase transition in random binary constraint satisfaction problems", *Theoretical Computer Science*, vol. 265, p. 265–283, 2001.

[SMI 05] SMITH B., STURDY P., "Value ordering for finding all solutions", *Proceedings of IJCAI'05*, p. 311–316, 2005.

[SMI 06] SMITH B., "Modelling", *Handbook of Constraint Programming*, Chapter 11, p. 377–406, Elsevier, 2006.

[STA 77] STALLMAN R., SUSSMAN G., "Forward reasoning and dependency directed backtracking in a system for computer-aided circuit analysis", *Artificial Intelligence*, vol. 9, p. 135–196, 1977.

[STE 80] STEELE G., The definition and implementation of a computer programming language based on constraints, Report num. AI-TR-595, MIT, 1980.

[STE 06] STERGIOU K., WALSH T., "Inverse consistencies for non-binary constraints", *Proceedings of ECAI'06*, p. 153–157, 2006.

[STE 07] STERGIOU K., "Strong inverse consistencies for non-binary CSPs", *Proceedings of ICTAI'07*, p. 215–222, 2007.

[STE 08] STERGIOU K., "Heuristics for dynamically adapting propagation", *Proceedings of ECAI'08*, 2008.

[SZE 05] SZEIDER S., "Backdoor sets for DLL subsolvers", *Journal of Automated Reasoning*, vol. 35, num. 1–3, p. 73–88, 2005.

[SZY 06] SZYMANEK R., O'SULIVAN B., "Guiding search using constraint-level advice", *Proceedings of ECAI'06*, p. 158–162, 2006.

[SZY 08] SZYMANEK R., LECOUTRE C., "Constraint-level advice for shaving", *Proceedings of ICLP'08*, p. 636–650, 2008.

[TAI 93] TAILLARD E., "Benchmarks for basic scheduling problems", *European journal of operations research*, vol. 64, p. 278–295, 1993.

[TEA 08] TEAM T. C., "Choco: an open source Java constraint programming library", *Proceedings of the third constraint solver competition*, p. 8–14, 2008.

[THO 00] THORNTON J., Constraint weighting local search for constraint satisfaction, PhD thesis, Griffith University, Australia, 2000.

[TSA 93] TSANG E., *Foundations of constraint satisfaction*, Academic Press, 1993.

[ULL 65] ULLMANN J., "Parallel recognition of idealised line characters", *Kybernetik/Biological Cybernetics*, vol. 2, num. 5, p. 221–226, 1965.

[ULL 66] ULLMANN J., "Associating parts of patterns", *Information and Control*, vol. 9, num. 6, p. 583–601, 1966.

[ULL 76] ULLMANN J., "An algorithm for subgraph isomorphism", *Journal of the ACM*, vol. 23, num. 1, p. 31–42, 1976.

[ULL 77] ULLMANN J., "A binary n-gram technique for automatic correction of substitution, deletion, insertion and reversal errors in words", *Computer Journal*, vol. 20, num. 2, p. 141–147, 1977.

[ULL 07] ULLMANN J., "Partition search for non-binary constraint satisfaction", *Information Science*, vol. 177, p. 3639–3678, 2007.

[VEM 92] VEMPATY N., "Solving constraint satisfaction problems using finite state automata", *Proceedings of AAAI'92*, p. 453–458, 1992.

[VER 94] VERFAILLIE G., SCHIEX T., "Dynamic backtracking for dynamic CSPs", *Proceedings of ECAI'94 workshop on constraint satisfaction issues raised by practical applications*, 1994.

[VER 99] VERFAILLIE G., MARTINEZ D., BESSIERE C., "A generic customizable framework for inverse local consistency", *Proceedings of AAAI'99*, p. 169–174, 1999.

[VER 06] VERROUST F., PRCOVIC N., "Solving partially symmetrical CSPs", *Proceedings of the workshop on Symmetry in Constraint Satisfaction Problems held with CP'06*, p. 25–30, 2006.

[VID 04] VIDAL V., "A lookahead strategy for heuristic search planning", *Proceedings of ICAPS'04*, p. 150–159, 2004.

[WAL 72] WALTZ D., Generating semantic descriptions from drawings of scenes with shadows, Report num. AI-TR-271, MIT, 1972.

[WAL 75] WALTZ D., "Understanding line drawings of scenes with shadows", *The Psychology of Computer Vision*, p. 19–91, McGraw-Hill, 1975.

[WAL 92] WALLACE R., FREUDER E., "Ordering heuristics for arc consistency algorithms", *Proceedings of AI/GI/VI'92*, p. 163–169, 1992.

[WAL 93] WALLACE R., "Why AC3 is almost always better than AC4 for establishing arc consistency in CSPs", *Proceedings of IJCAI'93*, p. 239–245, 1993.

[WAL 99]   WALSH T., "Search in a small world", *Proceedings of IJCAI'99*, p. 1172–1177, 1999.

[WAL 00]   WALSH T., "SAT v CSP", *Proceedings of CP'00*, p. 441–456, 2000.

[WAL 01]   WALSH T., Relational consistencies,   Report   num. APES report 28-2001, University of York, 2001.

[WAL 06a]   WALLACE R., "Heuristic policy analysis and efficiency assessment in constraint satisfaction search", *Proceedings of ICTAI'06*, p. 305–314, 2006.

[WAL 06b]   WALSH T., "General symmetry breaking constraints", *Proceedings of CP'06*, p. 650–664, 2006.

[WAL 08]   WALLACE R., GRIMES D., "Experimental studies of variable selection strategies based on constraint weights", *Journal of Algorithms*, vol. 63, num. 1–3, p. 114–129, 2008.

[WAT 98]   WATTS D., STROGATZ S., "Collective dynamics of 'small-world' networks", *Nature*, vol. 393, p. 440–442, 1998.

[WIL 94]   WILLIAMS C., HOGG T., "Exploiting the deep structure of constraint problems", *Artificial Intelligence*, vol. 70, p. 73–117, 1994.

[WIL 03a]   WILLIAMS R., GOMES C., SELMAN B., "Backdoors to typical case complexity", *Proceedings of IJCAI'03*, p. 1173–1178, 2003.

[WIL 03b]   WILLIAMS R., GOMES C., SELMAN B., "On the connections between backdoors, restarts, and heavy-tailedness in combinatorial search", *Proceedings of SAT'03*, 2003.

[WIL 05]   WILSON R., *Four Colors Suffice: How the Map Problem Was Solved*, Princeton University Press, 2005.

[WWW97]   World Wide Web Consortium, http://www.w3.org/XML/, Extensible markup language (xml), 1997.

[XU 00]   XU K., LI W., "Exact phase transitions in random constraint satisfaction problems", *Journal of Artificial Intelligence Research*, vol. 12, p. 93–103, 2000.

[XU 03]   XU K., LI W., Many hard examples in exact phase transitions with application to generating hard satisfiable instances, Report num. cs.CC/0302001, CoRR, 2003, Revised version in *Theoretical Computer Science*, vol. 355, p. 291–302, 2006.

[XU 05]   XU K., BOUSSEMART F., HEMERY F., LECOUTRE C., "A simple model to generate hard satisfiable instances", *Proceedings of IJCAI'05*, p. 337–342, 2005.

[XU 07]   XU K., BOUSSEMART F., HEMERY F., LECOUTRE C., "Random constraint satisfaction: easy generation of hard (satisfiable) instances", *Artificial Intelligence*, vol. 171, num. 8–9, p. 514–534, 2007.

[ZAB 90]   ZABIH R., "Some applications of graph bandwidth to constraint satisfaction problems", *Proceedings of AAAI'90*, p. 46–51, 1990.

[ZHA 01a]   ZHANG L., MADIGAN C., MOSKEWICZ M., MALIK S., "Efficient conflict driven learning in a Boolean satisfiability solver", *Proceedings of ICCAD'01*, p. 279–285, 2001.

[ZHA 01b]   ZHANG Y., YAP R., "Making AC3 an optimal algorithm", *Proceedings of IJCAI'01*, p. 316–321, 2001.

[ZHA 02a] ZHANG H., "A random jump strategy for combinatorial search", *Proceedings of AI&M'02*, 2002.

[ZHA 02b] ZHANG L., MALIK S., "The quest for efficient Boolean satisfiability solvers", *Proceedings of CADE'02*, p. 295–313, 2002.

[ZHA 03a] ZHANG L., MALIK S., "Extracting small unsatisfiable cores from unsatisfiable Boolean formulas", *Proceedings of SAT'03*, 2003.

[ZHA 03b] ZHANG Y., YAP R., "Consistency and set intersection", *Proceedings of IJCAI'03*, p. 263–270, 2003.

[ZHA 03c] ZHANG Y., YAP R., "Erratum: P. van Beek and R. Dechter's theorem on constraint looseness and local consistency", *Journal of the ACM*, vol. 50, num. 3, p. 277–279, 2003.

[ZHA 04] ZHANG Y., FREUDER E., "Tractable tree convex constraint networks", *Proceedings of AAAI'04*, p. 197–203, 2004.

[ZHA 06] ZHANG Y., YAP R., "Set intersection and consistency in constraint networks", *Journal of Artificial Intelligence Research*, vol. 27, p. 441–464, 2006.

[ZHA 08] ZHANG Y., FREUDER E., "Properties of tree convex constraints", *Artificial Intelligence*, vol. 172, num. 12–13, p. 1605–1612, 2008.

[ZOB 70] ZOBRIST A. L., A new hashing method with applications for game playing, Report num. 88, Computer Sciences Dept., Univ. of Wisconsin. Reprinted in *Int. Computer Chess Association Journal* 13(2):169–173 (1990)., 1970.

Index